Plantation Jamaica
1750–1850

Plantation Jamaica

Jamaica

1750–1850

Capital and Control in
a Colonial Economy

B. W. Higman

University of the West Indies Press
Jamaica • Barbados • Trinidad and Tobago

University of the West Indies Press
7A Gibraltar Hall Road   Mona
Kingston 7   Jamaica
www.uwipress.com

12 11 10 09 08   5 4 3 2 1

CATALOGUING IN PUBLICATION DATA

Higman, B. W., 1943–

Plantation Jamaica, 1750–1850: capital and control in a
colonial economy / B. W. Higman

p. cm.

Includes bibliographical references.

ISBN: 978-976-640-209-9 (paper)

1. Plantations – Jamaica – History – 18th century. 2. Plantations – Jamaica –
History – 19th century. 3. Plantations – Jamaica – Management.
4. Plantation owners – Jamaica – Economic conditions.
5. Golden Grove Estate (Jamaica). 6. Montpelier Estate (Jamaica). I. Title.

F1884.H46 2008   972.92

Cover illustration: Golden Grove Estate, St Thomas in the East, A. Duperly.
Reproduced by courtesy of the National Library of Jamaica.

Book and cover design by Robert Harris.
E-mail: roberth@cwjamaica.com

Set in Adobe Garamond 11/14 x 27

Printed in the United States of America.

For Howie

Contents

List of Illustrations / ix
Preface / xi

1. **Planters and Proprietors** / *1*

Part 1 Managers

2. **Managerial Hierarchies** / *15*

Absentees / *17*
Absenteeism / *22*
Managerial Alternatives / *29*
Terminologies / *32*
Defining the Attorney / *36*

3. **Planting Attorneys** / *41*

Regulation / *41*
Appointment / *44*
Qualifications / *47*
Functions / *49*
Numbers / *55*
Domains / *69*
Demography / *75*
Payment / *81*
Wealth / *84*
Status / *88*
The Typical Attorney / *91*

4. **Keeping Accounts** / *94*

Planters' Accounts / *95*
Merchants' Accounts / *102*
Planning and Projections / *109*

5. **Communicating** / *113*

Writing Technologies / *115*
Inland Post / *117*

Overseas Post / *121*
Speed / *128*
Communication and Correspondence / *131*

Part 2 Managing

6. Two Attorneys / *137*

Simon Taylor / *137*
Simon Taylor's Letters / *147*
Isaac Jackson / *151*
Isaac Jackson's Letters / *160*
Two Attorneys, Two Estates, Two Eras / *164*

7. Managing Golden Grove, 1765–1775 / *166*

Personnel / *168*
Defending Inheritance / *173*
Defending Boundaries / *176*
Water Wars / *180*
Building / *190*
Working Land / *194*
Working People / *197*
Trading / *205*
Book-keeping / *212*
Predicting and Planning / *216*
Assessment / *221*

8. Managing Montpelier, 1839–1843 / *227*

Montpelier's Managers / *231*
Workers and Wages / *234*
Rents and Renters / *247*
Sugar / *257*
Livestock / *262*
Profit and Loss / *267*
Assessment / *272*

9. Honour Among Thieves / *279*

Notes / *294*
Bibliography / *344*
Index / *367*

Illustrations

Figures

1.1   Jamaica: parishes and towns *c.*1830 / *2*

2.1   Plantation management hierarchy / *31*

3.1   Estates under attorneys, 1832 / *59*

3.2   Percentage of estates under attorneys, 1832 / *60*

3.3   Pens under attorneys, 1832 / *61*

3.4   Plantations under attorneys, 1832 / *61*

3.5   Percentage of slaves under attorneys, 1832 / *62*

3.6   Attorneys of distant properties, 1832 / *69*

3.7   Properties under John Salmon Jr, 1832 / *70*

3.8   Owners of ten or more properties with
          one attorney, 1832 / *71*

3.9   Properties under George Gordon, 1832 / *71*

3.10   Network of attorneys with William Miller, 1832 / *72*

3.11   Properties under William Miller, 1832 / *73*

3.12   Network of attorneys with Colin McKenzie and
          George W. Hamilton, 1832 / *74*

3.13   Properties under Joseph Gordon, 1832 / *75*

4.1   Sugar flow chart / *104*

5.1   Post roads, 1770 / *118*

5.2   Post roads, 1833 / *119*

5.3   Great Britain, ports and places / *123*

5.4   Sailing packet routes / *124*

5.5   Steamer packet routes, 1842 / *127*

5.6   Thames River, ports and places / *129*

6.1   Simon Taylor, his brother and family, *c.*1780 / *139*

6.2   Simon Taylor's Jamaica / *141*

6.3   Holland Estate, 1820 / *142*

6.4   Isaac Jackson's properties / *153*

7.1   Plantain Garden River stream net / *167*

7.2   Plantain Garden River valley and district / *168*

7.3   Plan of Golden Grove, 1788 / *169*

7.4   Golden Grove area patents, 1671–72 / *177*

7.5   Plantain Garden River mouth, at Holland, 1780 / *178*

7.6   Potosi river channels, 1818 / *182*

7.7   Golden Grove water system / *183*

7.8   Batchelors Hall Plantation, 1741 / *185*

7.9   Plan of Golden Grove, 1782 / *190*

7.10   Winchester weir, 1846 / *191*

7.11   Golden Grove yard, *c.*1845 / *193*

7.12   Capoose and gudgeon, *c.*1790 / *202*

8.1   Great River stream net / *229*

8.2   New Montpelier water system / *230*

8.3   Montpelier region / *236*

8.4   Montpelier Estate, 1820–43 / *256*

9.1   Distribution of sugar estates abandoned 1832–47,
        with and without attorneys / *283*

9.2   Percentage of sugar estates abandoned 1832–47
        under attorneys in 1832 / *284*

9.3   Distribution of coffee plantations under
        attorneys abandoned 1832–47 / *285*

Preface

Some of the questions that trouble historians seem almost as persistent and intractable as the central problems of philosophy and religion. In the history of the Caribbean, many of these abiding concerns have to do with the character of settlement and society, the exploitation of resources and people, the profits of the plantation economy, and the role of the region in the making of the modern world. Today, most Caribbean nations are seen as backwaters of the global economy, marginal contributors at best to the creation of capital and economic innovation. This was not always true, however, and the questions that have long preoccupied historians stem from attempts to measure and interpret the role of sugar and slavery in the building of the economic power of the empires of the British and the French, and the making of modern industrial enterprise. Much of the questioning began with contemporary thinkers, in the later eighteenth century, in debate over the profits of empire, the economic benefits of free trade and free labour, and the consumption and investment of income and capital.

In this book, I take up a small corner of this large field. At the core of my analysis is the character of the planter class and its relationship to the economy and society of the West Indies. Particularly in the case of the British colonial empire, the absenteeism of the planters, the management of their plantations by agents, and the export of profits and capital were all issues debated by contemporaries and remain important in the historiography. Much of the argument about management has, however, lacked empirical substance and failed to move beyond the often polemical statements of the commentators of the time. Recent work by Selwyn H. H. Carrington and Heather Cateau, in particular, has begun to build a more solid base, but there remains a lack of systematic work on the agents of plantation management. Many central questions remain to be posed and answered. How were West Indian plantations managed before and after the abolition of slavery? Who were the managers and how did they relate to proprietors, workers and merchants? What were the costs of communication and exchange? What was the economic and social impact of absentee-proprietorship? Was the system "efficient" in economic terms?

My aim is to offer a contribution to this discussion by looking in detail at Jamaica, the most important example of absentee-proprietorship and management through agents. The focus is firmly on the management of the plantation economy, underpinned by the imperial state but offering alternative opportunities for investment and demanding independent decisions by colonial capitalists. The first part of the book is concerned chiefly with the owners of plantations and their agents. I set out to chart the extent of absenteeism and the structure of the managerial hierarchy. Here I use sources which enable a comprehensive analysis of the system and I seek to look at the proprietors and their employers as classes. I am able to do this in most complete detail for 1832, at the very end of slavery, using the returns of registrations of slaves. Similar records exist for 1817 and every third year following, down to 1832, and much remains to be learned by their analysis. For earlier periods, my data are less systematic. Again, much remains to be discovered through study of the crop accounts and inventories.

The second part of the book is concerned with the management choices of planters, merchants and agents. Rather than attempting to be systematic, I offer two studies of particular attorneys and the plantations they managed. The first of the agents, Simon Taylor, is well known to historians. His management of Golden Grove Estate has also been written about to some extent, particularly by Betty Wood, and it is her recent edition of Simon Taylor's letters to his employer Chaloner Arcedeckne 1765–75 that I have depended on for my own analysis. The second attorney, Isaac Jackson, is much less well known. I mentioned him occasionally in my book *Montpelier, Jamaica*, published in 1998, but knew little of his management of that estate. He has come to light only recently, through the acquisition by the American Philosophical Society of three volumes of his letterbooks for the period 1839–43. I have depended on this material to offer an analysis of management at Montpelier in the post-slavery period.

My aim is to enable an understanding of the management practices of Taylor and Jackson, setting them in context, but more particularly seeking to test their behaviour against some of the general principles set out in the first part of the book. I try to do this through a close reading of their letters, using quite short runs of correspondence, to test and illustrate rather than to hope for anything like a comprehensive study. The narrative is presented in some detail because, in the light of the exiting historiography, I believe it is important to give as complete as possible a picture of the workings of the system of management in order to build the basis for an assessment of its efficiency. The plantations studied here – Montpelier and Golden Grove – are both well known to me, on the ground as well as in the archives, and I have spent many days driving and tramping across them, searching for material traces and doing archaeology. At the same time, I am well aware that within the complex landscapes of these regions hide nooks and crannies yet to be discovered. I am equally aware that there exist many more documents – letters, court records, legal papers, maps and plans, accounts – that might be applied to the study even of Golden Grove and Montpelier. For example, after my book was in proofs, I discovered in the Jamaica Archives a ninety-five-volume series of Powers of Attorney, stretching from 1686 to 1803, that includes the power granted by Chaloner Arcedeckne to Simon Taylor, Elizabeth Kersey and Malcolm Laing on 16 February 1765. Similarly, on the ground, I was able for the first time to find my way to the ruins of the Golden Grove great house. I would like to hope that this book will stimulate further research specific to these cases and more broadly on a comparative basis. This study has a heavy focus on sugar estates and their associated pens, and parallel studies of coffee plantations would seem an obvious next step in the analysis.

This is mainly economic history, but I attempt to approach the questions from a broadly social and moral point of view, with a firm eye on the alternatives and might-have-beens of Jamaican history as a means of understanding why what did happen happened. In order to achieve this goal, it is necessary to attempt to see the system largely from the perspective of the capitalist and manager. Their business was exploitation and part of my task is to assess how efficiently they carried out that enterprise. It is only by taking this perspective that it is possible to understand the working of the larger system of plantation economy and the role of enslaved and free workers within the society. The people who did the hard work of the plantations remain essentially voiceless in the narrative, reduced to the tools of capital and themselves literally human capital. It is a harsh story.

For helping me to think my way through these issues and providing me with relevant material, I thank John Aarons, Rafi Ahmad, Wilma Bailey, Dalea Bean, Trevor Burnard, Garry D. Carnegie, Heather Cateau, Michelle Craig, Kirsty Douglas, Richard Dunn, Eppie Edwards, Stan Engerman, Howard Johnson, Hannah Lowery, Kathleen Monteith, Philip D. Morgan, Wilfrid Prest, Verene Shepherd, Barry Smith, Gary Spraakman and Margaret Steven. Rod MacDonald got me started on this project by bringing to my attention the letters of Isaac Jackson, and Rob Cox and Martin Levitt of the American Philosophical Society library in Philadelphia kindly facilitated my use of the correspondence. The publication of the letters of Simon Taylor, in the edition prepared by Betty Wood and her colleagues T. R. Clayton and W. A. Speck, proved a wonderful conjunction, enabling the comparison that I have attempted, and I thank them for making the Taylor manuscripts better known and accessible.

This work was written in the History Program of the Research School of Social Sciences, at the Australian National University. I thank particularly Eric Richards, a visitor to the Program and an expert on the management of estates in eighteenth- and nineteenth-century Scotland, both for his unfailing interest in my project and for his detailed critique of the entire manuscript. Kay Dancey of the Cartography Unit in the Coombs Building at the Australian National University expertly prepared the maps and diagrams. David Eltis, David Oldroyd, Sarah M. S. Pearsall, Swithin Wilmot and Betty

Wood read various sections of the draft and answered my queries on particular areas of specialization. At the University of the West Indies Press, Shivaun Hearne and Linda Speth have been consistently encouraging and enthusiastic, even when my energies have gone in directions other than those they, and often I, had expected. My wife, Merle, as always, supported me throughout, reading what I wrote and listening to my obsessions. In spite of all the guidance and collective wisdom my friends have offered, I have sometimes ignored their advice and must take responsibility for what I have written.

I have modernized and simplified spelling and capitalization, for ease of reading. I trust those who disapprove of such practice will forgive me. Often, the original sources contain their own variant spellings. In referring to the proprietor of Golden Grove, I have used Arcedeckne (pronounced "Archdeacon") rather than Arcedekne. In referring to England, Wales, Scotland and Ireland, I have sometimes used "Great Britain" to comprehend the total, though England and Scotland were not constitutionally united until 1707 and the union of "Great Britain and Ireland" occurred only in 1801. Students seeking maps and plans in the National Library of Jamaica collection may find my parish file references unhelpful, since it has been systematically catalogued in the more than twenty years since I used the material, but hopefully the clues will be sufficient.

For permission to use material in their hands, I thank the National Library of Jamaica, the Jamaica Government Archives, the University of the West Indies Library at Mona, the British Library, the John Carter Brown Library, the Library of Congress and the American Philosophical Society. Figures 7.4 and 7.9 have been redrawn and are used with the permission of the Director of Information Services, University of Bristol. I thank the University of the West Indies Press for permission to use some material first published in my book *Montpelier, Jamaica* of 1998, and in my article "The Letterbooks of Isaac Jackson, Jamaican Planting Attorney, 1839–1843", *Journal of Caribbean History* 37 (2003): 317–29. If any issues of copyright remain outstanding, I would be happy to hear of them.

B. W. Higman

Chapter 1

Planters and Proprietors

In 1805 Jamaica exported almost one hundred thousand tons of sugar, more than any other country. In 1810 it led the world in coffee.[1] How were these impressive records achieved? The island's resource base was not substantial, occupying just 4,400 square miles and stretching 150 miles from west to east (Figure 1.1). Within that small space the proportion of level land with conditions of soil and climate suited to the cultivation of sugar was limited. Half of the island's area was higher than 1,000 feet above sea level. In the eastern end, the Blue Mountains rose to 7,402 feet and received heavy rainfall. There, conditions were ideal for coffee growing but most of the mountain land remained clothed by forest and the best sites were quickly occupied.

How did Jamaica's resources compare to those of its competitors at the turn of the nineteenth century? On a global scale, Jamaica could not compete with the output of much larger places, such as India and China, that produced raw sugar primarily for domestic consumption.[2] Only by committing more than 80 per cent of its product to international commerce was Jamaica able to become a leading exporter. In terms of the capacity to trade, being a small island had advantages, especially in the age of sail. No place in Jamaica was further than twenty-five miles from the coast and access to external markets was relatively rapid and cheap. Ports large and small were sprinkled around the coast. Kingston, the largest, had few equals in wealth or population in the British-American sphere to 1775 and supported a substantial merchant class.[3] Some plantations operated their own wharves. Ships that had crossed the Atlantic did business at all of these shipping places. But Jamaica was not the only island, not the only sugar producer with such efficient access to international markets.

Within the Caribbean, the centre of the eighteenth-century sugar trade, Jamaica had numerous rivals. In this field, Jamaica was larger than any other island-colony of the British and possessed a competitive proportion of

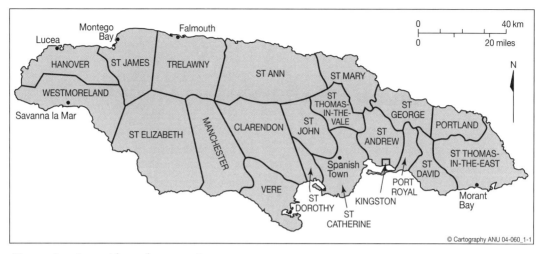

Figure 1.1 Jamaica: parishes and towns, *c.*1830

potential cane land. On the other hand, Jamaica lacked the extensive plains of its neighbours, the French colony of St Domingue one hundred miles to the east and the Spanish colony of Cuba ninety miles to the north. Its irrigation systems were less well developed than those of St Domingue, but Jamaica did have the advantage of good water resources. The island's streams and springs powered sugar and coffee mills, delivering the most efficient technologies available well into the nineteenth century. These natural and technological advantages of Jamaica, within the Caribbean context, were important but have only limited capacity to explain the island's impressive achievements in production for export.

Equally impressive was the productivity of the Jamaican people. In 1750 the population was 142,000, with enslaved people of African origin making up 90 per cent of the total and whites 9 per cent. In that year, per capita output was roughly £8.0 sterling in current money, more than half the total being derived from export earnings. The earliest year for comparative output data is 1770, when low estimates of per capita product give £13.2 for Jamaica, £10.7 for the thirteen mainland colonies of North America, and £10.0 for England and Wales. Jamaica's only real Caribbean rival was St Domingue, which produced more strongly down to the Revolution of 1791 but then fell away. In 1790 Jamaica produced 0.18 tons of sugar per capita, compared to 0.17 in St Domingue, but the French colony had a more diversified base. In Barbados the rate was only 0.10 tons. By 1800, with prices and production up, Jamaican per capita product doubled to £29.2 in current money, then declined to £14.0 by 1850, when the export sector was in retreat and the population 400,000.[4] Thus, particularly in the second half of the eighteenth century, Jamaica performed strongly not only by comparison with other plantation economies but also relative to the emerging industrial nations.

The comparison goes beyond simple measures of absolute output and productivity. In the second half of the eighteenth century, the mature stage of plantation slavery co-existed with the beginnings of the Industrial Revolution in Britain. Some historians, following the lead of Eric Williams and against Adam Smith, argue that the association was no accident, that the plantations were not a drain on Britain but rather contributed substantially to its capital stock, and that Britain's profits from the Atlantic system fed investment in industrialization. As producers of tropical staples, the West Indies were seen as "the mainstay of the Empire". As the largest of the plantation colonies in the middle of the eighteenth century, Jamaica was the "powerhouse" of the British imperial system and its governors the highest paid. On the other side of the argument it is contended that it is impossible to identify a vital, measurable contribution. The debate over these questions remains vigorous and, however difficult it may be to reach firm conclusions, locates Jamaica and the West Indies at the heart of the beginnings of the modern world.[5]

How can the high level of Jamaican productivity be explained? The striking association between productivity and the role of enslaved people in the labour force is an obvious starting point, as is the role of the high-value product sugar.[6] In 1800 Jamaica was a mature slave society, in which slavery dominated social relations, with nine of every ten people enslaved. This was a proportion significantly greater than the 33 per cent found in the United States South, the 30 per cent in Brazil and the 50 per cent in Cuba.[7] Jamaica's product depended almost entirely on the labour of enslaved people, in contrast to the virtual absence of slaves in industrializing Europe and the northern states of the United States, and the relatively smaller contribution of slave labour in most slave societies. In slavery, people had little or no choice in their employers, their sites of labour, their tasks, their hours and days of work, their conditions of labour, or their food, clothing and shelter. They were beaten and abused. These were principles and conditions common to the practice of slavery throughout the Americas, however, and in themselves they help little in explaining the comparatively high levels of productivity extracted in Jamaica.

Why were the enslaved people of Jamaica so productive compared to other enslaved people? What was different about slavery in Jamaica? Answers to these questions must be sought first in decisions made by slave owners and those who wished to be slave owners, the free people of Jamaica and Great Britain. The enslaved had no interest in high levels of production or productivity, since they had no share in the profits, but their lives were directly affected by the choices made by these slave-owning people. The most important of the choices had to do with the selection of crops, scale of production and system of management. The choices that were made were intimately linked with the levels of brutality associated with, and made possible by, different types of enterprise. The choices made in Jamaica created harsh forms, making great demands on the physical endurance of workers.

The owners of Jamaica's enslaved population chose to concentrate their resources on export crops. Even more important, they chose to focus on sugar and to establish plantations on a large scale in terms of area, workforce and output, and they employed the gang system of field labour. The consequences of these choices, worked out between 1670 and 1750, were far reaching. Jamaica's plantations, particularly those producing sugar, grew quickly to become some of the largest private agricultural enterprises in the world. The typical enslaved person in Jamaica belonged to a unit of more than 150 and one-quarter of the people lived on plantations of more than 250, creating the potential for hierarchical subdivision of the labour force.[8] By comparison, down to the middle of the nineteenth century, British industrial enterprises with workforces of more than two hundred were few and far between, most of them dependent on waterpower.[9] Sugar was not merely an agricultural enterprise but required also relatively elaborate technologies and substantial buildings. Further, the manipulation of these resources, physical and human, demanded a system of management that articulated the elements in an efficient and profitable way.

How did the planters of Jamaica manipulate and manage the resources of their plantations? By acquiring large landholdings, they were generally able to comprehend considerable topographical diversity. Thus the typical Jamaican sugar plantation or "estate" could often produce essential inputs from within its own boundaries. Timber used in building came from the woodland, limestone was excavated and burned in kilns for both building and sugar-making, food crops were grown on land not suited to cane or beyond the capacity of the planter to cultivate, and livestock were raised for use in draft and as power in the mills. An important feature was the "provision ground system" in which areas of land were allocated to the enslaved on which they were required to produce most of their own food, in the time they were not labouring for the planter. These plots provided the basis for an autonomous economy and an internal marketing system that effectively provisioned all sectors of the population. The possibilities varied from region to region and from plantation to plantation, but they created the potential for a more extensive and intensive employment of labour and the basis for internal transactions.

In addition, a series of independent sectors developed, producing commodities for exchange between units. The most important of these were the "pens" which produced livestock for sale to the sugar plantations as working stock and purchased old and meagre stock for fattening and the meat market. During slavery, the pens were numerous and prosperous, often with populations on the same scale as the smaller sugar estates. They did not themselves produce for export but provided an essential underpinning to the export staples sector that might otherwise have had to depend on imported livestock. "Plantations" and "settlements" producing minor export staples and commodities for domestic exchange flourished on the fringes but contributed relatively little to total product compared to the sugar and coffee sectors.[10] These systems of plantation economy had been worked out in detail by the middle of the eighteenth century.

Who were the planters of Jamaica and what made them so rich and powerful? At first, following the conquest of 1655, they were simply colonists or people "planted" in the island to establish the English settlement; the colony itself was thought of as a "plantation".[11] They were remade as planters by the sugar revolution that transformed colonial economy and society and transmogrified the concept of the plantation. It separated the "settler colonies" of the North American mainland from the "plantation colonies" of the tropical Caribbean. "Planters" and "plantations" survived in archaic forms in temperate settler colonies but it was the tropical agrarian system that became definitive.[12] Thus the plantation came to be understood as a unit of landholding and people-holding, each plantation a microcosm of colonization and each colony in turn shaped by this newly defined plantation. The principal features of plantation economy were found in the large scale of landholdings, dependence on enslaved and other forms of forced labour, hierarchical management, monoculture, export-orientation, high population densities, high ratios of African to European people, and high-value per capita output.[13] The plantation provided a model that was rapidly embraced by the colonists and made difficult if not impossible the consideration of alternatives.

By the middle of the eighteenth century, the sugar planters of Jamaica were some of the richest men in the world. Their incomes came from the manipulation of a complex agro-industrial technology, an integrated trade network and a brutal system of labour exploitation. Their wealth in turn derived from all of these resources but most particularly the ownership of human beings, the enslaved who worked in field and factory. It was slavery that made the planters rich.[14] More broadly, the riches of the planters were founded on an extremely unequal distribution of wealth, in which most people did not even have legal possession of their own bodies but rather were counted as part of the tradeable capital stock. In addition, the accumulation of properties enabled the bigger planters to take the wealth of the smaller members of the class. Thus the planters of Jamaica built a highly productive system in which per capita output was greater than almost anywhere else yet took to themselves the lion's share of the profits. The great wealth of the few depended on the poverty of the productive many. In 1750 the planter class was moving rapidly towards the peak of its power and prosperity. New plantations were still being established and new planters regularly added to the class, but by the 1780s the process of geographical expansion came close to its limits. Thereafter, there was contraction in some regions of the island, where topography and climate made the profitability of sugar marginal. This relative decline in sugar was balanced by the rapid expansion of coffee cultivation, occupying upland areas of Jamaica that had never been considered for sugar, and leading to the emergence of a new type of planter.

At the beginning of the nineteenth century, when Jamaica led the world in sugar and coffee exports, the systems of production and exchange were fully integrated and performing at levels close to their upper limits. The island's successes in production and productivity were short lived, dependent as they inevitably were on the relative failures of other places. In sugar, Jamaica itself did not equal its own record of 1805 until 1936 when several other places produced vastly more. St Domingue held the top place from 1750 to 1791, when the Revolution cut down slavery and sugar. The planters of Jamaica feared the Revolution might spread to Jamaica and destroy their plantation system, and these fears were well founded.[15] However, the next great Jamaican slave rebellion did not come until 1831 and was quickly followed by the formal abolition of slavery in 1834 and its effective end in 1838. Cuba, where slavery continued to 1886, soon emerged as the world leader in sugar, passing Jamaica by 1830. Brazil also went ahead, as did the mainland colony British Guiana by 1835.[16] Thus in terms of output Jamaica maintained a fragile supremacy from about 1790 to 1830, whereas the great period of planter prosperity occurred earlier in the second half of the eighteenth century.

Although the productive achievements of Jamaica's plantations around 1800 occurred in a context of uncertainty, the planters of Jamaica remained optimistic. The price of sugar had been increasing steadily for fifty years and had not begun the long decline it was to experience in the nineteenth century.[17] Between 1787 and 1793 the British government had underwritten two expensive voyages to the Pacific in order to bring the breadfruit to the West Indies to provide a secure food resource for the enslaved.[18] The optimism of planters and merchants was further demonstrated by the opening in 1802 of the West India Dock in London, an enterprise that prominently displayed the political influence of the group as a metropolitan mercantile lobby. On the other hand, the slave trade from Africa was already under attack and ended in 1808. How had the planters become so powerful a force within British imperial economy and why was their influence beginning to wane just as it seemed to reach its peak? These questions have occupied several generations of historians and interpretation depends on contested diagnoses of the health of the plantation slavery as a system. What is agreed is that down to the American Revolution, at the very least, the planters of Jamaica were rich and powerful. They spoke loudly of their political rights and liberty but understood that their situation was fundamentally different to that of their fellow colonists in British North America. They did not join the American Revolution because they knew that ultimately the preservation of their wealth and power depended on British imperial military force and because of their demographic weakness.[19]

Initially, slaves and masters had lived side by side. Quite quickly, however, by the beginning of the eighteenth century, some planters began to choose to live elsewhere. As they became rich, they sought to display their wealth and status on a different stage, performing for a metropolitan audience rather than the poor black Africans who increasingly made up the society of Plantation Jamaica. As well, they sought to distance themselves from the fear in which all whites lived, the very real expectation that they might be cut down by disease or murdered by the enslaved. The whites might also have had qualms about the brutality of the plantation, and the systematic application of terror they had themselves established and practised, but fear for their own lives was a vital driver of absenteeism.[20] In order to succeed as absentee-proprietors, to ensure the continuing profitability of their plant-ations and the efficient transfer of the wealth produced, the planters had to create an alternative system of management. They had to find substitutes willing to take the risks for a price. Some absentees divided their time between Jamaica and Britain, following ambiguous patterns of migration and residence, but they still required a system of delegated management. Even proprietors who remained in Jamaica often depended on such a system, because they owned multiple scattered estates or because they spent much of their time in town or simply preferred not to be directly responsible for the running of their enterprises.

The second half of the eighteenth century saw the beginning of a distinction between planter and proprietor. This distinction had its origins in the development of a specialized cadre of plantation managers. The members of this managerial hierarchy all came to think of themselves as "planters". They called themselves planters because "planting" was what they did, and some came to regard themselves as planters by "profession". They were not labourers but the managers of the supervisors of labour. On the other hand, the owners of the plantations increasingly distinguished themselves as "proprietors". They were not mere planters but the employers of planter managers, the owners of land and factories, the owners of people.

What choices faced the eighteenth-century proprietor and planter? Almost all members of the class saw the plantation as the most profitable agrarian system available to them and recognized sugar as the most profitable crop. Similarly, they took for granted the system of slavery as the most profitable labour regime. Those who were already proprietors needed to make decisions about how best to deploy the resources they commanded and how best to manage their properties. They also made choices about consumption, most importantly whether they should live in Jamaica or elsewhere. The decisions they made about residence had important consequences for the ways they might manage their plantations. For planters of the managerial class who were not yet proprietors, choices were made between employers and plantations, and between various investment possibilities once they accumulated sufficient capital to have aspirations of themselves becoming proprietors. The managerial class of planters also faced the daily choices that had to be made in fulfilling the demands of their employers, the range of decisions varying with their place in the hierarchy. It was the principal objective of the planters to "manage" the enslaved by means, however brutal, to extract the maximum labour from them for the maximum profit of the proprietor. Many managers came to enjoy the privileges of their position and lived comfortably in their way, contributing to the development of a creole society that had its own local logic and creative vigour.

The enslaved in turn faced daily decisions about how best to cope with the demands of the managers and, even if they were not resident, the proprietors. As workers, the enslaved could deploy various strategies to limit the quantum of labour extracted from them. They could also deploy strategies to exploit the resources of the plantation, and they could choose to rebel, escape or commit suicide. All of these tactics were used by the enslaved from time to time, in various combinations and situations. All of them had their particular hazards and rewards. The enslaved did not merely react to the "treatment" they received from their owners and managers, they also demonstrated agency in their resilience and creative life. The managers had to take account of the behaviour of the enslaved.

The obvious success of the planters of Jamaica in achieving high levels of production, productivity and wealth has not always been acknowledged by historians. Interpretations of the modes of management installed by the planter class are surrounded by a series of seeming paradoxes. On the one hand, the plantation has been characterized as dependent on outmoded systems of coerced labour, most obviously slavery. From this dependence, it has been argued, stemmed a failure to innovate and to allocate resources on rational principles. Alfred D. Chandler Jr, in his classic history of United States business, concludes only that "the southern plantation, although it required some subdivision of labor and some coordination of the activities of the work force, had little impact on the evolution of the management of modern business enterprise".[21] On the other hand, the sugar plantations of the eighteenth century have been seen as practising basic concepts of modern scientific management in the division of labour and specialization of tasks enabled by their large structured workforces, deployed in a coordinated and disciplined manner.[22] Further, the plantation, and particularly the plantation producing sugar, can be viewed as a precursor of the modern industrial factory, based on its scale of capital investment and output, technology, processing functions, and large labour force. This interpretation emphasizes the essential modernity of the plantation in slavery.[23] These ideas have recently been taken up by management studies theorists, some of whom now argue that the long-standing "denial" of the role of slavery and the capitalist plantation by their discipline has impoverished the history of modern management in both theory and practice.[24] Within the context of British Caribbean history, the work of Heather Cateau and Selwyn H. H. Carrington has maintained a strong critical focus on the role of management.[25]

An associated paradox is found in the alleged economic efficiency of slavery as a system of labour. The virtue or moral value of a technology does not, however, arise from its productivity or efficiency. Thus Robert William Fogel argues that slavery was not a morally neutral technology of labour management applied to evil ends but rather "intrinsically evil because its productive efficiency arose directly out of the oppression of its laborers".[26] It is not necessary to establish that slavery was unprofitable to the slave owner in order to condemn slavery as a system of labour. Similarly, slavery may coexist in what may seem an equally paradoxical fashion with concepts of progress, democracy and civilization.[27]

What were the conceptual foundations of "modern management" and how did they relate to the practice of plantation economy? The basic organizing principles were founded on a separation of ownership and management, and the division of labour. The fundamental ideas had to do with the theory and practice of specialization at several levels, from the international to the individual enterprise and the individual worker. Most importantly, special roles were found for the "manager" acting as agent or intermediary between the capitalist entrepreneur and the labour force of an enterprise.[28] The Jamaican sugar economy of the eighteenth century saw the development of these principles in the separation of proprietor (ownership) and planter (management), and in the articulation of a refined managerial hierarchy.

Theoretical approaches to the study of management were largely a product of twentieth-century conceptualizations. Even the idea of "management" was poorly developed down to the end of the nineteenth century and the notion of "executive" action hardly known. A coherent theory of the firm emerged only in the 1930s and the role of transaction costs in determining the firm's scale and internal organizing hierarchy came even later.[29] However, it can be argued that the fundamental tasks of the modern manager are not new but have their roots in early enterprise. Running a successful modern firm depends on the managing of production, marketing, finance and personnel, and dealing with risk and uncertainty in the context of the larger economy. Modern managers seek also to plan and to control performance. Early entrepreneurs and managers were happy when they were able to do all these things. More often than modern managers, however, they generally felt powerless in the face of external forces. Partly, this powerlessness reflected the typically small scale of operation and the inability of the entrepreneur to manipulate the macroeconomy. It also had to do with a general lack of information and measurement that made risk and uncertainty seem overwhelming. The development of theory went hand in hand with information gathering, efforts to measure inputs and outputs, the application of cost accounting, and the engineering of the workplace. Practice and theory benefited dramatically by the development of technologies that speeded up communication and made available vast quantities of data, and by experimentation that enabled the comparative measurement of different systems of working.

How did the planters of Jamaica manage risk and uncertainty and what were the managerial systems they adopted and adapted? They faced uncertainties of output and price, without access to insurance. Vagaries of weather, notably hurricane and storm, as well as pests and diseases, affected the quantity and quality of output. The major export crops, sugar and coffee, had relatively long gestation periods and thus decisions about the crops and areas to be cultivated had to be made far in advance of sale, so that prices could not easily be predicted. The storage of product in hopes of better prices was rarely an option, and producers depended on the marketing expertise of distant agents. Political decisions, beyond the control of the planter class, changed market conditions, and the political activity of the enslaved people on the plantations might disrupt or destroy the productive capacity. The planters of Jamaica operated on a large scale, particularly when they produced sugar, and they took the risks associated with producing a single crop, rather than diversifying output, in order to maximize returns. Other risks were associated with the manufacturing processes that were part of the work of the sugar or coffee plantation, with the hazards of mechanical breakdown and loss of power. When the finished products left the plantation, they faced the hazards of transport on land and sea, only now under insurance, and the vagaries of the market.

Plantation processing required a complex coordination of local and imported inputs and created a range of tasks that could be managed on "factory" lines. As one sugar planter observed in 1783, a West Indian sugar estate "may be properly compared to a manufacture", its profits depending entirely on the knowledge and experience of the manager, "and without these necessary requisition in a manager, it becomes the most unprofitable of all estates, and literally, a sinking-fund".[30] It was the sugar planters who led the way, argues Fogel, in developing "a new industrial labor discipline" that was "at once their greatest technological achievement, the foundation of their economic success, and the ugliest aspect of their system".[31] In Jamaica, more than one-half of the enslaved lived on plantations producing sugar. Equally important, the high rate of absentee-proprietorship that characterized Jamaica after 1750, founded on the profits of sugar and slavery, created the need for a class of intermediary managers without parallel in most of the Americas.[32] It was absenteeism producing a separation fundamental to the rise of modern management that created the foundations of Plantation Jamaica.

This leads to a final paradox. In the case of industrializing Europe and North America, the separation of ownership and management that underpinned the concept of modern management was seen as a positive thing, a rational solution to the distinctive demands of entrepreneurship and executive decision-making. In the case of the Jamaican plantation, on the other hand, separation has often been seen as harmful to the success of enterprise and frequently as an indicator of failure and a drain on resources. Rather than a paradox, the argument may simply be inconsistent and lacking in logic. Why should the Jamaican separation of ownership and management not be seen as an equally profitable, equally efficient solution? It is not a matter of equity, justice or morality. The planters of Jamaica were capitalists operating within the context of a capitalist colonial economy, always on the lookout for ways to increase private profit.

What was the Jamaican proprietor's solution to the problem of management and how did it come to been seen in a negative light? Where exactly was the locus of decision making?[33] To what extent were initiative and choice the monopoly of the metropolitan merchant and absentee-proprietor?

The proprietor's solution was to empower an attorney. By 1750 the "attorney" of Jamaica had emerged as a distinctive managerial type, placed at the head of a hierarchy of managers, supervisors and workers, and with the authority and power to make major business decisions on behalf of the proprietor. The attorney, the central figure in this book, was a colonial creole creation, a unique product of the separation of ownership and management that typified Jamaica between 1750 and 1850. The role was a product of the period of slavery but remained in place at abolition and necessarily provided the framework within which the transition to freedom was worked out. What were the sources of this innovation and how did it affect the profitability of plantations and the growth of the colonial economy of Plantation Jamaica?[34]

Part 1
Managers

Chapter 2

Managerial Hierarchies

How can the emergence of the Jamaican plantation attorney be explained? Most often, historians have seen the attorney as the inevitable if unwanted progeny of absenteeism. Douglas Hall, in a series of critical reflections on absenteeism published in 1964, argued simply, "As time went on and absentee-ownership generally increased, there began to appear in the colonies a class of professional estate-attorneys or managers, some of whom were also planters on their own account." Some of these attorneys, said Hall, "were individuals who, as they gained in knowledge and experience, became recognised as experts in their business". Such men were sought after and, by the middle of the nineteenth century, "jealous of their reputations and justly proud of their acknowledged expertise".[1] In Hall's account, the mechanisms that created the attorney and the chronology of the process remained hazy.

A more complete analysis of the origins of the system was offered by Richard Sheridan, who related attorneyship to the increasing complexity of plantation management. This complexity was not the product of absenteeism but emerged directly from the work of a large-scale sugar plantation. Sheridan presented his argument in the context of a broader discussion of "planters and plantership", arguing that the eighteenth-century sugar planter was "a complex personality; at once landlord, slave owner, farmer, manufacturer, and merchant". The planter, said Sheridan, "owned the land, slaves, and equipment; he supervised the labourers in the cultivation and processing of the sugar-cane; he purchased plantation supplies and consigned the final products to overseas merchants; he arranged for credit and loans".[2] Proof of the complexity of management was found in the publication of guides to plantership in all its elements, beginning in the middle of the eighteenth century and parallel to the flowering of a literature of agricultural improvement in Britain.[3]

The push to sugar monoculture led the planter to consider economies of scale and the composition of his investment in factories, machines, aqueducts and labour. As the workforce expanded, argued Sheridan, "the planter was no longer able to attend to day-to-day training, supervision and correction", and necessarily spent more of his time in "planning and co-ordination, buying and selling", exchanging information and perhaps taking an active role in local politics. It was no longer possible for an individual to efficiently supervise the diverse activities of the sugar estate, even when resident, and it "became necessary to develop a managerial hierarchy, each level of which attained some degree of specialization". In Sheridan's account, however, the managerial hierarchy did not include an attorney so long as the proprietor remained resident. It was permanent long-distance absenteeism that demanded an extensive delegation of authority. The planter no longer could make occasional and unexpected visits to his plantations, and thus lost the power of surveillance. Friends and relatives served as informal monitors but came to be supplanted by formally appointed "quasi-professional attorneys".[4] For Sheridan, then, managerial hierarchy was the inevitable consequence of technological complexity and scale, whereas the system of attorneyship only occurred when this was combined with long-term absenteeism.

Building on the argument of Sheridan, David W. Galenson contends that the "division of responsibility evidently appeared not only as a result of the complexity of managing large sugar plantations, but also as a solution to a severe principal-agent, or monitoring, problem that plagued absentee plantation owners in the seventeenth century". Galenson notes the advantage of having a resident friend, who could keep an eye on the overseer, but contends "the employment of not only a manager but also a resident attorney, who was typically compensated in part by a commission calculated as a percentage of the value of the plantation's exported crops, probably did much more to reduce cheating and shirking by the resident manager or overseer".[5] Once again, the ultimate origin of the attorney is found in absenteeism. In some cases, however, the employment of an attorney as monitor was not the result of a proprietor's choice. For example, the estates of infants, heirs, and the mentally incompetent might all be managed by attorneys, and an attorney might also be imposed by a mortgagee, through the courts, even when the proprietor remained on the plantation.[6] Thus it is possible to argue that the question of accountability existed independent of absentee-proprietorship.

The system of plantation attorneyship in Jamaica also had precedents in trade and governance. Beginning in the 1660s, the flourishing trade and commerce of Jamaica quickly attracted interest from metropolitan merchants, many of whom established "themselves or their representatives" at Port Royal. Michael Pawson and David Buisseret have compiled a table of "grants of powers of attorney" for the period 1664–74, covering sixty-three examples. Some of these grants were for merchants already at Port Royal, while others empowered attorneys sent out from England as factors or to recover particular debts. A smaller proportion originated in Barbados, Boston and Charleston. At Port Royal, the attorney necessarily "enjoyed a very wide liberty of action", with significant consequences for his English partner. Some of the attorneys worked for more than one metropolitan merchant, so that their interests might be diffused or even conflicting. It was these possible consequences that made necessary the formality of the legal relationship between the parties – the signed and sealed letters of attorney – even when they were family or "partners".[7] The later planting attorneys were also sometimes kin but rarely partners. Their relationships were more obviously hierarchical.

Pulling these arguments together, the sources of the system of attorneyship practised in Jamaica seem most likely to be found in complexity, accountability and absenteeism. It was complexity that created managerial hierarchy and the problem of monitoring. It was these demands that shaped the tasks of the attorney and gave him power and control. Without the exigencies of absentee-proprietorship, however, the role and significance of the attorney must have been more limited, less essential.

Absentees

Why did planter-proprietors become absentees? Most thought it a simple and obvious choice. Having struggled to establish their plantations as profitable enterprises, and having wound up the mechanism that would produce regular and reliable income, the British returned without regret to their home places. Jamaica was understood to be an unhealthy environment, lacking culture and opportunities for social advancement. The idea that the island was the proper site for a colony of English settlers was quickly abandoned, overtaken by slavery and the plantation. The home country was an irresistible magnet, with chances for investment, gentrification and aristocratic status. Down to the middle of the nineteenth century, and beyond, there were few people of "British" (English, Welsh, Scottish, Irish) origin who did not share the ambition to "return" to Britain and live British lives enabled by income drawn from their Jamaican properties. The resident planters were seen as failures, late developers or misfits.[8]

Absentees were of different types. First, some were people born in Britain who had migrated to Jamaica, established plantations and other enterprises there, and returned to Britain to live on the profits of those enterprises. Second, there were people of British ancestry born in Jamaica, creoles, who inherited or established plantations and migrated to Britain when their fortunes seemed sufficiently certain. Third, others were people born in Britain who acquired plantations in Jamaica by inheritance, marriage or purchase, but never saw their properties or made only fleeting visits to the island. This last group rarely thought of themselves as absentees. The first and second categories quickly came to the same view, embedding themselves in the English gentry and landscape.

With these components and these ambitions, it was certain absenteeism would continue to grow so long as investment in Jamaica's plantation economy remained profitable. Beginning pragmatically in the 1680s, by the 1740s it was regarded as normal that a planter, having made his fortune, would leave the island with his family and household goods and put his plantations in the hands of agents. By the 1750s the flaunting of fortunes in metropolitan England was engendering hostility from the landed gentry as well as City merchants and Parliament.[9]

How did Jamaica-born creoles who became absentees think of themselves? Many accepted the view that they were "sojourners" or intentional trans-atlantic transients who had simply taken more than one generation to get back to their true home. Even creoles who never became absentees often referred to Britain as "home" and indeed the notion was an encompassing one, parallel to the idea of Britannia as imperial ruler and Britain as the "mother" country.[10] It was a concept that made Britain home even for Britons born in "settler colonies". Absenteeism was not essential to the identification. Rich white Jamaicans of the eighteenth century could readily identify both Jamaica and Britain as "home". They could afford to travel and live in both places and adopted a transnational British-Atlantic culture that appears modern. If they died in Jamaica, some had their bodies shipped to Britain for burial. If they died in Britain, the body might be sent to Jamaica to be buried in a plantation mausoleum.[11]

The growth of absentee-proprietorship in Jamaica is difficult to chart in detail but the broad outlines seem clear enough. Absenteeism was always most common for sugar planters because sugar was the crop that produced the greatest wealth and the best opportunities for long-term financial success. The geographical spread of sugar and settlement continued over a century, however, so the building of fortunes and the potential for absenteeism were not uniform. For example, the late-settled parish of Hanover was said to have no absentees even in 1748 and, overall, resident sugar planters probably remained a majority in the sector down to the middle of the eighteenth century.[12] By 1775 one-third of the sugar estates of Jamaica were owned by absentees and those estates produced 40 per cent of the island's sugar and rum.[13] In 1832, immediately before the abolition of slavery, 54 per cent of the enslaved lived on properties owned by absentees, almost all of them residing outside Jamaica. Of the dominant sugar estates, 81 per cent belonged to non-resident proprietors.[14] John Stewart argued in 1823 that "most of the less opulent proprietors wisely reside in the island on their estates", and indeed they had no choice.[15] Stewart gave no idea, however, where the dividing line was located. Gad Heuman argues that absenteeism declined after 1838, with an increase in the proportion of white women living in the island, and "more absentees were forced to live in Jamaica because of the economic threat which emancipation posed to their survival".[16] On the other hand, the post-slavery period saw extensive abandonment of estates, thus reducing the possibilities of residence.

Enterprises producing crops other than sugar typically had lower levels of absenteeism, because they were less profitable. Coffee emerged as an important export crop in Jamaica only in the 1780s and failed to create major fortunes. According to returns made to the House of Assembly in 1799, only 9 per cent of the 686 "coffee settlements" in the island belonged to absentee-proprietors.[17] On the livestock-producing pens the rate of absenteeism was significantly lower than on sugar properties. Pen-keepers were more often creoles. However, in terms of the enslaved population and output, absentee-ownership was common because many of the bigger pens were owned by (absentee) sugar planters who operated them as elements of interdependent agricultural systems.

Outside of agriculture, the pattern of colonial government provided a parallel model of absenteeism. Many of the most important executive offices were held under patent direct from the Crown, the holders living in Britain and sharing the profits with deputies who performed the actual work in Jamaica. Included among these were the island secretary, surveyor-general and the registrar of the Court of Chancery. All received incomes comparable to those of absentee planters. As early as 1700 an act passed by the Assembly attempted to compel patentees to live in the island but the system persisted into the nineteenth century.[18] Even those officials who normally performed their duties in person sometimes became temporary absentees. For example, a collector of customs for the port of Kingston appointed in 1802 remained in the island only three months, then took leave of absence and contracted a merchant to do the work.[19] Thus the planters had prominent examples before them.

Was the pattern that developed in Jamaica unique? Certainly absenteeism was known in other regions of Plantation America but it rarely rivalled the Jamaican rate. The case that came closest was St Domingue in the boom decades before the Revolution. David Geggus argues that "the extent of absentee proprietorship is unknown and controversial, but in the plains it was probably as great as in the British islands".[20] The Revolution was followed by a dramatic flight, the planters leaving property in the hands of attorneys and managers. St Domingue is generally thought to be an exception, however, with absenteeism otherwise a unique characteristic of the British Caribbean.[21] In Brazil, the sugar planters were "a resident planter class", fundamentally "ruralized" by the eighteenth century. Hardly any of them lived in Europe, though some did live permanently or temporarily in nearby cities. When Brazilian planters owned multiple mills, they employed overseers or agents, but these were uncommon.[22] In the United States, Carter G. Woodson found only sixty-two holdings of more than one hundred slaves belonging to absentees in the census of 1830.[23]

Although it is not possible to prove Orlando Patterson's claim that Jamaica experienced a "degree of absenteeism which was greater than in any other slave colony in the New World", without doubt the level of absenteeism achieved by Jamaica's sugar planters in the later eighteenth century was at the extreme end of the scale.[24] As Richard Pares said, "Other absentee planters were nothing to them."[25] In Britain, their only conspicuously rich rivals were the East India nabobs. The nabobs, however, were generally mere sojourners, at least down to 1850, bringing home the fortunes they had made through tribute, trade and tax, and rarely maintaining enterprises in India.[26]

Apart from the planters and the nabobs, it was Ireland that typified absenteeism for most contemporaries in the British Atlantic. The Irish experience did come closer to the Jamaican pattern. In the middle of the nineteenth century, 46 per cent of "estates" in Ireland had resident landlords and a further 25 per cent belonged to owners who lived elsewhere in Ireland.[27] Jamaica's absenteeism around 1800 was substantially greater. For England, it is generally agreed that absenteeism increased among landowners from the later seventeenth into the early nineteenth century, paralleling the process in the West Indies. J. V. Beckett attributes this increase to the "development of the London season, annual meetings of Parliament, and the growth of the finance market" which drew "country gentlemen to London in larger numbers and for longer periods of time than at any previous period".[28] This was a world in which the absentee planters of Jamaica felt at home, even if their ancestry was Scottish or Irish.

What did Jamaican planters and merchants do when they became absentees? The merchants had the easiest transition, often setting up as metropolitan merchant-factors and continuing to trade plantation produce, shipping and investment. For example, Thomas Hughan described himself in 1808 as "a West India merchant, connected particularly with the island of Jamaica, and have been acquainted with its trade for the last twenty years and upwards". He had lived first in Jamaica, for twelve years, then ten years in London. Similarly, Robert Milligan had been "a West India merchant in London" for twenty-seven years, beginning in 1780, and having for the preceding twelve years been "a merchant at Kingston in Jamaica".[29] The Scots sometimes joined the "Glasgow merchant aristocracy" trading with the colonies and establishing their own "interest". Others established merchant houses in Bristol and Liverpool, but the great magnet was London.[30]

Some absentee planters saw themselves as the beneficiaries of "aristocratic capitalism" and settled down to a life of sybaritic idleness, occasionally cultured, often vulgar. They repatriated the wealth generated in the West Indies and wasted it. Many brought elements of slave society with them, most obviously in the enslaved people carried to Britain to serve as household domestics. Others invested profitably in British industries, giving a direct impetus to the Industrial Revolution.

Some absentees played politics. They were commonly equated with the political lobby group known as the "West India interest" or the "sugar interest". In eighteenth- and nineteenth-century British politics, at least down to the Reform Bill of 1832, interest groups had a vital role in the promotion of particular economic agendas. They represented both domestic and colonial communities, the best known being the landed interest, the East India interest and the West India interest. Between 1730 and the American Revolution, at least seventy "West Indians" had seats in the House of Commons, compared to only five from the North American colonies. Fifty of these West Indians were absentee-proprietors, the rest merchants, about half of them connected with Jamaica.[31]

The West India interest was, however, more broadly based than its absentee-planter membership. Many absentees joined the landed gentry and thus came to have both conflicting interests and supportive kin. The West India interest included also British merchants, located in London and the outports, whose business was directed at the West Indian colonies. Merchants and planters advocated their interests directly as members of Parliament. From 1775, the separate clubs and societies of planters and merchants were combined in the Committee of West India Planters and Merchants, which eventually became the West India Committee. Further, beginning in the 1730s, the resident proprietors themselves appointed official "colonial agents" to represent their causes to the British Parliament, government and Crown.[32]

Although the West India interest was not always united in its views, with occasional conflict between colonies and groups of colonies, between merchant and planter, and between absentee and resident, it did in its various transformations constitute a powerful influence. Andrew Jackson O'Shaughnessy has called it "the most powerful colonial lobby in London" around the time of the American Revolution.[33] The interest's numbers grew and its representation in Parliament did not peak until 1826, though its influence was by then much reduced. By the early nineteenth century, the balance of empire had shifted to the east, and the West India and East India interests were often rivals for imperial favours. Alongside this rivalry, both nabob and absentee planter were cast as vicious exploiters, and British public opinion increasingly turned against them.[34]

The existence of the West India interest did not depend completely on absenteeism but certainly much of its power derived from the presence in Britain of leading members of the planter class. The success of the interest in defending the wealth of that class was demonstrated most clearly in the long period of monopoly enjoyed in the British market and the military and naval defence of the islands. The West Indian colonies were given favoured treatment, over other British colonies as well as over foreign interests.

Through their political activism the absentee planters contributed to the defence of the system of sugar and slavery in ways they could never have achieved had they lived permanently in the colonies. The benefits they gained enabled them to reduce their costs and increase their income.[35] The sugar planters of Jamaica were vastly more wealthy than their North American colonial counterparts, and their personal fortunes compared strongly even with those of the British landed aristocracy.[36]

Other British colonists, notably the North Americans, were jealous of the success of the West Indians. In spite of the Jamaican colonists' long fight for political rights within the imperial system, absentee planters and merchants saw their interests as separate from those of the North Americans. They recognized economic interdependence but did not unite in opposition to the Stamp Act or in the larger constitutional claims made by the North Americans.[37] Supporting the metropolitan, imperial government, even in its struggle with fellow colonists, was in the long-term interest of both absentee and resident West Indian planters, most believed, even though their internal divisions were often as great as their conflict with other interest groups.

Absenteeism

The success of the Jamaican planters in achieving a high rate of absenteeism, with all its consequences, was surrounded by a vigorous critique. The absentee-proprietors' managerial agents, the attorneys, were drawn into this dialogue, and declared guilty by association. One arm of the critique came from government, another from the planters themselves. In the long run, the contemporary debate spilled over into the modern historiography, giving absenteeism a central role in determining the trajectory of social and economic development.

By the early eighteenth century, Jamaica's governors were complaining that a lack of potential candidates, caused by absenteeism, made representative government difficult. From 1700 the Assembly legislated to increase the size of the white population of the island but without effect. The Deficiency Act of 1718 imposed fines on planters who failed to have the required proportion of whites to enslaved on their properties, and sought to demand a higher ratio from absentee-proprietors (1:24) than from residents (1:30). In 1735 the rate was increased to 1:20 for absentees. The tax came to be seen as a punishment for non-residence. In 1748, however, the absentee interest in Britain was powerful enough to have the special tax disallowed as inequitable.[38] The Reverend George Wilson Bridges, writing in 1828, argued that "the patient colonists" sought only to levy "a fair and equitable tax upon the absentees, who enjoy the fruits of their land without participating in its troubles" and did so simply to get relief from the imposition of "intolerable taxes" by Britain.[39]

Edward Long, himself no more than a part-time resident, complained in 1774 that by the middle of the eighteenth century defaults under the deficiency laws came to be seen merely as a regular revenue. The consequent decline of white indentured servitude went together with an increased migration of proprietors to Britain and North America and a further depression of the demand for a secondary population of whites as artificers and shopkeepers, said Long. Instead of importing tutors, the children of planters were sent to England and Scotland for schooling, only a proportion returning to Jamaica. Between 1753 and 1776 at least fifty-three Jamaicans were schooled at Eton, more than twice the number from the whole of the North American colonies. All of this, argued Long, was loss to the "trade, navigation, and consumption of manufactures" not only in Jamaica but also in Britain, and he thought it "certain, that Great-Britain gains much more from the planter who lives in Jamaica, and disperses his income there, than she can possibly gain if he spends it in Great-Britain". Long also related his critique to plantation management, saying, "The residence of the planter necessarily occasioned a better attention to the management of his estate, the cultivation of more land, the increase of produce, and greater security of property in general." Further, he said, offering a local education would have "insured the attachment of the children to their native spot, and led them into an early knowledge of the planting business, and of the means by which their estates, when they should come to the enjoyment of them, might be preserved and improved".[40]

A paradox underlying this argument of Long was that he painted a generally negative picture of the (white) creole man and woman. Although he praised the creoles for their generosity, Long found them "possessed with a degree of supineness and indolence in their affairs, which renders them bad economists, and too frequently hurts their fortune and family". They were "addicted to expensive living, costly entertainments, dress, and equipage". If only the creoles had been "more abstemious in these respects, and more attentive to good husbandry on their plantations", wrote Long, "there are few who would not amass considerable fortunes, and render their posterity opulent". The problem was that they overextended their estates and sunk into debt.[41] Long's disdain was shared by contemporaries such as William Beckford, who left Jamaica in 1786 and spoke from the debtor's standpoint. He described the West Indian as indolent in mind and body, hot tempered, "desultory in action" and often a spendthrift. "For the interested bustles of life, for that industry that begets wealth, and that circumspection that knows how to keep it," wrote Beckford, "there is not a character in the world less adapted than a West-Indian."[42] However, it was these same people who would necessarily constitute the resident planter class, with all its supposed advantages of culture and managerial efficiency. Perhaps Beckford and Long supposed that those who had become absentees were somehow superior as a class but, brought back to Jamaica, surely a generation or two would have re-made them all in the creole mould. A much more fundamental transformation of society seemed essential – not merely the return of the absentees.

The argument that absentee ownership of assets and enterprises was deleterious to the "home" economy was not confined to critiques of the West Indian planter class. Ireland was commonly seen by the British as the linchpin of arguments for the negative impact of absenteeism and contemporaries often saw the "evil" of absenteeism as peculiarly Irish. From 1715 there had been an "absentee tax" on offices and pensions on the Irish establishment. The landlords of estates, having left to reside in England, collected rents in the 1770s of about six hundred thousand pounds per annum, or one-eighth of the total rental of Ireland. An abortive proposal made in 1773 for the taxing of these landowners was called by contemporaries the "absentee tax".[43] Absenteeism was widely resented in Ireland and the absentees themselves contributed to the critique, frequently extolling the advantages of residence, pointing in particular to the hazards of depending on agents. Maria Edgeworth's novel *The Absentee,* published in 1812, presented a political critique of absenteeism and Anglo-Irish relations, in which Edmund Burke appeared as the good agent of the absentee landlord.[44]

By the 1820s, however, a strong counter-argument had emerged in political economy, directed particularly at showing that absenteeism was not the cause of Irish distress. For example, J. R. McCulloch's 1825 "Essay showing the Erroneousness of the Prevailing Opinions in regard to Absenteeism" sought to prove that the level of demand for Irish commodities was unaffected by the place of residence of the landlords and that tenants were in fact better off under absentee-proprietors. Opposing the view advanced by Edward Long in relation to Jamaica, that because absentees spent their income in another country they deprived workers of employment at home, McCulloch applied free trade principles to conclude that "gentlemen who consume nothing in their families but what is brought from abroad, are quite as good, as useful, and as meritorious subjects, as they would be did they consume nothing but what is produced at home". As to productivity, McCulloch argued that "the estates of absentee proprietors . . . are better managed, and are occupied by a richer and better class of tenants, than those belonging to residents". Indeed, the absentee living in England had the advantage of being able to observe the superior systems of agricultural improvement employed there and the more advanced systems of tenancy and rents, rather than being bound by tradition. Later, in the 1850s, McCulloch recalled that his arguments had been met by a "loud burst of reprobation" but believed they were really just "a very obvious application of those free-trade principles which have since happily gained the ascendant".[45] The victory was not as easy as McCulloch thought it, however, and the belief that absenteeism was prejudicial to the prosperity and moral state of a country, particularly Ireland, long remained vigorous.[46]

Herman Merivale, in his Oxford Lectures on political economy delivered in 1839–41, argued that sugar and slavery had created an "unwholesome state of society" in Jamaica, because economies of scale concentrated ownership and inhibited the development of white settlement. The absenteeism that followed he regarded as "in some respects still worse". However, Merivale felt a pride that the English, peculiarly, developed a distaste for the "deep-rooted hard-heartedness and profligacy" of life in the slave colonies. Thus, he thought the wealthy planters became absentees for reasons that were at least partly moral. They might have had "no objection to enjoy the wealth derived from so impure a source", he conceded, but in spite of this inconsistency found it "not therefore altogether to be regretted that the race of Englishmen has not thriven and multiplied in our West Indian colonies".[47] This, somewhat ambiguously, made the British superior to the Spanish and French who lived comfortably amongst the enslaved.

Palgrave's *Dictionary of Political Economy,* first published in the 1890s, defined the "absentee" as a landed proprietor living away from his estate or country or, more generally, "any unproductive consumer who lives out of the country from which he derives his income". Examples mentioned were from Ireland, India and France. None came from the West Indies. In terms of assessing the impact of absenteeism, Palgrave sought "a just mean between two extremes – the popular fallacy and the paradox of McCulloch", and followed Nassau Senior in concluding that "in general the presence of men of large fortune is morally detrimental, and that of men of moderate fortune morally beneficial, to their immediate neighbourhood".[48] Thorstein Veblen's *Absentee Ownership* of 1923 made absenteeism the controlling factor in modern civilization, causing the wasteful use of industrial resources and the exploitation of labour. He favoured its abolition and the giving back of industry to the workers.[49]

It is an irony that by the end of the twentieth century "absenteeism" had come to mean primarily the failure of employees to turn up to work. It became a failure of labour rather than capital, punishable by sacking. In part, this shift reflected the global decline in agrarian landlordism, both absentee and resident, which occurred largely as a result of land reform programmes of the twentieth century. The critique of absentee entrepreneurship became engrossed in larger debates over globalization and the role of multinational corporations, in which modern management created an extreme separation between capital and labour. The takeover of local enterprise by foreign corporate capital became commonplace, shareholder interests diffused, and the family firm increasingly distanced from the cutting edge of the modern economy. The battle for resident proprietorship was lost, and the terms and terminology of the debate shifted radically away from the arguments that had for centuries surrounded absenteeism. Further, by the late twentieth century, condemnation of landlordism and latifundia became complicated, with these institutions increasingly seen as rational responses to economic backwardness rather than its cause.[50]

The notion of the worker as "absentee" had no place in eighteenth-century thought. Enslaved workers who left their masters for short or longer periods were hardly ever called absentees.[51] Rather, slave owners termed them "runaways" or "maroons" and modern historians have applied the systemic label "marronage" to behaviour now understood as resistance to the system of oppression. Few modern historians of the Caribbean have followed the twentieth-century shift, applying "absenteeism" to workers rather than landowners. An exception is Mary Turner, who has referred to enslaved people using "absenteeism" in negotiating improved work conditions with plantation managers. Her application of the term is part of a larger modernizing approach, seeing the enslaved also employing labour-relations tactics such as "appeals for mediation, and . . . collective bargaining that involved strike action".[52]

The modern historiography of the Caribbean, emerging in the early twentieth century, reflected its context in attributing to absentee-proprietorship a powerful negative role in economic and social development. The critique can be identified first in the work of the American historian Frank Wesley Pitman. Writing in 1917, he saw "the general absence from their estates of the highest class of planters" as the "feature of West India society that accentuated all the evils of a community resting on slavery". The absence of this class "left the islands impoverished for want of talent and leadership in public life, and of humane, conscientious, and responsible direction in private industry". On the plantations themselves, argued Pitman, the absence of proprietors "did much to promote that careless, cruel, and extravagant management . . . that became so frequent a subject of comment toward the middle of the eighteenth century". Pitman believed that life was harder for the enslaved under agents and overseers, leading to rebellion. Jamaica became a "wilderness of materialism". In 1927 Pitman published a paper dedicated to the topic: "The West Indian Absentee Planter as a British Colonial Type".[53] His argument was now more comparative but followed closely the earlier critique.

Lowell Joseph Ragatz, the other American pioneer historian of the West Indies, published his own special paper on the subject in 1931, "Absentee Landlordism in the British Caribbean, 1750–1833", without citing Pitman's contribution. Ragatz saw absenteeism as "an outstanding characteristic of British West Indian agriculture during the second half of the eighteenth century and the early nineteenth". Like Pitman, he thought the outcome "deplorable in the extreme", pointing particularly to the effects absenteeism had on colonial government, "the debasement of island society, and the passing of local pride and feeling". Ragatz also found absenteeism responsible for failure in the upkeep of roads, bridges and public buildings.[54]

The supposed ill effects of absenteeism began with the absentee-proprietor. The owner's non-residence was, however, simply an absence, with the alternative of residence having imponderable implications and outcomes. The other side of the coin was the presence of the attorney, the effective face of absenteeism, the manager with practical power. In the sphere of plantation economy, Ragatz attributed the worst effects of absenteeism to the self-interest of the attorneys and their lack of agricultural knowledge. The attorneys were themselves secondary absentees, he argued, rarely residing on the properties, even when they were planters in their own right. As a result, said Ragatz, "the overseers, men of low station and little learning, were in actual control". Management was extravagant, since "no one whose capital was at stake" was responsible for decisions and there was no concern for economy in the purchase of supplies. Longer term improvements were ignored, the owner depending on "a regular and steady income" rather than guarding his capital. "Buildings were allowed to fall into ruins," said Ragatz, "fields were tilled until exhausted and then left to grow up in weeds; properties bore the ungenteel signs of general neglect." These attitudes were exaggerated among the attorneys and overseers, who sought to force output and treat slaves harshly. There was no reason for them to be innovative, argued Ragatz, "all change was scoffed at while time-hallowed custom was obdurately followed".[55]

The broad outlines of the critique developed by Pitman and Ragatz proved appealing and persisted in much of the historical writing that followed. Thus Eric Williams in *Capitalism and Slavery* declared "absentee landlordism . . . the curse of the Caribbean". He saw no need to provide evidence for his broad condemnation that "plantations were left to be mismanaged by overseers and attorneys".[56] Richard Pares, in his *Merchants and Planters* of 1960, thought the effects of absenteeism were "in many ways fatal", encouraging a broad neglect of the future for the present, an attitude that ate into the plantation's profits. With proprietor and attorney each seeking to keep up a "princely establishment", absenteeism was a common cause of debt.[57]

Alongside the continuing critique of absenteeism, a questioning began to emerge. This questioning was largely the work of the Jamaican historian Douglas Hall and his paper of 1964, "Absentee-Proprietorship in the British West Indies, to about 1850". Hall claimed no more than a strict agnosticism, concluding that the matter was not cut and dried, that many exceptions and variations must have operated, and that management by an agent was not inevitably inferior to that of a resident proprietor. He did not find in favour of absenteeism and the system of attorneys but argued for further research and a recognition of the multiple variables involved. Although Hall's argument discomforted the traditional interpretation, it failed to dislodge it.

Little of the detailed research he thought essential to advancing the argument was undertaken. His critique was taken on board by some scholars but otherwise summarily dismissed or even ignored.[58]

In 1967 Orlando Patterson restated the basic ideas of Pitman and Ragatz, calling absenteeism the "basic and dominating element of Jamaican slave society", and "the root of all the evils of the system". It drained the island of potential leaders, undermined the development of education, led to the breakdown of religion, morality and the family, and contributed to the frequency of slave revolts, but, argued Patterson, "perhaps the most disastrous consequences of absenteeism were to be found in the gross mismanagement of the economic affairs of the island".[59] Brathwaite's alternative interpretation of Jamaican creole society, published in 1971, sailed much closer to Hall's critique. Brathwaite believed it was "very much to be doubted" that had the planters been residents rather than "handing their properties over to the clumsy mercies of attorneys and overseers, things would have been more efficient, more humane, certainly different".[60] Sheridan too, in 1971, though without mentioning Hall's article, implicitly accepted the caution against generalization and concluded that "not all absentees were the spendthrifts and idlers whose fictional counterparts populated the stage at Drury Lane when 'The West Indian' and 'The School for Scandal' were played".[61] In 2004 the debate was revived by Trevor Burnard, who effectively took up the challenge laid down by Hall forty years earlier and found that absenteeism was not uniformly socially and politically deleterious. Burnard preferred to "see white Jamaicans in the eighteenth century as genuinely trans-Atlantic people, connected to both Britain and Jamaica but not fully part of either polity".[62]

Interpretations of absenteeism elsewhere in the Caribbean have followed a similar path. Thus David Geggus in 1982, writing of St Domingue, argued that on the plains where sugar dominated, absenteeism "was responsible for draining away profits better spent in the colony", and that in the 1780s "absenteeism sapped the fibre of colonial society, increasing the damage done by difficult communications, a paucity of women, and a materialistic outlook". On the other hand, Geggus saw absenteeism creating a "trusteeship" that inducted merchants and lawyers into the plantocracy and thus proved "an integrative influence".[63] Seymour Drescher claimed that "France's premier colony of St Domingue had immense absentee holdings, yet it was by no means thought to be less efficient than the more 'resident' French islands of Martinique and Guadeloupe".[64]

Questioning of the negative interpretation of absenteeism has occurred also in the literature of Britain, beginning in the 1970s, and raised many of the points outlined by Hall for Jamaica. Occasionally, it is now argued, absenteeism resulted in the introduction of improved accounting methods, the absentees developing their own theoretical models, and ultimately increased profits. Absentees were not all conservative and many led the way in technological and investment innovation. More broadly, it can be argued that England's agricultural development occurred alongside the growth in absenteeism, from the later seventeenth century, suggesting the effect was not all negative.[65] Similarly, A. P. W. Malcolmson has argued that the root cause of Irish absenteeism was not so much a desire to leave behind the life of the provinces "but the fact that the landlords, particularly great landlords, married heiresses with estates remote from their own, and were inhibited by the principle of primogeniture from settling those estates on younger sons who might have lived on them". Aristocratic life of the eighteenth century was "peripatetic" and landowners who spent perhaps six months every two years on their Irish estates did not think of themselves as "absentees". Further, says Malcolmson, discussion "is bedevilled by the assumption that absenteeism implies improvidence and neglect".[66] All of these are points equally applicable to the absentee-proprietors of Jamaica.

Managerial Alternatives

What alternatives were available to the planter who chose to become an absentee? One option was to enter a partnership with an equal investor, leaving the partner to run the plantation. Partnerships had been used in the seventeenth century to build up the capital of an estate but these were mostly between a planter and a merchant, the planter acting as the resident agricultural manager, and the merchant supplying capital and marketing skills. Once the planter became an absentee, it was more difficult to carry on the enterprise as a partnership, and as absenteeism increased it became difficult to find a person to purchase the planter's share. Any successful planter was himself likely to wish to leave. By 1750 partnerships based on the residence of one or more of the partners were rarely viable, though joint ownership was common enough.[67]

Another alternative was to rent out the plantation. Most potential absentees regarded this as inferior even to partnership, knowing that tenancy almost inevitably led to disagreements over every aspect of management, and conflict over the distribution of profits and the need for investment. Here the problem was not simply that of finding a competent and honest tenant capable of running a plantation, one who did not himself wish to become absentee, but of keeping control of the estate's accounts and produce in what was an unequal relationship.

A third solution was to sell. Once again, the potential seller had to find an investor willing to purchase at a price high enough to justify losing the income stream built up by the planter. By 1750 most people possessed of such capital were either already absentees or wished to become so. Thus the purchaser was likely to face the same questions of management as the seller.[68] On balance, the planter who wished to become absentee calculated that he had most to gain by retaining his estate and operating an alternative mode of management. Whatever style of management he chose to operate at a distance had its risks and uncertainties.

How did the managerial possibilities open to the absentee differ from those facing the resident? For various reasons, even a resident proprietor might choose not to deal with the day-to-day running of his plantation, leaving the task to a hierarchy of supervisors. Samuel Gooding Barrett, who lived in Jamaica from 1838 to 1841, observed that there were resident proprietors who took "no active management of those estates".[69] As Douglas Hall pointed out in his questioning of the traditional critique of absenteeism, the resident might feel or actually be incompetent, or simply wish to maintain a distance and enjoy the fruits of his investment. Jamaica was not considered a healthy place for white people and many residents chose to protect themselves from weather and other hazards while at the same time living a life of indulgence, perhaps dissipation.

What of the resident who owned more than one property? Was he a better manager than an absentee? In 1842 Hinton Spalding, calling himself a "resident proprietor", said he owned four coffee plantations and a "breeding-pen or farm", spread from Manchester to St George. "I had the management of them all as the superintending manager", said Spalding, but he resided on a plantation in St George. Barrett owned four sugar estates and two pens, and lived on one of the pens. Scattered properties might belong to a merchant-factor, the merchant permanently resident in Kingston and depending on attorneys to manage his estates, while he himself managed other properties.[70]

Who were the people, other than the proprietor, who could be expected to manage and supervise? By the early eighteenth century, a refined hierarchy had been worked out and existed on any large sugar plantation (Figure 2.1). There was first of all the overseer, a man with general responsibility for the everyday planning and execution of productive activity. The proprietor might in theory play the part of the overseer, but to be effective the role demanded constant presence on the property, to ensure surveillance of the other white employees and of enslaved and indentured workers. The proprietor wanted to be able to be away from the plantation for extended periods, to visit other planters in their great houses, to go to town and to attend the House of Assembly, for example. Thus, by 1750 even a resident proprietor was likely to employ an overseer.

The lower ranks of the supervisory hierarchy, whether free or enslaved, were unlikely to yield people the proprietor might consider potential managers in his long-term absence. Certainly there were occasional reports of the enslaved keeping plantations running efficiently in the absence of their masters and the enslaved possessed extensive knowledge of the productive process. Thus Augustus Hardin Beaumont claimed in 1836 that in practice the overseers knew little of their plantations, that the effective management

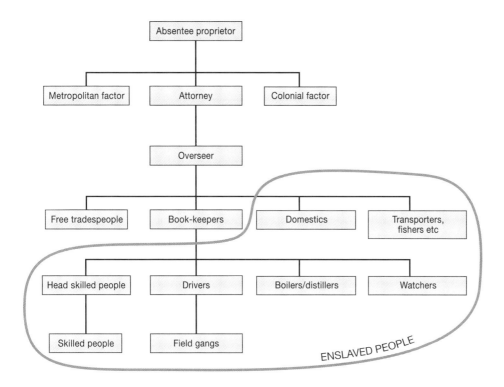

Figure 2.1 Plantation management hierarchy

was really in the hands of the black headmen, and that he knew "estates managed for weeks together entirely by the blacks, and very well managed".[71] The fictional Marly said the planter might remain a resident, rather than becoming an absentee, because he "would sooner entrust his estate to a negro than to an attorney" and had "a most decided hatred and antipathy to every sort of attornies".[72] Few of the enslaved were literate, however, and few had the knowledge of marketing and financial networks necessary to the enterprise, even if doing so had any attraction. Thus the planter who chose to be an absentee had to employ an individual to manage these matters of business, with the time and knowledge to deal with the many parts of what was a complex transnational enterprise. The person so employed was the attorney.

Would the system of attorneyship have emerged in the management of Jamaica's sugar estates if there had been no absentee ownership? If it is assumed that everything else remained the same – that the value and scale of the estates, and the concentration of ownership of geographically scattered properties had been as it was in 1750 or 1800 – something like attorneyship seems certain to have been essential. If the plantation economy had been less complex, in the manner argued by Sheridan, attorneys would have been less necessary. In this case, the proprietors would have been less wealthy, too, and unworried by principal-agent accounting problems. Complexity came before absenteeism, as a feature of Jamaica's sugar plantation economy, so must be attributed the primary role in the origins of the system of attorneys. If the proprietors had all been resident, the system would have been ordered differently, probably giving a larger role to the colonial merchant. There is no doubt that absenteeism helped make management by attorney the dominant element in the hierarchy. However, the system of attorneys was not the inevitable creation of absenteeism. Rather, attorneyship was the managerial technology that made successful (profitable) absenteeism possible. The managerial hierarchy had to be created first.

Terminologies

The *Dictionary of Jamaican English* edited by F. G. Cassidy and R. B. Le Page, first published in 1967, contains a substantial entry on the attorney, defining him as "one who manages a property for an absentee owner". The earliest citation offered by Cassidy and Le Page is from Long's *History* of 1774, occurring not in his chapter on agriculture but in the preceding general description of the island, in the section concerned with population. There, Long decried the relative decline of the white population of Jamaica, attributing it to growing absentee-proprietorship rather than a preference for the employment of enslaved people. The absentees' estates "were kept ill-provided with white servants, and the management resigned to one man, who in many cases acted in several attorneyships, and so became the only representative on the spot of six or eight different proprietors residing in Great-Britain". These estates, said Long, were "left without a due super-intendency, by the practice of employing one attorney to take the management of several different and distant properties".[73]

The Jamaican use of "attorney" was not unique. Equivalents can be found in the anglophone West Indian world. Contemporaries in the Leeward Islands did occasionally refer explicitly to attorneys but without giving them a large part in the system or discussing in any detail their functions. Sheridan, for example, claimed Dr Walter Tullideph acted as "an attorney for several absentee planters" in Antigua between 1739 and 1758, performing duties similar to those of the Jamaican attorney.[74] Goveia, describing the Leeward Islands at the end of the eighteenth century, indicated a hierarchy from absentee-proprietor to attorney, manager and overseer. In the early nineteenth century, the Demerara plantations of John Gladstone were said to be managed by an "attorney".[75] These historians' accounts seem, however, to be modelled on the Jamaican terminology. The "attorney" is absent from Richard Allsopp's 1996 *Dictionary of Caribbean English Usage*.

Unlike attorney, "overseer" had broad currency in the English-speaking regions of Plantation America. Generally, the overseer was the principal manager of a plantation, answering immediately to the owner whether resident or absentee. In Jamaica, the overseer lived on the plantation and, normally, had charge of just one property. J. B. Moreton, in 1790, said, "He who is chief in the superintendency of a plantation in Jamaica, is called an overseer; and in the Windward Islands [meaning all the islands to windward, including the Leeward Islands], a manager."[76] Similarly, in 1842 the Jamaican attorney Thomas McCornock stated, "The person who is called a manager in the Windward Islands, is an overseer in Jamaica."[77] Douglas Hall, however, claimed that "in other islands" the equivalent of the Jamaican absentee's attorney was usually called a "manager".[78] Allsopp's dictionary defines "overseer" as the general term for "a man who superintends several gangs of field labourers on a sugar-plantation".

In Jamaica, "overseer" became "obisha" by the late eighteenth century and "busha" by the early nineteenth. In modern Jamaica, busha survives as a form of address, indicating genial respect or serving to undermine an overbearing manner. "Master" and "massa" are also used, as are "mistress" and "missis", as friendly ways of recognizing equals, particularly those sharing a common adversity.

The antebellum South had a truncated management hierarchy. On the typical smallholding, where the proprietor was resident, the employment of an "overseer" depended on the wealth and status of the owner. The overseer, says William K. Scarborough, "was often little more than a glorified driver, charged with carrying out routine duties under the watchful eye of his employer". Outside the sugar zone, the overseer was generally the sole white employee on a Southern plantation. The only person other than the proprietor who might stand above the overseer was the "steward", a term derived from the English model, identifying the rough equivalent of the Jamaican attorney. According to Scarborough, the steward was "a person usually charged with the general oversight of two or more plantations owned by the same planter". Some of these stewards were "men who earned their livelihood serving as agents for members of the planter community", while others were "relatives or friends who performed a like service for absentee proprietors".[79] Another indicator of the persistence of English terminologies was the early use of "bailiff" to identify the overseer of a Southern plantation. The Southern steward was generally a salaried employee, well educated, behaving in a gentlemanly fashion and enjoying entry to respectable society. These were qualities rarely claimed for overseers but mirrored in the English steward of a great estate. The steward earned roughly twice as much as an overseer.[80]

A further anomalous linguistic transformation found on Jamaican plantations was the use of "book-keeper" to mean any (white) man employed as a supervisor answering to the overseer. As Beckford put it in 1788, "book-keepers are in subordinate command to the overseers", active in field and factory but having little to do with the keeping of books. Indeed, said

Beckford, many book-keepers were "so little deserving the name they bear, that so far from being able to calculate accounts they cannot many of them even read". Peter Marsden, also in 1788, called them "under-overseers". Marly was employed as "under book-keeper". Moreton explained that in Jamaica, "the overseer's deputies are called book-keepers; and in the Windward Islands overseer's or Negro-drivers".[81] In Jamaica, down to the middle of the eighteenth century, white men were sometimes referred to as "drivers" but this usage came to be replaced by "book-keeper". The "driver" and "driveress" were the people who worked below the book-keepers, on the bottom rung of the supervisory ladder. During slavery, the driver was almost always an enslaved person.[82]

Looking for the equivalents of the Jamaican "attorney" and "overseer" in the French and Spanish colonies is hazardous, falling foul of problems of translation. In St Domingue, before the Revolution, absentees were sometimes represented by a *procureur* ("attorney-at-law") who worked by commission and lived in town. Under the *procureur* was the *gérant* ("manager") who lived on the plantation and did the work of the Jamaican overseer. He supervised one or two *économes-surveillants* ("overseers") who were initiated into the plantation regime like the book-keepers of Jamaica. Most of these men were white. At first the *commandeurs* ("drivers") were also white but they soon came to be replaced by enslaved blacks, as in Jamaica.[83] In comparing Jamaica and St Domingue, the major confusion is with the "overseer", whose task in Jamaica was managing rather than overseeing, resulting in occasional references to "overlookers" rather than book-keepers. The usage of St Domingue was close to that of the eastern Caribbean.

The managerial and social hierarchy was paralleled by a hierarchy of punishment that determined who punished whom, how, when and why. Failures to perform, to meet the obligations of the system, were punished in different ways at different points on the ladder. Enslaved field workers, labouring slowly or without energy, might receive corporal punishment while at their tasks, feeling the lash of the driver. In some cases, this punishment while at work was ordered by the book-keeper or overseer. Greater failures, such as theft and marronage, might be punished by more formal floggings performed by the driver under the supervision of the overseer or public floggings and executions sanctioned by the colonial state. In turn, drivers might be punished on estates, flogged by other drivers under the eye of the overseer. White people, however, seem rarely to have suffered corporal punishment on plantations, whatever their failures. For the book-keeper, dismissal on short notice and being made to leave the plantation on foot was disgrace enough. The same applied to the overseer, though he generally owned a horse or mule so could leave with dignity.[84] The overseer was the lowest level of the hierarchy to concern the attorney. The planter-proprietor could dismiss attorney and merchant-factor but their corporal punishment or imprisonment was a matter for the state. Hangman's noose and gaol awaited people at all levels of the hierarchy but their rights in court differed substantially, and the kinds of crimes they might commit varied according to status and role in the system of labour, management and finance. Even proprietors could end up in a debtors' prison.

What was the origin of this Jamaican terminology for the managerial hierarchy of the plantation? An obvious source might be the estate systems of England, Scotland and Ireland, and other sugar regions of Plantation America. In seventeenth-century England, the manorial "lord" of a tenanted estate employed a "steward" to act as "constable", keep the courts, audit accounts and receive rents collected by a "bailiff". On very large estates, there might be a "receiver-general" receiving rent money from several "receivers" each responsible for a different part of the property, and the owner might have an "agent" in London. Between the lord and the receiver-general there was sometimes a "commissioner" drawn from the gentry. As English estate management became professionalized, in the eighteenth century, land "agents" and land "surveyors" were increasingly able to sell their advice and skills and might be employed on a permanent basis.[85]

Around 1750, argues Beckett, English practice was variable. The "model structure consisted of a single full-time steward or agent responsible for all the land in a geographically compact area, and with authority over subordinate officials". Where a landowner had scattered holdings, he might employ a chief agent or "auditor" with responsibility for the local agents on each holding. The auditor was often the family's solicitor, based in London. Landowners who could not afford a full-time steward but were absent from their estates for long periods sometimes employed a tenant farmer in the role or used an attorney.[86] According to Christopher Clay, professional agents were rare and had little impact before 1750, but "the rise of the professional steward, well educated, with a considerable knowledge not only of agricultural techniques, but also of surveying, land law, and accounting, undoubtedly improved the quality of management on estates large enough to justify his employment".[87]

In 1803 R. C. Dallas declared that the Jamaican "attorney of estates" was an "agent", and believed that "the duties annexed to his office are so similar to those of a steward in England, that were it not for the dissimilarity of executing them, and the dignity attendant on the former, I should pronounce them one and the same. But as this colonial stewardship is the surest road to imperial fortune, men of property and distinguished situation push eagerly for it."[88] This was, however, a usage that failed to achieve acceptance and other commentators disputed the correspondence of the duties of attorney and steward, seeing the domain of the attorney as more extensive and complex. The Jamaican attorney had no real rivals, whereas the British scene cast up more alternatives.

At the end of the eighteenth century, according to F. M. L. Thompson, "in terms of personal qualifications and status the steward who was in any sense a professional land agent worked in a field whose possession he was still disputing with others, principally attorneys and farmers, to whom estate management was a secondary occupation".[89] Beckett argues that the eighteenth century saw "the rise of the lawyer-steward", while "the nineteenth saw his replacement by the full-time land agent".[90] In the nineteenth century, writes Eric Richards, the land agent on a large estate presided over "a bureaucracy of bailiffs, stewards, ground officers, clerks, mineral managers and sub-agents of all sorts". The ranks might be extensively ramified, from drainage superintendent to clerk of works, head cashier and head gardener. The general tendency was for the "land agent" to replace the "steward".[91]

In Scotland, the great landlords of the eighteenth century rarely employed a man in the role of the English "land steward" but rather used a local part-time "factor" or "chamberlain" who made remittances to an urban "law-agent" for auditing or to a "general receiver" or "commissioner". From 1750 professional accountants were generally employed to conduct audits. More important, from about 1740 to 1810, Scottish landowners employed a substantial number of "land surveyors" who were directly responsible for the planning of a new land economy and the improvement of land management techniques.[92]

In Ireland, where absenteeism was rife, estate management was placed in the hands of "agents" and where a proprietor held scattered holdings one of these acted also as "chief agent". Many of these were recruited from personal friends, local solicitors (attorneys) and retired army officers, some of whom had served in the West Indies. Trust was a more important quality than any professional qualification. Malcolmson argues this resulted in the practice of employing as agents "generation after generation of a local family of some substance and social respectability".[93] Some landlords employed a full-time valuer, to fix rents, and a land surveyor. Bailiffs and clerks filled the lower ranks. On the largest estates, argues W. A. Maguire, "a centralized, departmentalized system of administration" emerged.[94]

This rapid survey of the terminologies of estate management employed in contemporary Britain offers little to explain the system developed in Jamaica. The plantation attorney of Jamaica seems truly to emerge as an original managerial type, performing a role and bearing a creole title peculiarly fashioned to meet the demands of a highly profitable sugar economy and its absentee-proprietors.

Defining the Attorney

Addressing their fellows in Jamaica, attorneys had no difficulty differentiating and naming their several statuses, roles and titles. The attorney invariably began by identifying himself a "planter". Thus William Shand, giving evidence before the House of Assembly of Jamaica in 1815, said he was "a planter, and has the direction of the estates of sundry absentees" and had been "for several years in the management of estates in the several parishes in the counties of Middlesex and Surrey". Joseph Green, before the same committee, said he was "a planter, and proprietor of a pen and coffee-plantation", and "attorney for several absent proprietors of sugar-estates and other properties". Robert William Harris stated, "He is a planter, and was placed early in life in that business, and regularly brought up to it, and is engaged in the management of his own plantation, and others as the attorney of absentees."[95] John Stewart, in 1823, said that "under the general name of planters are included proprietors, attorneys, overseers, and book-keepers".[96]

Outside Jamaica, the attorney often had difficulty explaining his role and occupation. He had the hardest task when in Britain, needing to distinguish himself from the English attorney-at-law as well as from the proprietors of estates. In 1842, for example, Thomas McCornock, recently come from Jamaica, told a select committee of the British Parliament that he had spent thirty-seven years in Jamaica, with the exception of eight months, "as a planter". He had lived at Golden Grove Estate, in St Thomas-in-the-East, for some thirty years beginning in 1812, the first eleven years as overseer and then "had the sole management as attorney". He was attorney for a further four properties in the district. He was a "planter" not a "proprietor". Pressed by his questioners, McCornock struggled to explain his precise role and place in the hierarchy of plantation management. To one he replied, "The person who is called a manager in the Windward Islands, is an overseer in Jamaica. I am the attorney. . . . and the proprietor of that fine property is now in London."[97]

Asked by a parliamentary committee in 1836 whether he had been "a proprietor of slaves", the attorney William Miller replied in the negative, saying he owned only "a few domestics". When next asked, "But you were not a planter?" Miller explained, "I am a planter by profession. I was agent for a number of proprietors, and managed their properties." He was not "a member of the legal profession", he said, nor of "any profession besides" that of planter.[98] Giving evidence before the same committee, Augustus Hardin Beaumont explained that he owned land and houses in Jamaica, where he had lived thirty years, but no slaves other than domestics. He had spent most of his boyhood there, brought up by his uncle who was a "proprietor". Beaumont "was bred a planter", and said, "It is usual in the West Indies to put the young men of a family to learn to be planters; I learnt the trade, or profession, or whatever else the business is called."[99]

On Jamaican memorials to the dead, the "attorney-at-law" was consistently distinguished from the "attorney".[100] Similarly, William Beckford, in 1788, stated that in Jamaica, "an attorney is a man who has a delegated power to act for principals in England; but is essentially different in practice from an attorney at law".[101] In 1835 Senior made clear that the "attorney" of Jamaica's plantations was unlikely ever to be a member of the legal profession, and that better terms for the attorney's role might be "agent or representative, factor or deputy".[102]

Even in England, as Andrew Long notes, " 'attorney' has not been a term of art". Increasingly, however, "the use of the term has tended to be limited to a particular type of agency, that in which from convenience or from necessity a person is formally appointed to act for and in the name of another in matters having specifically legal effect".[103] It is this specialized legal use that makes modern British historians sometimes still uncomfortable with the Jamaican use of "attorney", preferring to term them "planters' agents" or "managing 'attorneys' " to make crystal clear these men were managers not lawyers.[104]

The word "attorney" itself comes from "attorn", meaning simply to stand in the place of, and the attorney emerged in medieval England as a person appointed or allowed to appear in court on behalf of a litigant. The attorney was thus defined as an officer of the court and subject to close regulation, in contrast to the barrister who did not stand in his client's place but merely served as advocate before the judges. By the early seventeenth century attorneys were being lumped together with solicitors, who had themselves arisen to assist attorneys but worked outside the courts. Regulation began only in the eighteenth century. An act of 1729 required attorneys to be enrolled in one of the courts and serve an apprenticeship of five years, and this proved the foundation of their emergence as a respectable professional class. Eventually, the solicitor was to engross the attorney, in the English legal system, and the title of attorney disappeared with the Judicature Acts of 1873.[105] Jamaica followed English practice until Independence in 1962. Barristers and solicitors were fused in the Legal Profession Act of 1971 and all legal practitioners given the title "attorney-at-law". This is the modern Jamaican attorney.[106]

In the Jamaican legal system, between 1750 and 1850, the attorney-at-law was always English-trained and he was systematically differentiated from the creole institution of attorney. The two attorneys had their origins in the same concept, the representation of one person's interests by another, but beyond this fundamental relationship they had little in common. The Jamaican attorney took his title from the legal fact of being granted powers of attorney but rarely had legal qualifications. Rather, his apprenticeship was informal, derived from observation and experience in the management of land and labour or of commerce. It is hard to find examples of attorneys-at-law who expanded their field to become practical managers of Jamaican estates.

Although the eighteenth-century English attorney was defined strictly as a legal practitioner, there were developments in the second half of the century that came closer to matching the Jamaican pattern. In provincial England, argues Michael Miles, "the country attorney was metamorphosed from being little more than a conductor of lawsuits into a dispenser of a much greater variety of non-litigious services".[107] When employed by the landed class, attorneys might be responsible for, among other things, drawing up deeds, mortgages and conveyances, the buying and selling of land, pursuing the payment of rents by tenants, and serving ejectment notices. Here the attorneys encroached on work previously performed by barristers. They also came to offer financial advice and negotiate loans, playing a role in the development of the capital market. Some even became substantial money-lenders in their own right, lending on mortgages and bonds.[108] As Philip Aylett has observed, "The eighteenth-century attorney already contained elements of several other later professional men – land agents, stockbrokers, the company secretary, and others."[109] On the largest estates, the "land steward" was required to have full knowledge of agricultural practice, whereas the "court steward" and the "agent" or "estate agent" had legal backgrounds and provided legal services. Their functions were not always clearly distinguished, however, and in the later eighteenth century might be performed by the same person. Sometimes this was an attorney. The "country solicitors" of England, says Thompson, were "never ousted altogether from their stewardships of estates".[110] It was the English attorney's role in estate management that most closely approximated that of the Jamaican planting attorney but it was a role firmly established in the law.

The task of the Jamaican attorney was clearly distinguished from that of receiver, mortgagee, executor, trustee, administrator and guardian, though an individual might hold one or more of these legal positions at the same time as serving as attorney for a particular property. Henry Lowndes, asked in 1842 to describe his "occupation" in Jamaica, said he had "been there 27 years as a planter", and "had the charge of eight sugar plantations, in the parish of St Thomas-in-the-Vale, both as proprietor, trustee, attorney, and lessee".[111] "Agent" was similarly distinguished from "attorney", in Jamaican usage, the former restricted to the generic notion of agency rather than pointing towards the management of land resources. Thus in 1832 the registration return for Papine Estate was given in by Edward Jones as agent to the attorney Matthew Farquharson who served the owner James Beckford Wildman.[112]

The separate functions and backgrounds of agriculture and commerce led to a further refinement of definition. The term "planting attorney" appears to have emerged first in the 1820s. Thomas Roughley in 1823 said that some planters employed "two guardians on the spot; one termed the planting attorney, the other the commissary, factor, or mercantile attorney". In the same year, John Stewart wrote that some proprietors appointed "two attorneys, one to manage their mercantile, law, and other concerns, the other a professional planter, to superintend the agricultural duties of their plantations". Marly referred in 1828 to a "managing as well as planting attorney". In 1832 Governor Mulgrave described William Miller as "managing attorney of nearly a hundred estates".[113] Speaking of the early nineteenth century, W. J. Gardner wrote in 1873 that "the planting attorney ranked among the most important personages in the island". In some cases, "two attorneys were appointed to one property", he said, "one having care of its mercantile affairs, and the other superintending its cultivation".[114]

The terminology distinguishing "planting attorney" and "mercantile attorney" was rare among contemporaries. Although it has proved attractive to modern scholars, the distinction is often difficult to identify in the historical record. The practical separation of functions occurred much earlier than Roughley's explicit definition, beginning in the later eighteenth century. As Ward explains, "The custom developed of appointing estate managers as the second attorney – the 'planting attorney' – to work in partnership with the merchant for whom in the past this mark of confidence has usually been reserved."[115] Richard Pares used the term "merchant-attorneys". He found a "rising class of merchant-attorneys for absentee planters" working in eighteenth-century Jamaica, before the American Revolution, some of these "town agents" operating on a sufficiently large scale to maintain an interest in the trade with North America.[116] Roughley's observation that this division between the roles of planting and trading led to conflict among attorneys contains an element of truth.[117] The reason for the conflict can most often be traced to an absence of clear definition and delimitation, the planting attorney becoming the generic attorney.

Chapter 3

Planting Attorneys

The Jamaican attorney was fully empowered and fully responsible. His power was direct and singular. He served in the place of his principal with complete authority to act as agent on the principal's behalf. In theory, that authority could not be sub-delegated to other agents but, in order to cope with the hazards of death and distance, many proprietors chose to appoint multiple attorneys and to identify substitutes.[1]

Regulation

As a class, the proprietors sought protection under the law. Regulation of the Jamaican planting attorney followed recognition of absenteeism as a problem. Unlike the deficiency acts that sought to increase the white population of the island, however, the legislation directed at governing the attorneys was concerned above all with the prevention of accounting failures. Essentially, the government of Jamaica put in place another level of surveillance, in order to keep an eye on the attorney in the absence of the proprietor. Thus the legislation dealt with yet another element of the principal-agent problem as laid out by David W. Galenson in his discussion of the emergence of the attorney.[2]

Jamaican law governing attorneys was directed almost entirely at securing the finances of their employers. The legislation was not intended as a revenue measure. Nor did it make demands in terms of qualifications and experience. Other land management professionals, such as surveyors, were required to enter apprenticeships and take examinations in Jamaica as early as 1780, but persons could practise as attorneys quite freely.[3] What the Jamaican legislature sought to do was control the remuneration of attorneys and in addition ensure the accuracy of their accounts.

The fundamental laws directed at attorneys were passed by the Jamaican legislature in 1740 and 1751. They came near the beginning and the end of the administration of Edward Trelawny, who governed Jamaica from 1738 to 1752. Trelawny's was a long governorship and he proved more successful than most in managing the colony's complex factional disputes, in Council as well as Assembly. Legislation originated in the Assembly was very much a product of the interests of the resident planters and merchants who held sway in that chamber, and Trelawny supported efforts to tax absentees, increase the white population and ensure the defence of the island. However, Trelawny and the Assembly were no match for the absentee lobby and plans for differential taxation were disallowed.[4] The regulation of the attorneys, their accounting practices and their commissions were, however, matters of interest to the planter class generally, whether resident or absentee. The legislation originated in the Assembly, with the residents rather than the absentees, but the British government allowed it because it suited the absentees equally well.

The earliest legislation included the planting attorneys among a larger group of agents but gave them pride of place. In 1740 the Assembly introduced "An Act for preventing of frauds and breaches of trust by attornies or agents of persons absent from this island, and by trustees, guardians, executors and administrators, acting for and on the behalf of minors and others; and by mortgagees in possession of estates mortgaged; and sequestrators appointed by authority of the Court of Chancery".[5] Sheridan argues that it was growing absenteeism that induced this act.[6] Certainly it was explicitly directed at the estates of absentees but other varieties of agency, including the estates of residents, were also regulated by its provisions. Effectively, the act was designed to cover the actions of all persons who had the "management, care and direction" of properties other than their own and the authority to "receive or dispose of the rents, profits, produce, and increase of any real estate whatsoever, viz. plantations, pens, land, and pens of cattle, sugar-works, or other settlements, messuages or tenements, and of any Negroe or other slaves". To prevent "so great an evil" as the frauds that might be committed, attorneys were required "to render and exhibit in the Secretary's Office" in Spanish Town "a true and just account in writing upon their oath . . . or the oath of their overseer or principal servant managing under them, upon such estate, plantation or settlement, or other real estate". The form of the oath was set out in full. These accounts were to be recorded by the island secretary, and came to be known as crop accounts or accounts produce. The 1740 act built on legislation of 1737 directed at "the better preserving the public record of this island", that required the island secretary to transcribe any decayed and hurricane-damaged documents and to keep all "deeds, records, and alphabets in his Office, in good order and repair".[7]

The accounts demanded by the act of 1740 were required to report "all the rents, profits, produce and proceeds" of the properties. More obviously connected with the work of the planting attorney was the requirement that the accounts "particularly set forth the quantity of sugar, rum, molasses, cotton, ginger, coffee, indigo and cocoa produced and made in the preceding year". This clause pointed to the continuing importance of the minor export staples around 1740 but added no detail on the livestock that were traded internally. In the form of the oath, pimento was mentioned and indigo omitted, another indication of the drift of the economy. The accounts were to be for the calendar year and recorded with the island secretary no later than the following 25 March, commencing with the produce of the year 1740. Failure to deliver accounts on time was subject to a fine of one hundred pounds and the attorney's loss of his regular commission. The act of 1740 required that it be in force for three years and then to the closing of the next session of the Assembly but no longer.

When the act expired in 1744, it was allowed to lapse for seven years, suggesting a lack of urgency or enthusiasm for its provisions or simply a failure of government. It was, however, revived in full in 1751 and made perpetual, beginning with accounts for the year 1752. This revival was contained within a portmanteau "Act for making good and wholesome provisions, for raising and establishing the credit of this island".[8] The act began by declaring that "the welfare and prosperity of this island and the further settling thereof depends greatly upon the credit, and the enabling persons to borrow money on easy premiums for forbearance". As Richard Pares noted, it was "part of a comprehensive measure for improving the honest planter's title to land, for reducing the rate of interest, and for ensuring that absentees should be able to obtain diligent and qualified attorneys".[9] In particular, the act sought to secure creditors and encourage investment in Jamaica. More fundamentally, it attempted to establish a money economy by overturning earlier legislation that compelled creditors to take sugar and other produce in payment of debt, valued according to the prices of those commodities in Great Britain. The act also saw the requiring of crop accounts as "a further means of advancing and retrieving the credit of this island".

Equally important, the act of 1751 regulated the rate of commission. Generally, it saw the "large commissions taken and received" by agents as an "obstruction to the credit and settling of this island, and to the lending monies upon landed securities". Specifically, beginning in 1752, "all commissions of attornies, or agents of persons absent from this island" that derived from the "rents, profits, produce, and increase of any of the estates and interest for which they are or shall be respectively concerned", were "reduced to six pounds per cent including the factorage, commission for supplies made in this island for such real estates, for which such persons shall or may be concerned". Any attorney demanding or receiving more than this was made subject to a fine of one hundred pounds, recoverable in the Supreme Court. This regulation applied only to transactions within Jamaica and was not applied to "commissions for the sale of Negroes, or other commodities, sent to this island from Great Britain, or elsewhere".

A separate act of 1751 was directed at "the better regulating of the probate of deeds and conveyances, and letters of attorney executed off this island".[10] The Assembly introduced this legislation because

> doubts have arisen concerning the probate or acknowledgment of letters of attorney before the mayor or other chief magistrate of any city, borough, or town corporate in Great Britain, by one or more witnesses subscribing or the party acknowledging the same, whether such letters of attorney, . . . is or may be sufficient to authorise the person or persons nominated . . . to commence and prosecute any action or suit in any of the courts of law or equity in this island.

The act gave such letters of attorney full authority, and extended the same power to letters authorized in Ireland and the American colonies.

In revised and modified forms, the acts of 1740 and 1751 remained in force in Jamaica into the twentieth century, at least down to 1938. By 1904 the clauses governing the commissions of attorneys and the recording of crop accounts were contained in "The attorneys, executors and trustees (accounts and general) law". The requirements and the rates remained essentially unchanged from those legislated in the middle of the eighteenth century, but by 1938 planting attorneys had effectively disappeared and the last crop accounts were recorded in 1927.[11]

Appointment

The basis of the planting attorney's authority, as well as the origins of the Jamaican version of the title, lay in the granting of legal "powers of attorney" or "letters of attorney". Such powers of attorney were described in written documents, examples of which have survived in scattered archives.[12] Contemporaries occasionally referred specifically to "the planting power of attorney" granted to the "acting resident manager".[13] Increasingly, the legal requirement was that such written authority be both signed and sealed, and most of the powers of attorney for Jamaica were in fact sealed.[14] The practical purpose of the signed and sealed powers of attorney was both to invest the attorney with power to act as agent and to define the limits of the authority invested by the principal. The Jamaican planting attorney, said Bernard Martin Senior, "receives a regular power of attorney, which must be duly recorded in the office of the island secretary, before he can commence his operations".[15]

The more general the authority granted under power of attorney, the easier it was to allow for every eventuality and every possible chance of profit. Thus the form of words used in letters of attorney was broadly standard. The detailed instructions prepared by planters when the sugar plantation was a new variety of enterprise, in the late seventeenth century, were gradually replaced by broader statements, permitting maximum flexibility.[16] For example, the letter of attorney written by Benjamin Way on 23 December 1698 and formally enrolled in Jamaica on 3 April 1699 began:

> Know all men by these presents, that I Benjamin Way of London merchant have made ordained and authorized, and do make ordain authorize and in my place and stead by these presents put and constitute, Doctor Edward Smith of Spanish Town, in the Island of Jamaica and Mr. Samuel Bromley, of the same place, and in case of the death sickness or absence of either of them Thomas Nicholls of the said Island of Jamaica Esquire with the other of them as shall be then present jointly my true and lawful attorneys and deputies for me in my name and to my use, to ask demand levy sue for, recover, and receive by all lawful ways and means whatsoever of and from all and every person and persons whatsoever whom it doth, shall, or may concern, full true plain and perfect account and accounts in writing, and also all and every sum and sums of money, goods wares merchandizes, effects debts dues claims and demands whatsoever as are to me now due owing or belonging or to grow due owing and belonging from time to time.[17]

The attorneys were to pay Way's debts and sell for the best possible prices his "houses lands tenements servants negroes plantation and stock in Jamaica". Way provided no details of his existing property or interests in Jamaica but attempted to provide for all possible events affecting his wealth.

On 12 November 1724 Thomas Cowper, his wife Ann Cowper and Samuel Hill, "of the parish of St Margarets Westminster in the County of Middlesex", gave power of attorney to Edward Pennant and Henry Dawkins of Clarendon. The letter was signed and sealed in London and entered into the official record in Jamaica on 6 April 1725. In London, Ann Cowper was asked jointly to acknowledge the letter, and then "privately examined". She declared that "she executed the same deed or instrument freely willingly and of her own accord without any threat or any ways compelled thereto by her husband". Previously, in May 1724, Pennant and Dawkins had signed an indenture as "acting attorneys" to obtain surveys to settle a boundary dispute for the same proprietors, but how they were granted this acting authority is unclear. The "letter of attorney" gave Pennant and Dawkins full authority to buy and sell "these our plantation or plantations lands tenements and hereditaments", as well as livestock, utensils, and any "goods and chattels whatsoever". They were to seek the best purchasers and best prices. The Cowpers and Hill promised "to establish ratify stand to and allow all and whatsoever our said attorney or attorneys shall lawfully do or cause to be done . . . as fully and perfectly to all intents and purposes as if we our selfs were present and did the same actually in our own proper persons". Pennant and Dawkins were to ensure payment of all rents and debts, taking any necessary cases to the courts.[18] Although the powers granted under this letter of attorney were extensive, there was no mention of the agricultural or marketing activities that came to be fundamental to the role of the planting attorney.

The basic form of the letter of attorney changed little between 1700 and the beginning of the nineteenth century but more of them came to be directed at mortgaged estates and more of them addressed issues of production and marketing. In 1816, for example, "Alexander Edgar of Stockbridge near the city of Edinburgh in Scotland Esquire" appointed Richard Pusey and William Rhodes James of Spanish Town "jointly and severally my true and lawful attorneys and attorney" in Jamaica. They were to "enter into and take possession of any plantations pens lands tenements slaves and hereditaments cattle and stock" to which he was entitled as "owner mortgagee or otherwise". Pusey and James were to pursue disputes in the courts. Once they had possession, they were to "manage cultivate maintain and keep the same to the best advantage and in such manner as they or he shall think fit and most conducive to my interest". The proceeds were to be invested. They were to ship the produce of the plantations as directed by Edgar and "in default of such direction" do what they thought best.[19]

Occasionally, powers of attorney included more specific conditions. For example, a power of attorney sealed in 1816 for the management of Catherine Hall Estate required that its sugar and rum be consigned to John Henry Deffell and Company of London, as well as sending them the proceeds of any local sales.[20] Most sugar estates were covered by powers of attorney that were much less specific, allowing maximum flexibility in changing circumstances. The same applied to coffee plantations.[21] On the other hand, the "power of attorney to take possession of Hearts Ease Penn etc. in the island of Jamaica and receive the rents" called on the attorneys, Thomas James Brown and John Gale Vidal, to take possession of the property (located in St Catherine)

> and also all those thirteen slaves or Negroes known by the several names and descriptions following that is to say Juan a carpenter, Dian a stock woman, Billy cook, Abigail stock girl, Robert field Negro, Ned Johnson, Bessy housewench, Joavey sempstress, Johnny stable man, Bob waiting boy, Spight Bonelba washerwoman, Peggy washerwoman or by whatever other name or names or descriptions they may be now called or known together with the offspring issue and increase of the females.[22]

Such specificity was rare. The many changes that might occur between the preparation of a power of attorney and its execution meant that keeping all options open gave the attorney the greatest flexibility.

How were attorneys chosen? A proprietor leaving Jamaica to become an absentee might select an attorney in person and complete the legal requirements before departure. On the other hand, it was rare for an absentee to recruit an attorney in Britain and send him to Jamaica specifically to undertake plantation management without first serving with an overseer. There was too much to be learned. An absentee might, however, send a friend or relative to the island to deal with legal matters that then led into management. For example, John Dovaston was engaged in 1764, in England, by Richard and William Jones, to travel to Jamaica to recover rents in arrears on their share of Old Woman Savanna Plantation, Clarendon, and to let it at a higher rate. The resident joint owner, Smart Hale, proved unable to cover the debt in cash. Dovaston, who identified the law as his profession, threatened to divide the property and exploit his half. To prepare himself for the task, he set about learning the business of sugar-making. This was enough to encourage Hale to quickly find the money owed, borrowing from other planters. Dovaston granted a ten-year lease on Hale's moiety of the plantation and went back to England. Following a second visit to Jamaica, with a stop to investigate the plantations of St Kitts, Dovaston finally returned to England in 1774 and felt sufficiently qualified to prepare a manuscript, still unpublished, on plantation management titled "Agricultura Americana".[23]

Once the proprietor was resident outside Jamaica, the process became more complex and mediated. He could take advice from other absentees on the success of various practising attorneys or depend on information from merchants and friends. In the event of an attorney's death, the proprietor had to depend on prior arrangements with agents in Jamaica who quickly took responsibility for finding an interim or permanent manager. The high mortality experienced in Jamaica down to the middle of the nineteenth century resulted in rapid, though unpredictable, turnover. The sons of close kin were often sent to the colonies to learn the business of trade and planting.[24]

Qualifications

Who could be an attorney? In general legal principle, the agent needed only to be free and of sound mind. In theory, a child, an illiterate, or even a bankrupt could serve as an attorney. The planting attorney or land agent, however, had to satisfy much more rigid selection criteria. Although Eric Richards has argued that, in Britain, the lack of systematic professional training for the business of land agency meant "virtually anyone could set up as an agent", there were always vital rules governed by gender, age and skill.[25] The positions were wanted because of the profits to be had and the resulting competition served to select particular types of people.

In practice, down to 1838 at least, the planting attorneys of Jamaica were all male, adult, free and literate. Less rigid requirements were that they should be white, of long residence and recognized status in the society. Knowledge of plantation agriculture was an advantage but its lack might be balanced by other qualities. Contemporary critics and some modern historians have broadly doubted and disparaged the qualifications of the attorneys. Thus Beckford said that the attorneys "who professionally undertake the direction of Jamaica estates" ranged from "the ignorant to the intelligent, and from the responsible to the dependent". Further, he claimed, "those properties are, I think, in general the best managed, upon which the attorneys do not reside". Such non-resident attorneys, "acknowledging their ignorance of the cultivation of the soil, and of the various processes of sugar-making, have the modesty and sense to depend upon the scientific and the experienced, without any other interference perhaps than that of making them responsible for their conduct, and of discouraging and discarding the worthless, and of rewarding and confiding in the meritorious".[26]

In 1793 J. B. Moreton said the attorney "should have gone through all the painful toils and drudgeries of an overseer, for three or four years, and be an experienced planter, to be capable of doing justice". Senior argued that the attorney "ought to be thoroughly skilled in the planting line, as regards every product of the island; also to be well acquainted with the characters, customs, and management of the negro race". In addition, Senior listed a series of virtues: "His temper should be mild, his habits abstemious, his reputation unsullied, his heart proof against all temptations, (for much will he meet with to draw him from the strict path of honour and honesty,) and his mind bent solely on the advancement of his employer's interest." Senior believed that although the position "may have been disgraced by some individuals, certain it is, there have been, and still are, such men as above described". Even Beckford conceded that among the attorneys of Jamaica "there are many who hold the first places in the community, and who are independent legislators, useful magistrates, and men of property; and who are besides attentive and just to the interest of their employers, and respectable both in private and public life".[27]

In terms of their occupational backgrounds, Beckford said of the attorneys "some are merchants, some are doctors, some are lawyers, and some have even been indented servants". John Stewart, in 1823, said the attorney "may be a resident proprietor, a merchant, a lawyer, a medical man, or an old experienced overseer who has given proofs of ability and diligence in his quondam situation".[28] Modern historians have been harsher. Ragatz argued that most attorneys were "non-agriculturists" and that "physicians, lawyers, and even clergymen were at times given charge of estates". W. L. Burn said some of the attorneys "had no other than agricultural interests, but many of them were lawyers or merchants; and too often a power of attorney was granted to a man who had not skill and knowledge enough to carry out his duties". Sheridan noticed a similar variety of qualifications and believed some attorneys had been "planters on their own account, while others were merchants, physicians, lawyers, and even clergymen". Perhaps the most critical of the recent writers, Carrington argues that among estate managers "a limited number were agriculturists and possessed knowledge of plantership". He also contended that most attorneys were "trained legal personages".[29] This last statement seems certainly untrue for the plantation attorneys of Jamaica.

In order to practise in Jamaica, lawyers required English qualifications, but medical practitioners were equally likely to have been trained in Scotland. Jamaica followed the English legal system. According to Alan Karras, migrants trained in Scottish law sometimes arrived in Jamaica unaware they would have to serve fresh apprenticeships, and "most of these people quickly turned to estate management". These attorneys-at-law made the calculation that planting would prove more profitable than re-training. Most clerics were also British trained but it is hard to find examples of their becoming planting attorneys. O'Shaughnessy contends that a British education was typical for "local merchants and agents" and also "for such plantation offices as estate clerks, bookkeepers, overseers, and managers". The same applied to the training of skilled artisans. On the other hand, book-keepers and overseers were sometimes brought initially as gardeners.[30]

Although Jamaica's plantation attorneys saw themselves as professionals, they flourished in a period before institutional organization was common. They never established an association or set examinations for entry. In England, the nineteenth century saw a "professional and managerial revolution" on the great estates and by the 1850s land agency had become "a distinct profession". There, institutional organization came only in 1902 with the founding of the Land Agents Society and professional qualifying examinations were not introduced until the 1920s.[31] Elements of plantation attorneyship came to be part of the training offered by agricultural colleges in Jamaica from 1910 and by the Imperial College of Tropical Agriculture established in Trinidad in 1922, but by then attorneyship had been overtaken by many developments in commerce and management science.[32]

Functions

Modern accounts of the work of the attorney often have their origins in the negative picture painted by Roughley and the harsh views of the equally embittered and bankrupt creole William Beckford. In 1790 Beckford said:

> The business of an attorney, when residing [temporarily] upon the plantation, is to attend the overseer in a circuitous visit of the cane fields, and to obtain from him a calculation of what they may produce; and as his emoluments arise from the magnitude of the crops, his interest will point out the means of making them productive; and hence the exorbitant expence of hired labour will be added, to swell the lift of payments under which the planter already labours, and for which, in seasons of storms and famine, he may find it very difficult, if not impossible, to provide: the attorney having the means of payment in his own hands, may say "that charity begins at home", and provides for his own wants before he considers those of his employer.[33]

Similarly, Roughley's attorneys made only "a casual visit to the estates over which they presided, with lordly pomp". This was "seldom done oftener than once a-year, and the plantations were governed without being actually inspected". Predictions of fair prospects were dashed by "malignant caprice". The exhaustion of land and livestock, employment of "endless jobbing", great waste in supplies, and failures of delivery were all "solely the fault of the resident attorney, arising from his connivance or ignorance". There were some good and honest attorneys, said Roughley, but "five sixths of this class of representatives, are men who are engrossed by their own interested speculations, attentive to what will promote their own selfish views, making every other object within their grasp subservient to their ambition". The attorney turned on the "poor overseer" whenever things went awry and had an interest in sending the estate into debt and mortgage.[34] Roughley's experience was that of the unappreciated overseer.

What did attorneys really do? The list of tasks is in fact quite long and it is possible only to outline the main elements.[35] Duties differed between planting and mercantile attorneys, between periods, between crops, between regions, and between individuals. Chapters 7 and 8 detail the activities of two attorneys, Simon Taylor 1765–75 and Isaac Jackson 1839–43, providing a fuller account. In summary, the attorney's responsibilities included the appointment of overseers, regular inspections of the plantations, the sale and purchase of land and enslaved people, negotiating wages and rents with free workers, attending court, financial and planning advice, trading through local merchants and shippers, providing accounts and reports, and information on local political developments. The attorney was expected to see that the directions of his employer proprietor were implemented and to ensure the profitability of his investment.

In the first place, attorneys were normally responsible for the appointment and dismissal of overseers, and set their salaries. They might also hire bookkeepers and tradesmen but generally this was the realm of the overseer. Selecting an overseer depended on networked knowledge and some enquiry into their previous behaviour and supposed success. Thus William Shand, in 1832, stated, "No man of common sense employs an overseer without knowing his character, and without knowing whether he is capable of acting properly in the situation in which he is placed; it is of very great importance where a man is to be entrusted with the charge of negroes upon a property." As to the "kindness" of the overseer, Shand believed that "it is in the interest of the employer to make the negroes contented, and what is the interest of the employer is consistent with the duty of the manager".[36]

The attorney was expected to make regular visits to the estates in his charge. It was through these visits that he gained the capacity to make plans and proposals to be put to the owner. Philip Curtin claimed an attorney "might not visit all his estates more than once or twice a year".[37] In practice, as will become clear, most attorneys saw their estates much more often, though the few with really large domains must have had lower frequencies. Certainly some attorneys seem to have known the properties in detail and were capable of describing their territories. Moreton said the attorney "should visit the plantation frequently, pry into every hole and corner of it; surprise the manager when he least expected his coming", press into the cane-pieces to ensure they were properly trashed throughout, and stand for hours in the boiling house to observe and correct any deficiencies.[38] On these visits, the attorney was usually guided by the overseer, whose job it was to explain the state of the plantation. Thus, said William Taylor in 1832, the overseer was always the first and last man to see the attorney when he visited an estate. On the other hand, Taylor claimed some attorneys actually encouraged the enslaved to make complaints direct to them.[39] Closer to the view of Roughley was that of Augustus Hardin Beaumont, who in 1836, in the course of a wide-ranging attack on the capacities of the attorneys and overseers, claimed that "it is the rule with all planting attornies never to interfere with the details of an estate, and they know, in fact, nothing of them: it is left entirely to the overseer as long as the crop is made, and the negroes are not discontented; the planting attorney never interferes; it is a rule not to interfere".[40] If an absentee-proprietor came to Jamaica to visit his properties, it was the attorney who showed him around and directed his thoughts. It has been said that "the attorney rarely showed any enthusiasm at the prospect of a visit from the owner and was inclined to use one or other of the stock arguments to keep him an absentee", but evidence to support this claim is hard to find.[41]

The attorney was often required to undertake legal tasks for the absentee-proprietor. He had documents prepared, saw to their certification, and gave testimony in court. In addition, the attorney had a role in defending the boundaries of his employer's properties, hiring land surveyors to run lines and putting up boundary markers. Attorneys might be given responsibility for the sale and exchange of properties. Thus William Miller, asked in 1836 if he knew Dean's Valley Estate, replied, "I had the management of Dean's Valley, and sold it."[42] Enslaved and free people were sent to court at the direction of the attorney.

Attorneys, as the agents of absentee-proprietors, kept their distance from punishment, though they certainly ordered it when they sat in courts. The corporal punishment of enslaved people and apprentices was sometimes done by overseers and owners but generally through the medium of the driver.[43] On the other hand, Henry Bleby, in his *Death Struggles of Slavery,* published in 1853, did claim that the rebellion of 1831 showed its first signs at Salt Spring, in St James, in response to "an act of wanton oppression on the part of Mr. Grignon, the attorney for the property". While visiting the estate, Grignon "met a woman belonging to Salt Spring with a piece of sugar-cane in her hand, which he at once concluded to have been stolen from the adjacent cane-field. After punishing her himself on the spot, he took her back to the estate, to have her more severely flogged by the driver." The head driver refused, the woman being his wife. The second driver also refused, and "the people became dogged and sullen, and the attorney could not succeed in getting the woman further punished". However, other accounts of these events say the woman had an armful of canes, more than the customary quantity permitted, and that Grignon sought her whipping by the driver rather than punishing her himself.[44]

Agricultural planning for the short term was generally a matter of discussion between attorney and overseer, with the proprietor having a long-distance input. Important decisions to which the attorney contributed included the areas and locations on the plantation to be planted in particular crops, the rotation of plant canes and ratoons, the sequence of cutting the cane, the use of livestock, and the hiring of labour. After the abolition of slavery, it was the attorney who negotiated wages and rents. Attorneys hardly ever directly supervised labour in field or mill, unless they were also overseer for an estate.

Planning for the longer term was the province of the attorney and in this respect he acted as a respectful financial adviser to the proprietor. During slavery, the attorney advised on the purchase of enslaved people and the general principles of hiring labour. After slavery, the attorney made recommendations on the policy of rents and wages, and the tying of residence to labour on the plantation. Further, he made recommendations on the construction of buildings, including the factories, the sourcing of water and other forms of power. He also advised on the profitability of large-scale expansion, through the cutting of forest, the extension of the cane field, the establishment of additional factory sites and the acquisition of new lands to increase the proprietor's fortune.

Dealings with local merchants were conducted almost exclusively through the attorney. Where there was both planting attorney and mercantile attorney, it was the latter who had responsibility for the ordering of plantation supplies. Pares argued that the "merchant-attorneys" sometimes took the initiative in importing lumber and other plantation necessities, to supply plantations for which they were responsible.[45] Where there was only one attorney, he played this role and sent the orders to the proprietor's metropolitan factors. Local purchases of goods for plantation use were the realm of the attorney. The attorney was also fully responsible for sales of the plantation's produce within Jamaica, though he might work through a local merchant or, for small amounts, the overseer.

The shipment of sugar and rum, and other produce, was organized by the attorney. He chose the ships and ship captains, and the quantities to be committed to them. Occasionally, this led to conflict with proprietor and overseer. The attorney was responsible for seeing the lists of cargoes were sent to the proprietor or his metropolitan agent, and advising on sailing times so that insurance could be arranged.

Accounts were prepared by the attorney, based on information he collected himself and on information passed on by the overseer. It was the attorney who had to submit accounts to the proprietor and to the island secretary in the annual crop accounts. It was also his responsibility to inspect the plantation books but not to keep them.[46] The writing of letters and reports was a vital aspect of the attorney's work, as it was these documents that provided the absentee-proprietor with a picture of the plantation, its performance and condition. The frequency of communication is discussed in chapters 5 and 6, but it may be observed that attorneys seem to have been quite assiduous in keeping their employers informed, often showing a greater interest than the employers themselves. The outcome was a great deal of correspondence, particularly from the attorneys, explaining actions and reviewing prospects, and a variety of accounting records. When it suited or seemed appropriate the attorney might act with undue haste, from the proprietor's point of view. In other cases he could be overly "cautious" in waiting for "instructions from home before giving his consent".[47]

These, then, were the major tasks of the Jamaican attorney. How did they compare to the duties of stewards in Britain and the South? At the middle of the eighteenth century, the role of the steward on a great English estate varied with the scale of the property. Usually, says J. V. Beckett, "the steward was responsible for the home farm, the house, gardens and parks, for leasing farms, collecting rents, surveying boundaries, drawing up accounts, and supervising other employees". Occasionally, he might double as an election agent or manage industrial concerns. Where an aristocratic landlord was absentee, because of his multiple properties, the steward was "required to act as a substitute for the owner".[48] In nineteenth-century Britain, the land agent of a large estate had extensive managerial responsibilities. As Richards argues, "the great landed estate was one of the largest business enterprises of the Victorian economy", and in many ways its management was "more complex and subtle than that of a factory or railway company or house of commerce". The agent was empowered to "influence the direction and volume of agricultural investment, modify the entire social climate of an estate, manipulate electoral behaviour and greatly affect the level of efficiency and welfare in the landed community".[49]

Although the plantation system of Jamaica might reasonably be expected to have drawn for its model on the agricultural economy of Britain, it was in fact quite different. Between 1750 and 1850, as Avner Offer points out, English agriculture was dominated by "a three-class system" in which landowners leased their land to tenant farmers for a fixed annual rent and the tenants in turn relied on wage labour.[50] Around 1800, less than 20 per cent of the income from agriculture came from owner-occupiers and more than

80 per cent of the land was worked by tenants. This was a highly unusual pattern of rural land tenure, with fixed rent leases replacing other forms of tenure, such as sharecropping and lifetime leases.[51] Although landownership in England was highly concentrated, with near to one-half of the agricultural land held in estates of more than five thousand acres, relatively few of the great landowners chose to farm the land directly in hopes of high incomes.[52] The implications for management were substantial, particularly because it placed a premium on the value of land, in spite of the uncertainty of income, and effectively transferred the risk to the tenant farmer. The English land agent was typically a collector of rent, a bailiff. Thus the English landowner's income was secured in a way the Jamaican planter's never could be, and the planter, by comprehensively controlling the resources of land and labour, took responsibility for a wide range of risks in hopes of great profits.

The steward of the United States South came closer to performing the tasks of the Jamaican attorney but the South followed neither the English nor the Jamaican models of land tenure. Small-scale landownership was common and the ownership of enslaved people widespread. Great estates were relatively few but where they did exist, argues Scarborough, it was the steward's responsibility to "take orders for plantation supplies, advise his employer of necessary work to be undertaken, supervise the overseers of plantations under his direction, introduce improved methods of planting or managing, and keep the proprietor informed of the progress of plantation affairs".[53]

The Jamaican attorney did a good deal more than the Southern steward or the English land agent, and he was vastly more visible in island society and economy. The attorneys had a clear awareness of the extent of their power and value. When a questioner at a British parliamentary enquiry in 1832 asked William Shand whether he thought "any management by an agent can be very profitable where an owner lives on one side of the Atlantic and the agent on the other", he responded positively. Shand argued that it might well be "more profitable than if the owner lived there", and offered good reasons why "an agent may manage West India property much better than the principal himself". Next he was asked, "Do you think a gentleman living constantly in London, and having a large farm in Scotland managed by a bailiff, he never residing there, or inspecting the farm himself, is likely to derive much profit from that large farm?" Shand readily opined that such a "gentleman farmer" might not make money as an absentee, "but in planting we have found it otherwise; in the colonies the business of a planter embraces more than that of a farmer of this country, and it requires a man to attend to it from early life to know the routine of management of an estate". The Jamaican attorney required a greater store of knowledge than the bailiff, said Shand, and "the business of a planter embraces a great deal more; he is not only a farmer, but he is a manufacturer of the article, and a species of manufacture which requires considerable skill and attention".[54]

Numbers

Sweeping statements on the proportions of Jamaican estates in the hands of attorneys are common enough. Solid numbers are rare. Stewart, in 1823, stated that "almost all the great proprietors reside in Great Britain, leaving their estates to the care and management of agents, or attorneys, as they are here called".[55] Similarly, Burn wrote that in the early nineteenth century the "typical sugar estate" was "owned, in all probability, by an absentee and under the care of a man who held a power of attorney to act for the proprietor".[56] More generally, Carrington argues that "by the end of the eighteenth century, a class of managers, and/or attorneys, operated most British Caribbean estates".[57]

In the long-term, the rise of the attorney is generally seen as matching the growth of absentee-proprietorship, though possibly becoming less common as the plantation economy declined in the nineteenth century, particularly the 1820s.[58] Similarly, the abolition of slavery is thought to have been quickly followed by a fall in the proportion of estates under attorneys, parallel to the supposed decline in absenteeism. The first complete census of Jamaica, taken in 1844, offered no specific occupational category for attorneys. Probably they were among the 3,987 "planters". In subsequent censuses only the eccentric listings of 1861 identified attorneys, finding just two "planting attorneys".[59] Anthony Trollope, travelling in Jamaica in 1858, said, "Some estates there are, and they are not many, which are still worked by the agents – attorneys is the proper word – of rich proprietors in England; of men so rich that they have been able to bear the continual drain of properties that for years have been always losing – of men who had wealth and spirit to endure this."[60] Thomas Holt argues that by the later nineteenth century estate attorneys "practically disappeared". Attorneys managed "two-thirds of the estates in 1881 but only one-third in 1911". Holt also contends that the metropolitan merchant-factors lost their role in marketing and supplying the estates. Local traders now did most of the marketing of sugar and "rum estates" came to dominate in several regions of Jamaica. Local corporations and investors actively bought up plantations, only to be displaced by metropolitan capital when the sugar economy revived in the 1920s.[61]

In 1937 the *Handbook of Jamaica* identified an "attorney or manager" for each of the thirty-four functioning sugar estates but several of these were resident managers, managing directors or managing trustees. How many of these men were commonly called "attorney" is unknown. A few may have operated along the old lines, representing more than one estate. Others, such as the resident manager for the West Indies Sugar Company, were responsible for series of estates that were being actively formed into new combines. By 1950, when the number of estates was reduced to twenty-four, the title of this *Handbook* column had become "general managers, managers, etc." and included only three "attorneys". By 1952 the attorneys had all gone, overtaken by the "managing director".[62] Something similar happened in the listing of banana, coffee and cocoa cultivations and grazing pens, the column called "attorney of owner" disappearing after 1950.

Only one modern attempt to calculate the numbers of attorneys in Jamaica between 1750 and 1850 is known. Kathleen Mary Butler, in her 1995 work on the distribution of compensation payments, published a count of 152 "properties administered by attorneys" in the period 1823–43 and named the twelve individual attorneys responsible. Her sources for this count are described as "deeds and conveyances" and "slave registers", but precisely how the list was arrived at is not clear.[63] Probably it is intended to be illustrative. It is not a complete count.

Firm estimates of the numbers of attorneys operating in Jamaica in the early nineteenth century may be obtained from the returns of registrations of slaves. These records began in 1817 and were collected triennially down to 1832. Only the final registration, the one taken closest to the time of abolition, is analysed here. Attorneys are identified as the "givers in" of returns for slaves which they did not themselves own. They were not the only people to make returns for others; guardians and parents did so for children and trustees for deceased owners, for example. Agents and overseers made some of the returns for their employers. Only those givers-in explicitly described as attorneys are counted here. Applying this definition, the number of slave-holdings returned by attorneys in 1832 was 1,125, or 9 per cent of the total. The number of slaves included in the returns made by attorneys was 140,586, or 45 per cent of the total slave population. The total number of persons making returns as attorneys was 423, many of them acting for more than one owner and joining in a variety of partnerships.

Not all of the 1,125 slave-holdings returned by attorneys were substantial agricultural units. Returns were made by "attorneys" for small urban units and minor rural settlements or small numbers of slaves belonging to a larger property managed by its owner.[64] All of these givers-in held powers of attorney, so met the legal definition but failed to satisfy the Jamaican definition of planting attorney. Separating the plantation attorneys from the general mass of attorneys can be achieved by using the names attached to the properties, as stated in the returns themselves and in the related claims for compensation.[65] A strict definition is provided by taking only those properties named as estates, pens and plantations. This winnows out the marginal cases. The resulting count is 745 properties in the hands of attorneys in Jamaica in 1832, made up of 467 estates, 146 pens and 132 plantations. Excluded are unnamed holdings (204), town holdings (169), settlements (4) and wharves (3). These 380 units accounted for only 7,841 slaves, compared to the 132,745 on the estates, pens and plantations. It was the agricultural units that mattered in terms of the system of attorneyship. In the analysis that follows only the 745 estates, pens and plantations are considered.

The number of people serving as attorneys and the number of proprietors served are harder to derive because of multiple ownership and attorneyship. Taking together individuals and partnerships, the number of attorneys managing estates, pens and plantations in 1832 was exactly two hundred, each of whom managed an average 3.7 properties. The two hundred attorneys were employed by a total 473 proprietors.[66] Of the proprietors, 70 per cent held only one property, 17 per cent two properties, and only 4 per cent five or more. In terms of the properties, 16 per cent of the total managed by attorneys belonged to owners of five or more units. The largest holdings consisted of 10 properties, four men owning this many: Neill Malcolm, Philip John Miles, and the late James Dawkins and John Tharp.

How did the properties controlled by attorneys compare with those in the hands of resident proprietors and other kinds of agents? Overall, the mean slave population of the units under attorneys was 178 (Standard Deviation 110). On sugar estates, the mean was 220 slaves on attorney-run properties, compared to 228 for all estates included in the returns of registrations of slaves for 1832. The means for pens were 101 and 99, and for plantations 117 and 100, respectively.[67] The difference between estates managed by attorneys and resident-proprietors was insignificant, chiefly because the former made up such a large proportion of the whole. The data do not permit a precise comparison of pens and plantations, partly because of problems of definition, but an inclusive approach would show the absentee properties to be substantially larger than those of residents.

Was there a geographical concentration of attorney-managed properties, or were residents and absentees intermixed? As expected, the distribution of sugar estates under attorneys matched closely the overall distribution of all estates in 1832 (Figure 3.1 and Table 3.1). There were, however, some small regions in which absentees dominated almost exclusively. The most striking of these were in southern Vere and along the Plantain Garden River of St Thomas-in-the-East, two areas renowned for their productive soils, as well as the not so well-endowed western corner of St Thomas-in-the-Vale and the hinterland of Falmouth in Trelawny (Figure 3.2). Resident sugar estate proprietors, on the other hand, dominated most obviously in interior St James and along the coast of St Ann. Outside these areas of local dominance, the estates of absentees and residents were intermixed without clear pattern. The spatial distribution of pens managed by attorneys also matched fairly closely the overall pattern, except for the semi-urbanized zone stretching from Spanish Town to Kingston where the "pen" served a different function and was generally small scale (Figure 3.3). The same applies to plantations. The most productive coffee plantations of the Blue Mountain zone had a relatively high rate of attorneyship, as did the more marginal

Table 3.1 Estates, Pens and Plantations Managed by Attorneys, 1832

Parish	Estates	Pens	Plantations	Total
Westmoreland	36	13	1	50
Hanover	54	11	1	66
St James	54	7	1	62
Trelawny	67	7	2	76
St Elizabeth	15	20	13	48
Manchester	3	2	35	40
St Ann	19	22	9	50
Clarendon	30	10	7	47
Vere	22	1	1	24
St Dorothy	8	6	0	14
St Thomas-in-the-Vale	18	4	5	27
St John	7	1	3	11
St Catherine	4	12	0	16
St Mary	47	12	8	67
St Andrew	8	6	9	23
Port Royal	3	2	13	18
St David	6	2	7	15
St George	10	1	6	17
Portland	9	0	3	12
St Thomas-in-the-East	47	7	8	62
Total	467	146	132	745

Source: Returns of Registrations of Slaves (Jamaica Archives, Spanish Town).

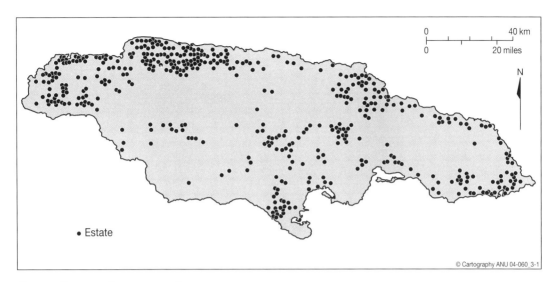

Figure 3.1 Estates under attorneys, 1832

properties of southern St Elizabeth, whereas attorneys were relatively rare in St Mary and St George (Figure 3.4).[68]

Another way of looking at spatial variations in the dominance of attorneys and resident proprietors is to consider the proportion of the enslaved population living under these different regimes. The overall importance of sugar and the sector's dependence on attorneys underlies the pattern for 1832, shown in Figure 3.5, but significant contrasts emerge. Interior regions, marginal to the plantation economy, tended to have few attorney-managed properties, but these zones generally had low population densities and merged into unpeopled territory. More broadly, areas of low population density were the least likely to be dominated by attorneys, reflecting directly the scale and structure of slave-holding and the agricultural economy. Parishes such as St Elizabeth had pockets of attorneyship, in the sugar and coffee areas, but also extensive districts of resident, small-scale proprietorship.[69]

Did proprietors owning more than one property employ multiple attorneys? Generally, regardless of the number of properties they owned, proprietors seem to have preferred to deal with a single attorney or partnership. It was easier to correspond with an individual attorney who knew all of the proprietor's business. In 1832 only 7 per cent of proprietors using attorneys employed two or more. Most of these used just two attorneys and half of the owners held only two properties in any case. Similarly, three of the four proprietors who employed three attorneys had only three properties each, the fourth having ten. On the other hand, the two proprietors who employed four attorneys owned eight and nine properties. Employing multiple attorneys was partly a means of taking advantage of

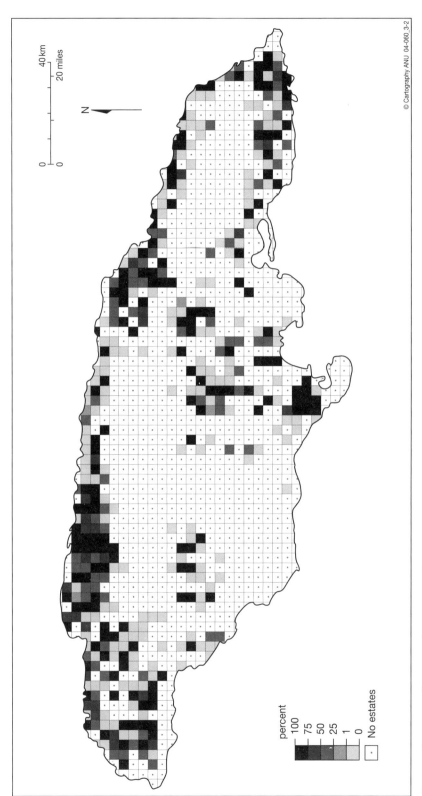

Figure 3.2 Percentage of estates under attorneys, 1832

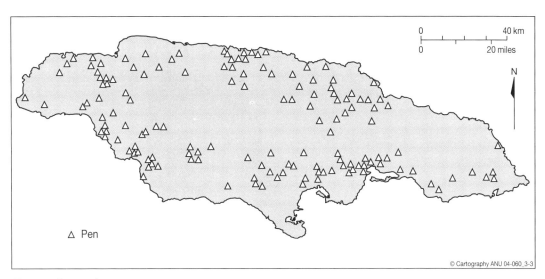

Figure 3.3 Pens under attorneys, 1832

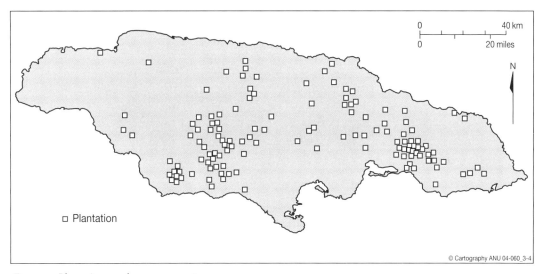

Figure 3.4 Plantations under attorneys, 1832

specialized knowledge and partly an insurance against sickness and death. For example, in 1781 the absentee John Pennant appointed Alexander Falconer to act jointly with William Atherton in the event of the death of the chief attorney for his Clarendon properties, John Shickle. Pennant himself was to die the following year and was strong enough only to make his mark on the power of attorney granted to Falconer. Shickle also died in 1782, of fever.[70] Making arrangements for the future was essential.

Why did proprietors employ different attorneys for their various properties? One reason was to ensure the attorney lived close to the property

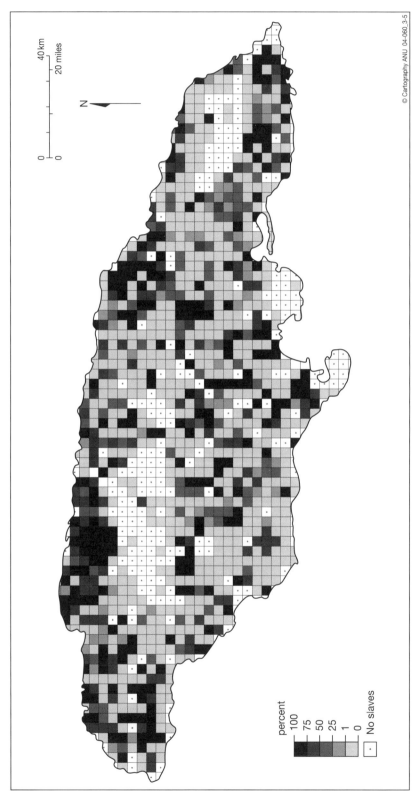

Figure 3.5 Percentage of slaves under attorneys, 1832

he managed and was not stretched in his dealings. In 1842 Ralph Bernal, a London West India merchant who had never visited Jamaica, explained that it had "always been my object, to give the management of my properties to persons who resided upon the property, not to any large overpowering attorney". He employed Francis McCook, who sat in the Assembly as member for St Dorothy, a man of integrity, ability and practical experience, but "certainly not a man of great property, or a man who may be considered as a leviathan of an attorney".[71] Thus a proprietor might employ a different attorney for each of his or her properties, ensuring each was a resident or near-neighbour. At the same time, however, each of these attorneys might serve several masters.

How many proprietors might an attorney serve at the same time and how many separate properties might he manage? According to Gad Heuman, "attorneys frequently had more than one plantation under their supervision". Similarly, Burn argued that, around the time of the abolition of slavery, it was "unusual to find an attorney who was responsible only for one property, that on which he resided; usual to find him responsible for a number of properties, living on one and visiting the others from time to time". And Curtin said, "An attorney might manage one estate, but more often he held attorneyships for several different proprietors and managed more – sometimes as many as fifteen or twenty."[72] This view seems to derive largely from the opinion of Stewart, who claimed in 1823 that "an attorney has sometimes fifteen or twenty estates, belonging to different proprietors, under his sole care". Stewart also claimed that some of these properties were so distant from one another that "the attorney employs a sub-agent to overlook the management of the remote estates, he himself paying them a visit once a-year".[73] More realistically, Brathwaite contends that attorneys in charge of fifteen to twenty estates were rare and that "more usual" was the attorney managing five to six plantations. He also argued that after the abolition of the Atlantic slave trade "attorneys were confined to a few manageable properties".[74]

In fact, most attorneys served only one master. Almost half (eighty-eight) of the two hundred attorneys in 1832 managed just one property and dealt with one owner or corporate group. A further twenty-seven managed more than one property but did so for a single owner. Thus, overall, 58 per cent of the attorneys were employed by a single proprietor, managing as many as seven properties for that one owner. These properties, however, accounted for only 22 per cent of the total managed by attorneys. Of the total 745 estates, pens and plantations controlled by attorneys in 1832, less than a quarter (166) of the properties were managed by an attorney responsible to a single proprietor.

Properties managed by attorneys dealing with just one estate, plantation or pen were swamped by properties under the control of attorneys working for multiple employers and managing multiple properties. Hence the persisting perception of the attorney as a man with a substantial network of power and enterprise. Holt's claim that "the most influential attorneys managed between twenty and thirty properties, thus representing a number of absentees", comes closer to the truth but even then the scale of operation is exaggerated.[75] In 1832 only four attorneys were responsible for twenty or more properties: William Miller with thirty-six; Joseph Gordon with twenty-two; John Salmon Jr, twenty-two; and George Gordon, twenty. The numbers given in Table 3.2 include only properties for which an attorney was the first-named in the returns of registrations of slaves for 1832, in order to avoid double-counting.[76] Only 26 per cent of attorneys looked after five or more properties, but these managed 489 properties or 66 per cent of the total under attorneys. It is these fifty-two attorneys who stand out in the historical record because of their wealth and associated social and political power. They were far from typical of the planting attorneys as a class but they dominated the system.

The "large" attorneys can be further divided into two groups, those with five to nine properties and those with ten or more. In 1832 there were thirty-five attorneys in the first group and seventeen in the second (Table 3.2). For those managing ten or more properties, the mean number of properties managed was 14.5, compared to 6.9 for those with five to nine and 3.7 for all two hundred attorneys. Taking all of the properties managed by attorneys in 1832, there was a very neat distribution between the different groups of attorneys. The large attorneys (managing ten or more properties), the middling (five to nine) and the small (one to four) were each collectively responsible for almost exactly one-third of the total. In terms of the enslaved population on these properties, however, the large attorneys were responsible for 37 per cent, the middling 33 per cent, and the small only 30 per cent. More interesting is the distribution among different types of properties. Thus, the three groups of attorneys managed much the same proportion of sugar estates (one-third) but the large attorneys had a bigger share of the pens (43 per cent) and a lesser proportion of the plantations producing coffee and pimento (20 per cent). The typical large attorney managed 9.2 estates, 3.7 pens, and 1.6 plantations, whereas the middling attorneys had 4.3, 1.3 and 1.3, respectively. As noted earlier, this pattern occurred because many pens were operated as integrated elements of larger agrarian complexes belonging to absentees, so they came as part of a package of properties. Independent pens tended to belong to residents. The odd man out was John Salmon Jr, based in St Elizabeth, with eleven pens, seven plantations and just four estates. Only Duncan Robertson, also in St Elizabeth, and John Davy of Manchester managed plantations exclusively. At the other end of the scale was William Miller with twenty-six estates, eight pens and two plantations, on which lived seventy-seven hundred enslaved people. Miller was popularly known as "Attorney General", while Joseph Gordon who managed twenty-two properties was called "the prince of the planting attorneys in Jamaica".[77]

Was there change in the numbers of properties managed by a single attorney? In 1796 there were said to be 606 sugar estates in the hands of 193 attorneys.[78] This is significantly more than the 467 estates found in 1832, and slightly less than the two hundred attorneys in that year. However, at 3.1 the mean number of estates in the hands of an attorney was not dramatically different. The findings for 1832 can also be roughly compared with those of Alan Karras for St Ann, derived from the registration returns for 1817. Karras identified forty-eight attorneys in the parish, twenty-seven of them (56 per cent) managing only one property each, seventeen managing two or three (35 per cent) and four attorneys a larger number.[79] In 1832 there was a total of fifty properties in the hands of attorneys in St Ann. Again, this suggests some retreat of the system. The anecdotal testimony points in the same direction.

Peter Marsden, in 1788, complained that the attorneys "too often have a multiplicity of business in various places to attend sufficiently to their great charge", and thought it would be "a good regulation to confine the attorneys more to their plantations, which would increase their number, and be the means of keeping the estates in better order". In 1807 William Mitchell, who had lived in Jamaica for nearly forty years, said he had managed "perhaps 16 or 18 at a time" in different parts of the island, but added, "I was not so much in that line as others." He was himself owner of four estates and "about 1,300 Negroes". John Blackburn lived in Jamaica for thirty-two years, down to 1807, having about thirty plantations under his "care and management".[80] Further evidence of larger numbers of estates under the management of a single attorney comes from statements made to the House of Assembly in 1815, when it enquired into the British government's proposal for the registration of slaves. It took evidence from many men, including seven attorneys. For example, Francis Graham told the committee that "he represents solely and in part forty-nine sugar-estates, nineteen pens, and ten other plantations, on which there are about thirteen thousand negroes; and that he possesses a sugar-estate, called Tulloch, with about four hundred and fifty negroes, and holds jointly with Lord Carrington the Farm pen, with about two hundred and fifty negroes". He had lived in Jamaica since 1797, with a break of eleven months, and believed that "the line in life he has followed" had given him a broad knowledge of most of the parishes.[81] Gardner in 1873 said, "The number of great attorneys, as those having many estates under their care were called, diminished somewhat in later years [of slavery], and more frequently only a few estates were entrusted to the same individual."[82] These examples suggest perhaps greater domains before the abolition of the slave trade, but more solid evidence is needed.

The more properties under an attorney's care, the more likely he was to have multiple employers. William Miller, with thirty-six properties in 1832, had twenty-two separate employers. Some twenty-seven of the two hundred

Table 3.2 Attorneys Managing Five or More Properties, 1832

Attorney	Number of Properties				Total slaves	Main parish
	Estates	Pens	Plantations	Total		
John Anderson	2	2	3	7	982	Ann
John Ashley	4	0	1	5	1,345	Vere
Alexander Bayley	6	1	2	9	1,530	John
Thomas J. Bernard	8	3	0	11	2,217	Clarendon
John Blair	7	6	1	14	2,767	Mary
Thomas Blakely	5	1	1	7	1,350	Thomas East
Hamilton Brown	6	4	1	11	1,380	Ann
Archibald Campbell	5	2	0	7	985	Westmoreland
William Carey	9	2	0	11	2,288	Trelawny
Edward Clouston	4	2	2	8	1,046	Thomas Vale
Henry Cox	3	1	2	6	483	Mary
James Daly	2	1	2	5	828	Elizabeth
John Davy	0	0	5	5	642	Manchester
Robert Fairweather	6	5	2	13	2,332	Mary
James Forsyth	5	1	3	9	1,177	Thomas East
Thomas Glen	4	1	0	5	672	James
George Gordon	17	3	0	20	4,310	Hanover
Joseph Gordon	15	5	2	22	4,704	Catherine
William Gordon	6	2	0	8	1,638	Hanover
John Griffith	0	4	5	9	1,212	Manchester
John Gunn	5	0	0	5	1,163	James
George William Hamilton	5	0	2	7	1,583	Thomas Vale
Thomas Hine	4	1	0	5	442	Trelawny
Lawrence Hislop	6	1	0	7	1,396	Trelawny
Henry Hunter	5	1	2	8	1,257	James
John Irving	5	2	0	7	945	Hanover
William Jackson	6	3	2	11	1,991	Dorothy
William M. Kerr	5	1	2	8	1,702	James

Table 3.2 continues

Table 3.2 Attorneys Managing Five or More Properties, 1832 *(cont'd)*

Attorney	Number of properties				Total slaves	Main parish
	Estates	Pens	Plantations	Total		
William Lambie	8	1	1	10	2,305	Mary
James Lawson	5	4	0	9	1,530	Westmoreland
Thomas McCornock	5	2	0	7	2,435	Thomas East
James MacDonald	8	2	1	11	2,147	Mary
James McDonald	8	0	1	9	1,978	Trelawny
Colin McKenzie	3	2	0	5	950	Mary
Alexander McWilliam	3	2	1	6	1,083	Clarendon
John Mais	2	0	3	5	519	Portland
William Miller	26	8	2	36	7,700	Trelawny
Matthew Mitchell	6	2	0	8	1,408	Trelawny
Charles O'Connor	4	1	0	5	884	James
George Hibbert Oates	5	3	0	8	1,851	Hanover
John Oldham	6	1	3	10	1,581	Mary
William Reeves	6	0	0	6	963	Trelawny
William Reynolds	5	0	0	5	726	Trelawny
William Ridgard	6	1	1	8	1,922	Elizabeth
Duncan Robertson	0	0	7	7	772	Elizabeth
John Salmon Jr	4	11	7	22	3,003	Elizabeth
Charles Scott	10	1	0	11	2,323	Thomas East
Simon Taylor	7	0	5	12	2,624	David
William Tharp	7	4	0	11	2,640	Trelawny
James Wright Turner	7	2	0	9	1,821	Clarendon
James Matthew Whyte	6	1	1	8	1,978	Thomas East
Joseph Stone Williams	7	4	0	11	2,701	Westmoreland
Total	309	107	73	489	92,211	

Source: Returns of Registrations of Slaves (Jamaica Archives, Spanish Town).

planting attorneys had five or more employers and they dealt with 310 properties. To a large extent, this group overlapped with the realm of the fifty-two attorneys controlling five or more properties. The difference occurred among a small number of attorneys dealing with only two, three or four employers but managing ten or more properties.

Why would a proprietor employ an attorney who was already busy? In the first place, such an attorney had a profile, a reputation, a proven record. In more practical terms, the large attorney had the advantage of extensive networks, in law and government, in the merchant class, and among penkeepers and planters with whom useful trade could happen. On the other hand, if the person appointed was a proprietor in his own right, conflict of interest might arise. This was resolved in various ways, the solution depending on the scale of the attorneyship and perhaps the status of the proprietor. Thus, when in 1805 Rowland Fearon took over as attorney for Lord Penrhyn, he sent a long letter explaining that the management of his own properties had been handed over to his brother and that he would therefore be able to devote all his time to the business of his new employer.[83]

How common were joint attorneyships? Taking only the estates, plantations and pens managed by attorneys in 1832, some 620 properties were in the hands of an individual, 81 per cent of the total. Another 102 (14 per cent) were managed jointly by two attorneys, 21 by three, and 2 by four. The preference to work alone was expressed in this pattern and it was a saving to the employer. Joint attorneyships were not generally a product of the number of properties managed, though might prove useful where scattered distant units were involved.[84] Some of the joint attorneyships, though certainly not all, seem to have combined a "planting" with a "mercantile" attorney.

How did the attorneys compare with local and metropolitan merchant-factors in the scale of their operations? In 1807 Andrew Wedderburn, who described himself as a "West India merchant, principally connected with the island of Jamaica", said that the accounts of eight estates "annually passed through my hands as a factor, so as accurately to judge of all the expences incurred in the conducting of a sugar plantation". Wedderburn, based in London, had never been to the West Indies but expressed opinions based on his "general knowledge of the situation of West India estates, acquired by conversation with persons who have been long resident in the islands".[85] In 1808 George Hibbert said he was "a partner in two distinct houses, trading with the island of Jamaica particularly, and in a small degree with Barbadoes". The total annual import dealt with by the two houses was eight to ten thousand hogsheads of sugar, the product of perhaps thirty different estates. His uncle Thomas, son of a Manchester merchant, had set up in Kingston as a middleman, traded in slaves from Africa and purchased a plantation, where he died in 1780. George Hibbert, born 1757, never visited Jamaica, but became a leading advocate of the colony, the slave trade and slavery.[86] His business was more extensive than that of most Jamaican attorneys, whereas Wedderburn worked on a larger Atlantic stage. A large sample is needed to make a certain comparison but it was rarely functional for a metropolitan merchant to deal with a small number of overseas enterprises.

Domains

A common reason for employing different attorneys was distance. The most celebrated example is that of Matthew Gregory Lewis, whose two estates were in the hands of his executors in 1832: Cornwall Estate in Westmoreland was managed by Henry Waite Plummer, and Hordley Estate in St Thomas-in-the-East by Charles Scott (Figure 3.6). From Cornwall to Hordley was about 150 miles, a journey that took him six days by carriage.[87] An attorney on horseback or sailing along the coast might have moved more quickly but the distance was sufficient to prohibit employing a single attorney for both. Cornwall was Plummer's sole responsibility, whereas Scott was attorney for ten estates and a pen. Another proprietor, the Earl of Balcarres employed Robert Fairweather as attorney for his plantation in St George and John Salmon Jr for his two pens in Manchester. Fairweather had seven other employers, Salmon nineteen more (Figure 3.7). The same applied on a larger scale to Sir Simon Haughton Clarke who owned nine properties and registered 2,306 slaves in 1832. In the western parishes of Hanover and Westmoreland, Clarke's three estates and one pen were in the hands of William Gordon; his St James estate was managed by John Gunn; two estates and a pen in Trelawny by Lawrence Hislop; and in the east his St Mary estate had Alexander Forsyth as attorney. All of Clarke's attorneys were busy: Gunn had five other employers, Hislop had four, Gordon two, Forsyth one.

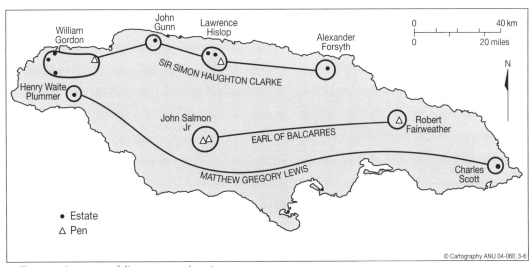

Figure 3.6 Attorneys of distant properties, 1832

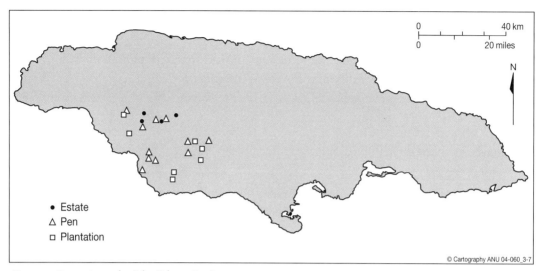

Figure 3.7 Properties under John Salmon Jr, 1832

In these ways, attorneys built up their own domains. They came to be important in a district, but never had exclusive control of all the properties in it. There was much overlapping. On the other hand, the owner of two or more neighbouring estates occasionally employed a different attorney for each, perhaps honouring long-standing contracts or simply hedging his bets. The largest proprietors similarly tended to build up domains in particular parishes or districts so that it was possible for a single attorney to manage all of their properties.

The solidity of these proprietorial territories may have reflected the role of the attorney in recommending acquisitions and the preference of a proprietor not to spread beyond the bounds of a space that could be efficiently managed by an existing attorney. Thus, in 1832, nine of Neill Malcolm's ten estates and pens were in Hanover and the other was located just over the border in the neighbouring parish of Westmoreland (Figure 3.8). All of these properties were in the hands of George Gordon, whose domain spread more widely, including St James (Figure 3.9). Similarly, all of the late John Tharp's ten estates and pens were in Trelawny with the exception of one pen across the border in St Ann, all of them managed by William Tharp. The rather more dispersed properties of James Dawkins were in the hands of a single team of attorneys, Thomas J. Bernard and William G. Stewart.

William Miller was sole attorney for twenty-six properties in 1832 but allied himself with William Reeves for one estate and with George Marrett for seven (Figure 3.10). Reeves was sole attorney for another six properties and Marrett for one. Miller and Marrett joined Wilkin Cooper and Bernard Schusmidt to make the only four-man attorneyship of 1832, with responsibility for Etingdon and Hyde Hall Estates in Trelawny, as well as

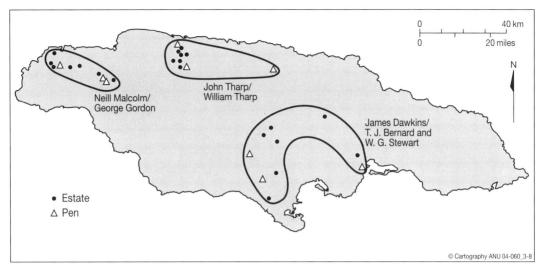

Figure 3.8 Owners of ten or more properties with one attorney, 1832

"Glamorgan and Cedar Spring", a nearby holding not distinguished in the records as estate, pen or plantation. In all of these joint attorneyships, Miller was the first named partner. He also associated himself with other attorneys as second-named partner, notably Robert Fairweather who had a large attorneyship of his own and with Thomas Hine who was in charge of no other properties. Mapping the distribution of the properties associated with Miller produces no clear pattern (Figure 3.11). His primary and secondary attorneyships were intermixed, with a concentration of partnerships close to his home base in Falmouth, so that the distance factor seems unable to

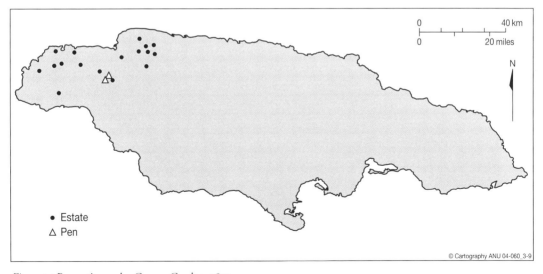

Figure 3.9 Properties under George Gordon, 1832

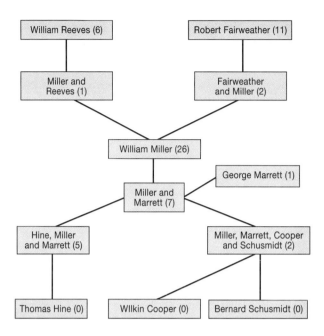

Figure 3.10 Network of attorneys with William Miller, 1832. (Numbers in parentheses indicate the number of properties managed by that person or partnership. Zero means the person was sole attorney for no property.)

explain the rationale for shared responsibility. By 1832 Miller had been an attorney for thirty-three years and in order to understand the structure of his partnerships it would be necessary to trace the process of accumulation of employers and properties.[88] Some of these partnerships may have been constituted by associating a planting attorney with a mercantile attorney.

In addition to the estates, pens and plantations for which Miller was attorney, he served as agent, mortgagee, receiver (appointed by the Court of Chancery) and executor for holdings large and small. He also returned ten slaves in 1832 as tenant of Thomas B. Hamilton, an "unrepresented absentee", on Pemberton Estate. Giving evidence in 1836, Miller claimed to have had forty-eight "properties" under his care at the beginning of the apprenticeship in 1834, with a population of more than ten thousand apprentices. In reaching this total, probably he included those for which he was second-named attorney as well as the thirty-six listed in Table 3.2 for which he was named first. Asked if he paid the estates "frequent personal visits", he said, "I did as often as I could." Shortly before coming to England in the middle of 1835, he had made "a tour . . . of a great part of the island, the last visit I paid to my concerns, and I was rather particular, as I was coming to England, in taking notes of the state of cultivation of different parishes".[89] He must have known he would be interrogated.

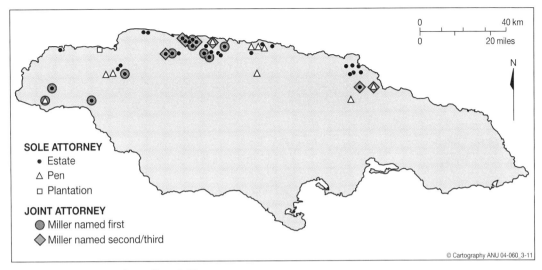

Figure 3.11 Properties under William Miller, 1832

Miller's network of attorneyships was large but less extensively ramified than some. He was connected with only six other men, all of whom worked exclusively with him. Another attorney, George William Hamilton, worked jointly with seven men for a smaller number of properties but, through his partnership with Colin McKenzie, had networked links to a total of nineteen attorneys, spreading out in many directions (Figure 3.12). It was this kind of ramified interconnection that enabled attorneys to manage local exchange and to share information, as well as providing the basis for favours and fraud.

Where did attorneys make their residences? The mercantile attorneys seem almost always to have lived in the port towns, even when they themselves owned estates. On the other hand, the planting attorneys who owned plantations in their own right generally lived on one of those plantations. For example, the creole William Murray stated in 1815 that he had lived almost twenty years on his own large sugar plantation in St James, but also held "considerable property in right of his wife, in the parishes of Clarendon and Vere, and has the management of several estates belonging to his friends in England".[90] Those who did not own plantations often lived on one of the properties for which they served as attorney. By making his residence in an absentee's great house, the attorney visibly established his commanding place in the social order. He might do so without charge or he might rent an unoccupied "princely mansion" on a plantation.[91] Others, like William Miller, preferred to live in a port town. Beckford in 1790 said that "some attornies are resident at the opposite parts of the island to those in which the properties for which they are engaged are placed".[92] This may have applied where a friend or relative took on the role of attorney but it is hard to find examples among the professionals. Miller's closest rival, Joseph Gordon, did have charge of

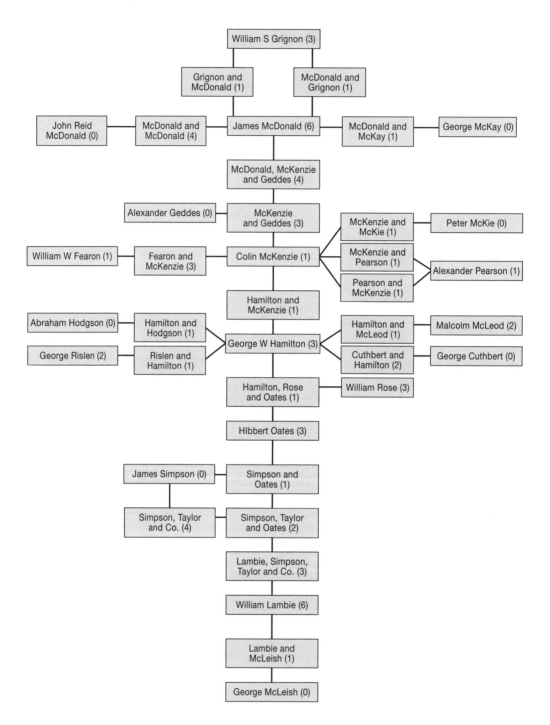

Figure 3.12 Network of attorneys with Colin McKenzie and George W. Hamilton, 1832. (Numbers in parentheses indicate the number of properties managed by that person or partnership. Zero means the person was sole attorney for no property.)

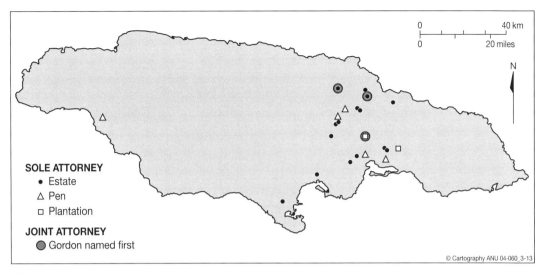

SOLE ATTORNEY
• Estate
△ Pen
□ Plantation

JOINT ATTORNEY
◉ Gordon named first

© Cartography ANU 04-060_3-13

Figure 3.13 Properties under Joseph Gordon, 1832

some distant outlying properties, but the great majority of his attorneyship was within a day's ride of his residence, Delacree Pen in St Andrew (Figure 3.13).

Occasionally, attorneys may have exaggerated the extent of their domains, eager to demonstrate the comprehensiveness of their knowledge of the island. Thus David Richards, who had managed "sundry plantations as attorney and receiver", said in 1815 that his "principal residence" was in Trelawny but he had "charge of estates in St James and Hanover, St Thomas in the East, and St George".[93] Shand, giving testimony to the British Parliament's Select Committee on the Extinction of Slavery in 1832, stated he had lived in Jamaica from 1791 to 1823, and again from 1825 to 1826, managing estates in "almost every parish". Some eighteen to twenty thousand enslaved people lived on these properties, he said, providing him "an opportunity of being acquainted with the negro character".[94]

Demography

Systematic data on the demography of the attorneys are difficult to compile, particularly because many of them were born and/or died in places other than Jamaica. The most accessible source is Philip Wright's comprehensive collection of inscriptions from surviving headstones and memorials to the dead in Jamaica's churches and churchyards, covering the period down to about 1880 when civil registration of births and deaths was introduced. Wright's work includes 3,092 memorials with information on roughly 4,370 individuals, almost all of whom died in Jamaica. Of the two hundred attorneys known to be active in Jamaica in 1832, some fifty-four appear in the collection. The missing persons may have died outside Jamaica or simply not been memorialized. Probably some memorials have perished. The population included in Wright's collection was almost entirely white and free, but even among the wealthy, memorials are known only for a relatively small number.

How typical of the attorneys of 1832 were the fifty-four memorialized? They tended towards the higher end of the scale, managing an average 5.3 properties and 993 slaves. Almost half of the memorialized managed five or more properties, and nineteen of them appear among the fifty-two attorneys managing five or more properties listed in Table 3.2. The memorialized had charge of 38 per cent of the properties under attorneys in 1832 and were firmly aligned with the sugar-livestock sector. Thus, although the memorialized made up only 27 per cent of the two hundred attorneys, they had control of 40 per cent of the enslaved people living on properties managed by attorneys. Overall, the memorialized attorneys accounted for a significant and influential slice of the attorney population, but were weighted towards the wealthier end of the system.

All of the fifty-four memorialized were men, as were all two hundred planting attorneys of 1832. Women did take effective control of plantations and merchant houses, particularly in the first years of widowhood, but generally were forced to work through intermediaries. They could more easily have legal ownership of a plantation than be given the job of managing one. Even ownership of property was made difficult by inheritance law and practice, with preference to sons over widows. The chances of women managing plantation property in Jamaica declined after 1700.[95] There is no indication of a woman formally employed as an overseer or planting attorney.

The average age of the memorialized attorneys, in 1832, was fifty years, ranging from twenty-six (born 1806) to seventy-four (born 1758). Two-thirds of the properties in the sample were managed by attorneys aged between forty and fifty-three, and half of the attorneys fell into this age range. The general tendency was for young men to be given charge of properties only after having already proved themselves as overseers or factors. Some began their managerial careers among the book-keepers. After forty years of age, they might rapidly acquire a large domain but those who survived beyond sixty saw their responsibilities dwindle.

Were attorneys long-lived? The mean year of death for the memorialized attorneys was 1847, so they typically lived on another fifteen years after 1832, with the longest lived surviving to 1875. Average age at death was sixty-four years (Standard Deviation 15). The attorneys had the advantage of having successfully survived the initial seasoning period and the hazards faced by newcomers. They entered the population of attorneys only after they reached their late twenties. On the other hand, their reputed dissipation seems not to have cut them down.

Few memorials identified birthplaces. Only one mentioned a Jamaican origin, this a mural tablet in St Paul's Church, Chapelton, in the parish of Clarendon, for "James Wright Turner Esq., b. in this parish 22 Aug. 1799 and died in it 14 Nov. 1840".[96] Similarly, only one memorial identified a birthplace in England (William Ridgard of Gainsborough, Lincolnshire) and one a place in Ireland (Hamilton Brown of County Antrim). More common were Scottish sites. Two were born in "Scotland" (Thomas McCornock of Dumfries and John McCreath of Kirkcudbrightshire) and two in "North Britain" (Colin McKenzie of Ross-shire and Evan MacPherson of Inverness-shire). Another twelve of the memorialized attorneys had "Scottish" names, confirming the common view that the attorneys (and overseers) of Jamaica were dominated by men from Scotland.[97] On the other hand, silence may point to Jamaican birth, so the role of creoles remains hard to pin down.

The dominance of the Scots was often remarked upon by contemporaries. Lady Nugent, soon after her arrival in Jamaica in 1801, bravely declared that "almost all the agents, attorneys, merchants and shopkeepers, are of that country [Scotland], and really do deserve to thrive in this, they are so industrious".[98] Sheridan believed "the greater number of attorneys" were Scots. He argued that their success as overseers, attorneys and factors had something to do with their "clannish disposition", and the necessity of networking. English contemporaries sometimes thought their clannishness "pitiful". Not all of them maintained their "Scottishness", however, particularly those of the middle class who aspired to a refinement associated with the world of the English.[99] The Scots also played a significant role in estate management within England itself. Shand, giving evidence in 1832, was asked, "What advantage has a Scotchman coming over from Scotland at 22 years of age over a person of colour in Jamaica at 24, in respect to the management of an estate?" With a sweeping disparagement of the creole character, Shand replied, "There is something different in his temperament and habits which render him more steady and more competent to business of that kind than a native of Jamaica, especially a person of colour."[100] Here Shand bundled together creoles of all sorts as ill-fitted for management.

In 1836 the creole Beaumont advocated the superior knowledge of the creole Jamaica-raised man over the Scotchman, defending his own claims to knowledge of the situation of "the negro". Disparaging the capacity of the "planting attorney", he told a parliamentary committee that "there is no set of men who really do know less about the active managing of an estate than planting attornies do, although these gentlemen are put forward as persons who must have an immense deal of knowledge upon the subject". The reason, said Beaumont, was that "persons who are called *par excellence* planters and planting attornies, in general have been young men sent from Scotland, and are occasionally the sons of Jamaica proprietors, born in the island". The latter, as in Beaumont's own case, "being brought up very much amongst the negroes, know their habits, their romances, . . . their superstitions and opinions". On the other hand, he said, "an imported planter knows nothing but how the greatest quantity of sugar is to be obtained out of the greatest quantity of labour".[101]

Were any of the attorneys "free men of colour"? The data are sometimes tantalizing but the memorials provide no solid reasons to doubt the assumption that they were all white. Benjamin Scott Moncrieffe, a free coloured man granted privileged status, is known to have acted as attorney but did not appear in the slave registration returns as such.[102] H. P. Jacobs contended that the title "Esquire" was used almost exclusively for white men in the period.[103] Some twenty-three of the fifty-four memorialized attorneys were given the Esquire label, and another ten "Hon", but most of the remainder were simply described by their names and should not be presumed to necessarily lack status. Lower down the hierarchy, in 1832 Shand said it was not customary for people of colour to be employed as overseers or book-keepers on estates and plantations, "as they were not found to make good managers in general". On the other hand, Matthew Gregory Lewis in 1816 did claim to observe young brown men as "clerks and book-keepers".[104]

Memorials that were silent on birthplace sometimes mentioned the number of years an attorney had spent in Jamaica, indicating birth outside the island. Six cases in the sample referred to "long residence", from forty to sixty years. These men had come to the island when they were nineteen to twenty-three years of age. Adding these to the explicit memorials, at least one-quarter of the attorneys of 1832 were born outside Jamaica. There is no doubt that British-born men predominated, the great majority moving to the island in their early twenties. Some who grew up through the ranks of the Jamaican planting system came to Jamaica even younger. Thus Richard Pennant wrote to his Clarendon attorney in 1781 saying, "I have sent three boys by Captain Carr. They will understand accounts very well – they are very good lads . . . they are about thirteen."[105] Shand, asked in 1815 whether he thought the enslaved people of Jamaica presented "the appearance of a contented peasantry", responded that he had "left Europe so early after his education was completed, that he has little recollection of the state of the labouring population".[106] Hope Masterton Waddell, evangelist with the Church of Scotland Missionary Society, described William Miller as a man who "had gone from Scotland in the lowest capacity, and had risen to almost the highest position in the colony", while Burn later said Miller had "come from Scotland, a working man, with nothing but his ability to rely on".[107]

Beyond these indications of birthplace, the memorials provide few clues to the education, background and earlier activities of the attorneys. James Brydon (1763–1840) of Kingston was described as a "merchant". Charles MacGlashan (1760–1834) was formerly a surgeon in the Royal Navy and "long a medical practitioner" in St Andrew. These two men were, however, planting attorneys only in a marginal way.

Waddell observed of the white men of Jamaica that "from the attorney down, all were unmarried, yet all had families". He did encounter some exceptions, however, such as the attorney of Running Gut estate, the property of an absentee living in Scotland, "a respectable married man, a rare character in those days, who with his wife attended Hampden Church".[108] Of the memorialized attorneys, fifteen (28 per cent) were attributed a wife, identified either on the attorney's own memorial or on a separate tablet, sometimes appearing as a widow. Occasionally, a second wife was mentioned, generally when the first had died young. Age at death for the attorney's wives averaged forty-one years but half of them died before reaching thirty. The memorials were silent on age at marriage, but the gap between husband and wife was often wide. In the few known cases, the attorney was typically more than twenty years older than his wife. The extreme case was Duncan Robertson. When his first wife Bridget died in 1831 she was only eighteen and he was fifty; the second son of his second wife Elizabeth Frances died in 1844 aged five but she bore another four sons before Duncan died in 1850.[109] The general pattern appears to be that those attorneys who married did so in their forties, when they had established their domains, and that they married much younger women, in their teens or twenties.

Where did the attorneys find their wives? The youth of the women and the sedentary character of life of the attorneys suggest that many of the wives were creoles, the Jamaica-born daughters of white parents. If any of their wives were "free women of colour" the memorials are silent on the matter. Occasionally, they were the daughters of other attorneys. Thus Duncan Robertson's first wife Bridget was the daughter of James Daly of St Elizabeth. Daly was attorney for two estates, a pen and two plantations, in St Elizabeth and Manchester; Robertson for seven plantations in the same parishes. Similarly, Angelina Israel Fearon, who died in 1819 aged twenty-three and was buried in the yard of Vere Parish Church, at Alley, was "wife of [attorney] William Wheeler Fearon Esq. of Clarendon, and daughter of the late Paul Christian Esq. of Vere". On the other hand, some of the Scots attorneys acquired wives from their homeland. For example, the attorney William Lambie's wife Elizabeth, who died in Kingston in 1821 aged twenty-three, was "daughter of Patrick Crichton Esq. of the City of Edinburgh".[110] Lambie was by 1832 attorney for ten large properties in the eastern end of the island. Another Scot, Duncan McCallum, was attorney for Bogg Pen in St Ann and buried his wife on the property: "Margaret McCallum, only daughter of Robert Gardner Esq., Irvine in Ayrshire, NB [North Britain], who after being happily married to Duncan McCallum of the island of Jamaica, d. 27 Jan. 1830 aged 29; her residence in the island was only 11 weeks." Duncan himself died in 1833, aged thirty-nine, and was buried nearby at Trafalgar.[111]

Children were less likely than wives to appear on memorials. Whereas 28 per cent of the attorneys were attributed wives, only 20 per cent had children associated with them. Duncan Robertson had the most, six sons, five of whom survived him. Often the children mentioned on memorials died young and sometimes they had been carried off together. Thus Robert Cron, attorney for three estates, inscribed a tomb at Carlton in St James, in memory of "Anna, Jemima, and Jessie, three infant daughters of Robert and Anna Cron; the two former d. on the eve of Christmas 1831, being the period when the fatal rebellion of that date broke out in this island; the last d. two days afterwards".[112] Thomas James Bernard, attorney for eight estates and three pens, buried three children at his property Bona Vista in St James, born in 1823, 1824 and 1827 (without mention of a mother or wife) and two in the yard of Spanish Town Cathedral, born in 1828 and 1832 (daughters of himself and his wife Theodora Foulkes).[113] None of these five children survived more than six years.

Overall, twenty of the fifty-four memorialized attorneys were associated with wives and/or children. Of these, nine had a wife but no children, six had both wife and children, and five had children but no wife. These numbers derive from what the memorials say explicitly. Only in a few cases, where memorials were erected by "friends" rather than kin, can it be presumed the attorneys died without publicly acknowledged family connections in the free community.

Attorneys were perhaps less notorious than overseers as the fathers of children by enslaved and free coloured women but it is certain that they fathered many children. In 1816 Matthew Gregory Lewis observed in Montego Bay an exclusive ball held by "brown ladies and gentlemen", the women mostly "the natural daughters of attorneys and overseers".[114] Some of the children whose deaths were memorialized may have been coloured. Often the attorneys, and white men generally, were reluctant to acknowledge paternity of children born of enslaved and free coloured women. The attorneys' relationships with these women and their children ranged across a wide spectrum, from rape and disavowal to varieties of acceptance and affection. Moreton claimed in 1793 that it was "common for an attorney to keep a favourite black or mulatta girl on every estate, which the managers are obliged to pamper and indulge like godesses". When visiting his estates, said Moreton, the attorney "commonly invites a few dissipated gentlemen to spend a few days with him", and required the overseer to "procure some of the finest young wenches for the gentlemen".[115] Simon Taylor, whose life is sketched in chapter 6, figures prominently in accounts of the unmarried attorney's sexuality, just as Thomas Thistlewood has come to represent the complex behaviour of the overseer class.[116] Occasionally, the attorney might send a mulatto child to Scotland or England, even accompanied by a maid, for education.[117]

George William Gordon, who was to become a national hero, was the son of Joseph Gordon, already noticed as one of the leading attorneys in 1832, and an enslaved woman of Cherry Garden. Joseph and the enslaved woman had three children, all of whom were manumitted. George was taught to read and write and to keep accounts, and became himself a merchant and planter. Joseph later married a white woman, a widow, and they had children. He was a member of the Assembly for St Andrew and was appointed custos during the apprenticeship. After abolition, Joseph's business declined and he and his white family left Jamaica, with George holding power of attorney and expected to send his father five hundred pounds each year.[118]

Payment

For most of the eighteenth century, attorneys were employed on commission. The rate was set at 6 per cent by the act of 1751. In practice, the exact amount of the commission and the basis on which it was calculated were more variable. J. R. Ward claims that soon after 1740 "the maximum rate of attorney's commission chargeable in the colony was reduced by law from 10 per cent on shipments to 6 per cent" but also contends that this regulation became fully effective only in the 1760s.[119] Edward Long said the incomes of absentees were "abridged by the commission of *6l. per cent.* paid to their agents in Jamaica, for managing their affairs", and Beckford that attorneys drew "6 per cent upon the produce of the plantation". Senior in 1835 also understood 6 per cent on the annual proceeds as the regular emolument of the attorney.[120]

By the 1790s, however, some attorneys were paid only 5 per cent and salaries began to replace commissions. Thus Moreton in 1793 believed the attorney "charges five per cent commission on the net proceeds of the shipments", and in 1823 Roughley said both planting and mercantile attorney received "a commission of five per cent on all sales or net proceeds". John Stewart, the same year, referred to "a commission of five per cent on all sales and purchases". Gardner in 1873 said of the early nineteenth century that "the general mode of remuneration was five or six per cent on the purchases and sales".[121] These pieces of evidence suggest that 6 per cent was the usual rate in the second half of the eighteenth century, and that after 1800 attorneys increasingly accepted 5 per cent.[122]

What exactly was the commission charged on? Here there is more significant disagreement among writers, contemporary and modern. Long was vague. Beckford said it was charged on "the produce of the plantation", R. C. Dallas in 1803 "all the produce of an estate", and Stewart in 1823 "all sales and purchases (the crop being valued at the existing current prices)". Attorneys in the 1840s referred to "commissions upon the gross produce".[123] Perhaps the clearest statement came from Senior in 1835, who said the attorney's emoluments arise from the annual proceeds of the property, on which he receives six per cent; consequently, should the sugar and rum exported realize £1,000, the attorney draws for £60. If from a penn, stock and wood should be disposed of, or hired labour furnished to the extent of £1,000 currency, the attorney charges, in his annual current account with the proprietor, the sum of £60 as his commission.[124]

Twentieth-century historians also differ. Burn said the commission was based on "gross sales", Curtin "the sale price on each crop shipped", Sheridan "the annual produce" or "the gross value of the produce of the plantations in his care", and Ward "on shipments".[125] The most plausible conclusion is that the commission was in practice charged on the value of sales of plantation produce, whether those sales occurred in Jamaica or in overseas markets.

Some attorneys had contracts which were more precise. For example, in 1810 a case came to court, in which an attorney was accused of overcharging by claiming 6 per cent on gross sales of sugar in Britain, including the cost of shipping, duties and other charges, whereas he was due only 5 per cent on net proceeds on sales in Britain or Jamaica. The planter was awarded damages.[126]

Salaries began to displace commissions at the end of the eighteenth century, in order no doubt to prevent such disputes and opportunities for fraud and siphoning. Dallas, in 1803, considered salaries a recent innovation. He said there were both "six per cent attornies, and salaried attornies", the latter "paid a certain stipend by some unincumbered proprietors, who have lately discovered that a steward in Jamaica may be hired like a steward in England, by which several thousand pounds a year are saved". The salaried attorney was, said Dallas, "often a plain plodding man", belonging to a different class. He might deserve respect, "but the high airs and rapid flights to fortune of the six per centers are out of his walk".[127] In fact, salaries had not then completely replaced payment by commission in Britain, but the trend was strong. Several commentators suggest that salaries became more usual after the abolition of the slave trade in 1808. Ward places the move to salaries in the 1820s, and that may be when the balance shifted. Stewart in 1823 said that "many now go upon the plan of allowing a stipulated salary to their attorneys, and no perquisite beyond that, and of confining them to the management of their estates only".[128] By 1842 the attorney Henry Lowndes, who reported receiving a salary of £150 sterling, could say that although legally still paid by "commissions upon the gross produce" the "usual remuneration is now by salaries". Salaries do seem to have been common by the 1840s, though some of the great attorneys are said to have refused them.[129]

Contemporary critics regularly complained that the system of payment through commission resulted in inefficiencies and fraud.[130] Modern writers have repeated these arguments. For example, Burn believed payment by commission "an unfortunate system" because it encouraged the attorney "to do everything possible to increase the present output of the estate, not only at the expense of the over-tasked slaves but of the future yield of the land".

The system offered no incentives "to rest old land or to bring new under cultivation", and at the same time "encouraged the attorney to be careless about the expenses which would have to be taken into account before the owner's net profit could be arrived at".[131] The attorney could make a fortune by buying and selling through his own estate or business, or give work to his own jobbing gang, or use estate resources such as carts for his own enterprises. Similarly, Curtin believed the attorney's commission placed "an enormous drain on the income from the property, and the method of payment was not one to encourage an interest in the long-term productivity of the estate". It created "immense opportunities for illegal and semi-legal practices that would increase his income".[132]

How much could an attorney make? His expenses were said to be few. He needed only to employ a clerk to prepare accounts and keep books, find an office or "counting room", and have means of transport. If he was lucky, he could get most of this from the existing resources of an estate on which he made his residence. Curtin believed "the planting attorneys were the wealthiest men in Jamaica", and those with several employers "might have an annual income of eight to ten thousand pounds currency".[133] Brathwaite argued similarly that a "really big attorney" representing fifteen to twenty plantations "was a nabob in his own right, with a yearly income of from £8,000 to £10,000".[134] This was more than the "average proprietor" could expect, and less affected by bad seasons and hard times. How typical were these annual incomes of £8,000 to £10,000? In 1796 the 193 attorneys who managed 606 sugar estates earned commissions exceeding £240,000 annually.[135] This gives an average £1,244 per attorney, and an average £396 paid by each estate. Certainly some attorneys did better than this, and others worse. To earn £10,000, at these rates, an attorney had to manage twenty-five "average" estates. Only the attorney able to pick and choose, and able to build up a domain composed of the most profitable properties, could expect to earn so much from a smaller number.

How did the incomes of attorneys rank within Jamaica? Beckford thought there was "not a profession in the country so much sought after". Gardner said of the early nineteenth century that in the estate economy, "the attorney's was the most lucrative post". Senior, on the other hand, said of the attorney, "If he derives no advantages, (but this is rare indeed) in various other ways under his own immediate control, from the property he has the management of to the detriment of his employer, he certainly is not overpaid."[136] He wrote in the 1830s when prices, and hence commissions, were substantially less than they had been in the 1790s. How did they compare with those of merchants, planters and overseers? The salaries of overseers, the next level down in the hierarchy of management, were substantially less than the commissions or salaries earned by attorneys. After about 1820, however, the gap was rapidly reduced. Before the American Revolution an overseer might earn £85 sterling but by 1790 he was making £125. By the early nineteenth century, he could expect £150 to £200 currency, with house and sustenance.[137] Henry Lowndes said in 1842 that the usual rate for overseers was £300 sterling, though he knew an estate on which the overseer was a black man, formerly enslaved, and paid just £60 sterling.[138] When George Scotland estimated the annual incomes of the major occupational groups found in 1847, he put merchants on top at £700, then "planting attorneys" at £600, then bankers, public servants and professional people all at £500, ministers of religion £400, and surveyors, tavernkeepers and storekeepers £300.[139] Even after the abolition of slavery, the attorneys were near the top of the scale, though then earning only perhaps twice as much as an overseer.

How did the incomes of Jamaica's planting attorneys compare with those of their counterparts in Britain? Only the steward of a very big English estate might expect a salary of £1,000 sterling in the 1790s, and £300 to £400 was more common even on the larger estates. On smaller properties he might make only £100. Overall, salaries increased along with the inflation of the Napoleonic Wars, and continued to increase thereafter as the semi-professional steward was replaced by the newly professionalized manager, the land agent. Even then, however, few could expect more than £1,000. Agents on Irish estates in the early nineteenth century generally were paid 4 or 5 per cent of rents received, but those on salary could expect only about £400.[140] Overall, and particularly during the period of slavery, the attorneys of Jamaica were substantially better paid.

Wealth

The transition from attorney to mortgagee, receiver and owner was a route frequently mapped out by critics of absenteeism. Attorneys possessed property in their own right, however, without always following this path. Some were proprietors before they were attorneys. Many moved up through the system of plantation management and capped their financial success with ownership of land and people. No doubt the success of the attorney in acquiring land depended not only on his ability to accumulate funds but also on the low prices he might pay for plantation property. More broadly, Moreton complained in 1793 that "executors, administrators, and attornies to estates, often accumulate larger fortunes than the heirs or proprietors". A man could obtain the attorneyship of an estate by lending a small amount of money to a planter in distress, then possess the entire property. A planter in this situation, said Moreton, was better advised to sell his estate at once rather than take a mortgage.[141] The attorney might himself contribute to depressing prices. Critics said that "the attorneys had an interest in the failure of the apprenticeship system since distress and discontent in Jamaica might induce the distant proprietor to sell to his representative at a low price". Further, wrote Burn, there were stories of "absentees who had come to Jamaica unannounced to find flourishing and prosperous an estate which the attorney had described as in the last stages of decay, fit only to be sold".[142]

The extent of the attorneys' landownership has not been charted systematically and would prove a difficult task. The numbers of enslaved people they owned can, however, be established directly from the registration returns for 1832, providing an indicator of the attorneys' wealth. Some attorneys owned no slaves in their own right, depending on and exploiting those of their absentee employers. Among the larger attorneys, John Blair, William Carey and George Gordon seem to fit this pattern. John Oldham owned 2 slaves on Agualta Vale Pen, in St Mary, but he was not attorney for that property.[143] Walter George Stewart owned 11 slaves at Bernard Lodge in St Catherine, 10 of them in right of is wife, while Thomas James Bernard owned 18 slaves at Bernard Lodge as well as holding 33 under agreement to purchase from Adam Hogg. James Forsyth owned only 6 slaves in his own right, at Richmond Pen in St Andrew, but was trustee for his wife for a further 112 slaves.

William Miller, the largest of the attorneys in 1832, owned no estates, pens or plantations, and held only 12 domestic slaves in Falmouth where he lived.[144] How he spent and invested his considerable income remains to be established. William Tharp owned only 5 slaves, in Falmouth. Miller's main partner George Marrett owned 10, at Ashton, just east of Duncans and about ten miles from Falmouth, close to the post road that ran along the north coast. Marrett died at Ashton Pen in 1851. Miller's minor partner Robert Fairweather owned 37 slaves at Industry Plantation in St Mary.

Some attorneys held enslaved people on the properties for which they acted and on which they presumably lived. Thus Charles Scott owned 59 slaves attached to Hordley Estate in St Thomas-in-the-East in 1832 and was attorney for the executors of Matthew Gregory Lewis for 242 slaves. William Lambie owned 19 slaves on Friendship Estate in the same parish and, with Charles Scott, was joint owner and agent for the heirs of Dr Irving who held 158 slaves at Friendship. John Salmon Jr owned 7 slaves on New Savanna Pen, St Elizabeth, a property for which he served as attorney, with 117 slaves belonging to John Salmon (probably his father).

More than one-third of the memorials erected to the attorneys of 1832 associate the attorney with a particular place, suggesting residence and perhaps ownership. Joseph Stone Williams (1779–1836), for example, was "of Carawina Estate and Anglesea Pen".[145] Occasionally the association was more precise. Thus William Reynolds (1785–1833) was "proprietor" of Catherine Mount Estate in St James, and Alexander Bayley (1772–1832) "proprietor" of Woodhall in St Dorothy. The registrations of slaves for 1832 found 168 slaves at Woodhall Estate, the return made by Alexander Bayley in right of his wife.

Not all attorneys made and retained large fortunes. For example, in 1832

Henry Cox, aged twenty-nine or thirty years of age, was attorney for properties with a total of 747 enslaved people living on them. All of these properties belonged to his father-in-law, the Honourable Abraham Hodgson, the member of the Assembly who in 1832 was sent, along with the Speaker, Richard Barrett, to London to talk to the West India interest and negotiate with the British government on legislation directed at the control of sectarians in Jamaica and the abolition of slavery. Hodgson was away for more than a year, returning to Jamaica only in late 1833. The governor at the introduction of the apprenticeship, Lord Sligo, described Hodgson as "the cleverest and wealthiest man in the House", and an "independent, but bigoted, old planter".[146] In St Mary, Cox managed Tower Hill Estate, Halifax Estate, Huddersfield Plantation, Saltrum Plantation, and, in St Ann, Albion and Halifax Pen. Butler says, "Cox registered the slaves and supervised the white employees but it is unlikely that Hodgson gave him any control over the financial concerns of the estates."[147] Butler's assessment stems from the fact that Cox was indebted to Hodgson. On the other hand, it is improbable that Cox would be given power of attorney for such limited objectives and, at least while Hodgson was overseas, Cox must have held wider authority. Cox himself owned three sugar estates in 1832, all of them in St Mary: Industry, Epping and Spring Garden. Matching the pattern for Hodgson, Cox also possessed pens in St Ann: Mammee Ridge and Friendship. Altogether, Cox owned 749 enslaved people. Although Cox owned more slaves, he seems to have been heavily indebted to his father-in-law and all of the compensation money paid for his people (£16,400) went to Hodgson (who was paid a total of £31,374).[148]

Sligo described Cox as "very poor".[149] When he died in 1855, aged fifty-two years, he was described on his slab in the floor of the St Ann's Bay Parish Church as "of Content in the Parish of St. Ann".[150] His sole executor was his widow Margaret Cox. When she showed the appraisers his personal property for the purposes of inventory, it came to just £196. The most valuable item was the silver, in spoons and forks, weighing 270 ounces and valued at £60. Many of the other things were described as "old". There was an old carriage and harness, four old horses, one old mule, two old sideboards, one old wardrobe, an old liquor stand, an old sofa table, nineteen old chairs, old books, four old pictures, four old plated candlesticks, an old servant's saddle, an old pimento fanner, an old drip stand, and an old safe. The items not termed old included bedsteads and bedding, common washstands, toilet tables, commodes, bidet stands, looking glasses, sofas, a dining table, cedar side tables, a Spanish chair, a settee, a small table clock, a hat rack, and sundry crockery, glassware and kitchen utensils.[151]

Somewhat more successful was John Mais. In 1815 Mais stated that he was "a merchant in the city of Kingston, and proprietor of a coffee-plantation in the parish of St. Andrew, and has charge of several others in the same and other parishes". He had been "acquainted" with Jamaica since 1792 and coffee since 1799.[152] In 1832 Mais owned Hall's Delight Estate and Mount Pellier and Mount James, in St Andrew, with 287 enslaved people, including 13 on behalf of his mother, a widow living in Great Britain. He was also receiver for Hall Green Plantation, in the same parish.[153] Mais maintained his base in St Andrew but also took attorneyships for properties further afield. In 1832 he was attorney for a series of proprietors, the owners of 603 enslaved persons. He was responsible for Mount Prospect Plantation in St Andrew, Westphalia Plantation in Port Royal, and Clear Mount in St Catherine, all belonging to William Parke, and Mount Idalia Plantation in St John in the hands of Elizabeth Clark, executrix to George Clark (or Clarke). Mais was also attorney in 1832 for Thomas Nash Kemble's two Portland sugar estates, Hope and Cold Harbour. For all of these properties, Mais was sole attorney. He joined with John Fowles as joint attorney for two plantations, Good Hope in St George and Penlyne Castle high in the hills of St David. Thus Mais kept a strong association with coffee planting at the same time as spreading into sugar. When he died in 1855, his property was appraised by John Fowles (Jr) and Peter John Ferron. Mais was described in the inventory they prepared as "late of the parish of St Andrew Esquire deceased". His executors were Edward Mais and Stephen Weise Mais, probably his sons. His personal property was appraised at £29,815, a substantial sum, but all of it composed of debts. The largest amount was due from Robert Paterson (£19,085), followed by John Fowles and Son (£4,300), and presumably his former partner and the appraiser, the estate of A. D'Meynard (£3,560), and "Samuel and Peter Sheppard Indian coast" (£2,870).[154] The inventory is silent on any goods and chattels Mais might have accumulated over his long life.

Other attorneys owned agricultural properties in their own right and, generally, lived on one of them. In 1832 James McDonald owned 11 slaves on Coffee Hall, his own small plantation, in Trelawny. Joseph Gordon owned Delacree Pen in St Andrew, with 69 slaves, as well as 21 on the sugar estates Spring and Barbican. William Reynolds owned Catherine Mount Estate, St James, with 131 slaves in 1832. Hamilton Brown owned Colliston Pen, Minard Pen, Antrim and Grier Park, all in St Ann, with 436 slaves, and was lessee of Beverly with another 28. Simon Taylor, of 1832, owned the Constant Spring Estate in St Andrew, with 317 slaves, held 2 slaves in his own right in Kingston and co-owned another 23 with Simpson Taylor and Company. Taylor had purchased Constant Spring, sometime between 1829 and the middle of 1832, at a public sale conducted by decree of the Court of Chancery in the case Belisario versus Lindo.[155] William Jackson owned 925 slaves, distributed between his three plantations in St John (Cedar Mount, Garden Hill, and Mendes) and his plantation (Blue Hole) and two pens (Bannister and Retreat) in St Dorothy.

Joseph Stone Williams owned all of Carawina Estate (a small proportion jointly with his wife), Anglesea Pen and Cairncurran Settlement in Westmoreland. When he died in 1836 his personal property was appraised at £103,786, more than half of the total in "public funds of Great Britain" in the hands of the factors Colville and Company. Debts owed made up another substantial proportion of the whole. The unexpired terms of the apprentices on the three properties came to £12,941. In 1832, at the last registration of slaves, Williams owned 504 people, the greater proportion at the sugar plantation Carawina.[156] Where Williams lived is uncertain but Carawina had at least an overseer's house, book-keepers' apartments, still-house, plantation stores, and hospital. The material goods housed in those buildings and elsewhere are described in rich and lengthy detail in the inventory, providing a picture both of the technologies of the plantation and the social and cultural life of the attorney. No buildings were identified in the inventory for Anglesea Pen, but the list of household goods suggests that was probably where Williams lived and it was there that he had his writing desks.[157]

Status

Of the fifty-four memorialized attorneys of 1832, nine were identified as "The Honourable", meaning they were elected or nominated members of government. Another five were described as members of the Assembly (sometimes called "the Honourable House of Assembly") without themselves receiving the "Honourable" label. Eleven of the memorialized attorneys were elected to represent their parishes in the Assembly and three were chosen by the governor to sit in the Legislative Council. James Gayleard (1780–1855) was president of the Council for seventeen years, and Walter George Stewart (1801–64) "Clerk of the Council in its legislative capacity".[158] Both of these men were buried in the churchyard of Spanish Town Cathedral. John Gale Vidal (1792–1850) was clerk of the Assembly, and the mural in his honour in Spanish Town Cathedral was "erected by the Assembly as a tribute to one who for 29 years served them with zeal and fidelity".[159] Stewart was an attorney on a large scale, but Gayleard and Vidal were minor players. Of the attorneys of 1832 known from their memorials to be members of Assembly or Council, the most substantial managers were Hamilton Brown, Thomas McCornock, Thomas McNeil, Duncan Robertson and Joseph Stone Williams.

The House of Assembly, at the time of the abolition of slavery, was made up of forty-seven members, two elected from each parish and one from each of Spanish Town, Kingston and Port Royal. Candidates had to be free males, possessing freehold property of at least £300 or other property valuing £3,000, or pay £10 or more in annual taxes. The Legislative Council normally had just seven members, most of them ex-officio and the others appointed by the governor. From the middle of the eighteenth century, the Assembly had established itself as the originator of all legislation in Jamaica, often coming in conflict with governor, Council, Crown and Colonial Office.[160] Given no choice, it even passed its own act to abolish slavery. The Assembly's acts were subjected to pressure from the British Parliament but the members' legislative role served them as a primary tool in the management of the economic and social life of the island. Thus the attorneys who sat in the House sought to use it to preserve the dominance of the plantation system and to place the greatest possible pressure on workers, slave and free. Governors often remarked on the strength of the attorneys in the Assembly, particularly during the transition from slavery to freedom, and appointed some to the Council as moderating influences and conduits to their absentee employers. On the other hand, a powerful member of Council such as William Miller, going into opposition, could make life difficult for a governor.[161] After 1838, the changing composition of the Assembly's membership and electorate reduced the representation of the planting interest, but down to 1865 and the introduction of Crown Colony government the attorneys remained a powerful force.

A second arm of state power manipulated by the attorneys, and the planting interest generally, was the application of the law through courts and magistracy. Six of the memorialized attorneys of 1832 held the parochial office of custos rotulorum, serving as chief magistrate for their parish, having charge of the appointment of magistrates, chairing the Vestry, and giving advice to the governor. Most of these custodes were also members of Assembly or Council. Thomas McCornock, custos for St Thomas-in-the-East, built a chapel at Golden Grove before the end of slavery, but, said H. P. Jacobs, was "associated with various reactionary policies as an Assemblyman". For reasons unknown, McCornock committed suicide in 1848.[162] Joseph Stone Williams, who died in 1836, was both custos of Westmoreland and "for many years one of the Assistant Judges in the Cornwall Assize Court".[163] Another three of the attorneys served as magistrates, while Gayleard was a master of the Court of Chancery and James Farmer Cargill (died 1871) became judge of the Supreme Court. Other attorneys, lacking memorials, were custodes.[164] William Miller was custos for Trelawny for two terms. He explained in 1836 that "being one of the Legislative Council made me a magistrate in every parish in the island", and he had served as a magistrate of several parishes for perhaps twenty years.[165]

In addition to these legislative and juridical roles, attorneys held positions significant to the management of the plantation economy. Walter George Stewart was for thirty-three years island secretary and in this office held formal responsibility, *inter alia,* for the public collection of accounts produce, accounts current, and returns of registrations of slaves. Stewart was also clerk of the Legislative Council and at his death in 1864 a member of the Privy Council.[166] During his almost sixty years in Jamaica, Alexander Barclay (1784–1864) was custos and member of Assembly for St Thomas-in-the-East, and "Receiver General for the Island". He had been appointed receiver-general in 1848, the year he, with George William Gordon, audited the failed Planters' Bank. In 1826 Barclay published a defence of slavery but, "when he saw that emancipation was inevitable", said Jacobs, "made proposals for the amelioration of the apprenticeship system".[167]

Attorneys also exercised their authority through the militia, taking up arms against Jamaica's freedom fighters. Six of the memorialized attorneys of 1832 held the rank of major general and commanded parish regiments. Most if not all of them had active roles in the slave rebellion of 1831 that had its epicentre in St James. Duncan Robertson's memorial, erected in Black River Parish Church by the "inhabitants of the parish" following his death in 1850, made reference to his twenty-four years as custos, twenty years as major general and thirteen years on Council. "As General of Militia," proclaimed the plaque, "the essential service he rendered his country in assisting to quell the rebellion of 1831 will long be remembered."[168] John Gunn, for whom there is no memorial, proved himself a brutal lieutenant during the rebellion of 1831–32. And Grignon, whose actions as attorney at Salt Spring prefaced the rebellion, commanded the Western Interior Regiment in its pitched battle at Montpelier.[169]

Memorials erected for attorneys who died in the island often referred to their public political roles. Thus a mural in the parish church of Savanna-la-Mar, commemorating Joseph Stone Williams who died in 1836, described him as "Custos Rotulorum of the parish and for many years one of the Assistant Judges in the Cornwall Assize Court, twice elected to represent his parish in the House of Assembly".[170] Hamilton Brown's headstone in the yard of St Mark's Church, St Ann, recording his death in 1843, noted that he had represented his parish in the Assembly for twenty-two years: "His name will long be cherished by a grateful community who for nearly half a century experienced the benefits of his generous mind and warm heart."[171] Brown's role as leader of the reactionary Colonial Church Union was not mentioned. Not everyone in the "community" was grateful, however. As a Baptist asked an election meeting in St Ann in 1840, "Who shall we send to represent us? Shall we send Hamilton Brown and Dr. Barnett; these fornicators; these oppressors; these robbers of the people's rights and privileges?"[172]

In spite of the specialization of the planting attorneys of Jamaica and the common use of "attorney" as a term of identification, the word rarely appeared on memorials. Indeed, only one of the memorials in the 1832 sample used it. This was the tomb of Thomas McCornock (1786–1848): "For upwards of 40 years he was manager and attorney of Golden Grove Estate."[173] Only one other memorial in Wright's collection, not part of the sample, uses the word: Thomas Thomson (1819–75) of Portland was "proprietor of Passley Garden, also attorney and manager of Low Leyton Estate".[174] Less direct was the memorial for the attorney Charles O'Connor (1772–1839), the mural tablet in the parish church of St James placed there "by his friends in testimony of their sense of his services in the management of their estates during a period of unparalleled difficulty".[175] More inclusive was the mural for the Jamaica-born attorney James Wright Turner, erected in 1840 in St Paul's Church, Chapelton:

> He was many years its [Clarendon's] representative in the island Assembly, and would have continued in that and many other of the highest offices but from a sense of the duties which he owed to the many persons who had entrusted their properties to his management. This tablet . . . is the combined offering of profound grief and affectionate regard on the part of a very numerous body of persons of all classes and conditions, from the labourer who worked under his orders to the beloved and munificent Governor of the island, Sir Charles Metcalfe.[176]

If the sparing use of "attorney" on the memorials seems significant, perhaps suggesting a reluctance to identify with the role, it is worth noting that use of "overseer" was just as rare for that much larger class of managers. So was "planter".[177]

Marly, taking the book-keeper's perspective, drew a starkly divided hierarchy of managers, in which the overseer often thought the book-keeper "a species very little raised above the negro", while the overseer's "weight with the attorney is not near so great as they themselves imagine, and their situation is equally precarious with that of those under them". Then there was the resident planter-proprietor "old Mr Marly who bore such a hatred to attornies that he never would associate with them".[178] Reflecting these opinions, Curtin has argued that the managerial hierarchy that developed in Jamaica was the basis of the social order. Thus "the three grades of planter – attorney, overseer, and bookkeeper – tended to form three separate social classes". The attorneys thought themselves "vastly superior to overseers, and overseers tried to keep a similar class line between themselves and the bookkeepers".[179] On the other hand, Trevor Burnard locates attorneys with several properties under their management as belonging to the "plantation elite".[180] Because planters might be both proprietors and attorneys, and because they had political power within the colonial state, they shared a capitalist advantage as well as social superiority. As people living in a slave society, the white men of Jamaica were uncomfortable allies in distinguishing themselves from blacks and the enslaved majority, a position they surrendered only partially and reluctantly after abolition.

The Typical Attorney

The stereotypical attorney, as painted by contemporary critics and many modern historians, was a self-important man who lacked practical knowledge of plantation agriculture and sugar-making, but defrauded his employers of their just profits in order to feather his own bed. He lived a far distance from the properties he was supposed to manage and rarely visited them. When he did, it was for his own pleasure and at the expense of the proprietor.

Thus William Beckford, ready as always with a flowery passage, said the attorney with numerous properties under him, was "followed about the country with a retinue of carriages, of servants, and of horses, which shake the ground as they thunder along; and when he arrives upon the plantation, the command goes forth, to catch and kill; the table is covered with profusion, and few are suffered to go empty, I had almost said sober, away".[181] The profession of attorney was the most profitable in Jamaica, Beckford claimed, but marked by "the greatest mediocrity of talents". The attorney's functions did not "require thought, or insist upon action", he said, so could be "equally exercised by the vacant and inactive". All the attorney really needed was "confidence and protection from home, an hospitable way of life in the island, a costly table, a full cellar, and good attendance; and if you have besides an easy carriage, and an ambling horse, 'all the rest shall be added unto you' ".[182] R. R. Madden in 1835 described a

> nabob of a planting attorney – a comfortable, well-conditioned, good-humoured-looking man; for your planting attorney is generally a fat, sleek, well-fed, demure-featured gentleman, with a good deal of what the Irish people call cuteness about the mouth, lurking especially about its angles, but not sufficient to predominate over a hilarious expression of the eye, in which fun and frankness of disposition is mingled with shrewdness.[183]

What was the reality? The typical attorney between 1750 and 1850 was a literate white man aged in his forties or fifties, who had lived in Jamaica for a decade or more and had made his way up the managerial hierarchy. His knowledge was generally derived from employment in supervisory roles on sugar estates. He was responsible for just one property and answered to one proprietor.

Beyond these common characteristics the attorneys are better understood as a series of types, varying according to the properties they managed as well as their individual temperaments. Although the typical attorney was in charge of only one property, the majority of the plantations under attorneys were managed by men with multiple employers. A relatively small but prominent group of "large" or "great" attorneys, just fifty-two of them in 1832, each had responsibility for five or more properties. Generally, the properties for which they were responsible were located in a clearly defined small region or domain. Planting attorneys were much more visible than the mercantile variety and dominated the system. They were more likely to accept salaries and less likely to live in a port town. Creoles were less common among the attorneys than the British-born, with the Scottish predominating. Some lived with white wives and children, marrying late in life. Some accumulated great wealth, others had less success. The most wealthy of the great attorneys sat in Assembly and Council. Some were appointed custodes and some held significant public offices. They had power in the courts, though lacking legal qualifications, and commanded the militia.

Compared to his stereotype, the typical attorney was a man equipped by practical experience to deal with the demands of plantation management rooted in his district. The large attorney also possessed political and legal power and influence that might benefit his employers. None of this is surprising, in the sense that absentee and resident proprietors seeking agents to manage their investments had an interest in appointing people qualified to serve them efficiently. However, the profitable operation of the system depended on more than finding men willing and able to exploit human and physical resources through harsh management. The proprietor had final authority in the deployment of capital and resources, but the attorney necessarily had responsibility for many areas of management, and opportunities barely dreamed of by the modern stockbroker. In order to monitor and ensure profitability, the absentee-proprietor needed also efficient modes of accounting and communication.

Chapter 4

Keeping Accounts

Accountability was at the core of the system of attorneyship. Absentees, unable to observe directly the condition of their property and its transactions, depended heavily on accounting documents, letters, written reports, lists and land surveys to safeguard their interests against dishonest practice by tracking rights and obligations, and to take the measure of their wealth and income. Indeed, as Galenson argues, the attorney was part of the solution to managerial fraud and financial inefficiency.[1] It was payment by commission that distinguished the attorney from the overseer and gave him an interest in ensuring the accurate and full reporting of transactions.

The regulation of Jamaica's attorneys, beginning with the law of 1740, was directed primarily at ensuring the honest reporting of plantation accounts and the fixing of rates of commission. Absenteeism and the role of credit (and book debt) had important economic consequences, and written accounts had legal significance as evidence in courts.[2] In this system, the accounts kept by overseers, attorneys and merchants were both an essential record and a key source of information for projections and planning. The exchange of management information depended, in turn, on the exploitation of available communication technologies. Down to 1850 absentee planters had little alternative to reliance on the accounts they received in the post.

The role of accounting and accountants was long viewed in neutral and amoral terms. Scholars wrote accounting history from a technical point of view, concerned above all to identify the origins of particular methods of book-keeping. Recently, this focus has been challenged by "critical accounting". In this approach, accounting and accountants are placed more firmly in their historical contexts and assessed in terms of their social roles. For example, accountants are accused of complicity in the reprehensible management of fundamentally immoral varieties of labour control and the exploitation of resources generally. Studies of plantation slavery fall naturally within the net of this approach. The keepers of accounts are seen as active agents in the efficient and profitable exploitation of enslaved people, not merely the keepers of record. This critical approach to accounting reflects debates that occupied economic and social historians, beginning in the 1960s, and may be seen as parallel to the paradoxical role of slavery in the development of the theory and practice of modern management.[3]

Planters' Accounts

The place of plantation practice within the accounting history of the West Indies remains poorly understood. Marcia Annisette has argued that, specifically in the case of Trinidad and Tobago, "there was little need for financial accounting in the plantation economy", chiefly because "all sales and purchase transactions relating to plantation agriculture were conducted by a merchant house in England, and it was there, and not in the colony, where detailed financial records of transactions were maintained. Sugar plantations merely kept records of shipments to merchants for later reconciliation with merchant records." Before emancipation, says Annisette, "plantation commodity flows were not accompanied by money flows", and there was therefore "little basis for accounting calculation". Abolition was followed by the introduction of money and banks, and the "importing" of accounting labour and skills.[4] This is too simple an interpretation. Certainly in the case of Jamaica, plantation accounts, created in the island, did play a significant role in the managing of the plantation economy.

The accounting documents created by Jamaica's plantation managers changed over time, responding in part at least to the needs of absentee-proprietors, their merchants and agents. There was a significant difference between the seventeenth and eighteenth centuries, marking the growing dominance of attorneyship. On the plantations and in the counting-houses of the merchant-factors, clerks increasingly did the job of writing the letters and keeping the account books. The degree of specialization of tasks increased along with the scale of enterprise, the sugar planters of Jamaica and their merchants being at the top end of development. Ward argues that the second half of the eighteenth century saw a significant improvement of "reporting and record-keeping" standards, most absentees receiving regular accounts. Plantations began to keep daily work journals. Further, says Ward, absentees "sought to widen the range of information by corresponding with the subordinate overseers who had day-to-day charge of individual plantations", and this in turn gave rise to the appointment of "planting attorneys".[5]

Planters could choose from a variety of accounting models. The most obvious was the ancient "master and steward" or "charge and discharge" system, used to administer large estates in Britain to the end of the eighteenth century. The method was designed to ensure the preparation of periodic statements, showing what the steward had received and disbursed. Most writers on accounting history distinguish between charge and discharge and double-entry, seeing the latter associated with estate accounts only in the nineteenth century. Sidney Pollard, however, argues that the bilateral version of charge and discharge was a system "based on double-entry book-keeping, but of a particular kind". On the debit or "charge" side were placed "all the receipts of the agent on behalf of his master". These were expressed first both in money and in kind, but by about 1800 usually only in money. On the credit side the "discharge" enumerated "all the payments made, including the contributions towards the upkeep of the master's household and cash payments to him, leaving as balance usually cash still in the hands of the agent, or, more rarely, the sum due to the agent from his master".[6] Christopher J. Napier, on the other hand, warns that an "estate account in bilateral form might be part of an integrated double-entry system, but is more likely to be a summary statement, in charge and discharge form, of a record of receipts and payments". Profit and loss accounts, cost analysis, and balance sheets are hard to find in British estate accounts down to 1800, though there are important exceptions. In any case, the emphasis on double-entry may be misplaced. Napier concludes that "double-entry, as a recording system, was not regarded as providing significantly greater control over the actions of estate officials than the traditional charge and discharge system". Similarly, David Oldroyd argues that "the bilateral recording of cash transactions was probably preferred because it was simpler and more versatile" than double-entry.[7]

On the great estates of England, according to F. M. L. Thompson, "the apparatus of journals, ledgers and double entry, segregation of estate, household and personal expenditure, and separation of capital and income accounts, co-existed at the end of the eighteenth century with direct descendants of medieval practice". The latter included using "the terminology of charge and discharge accounts, . . . which effectively concealed his real financial situation from the owner even if it served to square the accounts of the steward". The tendency was for estate managers to seek "maximum physical output" rather than "maximum financial return from outlay".[8] The main achievement of the bilateral charge and discharge system was its ability to detect fraud by employees, but it also offered a kind of "elaborate cash account" and a rough check on the "efficiency" of the estate by enabling comparison over time. With these materials, further work could have provided measures of the profitability of particular enterprises or products of an estate, but such "charge and discharge" accounts were rarely analysed in this way. Thus the inputs and outputs associated with a particular field or wood were not easily understood. Similarly, the method was incapable of providing a direct check on returns from capital investments or technological innovations.[9]

Plantation Jamaica

Much the same applied to plantation accounts, though planters did regularly measure and record on maps or in accounts the yield of cane-pieces (fields) and their state in the cycle. Occasionally, they related yields to the amounts of manure applied, mapping the outcome in detail over a period of years.[10] In spite of the complexity of the productive processes and the emphasis on efficiency practised on sugar plantations, double-entry accounting systems seem to have been rare. On the other hand, Joseph R. Razek found that a number of Louisiana sugar plantations had by the 1830s begun to employ "a hybrid accounting system, using elements of cash and accrual and single and double-entry book-keeping". The variation within this system seems to have originated with the source of the transaction. Items coming from a merchant were more likely to be recorded in double-entry. The system had little interest in the preparation of a balance sheet.[11]

What were the major kinds of accounts kept by planter and attorney? Most were written into "books" with a variety of names. Copies, summaries and reports were generally extracted on loose sheets. The latter included the public crop accounts and accounts current. The attorney was interested in some of this information and sought it for his own records, for transmission to his absentee employers and metropolitan merchants, and legal deposit. The books themselves remained on the properties, however, sometimes curated for many decades after their production. The most common books of account were the diary, journal and account book. Some plantations kept separate boiling-house books and still-house books, but these often had overlapping titles. According to the leading Scottish accounting textbooks of *circa* 1750, published by William Gordon and John Mair, three main types of books were kept: the boiling-house book (containing a daily record of the sugar potted), the still-house book (an account of the amount of rum produced), and the plantation book (listing produce sent off the estate, goods acquired, and the numbers of free and slave people on the property). All of these might be inspected by overseer and attorney, though questions of accountability remained. Most absentee-proprietors seem to have been satisfied by annual sets of accounts. On the other hand, the absentee planter Richard Pennant, taking over from his father John in 1781, directed the attorney of his Clarendon estates to supply "twice-yearly accounts" as done for Henry Dawkins.[12]

Roughley in 1823 emphasized the importance of the attorney keeping "fair and equitable accounts of the various transactions of the estate, with respect to its culture and incidental transactions, in as simple a manner as the nature of things will admit of". The attorney was to provide the proprietor with accounts to the end of each year "in plain legible terms". Roughley mentioned first "a list of the slaves and stock, with their increase and decrease". Next, he moved on to a statement of the cultivation, showing the acres in plant and ratoon canes and the yields achieved in sugar and rum. He also required a list of the white people on the estate, detailing their occupations and salaries. The "island accounts", shipments, and disposal of the produce were to be laid out, along with the quantities remaining on hand and the accounts left to be settled. So too were the annual allocations of clothing and provisions, the jobbing and tradesmen's accounts. Roughley thought all of these "simple accounts", easily kept and transcribed.[13]

The plantation "diary" was a book in which daily transactions and activities might be recorded. Few examples seem to have survived, though "diaries" of boiling-house production are occasionally found within more comprehensively named account books. On the other hand, William Miller claimed in 1836 that every property under his management sent him "a diary every week of the actual transactions during the week".[14]

Journals sometimes contained information overlapping that in a diary but generally included inventories, lists and a record of cash transactions. The journals of sugar estates often included lists of enslaved workers, and daily notes on the distribution of labour, tasks and the weather.[15] The journal's function was similar to that of the more inclusive "account book". On coffee plantations, said Laborie in 1798, "the object of the journal" was to make available the records of any "administrator" but more commonly to enable the resident planter "to balance accounts with himself, and to be able to refer to notes upon occasion". Laborie believed

> the journal must contain a state of the negroes and cattle, a state of the births and deaths, the number, dates, and various kinds of plantations, the daily works and employment of the negroes, ordinary as well as extraordinary; the state of the crops day by day; the deliveries of coffee, as well as the price of sale and amount, as stated in the [local] factor's letters; lastly, the state of the provisions received, and of the tools, utensils, and cloaths delivered to the negroes.[16]

The journal or account book sometimes included lists of enslaved people valued in money terms according to principles that were rarely made explicit but depended primarily on age, sex, colour, health, skill and temperament. These valuations were essentially predictions of the productive potential of the enslaved and of the prices they might be sold for in the market. Similar principles were applied to livestock. It was more common, however, for the characteristics of enslaved people and of livestock to be listed in account books without any statement of value. The births, deaths, purchases and manumissions of enslaved people were listed as "increase and decrease" in charge-and-discharge format.[17]

The "account book" for Old Montpelier Estate for the years 1824–28 was typical of this type of record on sugar plantations.[18] It contains copies of official returns, including returns to the vestry for taxation purposes (poll tax and deficiency saving). There are extensive lists of the enslaved people, with comments on their health and "disposition" as well as their occupations, and the "increase and decrease" among them. Livestock were listed in much the same way. These lists were annual, serving the purposes of the estate rather than the official registration returns that were made every three years. There were also detailed lists of distributions to the enslaved of cloth, clothing, tools and utensils. The salaries of overseers and book-keepers and free tradesmen, and all purchases and debts were recorded. The annual supplies received from England were listed in detail, in quantity and value, copied from the bills of lading sent from London. The estate account book also included the costs of freight and primage, the preparation of bills of lading, export duty, a proportion of custom house costs, porterage, cartage and wharfage, and insurance from London to Jamaica. To maintain the record, Old Montpelier imported in 1824 two folio ruled books. For 1841 Montpelier imported from Britain "2 two-quire account books ruled with faint lines".[19]

An important feature of the Old Montpelier account book was its careful recording of intraplantation transactions. For example, "Montpelier Farm", which was located within the boundaries of Old Montpelier, was paid by the estate for yams, cocos and plantains supplied as provisions. Cattle were sometimes purchased from the enslaved people who were allowed to pasture their animals on estate lands. Transactions between Old and New Montpelier and Shettlewood Pen, all of which shared a continuous block of land and belonged to one owner with a single attorney, but had separate overseers, were also recorded. Old Montpelier also maintained a "borrowing and lending account", for things as diverse as wood and iron hoops, fire bricks, blankets and arsenic, but this extended beyond the three properties. The crop accounts for Old Montpelier, New Montpelier and Shettlewood similarly recorded their transactions with one another.

The Old Montpelier account book included a "boiling house diary". It appeared first in 1827 and provided daily and weekly summaries of the number of pans of juice boiled (large pans, small pans and skips), the gallons of liquor boiled, and the numbers of hogsheads and tierces (casks containing, respectively, about two thousand and thirteen hundred pounds) filled with sugar. These statistics were related to the pieces being cut (listed by name), the area cut, and the yield in hogsheads per piece. There was also a weekly calculation of gallons of liquor to the hogshead, though this was not linked directly to particular pieces. The "quality" of the canes cut was recorded, meaning simply whether they were plants or ratoons (secondary growth), along with remarks on the weather. The movement of sugar to the wharf was recorded, and a summary of the "disposal" of the "sugar and rum crop" prepared that would have served as a preliminary to the official accounts produce. Although rum was included in this final summary, it is significant that no attempt was made to measure and record the outcome for the distillery to match the boiling-house diary. In these ways, the Old Montpelier account book supplied elements that could be fed into calculations of costs and productivity based on a crude form of partial double-entry.

The "crop accounts" required by the state under the law of 1740 were confined to a statement of the disposal of the plantation's produce and stock, as noted in the previous chapter. Most attention was given to the commodities exported, listing in detail the quantities shipped on particular vessels. The prices attributed to these commodities seem generally to have been prospective. Local sales, exchange and gifts were also described in terms of value and receiver, and here the values could be much more precise. The crop accounts said nothing about expenditure and this was not their purpose.

In contrast, the "accounts current" formally deposited with the island secretary covered both expenditure and receipts. They matched the accounts current prepared by attorneys and sent, along with the crop accounts, to their employers. According to Carrington, " 'Accounts current' began initially as short-term debts and were normally established for recording the sale of West Indian commodities to offset the purchase of British goods and services. These [debts] were held by merchants or factors, locally and in Britain." As the prosperity of the islands declined, he contends, the debts increased and were rolled into mortgages.[20] The mortgage was used throughout the eighteenth century, however, and offered one of the most efficient ways of mobilizing investment capital by long-term borrowing and lending. It was not so much an indicator of penury as a means of using land to secure debt, and this was often negotiated through the attorney. There were many disputes, however, giving a vastly increased role to the Court of Chancery, and mortgages became a subject of much importance in Jamaica in the longer term.[21]

What the accounting system of the typical Jamaican plantation lacked was the ledger. In the ledger, expenditure could be sorted into its different elements or categories and disconnected from the particularity of individual accounts and chronologies. It provided a means of thinking in an abstract and analytical manner about the efficiency and profitability of an enterprise, a way of tracing the contributions of specific elements rather than simply looking at gross outcomes. The ledger also served to provide a legal record of rights and obligations. The lack of the ledger made it difficult for the planting attorney to appreciate the pattern of spending in a cost accounting framework. He could not properly measure the cost of hired labour, the manuring of cane-pieces or the transport of canes, for example, though he might have a rough idea in his head of all these things in proportional terms. The lack of a ledger also made it difficult to draw up a balance sheet. This was in any case an impossibility because the attorney lacked the necessary information on income. Knowledge of receipts was only partly the province of the planting attorney. A local merchant might know more of it, but most of the necessary information appeared only on the books of the commission agent, and it was the metropolitan factor who was therefore in the best position to create more complete accounts.

Asked by a British parliamentary select committee in 1842 to estimate the price sugar needed to fetch in order to keep the estates afloat, the attorney Thomas McCornock conjectured twenty-five to thirty-five shillings per hundredweight, but added, "That is a question more likely to be answered by a merchant than by me, as a planter, for we have nothing to do with the accounts in London, nor the expenses or prices of produce there." He did not possess the knowledge necessary to answer precisely or, at least, said McCornock, "I am not so competent to give it as a merchant or a proprietor." He did keep his own set of accounts, but all requests for supplies from outside Jamaica were made to the proprietor who in turn had them filled by the agency of a merchant or broker.[22]

Claims of ignorance were sometimes countered by accusations of collusion. For example, when John W. Cooper was sent from England in 1834 to report on Lyssons and Holland estates, he recommended a substantial reduction in the profits of the metropolitan agents because he believed there was "too good an understanding between them and attorneys in general". The attorney for both Lyssons and Holland was McCornock, who lived at nearby Golden Grove where he had been overseer from 1812 to 1823 and attorney thereafter. Cooper found that the estate accounts were made up on the last day of December, and "a bill for the balance is drawn upon the proprietor's agent in London as early in January as the accounts can be closed". However, the salaries of the overseer and tradesmen were not paid until the following August and "then paid with a bill on the agents at 3 months after sight". McCornock, said Cooper, charged a high rate of interest on these salaries, as though they had been paid when due. Cooper saw further evidence of collusion between attorneys and agents in the fact that when goods were ordered for the estate they were not bargained for but simply paid out in the same way as salaries. "These practices I believe are common in Jamaica," said Cooper, "but in England it would be called down right roguery." He thought it odd that "white persons on all estates in Jamaica are fed and provided with bed linen at the expense of the owner", and added, "I noticed, when at Golden Grove [dining, no doubt, with McCornock], that not only linen but also the plate of which there was a glittering display, had upon it the mark of the Estate."[23]

The accounting record shifted to the books of the commission agent once the planter's sugar was on board ship. The captain of the vessel had in hand the bill of lading, listing in detail the containers entrusted to him, and a copy was transmitted separately by the attorney to the commission agent. The metropolitan merchant collected the proceeds from sales, then deducted freight charges, commissions to brokers and themselves, and payments on interest or capital due from the planter. The balance was either paid or kept on the planter's account. As Hall noted, "Unless absentee-owners or merchants supplied the necessary information, estate accounts kept by resident managers were restricted to local dealings followed by a statement of the produce shipped." The attorney might possess more accounting information than the overseer but he too had only a vague notion of how the profits of the estate related to the broader financial state of the absentee-proprietor. Any estimates he might make were vulnerable to the indeterminacy of imputed prices. For all parties, there was a fundamental problem of "incalculability" that went beyond the uncertainty typical of any enterprise.[24]

Merchants' Accounts

Merchants came in various guises and kept accounts matched to their different roles and locations. In some cases, continuing into the seventeenth century, merchants travelled on ships along with their own goods, taking direct responsibility for all aspects of transactions in the home and foreign market. They might also own the ship in which they travelled. Others employed supercargoes who acted as agents, travelling to foreign places on behalf of the merchant and having responsibility for sales and the preparation of the homeward cargo. More common by the eighteenth century was the employment of a factor or merchant's agent, empowered by letter of attorney, to reside in a foreign port and undertake all of the commercial business of the principal, and paid by commission, much like the planter's attorney. Also like the planter's attorney, the colonial factor might relatively easily commit frauds, located as he was far away in space and time from the eyes of his principal. The factor thus gained a reputation for embezzlement by inflating expenses and carrying on his own private business under the same roof. As Ray Bert Westerfield argued, the best corrective to such behaviour was "a prescribed system of accounting and provisions for close inspection of accounts".[25] Factors, particularly those located in the metropolitan ports, were best able to operate successfully when they gained sufficient scale and reputation to be able to give credit and to reliably honour bills of exchange drawn on them.

The ownership or legal responsibility for plantation produce passed through a number of hands, as set out in Figure 4.1. Within Jamaica, rum, livestock and small quantities of sugar might be sold from estates direct to colonial consumers. The persons with authority to sell or exchange these commodities were the proprietors, attorneys and overseers, and accounting for these transactions was a matter for the plantation books. Pens, whether owned by absentees or residents, traded the great majority of their produce within the island, only occasionally making use of merchants. Coffee plantations, on the other hand, exported most of their crop but chose to do so through Kingston merchants. The difference between coffee and sugar was that coffee came in much smaller volumes and the plantations were typically distant from ports and wharves.[26] Estates were often able to contract directly with ship captains for the export of their sugar and rum, using their own wharves and sometimes even their own ships. These arrangements were made directly by the planting attorney or overseer. When this did not happen, a local merchant or mercantile attorney had responsibility for the identification of ships to carry the produce and sometimes physically moved the goods to Kingston, by land or sea, for re-shipment or local sale. Once on board ship, commodities were consigned to particular metropolitan merchants, who began their accounting record on the basis of bills of lading or advance notice of the need to insure.

What was the role of the metropolitan commission agent? He insured cargoes on advice from attorneys, received the planter's commodities from ships arriving in port, paid customs duties, arranged storage in warehouses and looked after final sale. He purchased supplies requested for the plantations, responding to orders placed by absentee planters who passed them on from the attorney who in turn depended on the overseer to prepare the details. He might also charter and insure ships, on his own account or in partnership with planters, ship captains and other merchants.[27]

Of vital importance was the collection and sharing of news about markets and political matters. On occasion, the metropolitan commission agent recruited artisans and indentured servants, and in the case of resident-proprietors arranged the schooling of children. In addition to these commercial and mercantile duties, the metropolitan factor also served as the planter's banker. He advanced credit on the goods he shipped out, buying the goods cash and charging the planter interest. He recognized the planter's bills of exchange, took secured and unsecured loans, and made investments in British enterprises, on the planter's behalf. Even though a single metropolitan counting-house might have as many as forty correspondents, close ties were developed, stretching across business and family matters, for both resident and absentee planters.[28]

Sugar sold in the metropolitan markets rarely went to public auction. Most often, the sugar was distributed through a broker or "sugar buyer", though occasionally a merchant-house might "higgle" its produce directly with the retail grocers or refiners in the British port cities. The job of the sugar broker was to act as middleman between the commission agent and the refiners and grocers, who were the major buyers, and the re-exporters and speculators, thus breaking the bulk of the planter's shipment (Figure 4.1). The refiners were numerous and the grocers even more so. The broker sought out these small scale processors and retailers, and provided samples of the available sugars. He was paid by commission, never actually owning the sugar. The prices obtained by the broker depended on his knowledge and

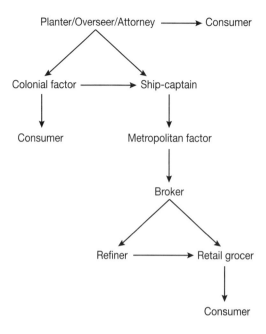

Planter/Overseer/Attorney ⟶ Consumer

Colonial factor ⟶ Ship-captain

Consumer

Metropolitan factor

Broker

Refiner ⟶ Retail grocer

Consumer

Figure 4.1 Sugar flow chart

ability to access the market as well as the quality of the sugar. Factors preferred to "sell rather than keep" because they had to advance payment on duties and freight, as well as give credit of two months to buyers. They needed to be cashed up from sales of sugar in order to meet bills of exchange drawn by planters and attorneys that might follow soon behind. When the planter's debt led in turn to the merchant seeking credit from his sugar broker, complained Beckford, "the sugars which he [the merchant] has had orders to insure, are sold to disadvantage before their arrival, or the samples, when purchased, are averaged at a price very far below their real value".[29] The merchant might also force a sale and take a lower price, in order to meet bills drawn on him, and sometimes this meant selling the sugars of planters other than those of the correspondent responsible for the bill of exchange. Successful metropolitan factors generally sought to push ahead by shipping and selling as quickly as possible, not waiting for events and uncertainties to overtake them.[30]

Sugar prices depended on quality. The major identifier of quality was colour, ranging from "brown" to "middling", "fine" and "very fine". This practice resulted in absentee planters complaining of the colours of their sugars on reaching the metropolitan market. When Lord Penrhyn complained in 1805, he was told by his attorney Rowland Fearon that "the quality and colour of sugar frequently depend on the soil; some pieces of land will make a fair strong body, others will not, and take a great deal of boiling", and that colour was also affected by "very wet seasons", especially if the cane was grown on clay soils.[31] Individual hogsheads from a single planter's shipment could fetch quite different prices and even different parts of the same cask might vary in colour and quality, as curing occurred unevenly, and buyers could expect a rebate if the cask did not match the sample. Further, the price paid for a single planter's sugar might be averaged over several hogsheads. When the role of the refiners increased in the British market after 1750, as consumers demanded "improved sugar", sales of small lots decreased, and the planter suffered (or benefited) by greater averaging. Merchants put together lots of fifty to sixty hogsheads of differing qualities. This practice may have pushed up average prices, but did not treat planters equitably and led them to demand that their sugars be sold unmixed.[32]

In the management of risk, most planters confined themselves to the insurance of cargoes on ships crossing from Jamaica to Britain, depending on their metropolitan merchants to take the necessary action. Down to 1775 insurance on shipping was relatively cheap, as were freights and duties. These low charges were partly the product of lobbying by the West India interest, led by London merchants. However, ships sailing in Jamaican waters always paid premium insurance rates. In the 1720s, a decade of peace, the rates were between 2.5 and 3.0 per cent from English ports to Jamaica, compared to the common 2 per cent to other ports, and the return from Jamaica was charged at 4 per cent. By the period 1765–75, however, insurance on the Jamaica–England route had dropped to between 3.0 and 3.5 per cent. War and the threat of war increased costs. In 1804, during the war with Napoleon, insurance on cargoes from Jamaica was as high as 10 per cent, down to 1 August, though less if the vessel sailed with a convoy. In 1799 it might reach 15 per cent.[33] Attorneys complained of the increasing cost of insurance in the 1790s, rising from 2 to 11 per cent of gross earnings on sugar. Increases in British import duties were also much complained of, the duty on sugar increasing fivefold between 1776 and the abolition of the Atlantic slave trade.[34]

Insurance was a touchy subject. The decision to insure was always that of the proprietor or his metropolitan factor but the attorney offered advice and opinion. By the eighteenth century, the habit of insurance against risks at sea was widely accepted by merchants and shipowners but the absentee planter was sometimes willing to take a chance. The British marine insurance industry was closely regulated, particularly between 1720 and 1820, with Lloyd's having few substantial competitors. In spite of its near monopoly, Lloyd's provided an efficient service, based on its effective communication network and concentration of brokers and underwriters. Further, a system of mutual cooperation developed between underwriters, because many were themselves merchants anxious to get equitable rates for their own commodity shipments.[35] Every year, insurance rates were doubled after 1 August, the day marking the onset of the hurricane season. This fixed the effective end of the crop. Sugar cargoes could not then be found and vessels spent long periods waiting in port. Metropolitan factors did their best to ensure their ships were in the right port at the right time, working on an Atlantic scale.[36] It required careful planning in the midst of so many imponderables.

How much did commission agents charge for their services? Beckford said, "The merchant's commission is ½ per cent upon insurances, 2½ per cent upon all the produce which is addressed to his house for sale, and ½ per cent upon what he pays." Advances paid 5 per cent interest, he said, "and it is the custom to carry the interest to the principal every year, and thus make it an augmenting sum". Beckford saw debt as a burden, saying the planter indebted to his merchant suffered "many pecuniary mortifications and disappointments".[37]

What kinds of books were kept by metropolitan commission agents? Most important were the invoice book, waste book, journal, ledger and sales book. The waste book contained the daily record, including the cash book, listing transactions in chronological order and, at least in theory, immediately they occurred. In the journal were posted the transactions recorded in the waste book, prepared for the ledger by being attributed to their appropriate debtors and creditors. The ledger was described in 1771 as "the principal book wherein all the several articles of each particular account, that lie scattered in the other books according to their dates, are collected and placed together, in spaces allotted for them, in such manner, that the opposite parts of every account are set directly fronting one another, on opposite sides of the same folio". This was double-entry. In order to follow the complex lines of particular elements within the ledger, indexes or alphabets were created.[38]

One London commission agent said in 1754 that his work involved "driving the quill or pouring over books of accounts".[39] Pollard argues that in eighteenth-century Britain the system of the counting-house was probably the most important source of accounting practice, "for not only had it developed double-entry book-keeping, the logical basis of all widely used systems, but it had also had to grapple at an early stage with the problems of large-scale enterprise, and the supervision of businesses at a distance; that is to say, it had to aid in the management of firms too complex to be directly controlled by a single head".[40] In this model, the absentee-owned sugar estate with its managerial hierarchy had a central place.

How did the commission system work in the midst of uncertainty? It depended above all on the reliable acceptance of bills of exchange. Before such bills were instituted, the machinery of exchange was much more cumbersome and international trade costly and constrained. Barter and the measurement of value in commodities (generally sugar and rum) persisted in Jamaica, in spite of legislation designed to prohibit such exchange, but overall it was a money economy. Coin played an important role, particularly in the internal marketing system dominated by enslaved people. In the oceanic-export trades, it was the bill of exchange that mattered most. Although coin remained the most secure medium, down to the early nineteenth century, its bulk and weight made it costly to transport and protect, and there were always questions of purity that required assay.[41] In Jamaica, Spanish coin was more important than British but by the 1820s the metallic currency proved insufficient for the island's trade and the Assembly began to issue notes or "island checks" for government business. In 1825 sterling was declared legal tender but currency remained dominant (at the rate of £1.4 currency to £1 sterling). The abolition of slavery increased the need to pay wages and created a great demand for coin. From the end of 1840, sterling became the currency of Jamaica. Note-issuing banks were established. Some planters paid wages in tokens.[42]

The bill of exchange had many advantages over coin. It operated somewhat like a modern traveller's cheque, ordering a person in a distant place to pay a specified amount in the currency of that place. One person drew on another for a sum payable to a third person. The system depended on trust in the ability and willingness of the person at the other end (the acceptor) to take responsibility for payment. If the acceptor refused to honour the bill, the payment failed. The commission system was an ideal site for transfer by bills of exchange, with established merchant-factors necessarily doing their best to honour bills drawn on them in order to maintain their place in what was a competitive market. Merchants who failed to honour bills were quickly ostracized by their fellows. The commission system in turn tied the planter to a particular merchant. Bills of exchange might be transferred by endorsement, increasing their flow, but again the commission system tended to limit circulation.[43]

It has been argued that the commission agent, by acting as a clearing house and making extensive use of the bill of exchange, slowed the development of metropolitan banking. The large proportion of book-debt along with the circulation of bills of exchange served to reduce the need for clumsy cash transfers. As well as bills of exchange, planters occasionally used direct drafts, drawn on their own accounts, and hoped by doing so to avoid the payment of commissions. In 1750, the year before the regulation of the commissions of attorneys was established, an act was passed in Jamaica to "establish the credit of foreign bills of exchange, by compelling the payment of interest thereon after judgment".[44] This legislation was introduced by the Assembly because "the trade and credit of this island hath suffered greatly by the too frequent protests of foreign bills of exchange drawn in this island", and the resulting delay in payment.

In the book-keeping of the metropolitan merchant, an account was kept that showed, on the credit side, all the bills of exchange drawn on planters, other correspondents and factors, and on the debit side all the bills that had been accepted or protested or were still outstanding. Additional accounts were kept detailing the status of cash and goods, other types of bills, stock and ships. The merchant's account current included, on the debit side, all the money in his hands received by sales of sugar and other commodities, as well as remittances and transfers. On the credit side were payments and remittances he had made and the debts owed him by planters and other traders. The merchant's balance depended on rates of exchange, which could earn a profit or a loss. The merchant's overall profit and loss account was derived from the closing of the journal and ledger.[45]

A major issue in plantation accounting during the period of slavery was the allocation of the costs of purchasing enslaved people against future revenues. The planters regarded these purchases as part of the necessary outlay to maintain the labour force, taking for granted a constant rate of attrition. The general principle followed by planters, and attorneys, was to hope to cover local and North American expenses from the sale of rum and molasses, leaving the entire sugar crop for export to metropolitan markets. Proceeds from the sale of sugar were applied to the proprietor's income. The attorney could then give bills of exchange, drawn on the commission agent, in payment for purchases of enslaved people. Indeed, it has been argued that it was the planter's indebtedness to the metropolitan factor, created by the need to cover the cost of slave purchases from future sugar shipments, beginning in the 1670s, that created the "commission system" that tied planters to particular metropolitan merchants over the long term. According to K. G. Davies, the system "was in origin the method of disposal for the sugar produced by the large, intensively cultivated, highly capitalized estate". It also made it difficult for planters to make sales of produce in the Jamaican market, since their sugar was committed to paying off debts and the metropolitan merchants had little trust in the bills of exchange the planters might negotiate in the colony.[46]

Although the purchase of slaves proved a continuing cost to the planter, and although attorneys sometimes encouraged proprietors to make regular annual purchases, few followed this practice. As Pares argued, planters rarely "faced the necessity of including this charge as a recurrent item in their budgets; this was because most of them bought slaves not regularly but in great gulps now and then, so that the cost figures rather as an emergency outlay of capital". Similarly, Carrington contends that although "the planters felt compelled to own their labour force, it is not clear from their accounts or other records whether or not they maintained a clear-cut long-term evaluation of their labour needs and how slave purchases were to be made, based on their financial position and crop prospects".[47]

When profits were slim, absentees commonly counselled their attorneys against buying and said they were "not sending money to the West Indies to purchase slaves".[48] Beckford advocated that the purchaser of a slave should have "the liberality to consider, that the merchant must make good his purchase at home, whatever disappointments he may meet with from abroad". Failure could lead to ruin for the merchant. Too many planters, he believed, were tempted by twelve or eighteen months' credit. Interest was charged at 6 per cent. When a planter failed to pay on time, the merchant might have executed a writ of *venditioni exponas*, under which slaves would be sold for a fraction of the original price.[49] In this account, Beckford might seem to be identifying both proprietor and attorney as irresponsible, but for the absentee planter and for the metropolitan factor it was most often the independent actions of the attorney that led to such an outcome.

Planning and Projections

The essential relationship between labour and the commission system, throughout the period of slavery and most particularly in the period of the slave trade, gave the metropolitan factor considerable capacity to influence planning by planter and attorney. Part of the metropolitan factor's power stemmed from his management of the proprietor's accounts, whether he be absentee or resident. The alternative to purchasing enslaved people was the hiring of gangs on a short-term basis. Here the metropolitan merchant had much less immediate control. Payments for hired workers were part of a plantation's internal accounts and appeared on the crop accounts only if the property hired out its own people. Attorneys generally followed their employers' orders in the purchase of enslaved people, and they did so at least in part because the plantation lacked the financial resources to cover large payments. The attorney could not risk drawing bills of exchange he knew the proprietor's metropolitan account was unable to cover. On the other hand, there was often dispute between attorney and absentee-proprietor over the hiring of gangs to work in place of existing or potential plantation labourers. Generally, it was the attorney who made the decision to hire, though he might simply follow the advice of an overseer. Proprietors complained about the cost of hiring as much as the cost of purchasing from the slave ships. An absentee could fight against the system but mostly the attorneys went ahead and hired the labour anyway, presenting the owner with a *fait accompli*.[50]

Occasionally, a proprietor sought detailed accounting projections before agreeing to purchase or hire. For example, in April 1787 Lord Penrhyn (Richard Pennant), who owned estates in Clarendon, told his attorney, "You say the negroes are hard pushed to do the work of the estate – I certainly do not wish to push them hard – I wish them to live comfortably and happily – and I had rather pay some hired labour than to press them too much." However, when the attorney Alexander Falconer proposed purchasing rather than hiring, Penrhyn responded:

> You recommended purchasing a gang of workers in order to make 200 hogsheads. But will you first of all inform me – a gang of how many workers will be wanted, to make 200 hogsheads. How many acres would such a gang, added to my own, plant in one season – and how many acres of plants will be sufficient to make 200 hogsheads and will you likewise tell me, whether you could buy me such a gang of workers, in May or June . . . When you have furnished me with answers to these questions, I will write further to you on this report.

Penrhyn considered May or June the vital months, in order to plant in time to produce sugar that would enable payment for the enslaved workers by three instalments, in June of 1789, 1790 and 1791.[51]

The emergence of anti-slavery movements in the later eighteenth century induced planters to think more abstractly about the costs of labour. First of all, they began to discuss the relative costs of purchasing enslaved workers as against the creation of enslaved populations that were demographically self-sustaining. A variety of calculations were produced. Most of these were theoretical rather than based on long-term records or the careful measurement of labour inputs, but they did demonstrate an understanding of the accounting framework. For example, calculations of "the cost of bringing a slave child to the working age of fourteen years" included elements such as the loss of the mother's labour and the special allowances she was given, medical attendance, maintenance and clothing, local taxes, compound interest on all this expenditure over fourteen years, and insurance on the enslaved child.[52]

After the abolition of the slave trade, attention shifted gradually to the comparative costs of enslaved and free labour. Here a fundamental accounting issue arose, as Douglas Hall argued, in that the comparison made by the planters was really between the costs of "capital equipment and of labour". Enslavement made the person property – capital, chattel, personalty – to be bought and sold and employed in a variety of tasks. In these terms, the planters were correct in putting together in their accounts enslaved people and livestock, or "negroes and cattle" as they generally wrote. In practice, the planters thought of neither man nor beast as "labourer" but regarded both as "capital".[53] As the absentee Richard Pennant told his attorney in 1783, "I am glad to hear the Negroes are well. The hearing a good account of them, and of the Cattle, always give pleasure."[54] "Negroes" and "Cattle" were equally likely to be given capital letters. Some strands of British radical thought of the early nineteenth century had begun to construct non-human animals as belonging to the working class but this was a development completely contrary to the ideas of the planters.[55] Their view of the world was one in which specific classes of humanity might be accounted equivalent to livestock, denying a broader proletarianization. This was an assumption that might be argued with or without the acceptance of a crude racism.

The planters of Jamaica had heavy investment in capital, particularly because of the system of slavery, yet generally lacked the accounting information needed for capital accounting. One way of dealing with risk was to seek insurance but this depended on having a good idea of the probabilities. By the early nineteenth century, there were schemes for the insurance of the lives of enslaved people, the rates sometimes being calculated from life tables derived from the registration data collected from the owners for identification purposes. How many planters took up these schemes is uncertain. Absentee planters anxious to expand their cultivation and output were constantly reminded by their attorneys that "nothing can be done without negroes".[56]

How theoretically did planters, merchants and attorneys think about the problem of accounting for plantation profits? Certainly they had an abstract concept of the costs of distance and movement. Intraplantation transport costs were a significant factor in determining overall profitability, the optimum size of plantation units and the internal layout of the plantation. Thus the cost of hauling cane from distant pieces to a central mill determined the scale of the factory as well as the plantation's acreage or cane field. Travel costs, particularly for gangs walking to their work sites, placed similar constraints on overall scale.[57] On the other hand, Jamaica's plantation managers failed to turn this understanding into a careful system of practical cost accounting or theory of marginal productivity in the way a handful of European agricultural thinkers were beginning to do in the early nineteenth century.[58]

What models might the Jamaican planter draw on in his attempt to most profitably exploit his resources of land and labour? The most obvious was that of British estate management. Beginning in the seventeenth century, the great landowners of Britain did sometimes prepare explicit statements of policy. They did so with a faith in the future, taking the long view for their estates and their families by laying out objectives they themselves might never see fulfilled. They built with an eye to the very long term, planted trees that could take centuries to mature and laid out legal settlements that were to last long after them, determining the futures of their heirs, their sons and grandsons. They wished to ensure the wise use of inheritances. When such men prepared detailed written directions for those who would follow, they often associated these with books of land surveys, deeds, inventories and other legal records that might be used in preserving the integrity of the domain. Such collections of documents became more common in the eighteenth century.[59] They were individual testimonies, built on establishing the legal tenure and productivity of particular estates.

Down to the 1780s, the planter class of Jamaica invested a similar faith in the future, building on a large and expensive scale, and assuming longevity for the moral order. Thus the British collations of estate records had their counterparts in Jamaica and their creation became increasingly important as absenteeism distanced the planter from his property. The Dawkins Papers are perhaps the best known of such collections for Jamaica, consisting of seventeen folio volumes of title deeds and indentures, plats and plans, and plantation accounts, stretching from 1660 to 1812.[60] Absentee planters, especially those who had never seen their estates, often asked their managers to provide detailed plans of their plantations, setting out the boundaries and size of each piece, the crops grown and their place in the cycle of ratooning and rotation.[61]

Planters used plantation mapping to plan far in advance the rotation of plant and ratoon crops, with an eye to maintaining production and labour inputs over the coming five or six years, even if they lacked a cost-accounting framework beyond keeping track of the production of individual pieces. They knew that the yield of ratoons declined over time but also reached maturity earlier than plant canes. Thus a long-term cropping plan was needed both for the timetabling of cultivation and planting and for the scheduling of cutting. Ratoons were sometimes continued into their twentieth year. It was also necessary to begin cutting, as far as possible, in the most distant pieces in order to do the least damage to the plantation roads. Practical planters, attorneys and overseers had an eye for the seasons, knowing the impossibility of attempting to take off the crop in the wettest months, when carts got bogged and illness followed exposure. They had more than an inkling of the annual variability in crop yields that might result from local differences in climate and drainage, soil and topography, and crop characteristics. The scale and complexity of the system, however, put the efficient exploitation of this knowledge beyond their scope and capacity as managers. They lacked the necessary long series of historical productivity data and the computing power to properly analyse them.[62] They could only guess where best to start the crop and how to order the cutting of the pieces, based on experience that was often of shallow time-depth.

Sugar planters should have been as interested in measuring efficiencies in the mill as in the field. Certainly they often expressed a concern for innovation, particularly in the improvement of water mills and, after 1750, the application of steam. However, down to the end of the eighteenth century, few attempted to measure the ratio of juice to cane or to test the crushing rates of different technologies in terms of cost. This lack of concern is probably explained by the need to balance crushing against cutting and carting rates. An improved crushing rate was helpful only if cane could be supplied to meet the demand and only if the distribution of labour matched the pattern. Thus, as under slavery, a fixed labour force had to be concentrated in the most labour-demanding areas and spread over the year. Hence the emphasis on taking off the crop rather than on the efficiency of mill or boiler. Planters had a notion of the optimum size of a plantation, and the range of acceptable levels of production and labour, though without possessing a clear understanding of the concept of economies of scale.[63]

Uncertainty and the lack of necessary accounting information introduced a fundamental difficulty to plantation management. Absentee, attorney and merchant-factor might each possess valuable information regarding the state of a plantation but fail to share it. Risk was, therefore, a vital but imponderable factor in the management of Plantation Jamaica. Communication was crucial to the sharing of knowledge and to accountability.

Chapter 5

Communicating

For the planting attorney and the merchant, literacy was essential. Communication between absentee-proprietor and attorney was conducted almost entirely in writing. Before the telephone, there was no practical alternative. The absentee might send a friend or relative to talk with an attorney or overseer, or even visit a property in person, but this was unusual. Visits were time consuming and costly. Successful absentees, those who could enjoy the wealth and leisure created by their plantation workers, were men and women who could rely on their representatives in Jamaica and could deal with matters of management simply by regular written correspondence. The letters of the attorneys were central to the practice of accountability and can only artificially be separated from the "accounts" they regularly enclosed.[1]

During the period of slavery, reading and writing technologies were jealously confined to the managerial classes of free people. Written documents were fundamental to the contractual side of their business at every stage. When Thomas Thistlewood sailed from England to Jamaica in 1750 he carried with him letters of introduction. On taking up the position of pen-keeper, he received formal letters of appointment, confirming his status, setting his salary and perquisites, and defining his responsibilities of supervision and accounting. On discharge, overseers and book-keepers were given signed and dated notes, confirming their status. Good service could be followed by a glowing testimonial, a letter of reference, valuable in obtaining further employment and rising up the ladder of management. Thistlewood regularly sent and received correspondence with other whites. Sometimes these notes and letters were delivered by whites but most came by the hand of enslaved persons, travelling on foot, horseback or by canoe. Letters were entrusted to enslaved people even during times of open revolt. Thistlewood sometimes wrote on behalf of enslaved people who wished to communicate with other overseers. He also provided written tickets, to be carried by the enslaved when travelling as proof of permission to leave the plantation.[2] The presumption was always that the enslaved could not read or write.

Instructions from attorney to overseer were generally communicated orally. The same applied down through the hierarchy of plantation management, from overseers to book-keepers, headmen, drivers and workers. English was the language of attorneys, overseers and book-keepers. Africa-born enslaved people spoke African languages and required translation until they had learned the creole language of command. With the growth of the creole population, Jamaican English evolved and gradually became the language most spoken and heard throughout the society. After slavery, negotiations over rents and wages between attorneys and plantation workers similarly depended on the spoken word, though agreements were often written down for legal purposes and read aloud. Attorneys also required that their overseers read out written demands, as for example when they served notices to quit, for failure to pay rent or labour on an estate, that might lead to the courthouse. General literacy was not essential to the functioning of the system.

In plantation management, it was communication between attorney, overseer, merchant and proprietor that mattered most in deciding the pattern of enterprise and exploitation. Some of these managers were separated by considerable distances, notably absentee-proprietor and attorney, on opposite sides of the Atlantic. The communication technologies available between 1750 and 1850 were "slow" in the sense that many important decisions had to be made before there was time to receive responses to questions and it was necessary therefore to give considerable power to attorneys. The telegraph did not reach Jamaica until after 1850. Every message had to be carried by a ship. Overseers were given responsibility for few decisions with significant long-term consequences and commitments of capital. By contrast, attorneys frequently made major management decisions and often acted before receiving confirmation or instructions from their employers. Planters and merchants were well aware of the necessity of patience in dealing with the uncertainties of the sugar trade with Jamaica. This need extended far beyond the technologies of communication. By the middle of the eighteenth century merchants came to accept the unpredictability and slowness of remittances. Thus the London factor Alexander Grant, who lived many years in Jamaica, saw the business as "slow and dilatory" with "no remedy but perseverance and patience".[3] Communication was just one element contributing to this slowness and uncertainty.

Often, absentee-proprietor and attorney were unknown to one another and met only in their correspondence. Proprietors might never visit Jamaica and creole attorneys might never see Britain. This gave added significance to the written documents, the reports and accounts that they exchanged. Thus in 1842 the London merchant Ralph Bernal, who had never visited his estates in Jamaica, could claim, "I know a great deal about the general management [of my estates], having from my earliest childhood heard so much about it, and having corresponded from very early years; I know almost every thing that goes on." Another proprietor who had never been to Jamaica was Neill Malcolm, the extensive owner of estates in Hanover, who said in 1842 that he was "in the habit of receiving constant communications" from his agent, Daniel Sinclair, who had lived in Jamaica for twenty-five years, and sought "every information" he could get.[4]

Writing Technologies

Down to the middle of the nineteenth century, writing was done by hand using a quill made from a bird's feather dipped in ink mixed from powder. Feathers were taken from geese, crows and other birds. The feathers second or third from the end of the wing were generally found to have the largest and roundest barrels, and therefore be best for writing. When quills became soft, producing blotchy letters, they could be hardened by heat and cut to renew the sharpness of the tool and the writing. Black ink was made from powdered galls (the tough protuberances on plants, particularly oak trees), infused in freshwater, mixed with copperas or green vitriol (ironstone dissolved in sulphur to make a salt) and gum arabic. The dry, powdered ink was then stored for use when it was mixed with water. Jamaican planters and merchants imported both ink powder (in "papers") and quills. An estate could use fifty quills in a year.[5]

Most writing was on "linen or European" paper though parchment was also used for some legal documents into the eighteenth century. Parchment was made from the skins of sheep or goats, treated with lime, dehaired and defleshed, dried, stretched and scraped, to make it as thin as possible. Most of the parchment used in Jamaica was imported. So too was the paper, all of it made by hand from linen or hemp rags until the nineteenth century when wood was substituted and machines took over. For 1841 Montpelier Estate imported "12 quires large thick post, with faint lines" and "12 quires fine foolscap paper".[6] A quire consisted of two dozen uniform sheets, giving a total of 576 for the year's correspondence and accounts.

Correspondents commonly had copies of their own letters transcribed into bound letterbooks. These were the outgoing letters. Copying was done by hand, just as for the originals, down to the middle of the nineteenth when press copying began to become common. Press copying enabled the transfer of ink from the original letter to a moistened flimsy sheet in a bound book. However made, copies of outgoing letters were essential as a record of what had been said and when, and often had legal value. Occasionally, incoming letters were copied into books, but it was the outgoing correspondence that was most carefully preserved by the sender because the original letter had to be posted. Incoming letters could simply be folded and stored in pigeonholes or tied up in bundles.[7]

Transcription was costly, often being performed by a salaried clerk. An attorney could afford to employ a clerk, if he had sufficient business, but an overseer would generally do his own copying. The "book-keepers" on Jamaican plantations performed duties in the field and were not necessarily literate. Most of the surviving copies of letters written by attorneys are to be found in transcription in letterbooks created in Jamaica or in bundles preserved by British proprietors and merchants. Occasionally, an absentee-proprietor transcribed into a book the letters received from attorneys along with his outgoing letters. For example, the owners of Georgia Estate, St Thomas-in-the-East, created three volumes of letters and accounts over the period 1805–35. These included the letters of Francis Graham, who was attorney until his death in 1820; George William Hamilton, who acted for Graham in 1812–13 and again in 1820; John McKenzie, who was attorney from 1822 until his death in 1832; and Charles Scott, one of the larger attorneys in the last years of slavery, together with letters written by and on behalf of the English owners.[8]

When the writing and transcribing was complete, the letter was folded and placed in an envelope. The envelope might be sealed with melted wax or a moistened wafer. Sealing wafers were made from fine flour, egg white, isinglass (fish glue) and yeast, beaten to a batter and formed into thin discs, and dried in an oven. They were regularly imported as part of the store of plantation supplies, and used to attach sheets of paper one to another as well as seal envelopes. In 1816 Matthew Gregory Lewis, reflecting on the ubiquity of wildlife in Jamaica, said, "Yesterday I wanted to send away a note in a great hurry, snatched up a wafer, and was on the point of putting it into my mouth, when I felt it move, and found it to be a cockroach, which had worked its way into the wafer-box."[9]

The diffusion of information within Jamaica also used printed media, notably newspapers that circulated along with the letter-post. Newspapers emerged as important sources of commercial information during the seventeenth century and commerce remained the driving force behind most journals down to the middle of the nineteenth century. They proliferated in the eighteenth century, reacting both to the improvement of postal technologies and the demand for commercial information in the Atlantic economy. The arrival of English newspapers was a significant event in Jamaica, bringing the first news of major political and commercial developments, the deaths of monarchs and states of war and peace. The news brought to Jamaica was dated only a few days more than the length of the vessel's voyage. The numerous local newspapers published in Jamaica regularly devoted their front pages to advice on the arrival of ships and advertised cargoes for sale. Down to the abolition of the slave trade, it was the arrival of ships from Africa that dominated, with political news coming later. Most of these newspapers were weeklies, but Kingston had some dailies by the 1790s, and for a year or two the *Kingston Mercantile Advertiser* appeared on alternate days.[10]

Printed laws were posted in public places and notices were sometimes read out in churches and courts. The 1740 act regulating attorneys and calling for the recording of crop accounts required that the island secretary should have copies of the act printed "and sent to the Custos or Chief Magistrate in each parish, to be read quarterly in the Vestry, and at each quarter-sessions".[11]

Inland Post

How quickly and efficiently could messages and information be transmitted within Jamaica? The speed of communication depended first of all on the technologies available for movement on land and water. Down to the early nineteenth century, travel on land was either on foot, on riding animals, or in animal-drawn carriages. Steam traction was applied to railways only on a small scale. Travel times depended principally on the state of the roads. Rivers, canals and trenches with adequate draft for small craft were used in parts of the island, as was travel along the coast, and these carried news as well as commodities.[12] Messages were carried along all of these routes, sometimes informally but increasingly by the postal systems created and regulated by the colonial state.

The postal system of Jamaica was an adjunct of the British imperial network. In the eighteenth century, the principals of the British colonial post offices were appointed by the British postmaster-general and sometimes called his deputies. Such appointments were a matter of patronage but in most colonies of small value. Jamaica was the exception, the postmaster's place worth £1,000 or £1,200 sterling per annum. The importance of the Jamaican post office in the British imperial system matched the wealth of the colony and the great amount of correspondence it generated both internally and externally. As Edward Long commented, "the extensive correspondence carried on by letter with merchants, absentees, and others; the frequent orders for insurance and for goods, the transmission-invoices, bills of lading, bills of exchange and accompts, with duplicates" produced a considerable revenue estimated at not less than £6,000 sterling annually.[13] The attorneys were at the centre of this correspondence. Much of it crossed the Atlantic but most began its journey in the internal postal system.

The mails of Jamaica were carried on designated "post roads". Around 1770 there were three routes, called the northside, southside and windward post roads, all of them centred in Kingston (Figure 5.1). Although the southside and northside posts both passed through Spanish Town, they commenced in Kingston. After crossing the island from Spanish Town, the

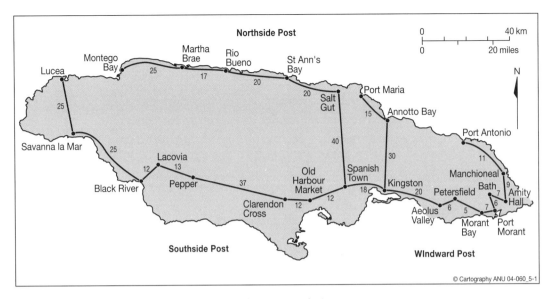

Figure 5.1 Post roads, 1770. (The numbers indicate distance in miles.)

northside post clung close to the coast, passing through the great zones of
sugar production, in which a large proportion were managed by attorneys,
and terminated in Montego Bay. The southside post road followed a more
consistently inland route, even passing through Old Harbour Market which
was a minor settlement compared to Old Harbour Bay. It eventually reached
the ports of Black River and Savanna-la-Mar and then crossed the island to
the northside port of Lucea. The route passed directly through the developed
sugar regions, with Clarendon Cross (the location of Lime Savanna post
office, known after 1850 as Four Paths) roughly intersecting the numerous
plantations of Vere and upper Clarendon.[14] The northside post to Port Maria
was unconnected with the route to Montego Bay but crossed the
mountainous backbone and passed through relatively few plantations until
reaching the densely settled areas of St Mary. Finally, the windward post road
zigzagged through the well-developed absentee-owned sugar estates of
St Thomas-in-the-East and swung around to Port Antonio.

Postal charges were determined by distance, as measured along the post
roads (Figure 5.1). Around 1770 there were three separate inland rates,
covering postage up to sixty miles, sixty-one to one hundred miles, and longer
distances. Items posted up to sixty miles paid 7½d currency for a single sheet,
1s 3d for a double or treble, and 1s 10½d per ounce.[15]

The network of post roads was gradually redesigned to reflect changes in
the distribution of production. The peak export years for sugar and coffee,
1805 and 1810, marked a greatly increased flow of correspondence, and when
the London postal authorities attempted to close down some of the Jamaican
post offices in 1814 there was much protest.[16] By 1833, immediately before the

abolition of slavery, the separation between northside and southside routes had been rationalized, the southside (western) post terminating at Savanna-la-Mar and the windward post going only as far as Manchioneal (Figure 5.2). Two routes then crossed the island directly from Kingston, passing through areas dominated by the new coffee plantations (though already in decline by 1833) and terminating in Port Maria and Port Antonio. The main northside post now pushed further west from Spanish Town, crossed Mount Diablo to St Ann's Bay, and travelled along the coast as far as Green Island. Jamaica then had "an internal post communication once a week to and from Kingston to other quarters of the island (daily only from Spanish Town, the capital)".[17]

The condition of the island's road surfaces was a regular cause for complaint, beginning in the eighteenth century and persisting much longer. Long devoted an entire chapter of his *History of Jamaica* to the subject, arguing that it was "principally from the want of good roads that the planting interest in Jamaica has not advanced more rapidly".[18] The reality was that the condition of the road surface varied from place to place and season to season. As Douglas Hall observed, "The post roads . . . were not good roads and were often impassable during wet weather, but they were the main highways of the Island."[19] Anthony Trollope travelled the post roads during his visit of 1858–59, as part of his investigation of the operation of the post office in Jamaica. He found the roads "through the greater part of the island . . . very bad indeed", but considered those of the north coast superior to the southern routes.[20]

Who carried the mails on the post roads and by what form of carriage? During slavery, enslaved people were used for many tasks that involved

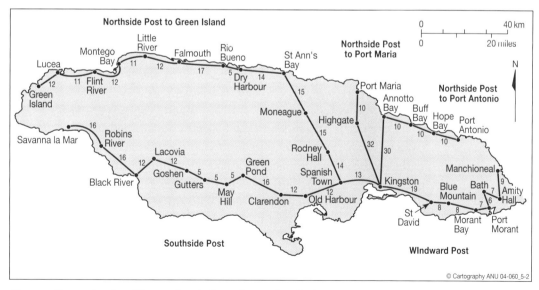

Figure 5.2 Post roads, 1833. (The numbers indicate distance in miles.)

security and trust, and they were the postmen. Letters and other mail were packed by the post office into canvas bags and then leather cases, wrapped with a chain and sealed. Even when the politically sensitive stamps arrived in Jamaica under the Stamp Act of 1765, it was enslaved people who "carted the stamps overland for more than ten miles without interference".[21] In 1814 it was complained that enslaved people could not give evidence in cases of robbery and that, because they travelled on foot, deliveries to Windward were slow.[22] In 1838 James MacQueen referred to the use of "special messengers" sent by planters and merchants to carry messages from place to place, at the cost of several days' labour, compared to the relative cheapness of an efficient internal post, and warned of the greatly increased cost that would follow the end of the apprenticeship.[23] The postmen generally rode mules. On his sketch made at Lime Savanna post office in 1815, William Berryman wrote, "Leeward post from tollgate Mile Gully to Kingston, 47 miles by the same mules."[24] Two saddled mules appear, but there may have been only one rider. Other sketches suggest that the heavy saddlebags made it efficient to have just one rider and that sometimes a pack mule might be led rather than ridden. After 1838, postmen were armed with pistols.[25]

Coastal shipping was used to move goods whenever possible but seems never to have been considered an option for the mail. The basic reason was that the post would still require delivery to inland plantations and the roads offered a denser coverage. The choice also suggests that the roads were not as inferior as contemporaries sometimes suggested. Lady Nugent, accompanying the governor on an island tour in 1802, noted when she reached Falmouth that Admiral Duckworth had sent a squadron "to attend us round the coast". They had not, however, made use of the ships, "the state of the roads" never obliging them to do so. Crossing the island from Montego Bay to Savanna-la-Mar, she found "the roads tolerably good", and moving on towards Black River, they were "uncommonly good".[26] Elsewhere, she encountered roads both terrifying and "unusually good".[27]

Kingston was the dominant port of Jamaica and ships bearing letters were most likely to dock there. Customs houses were first established in the outports of Montego Bay, Savanna-la-Mar and Port Antonio only in 1758, and before that trade was largely funnelled through Kingston. Montego Bay, Savanna-la-Mar and Lucea were opened as free ports in 1766 but Kingston was by far the most important.[28] Long in 1774 thought "the traffic carried on by captains of ships, and other transient dealers" at Montego Bay, Savanna-la-Mar and St Ann's Bay about one-fifth of that at Kingston, with much smaller proportions at Old Harbour, Lucea, Black River and Carlisle Bay. Post offices came before the declaration of free port status, however. Savanna-la-Mar, for example, had one by 1761. By 1840 there were forty-two post offices.[29]

How quickly did messages move along the post roads? Long said, "The several mails are dispatched from Kingston but once a week; and, if a merchant there sends a letter by this conveyance to his correspondent at Savannah la Mar, he must wait twelve days before he can receive an answer." The postmaster, he believed, could do little to speed the mail "until the roads shall be further improved, and the country better peopled".[30] Around 1810, a postman riding one mule and leading another laden with packs could cover seventy miles in twenty-four hours. Mail sent from Montego Bay to Kingston could be delivered within thirty hours.[31] Other travellers seem to have moved more slowly, rarely exceeding fifty miles per day.[32] The inland post might have been considered expensive but it moved speedily, demonstrating its significance in the planters' desire to manage communication efficiently.

Public transport was limited to road travel between the major centres until the coming of the railway that linked Kingston and Spanish Town in 1845. In the 1780s there were "public conveyances" between Kingston and Spanish Town, and Spanish Town to Passage Fort, the latter journey of six miles costing twelve shillings sterling. At these rates, the wealthy used their own carriages and the poor travelled by foot. On the other hand, the post-slavery period saw significant reductions in the cost of inland postage, with the rate for printed papers brought down to one penny per ounce and the halving of the letter rate in 1843.[33]

Overseas Post

In the managing of Plantation Jamaica, communication with England was the vital link, for governors, traders and planters. The transmission of their messages across the Atlantic was effectively controlled by the English post office and in some periods the Admiralty. The English conquest of Jamaica was followed in 1660 by a new Post Office Act which united the domestic and foreign offices under a single postmaster-general, but the Foreign Post Office, as it was known, was in practice a distinct establishment. This form of organization, establishing the framework for a persistent monopoly, survived until the reforms of 1839.[34]

Naval and merchant ships sailed unscheduled and indirect routes. In this unregulated system, "ship letters" were entrusted to the masters of vessels and collected informally. The captain would simply hang a bag on a hook in a tavern, coffee house or merchant's rooms, since he was entitled to carry free of charge any letters dealing with the cargo of his vessel. In practice, the captains did charge for carrying ship letters but the amount was considered small. In Jamaica, these were received informally until 1671 when a marshal was given responsibility for collecting all incoming mail and displaying a list of the addressees. In 1683 a letter office was established to collect and distribute local mail as well as ship letters. On their entry to England, ship letters were delivered to postmasters in any port where the vessel happened to anchor. Beginning around 1700 it became customary to pay ship captains one penny for each letter delivered, but the post office rarely succeeded in securing all incoming letters and the majority of letters leaving England did not pay the penny. Thistlewood recorded that in 1770 he "put the following [three] letters in Captain Richardson's bag", and listed their contents in detail but made no reference to paying any charges.[35]

An alternative to this rather chaotic system was found in contracting the mails to private ships or "packet boats". From the beginning, this was seen as a means of facilitating trade and commerce, and ensuring imperial security, rather than a profitable source of revenue. Packet boats, carrying mail, passengers and cargo on a regular and fixed route, were first proposed in the 1680s but limited to European ports. In 1702 Edmund Dummer, formerly surveyor of the Navy for the British Admiralty, outlined a scheme "for settling a monthly intelligence between England and the Island Plantations in the West Indies". The system was to use four vessels, each to complete the round trip in one hundred days, "wind and weather permitting", including a stay of ten days in Jamaica and shorter stays in Barbados, Antigua, Montserrat, St Kitts and Nevis. Postmasters were appointed by Dummer in each of the island colonies. At the English end of the journey, wagons hauled the mailbags across country from Falmouth to London, travelling at two to three miles per hour (Figure 5.3). The cost of posting a letter was to be one shilling threepence, the revenue belonging to Her Majesty's Service. Several of the packet boats were taken by privateers, however, and the letter postage and passenger fares proved insufficient to produce a profit for the contractor. The boats could accommodate only limited cargo and had to adhere to a strict schedule in port, making it difficult to accumulate goods and passengers, but at the same time had to carry guns. The service lapsed in 1711 and the mails returned to the merchantmen and warships. Postage rates increased.[36]

Dummer's scheme was not regarded a complete failure and served as a model for future enterprises. In 1712 the Lords of the Treasury described Dummer's packets as "a very good service to Her Majesty and her subjects, particularly to such who were concerned in trade to and from the West Indies, or who had settlements or estates there". The following year the postmaster-general said that "it was not only useful to merchants in England and the West Indies by giving them early intelligence of the disposal of their property, but also to the Government at home by bringing prompt advice of all occurrences in the islands".[37] Even more important in the long run, the regularity of correspondence made possible by the packets encouraged more frequent letter writing and placed pressure on managers to communicate. It became reasonable for correspondents to complain of the failures of their counterparts to write when the opportunity arose. The packets gave rise to the notion that the monthly letter was a reasonable expectation.[38] Thus the

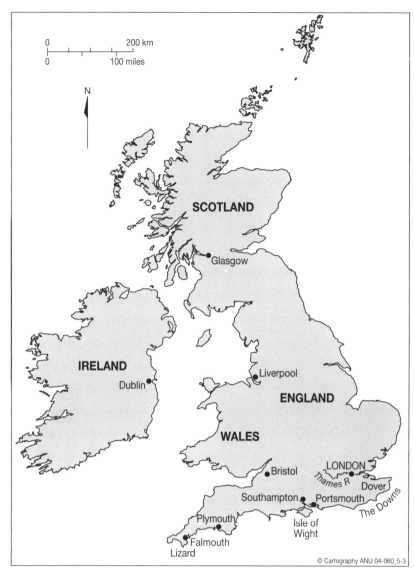

Figure 5.3 Great Britain, ports and places

post acted as a spur to the growing absenteeism of the 1740s and underpinned the system of attorneyship and its regulation.

Monthly packet post to the West Indies and, for the first time, the North American colonies was revived in 1745 but again proved unprofitable and was closed in 1749. The threat of war with France, however, resulted in resumption of the service in 1755, the contractors guaranteed an income by subsidy from the post office. Packet boat captains had the benefit of fares paid by passengers and contractors made fat profits.[39] The experience of the Seven

Years War, ending in 1763, was even more costly than the earlier experiments but from then on the packet boats became permanent, for military and political reasons. In 1765 postage was fixed at 4d for a single sheet of paper, rising gradually to 1s 4d per ounce for packets. Postage from Jamaica to England was set by law at 1s 6d sterling for a single sheet, 3s for a double, 4s 6d for a treble, and 6s per ounce. It was not cheap.[40]

In the new system, Jamaica had an important place, because of its relative economic weight and strategic western location within the Caribbean. It became a hub for less significant British colonies, including some on the North American mainland, the packet boats being required to return direct from Jamaica to the focal English port Falmouth (Figure 5.4). Various problems of navigation and communication made it difficult to maintain a regular schedule, particularly during time of war, but the service was more reliable than the alternatives for the typical merchant and attorney. It facilitated the more efficient circulation of business information, not only by speeding the delivery of letters and documents but also by carrying newspapers which contained detailed reports on markets and the arrivals and departures of vessels.[41]

The American Revolution severely tested the packet boat service but equally demonstrated its importance to the management of empire. The West

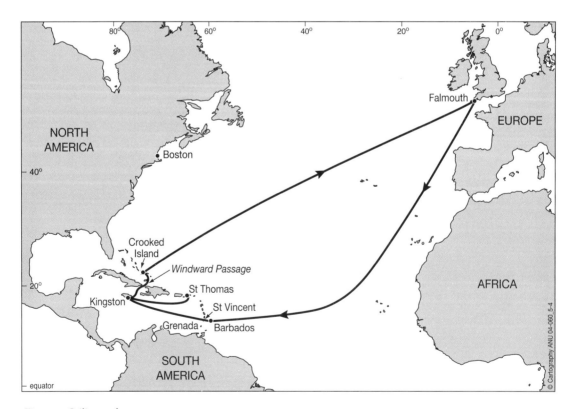

Figure 5.4 Sailing packet routes

Indies remained central and communications were expanded rather than contracted, as the number of British colonies in the eastern Caribbean increased. The monthly packet was replaced by a fortnightly service, one of the vessels now fully committed to Jamaica. By 1793 the British Post Office was using ten packet boats to serve the West Indies, five of them on the direct route to Jamaica. The Jamaica packet sailed from Falmouth on the first Wednesday of each month. It called at Barbados but immediately sailed on to Jamaica and returned to Falmouth by the Bahamas (Crooked Island). The second boat, the Leeward Island packet, departed on the third Wednesday of each month for Barbados and the Leewards. In Jamaica, the postmaster was responsible for delivery of letters. Items not delivered after three weeks were returned to England, marked with the reason, such as "Not to be found", "Dead", "Gone away" or "Refused". The outgoing letters were put into bags, according to their destinations, with the postage paid or due marked on each letter. Around 1790, the total number of letters carried each month averaged six thousand for all of the islands.[42]

During the Napoleonic Wars, the French captured forty-six packet boats and ten mail schooners used in the eastern Caribbean, making the system hazardous and costly. The merchants recommended the packet service be assigned to the Admiralty and by 1812 naval vessels were being used when packets were not available. Following the end of war in 1815, more use was made of circulating mail-boats, collecting the post from various outlying ports and bringing them to the hubs. In 1820 the Jamaica packet stopped at Barbados only twenty-four hours, then proceeded to St Vincent and Grenada to land the mails, and on to Kingston. It was recommended then that the stopping time at Barbados be reduced to twelve hours and that the packets not be detained, for any reason, by governors or other officials. The packet letter rate was one shilling twopence, plus the inland rate to London of one shilling. Letters posted in Jamaica had also to prepay the inland postage to Kingston.[43]

Within Britain, the incoming Atlantic mails were hauled by coach from Falmouth to London and then distributed along the "post roads" by coach or horse, and by water to Ireland. Steam-powered packet boats were introduced on the Irish sector beginning in 1821.[44] The outgoing Atlantic mails were made up in London on the first Wednesday of each month, carted to Falmouth, and despatched on the Jamaica packet on the following Saturday morning. In 1823 responsibility for the mails from Falmouth was formally transferred from the post office to the Admiralty. The reasons had to do with defence and the patrolling of the seas, as well as a desire to suppress the smuggling in which many packet boats engaged. Existing contractors were permitted to continue, however, so the immediate impact of the transfer was minor. The number of vessels increased quickly to thirty-nine, including seventeen private operators. The route followed by the Jamaica packet remained unchanged down to 1832: Falmouth–Barbados–St Vincent–Grenada–Jamaica–Crooked Island–Falmouth.[45]

As early as 1824 a prospectus was published in the newspapers of the eastern Caribbean offering shares in "the Steam Boat Company of the Windward West India Islands".[46] By 1834 the Admiralty was operating steam mail-boats within the Caribbean, moving mails between Jamaica and the Danish island of St Thomas, enabling the Leeward Island packet to collect Jamaican mails on its return voyage via St Thomas. Barbados, sometimes called "the porter's lodge of the British West Indies", remained the first port of call and the packets followed a scheduled two-weekly service, the round trip taking twelve weeks. By 1836 the Jamaica packet transferred its mail to a steam packet at Barbados and sailed to St Thomas. The steam packet carried the mails to Jamaica, stayed there four days, then proceeded to St Thomas, taking a total of fifteen days and providing a more reliable service than offered by sail. The sailing packet waited an unlimited time in St Thomas to receive the mails from Jamaica. The Leeward Island packet, on the other hand, waited only twenty-four hours, occasionally missing the mails from Jamaica. In early 1838 it was proposed that the "important island" of Jamaica be guaranteed a fortnightly service by increasing the power of the steam packets to St Thomas.[47]

The first completely successful crossings of the Atlantic by steam in April and May 1838 were quickly followed by the incorporation of the Royal Mail Steam Packet Company in September 1839. The preamble to its charter stated that it was "expedient that the transmission of the mails for the conveyance of the letters from Great Britain to the West Indies and elsewhere should be conducted through the medium of a regular succession of steam or other vessels, to be specially employed for that purpose", and that these "should be furnished through the medium of merchants and other persons of capital".[48] The concept behind the proposed service was advocated by James MacQueen, a Scots entrepreneur who had first worked as overseer of a sugar plantation in Grenada. His ideas were taken up by the Committee of West India Planters and Merchants. Led by Andrew Colvile, the committee sent a memorial to the Lords of the Treasury in 1837, complaining of the irregularity and uncertainty of communication with the West Indies under the existing packet service and the resulting exposure to risk suffered by the planters in failures of insurance. The eventual incorporation of the company, with MacQueen as general manager, followed directly from the advocacy of the committee.[49]

Specially built paddle steamers were introduced to the Caribbean early in 1842, following carefully specified routes, with advertised sailing times. They departed England on the third and seventeenth days of each month. Initially these routes were rather roundabout. The main steamer went first to Barbados, then Grenada, St Croix, St Thomas, Mole St Nicholas (Haiti),

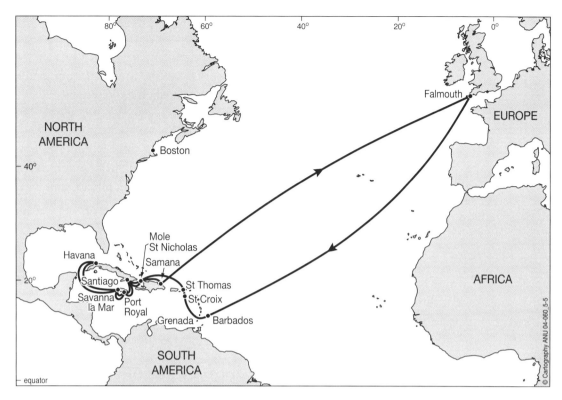

Figure 5.5 Steamer packet routes, 1842

Santiago (Cuba), Port Royal (Jamaica), Savanna-la-Mar (Jamaica), Havana, then back to Savanna-la-Mar, Port Royal, Santiago, Mole St Nicholas, Samana and, finally, England (Figure 5.5). Secondary steamers worked out of Barbados and Grenada. Initially, the steam packets were required to operate via Falmouth and the Admiralty maintained its role, but the Royal Mail quickly established Southampton as its base. The steamers carried passengers as well as post but no freight other than specie.[50]

In 1846 a new system of communication, combining steam railways with steam shipping, was proposed by Edward McGeachy, a Jamaican land surveyor.[51] The proposal depended on an easy passage across the Panama Isthmus, which McGeachy had crossed in 1845 together with a representative of the Royal Mail Steam Packet Company. McGeachy saw this link giving Jamaica an even greater focal position. Ships from the Pacific, including Australia and New Zealand, would steam to Panama where the mails would be carried across the isthmus. From the Caribbean shore they would go by ship to Kingston, then by railway across Jamaica to the western end of the island, ship to Batabano in Cuba, railway to Havana, steamer to Tampa (Florida), railway to Halifax (Nova Scotia), and finally ship to England. McGeachy estimated that under this system, mail from Jamaica could reach New York in five or six days and Ireland in fourteen days and five hours. He estimated the speed of steam ships at ten miles per hour and steam trains thirty miles per hour.[52] "Time is above all price", wrote McGeachy, "and to economize it in every practicable way is obviously a desideratum in the present advancement of the world".[53] His ideas fell on stony ground.

The steam packet routes remained little changed until the 1860s. On Trollope's recommendation, the post office was placed under the control of the Jamaica legislature, making it independent of the General Post Office in London. Jamaica issued its first postage stamps in 1860, having introduced the use of British stamps only in 1858. As the government service improved, the old system of ship letters diminished and eventually disappeared.[54]

Speed

How long exactly did it take for messages to travel between Jamaica and Britain and did the interval change significantly over time? Ship letters moved the most slowly because merchant shipping was almost always slower than the specialized packet boats. In the 1730s the voyage by merchant ship from England to Jamaica took almost 70 days and the return 100 days.[55] By the 1780s the times were reduced to 62 and 67 days, respectively.[56] The merchant ships also spent many days waiting in port to collect cargoes and undertake repairs. In terms of round-trip voyages between English and Jamaican ports, in the 1780s the number of days varied from 294 for a vessel of 100 tons to 397 days for a vessel of 600 tons. More time was spent in port than on the sea. Ships might spend 95 days in port in Jamaica, and 110 days in London.[57] This did not matter much for the transmission of letters, however, so long as a ship sailed soon after a letter was committed to it and the vessel was a good sailer. Naval ships travelled at about the same rate as merchant vessels. In every case, the passage from England to Jamaica was quicker than the return because of the different conditions of wind and current. This was unusual. As Ian K. Steele observes, "Jamaica was the only colony that could hear from England more quickly than a ship could take an answer back."[58] Steam speeded the voyages of merchant and naval ships just as it did those of the packet boats.

Average times served only as a guide to the senders and receivers of letters. The experience of individual voyagers varied substantially. For example, in 1750 Thistlewood travelled on the *Flying Flamborough,* a merchant vessel of 350 tons. The ship left Gravesend in bad weather on 3 February and did not pass the Isle of Wight until 2 March, eventually reaching Kingston on 24 April, a voyage of 80 days.[59] In 1801 Lady Nugent sailed from Spithead (Portsmouth) on a frigate of thirty-six guns and got to Kingston in 65 days. Her return voyage in 1805, in a convoy, took 67 days.[60] The absentee planter Matthew Gregory Lewis embarked at Gravesend in 1815 on a ship of 600 tons, formerly in East India service, and reached Black River in just 53 days.[61]

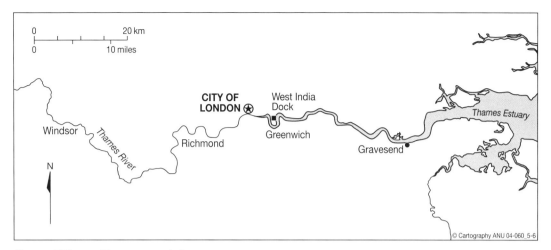

Figure 5.6 Thames River, ports and places

The difference between this voyage and that of Thistlewood in 1750 had little to do with any new technologies but consisted almost entirely in the slowness of Thistlewood's ship in reaching the Isle of Wight (Figures 5.3 and 5.6). Nugent avoided this stretch by starting from Portsmouth. After just three months in Jamaica, Lewis left for England on 1 April 1816, departing Black River on the same ship as he had come out on, with a cargo of sugar and rum. They sailed by the Cayman Islands and the Gulf of Florida, reaching Gravesend in 66 days.[62] The round trip totalled 197 days. A year and a half later, in 1817 Lewis embarked once more at Gravesend, travelling again on the same ship with the same captain. This time the voyage to Jamaica took 86 days, even longer than Thistlewood in 1750.[63] Lewis died on the return voyage to England, in 1818. Letters carried on any of these ships would have had quite different experiences.

How did the Jamaica–England routes compare with contemporary voyaging? In the Atlantic slave trade of the eighteenth century, ships typically took about 93 days to reach Africa, spent 138 days on the coast, 77 days on the crossing to the Caribbean, and 81 days on the return voyage from Jamaica to London.[64] Thus they were not particularly competitive. Whatever the speed of the slave trade ships, there is little to suggest that they were used commonly to carry letters from Jamaica to Britain after 1750. An important reason for this may be that the slave trade ships ceased to be important carriers of plantation produce and that the commodity and people trades were effectively separated in this period.

A fundamental disadvantage of the merchant ships was that they followed seasonal rhythms. They were common during the months when the sugar crop became available for export and the weather favourable for sailing, hard to find in the hurricane season. The peak months for sailings from Jamaican ports were April, May, June and July. In the 1780s almost 90 per cent of sailings occurred in these four months.[65] Large vessels had an advantage in sailing time, whereas smaller vessels spent much less time in port. Thus sending a letter on a large merchant vessel gave a slight edge, if one could be found sailing at the time needed. For example, on 3 March 1803 Governor Nugent received despatches by the packet and wrote responses the following day "to be sent off by a merchant ship immediately, and not by the regular packet".[66] Vessel size increased steadily during the eighteenth century. In the direct trade between Jamaica and Bristol, for example, Kenneth Morgan found an average increase from 101 tons in the 1730s to 265 tons in the 1790s. Ships trading from London were always larger. In addition to increased size, other improvements in ship design helped reduce sailing times.[67]

How much faster were the packet boats? On fifty-three voyages between 1702 and 1711 the average round trip took 113 days, including 33 days from England (Falmouth) to Barbados and 43 days from Jamaica to England.[68] The packet boats were quick to adopt superior technologies. Beginning in the 1770s their wooden hulls were sheathed in copper, creating a smoother passage through the water, reducing the sailing time from Jamaica to Falmouth to about 50 days. By the 1780s it was ordered that all newly built packet boats be copper sheathed.[69] In 1787 the Admiralty estimated the travel time at: Falmouth–Barbados, 30 to 35 days; Barbados–Kingston, 5 days, stay in Kingston 2 days; Kingston–Falmouth, 44 days.[70] Actual travel time Falmouth–Jamaica for sixty-one packet voyages 1781–88 averaged 42 days, with a range of 29 to 55 days, whereas the return took 47 days (ranging between 31 and 69 days).[71] On 31 December 1802 Lady Nugent reported receiving "papers as late as the 23rd of November", thinking a passage of 38 days exceptionally speedy, and it certainly was, compared to her own experience.[72] New 170–ton packets built at the beginning of the Napoleonic War were even faster, making the round trip to the West Indies in as little as seven weeks. However, some of the apparent relative speed of the packet boats compared to the merchant vessels resulted from differences in the point of embarkation (Figure 5.6). The merchants started counting the days from Gravesend or (from 1802) the West India Dock, on the Thames immediately downriver of the City of London, whereas the packets began from Falmouth or Southampton, avoiding the notoriously slow sailing around the southeastern coast.[73]

The merchants of Jamaica sometimes complained of poor service, and sent a memorial to the post office in 1798 saying the average passage from Falmouth to Jamaica was then 45 days and the return 53 days.[74] On the other hand, the Kingston merchants were willing to use their influence to delay the departure of the packet boat when it suited. For example, Lady Nugent noted on 8 August 1801, "Begin letters to England at 6 o'clock, but find that, at the request of the merchants, General N. had ordered the packet to be delayed, till the 17th."[75] The effect was to slow the journey of the packet. Thus it increased the time taken by letters already written and waiting at the post office but at the same time speeded the last-minute letters that otherwise would have had to wait another two or more weeks.

To summarize the available indications, the travel times of the sailing packets remained fairly constant throughout the eighteenth century and into the early nineteenth century. These boats took about 42 days from England to Jamaica via Barbados, and 47 days to return to England via the Windward Passage. The round trip was completed in about 110 days.[76] By the 1850s the times were radically reduced, steam packets travelling via St Thomas taking only about 20 days to reach Kingston from Falmouth, England.[77] By 1914 ships travelling direct from England to Kingston took 10 to 11 days.[78]

The most dramatic reduction in travel times occurred around 1840, with the adoption of steam. At first, steam power was used in combination with sail, as an auxiliary when the wind failed. Thus steam not only increased speed across the water but also improved reliability and predictability, which were vital factors in communication of matters such as advice for insurance of sugar cargoes. On the other hand, steam without the packet boat system would have offered much less to attorney and proprietor. Frequency mattered even more than speed and reliability. Thus the existence of the packets throughout the eighteenth and nineteenth centuries was the most important benefit. Once sail was combined with steam, the system possessed speed and reliability as well as frequency and regularity. Answers to questions sent across the Atlantic could be expected within three months in 1750. This pattern changed little down to the abolition of slavery but by 1850 the time had been reduced to six weeks. It was the packet boats that dramatically reduced the level of uncertainty, bringing predictability to reasonable expectations. However quickly or slowly they travelled, the sighting of the packet boat was enough to stir colonial enthusiasms and fears. News of the arrival of a packet was generally known several hours in advance of the arrival of the letters from it. Watchers in Kingston spied ships as they approached the entrance to the harbour, long before they anchored.[79]

Communication and Correspondence

In communication between attorney and proprietor, the two main factors were speed of travel and promptness of writing. Letters and accounts might be delivered speedily yet lie unanswered for extended periods, missing the opportunities of a series of ships. Prolonged silences of several months were not uncommon among absentees, resulting from their desire to live lives of leisure or simply reflecting the confidence they had in the men appointed to manage their interests.[80] An attorney wishing to postpone answering a difficult question or delaying bad news might succeed for several weeks or even months, but the absentees generally had their own larger network of correspondents and found out eventually. Clare Taylor has argued that newly absentee proprietors tended to write long letters of advice to their attorneys, then, as the years passed, gradually write less and seek less information from their managers as the picture of the plantation grew increasingly dim and they sought to insert themselves into the landed gentry and leave behind their distant and increasingly uncomfortable colonial wealth and creole manners.[81] This was not always the case, however, and fits poorly the examples discussed in the next chapter.

Sailing contracts routinely contained the clause "wind and weather permitting", to signal the necessity of variations in route as well as expected arrival times. The ability of absentee planter and resident attorney to communicate effectively was made unpredictable by these factors. The uncertainty of the delivery of directives and recommendations was more important than the average time taken by the average vessel to cross the Atlantic. Delay and uncertainty were compounded by the failure of absentees and attorneys to write at the first available opportunity, and the unreliability of sea passages perhaps excused or encouraged this attitude. Absentee, attorney and merchant-factor might each possess valuable information regarding the state of a plantation but fail to share what they knew.

The underlying uncertainty of the postal system also meant that a writer could not assume their message had been received. Duplicates were often sent on following vessels and information repeated, and correspondents were generally meticulous about advising what they had received and sent, and noted periods when they received no letters. The attorneys commonly had their letters copied into letterbooks, to ensure they had a precise record. However, the effect of this practice was to place further pressure on the clerk doing the copying, especially when the letters were long and included numerous accounts and other enclosures. The desire to catch the post meant there might be little time for proofreading and often enclosures were not copied. In such cases, the attorney had to rely on rough drafts. However, the correspondence of the attorneys Simon Taylor and Isaac Jackson – discussed in the next chapter – suggests few examples of important messages or instructions going missing, and few cases where delays in the transmission of information resulted in financial loss to the proprietors.[82]

In the context of the British imperial system, communication with the Caribbean colonies was relatively rapid. In the era before steam, movement on water was almost always potentially speedier than movement over land. Rather than being isolated, the small island colonies of the West Indies were easily accessible and open to information flows. They had advantages not shared by the interior settlements of colonial America, for example, even though the North Atlantic crossing was shorter. Around 1810, packets sailed from New York to England in just twenty days, but overland transport substantially delayed communication.[83] Similarly, the West Indian plantations were much closer to their metropolitan managers than the British colonies of the East. Down to the 1830s, a letter to India might take five to eight months to reach its reader and the sender could wait two years for a response.[84]

If the relative speed and regularity of communication between Jamaica and Britain was a significant factor contributing to the growth of absenteeism and attorneyship, the efficiency of the system depended on the willingness of principal and agent to write. The pattern of letter writing by attorney and proprietor is difficult to measure systematically, because the necessary documentary materials are rare and under-analysed. This means that it is hard to assess the potential three-month response period in 1750 in terms of its impact on decision making in plantation management. What particular decisions had to be made by the attorney because he could not wait on an answer from the proprietor? What difference did the reduced potential response time of six weeks, achieved by 1850, make? In order to answer these questions it is necessary first to analyse the actual pattern of letter writing and, second, to dissect the content of the letters. The following chapters take these issues as their major tasks, using the examples provided by two attorneys – Simon Taylor and Isaac Jackson – and the letters they wrote to their absentee principals.

Part 2
Managing

Chapter 6

Two Attorneys

Many of the men employed as attorneys seem likely to remain shadowy figures, known only as members of a class. Some take on a little personality from brief appearances in the historical record when, for example, they are found giving evidence before select committees or having their property inventoried. Only occasionally do individuals emerge in more complete character, providing details of their actions as managers and of their social lives. These few are known most often from their correspondence, the collections of letters created through the process of communication between attorney and absentee-proprietor. Their letters take on a particular historical value because of the necessity, generated by distance, to explain in detail what the principal could not observe and often did not understand.

Among the attorneys for whom such collections of correspondence are available, two offer themselves as contrasting examples. The first, Simon Taylor, represents the era of planter prosperity in the letters he wrote between 1765 and 1775 to the absentee Chaloner Arcedeckne.[1] The second, Isaac Jackson, served as attorney to Lord Seaford in the period immediately following the abolition of slavery. The surviving letters of Jackson to Seaford cover the vital years 1839 to 1843.[2] Both Taylor and Jackson had other employers than these, dealt with other properties and wrote many more letters.[3] But Taylor's management of Arcedeckne's Golden Grove and Jackson's management of Seaford's Montpelier are best documented.

Simon Taylor

Simon Taylor (1740–1813) was born and died in Jamaica. During his seventy-three years he rarely left the island. According to James Hakewill, Taylor went to England only once after his schooling.[4] He was no absentee. The details of his life are relatively well known, thanks to the visibility given him by his wealth, the extent of his correspondence and his political influence.[5] Philip Wright, in 1966, observed that "it was said of him [Taylor] that he exercised greater influence in Jamaica, and for a longer period, than any other individual". Richard Sheridan repeated Wright's assessment and labelled Taylor a "sugar tycoon", for many years "a leading plantation attorney for absentee proprietors". Betty Wood and T. R. Clayton, writing in 1985, described Taylor as "arguably the most important planter in late eighteenth-century Jamaica".[6]

White contemporaries were impressed by Taylor's wealth and power. Governor Nugent, making abbreviated notes in 1806, described Taylor, then aged sixty-six, as

> by much the richest proprietor in the island, and in the habit of accumulating money, so as to make his nephew and heir (Sir Simon Taylor) one of the most wealthy subjects of His Majesty. In strong opposition to Government at present and violent in his language against the King's Ministers, for their conduct towards Jamaica. He has great influence in the Assembly, but is nearly superannuated.[7]

Simon Taylor was member of the House of Assembly for Kingston 1763–81, and for St Thomas-in-the-East 1784–1810; custos for St Thomas-in-the-East 1774–1813; lieutenant-general of militia; and chief justice of the Court of Common Pleas.[8]

After slavery, Taylor's character and political influence came into question. Thus in 1873 the Reverend W. J. Gardner described Taylor as "a man of degraded habits, though possessed of many estates, and the attorney for several absentees". Taylor, said Gardner, developed "a great hatred to the Wesleyans, and having failed in shutting them out from St Thomas, of which parish he was custos, he determined, if possible, to restrain them by legislative enactment". In 1802 he moved against the missionaries, pushing for the control of preaching. Of Taylor, Gardner concluded, "Perhaps no planter was ever possessed of more power than this imperious, vulgar man."[9] Taylor's importance and wealth existed within the context of slave society, a system of oppression he exploited to the limit.

Lady Nugent, in 1802, wrote in her journal that "Mr. Taylor is the richest man in the island, and piques himself upon making his nephew, Sir Simon Taylor, who is now in Germany, the richest Commoner in England, which he says he shall be, at *his* death".[10] In 1814, a year after the death of Simon Taylor, the nephew, whose full name was Sir Simon Richard Brissett Taylor, erected a memorial at the family estate Lyssons, near Morant Bay, commemorating his father and uncle. The memorial stated that Sir Simon's father, Sir John Taylor (1745–86), the younger brother of Simon Taylor the attorney, had died "during a visit to his estates in this island" (Figure 6.1). The uncle, Simon Taylor, was described as "a loyal subject, a firm friend, and an honest man", who had led "an active life, during which he faithfully and ably filled the

Figure 6.1 Simon Taylor (seated left), with his brother, Sir John Taylor, and John's wife, Elizabeth Haughton, and their children, *c.*1780. From a photograph of a pastel by Daniel Gardner, National Library of Jamaica.

highest offices of civil and military duty in this island". The memorialist and heir, Sir Simon, lived only into the next year, dying in 1815 aged thirty.[11]

Simon Taylor first became an attorney while still a young man, gaining directly from experience in his father's merchant business. The father, Patrick, had come to Jamaica from Scotland. Some accounts say he was a carpenter. He established himself as a substantial Kingston merchant and married the daughter of a Caymanas planter. John, the younger son and Simon's brother, married the daughter and heir of Philip Haughton, another planter. When Patrick died in 1759, Simon inherited both his father's substantial accumulated wealth and his list of planter clients. The personalty totalled £51,751 sterling on paper. Most of this wealth, however, consisted of debt. Among the planter debtors, one of the largest was Andrew Arcedeckne, owner of Golden Grove Estate in St Thomas-in-the-East.[12] Andrew was a resident proprietor but it was with his absentee son Chaloner that Taylor would correspond about Golden Grove, beginning in 1765.

To the attorneyship of Golden Grove, Simon Taylor quickly added other properties. A complete list is difficult to compile. In a letter to Chaloner Arcedeckne, Taylor mentioned in 1769 that he had the management of two estates in the Blue Mountain Valley, assuring Arcedeckne "intend being at windward almost the whole crop time and pay my greatest attention to yours and the other properties I have care of there". Taylor also extended the Kingston mercantile enterprise established by his father. In 1764 or 1765 he entered partnership with his brother-in-law Robert Graham, founding the merchant house of Taylor and Graham. Born in Scotland in 1735, Graham had migrated to Jamaica in 1752, marrying Taylor's sister Anne in 1763. The partnership continued until 1770 or 1771 when Graham inherited a Scottish estate, Ardoch.[13]

Taylor's income from attorneyships and trade was considerable. In 1771 he purchased Holland Estate, on the north side of the Plantain Garden River and just beyond Arcedeckne's Golden Grove. Taylor told Arcedeckne, "I always wanted to be in your neighbourhood in Plantain Garden River that we might be near one another, and not to have far to go to smoke a pipe together."[14] He also bought Moro Pen, part of Hordley Estate, in the hills immediately to the west, renaming it Holland Park.[15] Two years before, in 1769, Taylor had encouraged Arcedeckne to extend his estates, suggesting specifically that he might consider acquiring Holland.[16] Now Taylor said, "I have given an amazing sum of money for it, no less than £100,000 sterling", to be paid over fourteen years, the first six without interest at £10,000 per annum. The estate had "2 water and 1 windmill in order, the works in repair, 400 Negroes, 100 mules, and 100 head of cattle". In the crop of 1772 Taylor expected to cut 430 acres of cane and make five hundred hogsheads of sugar. At this scale, Holland was a close rival to Golden Grove. Arcedeckne must have wondered at Taylor's good fortune and the extent to which Golden Grove had been a contributor. On top of this, Taylor sought the lease of a detached piece of land belonging to Golden Grove, in the territory of Holland, and already rented out, to plant cane and establish a plantain walk.[17]

When he died, at Port Royal in 1813, Taylor owned four sugar estates and three pens spread widely across the island. Two of the estates, Lyssons and Holland, were in St Thomas-in-the-East; Llanrumney in St Mary; and

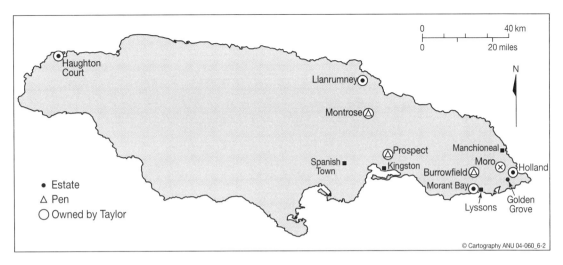

Figure 6.2 Simon Taylor's Jamaica

Haughton Court in Hanover (Figure 6.2). The pens were Prospect in St Andrew, Burrowfield in St Thomas-in-the-East, and Montrose in St Mary. Taylor owned 2,228 enslaved people. He had his own ship, the *West Indian*, and an island schooner for trade. All told, his personal property was valued at £739,207 sterling, almost fifteen times the amount left by his father fifty years before. Taylor's wealth in realty (land and buildings), when added to the personalty, totalled an estimated £1 million sterling. Of this amount, roughly 40 per cent consisted of the personalty and realty on his estates and pens. The remainder came from investments, other property and debts owed. Nugent's assertion that Taylor was the richest Jamaican of his time seems secure.[18] His estate was, for example, much larger than the £362,262 left by his creole friend John Tharp in 1804.[19] Not only was Taylor one of the richest of all Jamaican planters, his fortune placed him at the very top of the scale among the landed aristocracy of contemporary England.[20] His income was equally large, about £47,000 sterling per annum, with only £3,000 derived from commission earned as attorney. Thus, although Taylor was one of the most active attorneys in his time, the greater part of his prime income came from direct investments in sugar, pens and slaves, and from trade. He was in a position to decline attorneyships that did not suit his interests or personal connections.[21]

Taylor lived most permanently at Prospect Pen, close to Kingston. He bought the pen in 1785 for £3,200 currency. The dwelling house was described as a "capital mansion" and sat on 128 acres. Following Taylor's death, the furniture and effects were sold at public auction, including everything from his gold snuff box to an old chaise and chariot.[22] At Llanrumney Estate in St Mary, the "overseer's house" included a room identified in the inventory as

"Mr. Taylor's room", containing a bed with two mattresses, sheets, counterpane, bolster and mosquito net, a table and wash hand stand, a chamber chair and pot, a night chair, and an old looking glass.[23] Montrose Pen, on the other hand, had a "great house" as well as overseer's house, and was rather more elaborately equipped.[24] Holland also had a great house, with six bedrooms, a dining room, a breakfast room, a back hall (used as a store for the household silver and kitchen utensils), and stores for salt provisions and other food supplies and tools (Figure 6.3). The total value of the personalty at Holland was £58,931, the enslaved people accounting for £50,150, leaving aside the value of the realty in land, crops and buildings.[25]

Holland was one of Jamaica's largest sugar estates. Some 610 enslaved people lived there at the time of Taylor's death. There were slightly more females than males. Of the females, 133 worked in the field but only one was a supervisor, the "driveress" of the small gang. Only half as many males worked in the field, though males held the occupations of head driver, second driver, third driver, fourth driver and driver for the "yaws negroes", while 22 men worked as carpenters, 15 as masons, 14 as coopers and another 14 in the sugar factory.[26]

Taylor's wealth, founded on the labour of these enslaved people, enabled him to live a life of indulgence in the midst of his active practice of management. He took advantage of his power in ways that disconcerted even some of the contemporary white males with whom he dealt. He was no pro-slavery

Figure 6.3 Holland Estate, 1820, by James Hakewill. National Library of Jamaica.

ideologue but a man who took for granted the system of exploitation he operated. In 1784, contemplating a visit to England, Taylor wrote, "I have been so long here that I do not believe the English customs and formality, with the routine of dissipation that prevails there, would at all suit me."[27] He might be a creole white male, but it was the English rather than himself whom he saw as debauched and unattractive. From the other side, Governor Nugent noted in 1806 that Taylor had the "most extraordinary manners and lives principally with overseers of estates and masters of merchant vessels; but he has had an excellent education, is well informed and is a warm friend to those he takes by the hand. He is also very hospitable and civilised occasionally, but is said to be most inveterate in his dislikes."[28]

Lady Nugent was similarly shocked and enchanted. In March 1802 she travelled with "an enormous cavalcade" from King's House to Prospect Pen. There she had dinner: "A most profuse and overloaded table, and a shoulder of wild boar stewed, with forced meat, &c. as an ornament to the centre of the table." During the course of this vulgar display, "Mr. Simon Taylor and I became the greatest friends", said Nugent. But after extracting herself from the all-male party, she "took tea in my own room, surrounded by the black, brown and yellow ladies of the house, and heard a great deal of its private history". The party travelled on to St David and St Thomas-in-the-East, including visits to properties in which Taylor had an interest: Albion, Lyssons, Golden Grove and Holland. In the course of the journey, Nugent noted that "Mr. Taylor is an old bachelor, and detests the society of women, but I have worked a reform, for he never leaves me an instant, and attends to all my wants and wishes". At Golden Grove, she was "every instant interrupted by mulatto ladies", and was told by the "housekeeper" that Taylor "had a numerous family, some almost on every one of his estates". After a series of profuse meals, Nugent's party headed north, taking leave of Taylor. Nugent wrote, "When I expressed my regret at parting with Mr. Simon Taylor, he said, 'I am very sorry, too, Ma'am, but good Almighty God, I must go home and cool coppers.' " Nugent at first understood this as a literal reference to the boiling house, but learned it was a creole expression meaning he should "be abstemious, after so much feasting".[29]

It was not the first time Taylor had been responsible for guiding the colonial chiefs through his territory. In 1769, before he became custos, he had written from Manchioneal saying, "Have been obliged to attend on the Governor and his family who are in this parish [St Thomas-in-the-East] at present for these 14 days past." They had dined at Golden Grove. Tantalizingly, Taylor told Chaloner Arcedeckne, "I must see the Governor and his family embark at Manchioneal for St Marys on a challenge from the ladys and a promise I made to them on board."[30]

Lady Nugent encountered Taylor often during the years following the tour of 1802. When leaving Jamaica in 1805 his farewell led her to observe,

I was as much surprised as affected by his manner, for he has the character of loving nothing but his money; and yet I have experienced such continued kindness from him, that he has shown me almost the affection of a father. Indeed, I feel that I know him much better than the world does, and shall always feel gratefully affectionate towards him.[31]

Taylor occasionally reflected on marriage and its place in the slave society of Jamaica. In 1768, when he was twenty-eight, he responded to a query from Arcedeckne, saying, "In regard to matrimony I have as yet no thoughts of it." He had himself been encouraging Arcedeckne to find a wife in order to secure his inheritance. After all, wrote Taylor, "You that are in so fair a climate must want a wife more than one who have been so long in this hot country and consequently excessively relaxed." Getting closer to his own sexual life, he added, "As I am on the subject there has been the devil to pay between two disbanded Councillors viz. Bayly and Kennion about the latters having debauched the others quadroon girl. Bayly says he is very glad he did not catch them in bed together or he would have been under the necessity of putting him to death."[32] Occasionally, Taylor referred to men taking white wives in Jamaica, but in September 1765, apparently in the context of a breach of promise judgement, he agreed with Arcedeckne that "it is very dangerous for young fellows to think of matrimony". In the same letter, he told Taylor, "There is a report that on Friday last a licence was taken out for our friend Rose Price and one Miss Patrick a writing master's daughter at Spanish [Town] and without a shilling but that Rose set out the next day for the Red Hills with his black wife." Rose was the eldest son of the resident planter Sir Charles Price ("The Patriot") of Worthy Park Estate. Taylor thought that for Rose to "play the fool so egregiously" was to risk his inheritance.[33]

In 1771 Taylor mentioned a Dr Collins who had lived formerly on Golden Grove and "kept a wench . . . named Catharine", with whom he had had three children. Collins left money and directions in his will to purchase their freedom. Taylor remarked, "He gave himself no trouble about it in his life but by his will he mentioned it, and desires they may be bought." Arcedeckne, their owner, raised objections, but his mother and Taylor favoured manumission.[34] In 1773 Taylor again encouraged the reluctant Arcedeckne to find a wife, "you who are in the land of beauties". For himself, said Taylor, "There are none my way but Mauritanians and their issue being in a manner a constant accident in the country and have no opportunity of seeing of but seldom indeed."[35]

When Taylor was much older, he had news in 1801 from his friend the absentee planter John Tharp, that his young second wife Ann had betrayed the marriage bed and slept with Tharp's son-in-law, the Reverend Richard Burton Burton Phillipson. The affair occurred in England but both John and

Ann were Jamaica-born and married in the island. Ann was pregnant with Phillipson's child. Tharp, born 1744, was just four years younger than Taylor. Taylor told his sister-in-law that the cuckolding "must serve as a lesson to me never to think of marrying a young girl for tho I am past one period of my life when people fall in love I am approaching another namely sixty-four when old men marry their cookmaids but I hope I shall avoid that piece of folly or rather insanity". Taylor had then lived nearly thirty years with his free black or coloured housekeeper, Grace Donne.[36] Tharp too had Jamaican mistresses. In 1767, two years before Taylor bought Holland, Tharp acquired Good Hope Estate in Trelawny for £74,000, making it his residence and building around it an extended network of estates and pens, with a very large population of enslaved people.[37] In 1795, soon after his marriage to Ann, and at the age of fifty-one, he left Jamaica to settle on an estate in Cambridge-shire. It cost him £40,000. According to Sarah M. S. Pearsall, Tharp sought also "to escape the challenges of overseeing estates in Jamaica". When the scandal broke, however, Tharp quickly sought "comfort and safety in Jamaica", returning to Good Hope in 1802. He died there in 1804.[38] Taylor must have seen Tharp's discomfort and embarrassment as the product of a series of avoidable mistakes.

Although Taylor never chanced marriage or attempted to insert himself into the English gentry, he did establish a strong metropolitan base for his fortune. Of his total estimated wealth of £1 million sterling at his death in 1813, a little over half came from assets in England. Part of this amount consisted of debts owed by London and Bristol commission agents, but £380,680 was in investments in consolidated annuities (consols) and other public funds. However, as Sheridan commented, "The fact that Taylor's stock purchases were concentrated in the seven months just prior to his death suggests that he was concerned to liquidate a large part of his estate." The expected annual interest on the consols amounted to more than £18,000.[39] Shifting the centre of gravity of his fortune away from Jamaica to the safe haven of British public funds might be seen as a reaction to the abolition of the Atlantic slave trade, in which Taylor had been a great believer as the foundation of plantation wealth. If so, he acted slowly. It is more probable that he chose to move his money closer to the beneficiaries of his estate.

In addition to this last-minute investment in British funds, Sheridan surmised that Taylor had established, in about 1799, an interest in a London merchant house. This was the firm of (Robert) Taylor and (James) Renny of Billiter Square. Sheridan further suggested that Robert Taylor was a cousin of Simon Taylor. However, the nature and extent of Taylor's "interest" remains unclear. What is certain is that in 1795 Simon Taylor appointed as his attorneys "Robert Taylor of Ember Court in the County of Surry Esquire and John Taylor of the City of Glasgow Esquire".[40] The letter of attorney was drawn up on parchment and proved by the chief justice of Jamaica, in the office of "George Atkinson, Secretary and Notary Public of Jamaica, resident in Spanish Town". The letter stated that Simon Taylor did

> make ordain constitute and appoint and in my place and stead depute and put the said Robert Taylor and John Taylor and each of them my true and lawful Attornies and Attorney for me and in my name place and stead and for my use and benefit to ask demand sue for and by all lawful ways and means recover obtain and receive of and from all and every or any person or persons whomsoever residing or being in Great Britain whom it doth shall or may concern to pay the same all and every such sum and sums of money as now are due and owing and which shall or may at any time or times hereafter grow due and owing and become payable to me upon any account whatsoever.

The letter further authorized Robert Taylor and John Taylor to draw bills of exchange in Simon Taylor's or their own names, and to accept bills, drafts and promissory notes indebted to him, and "to indorse and sign my name upon any bill or bills of exchange or any promissory note or notes made payable to me or my order". It gave the attorneys, at "their free will and pleasure to take care of and manage or let in such manner as they or either of them shall think proper and most to my advantage", all the "hereditaments estates and premises whereof or wherein I now have or at any time or times hereafter shall or may have any estate right title or interest". They were to "receive and take the rents issues profits and produce thereof . . . and in my name to sell and dispose of all or any part or parts of such hereditaments and premises as shall or may be saleable by me . . . for the best price or prices that can or may be had or gotten". The resulting funds were to be lent or placed at interest, and reinvested when paid. The attorneys could undertake "mortgages of freehold or copyhold lands tenements and hereditaments free from incumbrances in any part of Great Britain or the Principality of Wales". Robert and John had authority to sue for money due from rents and mortgages, to appear in court and undertake arbitration on Simon's behalf. It was a broad power of attorney, effectively establishing Robert and John as Simon's investment bankers in Britain, but without any clear suggestion that their business relationship was connected to trade or a London merchant house.

Whatever Simon Taylor's investments in Great Britain and his interest in metropolitan mercantile enterprise, the essential foundation of his fortune derived from his exploitation of the resources of Jamaica and the labour of enslaved Africans. In the longer term, however, Sheridan argues that Taylor's wealth was "probably derived chiefly from his services as a plantation attorney for absentee proprietors".[41] It was the commission and opportunities created by his work as both mercantile and planting attorney, beginning with the business inherited from his father, that laid the foundations.

Simon Taylor's Letters

Among Simon Taylor's various clients and employers, two of the most important were Andrew Arcedeckne and his son Chaloner, the owners of Golden Grove. It is the correspondence between Taylor and Chaloner Arcedeckne for the years 1765 to 1775 that is subjected to close scrutiny here and in the next chapter. As noted above, although Andrew Arcedeckne was a resident proprietor, he employed the Kingston merchant Patrick Taylor as attorney. The estate and the business of attorney descended to the sons, Chaloner and Simon.

Andrew Arcedeckne (pronounced and sometimes written "Archdeacon") was born in 1681 and migrated to Jamaica in 1716. Described by George Metcalf as "an Irish lawyer", he suffered by his Roman Catholic ancestry and education, and in Jamaica was maligned as a papist though officially declared a "loyal protestant". In Jamaica, Andrew served as attorney-general for a year and had a seat in the Assembly from 1718 to 1757, representing the parish of St Catherine, generally opposing the governor. He accumulated 12,700 acres and early took up land in St Thomas-in-the-East, where he developed Golden Grove as a sugar plantation.[42] He became possessed of "very considerable real and personal estate" in Jamaica.[43] When Andrew died in 1763, he left his wife Elizabeth (Kearsey) and their two children. Elizabeth was a widow when Andrew hired her as housekeeper, then married her. They had their first child Anne in 1738 or 1739 and their son Chaloner in 1743 or 1744. The children erected a mural tablet in the Spanish Town Cathedral, memorializing "Andrew Arcedeckne Esq., a native of the Kingdom of Ireland, many years barrister at law, and representative of this town in the General Assembly of the island". The five packing cases containing the monument, shipped by the London merchant house of Long Drake and Long, were received by Simon Taylor in 1769.[44] Elizabeth lived on in Jamaica until 1778.

Chaloner Arcedeckne inherited Golden Grove but travelled to England early in 1765, when he was twenty-one or twenty-two years of age, and established himself as an absentee-proprietor living at Glevering Hall in Suffolk. Simon Taylor, himself just twenty-five years old, had already been made attorney for Golden Grove. Both men, born in Jamaica, had been educated at Eton. Thus began their extended correspondence, which continued until the death of Arcedeckne in 1809.[45]

It was only in retrospect that Chaloner Arcedeckne's long-term absenteeism seemed inevitable. At first, after he had been away from Jamaica just a few months, Taylor could write to tell him that a seat in the Assembly was his as soon as he returned to the island. Friends and family wished to advertise his candidature in July 1765. Chaloner had already held a seat in the Assembly, elected when he was just twenty and recently returned to Jamaica from his schooling in England.[46] In expectation of his coming back again, Taylor began the building of a great house for him, on Golden Grove. Taylor expected him to come in 1766 and kept a pipe of wine ageing in readiness.[47]

The consequence of this uncertainty was that Taylor had to be prepared for Arcedeckne's early return, and perhaps the end of his attorneyship, as much as he saw the possibility of long-term responsibility. Only gradually did it become clear that Arcedeckne would not come back to Jamaica to live, failing to set sail even when the great house seemed almost ready for him in 1771. The following year, Arcedeckne asked Taylor to send his library to him in London. His aunt had been taking care of the books in Spanish Town.[48] By then, Taylor must have known he had a free hand and long-term charge of the management of Golden Grove.

Taylor's correspondence with Arcedeckne contained much discussion of Jamaican politics and people, intermixed with the details of management. The relationship was founded on friendship as well as business. Taylor went out of his way to assure Arcedeckne that his attorneys were concerned for the profits of the property and that he would "take as much care of as my own".[49] He gathered information wherever he could, for the benefit of his own properties as well as those he managed. In 1767, for example, Taylor travelled to St Domingue "to see how they make sugar there and what sort of country it was". He told Arcedeckne that he had "a tolerable pleasant trip but found nothing could be learned from them but the art of watering their lands".[50]

Between 1765 and 1775 Simon Taylor sent at least sixty-eight letters to Chaloner Arcedeckne and sixteen to his brother-in-law Benjamin Cowell (1767–69). These eighty-four letters have been published in an edition prepared by Betty Wood. Many more letters survive for the period beyond 1775 but have not been published.[51] The collected edition for 1765–75 includes only Taylor's letters, sent from Jamaica. He mentioned receiving forty-six in return, from Arcedeckne and Cowell, but the contents of these letters is not generally known.[52] Cowell served as Arcedeckne's attorney in Britain while he was touring France and Italy in 1767–69. Taylor agreed to send to Cowell "whatever bills are designed for Europe and supplies for the estate", as well as bills of lading, and "the accounts" to Arcedeckne. "You may depend on my punctually executing your orders and letting him know every thing that occurs", Taylor told Arcedeckne. Taylor and Graham wrote separately to Cowell saying, "Our mutual friend Mr. Arcedekne has acquainted our ST [Simon Taylor] that he intends to return to the South of France and has left you his attorney in his absence. Therefore think it but our duty to inform you of every thing about his affairs here."[53]

Occasionally, Taylor sent as many as five letters before mentioning having anything from Arcedeckne or Cowell. Some of Arcedeckne's long silences resulted from his travels, including his move from Jamaica to England at the beginning of 1765 and his later tours in France and Italy. In forty-nine of his eighty-four letters Taylor states explicitly that nothing fresh has reached him or makes no mention of it. On the other hand, on ten occasions he responded to more than one letter. At the extreme, on 25 January 1773 Taylor acknowledged a total of four letters from Arcedeckne, dated 20 and 27 August, 3 September and 8 October.[54]

The disproportion between the number of letters sent and received by Taylor demonstrates at least that as attorney he showed more interest and had more to report than the absentee-proprietor. The difference is not explained by Arcedeckne's temporary dependence on Cowell as attorney, since Cowell was overall a more frequent correspondent than Arcedeckne. Taylor expected little from Arcedeckne while he was touring France and Italy. Thus, on 25 March 1768, Taylor wrote, "Since my last to you [3 October 1767] have not had the pleasure of hearing from you which indeed I did not expect, and as am uncertain where this will meet you, write chiefly to shew you that am still in the land of the living."[55] Arcedeckne had in fact sent a letter on 3 March from Naples but Taylor did not receive it until 25 July.[56] In the meantime, occasional letters from Arcedeckne to Taylor were forwarded by Cowell.[57] In June 1769 Taylor outlined the contents of several letters he had sent previously to Arcedeckne, in order to allay his fears on various issues, and listed the dates of those letters. "I am very sorry you should imagine that you are forgot", said Taylor, never meaning "to give you the least reason for complaining [and] for the future will write oftener to you".[58]

Taylor's output of letters was rather erratic. The mean interval between his letters to Arcedeckne (and Cowell) was 38 days and the median 21, but around these general tendencies he varied enormously. At times he was prolific, sending three or even four letters in a single month. Overall, 18 per cent of his letters were written within less than 10 days of one another. Occasionally, when responsibilities were split between Arcedeckne (accounts) and Cowell (bills of lading and requisitions for plantation supplies), Taylor would write two letters on the same day. One of these might be addressed to Cowell, enclosing a letter to be forwarded to Arcedeckne. On other occasions, Cowell himself communicated to Arcedeckne the contents of a letter from Taylor.[59] On the other hand, the frequency distribution had a long tail stretching out to a maximum of 157 days or more than five months. Some of the long gaps between letters related to Arcedeckne's absences from home but others seem simply to represent a hiatus.

Taking all of Taylor's letters which acknowledged correspondence from Arcedeckne or Cowell, the mean interval between their writing and Taylor responding was 116 days and the median 110. The fastest letter arrived in 55 days and the slowest, posted in France in August 1769, took 189 days. This may be compared with the average speed of the packet boats that reached Jamaica from England in 42 days. Ignoring Arcedeckne's letters from France and Italy, and taking only those sent from England, reduces the mean to 110 days and the median to 100. Ignoring the accumulated letters and taking only the most recently received messages further speeds the correspondence, to give a mean of 97 days and a median of 95, but leaves the typical interval at about fourteen weeks.

How quickly did Taylor respond? The speediest letter, the one that reached him in 55 days, Taylor answered the day after he received it. On 20 March 1769 he replied to a letter "this minute received" in order to counter Arcedeckne's "concern and uneasiness . . . which makes me not delay a single minute in informing you, which I do with the greatest pleasure, that your apprehensions are a good deal imaginary".[60] The time taken for letters to reach Arcedeckne (or Cowell) from Jamaica is hard to establish since the available observations are few. In 1765 Taylor noted that his letter of 26 March had reached Arcedeckne by 20 June, some 86 days.[61] On 2 June 1769 Taylor told Cowell he had received Cowell's of 8 April which reported not having received Taylor's of 27 January, or 71 days and still waiting.[62] Two letters posted by Taylor in 1773, one in January the other in September, took 67 and 135 days respectively to reach Arcedeckne.[63] The following year Taylor's of 12 March reached Arcedeckne by 15 June, some 95 days later.[64] These four examples suggest that the mail moved more rapidly east than west across the Atlantic, but generally the reverse was true.[65] Typically, Taylor had to wait at least six months to get an answer from Arcedeckne, twice the potential three months offered by the speedy packet boats.

Taylor had no great faith in the reliability of the mail across the Atlantic. He regularly sent copies of letters previously transmitted, the earlier messages copied into the text of the current letter. Occasionally he sent more than one copy. For example, on 23 April 1765 he sent a letter with an account of floods at Arcedeckne's plantation Golden Grove. The same account was written into his letter of 30 April and then enclosed with his letter of 15 June along with copies of two other letters.[66] For various reasons, ships reached England out of sequence, creating financial problems. On 2 May 1767 Taylor told Arcedeckne,

> Your letter of 3rd January acquaints me that you have received several of my letters and a bill of lading for the sugars on board the Sally and that mine by the *Dreadnought* arrived first tho' the last in date for which I am very sorry on account of your insurance but hear she is put in to Carolina so she is not lost and in all probability the sugars on board her will come to a good market.[67]

Some of Taylor's letters travelled on packet boats but others by merchant ships and men of war.[68] Those sent by merchant men sometimes went to Bristol and Liverpool rather than London.[69] Occasionally he received his letters via Montego Bay.[70] Although Taylor did not include in his letters information on the cost of postage, he did make the interesting comment in

January 1769 that "the postage of a large packet comes to much by a man of war that shall enclose your accounts for 1768 by the merchant man for London".[71] In 1767, when he was busy preparing the accounts for 1766, he told Arcedeckne he would send them by a merchantman sailing from Kingston under Captain Barnett, adding, "his bag is advertised to be taken down the day after tomorrow".[72]

Taylor addressed most of his letters from Kingston, where he lived nearby at Prospect Pen, but occasionally he wrote from his St Thomas-in-the-East plantations, Lyssons and Holland, and from Manchioneal. Golden Grove was located close to Holland, making it easy for Taylor to visit and talk directly to the overseer John Kelly. Taylor did, however, mention receiving letters from Kelly reporting on the weather, the state of the crops and sugar shipments, and Arcedeckne sometimes wrote directly to Kelly with instructions. In addition to his letters to Arcedeckne and Cowell, Taylor also wrote to London merchants regarding shipments and insurance, sending them the bills of lading and merely advising Arcedeckne that he had done so.[73] Taylor regularly enclosed documents such as current accounts and inventories for Golden Grove. Sometimes he enclosed letters from other people, such as Arcedeckne's mother, Elizabeth Kearsey, who lived in Spanish Town.[74]

Taylor's letters of 1765–75, in the edition published by Wood and derived from the Vanneck Papers at the Cambridge University Library, survive only as originals.[75] There is nothing to suggest Taylor had them copied into a letterbook, though he certainly had a record of the letters sent so that he could refer to them by date and detail their contents.[76] Copies were also needed in order to send the duplicates which so often went with later letters. The copies kept by Taylor seem to have been somewhat rough-and-ready. For example, Taylor wrote to Arcedeckne on 16 April 1770 in which he claimed to copy part of a letter written to Cowell on 14 April 1769. Although the general drift of this purported duplicate was the same as in the original, the wording and some of the numbers differed.[77]

No doubt there was at least one clerk working in the house of Taylor and Graham in Kingston, with responsibility for copying letters, but Taylor did not always write from Kingston and may sometimes have used ships sailing direct from eastern ports. There are no references in the letters to a clerk travelling with him on his various tours of inspection. He seems to have done much of his own copying and spent many hours writing.[78] Taylor's prose was fluid, phrases and sentences rushing out in a barely controlled chaos that suggests he himself was responsible for the writing as well as the words.

Isaac Jackson

Whereas the life of Simon Taylor has long been well known to historians, quite independent of his correspondence and generally without reference to it, Isaac Jackson has come to prominence largely through the recent discovery of the letterbooks he kept as attorney between 1839–43.[79] The two attorneys lived in different times, their letters separated by almost three generations, by the American Revolution and abolition. Jackson is of particular interest because one of the proprietors for whom he worked as attorney was Lord Seaford, owner of the well-documented and closely studied Montpelier Estate and Shettlewood Pen in western Jamaica.[80] The surviving letters of Jackson also give him importance because they provide an account of the immediate post-slavery period and the many negotiations and adjustments demanded of those who had been enslaved and those who had been their masters and of the particular role of the attorney in that transition. It was a time of dramatic challenge and change in management.

Jackson was born in 1796 or 1797 but whether in Jamaica or England is uncertain. In his letters, he referred specifically to events that occurred in Jamaica in 1821, so he must have been living in the island by his twenty-fifth birthday at least. In 1843 he used the term "home" to refer to England and mentioned having himself seen the "hoe harrow" in use on farms in Cumberland, northern England.[81] It seems most likely that he came to Jamaica from England as a young man and rose steadily through the ranks of management, starting perhaps as a book-keeper.

By the last years of slavery, Jackson was both attorney and overseer for Copse Estate, a sugar plantation owned by Alexander Campbell.[82] Jackson was not then attorney for any other property and indeed could not serve effectively while resident overseer at Copse. He does not seem to have owned any enslaved persons but there were 378 living on the estate at the final registration in 1832. Copse was a centre of the great rebellion that broke out in December 1831. Its buildings were burned.[83] Three enslaved people belonging to Copse were shot by order of courts martial, five were executed by sentence of slave courts, two shot by the militia and one by the Maroons. One rebel drowned himself. Nearby Montpelier and Shettlewood, Seaford's properties, were also engulfed by the rebellion. Jackson took part in its suppression, holding the rank of lieutenant colonel in the Western Interior Regiment. He later became a magistrate for the parishes of Hanover and St James, and a member of the Legislative Council.[84]

In the years following 1838, Jackson emerged quickly as a leading attorney, building on a reputation established during the apprenticeship. He was "personally liked" and proved successful "on estates managed by unpopular planters or where long-established prejudices existed on the basis of past grievances".[85] His conciliatory approach and willingness to negotiate contrasted with the iron hand of the likes of the great attorney William Miller who ruled Montpelier over the last twenty years of slavery. Jackson's rapid rise to power and influence in plantation management came as he approached forty, a pattern typical of those who rose through the ranks, but in strong contrast to the precocious Simon Taylor. In October 1835 Jackson was described as "manager" of Copse and already attorney for estates with more than nine hundred apprentices.[86] In 1836, before he became attorney for Montpelier Estate, Jackson was added to the group of commissioners for Seaford Township, a community of German immigrants established by Lord Seaford.[87] By August 1839, when the letterbooks commence, Jackson was attorney for eight sugar estates and a livestock pen (Figure 6.4). In the parish of Hanover he was responsible for Copse (still the property of Alexander Campbell), Flint River (Edmund Gardiner), Tryall (Robert Allen), Belvidere (Roger Kynaston Jr), and four properties belonging to William H. Heaven (Golden Grove, Silver Grove and Beans estates, and Ramble Pen). In Trelawny, Jackson was attorney for Gibraltar, another property of Alexander Campbell, held as executor of the late John Campbell. Jackson remained attorney for all of these properties throughout the period of the letterbooks. Copse and Flint River he would eventually own. All were substantial properties, the owners receiving compensation for 1,841 enslaved people in 1834. Jackson began to think he had as much as he could cope with.

Lord Seaford wrote to Jackson on 1 July 1839 offering him the attorneyship of Montpelier and Shettlewood. He declined the offer. In a letter to Seaford dated 14 August 1839, Jackson explained that

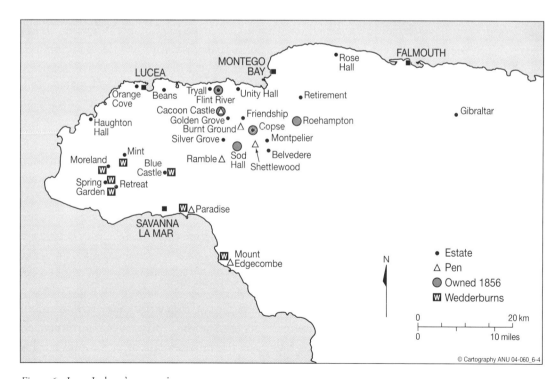

Figure 6.4 Isaac Jackson's properties

in consequence of the unexpected call upon me by Mr. David Lyon of London to act as joint attorney [with C. Paterson] for the Wedderburns' properties in Westmoreland, which has placed me under the obligation of superintending them until that gentleman can make arrangements to relieve me, which cannot take place before the beginning of November, prevents me undertaking any more business in the meantime. After that period I shall be most happy to tender my services as sole attorney, but I am averse to being joined with any gentleman – well knowing that no two men possess the same opinion of the management of Negroes and property, which lead to confusion and ruin in the end, and have declined several attorneyships in consequence. I have indicated the purport of this letter to Mr. McNeil.[88]

This was Thomas McNeil, the attorney of Montpelier. The same day, Jackson sent a letter to Patrick Haughton James, saying he had just returned from a visit to the Wedderburns' properties. These were five sugar estates (Blue Castle, Mint, Moreland, Retreat and Spring Garden) and two pens (Mount Edgecombe and Paradise). The properties were almost as numerous as those Jackson was then managing. In 1832 the Wedderburn properties had been in the hands of Andrew Colvile (the promoter of the Royal Mail Steam Packet Company) and Alexander Seaton as executors and trustees, and under Joseph Stone Williams as attorney.[89] The founder of this dynastic plantation empire was James Wedderburn (1730–1807), who had migrated from Scotland to Jamaica and worked as a doctor in Westmoreland. In 1774 James married Isabella Blackburn, the great-grand-niece and heir of the last Lord Colvile of Ochiltree, and changed his name to Wedderburn-Colvile. When he died in 1807, he left an estate valued at more than three hundred thousand pounds currency. Andrew (1779–1856), son of James and Isabella, assumed the name Colvile by royal licence in 1814. He was a London sugar broker and a prominent shareholder in the Hudson's Bay Company.[90] It was Andrew who served as executor and trustee of "the Wedderburn properties" in 1832. It was also Andrew who in 1824 denied that Robert Wedderburn, the prominent radical thinker and author of *The Horrors of Slavery,* was his older brother, born 1762 the son of James and an enslaved woman, Rosanna.[91]

In 1839 things were not going well on the Wedderburn properties. Mint and Spring Garden had been in receivership for at least five years. Jackson found the expenditure far in advance of expected returns, the people of lower Westmoreland "not working well at all", and the pens understocked. He wrote on 14 August that he hoped soon to be relieved of the properties, saying, "The great distance from me prevents my bestowing that attention that such important properties demand, had they been more convenient I would be very happy to keep them." The most distant of the properties, Spring Garden, was thirty miles by road from Copse. Jackson told Patrick Haughton James he had visited Westmoreland "but have not time to write the parties interested this packet". On 3 September he told James, "I am again disappointed in writing Mr. Lyon on the state of the Wedderburn properties, should you see that gentleman pray say that I am doing my best although not writing." He eventually wrote to Lyon on 10 September.[92]

At the same time, Jackson did consider taking on further properties and did travel some long distances to look after those he already managed. He told James that Sir Simon Haughton Clarke "intends to leave me in charge of Cocoon and Retirement, they are both convenient to me and I hope to do them justice". He visited Gibraltar Estate, forty-five miles away in Trelawny, but the distance meant he also sent occasional letters to the overseer, Nicholas Tinling, giving detailed instructions and foreshadowing visits.[93]

In Jackson's second letter to Seaford, written on 10 September 1839, he made clear that Seaford had invited him specifically to "take charge of your properties so far as relates to cultivation and manufacture", which would have left marketing and finance to the other attorney. It is not certain who Seaford planned to appoint as Jackson's partner, but he may have had McNeil in mind. Jackson could find little good to say about McNeil and it may have been personal animosity as much as the question of principle that discouraged Jackson from agreeing to the joint appointment. In any case, his "sentiments" remained unchanged. "To do justice to your Lordship," Jackson told Seaford, "I can only act as sole attorney." Taking the opportunity to indirectly disparage McNeil, Jackson concluded saying, "I feel confident I could improve these important properties, that are at present in a most deplorable state and give your Lordship every satisfaction."[94]

Jackson wrote to David Lyon on the same day, reporting on Paradise and Mount Edgecombe, and complaining that two overseers had left his estates to go to work with McNeil, which "excites suspicion". Although Jackson regretted "being obliged to decline the management of these properties [the Wedderburns'] after being recommended by my respected friend Mr. James", he said that the "great distance" meant he could not "visit them more than once in eight weeks and remain one week upon them which is too little to do them the justice they require".[95] It was a time of great transformation, placing heavy demands on those managers, such as Jackson, willing to sit down with the people and negotiate systems of wages and rents that had few precedents. A property could not be effectively managed at arm's length. A few weeks later, Jackson thanked James "for having recommended me so highly to Messrs. Hawthorn and Shedden [London commission agents] who have sent me a power of attorney from Mrs. Gray for the management of Friendship; this property is so contiguous to me that I hope to have no trouble".[96] A sugar estate, Friendship shared a boundary with Copse. Writing to Hawthorn and Shedden, Jackson thanked them for their "mark of confidence, as well as our mutual friend Mr P. H. James, for the manner he has spoken of my abilities, which I fear he over rates". Typically, Jackson said he would do his "utmost for Mrs. Gray's Estate, which is now in a deplorable condition". He also thanked Hawthorn and Shedden "for your tender of services in London, which if necessary I shall not fail to avail myself of".[97]

Continuing his complaint about the actions of McNeil, Jackson told Alexander Campbell of problems at Copse at the end of September 1839. The people had struck work and he was sending out summonses for rent, to be tried in court at Lucea. The cause of the trouble, he said, was the high wages offered on Seaford's properties and McNeil's willingness to employ "any people, come from where they may". Indeed, he had tempted some of the Copse people to move to Shettlewood. "On this account," Jackson confided in Campbell, "I regret not accepting these properties when Lord Seaford offered me them and I then could have brought all the labourers in this district to my own terms."[98]

On 23 October 1839 Jackson acknowledged Seaford's power of attorney, sent with a letter dated 2 September, saying that "as soon as possible I will take possession of the properties". He hoped to do so by early November and promised that "on obtaining possession I shall give in detail a report of the state of every thing".[99] His willingness to accept the attorneyship related to his desire to control the district but did not mean that he had divested responsibility for the "distant" Wedderburn properties. He proposed Mr Glen of Blackheath to work with Paterson, "a most industrious young man", but told Lyon to "nominate the person you may think fit to join Mr. Paterson in the management of the properties".[100]

Jackson's failure to release himself from the Wedderburn attorneyship required him to appease his other employers. On the same day that he had written to Seaford agreeing to accept his properties, Jackson told Alexander Campbell that he would merely ride around the Wedderburns' properties every two months until the management was sorted out. "Rest assured," he wrote, "nothing will ever induce me to neglect your property being well aware that my own welfare and character will stand or fall with it." Jackson also told Campbell that he had received power of attorney for Seaford's properties. These "have long been a receptacle for the disaffected from here and all the neighbourhood and caused great dissatisfaction by giving high wages for little work". Being in charge gave him the power to correct this situation and "put my finger on a few of our [Copse] ladies who have been sitting down at Shettlewood, ever since they were freed".[101] Jackson wrote again to Campbell in the middle of November 1839, saying he would very soon take over from McNeil "and trust by doing so, you will not consider that I am lightly abandoning your interest. On the contrary I find that it has added to my influence with your people and will enable me to check squatting on Shettlewood, which some of our inferior people altho' good labourers are much disposed to do."[102]

Seaford offered Jackson a salary of six hundred pounds sterling. Jackson responded saying that "altho' small" the amount was "more than the present returns of the properties will warrant, but with it I shall be perfectly satisfied, until the increased returns of the estates might afford further remuneration". In following years, when the profits remained slim, Jackson proved undemanding relative to what Seaford was willing to offer in addition.[103] McNeil had encouraged Seaford to visit Jamaica. Jackson advised against it. He thought McNeil's motive "must have arisen from the conviction that he felt as to the deplorable state of the properties and that you might be personally convinced of it". A short visit would serve no purpose, said Jackson, and indeed, "might probably tend to alter such arrangements as might have previously been made and afford the people an opportunity of making increased demands upon you, which might be prejudicial to your Lordships interest".[104]

When Jackson wrote to McNeil asking him to propose a date for the transfer of possession, he took the opportunity to dispute some livestock and wharfage accounts, suggesting that McNeil was overcharging.[105] A week later, Jackson told Seaford he was still waiting on McNeil to give up possession,

> which I am daily expecting – from the tenor of his reply to mine of 24th ultimo requesting that he would give up possession at his earliest convenience, that gentleman informs me that "he would endeavour to have the accounts made up as early as possible, when he would inform me and if health permitted would be over to deliver up charge, and that the relief he experienced by the change was most gratifying".[106]

Four days after this, Jackson wrote to McNeil saying, "I beg that you will now name an early day" for the transfer "or give me a letter to the overseers" because it was "necessary that arrangements should be made for the future management of the properties and acted upon at once as the season for taking off crop is fast approaching". With this note Jackson enclosed a document regarding the price of mules as evidence, supporting his view that McNeil was overcharging.[107] McNeil seems to have been genuinely ill and Jackson accepted further delay, but he found time to tell Seaford, "You may be assured that I will have the accounts minutely examined before I make any settlement with him."[108]

Jackson finally received charge of Seaford's Montpelier and Shettlewood on 20 November 1839. On the same day, he wrote to Sir Simon Haughton Clarke saying he had received a power of attorney from Messrs Lightfoot and Robson of Leicester Square, London, for Retirement Estate and Cacoon Castle Pen. Jackson accepted the attorneyship.[109] Clarke visited Jamaica, arriving in May 1840, and quickly headed for Cacoon. He told Jackson that only immigration could save the plantations and that he planned to go to the United States to recruit free blacks.[110]

In his regular reports to his employers, Jackson never suggested that he had bitten off too large a contingent of properties or that he lacked the time needed to properly represent their interests. His letters detailed the state of the weather and the crops, experiments with new technologies, the availability of labour, negotiations over rents and wages, sales and shipments of produce, estate finances, local politics and his thoughts on immigration, the magistracy and the clergy. He transmitted bills of lading and advised on the need for insurance. He explained demands on the employer's accounts. Occasionally, he wrote to an overseer, ordering him to start or stop alterations to a mill or to sue defaulters for rents. He appeared at court on behalf of the properties. He challenged other attorneys and government officials. Like Simon Taylor, he entertained governors and sought their patronage.

For all of the properties in his attorneyship, Jackson prepared annual lists of supplies needed in the following year. These lists were transmitted to the metropolitan agents about six months in advance. In June 1840 Jackson followed this exercise for thirteen properties. The supplies for Montpelier Estate and Shettlewood Pen were to be landed at Montpelier Wharf, west of Montego Bay. Copse Estate, belonging to Alexander Campbell of Upper Thames Street and Woburn Place, London, also used Montpelier Wharf. Tryall Estate, property of Robert Allen of Cornhill, London, had its own. So did Flint River Estate, the property of Edmund Gardiner of Rimenham Lodge, Henley-upon-Thames. The orders for Friendship Estate were sent to the agents Hawthorn and Shedden, Lime Street Square, London, to be landed at the Welcome Wharf near Montego Bay. The properties of W. H. Heaven (Golden Grove, Silver Grove, Beans Estate, Ramble Pen, Burnt Ground Pen) were represented in England by Messrs Heaven and Company of Bristol, the goods to be sent to Flint River and Barbary Hill wharves. Belvidere Estate, belonging to Roger Kynaston Jr of St Helens Place, Bishop Gates Street, London, used the Sterling Wharf, near Montego Bay. Finally, Gibraltar Estate, represented by Stirling Gordon and Company of Glasgow, had its goods landed at Atkins Wharf, Rock, Trelawny. The following year, Haughton Hall Estate (Hawthorn and Shedden), forty miles away to the west near Green Island, was added to the list.[111]

Jackson maintained his residence at Copse and continued as attorney, but from 1840 surrendered the position of overseer to Thomas Ferguson.[112] In June 1841 Jackson told Seaford he intended "to spend a great deal of time" at Shettlewood, to keep an eye on things. It was in fact "a much more comfortable situation than Copse". However, he said, "I cannot with propriety make it my permanent residence, without first consulting Mr. Campbell and should he not sanction it, rest assured your Lordships interest shall not be lost sight of, neither shall I forget your Lordships more than liberal offer of remuneration in these unprofitable times for Jamaica property, when so few of them are meeting their contingencies." There is nothing to suggest Jackson ever moved to live on Montpelier or Shettlewood, but the suggestion hints at a shifting of allegiance.[113]

Plantation Jamaica

By the middle of 1842, when Jackson made up the lists of supplies needed for 1843, he had added to the properties under his control Orange Cove Estate (John Dawson) in Hanover and Rose Hall Estate (Hawthorn and Shedden) in St James. He soon added also Unity Hall Estate on the western edge of St James. Orange Cove was the property of Raines Waite Appleton and the executors of William Appleton, a mortgagee. Rose Hall had been in the hands of receivers. Unity Hall had belonged to James Galloway. By February 1843 Jackson was receiver for Orange Cove, Belvidere and Rose Hall. Gibraltar was then said to belong to the heirs of John Campbell. Alexander Campbell still owned Copse.[114]

When the letterbooks close in December 1843, Jackson was attorney for ten sugar estates in Hanover (Beans, Belvidere, Copse, Flint River, Friendship, Golden Grove, Haughton Hall, Orange Cove, Silver Grove and Tryall), four in St James (Montpelier, Retirement, Rose Hall and Unity Hall), and one in Trelawny (Gibraltar), as well as four pens in Hanover (Burnt Ground, Cacoon Castle, Ramble and Shettlewood).

How much Jackson earned for his toil is uncertain. Using his Montpelier salary as a guide, he might have made £5,000 sterling in 1843, with free lodging and grazing at Copse. This was more than many of the absentees he served were making at the time. Certainly Jackson was able to accumulate enough capital to build his own estate. His acquisition of land commenced shortly after the closure of the extant letterbooks in 1843. The transactions are known thanks to research in the land deeds carried out by Swithin Wilmot. The first known purchase occurred in 1846 when Jackson paid £240 for Shepherds Hall, a property of 80 acres to the west of his residence at Copse.[115] The same year he bought another interior Hanover property, jointly with John Gerrard, Kendall Settlement. It was cheaper, at £100 for 84 acres.[116] Jackson acquired his first estate, Bachelors Hall Sugar Estate, in 1848. Located in the Hanover coastal zone, it covered 662 acres and cost £2,200.[117] Jackson had not served as attorney for any of these properties. In 1849, however, he leased Haughton Hall Estate (620 acres) and Burnt Ground Pen (1,750 acres) from Philip Haughton James for whom he had acted as attorney since 1841. Both of these properties were in Hanover. Jackson's largest purchases occurred in 1850 and saw him spreading his reach into St James. In that parish, he paid the absentees William Sterling and Graham Russell £4,200 for a series of tracts, described as Roehampton Estate and Blarney (490 acres), land adjoining Roehampton (323 acres), Mafoota Bottom (400 acres), Mountain Settlement (74 acres) and Castle Pen (127 acres).[118] In Hanover, Jackson acquired Copse Estate from his first known employer, Alexander Campbell, along with the neighbouring Beverly Estate and Farm Pen. The total area of these three properties was 1,735 acres, for which Jackson paid £5,000.[119]

Jackson died on 3 August 1856 at Roehampton, the estate he acquired in 1850, in the parish of St James. He was buried the following day at Copse, across the Great River, in Hanover. Jackson's "nephew and successor" Richard Hind erected a tombstone in his honour. Its inscription declared Jackson "proprietor of the Copse, Sod Hall, Flint River and Roehampton Estates and Cocoon Castle Penn, the whole of which he acquired by his own industry and perseverance". The ethical justification seems self-conscious, a reaction to the contemporary critique that saw the attorney taking advantage of the planter-proprietors' misfortunes. Assuming this list of properties was complete, Jackson had disposed of several lots as well as acquiring more between 1846 and 1856. He spent less than £20,000 to accumulate near to ten thousand acres.

Jackson's tomb at Copse adjoined that of his daughter Ann, who died in 1863 aged thirty-two, and was probably born in 1831. She was to marry Richard Hind, Jackson's nephew and eventually also his executor. Ann's mother is unknown as are the parents of Richard. In the three years prior to the final registration of slaves taken in 1832, six mulatto and three quadroon children were born to women belonging to Copse, but there seems nothing to say that one of these was Ann or that Jackson fathered any of them.[120] His kinship remains to be untangled.

As Jackson's executor, on 22 January 1857 Hind showed the administrators, Henry Routledge and Daniel Duncan Fisher, "all and singular the goods and chattels rights and credits of Isaac Jackson" for inventory and appraisal. This was his personal property, not including his wealth in land and buildings. The total came to £5,500 currency, the largest element being £3,000 in book debts. The remainder was made up of £2,000 in "horned stock and mules on Copse and Roehampton", £100 in "cattle carts, wagons and dead stock on the two estates", £250 in "horses and carriages", and £150 in "household furniture and plate etc".[121]

Isaac Jackson's Letters

The three volumes of Jackson's letterbooks preserved at the American Philosophical Society in Philadelphia contain about 580 pages and 825 letters.[122] For each of his principal absentee correspondents there are about 50 letters. The first volume covers the period 1 August 1839 to 17 July 1840, the second 1 June 1841 to 10 May 1842, and the third 10 May 1842 to 21 December 1843. Thus there is a gap for the period July 1840 to May 1841. Jackson communicated with all of the proprietors who employed him as attorney, but the analysis here is confined to his correspondence with Lord Seaford.

Over the three and a half years covered by the letterbooks Jackson received fifty letters from Seaford and wrote fifty-one in response. The precise dates when letters were received by Jackson is generally unknown so it is only possible to calculate the interval between Seaford writing and Jackson replying. In eleven of his letters, Jackson told Seaford that he had not received anything from him since last writing. On the other hand, eight of Jackson's letters replied to sets of two or three received from Seaford. The latter either arrived close together or were allowed to accumulate until the next available packet. The mean interval between Seaford writing and Jackson replying was fifty days and the median fifty-one days or roughly seven weeks. The fastest of all Seaford's letters was replied to by Jackson in just thirty-one days while the slowest took seventy-one days. Taking only the most recently received letters answered by Jackson and ignoring the slow travellers or accumulated correspondence reduces the mean to forty-seven days and the median to fifty. Seaford and Jackson could expect answers to questions within about three months and hardly ever had to wait more than four.

This was twice as fast as the speed of correspondence between Simon Taylor and Chaloner Arcedeckne in the period 1765–75. Jackson also proved a much more regular and consistent writer than Taylor. The differences reflect the contrasting styles of the two attorneys but, more obviously, matched the doubling of the speed of the increasingly reliable packet boats under steam. Whereas the mean gap between letters was thirty-eight days for Taylor, Jackson produced one (to Seaford) every twenty-five days. More striking are differences in the frequency distributions. Taylor's median interval between letters was twenty-one days, shorter than the twenty-five achieved by Jackson, but Jackson never let more than forty-five days pass between letters and only 6 per cent of his letters were written within less than ten days of one another.

The increased reliability of the mail service was also evidenced by the rarity of Jackson sending copies of letters and the regularity with which Taylor had done so. However, Jackson could not assume a message had been received, and sometimes sent duplicates on following vessels and repeated information. Because of the uncertainty, he also noted periods when he received no new letters. For instance, Jackson told Seaford on 10 May 1842, "My last letter to your Lordship was dated 12th April. Two packets have since arrived but without any letter from you."[123] Failure to explicitly acknowledge a letter led the sender to believe it had not been received. When Seaford wrote to Jackson on 29 April 1843 he sent a copy of his letter of 12 December 1842, thinking this had gone missing for many months. Jackson responded, shamefaced but a little evasive, saying, "This letter was received in due course and I regret, through inadvertency it was not acknowledged at the proper time."[124]

Jackson's letters were more modern, more structured and formal, than those of Simon Taylor. Jackson lived in the age of the professional and took his position seriously. Sometimes, letters contained numbered questions, to assist and monitor answers, and Jackson came to use a system of marginal subheads for the same purpose. Most of his letters were matched to a sheet or two of foolscap paper, posted in an envelope, but bulky letters might require more than one package. For example, when Jackson received instructions from Seaford in October 1839, he acknowledged Seaford's "No. 1 and 2 of 2d September, accompanied with a power of attorney".[125]

Jackson employed a clerk to deal with the increasing volume of business he took on. The clerk is known only as "C. R.", applying the initials when he occasionally drafted a letter on behalf of Jackson.[126] For example, Jackson's letter of 26 August 1841, replying to Seaford's of 8 July, was composed by his clerk and ended "P.S. Mr. Jackson has been confined to his room for the past week with fever, having got wet several times of late, but he is much better today."[127] When Jackson next wrote more than a month later, on 28 September, he formally acknowledged Seaford's letters of 8 and 28 July and 9 August, saying, "The former of these letters was shortly replied to [by] my clerk on 26th August. I was then and when the last packet sailed labouring under a severe attack of fever but am now thank God quite recovered."[128] The copying of the letters into the letterbooks was the work of C. R. and this task placed further constraint on the time of writing. When the letters were long and numerous, and perhaps contained enclosures, there was great pressure on the copyist to complete his work. There might be little time for proofreading and often enclosures were not copied. Even some of the vital annual lists of supplies required by Jackson's properties were occasionally not copied, leaving blank pages in the letterbook. In such cases, the attorney must have had to rely on rough drafts, an unsatisfactory state of affairs which he would be reluctant to report to the employer.

Almost all of Jackson's letters were addressed from "Copse, Montego Bay, Jamaica". He chastised correspondents who failed to use this full address. Thus on 29 September 1839 he told Hawthorn and Shedden of London, "In future correspondence please address me as above." Jackson had just been given charge of Mrs Gray's Friendship Estate. He advised Hawthorn and Shedden, "I was only this morning put in possession of your esteemed favor of 15th August it having been addressed to me in Hanover, or I should have replied to it, by the mail that left Montego Bay last evening."[129] Occasionally, Jackson indicated he was writing from some other place. For example, a series of letters written in October 1841 had the "Copse" crossed out in the transcript. Jackson told Seaford, "I have come here [Montego Bay] to collect money where I have met with your Lordships letter of 7th September as I did not write by the last packet."[130] He also warned that necessary absences from home would delay his replies to letters received while away. On 2 August 1842, for example, he wrote, "I am on the eve of starting to Lucea to attend the Vestry and pay taxes and will not have an opportunity of answering any letters that may come by the packet which is hourly expected."[131] His employers similarly sent letters from unusual addresses while travelling. Thus Seaford sent a letter from Geneva in June 1842, but it reached Jackson in Jamaica within the normal sequence.[132] He had written from Florence in May, addressing the new governor, the Earl of Elgin, and introducing him to

Jackson, and did not return to England until August. His correspondence followed him.[133]

The arrival and imminent departure of the packet boat concentrated energies and regulated the timing of letters. Jackson frequently told Seaford that the need to get his letter on to the boat constrained his writing time. When he received the power of attorney for Montpelier, Jackson claimed, "By the present packet mail I have but time to say that as soon as possible I will take possession of the properties", though he then went on to discuss various matters in further paragraphs.[134] On 1 November 1842 Jackson sent Seaford a brief letter, saying, "I am obliged to close this letter in order to save the post."[135] On 30 May 1843 he said, "I have this moment received your Lordships letter of 29th April with its enclosures, but the early departure of the post will not admit of my answering it." Jackson did not formally acknowledge Seaford's letter of 29 April until he wrote again on 27 June.[136] On Sunday 29 September 1839, in the midst of writing a letter to Patrick Haughton James, Jackson said, "I have just been informed that the mail has come in and returned, so that I shall not get a letter forwarded by this packet, unless she is detained in town and this will reach in time."[137] The same day, Jackson told Alexander Campbell, "I have just been informed the packet post came in late on Friday night [the 27th] and returned last night. I write this which will go by Tuesdays post in the hopes it will reach Kingston before the packet sails." To this letter he added a postscript dated Tuesday 1 October.[138] Optimistic about his chances, Jackson wrote some more letters that day.

Although the introduction of the steamer packets improved the reliability and speed of the post, there were occasional breakdowns and delays. For example, Jackson commenced writing a letter on 17 October, assuming the packet was imminent, but added a postscript five days later, saying that "the long expected packet has at last arrived" bringing letters dated 1 September.[139] Longer delays could disturb the financial arrangements of planters and attorneys. Jackson regularly sent Seaford advice of the need to cover bills and asking him to honour such requests in favour of his local agent.[140] This enabled Jackson to cover his local debts, including the payment of wages. He allowed an appropriate time to pass before drawing on these transfers. However, on 1 December 1842 he told Seaford, "The packet which carried my letter of 19th August advising my bill for £700 sterling was detained on her passage for want of coals, and accounts for the bill and letter of advice being received the same day. I always endeavour to let the advice precede the bills I draw by one packet or more if possible."[141] Worse than delay was the loss of a vessel. Thus Jackson told Seaford at the end of May 1843 that "the steamer that took the 1st April mails was lost off Corunnu, with a great number of passengers". This was the *Solway* which sank after striking a reef at Corunna, Spain, just four months after its maiden voyage. It was the third of the ill-fated Royal Mail packet steamers to be lost.[142]

Two Attorneys, Two Estates, Two Eras

What did Taylor and Jackson have in common? Both of them died in Jamaica, having lived most of their lives there. Taylor was a committed creole, seeming never to find the life of the absentee or the culture of the English sufficiently attractive to make him think of leaving the island. Jackson, probably born in England, seems never to have left Jamaica once he had established himself. Neither Taylor nor Jackson married. Taylor had a long-term mistress, perhaps a free woman of colour, and children among the enslaved. Jackson had a daughter but whether her mother was enslaved or free is unknown. Both Taylor and Jackson acknowledged relatives living in Jamaica. Both left their estates to nephews.

Taylor and Jackson died rich. They owned roughly the same number of acres, about ten thousand each, but overall Taylor was much more wealthy because he also owned people. Jackson's acquisition of land began late in his life, whereas Taylor was born with a silver spoon, inheriting plantations as well as a merchant-house. These enterprises provided Taylor with a substantial income stream that enabled investment in further plantations. Jackson had to work his way up through the ranks, assuming his first attorneyship only when he reached the age of forty. Taylor was brought up by an attorney father and inherited absentee employers when he was barely twenty. He was able to use income earned as attorney from early in his career but it was not the essential foundation of his fortune. Jackson was much more the professional attorney, building his wealth almost exclusively on salaries and commissions.

Both Taylor and Jackson served several masters. But their most prominent employers, Arcedeckne and Seaford, dominated their managerial activity and, less certainly, their correspondence. Arcedeckne was Taylor's creole age-mate. Taylor gladly managed Golden Grove because of its great productivity and the returns it offered him. But he regarded Arcedeckne as effete and an unwilling entrepreneur. Taylor had no respect for the absentees who had been out of Jamaica so long that they knew little of the realities of life in a slave society, yet pretended to represent the interests of the planters in the metropolitan Parliament. Taylor always knew that it was his throat that would be cut when the enslaved took managerial life in their hands. As attorney, he protected the interests of his employers but knew he was the one risking the climate and doing the dangerous work of management, and believed he deserved a good share of the rewards. Jackson was almost thirty years younger than Seaford, who though a creole was by 1839 firmly inserted in the English aristocracy. Jackson was more deferential, more professional in his dealings. Letters to Seaford were sometimes concluded with the refrain "I have the honour to remain/My Lord/Your Lordships most obedient/Isaac

Jackson".[143] What Jackson thought of absentees is not clear. He corresponded more regularly and consistently than Taylor but was less open in his opinions. This was part of Jackson's professionalism.

Taylor's management of Golden Grove between 1765 and 1775 illustrates the system of plantation slavery in its mature and most profitable form. Pares called the period the "silver age" of West Indian history, inferior only to the "golden age" of the seventeenth-century sugar revolution. Metcalf went further, saying, "The years between the Seven Years War and the American Revolution marked a brief golden age for the plantocracy."[144] Taylor and Arcedeckne shared the many advantages of the period, with high prices for sugar in protected metropolitan markets, an unusual absence of hurricanes, good harvests, an active trade in enslaved people from Africa, little pressure for the humane treatment of enslaved people on the plantations, cheap supplies from the North American colonies, and relatively little competition from other Caribbean sugar producers. The planters were at the height of their political power and influence, both in the local Assembly and through the metropolitan interest lobby. The years 1765–75 offered great opportunities for the unfettered exploitation of people and resources, with great suffering for the enslaved and great profits for their masters.

Above all, Taylor had slavery and the Atlantic slave trade, which provided the basis of his wealth directly through legal property in people and through the exploitation of labour sanctioned and supported by the state. Jackson at Montpelier 1839–43, on the other hand, had the task of managing the establishment of a system of wage labour. People could not form part of his personal fortune and the extraction of labour was more expensive. Jackson was able to buy land because it had become cheap but equally it did not count for as much because it did not come with people. Whereas Taylor sought to make his brother's son the richest commoner in England, and came close to achieving his ambition, Jackson had no such grand ambitions for his nephew.

How did Taylor and Jackson differ from the mass of attorneys? Both of them managed more properties and possessed more wealth than the typical attorney. Taylor stands out more prominently from his contemporaries but was typical of his period in the way his attorneyship for Arcedeckne began with personal friendship and paralleled Taylor's career as planter and merchant. Jackson was also typical of his period, rising through the ranks of plantation management and seeing himself as a professional who became personally wealthy only by good fortune and only in his later years. Golden Grove and Montpelier, as sugar estates, similarly typified their periods but fell towards the large end of the scale in area, workforce and profits. Their management confronted Taylor and Jackson with quite different challenges, because of contrasts in the environments of the estates as well as the periods in which they can be followed most closely.

Chapter 7

Managing Golden Grove, 1765–1775

Golden Grove was one of a series of sugar estates strung along the floodplain of the Plantain Garden River. The estates took advantage of the rich soils of the alluvial flats and drew off the river's water to power their mills. The estates on the northern, mountainous side of the river combined much woodland with their level cane lands. Golden Grove lay to the south, with the river forming its northern boundary, and consisted almost entirely of level land. A few low hills jutted out in the south and west of the property, but most of its land was ideally suited to the cultivation of sugar cane. It has remained in cane to the present, sometimes sharing space with bananas and coconut palms.

The Plantain Garden River rushed and tumbled out of the mountains, gathering its water from steep narrow valleys. In its headwaters, the river carried coarse sediments and boulders. Browne, on his map of 1755, identified "The Source" of the Plantain Garden River, and here the annual rainfall averaged 200 inches. Just to the north, along the ridge of the Blue Mountains, it reached 250 inches. Frequent storms and occasional hurricanes produced dramatic accumulations of water that caused land slips and slides, and easily transported masses of clay, pebbles, large stones and even blocks of bedrock.[1] As the river levelled off, around Golden Valley, its capacity to move this coarse material was reduced and transport downstream occurred only in peak flow floods. Between Sunning Hill and Bath the river spread out, in braided streams that constantly shifted and re-formed, created by an abundant bedload and highly variable discharge. Here the heavier stones and sediments were deposited, with boulders and pebble bars scattered along the riverbed.[2]

Below Bath, few substantial streams entered the river and it flowed along the foot of the hills, guided by the Plantain Garden Fault (Figure 7.1). Here the river established a more permanent channel, meandering but maintaining its general form as it built up natural levees from the finer grained materials

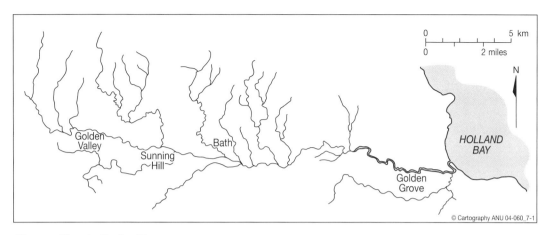

Figure 7.1 Plantain Garden River stream net

that it deposited on the banks. The surrounding floodplain, created from these same materials, spread out and entrenched the river. The floodplain's topography was formed by the long-term meandering of the channel and its overbank deposition patterns. The Plantain Garden River's channel was relatively wide and deep because of its high peak flows and intermittent extreme events. Its "rich banks", wrote Edward Long in 1774, were the site of "a succession of the finest sugar-plantations in the island". This was the territory of Golden Grove, the level, rich alluvials of the floodplain. The rainfall here was much less than in the mountains and now averages eighty-five inches. The climate of Taylor's period was cooler and moister than that of the present, however, with heavier dry-season rainfall. Travel was often impeded by storms and floods.[3]

Spreading south from the Plantain Garden River in a roughly rectangular shape, Golden Grove covered 1,925 acres (Figures 7.2–7.3). Craskell and Simpson's map of 1763 showed the works of Golden Grove located on the Negro River (earlier called "Muddy River"), which flowed east through Duckenfield and entered the Plantain Garden River near Holland Bay.[4] The earliest known plan of Golden Grove, made in 1788, showed the course of the Negro River but without naming it. The mill and other factory buildings were to the north of this stream and the houses of the enslaved people immediately to the south. The road from Stokes Hall, Port Morant and Kingston passed through the middle of this complex. West of the works, the channel widened and was described in 1788 as a lagoon. The plan also identified a second, smaller lagoon and three elongated ponds of shape similar to that of the lagoons, suggesting that they were prior streams. Golden Grove had its own pen, Batchelors Hall, higher up the Plantain Garden River, towards Bath, and it served to supply the cattle that were used in substantial numbers to haul carts and power sugar mills.[5]

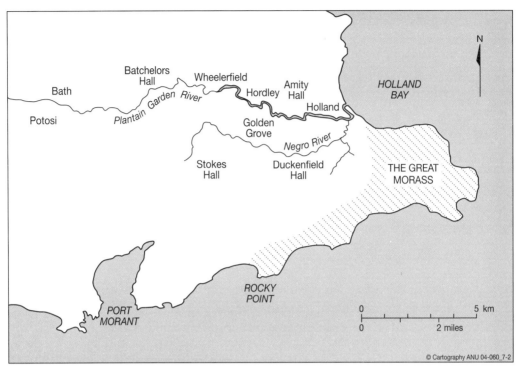

Figure 7.2 Plantain Garden River valley and district

Personnel

Andrew Arcedeckne established Golden Grove as a sugar estate in 1734. Formerly, the colonists and government had thought the area vulnerable to attack from "runaway and rebellious Negroes". To encourage and secure settlement, the Assembly in 1721 proposed clearing a road from the Plantain Garden River to the Rio Grande, to secure the area and provide access, and commissioners were appointed to purchase uncultivated land held by absentees and attorneys. Arcedeckne was one of the commissioners. His son Chaloner Arcedeckne inherited in 1765, and left Jamaica that year to live as an absentee-proprietor.[6] Simon Taylor became his attorney and the published correspondence between these two young men, continuing from 1765 to 1775, defines the period of study. At Golden Grove, the overseer throughout the period was John Kelly. These three – proprietor, attorney and overseer – continued in their roles beyond 1775, Kelly into the 1780s, Arcedeckne and Taylor even longer. All three were in communication with one another, but the published series of letters consists only of Taylor's letters to Chaloner and to Benjamin Cowell his brother-in-law (married to Chaloner's sister Anne) and London agent. Taylor regularly visited Golden Grove, staying there for

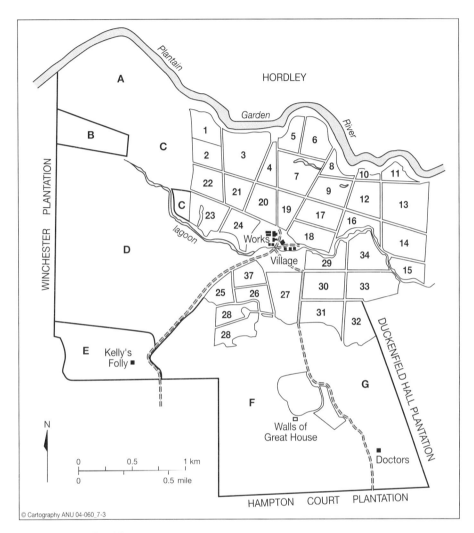

Figure 7.3 Plan of Golden Grove, 1788

Key: *1–36* Cane pieces; *A* Woodland; *B* Cocoas; *C* Common pasture; *D* Woodland, plantain walk, and Negro grounds; *E* Leased to Kelly; *F* Woodland and Negro grounds; *G* Ruinate pasture. Redrawn from National Library of Jamaica, Plans, St Thomas 12A.

several days at a time, combining these tours with visits to his own estate Lyssons, near Morant Bay, and, from 1771, Holland. On some occasions, he was specifically called by Kelly to deal with immediate issues.[7]

Arcedeckne gave Kelly fifty acres for life at Golden Grove and an additional hundred acres rent free. The plan of 1788 shows this land in the southwestern corner of the plantation, measured at seventy-six and a half acres and containing the site of "Kelly's Folly". A plan of 1782 called the place simply "Kelly".[8] He owned enslaved people and hired them to Golden Grove, charging one shilling threepence per day. Kelly might have asked more but, as Taylor explained in 1774, it was an advantage to Kelly, "for when working at Golden Grove his people slept in their own houses every night and were at home whereas being at a distance they lost time in going home to their houses in the evening and coming to their work in the morning".[9] In 1774 Kelly was appointed attorney for the neighbouring sugar plantation Duckenfield Hall, while remaining overseer at Golden Grove under Taylor as attorney.[10]

In making decisions, Taylor often took advice from Chaloner's mother Elizabeth who lived in Spanish Town until her death in 1778.[11] Indeed, Taylor told Arcedeckne in 1770, "I have all along made it my business to consult your mother on every piece of business concerning your affairs."[12] Elizabeth lived together with her widowed sister Frances Harris, Arcedeckne's aunt.[13] Taylor consulted her too, and concluded most of his letters to Arcedeckne saying mother and aunt were well and noting how recently he had seen them.

Taylor dealt also with Malcolm Laing (1718–81), a merchant-planter who had migrated to Jamaica from Britain and represented St Thomas-in-the-Vale in the House of Assembly in the 1770s. Taylor, writing to Arcedeckne, described Laing as "our mutual friend". Laing occasionally wrote directly to Arcedeckne and to Kelly with regard to Golden Grove business. He had power of attorney from Arcedeckne.[14]

Elizabeth, Frances and Laing were Taylor's (and Arcedeckne's) seniors. In several cases, the joint approval of Taylor, Laing and Elizabeth was required to permit action. All four had powers of attorney from Arcedeckne, as did, by the early 1770s, John Kelly. All five might sign important documents, such as bills of exchange, though it was not essential to have every signature. Where signatures were lacking from bills of exchange, Taylor sought to have all of the attorneys sign relevant receipts, to ensure the bills were honoured.[15]

Having five attorneys concerned with the business of a single estate was unusual. In the case of Arcedeckne, the proliferation began with a perceived need to protect his inheritance and interests. It continued as a result of the growing separation of functions between Taylor and Kelly, who became distinguished in practice as respectively "mercantile attorney" and "planting attorney", though the differentiation of functions was far from neat and complete.[16] In the long run, Taylor was Arcedeckne's primary attorney.

Arcedeckne's mother and aunt, and Laing, were all referred to by Taylor as Arcedeckne's attorneys, but effectively these three held legal powers of attorney without entering the realm of the Jamaican "attorney" in his fully formed character. They lived far from Golden Grove. Taylor, even if defined as a mercantile attorney, was a frequent visitor to Golden Grove, and a planter-proprietor in his own right who felt quite capable of making decisions about agricultural, manufacturing and labour choices. He saw himself, and was seen by Arcedeckne, as a prototype chief executive officer.

In terms of the cost of management, it seems the five people holding power of attorney, Taylor, Kelly, Laing, Elizabeth Kearsy and Frances Harris, each received a one-fifth share of the commission. Kelly's share was in addition to his salary and to what he made by hiring his slaves to the estate.[17]

The day-by-day management of Golden Grove was in the hands of Kelly as overseer. Arcedeckne had left him in the position when he departed Jamaica early in 1765. Towards the end of that year, Taylor wrote, "I have a real pleasure in acquainting you your overseer Kelly continues his diligence and industry and behaves extremely well indeed I see no one whatsoever goes on better."[18] In the same way that Taylor did not always follow the directions he received from Arcedeckne, however, the overseer might not always accept the views of the attorney. Such questioning of authority arose from several sources, ranging from differences of temperament to the consequences of distance and the need to make decisions on the spot. These variables provided a rich ground for potential conflict as well as necessitating practical consent and accommodation.

Taylor's first difficulty with Kelly came at the end of 1765, when he turned away the estate doctor. Taylor then told Arcedeckne that Kelly was "rather haughty to the white people and overbearing but to give him his due takes great care of the Negroes and manages your estate excessive well". Taylor thought it best for Kelly to "have doctor of his own choosing to reside on the estate provided he is capable".[19] Normally, the appointment of a resident medical practitioner to treat the enslaved would have been a matter for the attorney. Kelly chose a Dr Hayward and Taylor seemed satisfied.[20] In 1768 Taylor told Cowell that one hundred of the enslaved people at Golden Grove had been inoculated against smallpox by Hayward and none had died as a result. This was a matter on which, in principle, Arcedeckne or Cowell might have been asked to rule. "Indeed we did not think of inoculating without your orders," wrote Taylor, "but as every estate about did it we were absolutely obliged out of self preservation to do it."[21] In 1774, however, soon after Kelly took up the attorneyship of Duckenfield Hall, Arcedeckne expressed displeasure that Hayward was appointed doctor there as well as at Golden Grove. Arcedeckne was upset with the Nisbetts, the owners of Duckenfield, rather than Kelly. Hayward offered to surrender the post but Taylor encouraged him to "wait the arrival of another letter when you

[Arcedeckne] might not be quite so angry". Arcedeckne did calm down and subsequently consented to Hayward taking charge at Duckenfield.[22]

Kelly supervised the white book-keepers, some of whom moved on to positions as overseers. There were also white tradesmen, including carpenters and masons. Taylor recommended recruiting these from Scotland. However, he rarely mentioned book-keepers by name when writing to Arcedeckne and probably knew more about the temporary artisans. At the beginning of 1767 there were three white people on Golden Grove, as well as Kelly and the resident doctor. All of them were men, apparently unmarried, most of them probably British-born and aged between eighteen and fifty years.[23]

These four or five white managers of Golden Grove lived with a large enslaved population. In 1765 there were 371 enslaved workers on Golden Grove and Batchelors Hall. Males outnumbered females 191 to 180, and the population contained only small numbers of children and aged people. More than 80 per cent were adult men and women, suggesting that a large proportion had been brought to Jamaica in the Atlantic slave trade. The Africa-born proportion was significant and increased over the years to 1775. No doubt some of the enslaved were the children of the current white managers and certainly some were the children of previous white employees.[24] Neither Arcedeckne nor Taylor could have known all of these people by name, though they were provided with regular lists. Probably even Kelly the long-term overseer and his book-keepers knew only a proportion.

Management of the enslaved devolved to the drivers but only one such was named in Taylor's letters. In 1765, in the midst of an outbreak of smallpox, Taylor told Arcedeckne, "You buried a very fine fellow a driver named Humphrey within a few days ago."[25] Other enslaved people were mentioned by name because of their resistance to the order of the estate under slavery. Thus Philip, who escaped on the night of the great flood of April 1765, was described by Kelly as "a very old offender" and Taylor recommended he be brought to trial and "made an example of".[26] For reasons unknown, in 1769 Arcedeckne "agreed to allow Philander £5 per annum as long as he behaves well" and Taylor promised to pay him.[27] In 1771 Taylor told Arcedeckne of a "Dr. Collins who I believe formerly lived at Golden Grove [who] kept a wench belonging to you named Catharine, and had by her three sons whose names are, Johny Chapplin, Edward Kidvallede Collins and Isaac Collins". Dr Collins had died, leaving instructions for their manumission.[28]

At Batchelors Hall, Kelly had broad responsibility for the pastures and livestock but the property had its own manager. When Taylor visited in late 1765 he told Arcedeckne enigmatically, "The old Man there surprised me much with quantity of fine pasture you have there with so few Negroes." By 1769 the man in charge, one Kearney, was referred to as penkeeper. Exactly how many enslaved people lived at Batchelors Hall Pen in the 1760s is unknown, but they may have numbered close to one hundred.[29]

Defending Inheritance

Although Taylor's role as attorney was not centred on legal matters, he played an active part in protecting the interests of Arcedeckne on several fronts. Arcedeckne had his own solicitor in Jamaica, Robert Cooper Lee, a prominent lawyer, who took matters to court. Taylor kept a running brief, however, and Lee was away in London during 1773 and 1774. On one particular dispute, active in 1771, Taylor declared himself "not lawyer enough to judge" yet he had firm views and instigated searches in the public records for titles, patents and other papers to back his case.[30]

Taylor's principal duty was the protection of Arcedeckne's tenure of Golden Grove. His father Andrew's will, made in 1757, provided for an annual payment of five hundred pounds currency to Elizabeth Kearsey and a single payment of seven hundred pounds to Frances Harris. Ann, the daughter, was to have Swamps Estate, in St David, and Robert, a nephew, all of Andrew's property in St Mary. Chaloner, the son, received everything else, to be passed on "to the heirs of his body lawfully to be begotten, with remainder to the said Robert Arcedeckne in fee". According to the Chancery case filed in 1802 by Taylor as attorney, Chaloner "immediately entered into possession" of Golden Grove on the death of Andrew in 1763. Chaloner's inheritance was not straight-forward, however, with counter-claims and allegations of his illegitimacy creating fears for the future.[31]

Andrew Arcedeckne did not alter his will of 1757, but he did appoint trustees (one of them the nephew Robert Arcedeckne) in 1758, to have responsibility for his property, including Golden Grove. Chaloner did not reach the age of twenty-one until 1765. At the end of September 1766 an indenture or deed of lease and release (presumably designed to facilitate a mortgage) was prepared to resolve dispute over Andrew's will, by which Nicholas Arcedeckne (brother of Robert and nephew of Andrew) "as heir at law" agreed to confirm the will of 1757, giving Chaloner Golden Grove.[32] Nicholas Arcedeckne lived in Ireland. Another party to the deed, the Anglo-Irishman Nicholas Bourke, was a resident planter and also nephew of Andrew and cousin of Robert. Bourke had come to Jamaica around 1740 under the patronage of his uncle Andrew, quickly established himself as a planter, and married in 1748 Elizabeth, daughter of the chief justice Thomas Fearon. In 1754 he was elected as a member of the Assembly and played a leading role in the constitutional crisis of the 1760s.[33]

The deed of lease and release reached Jamaica early in 1767. In March, Taylor wrote to Chaloner Arcedeckne from Kingston, saying "Robin" (meaning Robert Arcedeckne) and "Bourke" had "executed the deed from N. Arcedekne in presence of Malcolm Laing and myself".[34] However, the deed "could not be recorded as it was not proved by the clerk that saw N.A. sign it, therefore it must go home again". Taylor heard the other parties, those who had disputed Chaloner's legitimacy and entitlement, were less than happy.[35]

Occasionally there were rumours of agents, including a "squire Burke", sent from Ireland "to take possession of Golden Grove". On a more trivial level, in 1765 a member of the Irish branch of Arcedeckne's family sent out a power of attorney to a firm of Kingston merchants to demand the balance due on two pipes of wine, an old debt from his father Andrew's estate. Taylor paid simply "to prevent their being able to say any ill natured thing which they be very inclinable to do".[36] At the same time, Taylor dealt with a series of cases in Chancery that involved Arcedeckne as trustee or guardian, sometimes inheriting the status from his father's estate. Taylor thought debts arising from Arcedeckne's father's estate had been cleared by 1768 but small claims continued to surface as late as 1770.[37] In dealing with these claims, Taylor sought to preserve the wealth Arcedeckne had inherited from his father, to ensure his continuing viability. For the future, there was the problem of Arcedeckne's own heirs.

Who would inherit Arcedeckne's estate? Had he died without children, Golden Grove would have reverted to his cousin Robert. The most effective solution to the settling of Arcedeckne's inheritance, Taylor advised, was marriage. In March 1767 Taylor told Arcedeckne, "I intended to send you home this year so much sugar as that you might make any settlement you pleased on any lady marry and then you would not give a single ryal for Robin's [Robert's] reversion."[38] In the meantime, Taylor sought to put in place the necessary legal documentation to defend any claims. Taylor took this action, apparently, at the bidding of Arcedeckne. Taylor told Arcedeckne he would speak to the island secretary, John Archer, "to get made out an office copy of all the deeds and other papers your father has been concerned in which was prevented by Robin [Robert]. It is a very necessary thing and may be of very great service in many respects." Taylor asked, "Do you think it necessary to have the titles of the lands which your father bought and has again sold?" At the same time, he "set about making out according to your desire a set of books of all your father's accounts and his answers to all bills in Chancery that he was concerned in on his own account and every other paper of consequence".[39] The work went slowly. In October 1767 Taylor reported that he had employed "a very capable man" to undertake the copying and would personally "overlook" the transcription of the accounts while he was in Spanish Town attending the Assembly. One part of the work had already been entered into a book. The following July, however, Taylor told Arcedeckne that his mother had "showed so much uneasiness and unwillingness" to cooperate in the process that Taylor "thought it much better to stop than run any risk of giving the old lady umbrage as she gave apparent signs of her disappointment of overhauling the old papers".[40]

Soon, towards the end of 1768, Robert was dead. He had travelled to New

York for his health and it was there he died. Although he was removed from the equation, the threat to Arcedeckne's property remained. Taylor believed Robert had "left half of the reversion of Golden Grove in case Mr. Chaloner Arcedeckne should die without children to Mr. Bourke to whom he has left the residium of the estate".[41] Robert left the bulk of his property, including a large plantation in St Mary, to Nicholas Bourke.[42] In October 1769 Taylor again encouraged Arcedeckne to marry, to disappoint his hopeful cousins, some of whom were putting about the rumour that he was dying. "I would do it really to vex them", said Taylor, having created his own rumour that Arcedeckne was then engaged to one Miss Jenkins. Arcedeckne was in fact "much out of order" and went to Bath (the English spa) to recover. Taylor thought that the returns of 1769 meant Arcedeckne had "as much money at home as would make a good settlement on any lady in England".[43]

Taylor returned to the subject of marriage in April 1771, telling Arcedeckne, "I wish you would think a little serious on that matter and do it as soon as possible, for I assure you I should be very sorry to see Robin [Robert] Arcedecknes heirs in possession of any part or parcel of what they want to defraud you of."[44] Taylor's Kingston merchant-partner Robert Graham travelled to England (with Mrs Graham), carrying a message from Arcedeckne's mother "to recommend matrimony to you".[45] When towards the end of 1772 Arcedeckne finally announced his intention, Taylor was happy, hoping for "heirs enough of your own to inherit your estate for the children of Bourke, and Bourke himself looked on Golden Grove as a matter that would of course be theirs".[46] Nicholas Bourke had died in 1771 leaving two sons and six daughters. According to the mural tablet erected to his memory in the Spanish Town Cathedral, Nicholas "came to Jamaica from Ireland about 1740 under the auspices of his maternal uncle Andrew Arcedeckne". At his death, Bourke owned two sugar estates and two pens, a house in Spanish Town, and almost five hundred enslaved people. His personalty was valued at nearly thirty-four thousand pounds. However, by early 1773 Arcedeckne had "given up all hopes or thoughts of marrying".[47]

Taylor also did his best to protect the property of Arcedeckne's aging mother Elizabeth and his chances of inheriting what she might leave. In 1771 Taylor encouraged Arcedeckne to come to Jamaica in order to settle her affairs. Taylor said Elizabeth "seems to break fast and is very old". She had made her will and appointed executors. Taylor trusted most of them but thought one, Charles Kelsall, "as great a villain as ever was hanged". He reminded Arcedeckne of "the advantage it was to you to be present at the death of your father" and believed Arcedeckne's presence would ensure the appointment of more reliable executors and secure the estate. Taylor recognized he was perhaps stepping over a line and told Arcedeckne he had heard the names of the executors "by mere accident . . . and my friendship for you is the occasion of my acquainting you of it".[48] Arcedeckne sent out a power of attorney for a Mr Welch, to thwart Kelsall, but Taylor found the power defective, "not being attested before the Lord Mayor, and under the City seal, or having one of the subscribing witnesses here to prove it before a judge". Taylor feared that Kelsall "might on her decease, possess himself of your [Arcedeckne's] house, papers, and effects which she has of yours under the power of attorney from you to her".[49]

Taylor developed a practical strategy, to rush to Arcedeckne's mother in Spanish Town on any news of her being sick and, should she die, take possession of house and papers as Arcedeckne's attorney, and turn Kelsall out of doors. Taylor persisted and apparently succeeded in his efforts to have Arcedeckne made an executor. Taylor talked separately to Arcedeckne's aunt, Frances Harris, but said she "desired me to tell you that you must excuse her not writing to you for if she did which she willingly would some of the Negroes etc about the house would tell your mother of it who she says would be jealous". In April 1774 Taylor told Arcedeckne, "Your aunt mentioned to me a few days ago that your mother took it unkind in you not writing to her for that she had only two letters from you since leaving the island and desired me to acquaint you of it." Arcedeckne wrote.[50]

In accepting responsibility for these legal and family matters, Taylor walked a fine line between friendship and business. Taylor's interest in securing Arcedeckne's inheritance and in ensuring his continuing tenure of Golden Grove was of course vital to his role as attorney and to his income. It was the foundation on which other aspects of management rested. Perhaps it carried Taylor towards the role of the attorney-at-law, though he was quick to protest his lack of legal knowledge. In more practical ways, Taylor took an active role in securing the tenurial boundaries of Golden Grove, and these carried him again towards the courts and the record offices. Here the competitors were generally neighbours rather than kin. Jamaican people early had a reputation for litigiousness, a reputation well deserved by the middle of the eighteenth century.[51]

Defending Boundaries

Estate boundaries were established legally through the making of plats and plans, and inscribed on the land itself in various ways by the use of markers such as earth banks, rocks, trees and streams. All of these lines and markers were the work of land surveyors. Taylor kept an eye open for them, knowing their presence meant trouble. When surveyors came on land without having given notice, Taylor empowered his overseers and book-keepers to "stop the chain" and even to impound the surveyors' staff and compass if they trespassed on territory to which he laid claim. Once boundary disputes reached the courts, however, surveyors had to be given entry to the lands in question, and their determination had weight.[52]

Golden Grove had been constituted by Andrew Arcedeckne, Chaloner's father, through the purchase of four adjacent runs of land patented by four separate men in 1671 and 1672, for a total of 2,150 acres.[53] The lines laid down by these seventeenth-century plats were based on surveying technologies less than perfect and imposed on a shifting land surface (Figure 7.4). It is not surprising they became lines of battle. Disputes over the tenure of parts of the land began as early as the 1730s, at the time of the establishment of the sugar works, when the land was already known as "Golden-grove Plantation".[54]

In 1765 Taylor was advised by Robert Arcedeckne, cousin of Chaloner, that the planter Henry Dawkins might claim "the land at the riversmouth". This was a lot at the mouth of the Plantain Garden River, part of the territory of Holland but disputed by Duckenfield Hall (Figure 7.5). Robert's advice was "to plead the law for quieting possession which is a law of this country for that he himself can prove 20 odd years possession and also told me he did not believe they could ever recover it from you".[55] The case reached Chancery in late 1766 but dragged on for years.[56] In January 1769 Taylor reported, "I hear nothing now about Dawkins's claim, they will never be able to get it from you and I hope by and by to see you have another estate as Kennion's Holland is there."[57] Arcedeckne seems not to have pondered seriously the possibility of extending his territory, however, and by early 1771 Taylor had himself acquired Holland.

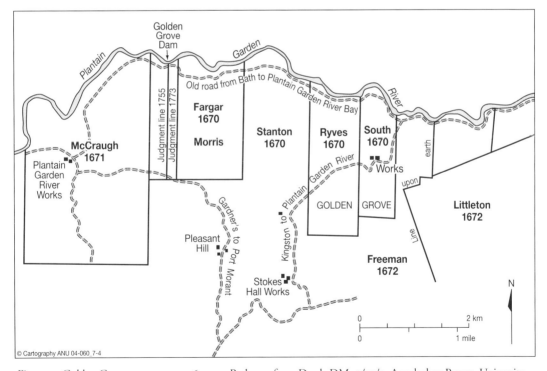

Figure 7.4 Golden Grove area patents, 1671–72. Redrawn from Deeds DM 41/92/2, Arcedeckne Papers, University of Bristol, Arts and Sciences Library, Special Collections.

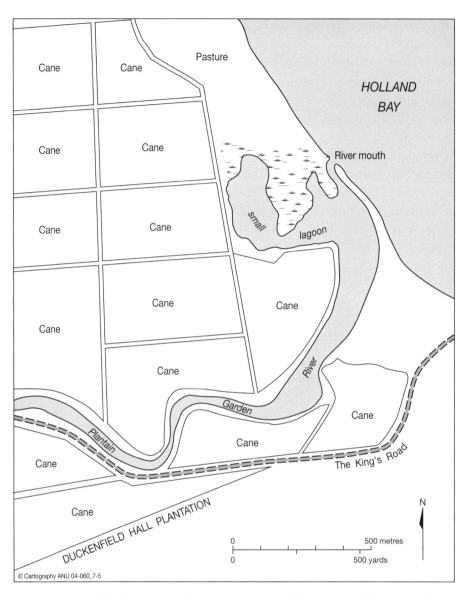

Figure 7.5 Plantain Garden River mouth, at Holland, 1780. Redrawn from "A Plan of Holland Plantation in the Parish of St. Thomas in the East the property of the Honourable Simon Taylor Esquire, surveyed in September 1780 by Smellie and Sheriff", National Library of Jamaica, Plans, St Thomas 12A.

Dawkins's attorneys applied pressure, bringing an ejectment order to court in the middle of 1771. Taylor remained confident, however, telling Arcedeckne, "Depend on it I will spare no pains to keep the land for you." In September, Taylor "went as much over the land at the river's mouth that is in dispute with Mr. Dawkins as I could". He found "the only valuable part of it" was ninety acres rented to Holland Estate, in fact the land Taylor had himself recently leased for canes and a plantain walk. As for the rest, it was "mere morass and quagmire".[58]

This inspection of the land, and perhaps his newfound self-interest, resulted in a very different approach. Taylor now told Arcedeckne, "As the land is not of that great value I always supposed it to be, and if Mr. Dawkins would give up his pretensions for a trifle, I would advise you to settle it with him, as the law suit will be very expensive on all sides."[59] Dawkins put about a rumour that Taylor was trying to buy the disputed land for himself but Taylor merely pursued the lease, hoping Arcedeckne and Dawkins would reach a settlement and deliver "a very great disappointment to the lawyers".[60] Finally, in March 1773 Taylor declared victory having found a document that proved Arcedeckne's father Andrew had obtained a deed of lease and release on the land. The document "was found out by chance by a man [Mr Brodie] who employs a great part of his time in hunting after old and obscure titles". The discovery cost Taylor two hundred pistoles or £169 sterling. Taylor increasingly believed that a fraud had been planned, to the extent of Brodie conspiring with the land surveyor John Rome, who had mapped the Dawkins family properties in Clarendon. Brodie was accused of offering to cut the vital document out of the book for one thousand pistoles. Dawkins had "acted a very dirty part" and his "prevarication" with regard to the title, said Taylor, was "equally infamous as his lie that I wrote to him to buy the land from him".[61]

Taylor opposed encroachment on the land of Golden Grove, even by legal rental. In 1769 David Milner of Wheelerfield, an estate on the north bank of the Plantain Garden River, went with Taylor to inspect a piece of Golden Grove, wishing to rent it as pasture. Milner claimed to have mentioned his wish to Arcedeckne. Taylor left the decision to Arcedeckne but noted long-term disadvantages in permitting such a foothold, particularly "if at any time hereafter you should think of extending your estate by putting up another set of works" when more pasture would be needed.[62] Taylor had expansion in mind for Arcedeckne, hoping that he would at least construct a second works on Golden Grove, even if he was reluctant to acquire new property. Exactly what Arcedeckne decided is unknown, but in February 1770 Taylor told him, "I acquainted Mr. Milner your determination about the land."[63] Nothing more was heard of the matter and it can be assumed the answer was negative.

Early in 1773 Arcedeckne proposed purchasing Winchester Pen, Golden Grove's western neighbour and in the direction of the land Milner had proposed renting and Taylor had seen as the potential site for a second works. Taylor must have been taken by surprise by this aberrant enthusiasm, telling Arcedeckne that Winchester would provide the basis for "a very fine estate" for "whomever you chose to leave it to". But Arcedeckne instantly got cold feet – "complaining of poverty," said Taylor – and pulled out of the deal.[64] Arcedeckne was less ambitious than his attorney.

Water Wars

The Jamaican sugar estate of the eighteenth century depended on water in three main ways. First, water was essential to the growth of the sugar cane, and for this purpose was obtained either from rain or irrigation. Second, it was the preferred source of power for driving sugar mills. Water was cheaper and more reliable than animal, wind or steam power, though often bearing a heavy establishment cost. It remained a subject of innovation well into the nineteenth century.[65] Third, water provided the cheapest surface for transport, within the island, wherever the necessary depth of channel was available. The outcome was that water resources became a matter of competition and conflict, even cooperation.

Rights to water were tied up with rights to land. This was the case with projects for the cutting of navigation routes through the "riversmouth" land. In July 1768 Taylor advised Arcedeckne that "Kennion and Tom Cussans want to cut through your river land to make a canal to the back of the stores and told Kelly you promised to let them but he told them he could do nothing without acquainting Laing your mother and self". John Kennion was owner of Holland Estate, lying on the north side of the Plantain Garden River with an eastern boundary on the shore of Holland Bay. Cussans owned Amity Hall Estate, immediately west of Holland, and Golden Grove's western bounder Winchester Pen.[66] At the beginning of 1769 Cussans left Jamaica with Taylor's brother John "for North America to take a tour of it", travelling to "the Lakes" and Quebec. John went on to England, Cussans to Corsica. The stores were the buildings at the bay where sugar and rum was stored awaiting shipment. Taylor made it clear he had no orders to let Kennion and Cussans make the cut, and asked Arcedeckne to "please let me know whether I am to permit them or not".[67]

At the end of 1771, after Taylor had purchased Holland for himself, he advised Arcedeckne that the attorney for Duckenfield Hall, Mr Winde, had made a similar request, seeking leave "to cut a canal through your land at the rivers mouth, to carry Duckenfield sugars to the stores at the Bay". Taylor had told Winde he saw no objection provided Arcedeckne was given the right to use the canal to carry Golden Grove sugar on canoes, at which Winde "seemed miffed".[68] Taylor repeated the argument in 1773, telling Arcedeckne he need not worry about the size or direction of the trench since the advantage of the navigation would be worth more to him than any effect on the land, but believing the owners of Duckenfield (the Nisbetts) would "rather forego the water carriage of their estate, than give you the right to go through it".[69]

The matter came up again in 1775, when Kelly had replaced Winde as attorney for Duckenfield Hall, and this time the proprietors were willing to grant the reciprocal "liberty of carrying your goods through that estate by which you would also have a water carriage for your goods to the barquader". Taylor now favoured granting permission to cut the canal, so long as Golden Grove was entitled to use it and a covenant drawn up, telling Arcedeckne, "It would be a very great ease to your cattle there being all the crop time two wains constantly carrying goods down and bringing up supplies and by the water carriage two boats and 4 negroes would do it which would be a considerable saving to your account."[70]

The water channelled through the Plantain Garden River valley was both blessing and curse to the agriculture of Golden Grove. The regularity of rainfall, compared to that of many other regions of the island that suffered drought, meant that irrigation was never considered. As Taylor told Arcedeckne in 1770, whereas most of Jamaica suffered a drought of many months, "in Plantain Garden River you have just rain enough to give plenty of water and make the canes flourish with out so much as either to hurt your roads or prevent the yielding of the canes".[71] Long similarly thought the district the most favoured in all Jamaica, because of its freedom from drought and its rich soil. He considered the "rich mould" of Vere its only rival, but concluded "the land on Plantain Garden River, being happily in a more seasonable situation, must be esteemed superior".[72]

If Golden Grove was relatively safe from drought, flood was another matter. The first occurred soon after Arcedeckne left Jamaica, in April 1765. At Golden Grove, five bridges, a wain and a floodgate were carried away, and the dam and trash houses "very much hurt". All of the salt provisions were spoiled and the staves, copperwood and empty puncheons washed away. Only two hills on the west of the estate stood out above the water. These details Taylor knew from a letter sent by Kelly, the overseer. Several days after the flood, the roads remained almost impassable but Taylor set out for Golden Grove, hoping to get the mill going.[73] Two years later, in May 1767, a "very great flood" saw most of Golden Grove under water. That November, heavy rain filled every gully, including, Taylor reported, "places where I never before saw the least stream of water". Once the water receded, "a very fine plant" was quickly put in, but the flood had undermined "the best mill" and "the trench that brings the water to the mill" was "very much injured".[74] On the other hand, Golden Grove was not subject to the disruption of cane fields and boundaries that occurred on estates bounding the Plantain Garden River in its upper, braided stretches, as recorded for example at Potosi (Figure 7.6).

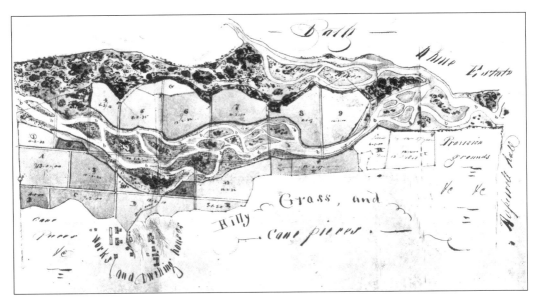

Figure 7.6 Potosi river channels, 1818

Key: *A–I* Level cane pieces not injured by the river [sixty-seven acres which may possibly be encroached on]; *1–12* Level cane pieces injured by the Plantain Garden River [one hundred acres carried away by the river]; *aaaa* Old course of the Plantain Garden River now grown up into bushes, weeds, etc.; *bbbb* Present course and the manner in which it is continually branching out. Part of "A Plan of All the Level Cane Pieces on Potosi Estate in the Parish of St. Thomas in the East, Jamaica; All said cane pieces bounding on Plantain Garden River, the former and present courses of which are represented and also the quantity of cane land carried away by it since the year 1813 but more especially in 1815 and the subsequent years to the present date; surveyed by Francis Ramsay, December 1818", National Library of Jamaica, Plans, St Thomas 12C.

May and October were the months normally associated with heavy rainfall. Planters expected to commence the crop only after the October rains had passed and did their best to take off as much as possible before May, though double insurance on shipping was not imposed until August when hurricanes loomed. In 1767, however, bad weather at Christmas meant they "could not put the mill about" at Golden Grove. Taylor commented that the weather had been "really dismal in that part of the country for 3 years last past and such as has never been known for 20 years before".[75] The years 1765–75 were unusually free of hurricanes, in strong contrast to the following decades and the series of hurricanes that hit Jamaica in 1781, 1782, 1784, 1785, 1786, 1790, 1791 and 1795. The great storms that affected Golden Grove were not related to the hurricane systems that hit other islands during the period.[76]

When Taylor told Arcedeckne of the need to replace floodgates, following the great floods of 1765 and 1767, he asked whether their being open had been the cause of the great flooding of the property. Taylor responded that the river had first broken its banks at other points and, in fact, "the river overflowed its banks every where and covered the whole vale". He had "given positive orders that the gate shall always be shut as soon as the rains begin to fall in April".[77]

Getting water to the site of the mill was a universal problem of management. Ideally, the mill was located in the centre of an estate, and if the mill was to be water-powered, water had to be brought to it.[78] For Golden Grove, the problem was that its best water source was the Plantain Garden River and, because of the flatness of the alluvial lands north and south of the river and the high banks that channelled the river in its lower reaches, it was necessary to find that source to the west. The cost of raising the water in the river to flow over the banks within the boundaries of Golden Grove would have been very great. The best option was a dam or weir upstream of Golden Grove's westernmost boundary. Further, in order to ensure a reliable and adequate flow of water, strong enough to drive the mill, it was necessary to lead the water from the river into a reservoir nearer to the mill. The cost of building an aqueduct from a point with sufficient elevation above the mill to drive an overshot wheel would also have been very great, resulting from the level topography and the difficulty of obtaining easily worked stone. Golden Grove, like most of the mills of the Plantain Garden River floodplain, used an undershot wheel. This was less efficient because it depended entirely on the kinetic energy of the stream that drove it, whereas the overshot variety used both the kinetic and potential energy of the water. The degree of efficiency achieved by an undershot wheel depended on the rapidity of flow, and a relatively fast flowing stream could be created by damming water in a reservoir then letting it out through a narrow channel as elevated as possible.[79] This was the technology used at Golden Grove (Figure 7.7).

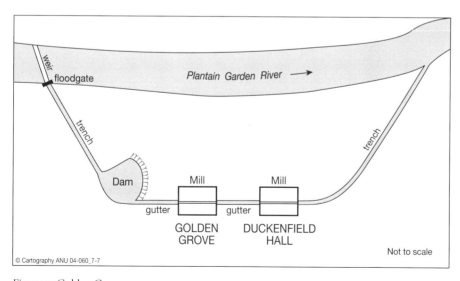

Figure 7.7 Golden Grove water system

The value of the water flowing in the Plantain Garden River, particularly as a source of power for the driving of mills, created the potential for conflict and competition among the planters located in the floodplain. Browne's map of 1755, based on surveys made between 1730 and 1749, identified eight "sugar works" below Bath, three on the north side of the river (the proprietors being "Pestel and Archdeacon" at the site of Batchelors Hall, Wheeler and "Cousons") and five to the south (Stuarton, Gardner, Morant, "Archdeacon" at the site of Golden Grove, and "Duckingfield").[80] Browne did not provide any clues as to the types of power employed. Batchelors Hall was described as a "plantation" on a plan of 1741, with about one hundred acres in cane and a "works". Land had recently been cleared for a plantain walk (Figure 7.8).[81] By the 1760s, however, any hopes of making it a profitable sugar estate had been abandoned and attention shifted to Golden Grove.

When Andrew Arcedeckne established his sugar works on Golden Grove in 1734 he "erected a dam, water mill, and other works thereon, and dug a canal to convey the water . . . which in several small streams flowed through" to the mill, and then on to the sugar mill at Duckenfield Hall.[82] In 1755 Andrew took his westside neighbour, Thomas Cussans, to court seeking ejectment as a result of encroachment by his Winchester Pen on Golden Grove lands. Surveyors were called in to run the lines of the original patents, and a new fixing laid down in 1758. Andrew recovered 285 acres. He then "found that the water conveyed by the canal formerly made was insufficient" and, together with Duckenfield Hall, "caused a flood-gate to be erected at the western extremity of the said land, so recovered", and dug a canal from the Plantain Garden River to the mills of Golden Grove and Duckenfield.[83]

Golden Grove and Duckenfield Hall shared a common trench and weir, and taking water from the Plantain Garden River necessarily required cooperation. Establishing and maintaining the system was a large-scale task, employing a substantial number of workers. Taylor told Arcedeckne and Cowell in January 1769 that "there have been 40 Negroes from your estate and as many from Duckenfield Hall for three weeks at work on the weir". The weir itself, stretched diagonally across the river to direct the flow from the northern bank across the deeper bed towards the shallower southern side, was "made of 5 or 6 rows of poles drove down and wattled together with river gravel etc thrown between". Taylor thought this construction strong enough, though it was often damaged in floods and in some years had to be repaired two or three times in order to raise the water. The immediate problem that required so much labour was "occasioned by the bottom of the arch [in which the floodgate hung] being at least five feet about [above] the surface of the river, so that they are obliged to raise it [the top of the weir] upwards of that to turn it in".[84]

The building of the weir changed the dynamics of flow and deposition in

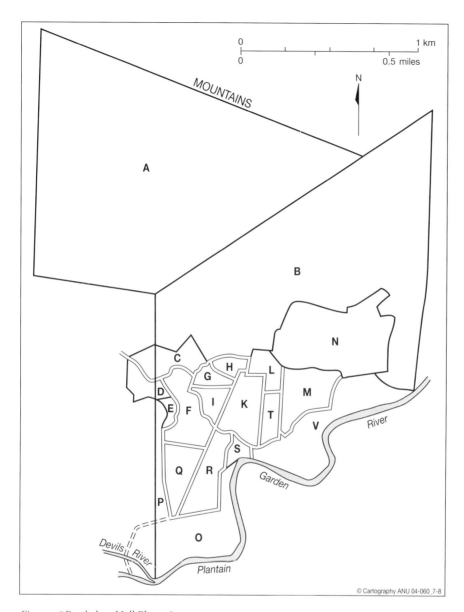

Figure 7.8 Batchelors Hall Plantation, 1741

Key: *A* Andrew Arcedeckne's patent for five hundred acres; *B* Robert Jacobs' patent for six hundred acres; *C* New fallen and planted in plantain walk; *D* Old plantain walk; *E* Pasture; *F–K* Canes; *L–M* Corn; *N* Great pasture; *O–P* Woodland; *Q–R* Canes; *S* Plantain walk; *T* Canes; *V* Wild canes by riverside. Redrawn from "A Plan of . . . Batchellors Hall Plantation at Plantain Garden River in the Parish of St. Thomas in the East, . . . April 1741, . . . by Bartholomew Brady, surveyor", National Library of Jamaica, Plans, St Thomas 12A.

the river channel. Flow accelerates over the top of a weir. Thus water that overtopped the Golden Grove weir and continued downriver initially created a crest or backwater curve that deposited sediment upstream and eroded the riverbed immediately downstream of the weir. It was this erosion that made the weir unstable. Once equilibrium was reached, sediment built up to a new level, but this took a long time and had little advantage in taking off the water into the canal. The large variations in discharge associated with the frequent flooding of the Plantain Garden River also created a hazard for the weir's stability and for the surrounding plain, making inundations more common.[85] Hence Arcedeckne's concern for the floodgate.

Taylor believed that the arch and its floodgate should have been built differently, constructed so that the foundation matched the level of the riverbed, with the trench dug deeper to take away the water efficiently. Until this was done properly and the trench faced with brick, he argued, "you will always be troubled for want of water". As it was, "the trench being cut through a rich loose mould the whole way is continually falling in after any heavy rain which were obliged to be continually throwing out to keep it open". Much of the water simply soaked away. Bricks to line the trench could be made from the mould dug from it, resulting in a much more efficient flow of water to the dam that held water for the mills. All of this constituted a major project, "a work of time", Taylor admitted, "and in the meantime must do as well as we can". He did not, however, offer any comments on optimum channel form or dimensions.[86]

In 1772 Cussans commenced an action in the Grand Court for ejectment, disputing the lines surveyed in 1758. Further claims caused the attorneys of Arcedeckne to fear that Cussans would stop up the floodgate and fill the canal. Golden Grove then, together with Duckenfield Hall, built a new floodgate on the bank of the Plantain Garden River, to the east of the disputed land, and dug a new canal. Cussans was simultaneously in dispute with his western neighbour, Plantain Garden River Estate, established on the patent of Dennis McCraugh.[87]

Relations between Golden Grove and Duckenfield were generally cooperative, sharing a weir and trench, and exploiting the same water. Even then, because Golden Grove held the upstream advantage, matters might become strained, as when in 1772, Taylor "dug a trench which I believe they will feel the inconveniency of, whenever the wet weather sets in".[88] The following year, in connection with the cutting of the navigation trench for Duckenfield Hall, Taylor told Arcedeckne he was mistaken on the question of the water used to turn the mills of that estate. Taylor argued, "I am sure they claim a property in the water and do not reckon they hold it by sufferance only, but as their right." Duckenfield had shared with Arcedeckne's father the cost of cutting the original trench from the Plantain Garden River and from 1758 or 1759 contributed labour to build up the weir. All of this gave them a right to the water, Taylor believed, "for if it does not and we have a right to direct the water from them at our pleasure, we can easily force them to dance to our pipe, and make them good neighbours in spite of their teeth by taking an opportunity of diverting the water from their mills when they have a quantity of canes there".[89]

The estates to the north of the river competed for the same resource, but shared no technologies with Golden Grove or Duckenfield Hall. In 1773, soon after the protracted dispute with Dawkins over the river-mouth land had been settled, Taylor and Arcedeckne found themselves locked in a new battle with Thomas Cussans, owner of Amity Hall estate, joined with Dr Matthew Gregory, owner of Hordley. Cussans sought possession of the land on which the weir was sited and the right to grant Arcedeckne use of its water for life at a peppercorn rent. Letters passed between Cussans, Arcedeckne, his mother, Kelly and Taylor. "As he [Cussans] and I are not at present very gracious", and because he did not wish to be "a fomentor of disputes between neighbours", Taylor told Arcedeckne, "whatever you choose to be done in the matter I am ready to follow your instructions". In March 1774 Taylor reported, "Your and my antagonist Mr. Cussans pushed exceeding hard to bring on the ejectment of the land at your dam but I got it starved off this court."[90]

Cussans, with Gregory, was still pursuing the ejectment of Arcedeckne from the land at his dam in 1774. Taylor advised Arcedeckne that "if Cussans gains the land they have a right to the place where your weir that takes in the water stands. Consequently even if they let you take it up they will only give you as much as they please under pretence that the rest is wanted for his mills and as the water first turns Dr. Gregorys mill he certainly will be a gainer." Therefore, Taylor promised to object strongly to the evidence of Gregory in the suit being brought to court. At the same time, Taylor confessed it was "very true that they have had a scarcity of water at Amity Hall this year owing chiefly to Mr. Kellys having taken in a greater deal more water than usual to keep the two mills about and having been a little wanton with it".[91]

Taylor argued that the rights of Golden Grove and Duckenfield superseded the entitlement of Amity Hall based on priority. He recognized that Amity Hall was the oldest mill in the district using the Plantain Garden River's water, having built a water mill "some years ago" when it was the joint property of Gregory and Cussans. As the first mill, Amity Hall therefore "had a right always to have sufficient water to turn it". It lost this right, according to Taylor, when in 1764–65 the property had been divided and a new works established at what became Hordley. Cussans then held Amity Hall and Gregory Hordley. Because the fall of water was shared by the two mills, a larger volume of water was needed from the river. Amity Hall had had a fall of twelve feet before the establishment of the mill at Hordley, which took half the fall. Taylor interpreted this to mean "the mill of Amity Hall had a prior right to a sufficient quantity of water to turn it when on the construction it was on in 1758 or 1759 but if it does it self an injury surely I do not think it can have a right to remedy itself by injuring you".[92]

The ejectment case came to court in May 1774 but a juror took ill and the trial was discontinued. Taylor reported, "Our friend Cussans was so very angry that he mentioned that he believed that the man was bribed to fall sick." Taylor confessed pleasure in the discomfiture of Cussans: "I did imagine that Cussans would have been found dangling in a garter the next morning but he has met with such disappointment in all his law matters that he is determined to leave the country and his law suits to be carried on by some more able General than himself." He was going "home" on the *Portland,* a man-of-war under Admiral Rodney.[93] Taylor warned Arcedeckne to expect a visit from Cussans, advising Arcedeckne "to act cautious with him for I look on him to be a man of weak head but very bad heart but if you agree what ever you direct me to do I will". The matter was complicated by Cussans having as one of his attorneys Malcolm Laing, who was also attorney to Arcedeckne. Taylor understood that Cussans stayed with Laing when visiting Kingston, and therefore thought it prudent not to tell Laing of the details of the case he planned to bring. It was at this time that Laing came to attention for his siphoning of funds from Worthy Park Estate, for which he was attorney.[94]

Taylor believed the real driver behind the battle over the weir was Gregory's desire to get water for Hordley. However, Taylor told Arcedeckne, with appropriate legal advice, "I can in two years make them dance to your pipe and they not have a drop of water to the mills of either Amity Hall or Hordley." His plan depended on the difference in height between the north and south banks of the Plantain Garden River. At the point where Amity Hall and Hordley took up the water, the north bank was higher, whereas the south was regularly encroached on by floods. Taylor therefore proposed driving an iron bar, to create a permanent landmark, at the high water mark during a flood on the south (Golden Grove) side of the river, establishing the point as part of Arcedeckne's property. If a right could then be established to prevent the making of a weir within this landmark, argued Taylor, the north bank claimants could not "raise the river to take it in their trench, and will be totally deprived (without your permission) of any water whatsoever".[95]

In spite of his cunning, Taylor claimed to be greatly disturbed by the dispute. He wrote to Arcedeckne at extraordinary length when accused of using it to his own ends, in order to increase the flow of water to his own estate, Holland.[96] Later, in September 1775, Taylor admitted he had been "in a good deal of agitation (when I wrote to you) at the infamous letters of that unhappy boy". Taylor believed he had by then won the battle of the weir and the water but, as to Cussans,

> I cannot say that I shall extend my compassion so far as even to pity him in the choice he has made of his wife for now what with his disappointments in this country, his lawsuits, the distraction of his affairs, his failing in his attempt to make you [Arcedeckne] a party to his malice by his unfair representations and such I wish to boot I think he has now the only alternatives of a pistol or a garter.

Cussans spared himself and when the published correspondence ends, in December 1775, the case was still to be settled in court.[97]

A resolution did emerge quite soon. In 1778 Cussans confirmed the right of Arcedeckne and his heirs to take up the water as before, and the two men agreed that "at all times when either of them should from the scarcity of water think it necessary to divide the waters for the use of Golden Grove plantation and of Amity Hall plantation", they would then take "an equal quantity for the benefit of their different mills". In order to enable this division, "proper floodgates" were to be constructed and kept in repair, "so as to gauge the water running towards the different mills to ascertain the quantity that neither might have more than the other without mutual consent". By 1782 Cussans had for "valuable consideration" granted rights to Duckenfield Hall to use the water after Golden Grove, and Arcedeckne confirmed Duckenfield's rights "in such manner as hath been usual and accustomed". Golden Grove was permitted to convey its water through Winchester in "the aqueduct gutter or trench now used for that purpose", and had the right to "repair or rebuild" the conduit as required, and to construct all necessary "dams dikes and wears sluices and floodgates" for the "turning and forcing" the water from the river. But no right was granted to raise the water in the dams "higher than hath been usual and accustomed". In order to carry out such works, Winchester was to give free access to Golden Grove's "servants workmen and slaves carts carriages and cattle", and Winchester was to do nothing to obstruct the flow of water through its lands.[98]

The dispute over the boundary between Golden Grove and Winchester also came closer to resolution. In 1779 an indenture between Arcedeckne and Cussans set out the various patents underlying the two estates (Figure 7.4).[99] It stated that Arcedeckne and Cussans were "desirous amicably to terminate and to put a final end" to their continuing "suits disputes and differences" and wished to establish the "just and proper fixings of the plats". Cussans and Arcedeckne committed themselves, and their heirs and assigns, to allow one another to occupy their lands without molestation or hindrance. The lines were to be "run and marked upon earth". Three stone pillars, placed at strategic points to increase the visibility of the boundaries, were to be erected and engraved "Golden Grove" on their eastern faces and "Winchester" on the western. Another indenture, signed and sealed by Cussans and Arcedeckne in 1782, committed fifty-four acres of Golden Grove land to Cussans for lease and ultimate purchase (Figure 7.9). Rather than a pen,

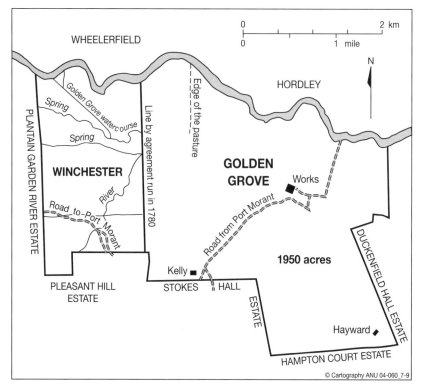

Figure 7.9 Plan of Golden Grove, 1782. Redrawn from Deeds DM 41/92/3, Arcedeckne Papers, University of Bristol, Arts and Sciences Library, Special Collections.

Winchester was now referred to as a "plantation and sugarwork".[100] The boundary dispute resurfaced after the death of Cussans, and was not firmly settled until 1826. A plan of "Winchester Estate" drawn in 1829, when the plantation was definitively a sugar producer, indicated the weir and canal that took water from the Plantain Garden River and sent it to drive the mill of Winchester and on into natural watercourses towards Golden Grove and Duckenfield.[101] A sketch of 1846 similarly detailed the construction of Winchester weir and how it led water into the "Winchester canal" (Figure 7.10).[102]

Building

As attorney, Taylor took a leading role in negotiating the construction of new buildings on Golden Grove as well as the replacement and repair of those damaged in storms and floods. He began with the mills, the most important elements in the productive process. Following the flood of 1765, a new cattle mill was constructed. Probably this replaced an existing cattle mill, though

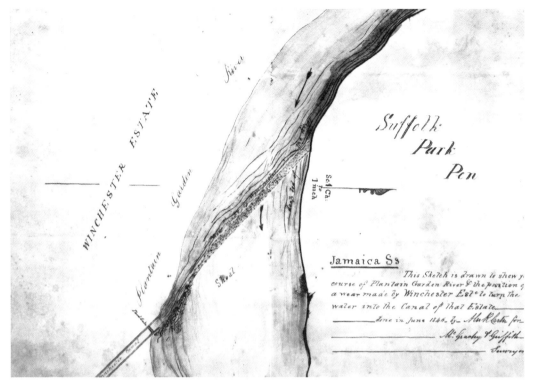

Figure 7.10 "A Sketch drawn to show the course of the Plantain Garden River and the position of a weir made by Winchester Estate to turn the water into the canal of that Estate, done in June 1846 by Alexander R. Carter for McGeachy and Griffiths, surveyors". National Library of Jamaica, Plans, St Thomas 3A.

Craskell and Simpson's map, based on surveys 1756–61, showed only a double watermill.[103] The cattle mill was always regarded as a backup, a substitute for watermills where they were normally available, and Taylor may have had in mind his struggles over water resources. A new distillery was also built. White tradesmen were employed, but Taylor recommended hiring "carpenter and mason Negroes" to save money. The new works were fully in place for the crop of 1767.[104] However, by early 1769 Taylor told Cowell, "I believe we shall be obliged almost to build a new mill after the crop" to replace one that was "very old and does almost nothing". A Mr Wynter, "one of the best mechanics in the country and a conscientious man", was brought "to examine her". The masons were put to work on it almost immediately.[105] Taylor asked Arcedeckne to ship a still with a capacity of one thousand gallons, and said that the coppers in the boiling house were "very old" and needed replacement. Rather than having them made of copper, Taylor requested twelve boilers of cast iron, "which we find to answer very well for every thing but clarifiers". Using iron would "save a great deal of money and the old coppers will buy or go very near to purchase the still". The "large still" and boilers were sent, though too late for the crop of 1770.[106]

The works buildings were the productive engine of the estate. Taylor's enthusiasm was overwhelmingly directed at their full functioning. He spent no more than few nights sleeping at Golden Grove and had no real enthusiasm for the building of a great house there. Arcedeckne ordered one built, however, for the day he might come back to Jamaica. Taylor did his best to follow directions. Arcedeckne began to talk about his desire to have a house built in mid-1765, when his return to Jamaica seemed imminent. In September, Taylor noted the tradesmen would need to construct first "a comfortable house for themselves and your bookkeepers for it has no occasion to be very large and then they will be able to build you a house for yourself according to your own liking".[107] Arcedeckne provided plans and shipped bricks. In November 1766, Taylor promised to "set about" the house after crop but confessed most of the bricks sent out by Arcedeckne had been used to complete the distillery. Taylor challenged Arcedeckne's desire for a house built of bricks, saying, "We can very easily get stone on the spot for it which will save the expense of bricks and last longer." The house was to be sited on a hill, with access by "a very good chaise road".[108] A year later, building had still not commenced, though the site had been cleared of timber and lime burned in preparation. The delay was caused by the need to plant canes and restore the works. Taylor continued to complain about the difficulty of building in brick but told Arcedeckne, "You may rest satisfied it shall soon be set about and every direction followed that is laid down in the plan except raising the foundation higher for it says 1 foot 8½." Taylor thought this too low.[109]

Taylor reported continuing delays, telling Cowell in March 1768, "We have not even yet begun on it neither are the window and door frames yet come out." Moving the required three hundred thousand bricks "would kill all the cattle on the estate to carry to the place where the house is to stand". Taylor repeated his argument that "we have no workmen in this country that can build with stone to the dimensions that the plan requires, that is to make the cornishes and raised work about the doors and windows, but shall set about the foundation and wait your orders. If we build it a plain front we can do it well enough."[110] The window and door frames reached Jamaica from England by July. Taylor had expected also the frame for the roof, but this was not sent. The house would be "set about directly after Christmas", and Taylor promised to "take care that it is conformable with Mr. Arcedecknes orders". Much stone had been collected and two large lime kilns burned. Once more, Taylor promised he would "take care that all your directions shall be followed" and hoped the house "will please you when you come over". Not everyone was happy with the project. Taylor said, "Both your mother and aunt have a great objection against the house for having no piazzas and want a Jamaica house built."[111]

By September 1770 the walls were finished and the roof begun.[112] What happened next is less than certain. Taylor stopped writing on the matter. Arcedeckne increasingly seemed an unlikely occupant, even as a casual visitor. The plan of the estate made in 1788 identifies "walls of great house" suggesting a half-finished shell on its way to becoming a ruin, much as it was to be for the next two hundred years.[113] When Lady Nugent visited Golden Grove in March 1802 she found "an excellent house, surrounded by sugar works, cocoa-nut trees, &c". This was not the great house built by Taylor for Arcedeckne on the hills to the south of the mill.[114] A later drawing of the Golden Grove mill yard and house derives from a daguerreotype by Adolphe Duperly, made about 1840 (Figure 7.11).[115]

In 1769 Arcedeckne agreed to give Dr Hayward a piece of land for a house. Hayward chose a lot a quarter of a mile to the east of the great house, in the hills towards Duckenfield, a site identified as "Hayward" on the plan of 1782 and "Doctors" on the plan of 1788. This house was built and occupied. In 1770 Dr Hayward drew up a plan for a new "hot house" or hospital for the enslaved, at a new location, and it is probable that this too was built and used.[116]

Taylor's correspondence with Arcedeckne devoted vastly more attention to the building of the great house, for its elusive single occupant, than to the houses of the hundreds of enslaved people on Golden Grove. The latter were

Figure 7.11 Golden Grove yard by Duperly, *c.*1845. National Library of Jamaica.

given time and materials to build their own houses, with occasional assistance from the plantation's carpenters, but otherwise the planter generally intervened little in the building process. In the flood of April 1765 Taylor said only that they saved themselves from drowning by getting on the roofs of their houses.[117] He said rather more in 1770 when he had purchased new workers. As soon as the crop was over, still six months away at the time of writing, they should be "set no other work than building houses for themselves that is a house for each of them and . . . making grounds for themselves". Taylor recognized this meant a loss of labour time but thought "by their being happy and contented it will very soon be made up".[118]

Working Land

Responsibility for decisions about the area and siting of planted crops was shared between attorney and overseer, the attorney having the greater authority and the absentee owner the last word. Rational choices depended on detailed knowledge of the land.

How well did Taylor know the land of Golden Grove and how far was he able to take an active role in making decisions about the manner of its cultivation? His correspondence with Arcedeckne contains relatively few clues. Taylor rarely mentioned the names of any of the cane-pieces but this may simply reflect his poor opinion of Arcedeckne's knowledge.[119] The earliest known plan of Golden Grove was based on a survey of 1788 (Figure 7.3). It is possible, though unlikely, that before the American Revolution there was no map to which Taylor or Arcedeckne could refer. Taylor did, however, advocate attention to putting in plant canes on a regular basis and the expansion of the area under cane. Over the years, he gradually began to provide more detail, suggesting a greater interest and understanding on his part, and perhaps also a growing need to inform an absentee whose knowledge of practical planting was limited and diminishing.

Whether the survey of 1788 was the idea of Taylor or Arcedeckne is unknown, but the resulting plan served as an important management tool. It showed a total of 1,925 acres, including 586 acres in canes planted in thirty-six numbered and named pieces. No other areas were named. Cane completely covered the northeastern third of the estate. To the west, near the river, there were large blocks of land in common pasture (more than half of it ruinate) and woodland. In the southwest corner were 417 acres in "plantain walk, Negro grounds and ruinate", as well as the area leased to Kelly and some "marshy ground covered with bush". Along the trench coming from Winchester was a coco piece of 33 acres, benefiting no doubt from occasional overflowings. The hills to the south, the site of Arcedeckne's great house, were also in provision grounds and woodland. The broad pattern of land use must have been much the same in the period 1765–75.

In September 1768, when Arcedeckne had been out of the island for more than three years, Taylor reported on a visit to Golden Grove, noting there were 182 acres in plant canes and 367 acres in ratoons, making 549 acres in cane, just 37 acres less than in 1788. Of the plant canes, more than half the total, 110 acres, had been planted in 1768. The following January, responding to a suggestion from Arcedeckne that they should try planting five canes to a hole, Taylor observed that when Kelly started at Golden Grove he had "planted rather too thin but now he puts in the clay land 3 canes in a hole and in the brick mould 4". Taylor found "the canes stand much better for the thick planting, they are not so luxuriant but they do not lodge so much". He promised to try five to a hole "but in my opinion 4 will do equally well".[120] Here Taylor and Arcedeckne traded ideas and information gleaned from others, no doubt, but demonstrated also a willingness to experiment. Lodged canes, lying down in the wet soil, were a problem at Golden Grove as elsewhere, particularly after flood rains, and anything that could be done to prevent this happening was productive. The trouble with lodged canes was that if they remained lying down they sent up fresh shoots that produced little sugar. At the beginning of 1773 Taylor feared great losses by the "black blast" (probably the disease smut) which covered the canes in a kind of soot but it was gone by the end of the year.[121]

The soil of Golden Grove was ideal for sugar growing. In 1765 Taylor described some of the soil then being holed, following the great flood of April, as "excessive rich" and expected to cut the canes when very young and cut again in the following year as ratoons.[122] Perhaps because of the regularly renewed fertility of the soils of the floodplain, Taylor never discussed with Arcedeckne the manuring of the cane-pieces that elsewhere proved so labour intensive a task for basket-carrying workers. For the same reasons, and because of the relatively small cattle herd of Golden Grove, he never proposed "fly-penning". A traditional practice that allowed for an interdependence of crops and animals and used on many Jamaican plantations, fly-penning involved the controlled rotation of livestock on the cane-pieces, pens and cattle being shifted about the space to supply an even spread of manure. It was a great advantage to Golden Grove not to have to apply manure, as where it was needed, planters believed, double the number of workers were required. The role of the Plantain Garden River was remarkable. The regular flooding of the land, said Long, covered the land with "a rich sediment of mud" and the canes grew "astonishingly luxuriant, requiring no other manure than what this river, like another Nile, so invariably deposits".[123]

Taylor talked occasionally of the need to extend the cultivation of food crops at Golden Grove. Thus in September 1765, apparently responding to a question from Arcedeckne, Taylor reported his certainty that a large quantity of ground provisions would be produced, "having long ago recommended it to Mr. Kelly and he told me he had both put in himself and made all the

Negroes put in a large quantity". In expectation of purchases of enslaved workers, Taylor said, "We have already made a plantain walk to have plenty whenever they come for nothing encourages Negroes more than great plenty of provisions and it is an utter impossibility for negroes to work without a belly full."[124] After visiting Golden Grove, however, Taylor became less confident, saying Kelly "told me without more Negroes it really was impossible to putt in much considering the many different things he was obliged to do together with having about twenty of the best hands constantly carrying lime and sand and filling the wains with stones etc".[125] Taylor and Kelly put the ball back in Arcedeckne's court, pointing to the demands of the building programme and the need for a larger enslaved workforce. Certainly Taylor did not order Kelly to change the priorities. In 1771 Taylor reported that seventy acres were being planted in provision crops for the newly purchased enslaved people at Golden Grove, with the "consent" of Arcedeckne's mother.[126]

Taylor sometimes countermanded instructions from Arcedeckne. In late 1765, for example, Taylor visited Batchelors Hall Pen and wrote to Arcedeckne saying, "Mr. Kelly told me you had ordered all the cows to be sold off but seventy as you did not apprehend you had pastures for more there." Taylor, however, found a surprising extent of "fine pastures". He ordered Kelly not to sell any cattle until the herd reached 300 head, well beyond the present 217, and told Arcedeckne there was "full sufficiency of pasture to keep 150 breeding cows there provided there should be 10 or fifteen more New Negroes putt on". Batchelors Hall would then "ease the contingencies on your estate greatly as you will always be able when you have that number not only to supply Golden Grove but also to sell 1200 or 1500£ worth annually from thence".[127] In this instance Taylor simply imposed his view, based on observations on the ground that were hard for Arcedeckne to challenge.

At the beginning of 1767 Taylor again reported that the cattle herd at Batchelors Hall was growing rapidly. He told Arcedeckne, "I had some thought of selling some of the steers but the fear of a wet crop has made me alter that resolution for fear of any accidents having so many canes to cut." A wet crop meant boggy soil and the necessity of strong animals, to pull the cane carts to the mills and wain the hogsheads to the wharf. After the crop, Taylor was, with Arcedeckne's approval, willing to sell some Golden Grove steers and gave orders "to keep up some of the old cows marked AA to fatten and sell off to the butchers". At the end of 1767, however, following the two great floods of that year, Taylor found that a number of cattle had died, "the continued rains giving the grass such a spring as purges the cattle to death".[128] Two years later, Taylor thought the cattle looked "thinner and rougher than they used to do though the pasture is pretty clean". He put the penkeeper on notice, though Kelly claimed he was "very sober and diligent". Taylor recommended planting Guinea grass as a way of providing "an opportunity of fattening all your old cows which are now lost", and ordered the feeding of herrings to the cattle to improve their condition.[129]

Working People

Manuals of plantation management generally gave a high priority to the "treatment" or "management" of enslaved people. In doing so, they covered topics such as the organization of workers into gangs ("sets or classes") and the selection and training of specialists, as well as food and housing.[130] Most of these manuals, however, were published after 1775, in the period of planter-led "amelioration" when effort was directed at increasing profits by improving the conditions of life of the enslaved and attempts to ensure the reproduction of the population. There was not much for Taylor to read, had he wanted to, in dealing with Golden Grove before the American Revolution. In any case, he had little to say on these topics in his correspondence with Arcedeckne. Probably he talked to Kelly but it was overwhelmingly the responsibility of the overseer to deal with discipline and work routines, and Taylor may have seen these as matters of "supervision" rather than matters of management.

Taylor did, however, have a great deal to say to Arcedeckne on the general strategy of labour supply and demand, and the long-term allocation of resources. He consistently advocated a policy of maintaining the enslaved workforce of Golden Grove by regular purchase of people from slave ships. He had a notion of the ratio of labour to expected yields and of the limits of endurance, the capacity of the human body to perform work. His understanding was located within the context of a brutal regime but based on observation and an appreciation of what went beyond the bounds of the possible. Often, he seems to have thought Arcedeckne lacked this necessary framework and that he had unreasonable expectations of what the enslaved people of Golden Grove might be asked to do.

Like most whites of his time, Taylor had few misconceptions about the fundamental role of terror in the maintenance of the slave system in Jamaica. Evidence that the enslaved people of the island hated their masters and their situation was hard to ignore, in rebellions and everyday resistance.[131] Taylor knew that he was as likely as any other white person to have his throat cut at any time. It was an understanding he rarely voiced explicitly. He did not express fear for his life. Within the region of Golden Grove, rebellion came closest at the end of 1765. Taylor told Arcedeckne of "an alarm of a rebellion in St. Marys when Matthew Byndloss and my overseer were both murdered by a parcel of new Negroes". The rebels shot Taylor's overseer and cut off his head. Buildings we set on fire but the more extensive rebellion that had been planned was thwarted. Rebels were pursued and killed in the woods and one man was burned. The public execution of rebellious people by burning and hanging in gibbets, as well as the placing of heads on poles, were common methods used by whites to instil fear. Apart from his graphic but matter-of-fact account of the outbreak of 1765, Taylor said little of any of this in writing to Arcedeckne, and he did not mention the application of terror to the people of Golden Grove. Taylor told Arcedeckne only that although the 1765 rebellion had been meant to spread across the island, "I do not find that any of the Negroes at windward had any knowledge of it".[132] Golden Grove was free of immediate threats, and the rebellion did not dampen Taylor's enthusiasm for risking investment in expansion and the purchase of "new Negroes" from slave ships.

Although Taylor believed Arcedeckne should invest more broadly, by establishing a second mill on Golden Grove or by acquiring another plantation, in the short and medium term Taylor concentrated his advocacy on the hire or purchase of additional enslaved workers. In April 1765, before the rebellion, he wrote, "Whenever get some more Negroes hope your Estate will net you as much as your most sanguine expectations can amount to at least it shall not be my fault if it does not."[133] It was Taylor's view that Golden Grove needed more enslaved workers to deal with the current crop and to enable the estate to bring in the canes early rather than late in the season. In order to achieve his goal, an early plant was necessary. He was confirmed in this view by the losses resulting from the flood of that month, the probability of damage and delay increasing through the year. In the short term, Taylor took Kelly's advice and hired slaves to keep the factory running at full pace. Taylor had no doubt about the wisdom of this approach "but did not choose to do it without consulting Mr. Laing who agreed that we should hire some Negroes".[134] Taylor told Arcedeckne he would have hired more but could not get them, because after the flood "the canes are so entangled they take double the quantity of cutters than if they were standing".[135] Hiring had to be done promptly in order to meet immediate needs, and Taylor as attorney was responsible for these decisions.

Whether or not to purchase enslaved workers was normally a decision for the proprietor. Buying people represented a major commitment of capital. Golden Grove bought twenty-four women in April 1765, and probably this purchase had been approved by Arcedeckne before he left Jamaica. Taylor thought them "very well looking but about 4 of them a little weak but will do very well".[136] He soon sought approval to buy more, saying, "If you think proper [I] intend purchasing 24 men about Christmas for it will be impossible to keep up the Estate at such great crops as it ought to make without it except by pushing your Negroes too much and killing them which am sure will not be for your advantage."[137] These "good able Negro men" would "pay for themselves by the greater quantity of sugar you will make for if we get them shall be almost able to keep both the mills about all night and one all day and be able to take off the crop in a reasonable time".[138]

In September 1765 Taylor told Arcedeckne he was "extremely glad that you seem to intend putting on some more Negroes".[139] There is nothing to suggest Arcedeckne became more certain. Taylor chose the moment to act. In November, he told Arcedeckne that a ship from Africa had arrived some weeks before and "as you were in excessive want of Negroes I thought you never could have a better opportunity of getting them than out of her especially as it was in our power to give you a choice and to let you have all men". So, Taylor had "consulted" with Arcedeckne's mother and Malcolm Laing and they "readily came into my sentiments". He had convinced them by arranging an effective twelve-month credit, during which the enslaved workers would be employed putting in a large coco piece as food security against hurricane and the loss of plantain trees. In arguing the case this way, Taylor was able to draw on Arcedeckne's own stated concern for the food supply and Kelly's contention that ground provisions could only be given priority if more labour was available. The new workers would also be used to advance the rebuilding of the works, another matter in contention with Arcedeckne. Taylor concluded the matter saying, "I really assure you I never bought Negroes on so advantageous terms for myself and you may depend on my doing every thing for you with as great a regard for your interest as I would for my own."[140] In all of this, however, Taylor never mentioned the number of enslaved people he had purchased (probably thirty to forty) or the price he had paid for them. Arcedeckne was left to discover this from separate documents or simply to wonder. At the end of 1766 he wrote prohibiting any further purchases until he was out of debt.[141]

Arcedeckne's mother, being made aware by Taylor that her son had ordered him not to buy, made a gift of enslaved workers in 1767. These were people in Kelly's jobbing gang. Taylor went to Golden Grove and purchased twenty of them for twelve hundred pounds, and had them branded with Arcedeckne's mark. Taylor told Arcedeckne, "I hope you will not think I acted wrong in this."[142] At the same time, Taylor continued to hire slaves in order to get in a spring plant. There were not enough enslaved people on the estate to achieve this as well as clean the cane fields and work the mill, "so as to make the estate profitable", said Taylor. This was another reason for delaying the building of Arcedeckne's great house. Taylor explained his choice to Cowell, saying, "Had I pushed both for a large plant and to build the house at the same time I should certainly have killed a good number of the Negroes which leaving humanity aside never could have been for the advantage of that gentle-man."[143]

Early in 1768 Taylor told Cowell that he hoped in future "to make the rum pay for the contingencies provided we do not buy negroes for the estate, but as Mr. Arcedeckne ordered none to be bought until his arrival here I do not think myself at liberty to buy any without ordered from him or you". He continued, "I assure you they are excessively wanted for to carry on the estate as it ought to be it will require upwards of 100 more working Negroes for there are a great number of old superannuated Negroes and young children there, and the whole Plantain Garden River is deemed unhealthy even in this country."[144] Long argued similarly that "Negroes on the plantations which border on Plantain Garden River are subject to frequent mortalities, especially if their huts are placed on the levels, which are damp, and annoyed by constant exhalations".[145] Taylor also wrote to Arcedeckne, then travelling in Europe, promising large crops in the future but emphasizing "you want a great many Negroes" and recommending the annual purchase of twenty people. This, he said, "would greatly hearten the rest and it will be impossible keeping the estate up to great crops without you do it".[146]

Even though there were 367 enslaved workers on Golden Grove in late 1768, Taylor believed the gang was too few, too "weak", to take off the crop of 549 acres without help. Taylor told Arcedeckne that everything else was in his favour. However, argued Taylor, "except you push it with some Negroes the estate will inevitably fall back and cost you a very large sum to bring up again". At the minimum, he should buy sixteen people each year from four different ships on twelve-month credit. Buying from different ships was a strategy to undermine the capacity of the enslaved to combine in rebellion. Probably, Taylor went personally to the ships to make his selection. Action was "absolutely necessary", he told Arcedeckne. The method proposed, said Taylor, would be both "the easiest and at the same time a very good way for to increase your strength without putting yourself to any very great expense at once".[147] Whether Cowell shared Arcedeckne's reluctance is not clear. This was territory for the proprietor to make his own decisions and mistakes.

Taylor claimed he sought not to push the matter, but told Arcedeckne in January 1769 that although very good crops were in prospect "without an addition of Negroes it will be impossible to keep the estate up". He repeated his idea of buying sixteen or twenty enslaved people each year, from four or five ships, "of the best countries and who have had the yaws if possible to be discovered". Within three years, said Taylor, the new slaves would be seasoned and pay their price. "For it is a pity and for after having such good lands and works the estate should fall off for want of a sufficient strength of Negroes, which if not put on must infallibly be the case", he concluded.[148]

Arcedeckne was eventually convinced. At the end of 1768 he wrote from Florence agreeing to purchase enslaved people for Golden Grove. Taylor responded briefly: "Am very glad you have consented to purchase some Negroes for the estate for it is otherwise impossible to keep it up there being work for 200 more working negroes than are on it without putting in an acre more of canes and by nursing weeding trashing them and tending the land it would yield infinitely better than it does now."[149] However, Taylor was delayed many months by slowness in the supply of enslaved people from

Africa. In October 1769 he told Arcedeckne, "There have been no Negroes arrive since your orders for buying more." Taylor would buy as soon as ships arrived, he assured Arcedeckne, as it was what he had "all along desired".[150] Only in February 1770 was Taylor able to report having purchased twelve enslaved men, "really very fine people". He hoped to buy more but still needed to hire workers to put in the spring plant. In order to justify the hiring, Taylor had sought and received approval from Arcedeckne's mother, "or would not have done it after what you wrote of not hiring negroes". Warming to his theme, Taylor told Arcedeckne, "I assure you on my word and honor the estate now and has ever since your being of age wanted £10000 worth of Negroes." Taylor did not relate this amount to any number of slaves but the money would have bought 150 to 200 people.[151]

Reflecting on the continuing demand for workers, Taylor thought it necessary to emphasize that "Negroes" wore out and needed replacement. "They are not steel or iron and we see neither gudgeons nor capooses can last in this country", he told Arcedeckne in 1770. He took his analogy from the vertical sugar mill. Gudgeons were the shafts let into the ends of the rollers. The gudgeon at the bottom of each roller rested on a hard metal capoose or pivot that rotated within a rigid metal housing mounted on the mill bed. The word "capoose" is a Jamaicanism. In 1790 J. B. Moreton said the rollers were supported on the mill bed "on small pieces of metal about the size and shape of whipping-tops, called capouses". Modern writers describe them as "the pivots on which the rollers in sugar mills formerly turned; they were shaped like cones rounded at the top and flanged below".[152] Gudgeon and capoose took the considerable stress created in the crushing of the canes in a mill made up of vertical rollers (Figure 7.12). As Bryan Edwards commented, although the sugar mill was "a very simple contrivance, great force is nevertheless requisite to make it overcome the resistance which it necessarily meets with". If overburdened, gudgeon and capoose became hot and snapped. When they snapped, everything came to a halt. Planters were warned that "gudgeons must always be well greased and cool".[153]

It was this pivotal role and inherent vulnerability that Taylor referred to when he told Arcedeckne the people on Golden Grove had long been worked "above their ability". If Golden Grove was his, said Taylor, he would use none of the estate's workers to dig cane holes for the next three years but in their stead hire jobbers. He reminded Arcedeckne that when Golden Grove had made 508 hogsheads, in his father's time, there had been 540 people on it, now there were fewer than 400. Taylor noted that the mill had begun work in December and would continue until August. "This is 8 months wherein the poor wretches do not get above 5 or at most 6 hours out of 24."[154]

In expressing himself this way, Taylor did not mean to suggest there was any fundamental fault in the system of slavery, its management or morality. His argument was not intended as an indictment of the plantation enterprise.

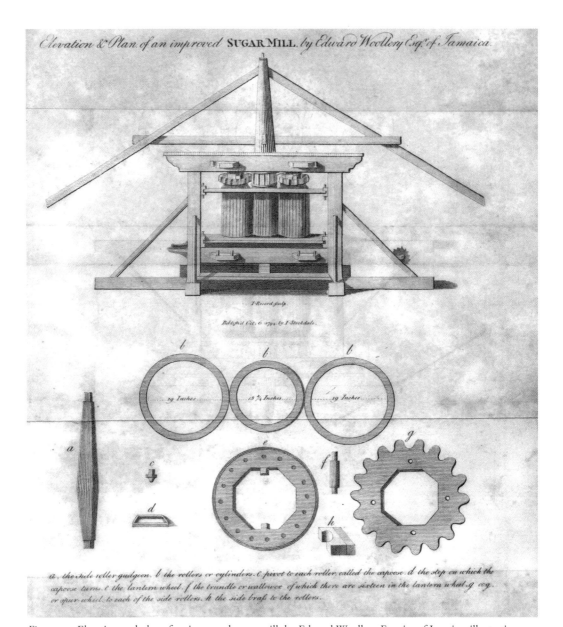

Figure 7.12 Elevation and plan of an improved sugar mill, by Edward Woollery Esquire of Jamaica, illustrating gudgeon (*a*) and capoose (*c*). Bryan Edwards, *The History, Civil and Commercial, of the British Colonies in the West Indies,* second ed. (1794), 2: facing 223.

Rather, he sought to bring home to Arcedeckne the inefficiency of the labour/population balance at Golden Grove. Taylor was arguing for the subjection of a larger number of people, under the same regime, but in a more productive long-term relationship to the labour demands of the property in order to maximize output and minimize unit costs. If only Golden Grove had "a proper number of negroes on it", he told Arcedeckne, the estate's profits "would exceed your most sanguine wishes".[155]

Taylor was not concerned about demographic stress or the "failure" of the enslaved population to reproduce itself. When Arcedeckne proposed that a larger proportion of women be purchased for Golden Grove, Taylor responded that the need was "infinitely more" for men. He explained that "there are many things which women cannot do, as cutting copperwood, wainmen, boilers, distillers, stokers, mulemen, etc.". Only if the total population was "sufficient" would the idea of increasing the proportion of women be workable. "Indeed it is a sort of miracle to conceive what they have done this year", Taylor wrote in July 1770. He had gone against orders in hiring slaves to cut copperwood and clean canes but saw it as essential to keeping up the estate "without murdering the Negroes".[156]

In March 1771 Taylor was busy buying enslaved people from ships in harbour at Kingston. He told Arcedeckne, "I do really want to do away with the hiring of Negroes, and this is the best time of year to buy new Negroes to be a little accustomed to the country before the bad weather sets in in September and October." He had bought sixteen for £952 currency (£680 sterling) and planned to buy another fourteen for Golden Grove.[157] The average price was £59 10s currency, close to the £60 paid Kelly in 1767, but Taylor did not offer averages or use them explicitly in any calculations or arguments. In May, Taylor reported from Kingston: "There is a Guinea man come in, but as the slaves rose on the coast of Guinea and murdered the captain many were drove over board and drowned I did not think it prudent to buy any for you out of her as they might be troublesome and think it better to wait a little till we can get some not quite so mutinous." This was the only time Taylor used the word "slaves" rather than "Negroes".[158]

Hiring continued at a high level. When Kelly received his salary of £300 in March 1773, he was paid an even larger amount, £566, for the hire of his enslaved gang to Golden Grove.[159] He owned roughly the number of enslaved people that Taylor thought Golden Grove needed. At the end of April, Kelly sought to sell to Arcedeckne the 140 people then in his possession. Taylor commented, "They have their houses and grounds on your land and consequently would suit you better than any person in the West Indies." They had all had the yaws and were fully seasoned. With such seasoned people, said Taylor, Golden Grove might expect crops of seven hundred hogsheads. "On my almost moral certainty of your agreeing to Kellys proposal," he wrote, "I have not nor will not buy any new negroes for the estate until I hear further from you on this subject."[160] Taylor told Arcedeckne, "You have always been complaining of poverty" but it was impossible to manage Golden Grove with greater frugality than currently practised and larger crops could be produced only with an expanded workforce. Arcedeckne agreed to the purchase. By March 1774 the deal had been closed, 120 enslaved people being purchased from Kelly for £8,714, payable in instalments down to 1778. The valuation was done by two merchant-planters, who added a percentage for houses and grounds even though these were located on lands belonging to Golden Grove. The average price was £72 12s, significantly above the prices paid earlier, though again Taylor did not make the calculation explicitly. Taylor told Arcedeckne, "I think them a prodigious acquisition to your estate and that you will not feel the purchase as you will by this means be enabled to enlarge your crop and save your capital and there will be no occasion of pushing so hard as we were formerly obliged to on the estate." At the same time, however, Taylor recommended to Arcedeckne "the purchase of 20 young Negroes annually to be bought for the use of the estate and by that means they will become as good as any creoles and very little risk in the seasoning of them and the yaws which is the most destructive thing in a wet country". Arcedeckne approved the plan.[161]

A year later, when Taylor was becoming increasingly testy about his role as attorney, he told Arcedeckne,

> I shall be obliged to you to giving your positive orders whether we are to put in any more canes at Golden Grove by jobbing as it will not be in my power to prevent it without your orders to me to that purpose for I do apprehend that the 100 Negroes were bought to prevent it and when I have your orders I stick to them literally without I see that your interest would materially suffer and then in that case I would do for you as I would do for myself.

When the price of sugar had fallen, said Taylor, he deferred purchasing the twenty slaves a year previously agreed, but now he asked Arcedeckne to "write to me on the matter fully".[162] Arcedeckne responded in June. What he said is unknown, Taylor noting only, "I shall show that part of your letter to Kelly when I see him regarding the hire of Negroes."[163]

If Arcedeckne prohibited hiring, his commands had little effect. At the end of 1775, Taylor reported simply that "Kelly has done a great deal of jobbing work on your estate and then tells me it is done". At the same time Taylor sought to explain to Arcedeckne the importance of the ratio of working people to working cattle, which went beyond the ratio of enslaved workers to cultivated land. A large expenditure on cattle was necessary in order to take off the crops. Taylor recognized that "more cattle more Negroes etc" was the way to increase output and profits, and indeed it was more or less what he had pushed for over the decade of his attorneyship, but now he asked

Arcedeckne for "positive orders whether you will have it continued or not". If Arcedeckne had been "married and had children to reap the advantages of putting on more Negroes increasing the quantity of your canes cattle and pasture and your improvements to go to whom you yourself pleased it would be very well". However, said Taylor, "for you to be continually advancing and keeping your self drained for perhaps those on the one side that you have no affection or regard for is the reason and motive of my mentioning it". The achievement of producing great amounts of sugar and rum was "certainly pleasing and adds both reputation and emolument to the agents", Taylor recognized, well aware that he was the principal agent and beneficiary. On the other hand, he continued, "I leave it to you to judge and consider whether you choose to have more sugar and rum than the natural strength of your estate will make." Taylor called this "a disagreeable theme" but called on Arcedeckne to "give me if you please positive orders and they must be obeyed for if more and more land is put in you must want 100 more Negroes 100 more steers and 2 or 300 more acres of land opened for pasturage at the same time". Uneasy at raising these matters, Taylor said, "I hope you will not conceive that there is any disagreement or jealousy whatsoever. I do it intently to know your sentiments that I may act in conformity to them and not be liable to blame or censure."[164]

Trading

As attorney, Taylor was in theory responsible for local exchange and for the shipping of export commodities. He might also make decisions about the proportions of Golden Grove's output that could be sold most profitably locally and overseas. In the local market, it was his task to find purchasers and to agree prices and conditions. In the export trade, however, he had no role in marketing and pricing, and his principal responsibility was to seek out ships. Often, particularly in time of war, it was a difficult task, and Taylor had to use every possible piece of intelligence and negotiating skill to get the proprietor's sugar and rum on board in good time.[165]

As was the general rule, Golden Grove's rum was much more likely than its sugar to be sold locally, because of differences in market demand and price. The proceeds from the rum were used to cover local debts. It was also commonly assumed by contemporaries that sugar and rum would be produced in the rough ratio of 2 hogsheads to 1 puncheon.[166] Golden Grove achieved a higher ratio, of 2.7 hogsheads of sugar to 1 puncheon of rum, so that using the rum to pay the local costs made possible even greater returns to the absentee. For example, in 1766 Golden Grove produced 472 hogsheads of sugar (averaging 1,652 pounds per hogshead) and 198 puncheons of rum (111 gallons each). Of the sugar, 372 hogsheads were shipped and 100 sold locally. Only 2 puncheons of rum were shipped. Three were used to replace losses by drainage, 13 were consumed on Golden Grove, and one was "paid" to Duckenfield and Wheelerfield Estates.[167] The following year, almost all of the sugar was shipped, and all of the rum sold locally.[168]

Taylor hoped that from 1768 sales of rum would completely cover local contingencies, so that Arcedeckne would get the sugar clear. Like most attorneys, Taylor generally expected to have authority in deciding how and where the rum should be sold. When experiments were tried in the shipping of Golden Grove rum to England, to test the waters, the idea did not come from Taylor. In July 1765 he told Arcedeckne that "Mr. Laing being very desirous to see how your rum would turn out in England told me he had given orders to Kelly to ship you thirty puncheons on board the *Susanna* Captain Baird who is now lying at Manchioneal". In the end, he could find only 9 puncheons.[169] In 1774 Arcedeckne intervened in the rum-making process, wanting an increase in the proof. Taylor was not happy. He told Arcedeckne, "I shall write to Mr. Kelly to make it to your proof tho it will be a loss for being so strong a great deal of the spirit must evaporate in the running off the spirit but as you desire it it must be done."[170] Later, Taylor told Arcedeckne, "I am glad to hear that you find a profit in making your rum strong and that it sells so well."[171]

Molasses, the other by-product of sugar-making, seems always to have been Taylor's responsibility. He regularly exchanged Golden Grove's molasses for staves, used in the making of casks, trading with North American ships. This cut into Golden Grove's rum output by limiting its raw material, but the molasses was the commodity most easily surrendered to ensure a supply of staves. Taylor used "Philadelphia staves" exclusively, saying they were "reckoned to be the best here", rather than mixing imported woods with staves from the Jamaican forests.[172] The "northward" trade ran smoothly and without much comment. In 1774, however, with trouble looming between Britain and the North American colonies, Taylor told Arcedeckne he had decided to take "the first good opportunity to get as many staves as will last you two years".[173] By June 1775 Taylor had purchased fifty thousand white oak staves and heading to make puncheons, and twenty thousand for hogsheads, enough for the next two years. Kelly was instructed on no account to lend out any staves to other estates. Taylor also bought tar. It was impossible to get lamp oil, he said, "but we can plant oil nuts". In December, Taylor reported securing from Philadelphia forty barrels of flour and "a parcel of lumber" for Golden Grove.[174]

Apart from the sugar, rum and molasses, Golden Grove's local trade was limited. In 1766 the estate sold seventy-eight hundred plantains, some empty puncheons, some livestock ("of the Estate and Batchelors Hall Pen") and some cloth (osnaburg and blanket). It also hired out some of the plantation's enslaved workers. The total income for 1766, as recorded in the crop account, was £15,249, only 3 per cent of the amount coming from items other than sugar and rum.[175] The pattern was much the same in 1767 but, because the crop was down, total income was estimated at £9,193, only marginally more than one-half the return in 1766.[176]

It was overseas trade that occupied most of Taylor's correspondence. His very first letter to Arcedeckne, dated 26 March 1765 and written from Kingston, began with the business of shipping. Taylor reported sending to the London factors Hilton and Biscoe, by convoy, invoices listing the individual weights of hogsheads of sugar shipped on two separate merchant vessels, the *Morant* under Captain Raffles and the *Brilliant* under Captain Millar. In addition to these invoices, Taylor supplied the bills of lading and asked Arcedeckne to obtain insurance coverage for the sugar through Hilton and Biscoe. Taylor and his merchant partner Robert Graham had sent the same advice independently, to ensure the orders got through. A third ship was on its way, the *Kingston* under Captain Ellis, with more sugar, and Taylor recommended obtaining insurance on this cargo also, in advance of the bills of lading.[177] Advices of this sort were the regular business of Taylor's correspondence during crop season.

On occasion, Taylor heard directly from Hilton and Biscoe, when they reported on the arrival of shipments and on the quality of the sugar received. In 1765, for example, they complained that the sugar had been shipped too green, resulting in a large proportion of "foot" in the bottoms of the hogsheads. Taylor expressed surprise at this but promised in future to cure them an additional six weeks before shipping.[178] Beginning in 1767 Arcedeckne agreed to have his sugar consigned direct to his brother-in-law Benjamin Cowell, who could then send the bills of lading to any merchant house he chose, cutting the link with Hilton and Biscoe. In 1768 the sugar was consigned to Beeston Long and Company.[179] In 1770, when Arcedeckne again left England for France, he ordered that his letters and accounts be sent to Long Drake and Long, the latest configuration of the firm of sugar factors and commission agents established by Beeston Long. Arcedeckne's bills of lading and requests for supplies went to Cowell.[180] Long Drake and Long retained their authority to 1775, when the published correspondence concludes. The firm was responsible for honouring bills of exchange drawn on Arcedeckne, most of them at ninety days' sight, and transmitted by Taylor as attorney.[181]

All of Golden Grove's sugar seems to have been shipped to London rather than any of the English outports. In October 1769 Taylor reported that he wished to ship more sugar but could find no ship for London either in Kingston or "at windward". Ship captains might alter their destinations to match the market. "One Edwards intended to go for London," wrote Taylor, "but found he could not get a load so changed his intentions to go to Bristol."[182] The lack of ships for London sometimes meant long delays and, once the hurricane-insurance period had begun in August, sugar might have to wait until February or March the following year when the shipping returned in quantity for the new crop.[183]

Although Taylor lacked knowledge of short-term movements in London sugar prices, he felt able to recommend not selling quickly in situations where it seemed the total product of Jamaica would fall short and so put upward pressure on the market. This was advice based on the collection of information from planters' expectations across the island. Some of Golden Grove's sugar was sold in the Jamaican market at good prices. When the crops were short, however, as in 1768, he exported every single cask.[184] Taylor also gleaned information about production levels in the other colonies of the British West Indies, well aware of the significance of competition in determining prices in the metropolitan markets. In 1765, reporting good prices in Kingston, he told Arcedeckne, "I apprehend also that sugar will rise with you as we hear here the crops in the Windward Islands are fallen very short."[185] The notion that it was a profitable strategy to hold sugar back from the market in hopes of future increases in price may have appealed to Taylor, and perhaps Arcedeckne, but it was counter to the instincts of the metropolitan commission agents who wished to clear their accounts as quickly as possible.[186]

The sugar produced by Golden Grove could be shipped most easily either from the wharves of Port Morant or the mouth of the Plantain Garden River (Figure 7.2). Taylor preferred the latter, since it saved the cost of overland carriage, but found ship captains reluctant to send for it there. Later, in 1802, Lady Nugent claimed there was "a good harbour at Rocky Point, for vessels to come up and take the sugars from the several estates, which are carried down Plantain-Garden River in boats".[187] Taylor tried hard to make this a condition of access to the sugar under his control. Hence his interest in the river-mouth land and access to canal routes through Duckenfield. Manchioneal, to the north, was also a shipping port but rarely used by Golden Grove because of the high cost of cartage over land. By 1769, when shipping was more plentiful, Taylor felt able to insist on ships collecting Golden Grove's sugar from the mouth of the Plantain Garden River at their expense. In 1770 Golden Grove built its own wharf at the river's mouth, so avoiding wharfinger charges.[188]

In theory, Taylor was fully responsible for the choice of vessels and captains on which to ship Golden Grove's sugar, but his power was occasionally challenged. Such challenge generally came from the overseer Kelly, on his way to obtaining his own power of attorney from Arcedeckne, and distinguishing himself as planting attorney from the mercantile Taylor. Although Taylor saw himself as much more of a generalist, with authority in all areas of planting as well as trading, he certainly thought his knowledge of commerce and shipping was superior to Kelly's. Worse, not knowing what Kelly was doing had its hazards. Thus, when in June 1769 Taylor found that Kelly had put thirty hogsheads on the *Morant Planter* under Captain Walter Power, Taylor told Cowell, "I did not intend to have shipped on him so soon which made me not write for insurance." Kelly sent the bill of lading direct to Cowell. What Taylor said to Kelly is not recorded. Kelly effectively stretched his authority from time to time with apparent impunity, but in this case Taylor was certainly not happy.[189] In April 1770 Taylor noted that he was unable to supply the weights of hogsheads shipped, though he had the bills of lading, saying Kelly had not supplied them. "As I doubt not but that Mr. Kelly will inform you of every thing relating to the estate," Taylor told Arcedeckne, "shall leave that to him."[190]

The development of this parallel correspondence obviously irked. Later in 1770, Taylor noted he had not even the bills of lading for some shipments and expected Kelly to send them direct to Arcedeckne, along with news of the estate. In July 1771 Taylor wrote, "We are now at work putting every thing in order for the next crop but as Mr. Kelly will no doubt write you every thing regarding the estate anything I say will only be a repetition of what he says."[191] Here Taylor may have expressed petulance or perhaps a confession that he had little to add to what Kelly could say about activities on the ground. When Taylor asked Kelly to send him a list of provisions needed for 1767, Kelly chose to send the request direct to Arcedeckne. Taylor let it pass and the practice became normal. On the other hand, when Kelly wanted to buy mules he asked Taylor and the attorney took on the task of finding a dozen creole animals.[192]

In managing risk, the choice whether or not to take insurance was always the province of the proprietor or commission agent. The responsibility of the attorney (or overseer) was simply to provide advice on the ships used, their captains and cargoes. At first Taylor generally told Arcedeckne directly, "You will be pleased to order the necessary insurance."[193] Sometimes he went further, recommending the security of insurance over the risk of substantial loss. He had his own interest in seeing the produce reached market. The risk might, however, be balanced against the cost of the insurance. For example, in September 1765, Taylor told Arcedeckne, "I entirely agree with you in making insurance it being so low and not worth running the risk of £1000 or 1500 for the sake of 3 per cent."[194] In some cases, the sugar was insured but not the rum.[195]

Taylor's advice on insurance was not always taken and gradually he became less insistent on the need. In part, his withdrawal reflected the way in which the reporting of shipping had shifted to Kelly. Thus in March 1775, when recording the names of ships, captains and cargoes, Taylor told Arcedeckne explicitly, "If you please to insure you may."[196] But when Taylor wrote again that September he said he was "glad to hear that you got and are pleased at my advice for insurance". It was just as well it had been taken, Taylor commented, as he had reports of the loss of the *Port Morant* "and I see by a letter from Messrs. Long Drake and Long to Mr. Kelly that you was insured which I am very glad".[197] Taylor promised to give "regular advice to insure or not as you please". With irony, he added that he was pleased "also to hear that you have made money by not having advice to insure".[198]

Risk could be managed by taking a chance on insurance. It could be reduced by choosing carefully the ships on which to send cargo and using reliable captains, and it could be spread by limiting the quantity of produce committed to a single vessel. As attorney, Taylor had only limited capacity in making these choices. He lacked full knowledge of all the variables that might affect the outcome, and he was pushed in different directions by proprietor, overseer and commission agent. Occasionally, Arcedeckne himself asked Taylor to ship with particular captains, and he complied.[199] At the beginning of 1775 he advised Arcedeckne to insure sugar sent by the *Morant Bay* under Captain Farr, saying, "I would not have put any on board her but you some years ago recommended him to me, not that I have the least disregard to the man but on the contrary a very great regard and esteem as being a very worthy honest good man, but I cannot say so much for his ship."[200]

An alternative to dependence on unreliable ships and incompetent captains was to invest directly in a vessel. Late in 1765 Taylor told Arcedeckne that a Captain Chisholm, brother of Malcolm Laing, planned to get a ship based in Morant Bay and sought partners in the venture. Taylor agreed to take a one-eighth share and encouraged Arcedeckne to participate, as "a very particular act of friendship". The advantage, said Taylor, was that the ship "would always be able to bring out all our provisions and perhaps some other freight which would load her out and she could always be dispatched to sail from hence the beginning of May". Arcedeckne took up a share.[201] It proved an investment with complications.

One hazard of owning a vessel was the temptation to ship large quantities of the plantation's produce on it, thus concentrating the risk of loss in a disaster. In April 1768 Taylor told Cowell he was waiting on the arrival of Chisholm and the *Golden Grove,* planning to ship one hundred hogsheads with him if the space was available. Normally, the hazards of shipping were spread by sending smaller consignments, and Taylor commented that "I would not willingly put so many on board of one vessel without he was pushed which I hope will not be the case". On the other hand, he told Cowell,

> Neither can I before he arrives give any promises to the other captains to ship on them for as Mr. Arcedeckne is concerned in that ship I would not by any means let her sail otherwise than full as the parish will fall short in the quantity of sugars and there are more ships this year at the Bay and Harbour [Morant Bay and Port Morant] than ever were before.[202]

Taylor had a more direct interest, of course, holding his own share in the venture. When the *Golden Grove* arrived, Taylor agreed to ship 80 hogsheads, the remainder to go on other vessels in lots as small as 20. In the end, Taylor reported in July, he sent 120 hogsheads of Golden Grove sugar with Chisholm. Twenty went on the *Morant Planter.* Taylor had hoped to ship another 30 on that vessel "but was prevented by three weeks excessive blowing weather so that no vessel could go in or come out of Plantain Garden River and when that ceased there was no vessel to be got on any account". Because of this, said Taylor, "I was obliged to order the last forty hogsheads to fill up the *Golden Grove* to be wained to Port Morant."[203]

After the *Golden Grove* had sailed and in the period when the threat of hurricane doubled insurance rates, Taylor reported to Cowell in September 1768 that a Captain Scrymsour had "shut out the remainder" of the Golden Grove crop, even though "we offered to wain them to Port Morant for him". Taylor noted, with appropriate acerbity, "We must remember him for another time." An alternative was to send the remainder of the hogsheads by the *York,* "but as she is an old New England built vessel and this is the most stormy time for a vessel to sail for Europe", Taylor declined. He next attempted to bring the hogsheads from Port Morant to Kingston by sugar drogger but these boats were scarce.[204] Droggers were small sailing vessels, capable of carrying cargoes from point to point around the coast, and, because they were equipped sufficiently well to travel further and were often manned by enslaved people, had to enter bonds before leaving port.[205] The lack of droggers led Taylor to ask a question of Cowell: "I should be glad to know if you would approve of my purchasing a small vessel for the use of the estate and buy sailor Negroes for her." Such an investment might not make much money, he admitted, but "it would be a means of never being disappointed as we could bring the sugars to the ships and save that freight and also send up in her whatever the estate wanted". Apparently, Taylor thought such a vessel might travel as far as Kingston. Taylor reminded Cowell that "until the war there was always a vessel kept by the estate which was then taken and since that time never had one".[206]

At the beginning of 1769 Taylor noted that no mention had been received of the arrival in England of Captain Chisholm or the *Golden Grove* and that everyone in Jamaica had assumed them lost at sea, together with the 120 hogsheads of Golden Grove sugar. Cowell had at least insured the original 80 hogsheads and Taylor hoped he had acted on the additional 40. If the *Golden Grove* was indeed sunk, which it proved to be, it was "exceeding unlucky", reflected Taylor. He hoped Arcedeckne had insured his eighth share in the ship but had himself "relied so much on her goodness that did not insure mine". On the other hand, they had been lucky in choosing not to send sugar on the *York,* since, in order to prevent sinking, that ship had been run ashore off Charleston, South Carolina, and every cask lost.[207] Arcedeckne eventually wrote from Florence, saying he had insurance of sixteen hundred pounds sterling on the *Golden Grove,* but directed Taylor never to ship more than 50 hogsheads on a single vessel. Taylor agreed, noting that the hogsheads they were using were large ones and asking Arcedeckne if he would like them made larger still.[208] Doing so, of course, meant more sugar committed to a single ship, but it was equally an economy in labour and in staves.

Some years later, at the beginning of 1773, Taylor expressed pleasure that Arcedeckne "intended sending another shallop out".[209] But by July the shallop, a small sailing boat, was wrecked on the east end of the island on its return from Port Morant, only the rigging, sails and anchors being saved. Another shallop employed by Golden Grove and Duckenfield Hall was lost with sugar in 1775, when the wind suddenly died away while negotiating the channel between the reefs at the mouth of the Plantain Garden River.[210]

Book-keeping

The most vital account, required of the attorney by both proprietor and state, was the crop account. Taylor's first crop account for Golden Grove covered the period from 20 February 1765 to 31 December 1765. It was sworn by Taylor on 23 March 1766 and entered by a clerk into the fourth liber (volume) of the island secretary's series of accounts produce on 21 April 1766. Taylor paid a fee of twenty-one shillings for the entry.[211] The prelude followed a standard formula:

> An account of the produce of Golden Grove Plantation in the parish of St. Thomas in the East belonging to Chaloner Arcedeckne Esquire according as the same came to the hands or knowledge of Simon Taylor one of the attorneys of the said Chaloner Arcedeckne Esquire from the 20th day of February 1765 to the thirty first day of December 1765.

At the end of the document, following the statement of accounts, came a formal "memorandum" stating:

> Personally appeared before me Simon Taylor of the parish of Kingston attorney to Chaloner Arcedecon Esquire on this 23 day of March one thousand seven hundred and sixty-six and made oath on the Holy Evangelists of Almighty God that to the best of his knowledge information and belief the account above written is a true and just account of the profits and produce of the above mentioned plantation called Golden Grove that did come to the knowledge and possession of him the said Simon Taylor attorney to Chaloner Arcedeckne Esquire for the time above specified and further this deponent saith not.

At the bottom of the account came the signatures of James Dawes, representing the island secretary, and Simon Taylor.

Between the prelude and the swearing came a statement of the disposal of the estate's output, beginning with the sugar. Most crop accounts, including later accounts for Golden Grove, listed the individual cargoes shipped. That for 1765 gave only totals. Some 297 hogsheads had been shipped, containing 482,632 pounds of sugar. The 1765 account was also unusual in providing a "valuation" of the shipment, £7,386 10s 6½d, presumably currency rather than sterling. Taylor, of course, could not know exactly how much the sugar would fetch when sold in London but the "valuation" gave him a number to use in planning and in the calculation of his commission. It was based on an average of 3.67d per pound, though this was not stated in the account and individual hogsheads would have contained sugars of different qualities and colours that commanded different prices. Nor did the account give the average weight of the hogsheads (1,625 pounds), though Taylor was well aware of the difference between typical and "heavy" hogsheads, and these were on the heavy end of the scale.[212] The hogsheads shipped by Golden Grove would have varied individually, according to the availability of staves and hoops, variations in cooperage, and differences in packing and drainage.

As well as the sugar shipped by Golden Grove, the crop account for 1765 listed 71 hogsheads and two tierces sold within the island, with a total weight of 120,152 pounds and an actual price of £2,054 16s 3¼d. These locally traded hogsheads were heavier on average (1,669 pounds) than those exported but the sugar was sold for significantly more (4.10d per pound) than the valuation applied to the shipped sugar. Adding together the value of the shipped sugar and the amount sold locally gave a total of £9,441 6s 9¾d. The account also listed a tierce of sugar delivered to Mrs Kearsy (Arcedeckne's mother) for which no price was paid. The final line for sugar in the 1765 crop account stated the total quantity disposed of: 368 hogsheads, three tierces, with a weight of 602,784 pounds.

Rum was listed next. Just 11 puncheons containing 1,100 gallons were shipped, valued at £154. Another 91 puncheons were sold locally, containing 10,351 gallons and bringing in £1,372 16s 10½d. One puncheon of rum was delivered free to Mrs Kearsey. For 11 empty puncheons the estate got £16 10s. The account offered a summary line: 103 puncheons containing 11,451 gallons of rum, worth (including the empty puncheons) £1,543 6s 10½d.

Finally, the Golden Grove crop account for 1765 listed the sale of 29 casks of molasses containing 2,852 gallons for £142 12s. Probably this was sold to a Kingston merchant rather than a North American ship captain. The entire account was then totalled, giving proceeds of £11,127 5s 8¼d. Two-thirds consisted of the hoped-for proceeds from sales in London.

The crop account for 1765 was typical of those produced by Taylor for Golden Grove, and similar to most such accounts. However, no standard format was set and various kinds of information appeared and disappeared. The later accounts for Golden Grove generally covered a complete calendar year. That for 1765 was abbreviated, beginning in February, probably because

Taylor became attorney only after Arcedeckne left Jamaica. The valuation of shipped produce was also somewhat unusual and Taylor gave up the attempt after a time, though he may have made his own private calculations to guess where things were heading. Measures of mass and volume also disappeared, perhaps because these were included initially only in order to estimate value. Rather, the crop accounts produced by Taylor increasingly turned towards identification and tracking, giving the names of the vessels on which sugar and rum were shipped, the names of their captains, and the names of the consignees, together with the numbers of hogsheads and puncheons sent on each ship. In this system, money largely disappeared, finding a place in the accounts only when goods were sold to individuals within Jamaica. Even rum consigned to Kingston merchants was not attributed a money value. As a result, the crop accounts no longer arrived at a money total, and purported to list only the "produce" and "how disposed of" rather than the "profits and produce".[213] The crop accounts had no ability in themselves to measure profit.

Taylor sent annual accounts to Arcedeckne, but the correspondence provides little detail about their contents. On 9 March 1767 he told Arcedeckne,

> I have sent you enclosed your accounts, viz. Golden Grove account your account current and the different accounts regarding Golden Grove that you may know on what accounts the sundry matters were paid to whom and for what, for the way I took that every thing might fully appear so as to be plainly understood and that you might know how your affairs stood and what wages were due.

Lists of slaves were included, with a balance sheet of births and deaths.[214] Taylor sent these accounts promptly. For example, the crop account for 1766 was sent two weeks before the formal swearing of the record in Spanish Town, and there is nothing to suggest discrepancies between the two copies of the account.[215] Arcedeckne did not always receive the complete accounts, however. Those for 1768 were not sent to him while travelling in Europe, "the packet being so large". He was simply given the balances, which went against him, and a brief summary by Cowell.[216]

Major demands, notably the purchase of enslaved workers, were generally handled by Arcedeckne or his metropolitan factors. Occasionally, however, Taylor attempted to pay such accounts directly within Jamaica, using funds in his hands to obtain discounts, rather than drawing on Arcedeckne, but difficulties of communication caused confusion.[217] In 1769 he was "pretty confident" that local sales of sugar and rum would "not only pay the contingencies of both but supply as many Negroes on Golden Grove as it will be prudent to put annually on or am much mistaken".[218] When he purchased slaves directly from slave ships, as he did in late 1765, he sought to delay payment by giving bills at eight months' sight, during which period sugar could be shipped and sold in time to cover the demands when they came due.[219]

In November 1766 Taylor told Arcedeckne, "I am afraid I shall be obliged to draw on you for about £800 this [Jamaican] currency in about three weeks." It was only "greatest necessity" that forced him to do so, said Taylor, knowing Arcedeckne had not "a great deal at home from the weight of the £5000 to your cousin and the supplies you sent out". When he wrote the following January, Taylor acknowledged letters from Arcedeckne "desiring me to pay myself out of any of your effects and not buy any more Negroes until you are out of debt". Taylor scotched the former, saying, "Do not let any matters between you and me give you the least concern for I shall always be happy in endeavouring to serve you and you may assure yourself you can at all times command me to my utmost extent of credit or fortune." In the end, Taylor found himself "absolutely forced" to draw a bill of exchange on Arcedeckne for £500 sterling, to the order of the Kingston merchants Reisset, Jaffray and Yelloly, dated 2 February 1767. He hoped this would not embarrass Arcedeckne, since sugar would reach the London market before the bill became due. Taylor recognized that Arcedeckne had had "immense expenses" but believed these were now behind him and hoped "for the future you will find the sweets of your estate".[220]

Demands on his account persisted, however, and Arcedeckne protested. In March 1768 Taylor told Cowell that he would be "obliged in the course of the crop to draw on you for about £1000 sterling to reimburse myself" but promised to "put it off as long as possible but at any rate will not draw until I ship sugars and not then if I can avoid it".[221] Taylor eventually drew bills for £1,000 at the beginning of July, when the sugar crop was being shipped, at ninety days sight.[222] Later, Arcedeckne complained that this proved an inconvenience, and Taylor responded that if he had known it would have "straightened you in the least would have put myself to any inconvenience rather than subject you to any, for I assure you there is nothing in my power but would do to serve you at all times and at all seasons".[223] In this way, Taylor reinforced his status as an equal, indeed a man possessed of superior resources, rather than a mere servant as attorney.

Arcedeckne was plagued by demands arising from his father's estate. In March 1768 Taylor wrote saying, "They are brought to this conclusion that I do not know of any debt now whatsoever that is due from your father's estate in the world or by you what is due to us."[224] This proved too optimistic a view, however, and in July, Taylor commented, "What you say is very just that Golden Grove has been a fund for paying of other peoples debts but am much afraid that the generality of those people or their representatives have nothing to refund." In the same letter, Taylor told Arcedeckne he owed £4,000 currency on his, Taylor's, account, but assured him the amount would be reduced in the future with no new building projects planned.[225] At the beginning of 1769, Taylor reported further demands resulting from mortgaged properties brought to market following the death of men with whom Arcedeckne's father had stood security. Taylor commented, "The old gentleman was very unlucky, almost every one he was security for deceived him and left him to pay their debts."[226] These continued to descend to the son. Arcedeckne, and Taylor, must have felt these unexpected demands made planning difficult by adding yet another layer of uncertainty.

Predicting and Planning

Taylor frequently mixed reports of current progress with thoughts on future prospects, but was well aware of the unpredictability of outcomes. In the short term, the weather was the most unreliable factor. On 16 April 1765, for example, he told Arcedeckne that he had spent three days at Golden Grove and "you are making as fine sugars there as it is possible for sugar to be and you will make a very fine crop in case the dry weather continues". Overall, "every thing in my opinion is in very good order and your Negroes happy".[227] A week later he wrote again, reporting that a "dismal flood of rain . . . has played the devil with almost all the estates in this parish". Taylor went to Golden Grove and prepared an on-the-spot report. "It is a very great loss to you," he told Arcedeckne, "for you had the appearance a fortnight ago of making the largest crop that was made from one estate in this island."[228] Taylor meant by this an output of 500 or more hogsheads of sugar. In the end, only 368 hogsheads were made and 110 puncheons of rum.[229]

Following this disappointment, Taylor was cautious of predicting the crop of 1766. The works were under repair and the weather uncertain. In November 1765, with the crop soon to commence, Taylor said only that he "never saw an estate in finer order" and was perhaps surprised by the actual production of 472 hogsheads of sugar (averaging 1,652 pounds per hogshead) and 198 puncheons of rum.[230] With the new and repaired works in place, he told Arcedeckne in November 1766, "you have now a set of the best works in the West Indies and capable of making you 800 hogsheads".[231] Taylor forecast 400 to 450 hogsheads for the coming crop. However, floods again affected the canes and undermined "the best mill".[232] Once more his prediction fell short and the crop of 1767 was absolutely down on the previous two years of Taylor's management, amounting to just 327 hogsheads of sugar and 126 puncheons of rum.[233] In 1768 the crop was even less at only 249 hogsheads. Taylor attributed this relative failure mainly to the weather, but looking forward to 1769 reported that "Kelly informs me that there is now the best appearance of a good crop that he has seen since he has been on the estate and we have had very good weather for sometime past".[234]

The beginning of 1769 brought a stocktaking and reassessment of the state of Golden Grove and its future profitability. Arcedeckne, aged twenty-six, was travelling in Europe, living a life of leisure. He had been out of Jamaica for four years, in possession of Golden Grove and settling his inheritance. Taylor, in his twenty-ninth year, was busy establishing his personal fortune, engaged in many ventures other than his attorneyship of Golden Grove. Kelly the overseer continued in place, having sold most of his jobbing gang to Arcedeckne, the enslaved workers now employed full-time on Golden Grove. A handful of other white men lived on the plantation, as book-keepers and tradesmen, rarely mentioned by name in Taylor's correspondence with Arcedeckne.[235] The 360 to 370 enslaved people were an equally unstable demographic group, a large proportion of them born in Africa, suffering heavy mortality and driven to the edge by the physical demands made on their labour. Taylor thought their number less than necessary for a productive estate.

On 27 January 1769 Taylor wrote from Kingston, responding to the most recent letter he had received from Arcedeckne. It was one of the longest and most systematic and reflective of Taylor's communications. Arcedeckne, writing from Venice on 2 August 1768, had noted the existing balance against him and hoped for better returns now that the "most considerable buildings" had been completed. "This is what I think you have the greatest right to expect," replied Taylor, "for you have been at a very great expense in your works and can assure you that nothing has been done to them more than was necessary." Nothing had been done extravagantly,

> but if you consider the low condition of the estate when you got possession of it, the expenses attending your law suit, the building of a new set of works, the demands against your fathers estate and the compromise at home, you will readily conceive how the crops have been disposed of which also from the very great and constant and uncommon severity of the rains have been less than might be expected not to say any thing of the two great floods which happened in that space of time.

The major expenditure for which Taylor held responsibility was the construction of the works but in this he had no choice he said, commenting, "Indeed had you on getting possession of the estate been £100,000 in debt you must either have built a set or thrown up the estate."[236]

Taylor, like most planters in the decade before the American Revolution, balanced an ever-present fear of slave rebellion against a long-term faith in the impregnability of the system, believing they inhabited a world in which slavery, mercantilism and privilege were secure for many generations. The works buildings were simply the most concrete evidence of this faith. Thus Taylor could tell Arcedeckne his sugar works at Golden Grove were "now built in a manner for ever provided no accident of fire etc, which God forbid should ever happen". With good weather and good crops in prospect, Taylor hoped all of this would put Arcedeckne "in good heart and spirits and also put you in mind of purchasing some Negroes as I hope it will do away your present objections". For the future, Arcedeckne could expect "a very large income coming in annually". There was no reason for him to cut back on his expenditure, said Taylor. "You have now chiefly to reap the advantage of your estate . . . and you can afford to live any where you choose yourself without renting it."[237]

In August 1769 Arcedeckne wrote from France, happy that his debt was lessened but concerned that the last crop had made only one thousand pounds and anxious to reduce the contingencies which consumed almost all of his produce. Taylor recited the difficulties of weather and disease but ultimately sheeted home the blame to a lack of labour power and resulting shortage of tradesmen and the necessity of hiring. Taylor pushed Arcedeckne to invest. For the long run he encouraged Arcedeckne to think of building a second set of works on the existing land of Golden Grove or establishing or buying a second property but, since this seemed unlikely, Taylor emphasized the need for an adequate force of enslaved people to enable reliable production projections. "You may depend on it I have always done, and always will do every thing in my power to serve you, and augment your property," said Taylor, "which I should have more improved had Negroes been put on as I recommended."[238] Thus the fault was Arcedeckne's, for timidity in investing and failing to accept the advice of his attorney.

The declining production experienced in the years 1767 and 1768 was turned around in 1769, with a crop of more than 350 hogsheads. Taylor wrote to Arcedeckne at the end of February 1770, saying the "impediment" to his marrying was now removed, with the prospect of 600 hogsheads in 1770, "so you will have money enough to make settlement on your wife and also on younger children".[239] In fact, the crop of 1770 finished at 630 hogsheads, exceeding Taylor's forecast, and "more than any estate ever yet made in this island".[240] In 1774 the Golden Grove crop was almost as much, 628 hogsheads.[241] In 1775 it reached 740 hogsheads, "the most extraordinary crop that ever was made on any one estate in Jamaica".[242] Although London sugar prices were down somewhat in 1775, Arcedeckne must have achieved gross receipts of close to fourteen thousand pounds sterling.[243]

The extraordinary output of 1775 marked a high point for planter and attorney, bringing the published letters of Simon Taylor to an optimistic close. Although Taylor was aware of the political trouble brewing in the Old Empire to the north, he devoted relatively little of his correspondence to the coming conflict.[244] By the middle of 1775, Taylor told Arcedeckne he found the dispute between Britain and the North American colonies "truly alarming" and unlikely to be settled without "a great deal of bloodshed". Probably the rebel colonies could be forced to submit, if confined to trade with Britain and the West Indian colonies, thought Taylor, but "wherever there is profit to be got there the Americans will send vessels". As to Jamaica, he believed the island could "do tolerable well without America" and hoped that "good will arise from evil". Jamaica had "land enough for provisions lumber etc.", and although the prices might prove higher there was the advantage that "the money that used to be paid to the Americans will rest among us and not be carried to Hispaniola to purchase sugar molasses and coffee there to smuggle into America to the ruin of our colonies". Taylor interpreted the revenue acts of which the Americans complained as designed to control their smuggling trade. On the other hand, he did favour caution on the purchase of new enslaved Africans until the impact of the "American disputes" became clearer.[245]

In December 1775, with the American War of Independence looming, Taylor was boldly predicting there need be no fear of a shortage of food supply. "Do not be afraid of wanting provisions for your Negroes," he told Arcedeckne, "I have constantly resided in Jamaica near 16 years and when there has been no hurricane know we can supply ourselves with provisions if we will but plant them."[246] He was wrong on this. The war, the associated trade embargoes, together with a string of hurricanes, resulted in widespread shortages and at least fifteen thousand deaths by starvation.[247] This experience gave the supply of food a much higher priority as a problem of management.

The decades following 1776 confronted Taylor and Arcedeckne with unexpected challenges. Taylor's faith in the permanence of the system in all its details was shaken. The reduction of shipping and the hazards of wartime threatened not only food supplies but also the export of sugar and rum and the Atlantic trade in enslaved people. Golden Grove's output remained substantial during and after the American Revolution but at much reduced levels.[248] Prices improved. In 1781 Taylor declared the American war threatened "everlasting ruin" to the whole of the British Empire, and he contemplated leaving Jamaica for some place where he would "not be held in Egyptian bondage". He complained of the sugar duties imposed by Parliament and the lack of military protection but was won round by Rodney's victory in 1782.[249]

For Golden Grove the consequence was that Taylor, consumed by the military and governmental issues of the moment, gave less time and thought to his role as attorney and thus provided the opportunity for the overseer Kelly to infringe even further on his authority. He and Hayward were dismissed in 1782.[250] Soon after, Taylor applied a new strategy to the expansion of the enslaved labour force. He maintained his belief in the need for a larger number of workers but began to advocate the virtues of "breeding" and the benefits to be gained by purchasing larger proportions of women. As always, Taylor had his eye to the longer term. He attacked the anti-slavery movement with a vengeance but took what he saw as practical steps to cope with the challenges to management of land and labour. He attempted both to increase fertility and reduce infant mortality.[251] Although the tendency was in this direction, the gap between deaths and births continued at Golden Grove down to the end of slavery.

Chaloner Arcedeckne died in 1809. His will provided that the profits of Golden Grove should be applied by his heirs to "annually purchase 50 Negro slaves or such other less number as might be necessary for the cultivation and working of the said plantation called Golden Grove always purchasing not less than 15 in number at any time".[252] This injunction sounded very much like the strategy advocated by Simon Taylor forty years before, but how it was to be carried through in the shadow of the abolition of the Atlantic trade in people remained to be seen. Having in mind the various possible options for Golden Grove, Arcedeckne instructed his trustees (one of whom was Simon Taylor) that in the event of the sale of the estate they were to invest the proceeds in property in Suffolk, the county in which he lived as absentee, or in the short term to purchase English public stocks or securities. It was the ultimate escape route for absentee capital and the strategy Taylor himself was soon to follow, transferring his wealth to the "home" which he claimed was not his place, in the months before his death in 1813.[253]

At the final registration of slaves, taken in 1832, Golden Grove and Batchelors Hall belonged to Andrew Arcedeckne, born 1780, son of the absentee and reluctant groom Chaloner. Andrew was Sheriff of Suffolk in 1819, and elected to represent the borough of Dunwich in the House of Commons in 1826 and 1830, when he was counted one of the West Indian interest or lobby, the defenders of slavery. In 1816 he married his first cousin Harriet, daughter of Francis Love Beckford, the absentee owner of Petersfield and Lincoln Estates in Westmoreland.[254]

Whereas Chaloner finally took Taylor's advice to marry, sometime between 1776 and 1780, he only partially followed his investment strategy. Neither Chaloner nor his son Andrew appear to have expanded their holdings of Jamaican property, owning the same estate and pen at the end of slavery as inherited from the elder Andrew seventy years before, in 1763.[255] They had, however, increased substantially the number of enslaved people on the properties. In 1832 there were 640 at Golden Grove and 122 at Batchelors Hall, and it is certain that, at least on the estate, the numbers had been significantly larger in the 1820s. The long-term growth did not result from natural increase, in spite of Arcedeckne's enthusiasm, but derived largely from purchases.[256] Taylor would have approved of this expansion of the enslaved labour force. Measured in hogsheads of sugar, the crop of 1832 amounted only to approximately 557 units, well down on the peak of the 1770s, when the enslaved population had been much less and Taylor saw the people pushed to the point of death.[257]

Assessment

How efficient and effective an attorney was Simon Taylor? His task at Golden Grove in the decade before the American Revolution was to manage a vicious system of labour exploitation and to extract the greatest possible product from the enslaved people forced to live and work on the estate. In terms of achieving that goal, he had almost everything in his favour, and he was successful. Output was brought to a maximum and the flow of profits to Chaloner Arcedeckne enabled him to live the life of a successful absentee. Neither Taylor nor Arcedeckne questioned the morality of their enterprise and pondered the harshness of the system only when there were implications for potential profits.

How powerful was Taylor? His employer held ultimate responsibility, and Taylor's first duty was to satisfy him. Failure to do so would have meant dismissal. Ensuring the satisfaction of Arcedeckne could, however, be approached in two distinct ways. On the one hand, Taylor could agree with everything Arcedeckne recommended and follow his directives to the letter. On the other, Taylor could seek to achieve satisfaction through production and profits. After all, the granting of power of attorney was intended to give full authority to the attorney to employ the resources of the proprietor to the greatest effect. Taylor employed both of these strategies, shifting from one to the other from time to time to keep Arcedeckne both happy and rich. Since Golden Grove was one of Taylor's first appointments as attorney he must have been determined to hold on to the post, partly for his own immediate financial benefit and partly to increase his own reputation as an effective attorney worthy of further responsibilities. Thus he was pulled between his desire to satisfy Arcedeckne and what he saw as the immediate management needs of Golden Grove. This tension inhibited Taylor's ability to follow what he saw as the most profitable strategies of investment and management.

As well as taking directions from Arcedeckne, Taylor had to work with two, sometimes four, other attorneys. He consulted with them on major investment questions. He seems to have had no great difficulty convincing Arcedeckne's mother and aunt of the force of his own arguments. He did nothing to discourage Arcedeckne's mother using her own money to cover the debts of her son or to stop her gifting him with enslaved workers for Golden Grove. Her acts of generosity often followed Taylor's recital of the difficulties faced by son and plantation. Malcolm Laing seems also to have been easily enough brought on side, though there was some falling out when Taylor suspected conflict of interest in the river-mouth land dispute with Thomas Cussans.

Working with John Kelly as overseer of Golden Grove proved much more difficult. Kelly gradually increased his areas of authority and eventually received power of attorney from Arcedeckne. Taylor resisted and complained of some of the ways in which Kelly took responsibilities normally assigned to the attorney, particularly in the areas of trade and shipping, but generally compromised. He did so partly because the functions of the planting attorney were still being worked out in the 1760s, partly because he had a growing portfolio of interests as attorney and as proprietor, and partly because distance made it difficult to control all the practicalities from Kingston or even Lyssons. Kelly himself became attorney for the neighbouring property Duckenfield Hall, no doubt partly on the basis of his success at Golden Grove, going further in making himself a competitor with Taylor.

Critics of absenteeism and attorneyship commonly identified a number of essential flaws in the theory and practice of the system, and pointed to failures of the typical attorney that effectively robbed the proprietor. The implicit contention is that resident proprietors, doing their own managing, would have made even greater profits both for themselves and for the island economy. The main elements of the argument relate to the qualifications and expertise of the attorneys, the frequency of their visits to the estates for which they were responsible, their practice of fraud and collusion, their manipulation of accounts, their failure to communicate, and their concern for the short term and the immediate pushing of profits.

How well did Taylor perform against these critical criteria? His correspondence shows a man well informed about the basic elements of plantation agriculture, based on his personal experience over an extended period. In 1775 he was still only thirty-five years of age but he had spent almost all of those years in Jamaica and the making of money, sugar and trade was his core business. If he advised Arcedeckne badly on any point it is not obvious that it held back profits. He travelled frequently through the southeastern corner of the island, observing numerous estates in different situations. He visited Golden Grove at least five or six times a year, sometimes staying for three nights. He knew the territory. Whether he defrauded Arcedeckne is harder to say. Perhaps he was so well recompensed that he had no need to bother. Taylor's acquisition of Holland was funded in part by the commission he earned and he had in any case his own plantations and his own merchant-house that directly fed his capital accumulation. He thought Arcedeckne lacked nerve in failing to purchase further estates and indeed did everything he could to encourage his employer to invest in land and enslaved people. It would seem far easier to build a case that Kelly the overseer drained funds from his employer. Taylor, as attorney, with his own personal fortune, had little need to collude with Kelly or manipulate the accounts of Golden Grove to his own benefit. He acted decisively in defending Arcedeckne's inheritance and the boundaries and water rights of Golden Grove. Taylor wrote quite often, certainly more often than Arcedeckne. Taylor was assiduous in transmitting accounts and did his best to ensure Arcedeckne's shipments were not exposed to risk. It was the proprietor rather than the attorney who seemed willing to take his chance on the high seas. As to the pushing of profits, people and production, it was Taylor who thought Golden Grove needed to be managed with an eye to the long term. Indeed, he criticized Arcedeckne for failures to see the consequences of his unwillingness to invest in the future.

Between 1765 and 1775 Golden Grove's production of sugar doubled. This massive increase, admittedly erratic and unsustained, was not matched by a doubling of the enslaved labour force. Nor was the area under cane increased more than marginally. How was it achieved? In part, it came from the hard-working and physical oppression of the enslaved, the purchase of people, and from hiring. It came also from the construction and maintenance of mills capable of dealing with the heavy throughput of canes, and ensuring a sufficient flow of water to drive them efficiently. Having in place numbers of livestock capable of moving the canes to the mill and waining the finished products to port was equally important. Maintaining a balance between plant canes and ratoons, and planning the spatial organization of cultivation and harvest contributed to high yields. In terms of management, the vital element lay in the coordination and manipulation of the complex. Golden Grove was a large enterprise, demanding a careful balancing and combining of technologies. Having in place a mill capable of producing eight hundred hogsheads was one thing; approaching that high level of output required management as well as hard driving.

How far was Taylor responsible for the success of Golden Grove as a productive estate? He had a coherent and dynamic vision of plantation management and investment. He set it out clearly enough and in sufficient detail for Arcedeckne to appreciate the plan and its potential mode of execution. In the broadest terms, Taylor advocated a policy of profit maximization, and of following a strategy of investment for the long term, based on expanded resources of land, works and labour. Within the existing bounds of Golden Grove, as inherited by Arcedeckne, Taylor promoted the building of works of increased capacity, the establishment of a second set of works, and a larger labour force of enslaved workers. This strategy began with a fixed area of land, a fixed proportion of potential cane land, and a somewhat less certain water resource. In order to maximize the exploitation of these resources, it followed that works should be constructed capable of processing the full quantity of cane the land could produce.

Economies of scale existed in the sugar factory but Taylor said nothing of them. In proposing the establishment of a second set of works on Golden Grove, however, he suggested the existing rebuilt complex, with a projected capacity of eight to nine hundred hogsheads, had reached an upper limit. Proposing a second works site also suggests an understanding of the costs of movement of people and of carts across the often muddy surfaces of the alluvial lands. Taylor talked explicitly of these advantages when discussing the movements of Kelly's jobbing gang. The practical principles of movement-minimization were well enough understood by contemporary planters, even if they had not made them part of a theory of space economy.[258]

In addition to these constraints of scale and movement, the sugar factories of the 1760s and 1770s were limited by their capacity to source and exploit the power needed to turn their mills. At Golden Grove, Taylor depended on water, though a cattle mill provided backup. Nearby Duckenfield and Holland had functioning windmills as did several other estates along the coast of St Thomas-in-the-East, but Golden Grove was just too flat and too far inland to be able to capture the breeze. Steam power was actively being developed as a means of driving sugar mills but Taylor never mentioned it. In 1766 the Jamaican millwright John Stewart was granted a patent for the invention of a steam-powered mill. It was proved in St Andrew in 1768 and Stewart rewarded by the Assembly. In 1769 Dugald Clark, a free coloured man of St Thomas-in-the-East, was granted a patent for an improved steam mill. It was also the year of James Watt's better-known patent.[259] Steam was soon to become a common source of power on Jamaican sugar estates, and the planters were indeed leading users of Boulton and Watt engines, but in the period to 1775 it was not a viable alternative. In concentrating his energies on the improvement of the water mills of Golden Grove, Taylor was exploiting the best resource available. He also introduced efficiencies to the boiling house and distillery, in materials and scale, but devoted little attention to convincing Arcedeckne of the need to adopt innovations in technology in field or factory. He said nothing of improving soil fertility through manuring, as done elsewhere, perhaps because the fertility of the Golden Grove lands made such concern unnecessary. Perhaps Taylor talked to Kelly about these matters without telling Arcedeckne of their dialogue, or perhaps Kelly told Arcedeckne of such things when he wrote his separate reports.

Taylor's central concern was investment in labour. He never questioned the superiority of enslaved African people as a workforce for Golden Grove. Nor did he wonder about potential alternatives. The period 1765–75 was one in which the principles had long been worked out by the planter class and the system had reached a kind of maturity. Indentured white labourers had effectively disappeared from the fields, with white people confined to employment in the trades and crafts and managerial supervision, including medical practice. The people who performed the hard labour in field and mill, and in transport, were all enslaved. Taylor saw the choices as limited. He promoted the use of enslaved tradesmen, in the place of whites, without much interest in saving deficiency taxes. Golden Grove could control the number of workers it exploited, and decide how many of them should be the property of the planter and how many hired from other owners, but every one of them was to be an enslaved person. In terms of numbers, Taylor repeatedly told Arcedeckne of his assessment that Golden Grove lacked sufficient workers to efficiently carry out all of the tasks of cultivation, processing and transport demanded by the potential level of production made possible by the estate's resources of land, water and works.

Beyond his advocacy of a substantially enlarged workforce composed of enslaved people, Taylor offered few suggestions on ways to increase the productivity of labour. He seems never to have considered the application of the task system, the allocation and measurement of work in terms of quantity and area rather than time. Had he done so, before 1776, he would have been very much ahead of his time. Few planters were experimenting with task work anywhere in the Caribbean, and it was only very slowly applied to sugar production in Jamaica. Taylor, by his silence, seems have been satisfied that the gang system of driven labour was the best he could devise. Certainly he believed the hours of work that could be extracted by this system approached the upper limit. When he compared "Negroes" to gudgeons and capooses, in 1770, he mentioned a regime that would have added up to more than five thousand hours per year in field and factory.[260] This was significantly more than the four thousand hours that became typical of Jamaican plantations by about 1830, following Amelioration and the closing of the Atlantic trade in enslaved people, and more than three times the hours of the modern factory worker.[261] Taylor argued that this regime was too harsh and, by causing heavy mortality, not in the interest of the proprietor. He did not prevent its practice, however, and it was the application of this extreme regime to the "poor wretches" of Golden Grove that produced the great crops of the early 1770s.

Taylor calculated implicit rough ratios of labourers to land, and labourers to product. Other planters did the same. Long, for example, employed the ratios one hogshead of sugar to one slave, one harvestable acre of sugar to one slave, and three plantation acres to one slave.[262] Taylor reminded Arcedeckne that in his father's time the ratio one hogshead to one slave had been respected but that by 1770 it had blown out to 1.3:1, and that the ratio of harvestable acres to slaves had gone to 1.5:1.[263] Taylor demonstrated in this way that Golden Grove was short of labour both to deal with the short-term demands of the crop, with a fixed plant of cane, and deficient for the future in its ability to extend the cultivation. He emphasized to Arcedeckne the possible consequences of pushing the enslaved beyond the bounds of the bearable. He did so not from any fundamental humanitarian concern but rather because he saw it as a costly policy in the longer run, an exhaustion of resources for the sake of immediate returns. Arcedeckne seems to have looked more towards the amount of his annual income. In this case, then, the attorney argued against the proprietor's apparent interest in short-term exploitation, an approach often attributed rather to the attorneys. However, at the same time as he argued for an increased labour force, Taylor did his best to encourage production in the shorter term, not being afraid to hire slaves even when Arcedeckne had explicitly prohibited doing so. What Taylor wanted for Arcedeckne, and for himself, was an enterprise with the largest possible enslaved labour force, the greatest possible resources of land and water, the greatest achievable production and profits. He wanted to be an efficient exploiter, on the largest possible scale.

Chapter 8

Managing Montpelier, 1839–1843

In his management of Montpelier in the years immediately following the abolition of slavery, Isaac Jackson faced a set of challenges very different from those of Simon Taylor at Golden Grove before the American Revolution.[1] It was much harder for Jackson to generate great profits. He lacked the many advantages Taylor possessed. After 1838, new ways of commanding labour had to be sought and new ways of increasing or at least maintaining the productivity of labour. The difference in the labour regime was crucial but it was not the only significant contrast. Montpelier was much larger than Golden Grove, spreading across almost ten thousand acres and incorporating a variety of land types. Rather than a level alluvial plain, Montpelier occupied an upland, interior ecological niche, a polje dissolved from limestone. The cane-pieces were surrounded by high hills, and smaller hillocks and rocky mounds jutted out irregularly. Although there were no persistent struggles over inheritance, boundaries, or rights to water, Montpelier saw new kinds of conflict. The customary rights of the people who had lived in the plantation villages during slavery and their tenure of houses, gardens and grounds became a matters of dispute. This new struggle was internal, centred on the people who lived on the estate rather than on the planter's relatives and neighbours.

Aside from these contrasts, Montpelier and Golden Grove had much in common. Montpelier had a boundary with a major stream, the Great River. The plantation was founded in 1739, just five years after Golden Grove, and the first sugar made in 1746. It was the conclusion of the Maroon War and the "quieting" of the region that led directly to the establishment of sugar at Montpelier, in much the same way that the treaties had encouraged the expansion of sugar-growing on the Plantain Garden River. In 1752 Montpelier became the property of John Ellis, father of Charles Rose Ellis (1771–1845) who lived to be the absentee-proprietor during Jackson's tenure as attorney. John Ellis was born in Jamaica and inherited from his father plantations in St Mary and St Thomas-in-the-Vale. He spent most of his time in St Mary and Spanish Town but visited Montpelier regularly and kept control of its accounts. With his wife, John Ellis sailed from Jamaica in 1782, probably on their way to becoming permanent absentees, but the ship went down. Like Chaloner Arcedeckne, the Jamaica-born Charles Rose Ellis was already at school in England. He definitively became an absentee, not returning to Montpelier until the estate was struck by the rebellion of Christmas 1831. He had been created Lord Seaford in 1826 and played a leading role in representing the West India interest in the British Parliament. Thus the attorneys of Montpelier had to deal with a long-term absentee-proprietor, a creole who had no adult experience of Jamaica's slave society or the making of sugar, a man who bought his way into the English gentry and aristocracy. Seaford knew even less than Arcedeckne the realities of slave society.

Unlike the Plantain Garden River, the Great River was deeply entrenched and unreliable (Figure 8.1). To take water from the Great River to power mills would have been very expensive, requiring lengthy aqueducts. Rather, Montpelier used a spring within the boundary of the estate, which enabled it to avoid disputes with neighbours. However, when John Ellis established a second set of sugar works the water came from a dammed spring on the western side of the Great River, in the parish of Hanover, and crossed the river in an elevated gutter (Figure 8.2). The New Works was established in 1775. Thus John Ellis, with a larger area of potential cane land than that found at Golden Grove, followed the aggressive approach advocated by Simon Taylor. Ellis was overall a more acquisitive planter than Arcedeckne. In 1792 he purchased the neighbouring property, Shettlewood, where the spring was located, and made it a pen to supply the livestock needs of the estate. Whereas Golden Grove and Batchelors Hall were four miles apart, Montpelier and Shettlewood together formed a solid block of territory. No sugar was grown on Shettlewood, the open pastures being composed of "common" grass or planted in Guinea grass. In the years following abolition, Shettlewood was to play a much more important role. This new role was initiated by the rebellion and the reorganization that followed, before Seaford contemplated the inevitability of abolition.

In February 1832 Seaford read in a Jamaican newspaper, then six weeks old, of the great rebellion of the enslaved that had engulfed western Jamaica. A few weeks later he had a letter from his attorney William Miller detailing the destruction at Montpelier and Shettlewood. Miller, like most of the attorneys, attributed the rebellion largely to the activities of Baptist missionaries, and indeed the rebellion came to be known as the Baptist War. Seaford had himself earlier placed on Montpelier a minister of the Church of England, to preach duty to the enslaved, but the teachings of the Baptists proved much more influential and the role of the parsons continued into the

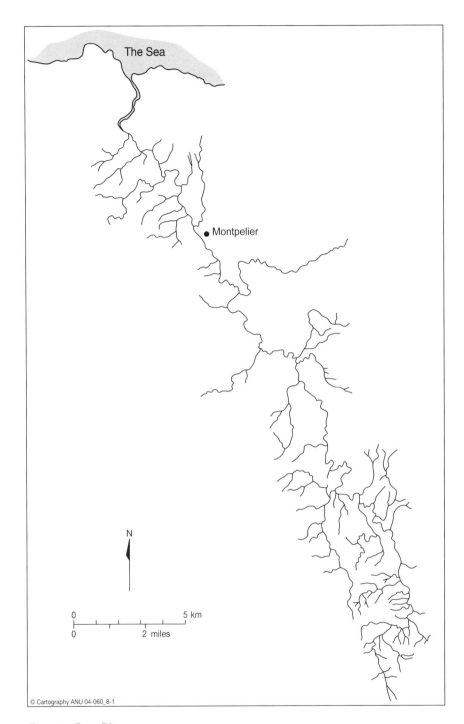

The Sea

Montpelier

N

0   5 km
0   2 miles

© Cartography ANU 04-060_8-1

Figure 8.1 Great River stream net

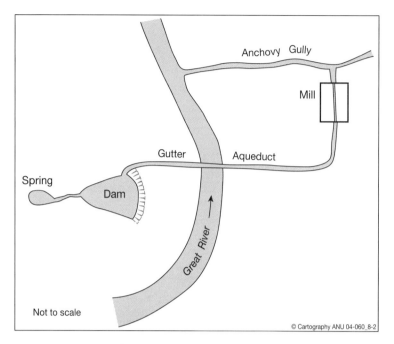

Anchovy Gully

Mill

Gutter   Aqueduct

Spring   Dam

Great River

Not to scale

© Cartography ANU 04-060_8-2

Figure 8.2 New Montpelier water system

post-slavery period.[2] By contrast, religion, in all its forms, seems never to have been a concern for Taylor at Golden Grove.

In April 1832 Seaford spoke in the House of Lords, in a debate on a petition presented by the West India interest. He referred to the Earl of Mulgrave, about to go to Jamaica as its new governor, "with the olive branch, that he might adopt conciliatory measures with the legislature of the island, bring back the slaves to subordination, and re-establish security of property, and, perhaps, restore that prosperity which had formerly existed". If this was optimism, it was guarded. Seaford's losses in the rebellion were estimated at forty-one thousand pounds sterling.[3] Miller sent a proposal for the rebuilding of the works at Montpelier and Seaford, for the first time in fifty years, decided to travel to Jamaica to see for himself.

By August, Seaford could write from Falmouth to his friend Frederick William Hervey, Marquess of Bristol, saying he had already spent a week at Montpelier, along with Miller, inspecting the damage done during the rebellion. They had discussed the options. Miller, said Seaford, "had upon further consideration, made a material alteration in the plan which [he] had originally proposed and which had also occurred to myself as the most advisable for the future arrangement of my Estates". The modified plan was "to restore the works at New Montpelier, instead of the Old Estate, as originally proposed, and to convert Old Montpelier into a breeding pen, to supply the New Estate with working cattle, of which they will require about 50 head annually, and to fatten this draft of old stock for the butchery". How the new supply of cattle from Old Montpelier would affect the existing supply and how a balance would be obtained, Seaford did not say. Miller, wrote Seaford, "explained it to me on the spot, and after examining it in all its details I have adopted it and sanctioned its immediate execution". Overall, the new plan was "very much preferable". Seaford reflected on the value of his presence in Jamaica, believing that had Miller needed "to wait for an answer from England, even if I could have made up my mind satisfactorily upon a written application, it would not have been possible to carry it into effect in time for this ensuing crop". He expected to lose ten thousand pounds on the crop of 1832 but had hopes for the future, particularly by matching the size of his enslaved labour force to the work required by estate and pen.[4] This was the system in place when slavery was abolished and the apprenticeship instituted.

Montpelier's Managers

The management of Montpelier during the transition from slavery to freedom was in the hands of four attorneys. They worked sequentially, each of them sole attorney. William Miller, the greatest of Jamaica's attorneys in the last decades of slavery, had served for Montpelier since 1812. He lived in Falmouth. When he left Jamaica in June 1835, he was replaced by his son Guy, who was in turn replaced by Thomas McNeil in July 1837. McNeil was attorney for the Westmoreland properties of Seaford's friend Lord Holland and lived at Paradise, twenty miles to the south. He lasted only until December 1839 when Isaac Jackson took over. Living at Copse, Shettlewood's northern neighbour, Jackson must have met Seaford when he visited Montpelier following the rebellion. In 1839 Jackson was forty-two years of age, much younger than his employer. Seaford married his second wife in October 1840 when he was sixty-nine. His first had died in 1803.[5] Jackson remained attorney of Copse but from 1840 surrendered the position of overseer to Thomas Ferguson.[6] In 1841 Jackson toyed with the idea of making Shettlewood his own residence but he never left Copse. Seaford died in 1845 but Jackson continued as attorney for Montpelier until 1850.[7]

At his appointment in 1839, Jackson told Seaford that he hoped to find overseers who had "the tact of managing the people easily".[8] He hired and fired overseers, and moved them from property to property in search of the best match. Only Thomas Patterson Gardner, the overseer for New Montpelier, where the sugar mill was located, held his position throughout 1839–43, the period covered by Jackson's letterbooks. At Shettlewood, Edward James Young was overseer in 1839 but by April 1840, Jackson was seeking to replace him. Jackson moved a Mr Godden from Shettlewood to Old Montpelier, though he remained responsible for keeping the accounts of the butchery. At the beginning of June, Jackson reported his dissatisfaction with Young's performance and denied him an increase in salary, but kept him on because "good overseers are very scarce".[9] A year later, in June 1841, Young had been dismissed and a Mr Shilletto placed in charge of Shettlewood. Shilletto lasted only to the end of 1842 when he was replaced as overseer by Edward Hudson Clark, "a person of experience".[10]

In addition to his hiring and firing of managers, Jackson also took a direct role in the employment of white men outside the managerial hierarchy. In 1840 he "engaged an excellent ploughman who had come out indented to Hyde Hall". On the other hand, he told Seaford that "Carson one of the indented servants and indolent bad character I have got rid of".[11] The attorney's personal interest in dealing with these lower ranks of white men mirrored the special treatment they had received on plantations during slavery.

More innovative was Jackson's incorporation of Montpelier's "headmen" into the managerial structure of the property. Simon Taylor hardly mentioned head people or headmen. After abolition, the distinction between supervision and management became more blurred and Jackson attributed higher statuses to some black and coloured men, though never disturbing the gender barriers. During slavery, the "head people" often played a role in the details of labour organization and received superior allocations of food, clothing, housing and other material goods. Thus Miller said in 1833 that the scheduling of shifts during crop season was "generally left among the head people . . . but it is always subject to the approval of the manager". At the same time, head people often gained a reputation for taking leading parts in rebellions. Of the eleven men of Montpelier tried for their role in the rebellion of 1831, for example, seven were headmen or skilled workers.[12] Thus Jackson took a measured risk in promoting headmen to managerial trust and in conducting wage and rent negotiations directly with them.

Because Jackson found it necessary to depend on the headmen as intermediaries, based on a recognition of their status in the internal social hierarchy of the estate, he paid some attention to ensuring their position. When he promoted headmen he paid them on a yearly rather than daily rate, sometimes calling their pay "wages" and other times "salaries". Penkeepers also received salaries and formed a secondary group of managers. Both headmen and penkeepers got advantages in rent-free housing and pasturage for their horses.[13] Jackson also sought to increase the authority of the headmen in more symbolic ways. For example, he told Seaford in 1841 that he had "asked the headmen for a description of the cloaks they required when they stated that they would be satisfied with any that your Lordship might think proper to send".[14] One of these headmen, Edward Payne, was "fully 6 feet high and will require a larger size than the others who are all men of middle stature". Payne, a black creole aged thirty-two, had lived at New Montpelier during slavery and was probably born there, the son of an African mother.[15]

Jackson also used the headmen as a conduit to government and proprietor. When Lord Elgin, the governor, visited Montpelier and slept a night at Shettlewood in March 1843, Jackson told Seaford, the "labourers . . . gave him a kind reception and the headmen waited on him the following morning requesting to be remembered to your Lordship and Lady Seaford promising an increased crop next year and accounting for the shortness of this, all of which his Excellency promised to convey to you by this packet".[16] Elgin reported optimistically on his tour, saying, "The peasantry . . . bore a cheerful and willing testimony to the comforts they enjoy, and the satisfactory understanding established between them and their employers."[17]

Jackson's boldest move was to replace the overseer of Montpelier Pen in March 1842, putting in his stead the headman. At the pen, Jackson told Seaford, "Finding no benefit resulting from keeping an overseer I have dismissed him and broke up the establishment and placed one of the head men there, who I expect will answer equally well and effect a saving to the property."[18] Seaford was intrigued by this solution and asked for more information. In July, Jackson told him that the headman was "Charles Lawrence Tharp who I consider the most influential person on your Lordships property and is head leader of the Baptist congregation to which all your people are attached". This was quite a reversal. Previously, Jackson had shared the planters' view that the Baptists were the root of all evil on the plantations and he had done no more than use evidence of membership of the church in order to identify troublemakers. Tharp was one of the headmen with whom Jackson had dealt directly in labour negotiations. Now he said of Tharp,

> He has all along afforded me great assistance and is more reasonable in his demands than any of the others, but from his activity in taking up their horses when trespassing and putting down other abuses, such as those who are cultivating provisions and not paying rent and others that no person could find out I can perceive that he is losing his influence that he before possessed and if not supported by the Minister he will lose his influence altogether, but I have reason to think Mr. Burchell is friendly disposed towards us.[19]

This was Thomas Burchell, the English Baptist parson who established congregations beginning in 1823 and was regarded by the planters as an instigator of the rebellion of 1831. His Montego Bay chapel was destroyed and he was forced to leave Jamaica, but returned in 1834 to found free villages.[20] By 1842, with the dynamics of labour and religion radically altered, Jackson liked to think Burchell, and Tharp, were now on the planter's side.

Some of the men on the edges of the management hierarchy created problems. During slavery, head people included drivers, skilled workers and craftsmen, but after 1838 headmen seem most often to have been in charge of field labour, the descendants of the drivers. In July 1841 Jackson told Seaford that he would "like to have had a present for John Stokes the distiller but I fear it would create jealousy amongst the people of colour and cause them to work at cross purposes, which alway[s] operates against the interest of the property". Stokes was a mulatto aged thirty-five, who lived at New Montpelier during slavery; by 1835 he was described as a "free carpenter", still living on the estate.[21] Somehow, he made the transition to distiller. He produced much rum, thanks to the large proportion of high-yielding plant canes cropped as well as his own "highly creditable" management of the distillery. As a reward, Jackson added to Stokes' salary of forty pounds old currency (about twenty-four pounds sterling) a doubloon (worth three pounds and four shillings). However, said Jackson, "his services having been over rated by others he does not appear satisfied and told my clerk he considered his services worth £60 and if this sum was given him he would expect £80 for the following year, there is no satisfying them with money".[22] Another man, Lewis Goodwin, a mill carpenter, was also given "a doubloon extra who has shown every disposition to give satisfaction". This was most likely Thomas Lewis Goodwin, a "sambo" man aged forty-nine, who had been head carpenter at Old Montpelier in the 1820s. Like John Stokes, by 1835 he was free, head carpenter on New Montpelier though living at Shettlewood.[23]

Workers and Wages

How did Jackson expect the managers and supervisors of Montpelier, at all levels, to behave? What did he expect from the people freed from slavery? Although he had little optimism for the new system of labour, writing in October 1839 Jackson advocated "the necessity of conciliation with firmness" as the only possible hope for the survival of the sugar estates.[24] "On visiting the properties," said Jackson, "many a time have I remonstrated with the laborers, on the great loss their master sustained by their indolence and neglect in the manufacture of the crop, fearful of saying something that might give offence which would have been a pretext for their withdrawing from work at once." He left such encounters, he claimed, "burning with suppressed rage at such heartless conduct".[25] The workers, Jackson remonstrated, lacked a moral concern for the failing fortunes of their former masters. It was an underlying assumption shared by planters, abolitionists and Colonial Office. Thus James Spedding, philosophical protégé of Henry Taylor, pondered in July 1839 "this most difficult and delicate task of securing to the negroes the enjoyment of real freedom, and at the same time making it their real interest, and making them feel and understand that it is their real interest, to remain in the condition of a labouring peasantry in the service of their former masters".[26]

Jackson and Seaford, like most planters of the time, seem to have hoped the organization of labour could go on much as it had done under slavery. Jackson, much more than Seaford, appreciated the weakness of his bargaining tools. Neither proprietor nor attorney considered the possibility of share-cropping as a means of ensuring the continuing production of sugar, but this was after all a system long discarded in England. Nor did they think of combining with their neighbours to establish a central mill in order to exploit economies of scale. These were radical alternatives, still too difficult to take seriously. On the other hand, Jackson and Seaford did contemplate the real possibility of abandoning sugar. They also chose to lease estate land in small plots with the hope of creating a pool of working people who could be employed for wages in the production of sugar. And they attempted to increase the productivity of labour through the task system, as well as to introduce new mechanical technologies.

How and where could Jackson and Seaford look for labour? There were four potential sources. The first candidates were the people who had lived as slaves on Montpelier and Shettlewood down to 1838. The population at the beginning of August was close to eight hundred, in three separate villages, and Jackson saw these as the most immediate source of workers.[27] Indeed, he thought of the village people as the estate's natural labour pool, bearing the primary moral responsibility to work for their former master. The second possible source of labour could be looked for in the people who had been enslaved to other owners on nearby properties. Montpelier was surrounded by plantations and pens, with a substantial population that it could compete for (Figure 8.3). However, the estate was relatively isolated and existed within an extensive woodland. Montpelier's immediate neighbours were few and similarly competitive. Third, workers might be sought from distant regions of Jamaica. During slavery, groups of people had been forced to move from parish to parish, but in the first years of freedom long-distance internal migration was uncommon and where people did move to new districts they generally did so to obtain freehold land, not to labour on plantations. The fourth way of recruiting labour was to find people outside the island and bring them to work on the estate. The global reach of the British Empire made this a real option, though an expensive one unless the state could be induced to underwrite the enterprise and the cost shifted to taxpayers.

The planters of Jamaica were commonly agreed that the fundamental problem in maintaining plantation agriculture was an absolute "shortage" of labour. Seaford and Jackson did not dissent. Whereas Taylor, during the period of the slave trade, thought in terms of Golden Grove as an enclosed pool of labour, which he needed only to top up from time to time, Jackson

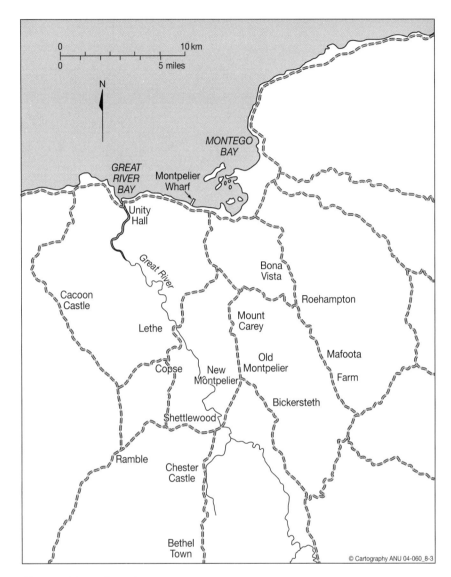

Figure 8.3 Montpelier region

had to think at a regional level with an eye to the alternatives that might attract away the people he hoped to employ. Successful competition with other estates might be achieved by offering higher wages or superior access to provision ground land but again there were risks in the ratchetting-up of competition. Jackson believed the pressure of population needed to achieve this goal was lacking. There were simply too few people in Jamaica at large. Thus in March 1840 he told Edmund Gardiner, absentee-proprietor of Flint River Estate in coastal Hanover, that "the want of labor arises as an unavoidable consequence from want of a sufficient population and from the facility of comfortable subsistence without continuously labouring for their masters, which the occupation of their provision grounds and various other means of procuring all the necessaries required afford them".[28]

Jackson supported his perception of a lack of population by advocating immigration. But the forms of immigration being tried in the period of the letterbooks did not strike him as appropriate. Jackson recognized the high cost of immigration schemes and said they were "very uncertain unless industrious good people are selected that have been accustomed to labor and coarse food in their native country".[29] All of the white immigrants proved failures, he believed, telling Alexander Campbell in June 1841 that they were "travelling from place to place apparently in great distress without shoes or stockings". He employed a few "at 1/6 sterling which is more than we can afford for the work they are able to perform", but thought "they all appear dissatisfied with the country and seek to return to their friends in poverty". Jackson's conclusion was simple: "Blacks I have no doubt will answer. But I am quite convinced that white labour never will."[30]

Seaford disagreed. Indeed, he was something of a true believer in immigration and he thought the best strategy was to bring in Europeans to provide an example of industrious labour and generate a pressure from the interior of the island that would keep the blacks on the estates. It was an old doctrine, associated with the notion of deficiency and the settlement schemes of Long before the American Revolution. Seaford had already established his credentials by the granting of land from his Montpelier Mountain property in Westmoreland as the site for a settlement of German immigrants in 1835. The settlement was named Seaford Town in his honour. Both Jackson and McNeil were township commissioners.[31] Jackson, for his part, had no enthusiasm for white workers and thought the Germans might soon leave Seaford Town, yet did not argue the point with his employer.[32] The settlement survived but Jackson saw it as a failure. He thought all white immigration useless.

On 29 October 1841 Jackson told Seaford that a ship had recently arrived at Montego Bay with 224 immigrants, "but I regret to say they are not the class of people that will ever benefit this island, but rather become a burthen".[33] This was the *Ceylon*, which had arrived from London on 18 October. The precise origins of the immigrants are uncertain, a report in the *Cornwall Chronicle* saying only, "Of the 224 in number all answer to their names with the exception of one man, who was indisposed, though not seriously." It is certain they were "European" and they might have been from England or Scotland. According to the *Cornwall Chronicle* they included only one "aged person" but "may be too many young children" who seemed not "calculated for the labour of this country". Some left the ship in Montego Bay but the others, "the agricultural portion", proceeded to Montpelier Wharf and then went to "a salubrious station in the St James mountains called Bona Vista" where an agent was to negotiate their employment.[34] Jackson, at the end of October, said "very few of them have been engaged as yet" and they were asking "most extravagant wages". The only immediate advantage he could see was that Shettlewood was supplying beef to them "at the Depot Buonavista near Roehampton", Montpelier's northeastern neighbour.[35]

If white immigrants were of no obvious use, Jackson did express a need for more labour. He favoured Africans. However, apparently because Seaford took a different view, Jackson did not actively pursue "liberated" Africans for Montpelier when the possibility arose in 1843. This occurred in spite of Seaford's influence with Governor Elgin. In May 1842 Seaford wrote, from Florence, to Elgin introducing Jackson and offering "whatever accommodation my very small habitation at Shettlewood can afford".[36] Jackson addressed Elgin in February 1843, enclosing the letter of introduction "from my constituent Lord Seaford" and saying he had hoped Elgin might have visited western Jamaica sooner, "when I should have had the honor of delivering it personally and made you a render of my services". Curiously, the purpose of Jackson's letter was not to advance the interests of Seaford but to seek his own appointment as colonel in the Western Interior Regiment of militia, which was to be re-formed, and "to obtain a supply of those Africans that are now shortly expected". He made the second request on behalf of thirteen properties for which he was attorney, seeking a total of 250 immigrants, but it was a list from which Seaford's properties were omitted.[37] It may be that Seaford had not sought a share of these potential workers but there is nothing in the correspondence to indicate any discussion of the possibility. Seaford had certainly shown a preference for trying white Europeans up to this point. More importantly perhaps, he did not see Montpelier or Shettlewood as suffering an absolute shortage of labour. The day after his letter to Elgin, Jackson wrote to Seaford without making mention of writing to Elgin or his actions in seeking Africans.[38] The lack of a viable immigrant labouring population on Montpelier, down to 1843, was certainly seen by Jackson as a disadvantage, but he had no power to recruit and had no support from Seaford. Jackson had to work with the people living at Montpelier and negotiate on their terms.

What choices faced the people formerly forced to live and work on Montpelier? They might continue to work on the estate, in return for wages and rights of residence, or they could choose to do estate work elsewhere, or decide not to perform any kind of plantation labour at all. Freedom meant that the people could move off Montpelier, to live in the village of some other plantation or perhaps in a town. The Assembly attempted to restrict such mobility, particularly through the Vagrancy Act of 1839, but the people found refuge in formal and informal free villages immediately beyond the boundaries of the estate, at Mount Carey, Chester Castle and Bickersteth.[39] Alternatively, they could establish themselves as farmers on lots of land, purchased or squatted on, near or far from Montpelier, making their livelihoods from their own products or combining these activities with occasional plantation wage labour. They could leave Jamaica. Few in fact migrated, either overseas or to towns, in the immediate post-slavery period and the potential labour pool of Jamaica grew somewhat in the years following abolition as the population began to reproduce itself.

Those who chose to remain resident in the villages of Montpelier and to offer themselves for labour in field and factory had other choices to make. They might offer themselves individually and attempt to work out their own terms and conditions, negotiating directly with the overseer, leaving cases of dispute to the headmen. They might form themselves into groups reminiscent of the system of gang labour in slavery and negotiate collectively. Or they might surrender negotiation to representatives, such as headmen or parsons, and accept whatever they could agree with the attorney. All of these approaches were tried. The possibility of individual negotiation increased with the status of a person's occupation. The potential worker could make choices about how many days to work in each week and which particular days, and whether to perform night work in the factory. Choices could be made about which particular tasks would be accepted and which refused. The amount of an acceptable wage had also to be determined and negotiated.[40] All of these were choices insecurely grounded in the experience and precedents of labour under slavery and their relative values generally had to be learned for the first time. Certainly they made the managerial task harder, from the attorney's point of view, both because of the range of alternatives and the difficulty of predicting the outcomes.

The first question for Jackson was how best to exploit the potential labour power of the people already resident on the property. He was well aware that the tasks required of sugar plantation workers were mostly unattractive and that the hours of work extracted under slavery were far beyond what a person would freely offer. Whereas slavery had given individual slave owners total power over the bodies of the people they owned, and an almost total power to decide tasks, hours and conditions of work, freedom required planters to find a new package of positive and negative incentives to labour. The planters now had a less complete control of the state and knew that the use of terror was no longer functional as the prime means of obtaining labour. The recalcitrant might be sent to the workhouse treadmill or to prison or be expelled from the estate, but these punishments were not efficient means of obtaining labour for the plantation's field and factory.

In order to recruit the labour needed to maintain sugar production at Montpelier, Jackson had to negotiate rates of wages, rights of residence, rents, hours and days of work on conditions sufficiently attractive to obtain labour from the existing estate population, and he had to avoid seeking to impose conditions that might have negative effects. Above all, he sought to retain the resident populations, and not to give the people cause to leave the estate, whether they left to work for some other planter or abandoned plantation labour altogether. The corollary of this strategy was to attempt to attract people from other plantations, by offering relatively attractive terms and conditions, to build up the potential labour pool for Montpelier. Jackson tried all of these methods.

From the very beginning of the post-slavery period, some of the resident population of Montpelier stopped performing specific tasks. Women quickly withdrew from some kinds of field work. In 1839 Jackson stated, "I find very few of the married women, which compose the greatest strength on each property, disposed to labour continuously, neither have I known one of them dig a cane hole since the commencement of freedom."[41] The following February, he said many women were also refusing to cut canes and some labourers refused to carry cut canes as "too hard work".[42] In 1843 he included in his order for supplies on Montpelier Estate "3 dozen womens hoes", but probably these were for the lighter work of weeding.[43]

Digging cane holes was particularly onerous. During slavery, as at Golden Grove, it was a task often allocated to jobbing gangs in order to save the health of an estate's population. At Montpelier, it was the practice to use people from Shettlewood to do this work. In the final year of the apprenticeship, Shettlewood workers dug 73,763 cane holes on Montpelier as part of their unpaid labour.[44] Jackson hoped he could induce some of the Old Works and Shettlewood people to work on Montpelier in sugar cultivation but lacked the capacity to force people to move to new tasks or to work where they did not choose. At the beginning of 1840, Seaford offered his own comments on "the unwillingness of the Old Works people to work on the New Works Estate".[45] The problem was that Old Montpelier was now a pen, while New Montpelier was the site of sugar-making. The work of cane field and sugar factory had always been less appealing than the labour of the pen. Jackson believed that "pen people . . . have always had plenty of time to themselves".[46] A strike by workers on Old and New Montpelier in January 1840, to obtain an advance of wages so that they could pay the increased rent and gain time to work their provision grounds, was not joined by Shettlewood people. By May, Jackson admitted that he had made no progress in shifting resources because the people "do not appear inclined to work on the Estate so long as there is employment for them on the Pen". Further, the Montpelier people were "opposed to them or any others working there". An obvious reason for this feeling was that outsiders might force down wage rates and increase competition for grounds, so the attitude had economic as well as social origins.[47]

How far was Jackson able to manage the daily supply of labour and its seasonal interruptions? His letters give few clues to expected or actual hours of work, apart from occasional references to special pleas for work at night in the factory. He tried to obtain agreement to a sixteen-hour five-day week during crop and five days every second week out of crop, but struggled to achieve regular work on Fridays and to combat the workers' desire for a four-day week. He was interested in regularity and continuity of labour but said little about the question, confining himself to complaints about seasonal fluctuations.

The brutal regime of night work that had produced so much sugar during slavery could not be maintained at Montpelier as a matter of course. It was a question of negotiation. In January 1842, for example, when production was interrupted by machine problems, Jackson took an optimistic view because "the labourers have agreed to work at night which I trust will induce others to follow their example and enable us to get off the crops more expeditiously than has been done since freedom commenced".[48] The May rains caused further mill stoppages but Jackson was proud to report that the "people" had honoured their promise to perform night work in the mill. He sought also to prove his concern and involvement through direct attention to the interests of Seaford during the crop, saying,

> I slept at Montpelier on Tuesday night and altho the rain began to fall about noon and continued until the evening the works people kept on until the canes were finished and took them until one or two oclock in the morning altho saturated with rain and working in mud. I really felt for them in the morning. There are several of the females who do not labor at all, others who prefer working grounds, but I cannot help saying take your people generally, they are as good as any I know of.[49]

This was high praise compared to the accusations of congenital laziness that came from the pens of most attorneys and the racist narrative which was soon to become the dominant discourse. Jackson's positive perceptions and indeed the willingness of the workers to engage in such hard labour for their former master was born in the bonding and camaraderie of "the crop", a shared experience with a tangible objective and an achievement in the face of natural adversity in which everyone involved could take pride. But there remained a great difference between such special effort, down to one or two in the morning, compared to the round-the-clock regime of the sugar mill during slavery.

The seasonal demands of the sugar estate did not mesh well with the seasonal labour needs of the provision grounds. Thus, while the rent of estate lands for settlements might help fund the wage bill and perhaps increase the available supply of labour, it equally created chances for people to make their own independent incomes synchronized with the seasons of the grounds and the markets. In the middle of March 1842, for example, when Jackson was relatively optimistic about the availability of estate workers, he told Seaford that "this is the season that the Negroes put in their own provisions which makes us short of labor at present and the weeding falls behind unless sharply looked after". He was trying to complete the sugar crop, but in addition to the shortage of labour, the rains had set in unusually early and the roadways were often impassable. Further, the canes had a high ratio of juice that required additional evaporation and additional fuel, which had become scarce. The wet weather made it difficult to dry the cane trash, the usual fuel, and Jackson had resorted to bamboos from Shettlewood.[50]

Seasonal holidays also affected labour supply and once again the pattern was not always synchronized with the demands of the sugar estate. Christmas was the major traditional break from plantation labour. After 1838 these holidays came to cover many more days. Writing on New Year's Day 1840, Jackson told Seaford he was "agreeably surprised" that some of the Montpelier and Shettlewood people had already turned out for work following the Christmas holidays that had commenced on 20 December. Work was about to resume in the factory.[51] At the beginning of December 1841 Jackson reported that heavy rain had left the canes green and unripe, but reported optimistically, "If the peoples promises can be relied on they are anxious to exert themselves to take off the crop. I therefore expect no difficulty."[52] From 1838 the Christmas holidays continued for ten to fourteen days at Montpelier, compared to the three or four days in slavery. The planters saw it as a substantial interruption at a crucial period of the crop cycle. Further, because the Christmas holiday fell shortly after the commencement of crop it forced Jackson to attempt to put the mill "about" earlier than he wished.

Added to Christmas was the 1 August holiday, the celebration of the anniversary of abolition, which also stretched over several days. When the August commemoration of the abolition of slavery arrived in 1842, Jackson noted that the "sectarian parsons are reaping a good harvest" amongst the people but thought the behaviour of the people was "orderly" and without the "uproarious mirth that formerly took place on such occasions". He was pleased to have got the cane field in order before the holidays started, however, "as it will be some time before they all resume work". On 19 August, Jackson noted that the estate had had "very little labor from the people since the 1st August holidays commenced".[53] This was typical, the holidays extending over two weeks in most parts of the island. For the estates, however, it mattered less than the Christmas holiday. Indeed, 1 August had long marked the end of the sugar crop, the beginning of double-insurance and the hurricane season, the time of "crop-over" celebrations. The planters were responsible for the choice of the date, to suit their convenience, and preferred 1 August to Christmas.[54]

How exactly were wages and the conditions of work negotiated? There was a good deal of formality and an appreciation of the importance of legal contract. Jackson, as attorney, had a central role. Overseers were sometimes responsible for agreeing wages with individual workers, within established parameters. Absentee-proprietors were able only to set out broad principles. Although wages and work, rent and residence, were closely bound, wages occupied much less of Jackson's correspondence than his struggles over rent. Wages were easier to set because there were firmer precedents. The rates paid for jobbers during slavery were well known and standard. Some enslaved people were allowed to practise self-hire, though this was most often an urban phenomena and apparently unknown at Montpelier. Jackson worried little about remuneration in kind, such as medical attendance and food, but devoted much ink to the provision grounds and the way in which they competed for the time and energies of Montpelier's workers. Much of his negotiation was mediated through the headmen.

What was the situation Jackson found at Montpelier when he took over as attorney? At the end of the apprenticeship, on 1 August 1838, McNeil had agreed wages and rents with the people of Montpelier "in the presence of their minister", the Baptist Thomas Burchell. Wages were calculated on the basis of an able person's nine-hour day being valued at one shilling eight pence. As to rent, said McNeil, "they were to pay only at the rate of 20s per annum rent for houses and grounds, say from the occupier or head of each family in possession of house and ground, with medical attendance, medicines and necessary nourishments supplied them as usually was done in slavery or apprenticeship". Apparently McNeil attempted to organize labour on the task system. There was a strike on 19 December 1838, the people demanding the end of task work and payment by the day only. Some had formed themselves into small gangs of six to eight people and thus commanded two shillings sixpence per day, the amount later complained of by Jackson. At the beginning of 1839 McNeil told Seaford that most of the workers did only one shilling threepence' worth of labour per day, saying "they are now freemen, and work as suits themselves". They were labouring hard in their provision grounds but idle in the cane fields, he complained.[55]

As soon as Jackson took over at Montpelier he sat down to begin negotiations on wages and rents. He associated most of his difficulties with the Baptist parsons, who instigated strikes, and the stipendiary magistrates, who undermined the resident planter class. However, he had hopes that "the Stipendiary Spaniels" would soon be dismissed and that the new governor, Metcalfe, would bring other benefits to the planters. On 3 December 1839, the day of Jackson's first report to Seaford, he told Alexander Campbell happily that the Baptists had quietened and were devoting themselves to "counselling the Negroes how to obtain high wages and avoid rent".[56]

Jackson was cautious in his negotiations on wages and particularly wary of the enthusiasm of some planters to reduce rates. He had seen examples where the strict application of an absentee-proprietor's instructions to do so had resulted in mass exodus. He believed that "the rate of wages can only be reduced imperceptibly, by keeping a small and highly cultivated canefield and confining expenditure to that alone and other requisite outlay". Further, Jackson contended that "the rate of wages cannot be reduced by any combination against the labourers who are as much aware of their strength as we are except by throwing up all the estates".[57] Workers rarely competed for wages, he said, being forbidden to do so by their friends, but combined to strike.[58] In November 1844, after the extant letterbooks cease, Seaford told Lady Holland that "my manager has been attempting to accomplish a reduction of wages, which has occasioned a strike on the part of the labourers".[59]

If it was difficult to reduce wages, it was easier to remove existing benefits in kind. Food, clothing and utensils were quickly removed from the list. Montpelier did maintain some responsibility for medical care, for several years. By October 1842, however, the arrangement was at an end, "the Doctor undertaking to collect the money himself and defray the customary expenses".[60] Jackson had earlier recommended that properties "discontinue paying for medical attendance upon the people excepting invalids, who are unable to pay for themselves". This was part of his plan for inducing wage labour by throwing the residents on their own resources.[61]

In February 1840 Jackson said some refused the wages offered on Montpelier and went to work on neighbouring estates. Others were demanding higher wages in order to increase the time available to cultivate their provision grounds. By May, however, the labourers of Shettlewood were planting grass at rates they had refused the year before and Jackson was collecting rents. He saw this as "a point gained".[62]

Denying access to the established provision grounds might have seemed an attractive option as a means of forcing wage labour, but it was never considered by Jackson or Seaford. Any such action would have quickly lost them the capacity to negotiate. The provision grounds remained a problem to proprietor and manager, and a substantial resource for the plantation populations. With his letter of 25 February 1840, Jackson sent Seaford a copy of the *Jamaica Despatch,* one of the island's larger newspapers, reporting a recent opinion of the attorney-general regarding rights to the possession of grounds "which will unsettle the people and do us a great deal of harm".[63] Seaford asked for details of the dimensions of the question but Jackson refused to be precise. The information was not readily available to him, with grounds located widely through the spreading lands of Montpelier and effectively hidden in its nooks and niches. According to Jackson,

> As respects the average size of Negro grounds it cannot be fairly stated. A man and wife of 1st class generally has, in standing provisions at least two acres. If 2nd class generally speaking has one acre. Single young men in many instances have equally as much as two of the 1st class. Married labourers, watchmen and grass cutters single about two acres, if married about three acres. There are instances

however on the property, particularly on Old Works of 4, 5, 6 and even a greater number of acres being kept in cultivation by married people.[64]

Neither Jackson nor the overseer knew the actual dimensions and locations of all of the grounds cultivated by the people on Montpelier. The lands of Old Montpelier, on which sugar had been effectively abandoned, provided the best sites and opportunities. The people took advantage of the ignorance of overseer and attorney, and used their own knowledge of the land to cultivate where they could. They also showed little fear in taking in grounds in full view.

The other side of the coin was that Jackson admitted "great difficulty" in getting rents "from those who do not work". He planned to sue some of them. He appreciated that this was a difficulty partly of the estate's own making and he was at pains to explain it to Seaford whose instinct was always to question expenditure and to be reluctant to commit resources to the payment of wages. The problem was that those who did not earn wages could claim they had no money to pay rent, and they could not be expected to pay if work opportunities were not provided by the estates. Thus, when Jackson reported to Seaford in June 1840 that the cane field had been cleaned of weeds and that he planned to start on the pastures, he admitted this would be "a heavy expense which your Lordship might not be disposed to do all at once, but I fear that if we do not give the people employment, they will squander about and we will not get the rents and perhaps not return when we again require them to go through the canefield".[65]

In all of this correspondence, Jackson provided surprisingly little specific information on actual rates of pay. This suggests a degree of short-term flexibility and negotiation, and variation between individuals and groups, in what was agreed. Probably Seaford felt left in the dark on these matters of expenditure and asked his own questions. In response, Jackson's letter of 21 June 1842 usefully set out the details of wages on Montpelier, including some surprises:

> Rate of pay. All field labourers are paid at the rate of 6d sterling per 100 roots of 4 ft square each root, which is 13/7 sterling per acre. An able man can when he exerts himself earn 2/6 per day, others do not earn more than 6d or 9d. Tradesmen and others that be tasked work 9 hours per day for which they are paid 1/6 sterling. We never have recourse to day labour when it can be avoided, as not 1 in 10 will labour faithfully, which causes much bickering and heart burning between them and the overseer, whose situation under the present system is no sinecure, neither is that of the book-keeper who measures and puts down all the work of each day.
>
> Headmans wages. Head Superintendant £16 sterling per annum the others £13 10/- sterling rent free and allowed pasturage for one horse in common. All other labourers pay rent and pasturage.[66]

Several points emerge from this statement. The first is the clear emphasis on task work. Jackson suggested that it was almost universal in the digging of cane holes, and what was true of Montpelier in 1842 seems to have been generally true of Jamaica. This was the work least favoured during slavery and the labour most likely to be allocated to jobbing gangs. The latter were generally employed on a task system, though it was the owner of the enslaved people who had collected the payment. During slavery, the median daily rate for cane holing by jobbers was two shillings sixpence currency, a close equivalence. One important feature of cane-holing was that the work was relatively easily measured and counted, and open to straightforward quality control. The number of cane holes expected of an "able man", roughly five hundred in a day, was high compared to expectations under slavery, even with prior preparation of the soil by ploughing.[67] Few would have been able to attain this rate.

The general rule was that task work was most likely to be practised where output could be quantified in terms of distance, area or volume. On sugar estates, these parameters could be applied to a variety of activities but often the accounting cost was too great to make it profitable, as hinted in Jackson's reference to the measuring and recording work of the book-keepers. On the other hand, the weeding of cane-pieces and the cleaning of pastures was harder to assess, and probably this work was more often paid by the day. As to the cutting of cane, Jackson gives no clues, but the pressure of the crop season and the high cost of measuring individual output meant this work was unlikely to fall within the task system. Work in the mill was also continuous and difficult to break into tasks, so day rates must have applied there as well. The same was true of haulage, security and domestic service. Jackson's note that tradesmen might be tasked for a fixed number of hours and a fixed amount of money, might appear confused, but is explained by the relating of jobs, such as the making of casks, to the expected daily rate of output.

Calculations based on Jackson's statement of 1842 suggest that the annual wages of a field worker, working four or five days for most weeks of the year at Montpelier, might amount to no more than two pounds at the bottom of the scale to ten pounds at the top. Tradesmen had more continuous employment and could make up to fourteen pounds, or roughly the same as a headman. The latter, however, was more certain of freedom from rents and pasturage. For the worker at the bottom of the scale, earning enough to cover the rents demanded by Montpelier might be impossible if they depended on wages alone. Although Jackson and Seaford must have been aware of this inadequacy, they never proposed raising wages substantially, even on an experimental basis to test the effect. No doubt they had in mind the trouble that followed attempts to reduce wages, and the competition between wage labour and the returns that could be gained from the cultivation of grounds.

Rents and Renters

Lord Seaford, shortly before he took ship for Jamaica in 1832, wrote privately to his friend and fellow absentee Lord Holland, saying that "what the Negroes look to, in freedom, is merely to be exempted from labour, or at least to continue to occupy their houses, and to cultivate their grounds, for their subsistence, without reckoning on having to pay rent for house or land".[68] This was an assumption that led to management policies making residence and access to gardens and grounds dependent on regular wage labour for the estate on which the worker lived and dependent on the payment of rent. By charging rent for house and grounds, planters believed, they could ensure the necessity of wage labour. McNeil's policy, supported by Seaford, was to eject those who refused to pay rent, believing this would ensure the freed population's return to wage labour on the estates. Seaford recommended a low rent on house and garden and a high rent on provision grounds, as a means of retaining workers on the estate and discouraging their focus on the grounds.[69] This was how things were at Montpelier down to July 1839 when Jackson was first offered the post of attorney.

Jackson approved this approach, at least until September 1839, and practised it on the properties already under his management. He believed that "the more the labourers are thrown upon their own resources the better will they labour" and advocated "a high rent to all persons not labouring for the property and a moderate one to those working".[70] When the workers of Copse struck for higher wages, Jackson resisted their claims and told Alexander Campbell that "rather than submit to it I will let them sit down for a while and sue them for rent, which will be the only way of bringing to their senses".[71] Jackson took a legalistic approach, well aware of the power of the magistrates. On all the estates under his control, he required that the overseers give notice of the scale of rents "by reading to each family".[72] In August 1839 he said that the people had "struck work on every property where rent has been demanded and enforced".[73] Gradually, however, "by suing a few of the most refractory" he hoped to establish a system of weekly payments.[74]

Between August and October 1839 Seaford radically revised his policy. He was not alone but represented part of the general pulling back from aggressive approaches that had proved disastrous as a means of retaining a labour force.[75] The most important element of his new approach was the separation of rent and estate labour. When Jackson took charge in December 1839, rent was no longer tied to estate labour but, equally, rent and renting became central to the estate's economy. Even before the transition, Jackson referred to a letter from Seaford, saying, "The other remarks made in your Lordships letter as to the great objection made by the people of both properties to paying rent and the most equitable mode of fixing it, shall have my best attention, so soon as Mr. McNeil gives me up possession."[76] Whereas Jackson's thinking had moved beyond a simple prohibition of residence for those who did not labour on the estate, connecting labour and residence through differential monetary claims, Seaford's proposal broke the nexus. Rents were to be based on the value of "house and tenement" and unrelated to the status of the occupant as worker. Similarly, provision grounds would be let to all comers, without any requirement of labour or residence. Seaford believed appropriate rents would be the equivalent of one day's labour, assuming a six-day week.[77]

Reporting on his initial negotiations with the people of Montpelier, in December 1839, Jackson indicated his difficulty with the system advocated by Seaford. He did not criticize the proposal directly. Rather, he told Seaford that although the "system of charging rent by valuation of house and land I admit the most equitable plan", it would be difficult to carry into effect "at this season of the year, when the people have already gathered in their yams crop and left their ground quite bare and of course of little value". Jackson recommended a tactic that took advantage of the crop cycle in the provision grounds and proposed applying the scheme in "July or August when provisions are in full bearing". However, said Jackson, "your people appear to prefer paying a weekly rent as is generally adopted in this district", set at three shillings four pence for the "head of the house" and one shilling eight pence and one shilling threepence for "first and second class inmates of the same house", respectively. He had proposed both of these schemes to the people

> but they wished a few days to consider them before giving an answer. I presume they wished this delay to consult their friends, who will not fail to tutor them properly. I expect an answer in two days, and should both of these offers be objectionable to the people, I will propose to lease them on the terms you propose for twelve months.

Things were going more smoothly at Shettlewood. There the "labourers" had "agreed to pay the above rent weekly and have all undertaken grass pieces to clean and are working cheerfully, although they had been doing very little work on the Pen for some time previous, neither have they paid the small rent of 1/8 per week that Mr McNeil demanded". He hoped "to get on well, at little expense, when the rent is regularly paid".[78]

On New Year's Day 1840 Jackson acknowledged letters from Seaford written in November, along with enclosures regarding rents. Jackson was now able to report the outcome of his negotiations with the people of Montpelier, concluded after the people had pondered. He thought he had done well enough: "I have had a hard bargain with your laborers to get them to pay rent, which three fourths of them have agreed to, viz. 2/6 grounds and 10d for house per week." He had effectively obtained the three shillings four pence rate he said was common throughout the district. At Shettlewood, the people had been "working and paying rent steadily ever since I fixed it". Thus, Jackson concluded, "I consider the system of rent now fairly established, which I hope will induce the people to give more labour to the Estate, if your Stipendiary Magistrates do not upset it."[79]

Within the month, Jackson was pointing the finger at the magistrates who had swiftly upset his carefully constructed bargain:

> Last week several of Old and New Works labourers struck work for an advance of wages, in order to meet the increased rent, finding they were much opposed to pay more than the former rent of 1/8 per week, and, that Mr. Finlayson told them in court that there was no law to allow the proprietor to demand an increased rent without giving six months notice. I agreed to charge no more than 1/8 per week rent, on all those working regularly upon the estate, which has had the effect of inducing them to resume work this week and I trust they will go on steadily during crop. I am satisfied were the present Stipendiary Magistrates Messrs Facey and Finlayson removed your properties would go on as well as any other in this district.[80]

Not only had Jackson been forced to back down on the rate of rent but he saw no alternative to linking labour to rent, the system Seaford wished to abandon but Jackson probably still hankered for. Jackson's reference to "your" stipendiary magistrates was a direct identification of the internal enemy. The power of the magistrates was all too visible on Montpelier, Jackson believed. A court was held in the military barracks by the Great River and Jackson recommended Seaford do away with it because it was "operating against the interest of your properties". In January 1840 Jackson lodged a formal complaint, saying the holding of the courts there brought "the disaffected people of the whole of that district among his [Seaford's] labouring population".[81] A month later, in February 1840, Jackson was still complaining of his fate at the hands of the magistrates. Workers persisted in refusing to pay more than one shilling eight pence in rent, "which they were put up to by Mr. Finlayson the special magistrate", who thus "upset my arrangement which was working well".[82] Fortuitously, the officers' quarters of the barracks in which the court was held were burned to the ground at the end of May. The fire was started by a "careless" person dropping a fire stick in the nearby grass piece on the way to his grounds. Previously, the barracks had housed troops during the rebellion of 1831–32 and from 1836 to the end of the apprenticeship they had been rented to the police. From early 1841 Montpelier Estate rented out a separate police station.[83]

Jackson believed that his ability to negotiate rent and wages was undermined not only by the stipendiary magistrates but also by the known views of Seaford and other absentees, and the consequent inducement to workers to take their grievances directly to the absentee-proprietors. Occasionally, however, pleas to the proprietor fell into the hands of the attorney. Thus, when Jackson wrote on 17 March 1840 he acknowledged a letter from Seaford "enclosing one from three men on behalf of all the other people on Montpelier Estate and Penn and Shettlewood". Jackson told Seaford with glee that "this letter will be of essential service to me in pointing out the leading characters on the three properties who attend the Baptist chapel, and possess great influence over the others. This influence they have hitherto exerted, in opposition to your Lordships interest and in support of their own." Jackson only mentioned two of the three by name, Tharp and Harvey. Charles Lawrence Tharp was to become headman at Montpelier Pen. The Harvey who signed the 1840 protest was probably George Harvey, a black creole aged thirty-five who had lived on Shettlewood Pen during slavery.[84] Jackson accused them of duplicity:

> Tharp and Harvey who sign their names as being willing to agree to the propositions contained in your Lordship's letter to Mr. McNeil and myself have repeatedly expressed themselves opposed to a valuation of houses and grounds, and agreed with me to pay 3/4 per week for house and grounds alone and to work five days per week in crop and five days each alternate week out of crop for such wages as might be agreed upon by them and the overseer, all cases of dispute to be settled by the head people, but, I am sorry to say they have not kept faith with me.

People not working for the estate were expected to pay rents of "6/8 per week for house and grounds and 5/- per week for grounds alone", but Jackson explained to Seaford that even though he "offered the highest rate of wages going many of the people refuse to work or pay more than 1/8 per week rent, for the best of all reasons that they can make more money by cultivating provisions than any wages the Estate can give for the cultivation of sugar".[85]

Few were willing to work on Fridays, the day before the markets, Jackson complained, making it impossible to complete the crop before the rains set in. He concluded that "nothing will check the evil until a limit is put to their present extensive grounds many of them having five and six acres of bearing provisions and falling [clearing] new land, which keeps themselves and any neighbours they can hire fully employed". In order to achieve this goal, he had "given them notice not to fall any new lands until they agree to work five days per week for the property and pay the value of the land in cultivation". He believed that some seemed "disposed to come to terms", while others paid no attention to his ruling and were "planting provisions, where it will interfere with the feeding of the stock". The overseer was to take the matter to court, hoping that the magistrates would declare it trespass and determine that the people had "no right to plant provisions in the pasture land, where it is required to feed the cattle". Jackson appealed to higher authority by getting the governor, Charles Metcalfe, "to visit the Montpeliers and speak to the people thinking that he might induce them to work five days per week, but they distinctly told him that they would not work more than four. He also told them they could not open new lands without my sanction which appeared to have no effect upon them." However, six people complained to the governor that the overseer "had fed cattle through their grounds" and in consequence had taken out summonses against the estate and were going to court. Jackson opined that these were the same people who had planted provisions in the pastures. He told Seaford, "The Governor is of opinion that the provisions are the true cause of all our difficulties."[86]

Montpelier was only one of the stops along Metcalfe's route when he travelled around Jamaica in February and March 1840 but he did report to the Colonial Office that Seaford's properties represented "one of the most remarkable instances of failure". Seaford himself, said Metcalfe, was "known to be one of the most kind considerate and generous proprietors" and served by "good managers". The "people", however, did not "work in sufficient numbers nor with sufficient steadiness" and were reluctant to pay rent even though Seaford had been "one of the first to enjoin the entire separation of the rent question from that of labour". Metcalfe was at a loss to explain the situation. Ultimately, he attributed the "ruin" of the properties "to the fact that on the broad lands belonging to them the people enjoy the use of unlimited or extensive grounds, which they cultivate for their own benefit, and that the necessary stimulus for labor on the properties, is consequently wanting".[87] Jackson told Campbell that he had breakfasted with the governor at Montpelier and that Metcalfe had "stated that the unlimited cultivation of provisions is the true cause of all our difficulties and that nothing but immigration to a great extent would remedy the evil".[88]

The case of trespass against the overseer, for feeding cattle on provisions planted in Yaws House piece, was dismissed by the court as not proven. Another charge against the estate was brought by Charles Palmer, a creole aged twenty-two and born on New Montpelier.[89] According to Jackson, Palmer "had refused to take the terms", paid only one shilling eight pence per week and worked elsewhere, but had "commenced opening and falling a quantity of wood land and planting provisions against orders". The overseer had "pulled out the yams plants", and Palmer then took him to court to recover damages. In this case, the magistrates split and Palmer was required to pay costs. Jackson saw both of these judgements as victories and believed they had the effect of encouraging more of the workers to turn out to field work.[90]

In spite of his successes in court, Jackson remained unable to settle the rent question. On 25 March 1840, a Wednesday, he told Seaford, "I have to meet your people tomorrow on the subject of rents. We were at it the whole of last Friday and could not come to terms."[91] Exactly how quickly they reached a resolution is unknown, but three weeks later, on 17 April 1840, Jackson was able to report a successful outcome, telling Seaford, "Your laborers have come to terms with me." He sent Seaford a copy of the agreement but sadly it was not transcribed in the letterbook. Jackson said,

It is a rough sketch hurriedly drawn out by myself in their presence, and it was to me a matter of surprise that the head people put their names to it at all, they are so fearful of being caught. This agreement is subject to your approval, although I do not think it would be binding on either party as it is not a legal document.

For my part I should be happy if they would adhere to it. So far, they have kept faith pretty well and will soon take off the small crop and put the cane field in good order and likewise the grass pieces that are at present in high ruinate, which will be attended with great expenses, but must be done if the estates are to be kept up.[92]

Jackson's letter quickly drifted off into the management of the livestock on Shettlewood and this was all he had to offer on what appeared a crucial negotiation.

The later correspondence of Jackson offers some clues to the details of the agreement. In his next letter, written on 12 May 1840, Jackson was able to tell Seaford that "since the agreement the laborers have been working pretty regular four days per week, which is quite sufficient to keep the present cane field in order, and they give less trouble than any I am concerned for at present which is very satisfactory". The "rents and pasturage" collected on Montpelier were then about ninety pounds per month and at Shettlewood twenty-four pounds, a substantial increase over the previous year.[93] He promised to supply in his next letter "a return of houses and gardens and provision grounds with the rent charged on each". More important, for understanding the agreement, he went on to say that "working or not the people refused to pay more than 1/8 per week from the time Mr. Finlayson told them which I was glad to get, neither would they again have given 3/4 per week had I not prevented them opening land until they agreed to pay it". It appears, then, that the agreement required payment of three shillings four pence per week for house and grounds, with the condition that the renters could establish additional provision grounds. The rent of three shillings four pence indicated a return to the rate Jackson thought he had established in January 1840. He hoped for better success in court, now that the agreement was in place, saying, "Hitherto it has been of no use to bring any case of rent before Mr. Finlayson. The chances were 20 to 1 against the master and invariably ended in unsettling the minds of the people."[94]

Details of the location and quality of the lands rented out are hard to find in Jackson's letters and there must have remained a good deal of indeterminacy in the measurement and control of resources. As to the houses in the villages, these were the responsibility of the proprietor. The letters contain occasional references to their improvement and maintenance. In 1841, for example, Montpelier Estate employed workers from the pen in "repairing labourers houses" and the following year Jackson noted the cost of "splitting upwards of 70 thousand shingles for repairs of labourers houses". Money was spent by the estate for workers "repairing fences, splitting shingles for labourers houses and reshingling same".[95] Jackson proposed putting a gate at the end of the "Negro houses" on Montpelier Pen, saying this "would prevent the stock from straying" and "have the further advantage of confining the peoples horses from straying on the pasture laid down for the Pen".[96] The horses grazed on common land close to the houses. Estate labourers sometimes paid separately for pasturage but generally the accounts included it with rents.

The difficulty of obtaining labourers from sources outside Montpelier led Jackson to nurture those he had. When he delivered the rent roll to Seaford in early June 1840 Jackson had argued that

> although many of them are not paying the value of the house and grounds they occupy, they refuse to pay more and so long as they continue to work as they are now doing, I would not like to make any alteration, for fear of disorganising them, they are at present working as steadily as any of their neighbours, and on as reasonable terms.[97]

These remarks suggest that Seaford was not happy with the arrangement and wished to revisit the system of charging rents according to valuation, something that Jackson found too hard and the people rejected out of hand. At the end of June, Jackson reiterated his view, telling Seaford, "The laborers seem satisfied with the agreement and I trust your Lordship will give it a fair trial." Jackson believed the labourers were "working more steadily" than they had been before the agreement, doing at least as well as those on neighbouring estates.[98]

While Jackson recognized that the estates were responsible for offering employment if the workers were to be expected to pay rent, at the same time he saw the rents as a major source of cash to pay wages. This was one of the reasons for his determination to collect rents, at least down to 1840, and his willingness to go to court. But enforcing dispossession of house and grounds raised other problems and Jackson therefore sought only to pursue individual cases, serving notices on the "worst" examples.[99] He feared unsettling the situation by intervening in disputes between headmen and workers, arguing (specifically in connection with Copse, in September 1841) that "they would not remain upon the property but would settle back in the mountains and form a nucleus for others of the Estate to settle down with". Similarly, he believed that "on each property there are several old persons and people of colour that we can get no rent from, but I have invariably found where they have been turned away they take all their families and friends along with them. Many properties have been almost thrown out of cultivation from the want of foresight in this matter." Here was the fear of a "flight from the estates" en masse and instant ruin for the planter.[100] Jackson had already seen it happen.

An alternative was to harness the flight to the benefit of Montpelier. Rather than attempting to retain and attract people to live in the former slave villages on the estate, and hoping their presence would result in plantation labour, new settlements could be established. It was an approach followed in the "free villages" of the missionaries and by some planters.[101] Seaford had already founded Seaford Town but that was designed for European immigrants and was not located on Montpelier. By the middle of 1840 he was pondering the possibilities of offering rented land rather than freehold. He had given land for a chapel, in 1839, close to the site of the Old Montpelier works and village, thinking this might serve as a nucleus, but no building had been put up.[102] Jackson thought the site good for a township so long as the land was sold in building lots, but doubted "many persons would be found to erect buildings upon land only rented". The problem was the low price of land, with woodland "selling at from £5 to £10 per acre and renting in good situations from 20/- to 40/- per acre per annum". He suggested that the "distant land of Old Montpelier might be made available in this way". Jackson told Seaford he would "consider these matters well and write you more fully on the subject". This is how Jackson concluded his letter of 24 June 1840, the last addressed to Seaford in the first volume of the surviving letterbooks.[103]

Jackson's further thoughts on the potential of new township populations and how the rent/labour issue worked itself out over the following months is not known because of the gap in the series of letterbooks. The accounts produce for the properties recorded a substantial decline in rent collections on Montpelier and Shettlewood in 1840–41, an overall reduction of 20 per cent, and the decline persisted into 1841–42.[104] What is certain is that the wage and rent questions ceased to be the preoccupations they had been down to the middle of 1840. Exactly when this change occurred cannot be established precisely but when Jackson's correspondence resumed he had nothing to say. His first letter to Seaford in the second volume of extant letterbooks was dated 15 June 1841 and entirely devoted to advice on the shipping of sugar, problems with overseers, the valuation of the properties for parish taxes, and financial matters.[105]

What accounted for Jackson's optimism? Had labour relations shifted as a result of broad acceptance of the ground rules laid down in 1840? Certainly Jackson said nothing to suggest any new system of rents and wages for those people living in the old villages of Montpelier and Shettlewood. He did, however, permit and encourage the establishment of new settlements. In February 1842 he reported:

> I have rented several small lots of land near Mafuta to the labourers from the adjoining properties for provision grounds @ £1 4/- sterling per acre a year to be paid in advance. Most of them have expressed a wish to have a lease of 7 years

which I hope your Lordship will accede to which would enable them to build upon it and prevent their running over the woodland. Cutting or otherwise destroying timbers I have prohibited unless for building upon the land rented.[106]

This was not exactly the plan favoured by Seaford, to create new townships peopled by potential labourers. Jackson may have seen it as a useful way of competing with neighbouring properties but it seems more likely to have been a scheme designed to create a cash flow that would help to pay the wage bill and to control the spread of provision grounds and forest clearance. Mafoota was in the hilly eastern edge of Montpelier, close to the boundary with Roehampton Estate, for which Jackson was not yet attorney (Figure 8.4). Jackson wrote again on the topic in May 1842, still optimistic. He told Seaford, "It is probable that at no distant period that a good revenue may be derived from renting the waste lands, provided leases of 8 or 10 years are granted them, so as to build upon the land, which will be beneficial to your Lordship."[107]

The "waste lands" of Montpelier Pen, in particular, were indeed extensive, covering more than three thousand acres of woods, ruinate and grounds on the northern and eastern borders of the property. Much of this land was essentially untrodden and inaccessible on horseback. Jackson thought it would "be necessary to keep a sharp look out so as to prevent them [the settlers] scorching the timbers as to destroy them".[108] By the end of June 1842, thirty-six acres had been rented at twenty-four shillings per acre per annum. Jackson looked forward to the establishment of "a fine settlement" from which would come labour for the sugar lands of the estate. In October, Jackson "had the surveyor running off the lots of land leased out and I hope shortly to forward a diagram". Towards the end of the year, Seaford proposed reducing the rents on leased land, but Jackson advised against this "as it would render those dissatisfied who have already paid their first years rent, neither would a reduced rent increase the number of settlers".[109] The accounts produce first listed income from rents of "land leased out" in 1842, at Montpelier Pen, which encompassed Mafoota. Montpelier Estate began leasing the following year.[110]

By February 1843 Jackson could tell Seaford there had been "numerous applications" for lots of land, the sale of which would contribute significantly to the estate's income as well as building up a labour supply. "A village has sprung up as if by magic at the Farm where 50 or 60 houses are erected and in the course of erection," wrote Jackson, "and we will soon have a population of two or three hundred people." He was in the process of "running off lots on the lines of Lethe where the Estate has been much trespassed on."[111] Lethe adjoined the northern boundary of New Montpelier, a vast extent of "woodland" measured at 720 acres in 1821. Farm was in the southeast corner of Old Montpelier, a settlement used to grow provision crops during slavery

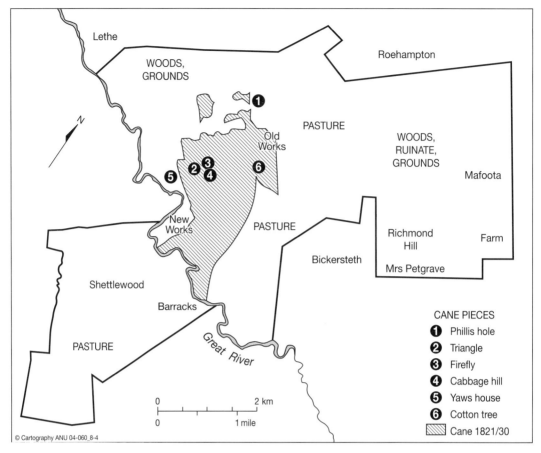

Figure 8.4 Montpelier Estate 1820–43. Based on "Plan of Old Montpelier and New Montpelier Estates, 1821", National Library of Jamaica, Plans, St James 12; "A Plan of Shettlewood Pen", n.d., National Library of Jamaica, Plans, Hanover 17; "A Plan of Shettlewood Pen situated in the Parish of Hanover and Island of Jamaica, the Property of the Honourable Lord Seaford, performed with alterations August 1830 [by] Morris and Cunningham, Surveyors", National Library of Jamaica, Plans, Hanover 17.

and a retreat for sick slaves, surrounded by an even larger area of woodland, estimated at 2,100 acres.[112]

The building up of the plantation population did not, however, bring all the benefits Jackson had hoped for. At the end of March 1843, in the midst of the sugar crop and facing declining yields and problems with the supply of water to the mill, he told Seaford that in spite of the "immense population that you have on the three properties" there were often too few workers to carry on the crop because the people were busy planting provisions. On the other hand, "during the periods of the year when they have no work in their own grounds we have frequently more than can be profitably employed". There was then 140 acres of land rented to ninety-seven people, "several of them have large families and we have every week applications for more lots". In the longer run, Jackson hoped that labour would be "more plentiful every year". Once again, the problem was not one of an absolute shortage of potential workers but an inequality in demand and supply. Jackson did not report trouble in collecting rents from the settlers. The rent on a larger slice of Montpelier, Richmond Hill, was not paid promptly by the long-term occupant Mrs Petgrave, however, even though she received "fully the amount from her settlers, not one of which has ever given us one days labor, but live solely by cultivating ginger and provisions".[113]

By May 1843 Jackson was referring to the settlement at Farm as "Mafuta Settlement", indicating that the area taken up stretched northwards through the eastern edge of Montpelier Pen, along the road leading to Roehampton. It had become "a flourishing village" of fifty to sixty houses either occupied or being built. Further, said Jackson, "Parson Burchell is putting up a school and others are opening shops and I fully expect we will soon have a population of 300. These will be a never failing source of labor and we have daily applications for more land from which I calculate upon an annual rental of from £200 to 300 in a short term."[114]

The income of the properties from the rent of houses and grounds and the lease of land to "labourers" peaked in 1839–40, declined in the following two years, then revived to almost reach the level of the early peak by 1843–44. The proportion of the income derived from leased land increased rapidly but did not rival that obtained from rent of houses and grounds at any time during the 1840s. Smaller sums came from the rent of a provision store, and Jackson sought to make money for Seaford through retailing. Montpelier Estate ran a "retail store" from the end of 1838, selling various commodities, including rum and tools, and made a small profit. Finding a reliable renter was difficult, said Jackson in 1842, because "the retail storekeepers have suffered much from over importations, and are generally very poor and not to be trusted and I must wait until a respectable tenant offers".[115]

Sugar

The combined sugar production of Old and New Montpelier peaked in 1810 at 753 tons, comparable to Golden Grove's 1775 peak, and remained as high as 662 tons in 1830. The rebellion of 1831 struck with the crop season barely underway. Seaford and Miller's decision to rebuild only one of the works, that at New Montpelier, and to abandon the site at Old Montpelier, pointed to a lack of faith in the future of sugar. Probably Seaford expected a reduction in output as a consequence of this concentration. At the same time, he certainly hoped sugar would remain a viable crop and that it was the best possible source of a substantial income. The uncertainties, however, made him anxious to have forward estimates and Jackson did his best to supply them, taking into account the relative proportions in plants and ratoons, piece by piece.

Sugar declined dramatically at Montpelier during the apprenticeship. When Jackson took charge, the overseer, Gardner, predicted an output of 118 hogsheads or about 105 tons. Jackson was sceptical, having told Campbell of Copse in September 1839 that, "notwithstanding the great expense of Lord Seaford's properties [his expenditure on wages], they are in a state of ruinate and I am confident will not make 100 hogsheads next crop". Jackson saw problems from vermin, a failure to plant some of the best cane-pieces, and labour.[116] There was also trouble with the mill because of a "great deficiency of water coming to the wheel", and Jackson employed "upwards of 30 hands" to repair the leaks by having the gutter "terraced" or plastered. The result was soon known, the crop being "small" and taken off quickly.[117] In the end, the crop of 1840 was less than half the quantity predicted by Gardner, coming to just 57 hogsheads of sugar and 30 puncheons of rum.[118] This was the long-term low for Montpelier, even less than in the year of the rebellion.

The area planted in cane contracted more slowly than the decline in production, reflecting the inertia created by ratooning. In December 1839 only 199 acres were in canes, less than one-third of the 870 acres of 1821 (481 acres at Old Montpelier and 389 acres at New Montpelier) when the properties were resurveyed at the order of Miller. All of the cane land was now attributed to New Montpelier, with 32 acres in plants, 89 acres in first ratoons, 43 acres in second ratoons, and 33 acres in third ratoons. Jackson complained that some of the best cane-pieces, located close to the works, were out of cultivation, and that the canes generally were short. "With the exception of three or four Guinea grass pastures and the canefield now in cultivation," he said, "Old and New Works are in ruinate for want of labour." He asked Seaford to send out new Wilkies four-horse, single-mould ploughs, to replace two that were broken, saying that the land had been hardened by dry weather and that the "people" were therefore increasingly reluctant to dig cane holes. Jackson hoped to increase the cane field by expanding the area under plant canes but commented that "it is no harm to allow the canefield to remain in ruinate until required for cropping, as it fertilizes the land and keeps down the smaller weeds". He admitted the fields "have not a good appearance, but we must not mind that, to avoid the expenses of cleaning them".[119]

In 1821 the lands of Old Montpelier spilled west of the main road across the level alluvials towards the Great River (Figure 8.4). After the rebuilding of 1832, at least some of the cane-pieces formerly within the bounds of Old Montpelier became part of the cane field of Montpelier Estate. For example, in 1842 Jackson reported that the crop had been taken from Firefly No. 1, Firefly No. 2, Triangle, and Cabbage Hill, former cane-pieces of Old Montpelier, and from the former common pasture Yaws House piece (Figure 8.4).[120] Jackson also complained of the quality of some of the land under cane. Of Shettlewood First Ratoons piece (located on Montpelier Estate), he said that it had never been properly cleaned and was plagued by rats, and "much trespassed upon by the pen stock and the laborers horses and hogs, several of the latter were killed in the canepiece after I took charge by my direction, a great quantity of the land is poor and unfit for canes".[121]

Looking forward to the crop of 1841, Jackson addressed the broader question of Montpelier's "future prospects". He told Seaford,

> I confess that I am at a loss to give your Lordship any thing like a correct idea, but it would not be unreasonable, to expect the estate to make 250 hogsheads of sugar annually, provided, the laborers will keep the mill about five days per week of 16 hours, and as they are settling down I hope to accomplish this, the ploughs and cattle are more than competent to establish a plant equal to this which ought to be 60 or 70 acres. Allowing the whole canefield to be 250 acres which if kept in a high state of cultivation would yield one hogshead per acre on an average, it would be a great waste of money and labour to put in more canes than can be kept in proper order, as the rats would destroy them all.[122]

Jackson's hope for 250 hogsheads represented a dramatic reduction from the last days of slavery, though the projected 250 acres seemed achievable. When the first shipment of the 1841 crop reached London, Seaford questioned its quality. Jackson implied that the cause was the early commencement of the crop, but hoped "that the remainder of the crop may turn out of better quality, both in grain and colour, as in the event of the estate making from 250 to 300 hogsheads sugar, we must commence before Christmas to enable us to finish in proper time". The final output was 152 hogsheads of sugar and 85 puncheons of rum, representing a big increase over 1840 but well short of Jackson's target.[123]

In spite of this failure, Jackson stuck by his objective of 250 hogsheads and predicted it again for the crop of 1842. He told Seaford he was supported in this opinion by "gentlemen of experience".[124] Jackson made determined preparations for the crop by having a new waterwheel built of "the hardest timbers", a new chimney erected at the boiling house and the "coppers rehung on an improved principle". Once again Jackson was worried about the likely quality of the sugar and the need to start crushing before the Christmas holiday. On 4 December 1841 he told Seaford they were ready to commence the crop "but the canes are very green and not ripe owing to the heavy seasons and many of the estates that have been about can with difficulty get the juice to granulate". He feared they could not make good sugar until there was some dry weather, "but however bad the prospects are we must try it".[125] Disaster struck in the middle of January when the main roller gudgeon of a mill purchased from Roehampton Estate collapsed and had to be replaced. Production was interrupted but the loss was balanced by Jackson's optimistic view of labour prospects resulting from the workers' agreement to work at night.[126] Jackson attempted to use as a replacement an old mill stored on the estate, but found that it "squeezed the canes so imperfectly that I called in an experienced engineer and millwright, who condemned it". Jackson then purchased a mill with an iron frame from Welcome Estate, eight miles to the west, paying two hundred pounds sterling, or just one-quarter its price new.[127]

In addition to the problems at the mill, strong winds and heavy rains caused the canes to become "lodged". Jackson and Gardner reduced the estimate and by February 1842 Jackson asked Seaford to arrange insurance for only 230 hogsheads and 120 puncheons, to be shipped by 1 August from Montego Bay, Falmouth or Lucea. In April, taking off the crop through persistent rain and threatened by plagues of rats, Jackson told Seaford they were 17 hogsheads behind the estimate of 116 for the pieces already harvested. Jackson hoped for better from the spring plants. A month later, in the middle of May, they were still behind. "The seasons have set in unusually soon," he told Seaford, "and it is with the greatest difficulty that we can proceed with the crop." The intervals, the narrow passages between the cane-pieces, had become almost impassable for the cattle-drawn cane carts, and the weather made it hard to find dry fuel. Jackson reduced his estimate to 200 hogsheads but told Seaford, "Your Lordship can rest assured, that I will do my utmost in such a trying situation over which I have no control."[128] Even this prediction proved too optimistic. The final result was only 173 hogsheads of sugar and 100 puncheons of rum. "This is deplorable," said Jackson, "but it has been the most unfavorable crop weather that I have ever experienced."[129]

Almost all of the output of 1842 was exported, with only trivial quantities of sugar and rum reserved for use on the estate. The only local sale, one hundred pounds of sugar, was to Shettlewood, an internal transaction.[130] The notion that local sales of rum should cover island expenses was a thing of the past. Molasses also disappeared, all of it being made into rum. Seaford, and Jackson, now sought to maximize metropolitan income by exporting everything possible. However, although Jamaica's output was reduced, finding shipping remained a task and sometimes a difficulty for the attorney. In June 1842 he shipped 45 hogsheads and 40 puncheons on the *Hopewell,* a vessel he had used the year before, saying, "Captain Selby has very kindly taken a larger proportion of rum than usual which other captains avoid when sugar is plentiful, as we are this year rather short of shipping." Jackson was fully responsible for sending bills of lading and making recommendations for insurance.[131]

The next crop, Jackson held back his predictions until the outcome seemed more certain. In January 1843 he predicted 186 hogsheads shipped, not far beyond the result for 1842, but well short of the 250 hogshead target.[132] By late March, however, he had to report poor yields, saying it was "a general complaint throughout this parish and Westmoreland and cannot fail to cause the cultivation being abandoned in many estates". There was also the seasonal problem of obtaining sufficient water from the spring and he stopped the mill to examine the gutter for leaks. "On putting about again," wrote Jackson, "the overseer was desirous of getting the mill house hands to work extra hours which they positively refused to do, which caused me to remonstrate with them on the impropriety of such conduct." Jackson spoke with authority and the workers started again the same night. He feared that "unless the people will work extra hours, the best crop weather will be lost".[133] In April, he reduced his estimate to 135 hogsheads but the final result came to 143 hogsheads of sugar and 74 puncheons of rum.[134] In August, Jackson responded to questions from Seaford regarding the "short crop", saying he was "somewhat at a loss to account for the great falling off from the estimate of this years crop". He attributed it to the "general inferiority of the ratoons, occasioned I have no doubt from the unfavourable weather of the preceding year and also from the delay in cutting some pieces when fit, occasioned by the mill in 1842". The decline in yield was common to estates throughout Hanover and Westmoreland, Jackson believed, and, along with the poor prices for sugar, foreshadowed their abandonment.[135]

Looking towards 1844, Jackson in August 1843 bravely predicted a crop of 190 to 200 hogsheads. He planned a large autumn plant but the bountiful supply of labour was not without its limits and he believed it not "prudent to extend the plant or canefield, beyond the means we possess of keeping it in a proper state of cultivation". He hoped for an increased supply of labour from the tenantry and, once they were settled, the time would be opportune for an extension of the cultivated area.[136] In September 1843 ploughing was underway for the fall plant, the weather mild, the winds light, the canes standing upright. The prospects were good, Jackson could report, "and we have no want of labor at present".[137] By November, however, the overseer had revised the estimate down by 16 hogsheads. This proved close to the mark, the final result, happening after the letterbooks conclude, amounting to 177 hogsheads of sugar.[138]

Although Jackson was optimistic about the willingness of the estate's people to work in field and factory, he was simultaneously investigating improved agricultural technologies to save on "manual labour". In 1843 he received a six-horse plough from England, hoping this would prove more useful. He also tried the "hoe harrow" for weeding the cane-pieces but found it wanting on stiff clay soils and wet lands and no substitute for weeding by hand.[139] Apparently Seaford was more enthusiastic and encouraged Jackson to seek out local models. Jackson travelled to Kingston especially to talk to the attorney Joseph Gordon regarding the hoe harrow. Jackson had ordered one from Gordon, with the latest improvements, saying he believed it was manufactured in Ayrshire and resembled ones he, Jackson, had seen in Cumberland. He favoured the "small plough" for the conditions at

Montpelier and hoped to borrow one for a trial.[140] A Mr Brockett had made a model light plough to be drawn by two mules that Jackson believed might save much labour. Behind the plough was "a first rate white ploughman who is paid 12/- per acre and is instructing one of our black people". On the other hand, Jackson rejected the clod roller believing it had no application at Montpelier. In October 1843 he was engaged in the fall plant, with thirty acres penned and "following up the pen with the plough as close as we can and planting it off". This was the fly-penning that Taylor seems not to have used on the more fertile soils of Golden Grove.[141]

Other innovations followed from the combination of field crops with livestock. In 1843 Jackson asked Seaford to consider "a description of wire used for fence in England which might be applied to great advantage in fencing the cane field from the pastures which is at present done with bamboos, at a great expense being so frequently to renew, owing to its perishable qualities in a damp atmosphere".[142] The use of imported wire would reduce dependence on the property's bamboo which could be used as fuel in the factory's furnaces in place of cane trash. The Montpelier trash house was too small to dry the material as quickly as needed in wet weather. This created a market for Shettlewood's bamboo but added to the cost of making sugar.[143]

Livestock

During slavery, the main purpose of Shettlewood was to breed the working stock needed to provide draught on the sugar estates. Its secondary function was to supply fresh meat to the white managerial staff of the estates and to sell meat to neighbouring properties. The livestock on Old and New Montpelier were used to power mills, to haul cane carts from field to factory, and to take casks to port. When they became old or "meagre" they were often returned to Shettlewood for fattening and slaughter. All of these animals were cattle. Small stock, such as poultry and pigs, were common in the villages, raised by the enslaved for consumption or sale. Shettlewood also raised horses and mules for use as riding animals. It worked together with Old and New Montpelier as a key element in an integrated system of production, balancing demands and maximizing overall productivity. Livestock were profitable but only in association with strong demand for draft animals from a productive sugar-growing sector.

For Jackson, the major choices facing him in 1839 stemmed from the changed balance between the units of Montpelier and the changed pattern of demand externally. In the first place, the conversion of Old Montpelier to a pen simultaneously increased the overall capacity of the properties to produce livestock and reduced the internal demand for working animals. By 1837 Old Montpelier had been renamed Montpelier Pen. The reduced output of sugar at New Montpelier also upset the balance, so that Jackson had to look to other estates for a market. The regional decline of sugar, however, made this difficult. Planter's stock was increasingly hard to sell. Before 1838, the whites on the estates had generally received allowances of food in kind, with generous helpings of beef, but after abolition got a money allowance, greatly reducing demand. To some extent, this loss was balanced by a new demand from the freed population, but the price of beef generally made it impossible for black people to become substantial and regular customers. Thus Jackson had to seek markets for both working cattle and fat cattle. This was a task that became increasingly important as the properties came more and more to rely on livestock for a major part of their income in the face of the rapidly shrinking output of sugar and rum.

When Jackson took over he found a total of 1,298 head of livestock on the properties, made up of 751 on Shettlewood Pen, 231 on Montpelier Estate, 279 on Montpelier Pen, and 37 recently imported from the Spanish Main. Shettlewood and Montpelier Pen were dominated by breeding cows (29 per cent of the livestock), calves (28 per cent), heifers and young steers (23 per cent), with smaller numbers of fattening stock, working stock and bulls. At Montpelier Estate, on the other hand, 98 per cent of the animals were working stock (steers, spayed heifers and mules). The "four-horse" ploughs were pulled by steers. The imported "Spanish stock" (four horses and thirty-three mares) were for breeding mules.[144]

What could be done to increase the carrying capacity and the productivity of the properties? A first approach was to clean the pastures of weeds and repair the fences, but for this work to be done money was required for wages, something Jackson found hard to convince Seaford about. It was also necessary to provide water in each pasture. At Montpelier Pen, said Jackson in 1840, "the grass pieces are in high ruinate and the walls in many places broken down".[145] Two years on, Seaford requested estimates of the projected carrying capacity of Montpelier Pen. Jackson took a month to respond in detail, saying he needed time to collect "the desired information of the extent of Guinea and common grass pastures and the quantity of stock it is capable of carrying to advantage".[146] He referred Seaford to "the plat of Montpelier Pen a duplicate of which I presume is in your possession", saying, however, that it gave "a very incorrect statement of the pastures". Some of the pieces identified on the plan as in Guinea grass were in fact in "high ruinate", having been cleaned only once since 1834 and lacking secure walls. Jackson's view was that Montpelier Pen was not "adapted for fattening but would answer well for a breeding pen". For this purpose, he proposed taking in "all of the pastures on the east side of the road from Great River bridge to the line at Miss Archers and from Phillis Hole on the other to the same line not going back from the Kings Road more than two grass pieces on the right hand side, which would include all the grass land to which any attention has been paid".

Elsewhere, the grass pieces had been neglected, and lacked walls and ponds. On the improved pastures, Jackson calculated that "one acre and a half of this land ought to carry one head of stock". At this time, Shettlewood carried over nine hundred head of livestock but Jackson believed Montpelier Pen could pasture no more than six hundred.[147] Jackson thought Shettlewood the best place for fattening, each pasture having its own water and properly walled. In September 1842 Jackson told Seaford he was proposing the enclosure of 1,076 acres of Montpelier Pen, with 735 acres in common grass and the rest in "St Marys or coarse grass". He thought "the Cotton Tree pieces Nos. 52, 53, 55 and 56 being within one fence is an excellent common and the Anchovy Gully stream gives a sufficient supply of water at all times for stock". East of Cotton Tree, towards the hills, said Jackson, were excellent glades and an extensive common.[148]

Seaford's letter to Jackson of 24 August 1842 included his ideas for Montpelier Pen. The details of Seaford's proposal for improvement are not known but the project appears to have been directed at further development of enclosed pasture, particularly in the wooded eastern stretches of the property, for the raising of working livestock for sale to estates. Jackson thought it very expensive and told Seaford that "the present state of W.I. affairs do not hold out much prospect of increase in the demand for planters cattle. I shall however give the subject due consideration and if any thing can be done to render the waste land available your Lordship may rely on my exertions to accomplish it."[149] Seaford was determined on his chosen direction and at the beginning of 1843 Jackson promised to carry out his wishes "as speedily as stock can be met with, on reasonable terms, and labor can be had to put up walls, without which we can not properly class the breeding stock, particularly the young heifers, that get to the bulls too soon". He had moved the heifers to Shettlewood, "until of proper age". Jackson told Seaford that some of the common pasture was "taken up by jointwood bush and guavas", invasive plants that flourished in ruinate lands. Much of the land must have been unknown territory to Jackson, having quickly grown up in thick forest though formerly in cultivation. He took advice from the workers: "The head mason states that there are several portions of walls to be found in the woods, but I cannot form an idea of the expense that it would take to enclose these pieces."[150]

At the beginning of 1843, there were 1,550 head of cattle on the properties, roughly 260 more than he had got from McNeil. Shettlewood Pen had the majority, 932 head, and Jackson believed it was already close to its maximum capacity, which he put at 1,000. By the end of April the number had passed 950 and, with the approval of Seaford, Jackson stopped buying stock for Montpelier Pen. On the other hand, he reported purchasing some 70 head of old cattle for fattening on Shettlewood where he had 20 fit for sale to the butcher.[151] Overall, within the period of the letterbooks, Jackson was successful in increasing the herd at Montpelier, through the management and improvement of the pastures.

Jackson also sought to improve the productivity of the pens by offering positive incentives such as special payments to leading workers. In 1841, for example, he told Seaford that Shettlewood had exhibited stock at the Hanover Agricultural Exhibition, where it "took the prize for planters steers and fat cattle amounting to £6 sterling which was given to the penkeepers". Jackson hoped that this annual show would encourage "great improvement among the penkeepers and overseers" and planned "to give a premium next year to the penkeeper who rears the greatest number of calves to the proportion of cows which I expect will have a good effect".[152] In 1842 Shettlewood won second prize for fat cattle and for planter's steers, while Montpelier Estate took second prize for working stock "which there was great competition for". Jackson believed the competition had "stirred up a spirit of emulation among the penkeepers, which will do much good".[153] He also sought to increase the income flowing to Seaford by tightening up on the overseers, who had previously been allowed to run large numbers of their own stock on the property's best grass.[154]

Although he did not share Seaford's enthusiasm for the raising of working stock, Jackson did his best to follow orders and improve output. He thought it a losing battle, not only because of the reduction of the market from estates but also because of competition from imports from the Spanish Main. When a cargo of cattle was landed at Falmouth in 1843, Jackson noted that "a great proportion" were "fit for work and of good size", and that if the trade developed it would "operate much against the pens". At the same time, the general failure of the sugar crop had reduced the capacity of the sugar estates to purchase working stock.[155] Orders for planter's cattle were few and far between. Estates that had been mortgaged were unlikely to make purchases and other properties would be abandoned. The only solution was to fatten the stock, wrote Jackson, and he was not afraid to move in this direction, since it would avoid "the long credit and risk on sales to the planters". He had sold planter's stock at seventeen to nineteen pounds in 1842 but told Seaford, "I prefer short credit in these distressed times among planters." Sales of working stock and fat cattle remained slow until the end of 1843.[156]

The market for fat stock also faced new challenges. Above all, Jackson complained bitterly of the new system of "overseer and bookkeepers allowance" in which money payments replaced allocations of food. He saw it as a self-inflicted wound. The new system, said Jackson when he took over Montpelier in 1839, had "ruined all the country butcheries".[157] He told Seaford,

> I do not approve of the present system of a money allowance in lieu of supplies to the white people, it is fast tending to demoralize the whole planting community

and without effecting any saving to the property as was intended. It is therefore my intention to recommend to your Lordship and others to give the amount in supplies and fresh beef that they are at present recurring, of which I will forward a list at the earliest opportunity. The overseers make the purchase of supplies a pretext for leaving home on all occasions and either become improvident or starve their book-keepers.[158]

Jackson's aims were both to control the behaviour of the lower level managers and to find a market for the beef produced by the pens. Keeping the overseers on the properties would prevent them "forming improper acquaintances". The cost of beef and flour would be less than the current money allowances.[159] He might also have argued that the properties would save on for imported foods. Seaford was not convinced and Jackson told him in September 1841 that "should your Lordship prefer a money allowance, it is only to withdraw the order for the overseers establishment from the list of supplies".[160] Jackson's preference eventually won the day. By early 1842 he could tell Seaford, "Now that the overseers are allowed a limited quantity of beef and paid by the estates they cannot live on saltfish hams etc as when they had a money allowance." He expected improved profits from the butchery and was looking out for "lean stock to fatten on the Pen".[161]

The other market Jackson sought to supply was the newly created wage-earning workforce. He had hopes for this market as a balance to that lost to the money allowances but feared it would not be sufficiently strong. In 1839 he said, "It is only by salting the great part of it and hawking it about the black people that one animal can be slaughtered on the Saturdays and does not pay." At first he was able to sell cattle direct to the working people, but reported by late 1839 that "the black people soon gave up purchasing fat stock finding it did not pay them". There was also a seasonal market for beef when the shipping began to arrive for the crop season. The 1839 Christmas market seems to have helped too, so that by New Year's Day Jackson could tell Seaford, "Fat stock goes off as fast as ready for the butcher."[162] A longer term solution to the problems faced by the meat market was the negotiation of local cooperation. Jackson believed he had achieved this by the end of February 1840 when he told Seaford that he had "arranged that Shettlewood kills each Wednesday and Ramble each Saturday, which enables each Pen to slaughter a good beast and dispose of it to good customers". This removed the need to corn meat, with the risk of spoilage and loss of weight, and saved the "expense of Negro labour in hawking it about and likewise incurring bad debts in order to get rid of it".[163]

Jackson kept a close eye on the price of beef. Early in 1842 he sold fat cattle to butcheries, including Green Vale in Manchester, more than forty miles distant. By March, however, he noted that beef maintained its price of seven and a half pence sterling per pound, "which is in favor of the pens", but the opportunity came when Shettlewood was understocked.[164] In May, Jackson told Seaford that "the Pen at present abounds with grass and I only regret that we had not more stock to feed it down", but the price of stock was "so high at present that I am unwilling to put your Lordship to the expense of purchasing". It was difficult to obtain "thin stock" for fattening, Jackson argued, because of the way the estates had responded to the pressures of the post-slavery economy. The scarcity occurred because older stock were "not being drafted off (so as to renew the herd every 10 years) regularly, but are worked as long as they are able". Jackson said this was a "ruinous system" because "if estates are to be carried on they must be stocked and the old ones regularly drafted off to keep up the herd".[165] Fattening stock were also hard to obtain, Jackson observed, because "the small pens in St Elizabeth and Manchester that formerly had so many stock are all in ruinate".[166] By February 1843 Jackson was looking to imports from Santo Domingo to supply fatteners.[167]

Profit and Loss

Old Montpelier, New Montpelier, Shettlewood, the Shettlewood butchery and Montpelier Wharf all kept separate sets of books. They transacted exchange with one another as well as with the wider world.[168] There was some consolidation of accounts, however, as sugar production became a less substantial component and management was simplified.

Even before replacing McNeil as attorney at Montpelier, Jackson found time to tell Seaford, "You may be assured that I will have the accounts minutely examined before I make any settlement with him."[169] When the accounts were settled, at the end of November 1839, McNeil was owed £1,629 currency and Jackson drew on Seaford for the amount. Various debts totalling £2,946 were owed to the Shettlewood butchery, to Montpelier Estate, Montpelier Wharf, and rents were due from Mrs Petgrave who leased Richmond Hill. Jackson set about collecting on accounts for beef purchased by neighbouring estates but told Seaford that the accounts had not been kept with "proper care" and that much of what was owed on transactions dating back as far as 1836 was "very doubtful". Jackson was still pursuing McNeil about the 1836–39 Shettlewood butchery accounts in April 1842.[170]

Jackson regularly submitted Montpelier and Shettlewood crop accounts to the island secretary's office in Spanish Town and sent copies to Seaford. These set out the gross income of the properties, detailing the quantities of commodities exported and local income. On the other hand, the Montpelier "accounts current" that recorded expenditure were submitted only to the scrutiny of Seaford. In May 1842 Jackson responded to a query from Seaford regarding the relationship between the accounts current and the accounts produce. Jackson explained that "the usual period for closing accounts for the year is now 1st August and for recording or rather making up crop accounts the 30th September so as to include the sales of planters stock and shipments of other produce". He promised in future to "make up my accounts and crop accounts to the same period, as your Lordship suggests". The crop accounts were thereafter fixed to 1 August.[171]

Seaford, for his part, regularly questioned expenditure on labour. Jackson found it necessary to explain that he, as attorney, had to advance money on account to pay the wage bill. He further explained items in the accounts showing the balances on labour and rents and in the hands of the overseer, and promised that "I shall in future send the overseers affidavits for the expenditure".[172] The vastly increased flow of cash in the wage-based post-slavery economy created accountability problems for absentee-proprietors, since it further distanced them from any ability to monitor income as well as expenditure and put cash in the hands of their employees.

Around the middle of each year, Jackson sent Seaford detailed lists of supplies required by the properties in the following year, things which could not be produced or purchased locally. These lists had to be approved by Seaford but in practice he seems not to have questioned the items and simply forwarded the lists to his London factor. The information provided by Jackson was generally precise. For example, in July 1840 he sent a long "list of supplies required for Montpelier Estate for the year 1841 forwarded to the Right Honourable Lord Seaford to be sent out and landed at Montpelier Wharf near Montego Bay, Jamaica". It included an order for 30,000 eight-penny cooper nails, 15,000 ten-penny cooper nails, 60,000 six-penny shingling nails, 15,000 ten-penny carpenter nails, 15,000 twenty-penny carpenter nails, 5,000 thirty-penny carpenter nails, and 10,000 seven-penny and eight-penny horseshoe nails. On top of all these nails, Jackson wanted puncheon hoops, chains, hoes, padlocks for gates, saws, files, rods, rivets, bars of iron, oils, paint, tar, pitch, coals, tallow, pump leather, cloth (osnaburg), shoes, hams and porter, among other things. Occasionally, the instructions were more complicated. For example, there was a note advising to "see that the bundles wood hoops are 'well wired' as in general they are short of the number charged in invoice, broken up and loss to Estate is great". In ordering two grindstones, it was stated that one was to be "charged to Shettlewood in lieu of one lent there from Old Works". The list of orders for Shettlewood was just as detailed and specific, with a note that one grindstone was "to repay Old Works". Items ordered specifically for the butchery included handsaws, knives of various lengths, a bolt of osnaburg and a "patent dial weighing machine with hook and scale".[173]

The following year, Jackson told Seaford that "the lists of supplies for 1842 are unavoidably heavy owing to the scanty supply for the last two or three years particularly the house establishment, such as linen, crockery ware, knives and forks". The pattern was much the same for 1843 except that

Jackson added a special list of medicines. The lists were drawn up by Jackson in close consultation with the overseers. He also sometimes consulted the headmen.[174]

A more active task required of Jackson as attorney was his advocacy with the parishes, to seek tax relief. In 1839 Seaford asked him to approach the vestries for a reduction in the assessment of land taxes. Jackson agreed to try, thinking the St James vestry might be generous in view of Seaford's "magnificent gift of lands" for the building of a chapel, but had little optimism.[175] The burden of the taxes resulting from the parish assessors' valuations loomed large as a threat to the viability of the properties. Jackson provided detailed information on the valuations and assessments for 1841. Shettlewood Pen, in the parish of Hanover, was valued at £15,633 sterling. The Montpelier properties were in St James. Montpelier Estate was valued at £23,271 sterling, Montpelier Pen £35,106, and Montpelier Wharf £1,000. The valuations included buildings. The reason that Montpelier Pen (Old Montpelier) was worth more than the estate (New Montpelier), where sugar production was then concentrated, was that the pen covered 4,750 acres and the estate only 2,372 acres. Montpelier Estate was valued at £9 16s per acre, whereas Montpelier Pen was worth only £7 8s per acre. These amounts can be compared to Jackson's statement a year before that woodland was selling for £5 to £10. The parish taxes were based on the annual value of the properties, calculated at 6 per cent of actual value. The total value of Seaford's properties in St James and Hanover was £75,010 sterling, making the annual value £4,500. Jackson thought the taxes would amount to at least £900 sterling, so payable at a rate of 20 per cent.[176]

In 1842 the tax account increased by £273, and had to be paid by 10 August in order to receive a 10 per cent discount.[177] Seaford apparently asked for an explanation of the method of valuation. Jackson told him,

> The principle on which the Assessors made their valuation of property is not generally known further than that a maximum and minimum value was fixed by the commissioners of account in different description of lands in cultivation and adding to the value of the land on sugar estates one half the amount for the value of the buildings the value of the pens and other settlements one third for buildings which makes the taxes fall heavy on properties that have large runs of land, so that the buildings however good or bad, their value is regulated by the value of the lands attached to them and therefore no just criterion of value.[178]

Montpelier Pen suffered most obviously by the application of these rules. On the other hand, Jackson thought Montpelier Wharf might have been valued as high as £1,500 sterling, and that in consequence the rent of £150 paid by Mr Whittingham in 1840 was fair. Early in May 1843 Jackson was able to tell Seaford that he had successfully appealed the assessors' valuation of Montpelier Pen and got it reduced from £35,106 to £10,000, "which the other tax payers do not at all relish". Because of this ill-feeling, said Jackson, "I consequently expect great opposition on 1st June when the valuation of the Estate will be appealed against."[179] His pessimism proved justified. The Appeal Court of 1 May was declared illegal and the original valuation had to stand. In August, he was trying for a reduction of taxes, appealing to Council.[180] Tax was also charged on the export of staple commodities, and Jackson was pleased to report, at the beginning of 1842, that the island export taxes had been reduced by 75 per cent. He believed, however, that the taxes on the planter remained heavy.[181]

In spite of these high valuations and heavy taxes, Seaford's properties were making a loss not a profit. Correspondence is not available on the result for 1840, the year when sugar production hit a low, but it was a heavy loss compared even to recent balances let alone the £20,000 sterling Seaford was said to have made before 1823.[182] At the end of 1841 the current account showed Seaford with a debit balance of £2,193 sterling. Almost all of the loss was incurred at Montpelier Estate, the sugar-producing property, which showed a debit of £3,622. Montpelier Pen lost £179, partly arising from the building of a new provision store on its lands. On the other hand, the wharf made £67 and Shettlewood £962 plus £221 from the butchery.[183] Jackson did his best to collect outstanding debts, he said, but there was no point suing most of the debtors because the "distress among the poor settlers is unprecedented this year". He had collected little of the debt from 1840 but believed "those who are worth powder and shot I will soon bring to a settlement". He did his best to avoid bad debts but some were unavoidable, as, for example, when an overseer owing money to the butchery died insolvent.[184]

Seaford had a series of queries. In July 1841 he asked for accounts setting out the average profit on fat cattle sold from the butchery. Jackson responded in September, saying,

> In answer to your Lordships observations on this head 8th July I beg to state that the cattle killed at the butchery are sold from the pen @ 30/- sterling per 100 lbs and retailed at 50/- giving a profit of 11/- per 100 lbs to cover expenses etc. Owing to the scarcity of fat cattle, beef has been raised to 7½ d sterling per lb or 62/6 per 100 lbs since 21 August and sold from the Pen @ 48/- which leaves 14/6 for retailing it but since the price has been raised the demand has slackened and it is with difficulty we can get off the smallest carcase. The people cannot do without beef and we will have them back as soon as they get through their small stock.[185]

In May 1842 Jackson answered queries regarding the balances on labour and rents, and explained how these related to the "balance in hands of the overseer". In order to avoid any misunderstanding, Jackson promised that he would "in future send the overseers affidavits for the expenditure". He kept to his word, regularly supplying "contingent account, in detail, crop account, affidavit of expenditure, increase and decrease of stock, and account current".[186]

Although the export of sugar and rum increased, things were worse in 1842, with a debit balance of £2,738.[187] Montpelier Pen was turning a small profit, with a credit balance of £293, but the balance of Shettlewood Pen fell to £391 and the butchery to £193, while the wharf remained stable at £70. All of these marginal credits were overwhelmed by the debit balance at Montpelier Estate that increased to £3,685. Seaford's metropolitan agents scrutinized the record but by the end of February 1843 Jackson received approval of his book-keeping and could say, "I am happy to learn that my accounts were found to be correct."[188]

The accounts for 1843 followed the pattern of earlier years, with a debit balance of £3,632 at Montpelier Estate far outweighing the credits of £449 at Montpelier Pen, £27 at Montpelier Wharf and £593 at Shettlewood. The reduced takings of the wharf Jackson "attributed to the general decline of business". He had sold planter's stock from Shettlewood but found little demand for fat cattle, particularly in Montego Bay. Overall, the final debit balance of £2,553 was only slightly better than the 1842 result. Once again, the whole of the loss occurred in sugar production.[189]

In spite of the losses made on the properties, Seaford was willing to consider increasing Jackson's salary. When offered £600 per annum in 1839 Jackson had said the amount was "more than the present returns of the properties will warrant", and was content to wait until improved profits justified an increase.[190] The expected improvement did not occur, however, and in 1842 Jackson told Seaford, "In consequence of the great falling off of the crop at Montpelier this season, I do not feel myself justified in charging the additional £100 currency this year, but in the event of the next crop proving more satisfactory I shall then avail myself of your Lordships liberality."[191] At the end of June 1843 Jackson told Seaford, with a measure of magnanimity,

> The conclusion that I came to on this subject was made under the full conviction that your Lordships properties could not afford any increase of my salary at present and that every possible means of economy should be resorted to, to enable you to continue the cultivation with any prospect of benefit. I cannot help saying, that my opinion is still the same, and that I am willing to abide by my own decision if it meets with your Lordships concurrence.[192]

Rather in the style of Simon Taylor, Jackson must have gained some pleasure from demonstrating his financial soundness in dealing with his still wealthy, but embattled, aristocratic employer.

Jackson proved his professionalism by taking responsibility for failures. In 1841, for example, when hides were allowed to rot at the Shettlewood butchery, Jackson attributed the error to the overseer Young, but told Seaford it was a matter "which either he or I must pay for, as it was a shameful neglect of his duty".[193] Jackson proved his liquidity by personally advancing money on account to pay for labour on the properties. This was, however, only short-term financing. In order to cover his advances and other accounts owed by the properties, Jackson regularly drew on Seaford through his local agent, just as Taylor had done for Arcedeckne. Thus in June 1841 Jackson noted that by the previous packet he had advised Seaford he would be obliged to draw for £700 sterling. These drafts were unavoidable, he said, as there was little hope of extracting money from the properties' debtors and the amounts due on planter's stock were "not payable till August and the banks refusing to discount any papers precludes the possibility of converting them into cash".[194] He soon needed more. In August, sending the final bills of lading for the 1841 crop, Jackson wrote, "I also beg to hand your Lordship a sketch of my account current with you to 1st August, as far as they can be correctly ascertained at present." The balance in Jackson's favour was £780. To cover this, he advised Seaford that "I shall draw on you in favor of C. Robinson for £800 sterling after the sailing of the packet on account of the same".[195] In 1842 and 1843 Jackson drew several times on Seaford, to cover spending on wages, salaries, taxes and other expenses.[196]

Assessment

Jackson's correspondence with Seaford, as contained in the known surviving letterbooks, ended on an optimistic note. The final letter, written by Jackson on 18 November 1843, acknowledged Seaford's of 14 October. Gardner, the long-term survivor as overseer at Montpelier Estate, estimated the forthcoming crop at 177 hogsheads. It was both a correct prediction and the largest crop since abolition. As well as this progress in production, Jackson had hopes for the estate's population and labour prospects.[197] His attitude was not unusual for the attorneys of the time and the experience of Montpelier fit quite well the pattern for many other sugar estates.

The years covered by Jackson's letters, 1839–43, fall within what several historians have labelled the "period of optimism" in post-slavery West Indian history. It was an optimism shared, though in unequal measure, by planters, freed people, humanitarians and Colonial Office. The sugar industry seemed capable of survival, allowing the maintenance of an entrenched plantation system, supplied with willing labour by people living in the old estate villages as well as in new townships, and providing the basis for a civilized Christian society. This was a conception of Jamaican society and economy in which the fundamental institutions remained firmly in place. Only the relationship of capital to labour was radically altered, hence the centrality of the conflict over rent and residence, wages and work. In *Free Jamaica,* Douglas Hall argued that "from the early 1840's until 1846 there was a spate of energy and enterprise among all classes. A general attitude of optimism and a noticeable pride in new accomplishment became evident, where previously pessimistic groans and unswerving attachment to traditional method had been the rule." This attitude, he contended, derived in large part from the separation of rents and wages, and "a rather uniform practice of charging one day's wage as the weekly rent for a cottage, and one day's wage as the weekly rent for the use of provision grounds". Richard Sheridan saw the Sugar Duties Act of 1846 as "a watershed between the period of optimism and innovation and that of pessimism and retrenchment". On the other hand, Philip Curtin saw the middle years of the 1840s as merely "a plateau in the long descent", and Thomas Holt recognized only a "brief bubble of optimism generated by the flow of compensation cash".[198]

When Seaford died on 1 July 1845 the bubble was not quite ready to burst. He would have known the crop of that year was less considerable than it had been in 1844 but Montpelier's sugar production then accelerated to exceed 200 hogsheads in every year down to 1850 and reached a peak of 375 hogsheads (about 337 tons) in 1848. The proprietor was then Lord Howard de Walden, Seaford's son, who spent two months at Montpelier in 1846 to observe the crop season. After 1850, however, failure of output combined with rapidly declining sugar prices and persistent losses on current account resulted in the abandonment of sugar in 1856, the year of Jackson's death.[199] Anthony Trollope, who travelled in Jamaica in 1858, described abolition and the removal of protection as a double blow that destroyed the industrious as well as the idle planter. "Ask the Gladstone family," said Trollope, "what proceeds have come from their Jamaica property since the protective duty was abolished. Let Lord Howard de Walden say how he has fared."[200]

In 1852, when Jackson had surrendered the attorneyship, Howard de Walden produced a ninety-page booklet, *General Instructions for Montpelier and Ellis Caymanas Estates in Jamaica*, in which he "observed that serious inconvenience often results from changes; that much which has been written from England becomes a dead letter after a change of either attorney or overseer; that quarrels and jealousies too frequently deprive useful subalterns of a knowledge not only of the wishes, but even of the positive injunctions of a proprietor". Further, "very few have the opportunity of studying and understanding the principle upon which their duties as well as operations should be based". Howard de Walden's object, he stated, was "to make known to all in authority on my estates, for their information and guidance, the general system which I will call upon them to carry out".[201] What he set out in the booklet was principally technical, with tables and diagrams, and little to do with the broader strategies of management, but he directed all of this information "to those on my estates, on whose intelligence, good-will, and zeal I rely". He sought to furnish the elements for understanding my personal views and wishes, trusting that, having the advantage of such knowledge, they may more cheerfully and with greater confidence undertake the duties incumbent upon them, in working out details as well as principle of enlightened practice (upon which the prosperity of a Jamaica estate henceforward must so much depend), than if left to be guided by mere verbal instructions and explanations signified from time to time on the spot.[202]

He called for an "annual report" to be made up at Christmas, providing "a general recapitulation . . . of all features of improvements, either in the condition of the peasantry or tenantry, or the works, or in regard to any operations, transactions, or occurrences, which may be characteristic of the expiring year".[203] Immediately after crop, he recommended, the state of all implements should be assessed and repairs undertaken, and it was then that "wants, remarks, and suggestions should be signified in correspondence".[204] Douglas Hall rightly thought this document unusual, saying many other planters "did not interfere so intelligently".[205]

Howard de Walden's book of instructions may be seen as a response to the need for a more closely regulated system of management or as a codification of the protocols put in place by Jackson. Whether Jackson contributed directly to its preparation or whether it was meant as a critique of Jackson's practice is unknown. How did Seaford rate Jackson's performance? Seaford seems never to have contemplated dismissing Jackson, whatever the level of production, the problems with labour or the lack of profits. Indeed, he was ready to increase Jackson's salary in the face of these failures. Seaford's knowledge of the fate of fellow absentees must have told him that he probably could not do better and that switching attorney was unlikely to change any of the fundamentals.

How well did Jackson perform as attorney? Just as for Taylor before the American Revolution and before the abolition of the Atlantic slave trade, Jackson's first responsibility was the making of profits for his employer. On this count he certainly failed but what more might he have done to follow different strategies with more positive results? It is easy enough to see that a more aggressive approach might have resulted in an even earlier abandonment of sugar and failure to increase production to the levels in fact achieved by 1850. The shift towards livestock meant reduced profits but held the land for Seaford. Montpelier was not abandoned and the property remained in the hands of Seaford's family for several more generations.

What more might Jackson have done to increase productivity? In terms of technology, Jackson did adopt a variety of new methods of cultivation and travelled the island to inspect implements and machines. He sought information on new methods of fencing, in order to separate crops and cattle, and practised manuring. He studied the capabilities of different fields and pieces with an eye to estimating their value for cane cultivation and their carrying capacity for livestock. He also developed a strategy for preserving a core cane supply area that would see Montpelier through its hardest days, and in the 1840s this proved quite successful.

What of the factory? Jackson generally did his best to keep the mill working by using the existing technologies and repairing what broke. He was, however, aware of modern instrumentation that enabled the transition from art to science in sugar-making. In June 1842, for example, Jackson ordered "a sacchrometer with set of tables" and "1 of Sykes hydrometers with tables calculated to 100° heat and ½ dozen spare glasses". These were relatively sophisticated instruments for determining the characteristics of sugar during the process of manufacture. The Sikes hydrometer had been invented in England in 1802, to measure the proof of spirits, and was established as the legal standard in 1816. The sacchrometer was a hydrometer designed specifically to determine the concentration of sugar in a solution. The glass tube, floated in the liquid, measured its density by the length of the stem immersed. Probably the idea to use them arose from the difficulties encountered with quality of grain and colour in the pre-Christmas phase of the crop.[206]

Jackson never made radical proposals, such as the erection of a steam mill. Seaford was similarly conservative on this score, anxious to limit his expenditure and fearful that sugar could not be saved at Montpelier. Neither Jackson nor Seaford were peculiarly backward for their time and water power remained a competitive technology for many decades. Within months of Seaford's death in 1845, his son Howard de Walden visited not only Montpelier but also another family sugar estate Ellis Caymanas, in St Catherine, and by April 1846 surveys were being made towards the establishment of a steam mill there. Ellis Caymanas was a smaller property than Montpelier but it lay in a larger plain with potential for centralized milling, much like Golden Grove's region. Perhaps Seaford had discussed this option with his son, as the best way to consolidate the family fortune.[207] Howard de Walden's *Instructions* of 1852 did not propose a steam mill for Montpelier and sugar production was quickly wound down there to effect a partial abandonment and a concentration of capital elsewhere.

Jackson's main problem, certainly down to 1843, was the cane supply and he saw this as the direct result of his inability to command labour. Without more cane a larger, more efficient mill would have been a wasted investment. How could Jackson have better increased the cane supply at Montpelier? He knew where he wanted to plant more cane and the best yielding cane-pieces had long been identified. The lack was labour to work the land. Fundamentally, Jackson believed Jamaica's population was simply too small to deliver the required number of workers on the required days at the wages the planter was willing to pay. He never proposed offering higher wages in order to achieve the wanted supply of labour, believing it impossible to compete with the peoples' provision grounds and desire for a lighter load. Because Montpelier was not the only property he managed, Jackson had also to avoid raising wages competitively and simply pushing up the district norm. Jackson was convinced that immigration was the only possible solution and advocated the employment of indentured Africans. Seaford opposed him, however, and promoted white immigrant settlements that Jackson thought a complete waste. Thus when Jackson had the opportunity to recruit Africans in 1843 he actively sought them for most of the properties for which he was attorney but not for Montpelier. What difference would a contingent of indentured Africans have made? The advantage would have been a core labour force, which the attorney and overseer could command without the uncertainty of continuing negotiations over rent and wages and without fear of strikes. Whether the presence of a gang of indentured labourers would have been enough to tip the balance is uncertain. After 1845 indentured Indians were in fact employed at Montpelier and this was the period of increased output, but, assuming they made a difference then, they delayed the abandonment of sugar only for a few years.

How well did Jackson negotiate wages and rents? Here again he was sometimes at odds with his employer. Initially, throughout 1839 and into early 1840, Jackson held to the view that residence should be tied to labour on the estate and that rents should be demanded aggressively in order to force wage labour on the plantation. Seaford's more liberal policy was not at first appealing to Jackson but he followed it as best he could and soon became a convert. By 1842 he was ahead of Seaford in promoting the settlement of "outsiders" on the properties, in order to attempt to build up a potential supply of labour or, if that failed, a substantial source of rent payments. Certainly, Jackson was successful in building up the population of Montpelier but he was less successful in the effective collection of rents. Probably he did as well as he could in negotiating wage rates, within the bounds of what Seaford and other planters were willing to offer and what was sufficient to entice potential plantation workers away from their provision grounds and alternative activities.

How well did Jackson perform against the criticisms commonly attached to attorneys? Certainly, he lived close to Montpelier and had a good working knowledge of the landscape and the operations of the estate. It was a vast sprawling space, however, and Jackson could not claim close knowledge of every niche and glade. How often he visited cannot be determined from his correspondence with Seaford but he must have been there much more often than Simon Taylor visited Golden Grove. Jackson slept occasionally at New Montpelier, to keep an eye on the operations of the mill, and considered living on the estate, at Shettlewood. He never proposed living in a distant town in the way Miller had done before him, residing in Falmouth, or Taylor, who had lived in Kingston. He possessed qualifications for his task that derived from his immediate experience as overseer on a sugar estate in the same district. He knew the land and the people. On the other hand, his experience was apparently completely rural and his network of contacts within the merchant world was more limited than in the cases of Taylor and Miller. Jackson had the advantage of closeness to Montego Bay, where the merchant class was much smaller than in Kingston, and he also knew Lucea and Falmouth and took advantage of shipping from all three ports. He had to deal only with a small crop, so the shipping needs were limited, but he appears to have negotiated successfully with ship captains to gain advantages.

There is no doubting Jackson's assiduity in correspondence with his principals. Occasionally he may have taken advantage of the increased speed and urgency of the post, dramatically raised around 1840, to delay answering difficult questions. His responses were, however, generally detailed and precise. His letters were organized in a professional way, arranged under subheads and mostly formal in style. Did he conceal fraud? Certainly livestock trading was commonly seen as the ideal way for attorney and overseer to strip profits from their absentee employers. No doubt Jackson might have been tempted by the opportunities. He was, however, determined in his exposure of the failings of others and the prices he recorded fell within the expected range for the time. Of the crop of 1841, he told Seaford explicitly, "I have no reason to think that any pilfering took place at the wharf or on its way to it."[208] The fact that he was taking a larger income from Montpelier than the profits achieved by Seaford was no secret and derived directly from his salary. Seaford would have been better off employing Jackson on commission but that was not a viable system in the period. Jackson's ability to purchase properties on some scale was no great surprise, reflecting the cheapness of the properties more than the extent of his resources.

Did Jackson push profits, with an eye on the short term and without regard to the long-term success of plantation and proprietor? This was a criticism regularly levelled at attorneys during slavery but it had less weight after 1838 because of the reduced capacity of the attorney to direct the destruction of human and physical resources. Jackson had limited power to destroy lives and extract extreme hours of labour. He showed some empathy when the people worked through the night in miserable conditions. His initial belief in the efficacy of an aggressive policy on rents and wages led in the direction of labour disputes and abandonment but he was quickly cured and came to realize that long-term viability depended on a spirit of conciliation. An argument might be made that it was in the crucial initial months of freedom that the struggle was lost, that the aggressive policy of McNeil and Seaford created an atmosphere in which the people of Montpelier saw their attachment to the plantation undermined. The challenge to their customary rights to house and ground changed everything.

Jackson was not then in charge at Montpelier, but it was a policy he approved and wished to maintain, and perhaps apply even more aggressively. Probably a more accommodating attitude would have been more successful in ensuring the continued residence of the village people. Whether this would have meant continued profits for Seaford is far less certain.

How powerful was Jackson as attorney? Several points of conflict with Seaford have been identified. Jackson may well have believed that had all of his strategies been followed Montpelier would have been more profitable, but the period in which he managed contained so many imponderables and uncertainties that conviction was difficult to sustain. He was the perfect attorney in always deferring to his employer and this deference was no doubt reinforced by the seniority and aristocracy of Seaford. On the other hand, Jackson had relatively great power to make decisions locally because of his refusal to accept any form of joint attorneyship. He had full authority as planting attorney and as mercantile attorney, and never faced the kind of intrusion Taylor experienced from the overseer Kelly at Golden Grove.

Chapter 9

Honour Among Thieves

. . . capital comes into the world soiled with mire from top to toe, and oozing blood from every pore.

Karl Marx, *Capital*

Were the attorneys of Jamaica good managers? In order to attempt an answer it is necessary first to wonder about the meaning and character of goodness and the definition of good management. Is it to be understood in terms of pure profit and, if not, what ethical standards are appropriate? The possibilities for conflict and contradiction were obvious enough to contemporaries and remain embedded in the historiography. The problem can be broken down into a series of questions, starting from different perspectives and different sets of assumptions. The answers do not necessarily fall into a neat pattern and this makes any attempt at an overall assessment of the role and significance of the attorneys hazardous.

In the first place, a critique can be applied from the perspective of the employers of the attorneys. How well did the agents perform the tasks expected of them by their principals? Were the attorneys efficient managers and did they maximize the profitability of their employers' investments in Jamaica? Would the proprietors have been better off without the attorneys and would absentee-proprietors have made greater profits if they had been residents? A second set of questions can be asked from the perspective of the Jamaican population at large. Would the economy have been more productive and would the wealth generated have been more equally distributed if there had been no attorneys? Would resources have been managed with an eye to the long term and sustainability? Would the working people of the plantations, enslaved and free, have had better lives if attorneys had been removed from the managerial hierarchy?

How could a planter-proprietor identify a good attorney? What exactly did he expect from an agent? Honesty was a valued quality, associated with the origins of the system of attorneyship in a desire for accountability. Criticism of the management practised by attorneys often begins with the defrauding of their principals. However, as Kamau Brathwaite argues, what employers demanded of a "good attorney" was not so much an unblemished character but simply that he should ship the greatest possible quantity of sugar and rum. Brathwaite concludes, "This, despite the details of their private lives, was their function, and this is what they did."[1] The emphasis on gross output conceals a critique of the attorney's impact on profitability and viability in the long term but future outcomes were in any event made imponderable by uncertainty and incalculability, for both planter and attorney.

How well did Simon Taylor and Isaac Jackson perform according to these criteria? In the short run, their principals, Chaloner Arcedeckne and Lord Seaford, expected the attorneys to maximize the flow of income from their properties, to ensure the security of their investments, and to endure the risks and inconveniences of their situation for a price. Taylor and Jackson satisfied them on these counts and successfully protected their employers' rights and interests. Probably, Taylor and Jackson shipped the greatest quantities possible for their particular periods and conditions. As attorneys, they took a positive approach to the making of profits and the exploitation of the resources and technologies available to them. They proved themselves assiduous in visiting the estates regularly and providing detailed accounts. They understood the details of sugar production and trade, recruited and dismissed supervisory personnel, and did what was in their power to increase the workforce. There is no evidence of fraud or dishonesty in their dealings. As absentees, Arcedeckne and Seaford could distance themselves from the everyday brutality of the plantation, but they were truly partners in the system of exploitation and indeed its principals. Thus they had little reason to complain of the vulgarity or harshness of the attorneys they employed. The social character of Taylor and Jackson seems not to have been a matter of moral concern to them.

The notion that the interests of the attorneys and their absentee employers were in perpetual conflict is difficult to accept.[2] In the first place, it was the system of attorneyship that made possible absenteeism. If the attorneys had not produced profits for their principals, the system would have collapsed and the absentees bankrupted. No doubt the absentees did not get every penny to which they felt entitled and no doubt most wished for greater incomes, but they made the calculation that the returns they did receive were sufficient to support them in the style they craved. Individual planters were bankrupted, of course, but this does not indicate the failure of the system overall. Most absentees, at least down to 1820, seem to have been happy enough with the returns produced for them. Few thought they could have done a better job and that it was worth their time to become resident planters. Few shifted their capital into other enterprises. In the period of the slave trade, most believed their investments were the most profitable open to them. The attorneys were their agents in achieving this outcome.

As social predators, the proprietors and the attorneys had entered into a pact that rewarded them for being honourable and loyal to one another for the sake of robbing other people who were not parties to the ethical contract. Thus proprietor and attorney could behave morally towards one another, without feeling guilt towards outsiders, the enslaved and the exploited free people. The attorney might risk defrauding his principal on a large scale, and no doubt some were tempted, but in the long run it was the rational self-interest of the attorney to respect and honour his partner in crime.[3] Similarly, a high-handed absentee, changing the rules and rewards in an arbitrary fashion, could not expect continued cooperation or substantial returns from an agent. In the same way, collusion between attorney and overseer, against the proprietor, was not in their long-term interest. Hence the solidarity of the various classes of whites within Jamaica and the willingness of the residents not to disturb the absentees in their leisure and luxury. The principal-agent relationship was not a simple dyad but rather a ramified network that meant self-interest could be pursued only within the limits of trust and moral hazard.[4]

While it is easy to agree with Selwyn H. H. Carrington that "it was efficiency of management above all else that, by the end of the eighteenth century, made the essential difference between those British West Indian estates that remained viable and those that did not", it is necessary to ask how this efficiency related to the presence and absence of attorneys and how important were differences in factor endowments.[5] Contemporary opinion cannot be trusted. As J. R. Ward says, critics of absenteeism believed it "quite beyond dispute that management through hired agents would be more expensive than resident ownership, and less capable of responding effectively to hard times".[6] In 1828 Marly quoted an old planter who "often used to say, it was his decided opinion, that a sugar planter would always prosper, if he only never placed trust in an attorneys".[7] Clare Taylor argued much the same in the 1980s, that "huge fortunes came to be made, but not usually by an absentee", and David Watts claimed "management efficiency normally declined markedly in the absence of the owner".[8] These are not systematically based conclusions.

Using the crop accounts, Richard B. Sheridan found that in 1775 absentees (and minors) owned 30 per cent of the sugar estates of Jamaica and that their properties produced 40 per cent of the island's sugar and rum.[9] The above-average performance of the absentees' estates was no doubt partly a function of scale but it was not obviously inhibited by management. Ward, studying a substantial range of examples, finds similarly that by the middle of the eighteenth century management had become more respectable, more efficient, more rewarding to the proprietor, and that in productivity terms there was no clear advantage to residence.[10]

How might long-term profitability and sustainability be measured? The ultimate failure, for planter and attorney, was the abandonment of a plantation. Loss followed by sale was one thing, abandonment another. "Abandonment" might be partial, indicating only the giving up of sugar or coffee production for less lucrative commodities, or it could be total in the sense that the proprietor abandoned all kinds of productive activity and gave up hope of sale, leaving the land to grow up in ruinate. Throughout the eighteenth century, abandonment occurred alongside expansion on the frontier. The process speeded up after 1838, however, and continued to the end of the nineteenth century. The difference after slavery was that the estates then abandoned were not balanced by the creation of new plantation settlements.[11]

Were the properties of absentees in the hands of attorneys more or less likely to be thrown up than those occupied by residents? In 1842 Samuel Gooding Barrett told a select committee of the British Parliament, "I believe that most of the estates that have been thrown up have been the estates of absentees."[12] On the surface, this seems likely to have been true, because there were many more estates managed by attorneys than occupied by residents. In 1832, 81 per cent of estates were in the hands of attorneys and 76 per cent of the enslaved people living on sugar estates were on properties managed by them. However, lists of sugar and coffee plantations abandoned between 1832 and 1847, collected by the House of Assembly, show otherwise.[13] Of the 140 estates listed as abandoned by 1847, only 54 (39 per cent) were managed by attorneys in 1832. Thus Barrett was wrong even about the absolute numbers. In terms of probabilities, the contrast was more striking, with 66 per cent of resident-managed estates abandoned but only 10 per cent of those under attorneys. Overall, 21 per cent of estates were abandoned between 1832 and 1847, though some shifted to products other than sugar. Old Montpelier was included in the list and it became a pen.

A different perspective is gained by looking at populations. Of the enslaved people on estates under attorneys in 1832, only 8 per cent belonged to properties with attorneys that were abandoned 1832–47, compared to 35 per cent of those on estates with resident proprietors. The resident estates that were abandoned had an average 151 enslaved people in 1832, whereas the estates run by attorneys that were abandoned had 178 people. The resident estates may have been abandoned partly because they had relatively small workforces and were less productive. Mapping the distribution of abandoned estates shows also that they tended to be located in marginal environments, contributing to their relative lack of success (Figures 9.1–9.2). Their ecological marginality equally made them vulnerable to peasant alternatives. The larger point is that sugar estates managed by attorneys proved significantly superior

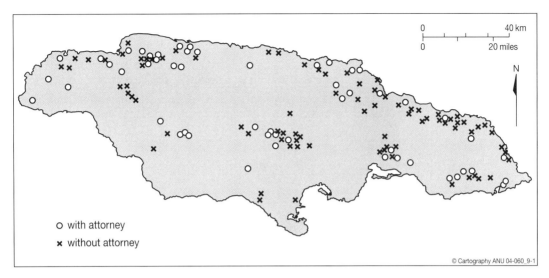

Figure 9.1 Distribution of sugar estates abandoned 1832–47, with and without attorneys

in their capacity to survive the ending of slavery, because they occupied the best sites and were on average more productive and profitable. The same applied to coffee, where only 6 per cent of the 462 plantations abandoned between 1832 and 1847 had been managed by attorneys in 1832 (Figure 9.3). Management by an attorney was an advantage not a burden.

How did the examples of Golden Grove and Montpelier fit this broad pattern of survival and abandonment? In the long run, their trajectories proved quite different. Golden Grove continued in sugar after abolition and beyond, and the proportion of its land area that was dominated by sugar increased. The site of the "Negro houses" during slavery was cleared and planted in cane, as were almost all the level areas formerly in woodland, provision grounds and pasture. Sugar covered the land much more completely than it had during slavery. Indentured immigrant labourers were brought from Africa and India, and workers came to be housed in barracks squeezed into narrow roadside lines. Golden Grove was the first estate in the Plantain Garden district to be attacked during the Morant Bay Rebellion of 1865, the people threatening to kill the overseer, Alexander Chisholm, and the attorney, Samuel Shortridge. These men escaped but the attorney of nearby Amity Hall was murdered.[14] Ownership of Golden Grove slipped from the hands of the Arcedecknes, passing to lessees then, by 1890, to the Boston Fruit Company. In 1925 a company incorporated in Scotland, Jamaica Sugar Estates Limited, built a massive modern central mill at Duckenfield that took all of the cane in the valley. Golden Grove came to be known as one of the poorest districts in Jamaica. Its dilapidated barracks survived to the end of the twentieth century, earning the epithet "Golden Grave".[15]

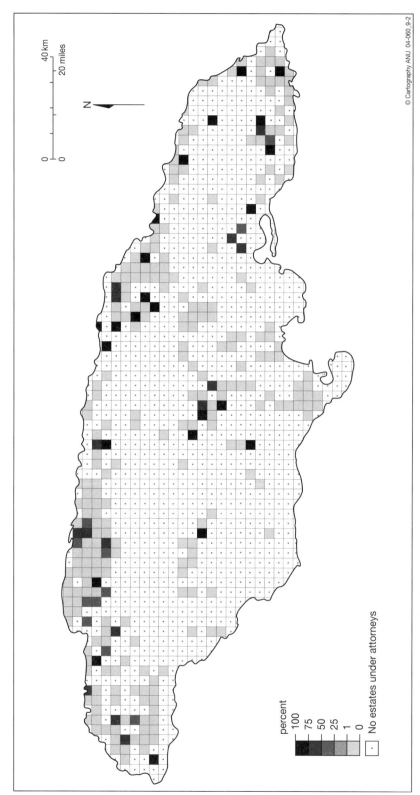

Figure 9.2 Percentage of sugar estates abandoned 1832–47 under attorneys in 1832

percent
100
75
50
25
1
0

No estates under attorneys

© Cartography ANU 04-060_9-2

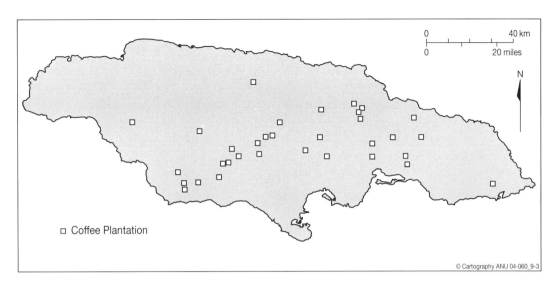

Figure 9.3 Distribution of coffee plantations under attorneys abandoned 1832–47

Montpelier abandoned sugar completely in 1856, never to return to the crop. The sites of the villages of the enslaved were abandoned and the property became one vast cattle pen. As the attorney John Blackburn predicted in 1807, the conversion of estates to pens would quickly prove ruinous to planter prosperity, because "the multiplication of pens, and decay of sugar works, would increase the number of cattle, and diminish the demand for them, and make the ruin tenfold".[16] At Montpelier, woodland and ruinate dominated the hills and pasture the former sugar lands. The property remained a single unit down to the 1970s, when it was purchased by government and partially subdivided. In the 1990s a large proportion was cleared once more and planted in orange groves, to extract juice for export.[17]

Why did Montpelier not follow the same path as Golden Grove? The reasons had more to do with conditions of soil and topography than with differences in management. The long-term retreat of sugar from the relatively marginal areas of Jamaica left only the most ecologically favoured areas viable. The much-praised virtues of the Plantain Garden River floodplain have kept it in sugar and its people in poverty. Management, absenteeism and the system of attorneyship went along with these outcomes but the business decisions that led to the differences between Golden Grove and Montpelier were necessarily made in the context of a larger range of factors and constraints.

Another way of looking at the success of the attorney as manager is to consider what happened when absentees became returning residents. The cost of management, through salaries and commissions paid to attorneys, overseers and factors, took 10 to 20 per cent of net revenue.[18] How much of this expenditure might have been saved by residence? The planter might easily save the salary of the attorney but doing without an overseer was harder to contemplate. The resident proprietor, playing a full role in the political and cultural life of the island as desired by the critics, would still need an overseer, and this would certainly have been the case where the proprietor owned multiple estates. Lord Seaford, for example, could not have run his scattered estates without overseers. Rose Price, who spent three years at Worthy Park Estate in the early 1790s, did dismiss both attorney and overseer but he had only one plantation to manage. He increased the amount of land in cane and the number of slaves, stopped hiring, and intensified the workload and close supervision. The outcome was mixed, with large increases in production coming only some years after his departure though attributable to practices he had put in place.[19] Price followed the essential message Taylor had given Arcedeckne, to buy people.

In some cases, attorneys admitted deficiencies in the system of management but passed the blame to the overseer. Simon Taylor provides an example of this attitude in his management of Golden Grove, sheeting home responsibility for unwanted expenditure to the overseer John Kelly. Taylor, in the role of proprietor as well as an attorney, was able to side morally with the absentee principal. Much the same happened on the Clarendon estates of Lord Penrhyn, where a new attorney dismissed two overseers for their "great excesses, extravagances and misdemeanours" under the previous agent. Of the overseers, the attorney told Penrhyn, "They do not think themselves menial servants. However, my Lord, I am a proprietor here and I hope and trust that I shall be able to show that I have a feeling for the absentee and that this class of man shall not, like so many vultures, feed on the vitals of their employer."[20] Others deflected blame from the attorneys to the metropolitan factors. Looking back from the vantage of 1848, Alexander Geddes said that, in the past, business between planter and merchant had been expensive and "in some measure unusual and unfair", meaning that the factors charged unreasonable commissions. "I consider that till public opinion forced the condition of those countries [the West Indies] upon the Government, and upon the proprietors, and upon merchants," said Geddes, "they looked upon them as mere mines of wealth from which to draw money."[21]

It is important not to make too strong a distinction between resident-proprietors and the attorneys of absentees. Most obviously, some of the residents were themselves attorneys and often became attorneys after rather than before taking up management for others. Simon Taylor is a good example of the type. Second, when attorneys purchased the properties of absentees, particularly after abolition, there was no necessary shift of personnel. The attorneys might experience some social mobility, joining the ranks of those thought potential candidates for public office, but they were the same men.

Did attorneys have an interest only in the short or medium term, or did they look more to the long run, and how did their management strategies compare with those of their employers? The example of Taylor and Arcedeckne points towards a far-seeing attorney and a cautious proprietor, in the optimistic decade before the American Revolution. To a lesser extent Jackson too had a larger view of the future than Seaford, though both faced great uncertainties and ultimate failure. Some absentees trusted their attorneys to make changes for the long run.[22]

How did the long-term health of the Jamaican plantation economy vary with changing levels of absenteeism? The period of most rapid growth in absenteeism began in 1740 and ended around 1790. This half-century comprehended most of the "silver age" or "era of prosperity" when profit-ability was at its peak. Indeed, it was the profitability of slavery and sugar that made possible the fulfilment of the planters' dream of absenteeism. The health of the plantation economy after 1790 is a more contentious matter, with opposed views argued forcefully on both sides. Ragatz and Williams see decline setting in soon after 1763, Carrington from 1776 or 1783, McCusker sometime after 1790, Ryden dates its commencement to around 1800, while Drescher believes it began only after 1815, after the abolition of the Atlantic slave trade, and Ward sees depression only in the 1820s.[23] In the case of Jamaica, the later dates are the most plausible.

Even in the 1820s, metropolitan merchants sometimes saw Jamaican property as a good investment. For example, the Liverpool merchant John Gladstone first acquired properties in the island in 1826. He had earlier taken up plantations in Demerara, and in 1823 one of these had been a prime site of the great insurrection of that year. According to S. G. Checkland, Gladstone "seems to have been kept in ignorance . . . by his attorney and manager" of "excessive labour and severe treatment". On the other hand, Gladstone had quickly switched from coffee to sugar and doubled the number of enslaved, with the consequence that "they were now required to work much harder".[24] At the beginning of 1833 he was worth £636,200 sterling, more than half of it in West Indian property, and his plantations returned 10 per cent. He defended slavery to the end but was a pioneer in the use of new technologies, increasing efficiency and profits wherever he could. He remained optimistic during the apprenticeship, pushing ahead by sending to India for indentured workers. By 1840, however, Gladstone had begun a reappraisal, leading to the sale of his plantations in both Demerara and Jamaica, and shifting investment away from imperial ventures.[25]

Were the attorneys active innovators? Overall, technological innovation moved ahead relatively easily on the estates of absentees and often the impulse for innovation came from the attorney and overseer rather than the proprietor.[26] Rather than conservatives, concludes Heather Cateau, the planters were rational innovators, choosing carefully between available options.[27] Probably, innovation in field and factory was equally likely to come from residents (proprietors or attorneys) seeing opportunities within the Jamaican environment, and from absentees taking advantage of methods and implements observed in the agricultural and industrial revolutions that surrounded them in Britain. The attorneys were often equally aware of these developments, through direct observation or by reading and listening, and made their own suggestions. Keith Mason has argued that "many absentees . . . proved either unable or reluctant to plan for the long-term welfare" of their plantations, even ignoring pleas from attorneys for construction and treating minor demands with parsimony.[28] Further, it was the larger attorneys, those serving several employers and managing a diversity of plantations under different conditions, who were the most likely to develop independent opinions and plans, and the most likely to take an active role in forming the ideas of the absentees.[29] Taylor and Jackson belonged to this category.

Perhaps mechanical invention was more likely to happen in the West Indies, where techniques evolved from practical knowledge of culture and environment, whereas the adoption of new machines was more likely to originate with absentees. For example, although Jamaica was the site of significant contributions to the application of steam power to agricultural processing, beginning with the experiments of 1768, by about 1800 the engines of Boulton and Watt had won the day and were imported in large numbers for the sugar industry.[30] One of the first to introduce steam, initially to pump water for irrigation and by 1806 to crush canes, was Lord Penrhyn, but the initial idea of using steam power on his Clarendon estates came from one of his attorneys in 1797, and the engine for crushing was ordered by another attorney in 1804. He was a leader in agricultural improvement in Britain and opened a slate quarry on his Welsh estate in 1785 where together with his agent he took an active role in management.[31]

Who initiated schemes for the increase of productivity and the harder working of the enslaved? Was it the absentee-proprietors or the attorneys? In the case of Golden Grove, it was generally the attorney, Taylor, who pushed for a larger enslaved labour force but he did so in order to meet the absentee owner's desire for greater production and profits. Taylor pointed out clearly and frequently the consequences of expecting greater output from the same number of hands. There was no attempt to conceal this outcome. It was generally the absentees who had unrealistic expectations about the productivity that could be achieved by their existing enslaved workforce, looking for returns that went beyond what was possible even within an oppressive system of slavery. Absentees often sought to stop the hiring of jobbing slaves, seeing the cost as a special charge on their accounts. Carrington contends the pattern of ownership put the absentee planters "at the mercy of a managerial class".[32] But hiring may be interpreted as a rational response to the labour market under slavery, and hiring jobbers to dig cane holes, the hardest work of the estate, writes Cateau, "was used as a means of preserving the permanent work force of the plantation".[33] Along with the task system, hiring introduced a flexibility to the supply of labour that did not exist within the established plantation system. Both tasking and hiring reduced supervision and transaction costs for the planter. Thus task work came to be fundamental to the system of labour at Montpelier, for example, after 1838. It was not so much the preferences of attorney and proprietor that drove this switch, however, but the active negotiation of the people they employed in field and factory.

What did the plantation workers of Jamaica, enslaved and free, make of absenteeism and the attorney? Often their own enforced residence on a particular plantation gave them a much longer knowledge of the family fortunes of their owners than that possessed by the white sojourners who passed through as overseers and attorneys. Probably the enslaved saw an irony in accusations of fraud between proprietor, attorney and overseer, the large-scale oppressors and exploiters, the true thieves and active transgressors of morality and justice. As Jamaicans say, "Tief from tief make god laugh", and "When black man tief, him tief half a bit [twopence farthing]; when backra tief, him tief whole estate."[34] The latter was first recorded as a proverb in 1873, but its application was as true for the eighteenth century as for the post-slavery period. In the same year, W. J. Gardner interpreted another proverb, "Massa's eye makes the horse grow fat", as more directly related to the system of absenteeism and attorneyship, saying, "Some shrewd old slave surely uttered this as the result of long observation of the comparative condition of estates belonging to resident or absentee proprietors."[35] Here Gardner sought to impose his own interpretation of relative profitability but perhaps the close observation of the enslaved led in an opposite direction.

Beyond these broadly moral perceptions, might enslaved persons have rationally preferred a resident proprietor to an absentee? What advantages might they see? Most discussions of this question relate to examples of previously absentee planters returning to their properties rather than cases of long-term residence. For example, Michael Craton, writing in the context of Rose Price's years at Worthy Park, claims that "slaves much preferred a master living in the Great House to a plantation run by an attorney and overseer for an absentee". Craton argues further that a resident master could intervene in internal conflict, between slave and overseer or driver, that scarce commodities were more likely to trickle down, and that "slaves even took pride in the style which their masters affected, as if such conspicuous consumption lent them reflected validity". The basis of Craton's claims is not clear, however, and the only source cited is the journal of Matthew Gregory Lewis.[36] Lewis complained of the amount of time he spent in conversation with his people, but presented his objectives as exclusively directed at improving their condition. Increasing productivity and profit was never his stated aim.[37] In this he was highly unusual. Owners and managers who claimed their primary objective to be the benefit of the enslaved were regarded by most proprietors as eccentric.[38] Planters of the later eighteenth century might see themselves as "improvers" – increasing the value of their land and resources, and having an interest in the welfare of their slaves – but those they labelled "reformers" were disparaged as fanatics or abolitionists, seeking to overthrow rather than regulate the entire system.[39]

Certainly Lewis was greeted with enthusiasm by the enslaved on his properties. When he left Hordley Estate in 1817, after a visit of just a few days, he was carried safely across the swollen Plantain Garden River by his people. He wrote, "who then left me, many with tears running down their cheeks, and all with thanks for the protection which I had shown them, and earnest entreaties that I would come to visit them another time".[40] Lewis dispensed favours and dealt with those who oppressed his people but ultimately was unsure how best to manage his properties profitably. Yet his experience was not unique. Thus the aging creole John Tharp, who returned to Jamaica in 1802 after an absence of seven years, told his son, "My Negroes have increased and are very happy, they kill me with their constant visits and attentions – it gives pleasure, though I am fatigued to death before the day is half gone, for I must talk and shake hands with every one of them."[41]

The short-term residence of absentee-proprietors gave the enslaved opportunities to appeal to their owners as individuals, seeing them as a soft touch for extra days, holidays, feasts, more food, better clothing and shorter working hours. It was overseer and attorney who came most visibly to symbolize the harshest exploitation.[42] In terms of the larger historical interpretation of absenteeism, however, there is a contradiction in this attitude. The expectations of the enslaved do not mesh with the idea that resident-proprietorship went together with increased productivity and profitability. The enslaved may well have been correct in thinking they were better off under a resident-proprietor because they saw this as their best chance of being able to work less hard and be treated less harshly.[43] They had no interest in working harder and producing more. It was the attorney and the overseer who ensured this happened.

Viewed from the proprietor's perspective, absenteeism and management through attorney and overseer may have been the most profitable choice. As anti-slavery sentiment increased, it also proved a useful moral choice for the proprietor. The system was a way of getting others to do the dirty work of managing, the hands-on exploitation and the implementation of the extreme demands on labour that contributed so substantially to profit. The proprietor could distance himself from the harsh regime of the plantation, claiming to want only happiness and comfort for his slaves, and seeing the harshness as practised by employees contracted of necessity. Overseers could easily be labelled "petty tyrants".[44] It also helped to construct attorney and overseer as the proprietor's own exploiters, creaming off part of the profit that was rightfully his, though the proprietor knew that ultimately he was part of the moral pact. Thus it can be argued the proprietors made the correct management choice in terms of maximizing their incomes. It was a choice counter to the interests of the enslaved.

The demographic experience of the enslaved seems not to have varied significantly according to whether they belonged to residents or absentees. What mattered most were the kind of crop they produced and the stage of settlement in which they found themselves. Mortality was always highest on sugar-producing properties and at its worst during the foundation stage of plantation development.[45] In Jamaica, the laying out of new plantations often happened while the owner was resident, but sugar was the great funder of absenteeism, so that in the long run being the property of an absentee went together with demographic disaster. By 1800 enslaved people living on sugar estates shared much the same fate, whether their owners were resident or managed through an attorney. Before 1750 the situation was worse, because of the initial conditions of settlement, but had little to do with absenteeism.[46] Within Jamaica, the most prominent example of positive natural increase on sugar estates was found in the parish of Vere, which also had one of the highest rates of management by attorney. Regionally, Vere looked rather like Barbados in terms of its agrarian regime and demographic performance, but Barbados had less absenteeism. British Guiana, on the other hand, closely approximated the Jamaican system of management and had heavy mortality that persisted beyond abolition.[47]

How different a place might Jamaica have been without absenteeism and without attorneys? Some contemporaries, recognizing flaws in the system of attorneyship, called for its reform. Thus R. C. Dallas, writing at the beginning of the nineteenth century, believed there needed to be some way to remove the attorney's temptation to spread himself over the management of too many estates, but saw no escape from this "incalculable evil" other than legislation to rein in the "great attornies". He recommended reducing the rate of commission and prohibiting attorneys' membership of Assembly and Council. More broadly, writing as he did in the shadow of the Maroon War and the St Domingue Revolution, Dallas implicitly linked the problem of the system of attorneyship to absenteeism and the lack of a prosperous and independent "middling class" of white people. The wealth and power of the attorneys contributed to the fundamental problem that "the great planters will swallow up the small ones; and that middling planters will dwindle and go in their turn". Dallas contended that the interests of "the overgrown planter", the great attorney and his metropolitan merchants clashed with "the general welfare of the island" in terms of its long-term prosperity and security.[48]

In his *Jamaica Planter's Guide* of 1823, Thomas Roughley proposed the replacement of the attorney by a "travelling agent" who would make an annual visit to the estates of his absentee employer. The agent would spend three months in the island, inspect all aspects of the estate, and carry back the full set of accounts and the list of supplies required for the coming year. Roughley thought his scheme would have wonderful effects on the white people on the estates, making them "assiduous, sober, and attentive".[49] He also saw substantial savings for the absentee-proprietors, who could group together to employ a single agent for a number of estates, with savings in expenditure in many other areas.[50] Ward has fairly styled Roughley's scheme "completely fanciful".[51] Other contemporaries, including William Knibb, proposed the abolition of attorneyships and the renting out of plantations to individuals.[52] Although partnerships had been relatively common during the first phase of plantation development, they became less easy to maintain once the burden of debt grew substantial or the need for finance too great. Tenants generally lacked adequate security and were difficult to dislodge, so renting was less attractive than selling a plantation.[53]

The outcome of tenancy would have been a resident planter class, but there was nothing in it to prevent individuals leasing a series of properties. The result would have been a continuing demand for agents to manage scattered plantations. As argued earlier, the attorneys gained their authority through the complexity of sugar production and marketing, and the need for accountability, rather than emerging as a simple reaction to absenteeism. More radical alternatives were possible, of course, but tended towards an economy in which the plantation was not the leading institution. For example, sharecropping, which had effectively disappeared in England by the eighteenth century, had its practical advocates in the West Indies in the 1840s.[54] In this system, people could have lived relatively independent economic lives, yet still been dependent on export crops and the planter's control of processing technologies. Production and processing might have been organized on a smaller scale.[55] Less likely to be considered before 1850 were systems of cane farming in which peasants owned their own land and cooperatives owned sugar mills.[56] Forms of agricultural agency, support and experiment might have been directed at improving the productivity of the peasant sector rather keeping that of the plantation system.[57] Socialism was another unlikely option before 1850 and experience was to show that it might in any case accommodate the plantation quite comfortably.

Most of these options harked back to the idea of a settler society. The white version of this model had failed by the end of the seventeenth century but there were still whites who looked with nostalgia on the lost opportunity to create in Jamaica a tropical New England. As Gardner put it in 1873, without sugar and the plantation, Jamaica would have been populated with "English towns and villages only changed so far as is requisite in semi-tropical climates, of farms and gardens covering the country, occupied by men to whom occupation is a necessity". He failed to notice that the black version of the settler society that became firmly rooted in Jamaica by the later nineteenth century was not so different from this ideal "gorgeous island home".[58] The generations of sons and daughters of the Africans carried to Jamaica, and forced to toil so profitably for the planters and their attorneys eventually made the land their own, of necessity. Some came to call it paradise.

In the real world of Plantation Jamaica between 1750 and 1850, no version of settler society was allowed to flourish. Under slavery, the provision ground and the internal marketing system foreshadowed peasant development but the growth of a creole economy had little chance. Plantation Jamaica was fundamentally a project opposed to common human goals and desires. That it was profitably imposed for the benefit of a small number of largely absentee principals was the most important index of the managerial success of the attorneys. The separation of capital and control, of ownership and management, was truly modern in its operational structure and efficiency. Rather than millstones around the necks of the proprietors, the attorneys were in large part their saviours. It was the management practised by the attorneys that squeezed the maximum possible product from the system and the people it oppressed. Together, proprietor and attorney created a system of management as modern as it was repugnant.

Notes

Chapter 1

1. Noel Deerr, *The History of Sugar* (London: Chapman and Hall, 1949–50), 1: 198; Mario Samper and Radin Fernando, "Historical Statistics of Coffee Production and Trade from 1700 to 1960", in *The Global Coffee Economy in Africa, Asia, and Latin America, 1500–1989,* ed. William Gervase Clarence-Smith and Steven Topik (Cambridge: Cambridge University Press, 2003), 412.

2. Deerr, *History of Sugar,* 1: 37, 59–60; J. H. Galloway, *The Sugar Cane Industry: An Historical Geography from Its Origins to 1914* (Cambridge: Cambridge University Press, 1989), 198–208.

3. Trevor Burnard, " 'The Grand Mart of the Island': The Economic Function of Kingston, Jamaica in the Mid-Eighteenth Century", in *Jamaica in Slavery and Freedom: History, Heritage and Culture,* ed. Kathleen E. A. Monteith and Glen Richards (Kingston: University of the West Indies Press, 2002), 225.

4. The Jamaica estimates assume a sugar price of £28 sterling per ton in 1750, £36 in 1770 and £50 in 1800, export production of 20,000, 36,000 and 100,000 tons of sugar, and total populations of 142,000, 200,000 and 350,000, respectively. The result is inflated by 1.2 to take account of other sugar estate output, notably rum. Sugar estates contributed only about 58 per cent of total output, so the estate value is multiplied by 1.7, including an allowance for provision crop production, to give a lower limit value. The 1850 estimate is from Gisela Eisner, converted to current money. Eisner assumed ground provisions produced for domestic consumption made up 27.7 per cent of gross domestic product in 1832. Eisner's estimates at 1910 prices have been converted to current money. Data on population and production do not always agree. See Deerr, *History of Sugar,* 1: 198, and 2: 531; Trevor Burnard, *Mastery, Tyranny, and Desire: Thomas Thistlewood and His Slaves in the Anglo-Jamaican World* (Chapel Hill: University of North Carolina Press, 2004), 14–16; Stanley L. Engerman and B. W. Higman, "The Demographic Structure of the Caribbean Slave Societies in the Eighteenth and Nineteenth Centuries", in *General History of the Caribbean,* vol. 3, *The Slave Societies of the Caribbean,* ed. Franklin W. Knight (London: UNESCO Publishing/Macmillan Education, 1997), 48; David Eltis, "The Slave Economies of the Caribbean: Structure, Performance, Evolution and Significance", ibid., 113;

B. W. Higman, *Slave Population and Economy in Jamaica, 1807–1834* (Cambridge: Cambridge University Press, 1976), 17, 215, 255–56; Gisela Eisner, *Jamaica, 1830–1930: A Study in Economic Growth* (Manchester: Manchester University Press, 1961), 9–11, 289, 375. For other places, see Alice Hanson Jones, *Wealth of a Nation to Be: The American Colonies on the Eve of the Revolution* (New York: Columbia University Press, 1980), 68; Robert E. Gallman, "Economic Growth and Structural Change in the Long Nineteenth Century", in *The Cambridge Economic History of the United States,* vol. 2, *The Long Nineteenth Century,* ed. Stanley L. Engerman and Robert E. Gallman (Cambridge: Cambridge University Press, 2000), 2–21; David Eltis, Frank D. Lewis and Kenneth L. Sokoloff, introduction to *Slavery in the Development of the Americas,* ed. David Eltis, Frank D. Lewis and Kenneth L. Sokoloff (Cambridge: Cambridge University Press, 2004), 9–12.

5. Eric Williams, *Capitalism and Slavery* (Chapel Hill: University of North Carolina Press, 1944), 105; George Metcalf, *Royal Government and Political Conflict in Jamaica 1729–1783* (London: Longmans, 1965), 2; Richard Pares, *Merchants and Planters* (*Economic History Review* supplement no. 4, 1960), 50; Adam Smith, *An Inquiry into the Nature and Causes of the Wealth of Nations* (1776), ed. Edwin Cannan (London: Methuen, 1961), 2: 101. For the later literature, see, *inter alia,* Richard B. Sheridan, "The Wealth of Jamaica in the Eighteenth Century", *Economic History Review* 18 (1965): 292–311; Robert Paul Thomas, "The Sugar Colonies of the Old Empire: Profit or Loss for Great Britain?" *Economic History Review* 21 (1968): 30–45; Richard B. Sheridan, "The Wealth of Jamaica in the Eighteenth Century: A Rejoinder", *Economic History Review* 21 (1968): 46–68; Stanley L. Engerman, "The Slave Trade and British Capital Formation in the Eighteenth Century: A Comment on the Williams Thesis", *Business History Review* 46 (1972): 430–43; Philip R. P. Coelho, "The Profitability of Imperialism: The British Experience in the West Indies, 1768–1772", *Explorations in Economic History* 10 (1973): 253–80; Kenneth Morgan, *Slavery, Atlantic Trade and the British Economy, 1660–1800* (Cambridge: Cambridge University Press, 2000), 58–60; S. D. Smith, "*Merchants and Planters* Revisited", *Economic History Review* 55 (2002): 460; David Eltis and Stanley L. Engerman, "The Importance of Slavery and the Slave Trade to Industrializing Britain", *Journal of Economic History* 60 (2000): 123–44; T. G. Burnard, " 'Prodigious Riches': The Wealth of Jamaica before the American Revolution", *Economic History Review* 54 (2001): 506; Joseph E. Inikori, *Africans and the Industrial Revolution in England: A Study in International Trade and Development* (Cambridge: Cambridge University Press, 2002); "Roundtable" on Inikori's work, *International Journal of Maritime History* 15 (2003): 279–361; Robert C. Allen, "Progress and Poverty in Early Modern Europe", *Economic History Review* 56 (2003): 403–43; Selwyn H. H. Carrington, *The Sugar Industry and the Abolition of the Slave Trade 1775–1810* (Gainesville: University Press of Florida, 2003); Burnard, *Mastery,* 13.

6. See, for example, Elizabeth B. Field-Hendrey and Lee A. Craig, "The Relative Efficiency of Free and Slave Agriculture in the Antebellum United States: A Stochastic Production Frontier Approach", in *Slavery in the Development of the Americas,* ed. David Eltis, Frank D. Lewis and Kenneth L. Sokoloff (Cambridge:

Cambridge University Press, 2004), 255–56; Robert William Fogel and Stanley L. Engerman, *Time on the Cross: The Economics of American Negro Slavery* (Boston: Little Brown, 1974), 1: 191–223; Robert William Fogel, *Without Consent or Contract: The Rise and Fall of American Slavery* (New York: W. W. Norton, 1989), 72–80.

7. B. W. Higman, "Demography", in *A Historical Guide to World Slavery*, ed. Seymour Drescher and Stanley L. Engerman (New York: Oxford University Press, 1998), 169–70.

8. Higman, *Slave Population and Economy*, 69; William Kauffman Scarborough, *Masters of the Big House: Elite Slaveholders of the Mid-Nineteenth-Century South* (Baton Rouge: Louisiana State University Press, 2003), 6.

9. Pat Hudson, "Industrial Organisation and Structure", in *Cambridge Economic History of Modern Britain*, vol. 1, *Industrialisation, 1700–1860*, ed. Roderick Floud and Paul Johnson (Cambridge: Cambridge University Press, 2004), 36–37.

10. B. W. Higman, *Jamaica Surveyed: Plantation Maps and Plans of the Eighteenth and Nineteenth Centuries* (Kingston: Institute of Jamaica Publications, 1988), 9–13.

11. Nicholas Canny, "The Origins of Empire: An Introduction", in *The Origins of Empire: British Overseas Enterprise to the Close of the Seventeenth Century*, ed. Nicholas Canny (Oxford: Oxford University Press, 1998), 8–11.

12. See, for example, Peter Karsten, *Between Law and Custom: "High" and "Low" Legal Cultures in the Lands of the British Diaspora – The United States, Canada, Australia, and New Zealand, 1600–1900* (Cambridge: Cambridge University Press, 2002), 305.

13. B. W. Higman, "The Sugar Revolution", *Economic History Review* 53 (2000): 213.

14. Sheridan, "Wealth of Jamaica", 292–311; Thomas, "Sugar Colonies", 30–45; Sheridan, "Rejoinder", 46–68; Burnard, "Prodigious Riches", 520–22.

15. David Geggus, "The Enigma of Jamaica in the 1790s: New Light on the Causes of Slave Rebellions", *William and Mary Quarterly* 44 (1987): 274–99.

16. Deerr, *History of Sugar*, 1: 112, 131, 193, 198, 239–40; Galloway, *Cane Sugar Industry*, 86, 151, 159.

17. Galloway, *Cane Sugar Industry*, 238.

18. David Mackay, "Banks, Bligh and Breadfruit", *New Zealand Journal of History* 8 (1974): 61–77; Richard B. Sheridan, "Captain Bligh, the Breadfruit, and the Botanic Gardens of Jamaica", *Journal of Caribbean History* 23 (1989): 28–50.

19. Jack P. Greene, "The Jamaica Privilege Controversy, 1764–66: An Episode in the Process of Constitutional Definition in the Early Modern British Empire", *Journal of Imperial and Commonwealth History* 22 (1994): 16–53; T. R. Clayton, "Sophistry, Security, and Socio-Political Structures in the American Revolution; or, Why Jamaica Did Not Rebel", *Historical Journal* 29 (1986): 319–44; Andrew J. O'Shaughnessy, *An Empire Divided: The American Revolution and the British Caribbean* (Philadelphia: University of Pennsylvania, 2000); Burnard, *Mastery*, 73–75.

20. Alan L. Karras, *Sojourners in the Sun: Scottish Migrants in Jamaica and the Chesapeake, 1740–1800* (Ithaca: Cornell University Press, 1992), 62; M. J. Steel, "A Philosophy of Fear: The World View of the Jamaican Plantocracy in a Comparative Perspective", *Journal of Caribbean History* 27 (1993): 1–20; Vincent Brown, "Spiritual Terror and Sacred Authority in Jamaican Slave Society", *Slavery and Abolition* 24 (2003): 24–53; Burnard, *Mastery*, 138–49.

21. Alfred D. Chandler Jr, *The Visible Hand: The Managerial Revolution in American Business* (Cambridge, Mass.: Harvard University Press, 1977), 64–66. Cf. Alfred D. Chandler Jr and Herman Daems, eds., *Managerial Hierarchies: Comparative Perspectives on the Rise of the Modern Industrial Enterprise* (Cambridge, Mass.: Harvard University Press, 1980); Mansel G. Blackford and K. Austin Kerr, *Business Enterprise in American History* (Boston: Houghton Mifflin Co., 1990), 34–36.

22. R. Keith Aufhauser, "Slavery and Scientific Management", *Journal of Economic History* 33 (1973): 811–24; Selwyn H. H. Carrington, "Management of Sugar Estates in the British West Indies at the End of the Eighteenth Century", *Journal of Caribbean History* 33 (1999): 27–53; Carrington, *Sugar Industry*; Heather Cateau, "Conservatism and Change Implementation in the British West Indian Sugar Industry 1750–1810", *Journal of Caribbean History* 29 (1995): 1–36.

23. Fogel and Engerman, *Time on the Cross*, 1: 201–8; Aufhauser, "Slavery and Scientific Management", 811–24; Heywood Fleisig, "Comment on Paper by Aufhauser", *Journal of Economic History* 34 (1974): 79–83; Jacob Metzer, "Rational Management, Modern Business Practices, and Economies of Scale in the Ante-Bellum Southern Plantations", *Explorations in Economic History* 12 (1975): 147; Fogel, *Without Consent or Contract*, 24; Sidney W. Mintz, *Sweetness and Power: The Place of Sugar in Modern History* (New York: Viking Penguin, 1985), 46–49; Robin Blackburn, *The Making of New World Slavery: From the Baroque to the Modern* (London: Verso, 1997), 333.

24. Bill Cooke, "The Denial of Slavery in Management Studies", *Journal of Management Studies* 40 (2003): 1895–1918.

25. Cateau, "Conservatism and Change", 1–36; Carrington, "Management of Sugar Estates", 27–53; Carrington, *Sugar Industry*.

26. Robert William Fogel, *The Slavery Debates, 1952–1990: A Retrospective* (Baton Rouge: Louisiana State University Press, 2003), 47.

27. David Brion Davis, *Slavery and Human Progress* (New York: Oxford University Press, 1984); Paul Finkelman, *Slavery and the Founders: Race and Liberty in the Age of Jefferson* (New York: M. E. Sharpe, 2001). Cf. M. I. Finley, *Economy and Society in Ancient Greece* (Harmondsworth: Penguin, 1983), 97–115.

28. Claude S. George Jr, *The History of Management Thought* (Englewood Cliffs, NJ: Prentice-Hall, 1968), 64–69.

29. George, *History of Management Thought*, 76; Oliver E. Williamson and Sidney G. Winter, eds., *The Nature of the Firm: Origins, Evolution, and Development* (New York: Oxford University Press, 1991); Stephen A. Marglin, "What Do Bosses Do? The Origins and Functions of Hierarchy in Capitalist Production", in *The Division of Labour: The Labour Process and Class-Struggle in Modern Capitalism*, ed. André Gorz (Atlantic Highlands, NJ: Humanities Press, 1976), 13–54.

30. Walter Nesbit, quoted in Carrington, "Management of Sugar Estates", 29.

31. Fogel, *Without Consent or Contract*, 25.

32. Lewis Cecil Gray, *History of Agriculture in the Southern United States to 1860* (Washington: Carnegie Institution of Washington, 1933), 1: 498; John J. McCusker and Russell R. Menard, *The Economy of British America, 1607–1789* (Chapel Hill: University of North Carolina Press, 1985), 183–86; Eugene D. Genovese, *Roll, Jordan, Roll: The World the Slaves Made* (New York: Pantheon

Books, 1974), 10–12; Fogel and Engerman, *Time on the Cross,* 1: 210–12; Scarborough, *Masters of the Big House,* 6.

33. C. Y. Thomas, "A Model of Pure Plantation Economy: Comment", *Social and Economic Studies* 17 (1968): 339. Cf. Lloyd Best, "Outlines of a Model of Pure Plantation Economy", *Social and Economic Studies* 17 (1968): 290–91.

34. For the idea of "Plantation America" in anthropology, sociology and economics, see Charles Wagley, "Plantation-America: A Culture Sphere", in *Caribbean Studies: A Symposium,* ed. Vera Rubin (Seattle: University of Washington Press, 1960), 3–13; *Plantation Systems of the New World* (Washington, DC: Pan American Union, 1959). For "Plantation Economy" see Best, "Outlines", 283–326; George L. Beckford, *Persistent Poverty: Underdevelopment in Plantation Economies of the Third World* (New York: Oxford University Press, 1972), 9; Hilary McD. Beckles, " 'The Williams Effect': Eric Williams's Capitalism and Slavery and the Growth of West Indian Political Economy", in *British Capitalism and Caribbean Slavery: The Legacy of Eric Williams,* ed. Barbara L. Solow and Stanley L. Engerman (Cambridge: Cambridge University Press, 1987), 302–16.

Chapter 2

1. Douglas Hall, "Absentee-Proprietorship in the British West Indies, to about 1850", *Jamaican Historical Review* 4 (1964): 23–24. Cf. Christopher J. Cowton and Andrew J. O'Shaughnessy, "Absentee Control of Sugar Plantations in the British West Indies", *Accounting and Business Research* 22 (1991): 35.

2. Richard B. Sheridan, *Sugar and Slavery: An Economic History of the British West Indies, 1623–1775* (Barbados: Caribbean Universities Press, 1974), 360.

3. See Richard B. Sheridan, "Samuel Martin, Innovating Sugar Planter of Antigua, 1750–1776", *Agricultural History* 34 (1960): 138; Ward Barrett, "Caribbean Sugar Production Standards in the Seventeenth and Eighteenth Centuries", in *Merchants and Scholars: Essays in the History of Exploration and Trade,* ed. John Parker (Minneapolis: University of Minnesota Press, 1965), 148; Edward Long, *The History of Jamaica* (London: T. Lowndes, 1774), 1: 435–38; John Dovaston, "Agricultura Americana, or Improvements in West-India Husbandry Considered" (Codex Eng 60, John Carter Brown Library, Providence, Rhode Island).

4. Sheridan, *Sugar and Slavery,* 362, 378; R. B. Sheridan, "Simon Taylor, Sugar Tycoon of Jamaica, 1740–1813", *Agricultural History* 45 (1971): 287.

5. David W. Galenson, *Traders, Planters, and Slaves: Market Behavior in Early English America* (Cambridge: Cambridge University Press, 1986), 139. Cf. Sheridan, *Sugar and Slavery,* 362.

6. William Beckford, *A Descriptive Account of the Island of Jamaica* (London: T. and J. Egerton, 1790), 2: 358–60. See also Richard B. Sheridan, "Planter and Historian: The Career of William Beckford of Jamaica and England, 1744–1799", *Jamai-can Historical Review* 4 (1964): 42; Edward Brathwaite, *The Development of Creole Society in Jamaica, 1770–1820* (Oxford: Oxford University Press, 1971), 131, 139.

7. Michael Pawson and David Buisseret, *Port Royal, Jamaica* (Oxford: Clarendon Press, 1975), 64, 158–67; Richard Grassby, *Kinship and Capitalism: Marriage,*

Family, and Business in the English-Speaking World, 1580–1740 (Cambridge: Cambridge University Press, 2001), 292–93.

8. Trevor Burnard, "A Failed Settler Society: Marriage and Demographic Failure in Early Jamaica", *Journal of Social History* 28 (1994): 63–82; Pares, *Merchants and Planters,* 38–44; David Watts, *The West Indies: Patterns of Development, Culture and Environmental Change since 1492* (Cambridge: Cambridge University Press, 1987), 352–53; Cowton and O'Shaughnessy, "Absentee Control", 34.

9. Frank W. Pitman, "The West Indian Absentee Planter as a British Colonial Type", *American Historical Association Pacific Coast Branch Proceedings* (1927): 118; Richard Pares, *War and Trade in the West Indies, 1739–1763* (Oxford: Clarendon Press, 1936), 508–9.

10. Karras, *Sojourners in the Sun,* 1–5; Betty Wood, ed., *The Letters of Simon Taylor of Jamaica to Chaloner Arcedekne, 1765–1775* (London: Cambridge University Press, for the Royal Historical Society, Camden Miscellany, vol. 35, 2002), 131–32; Isaac Jackson Letterbooks, vol. 3, Jackson to Seaford, 5 Oct. 1843 (American Philosophical Society, Philadelphia); Hall, "Absentee-Proprietorship", 27.

11. Douglas Hall, *In Miserable Slavery: Thomas Thistlewood in Jamaica, 1750–86* (London: Macmillan, 1989), 233, 257. Cf. Sarah M. S. Pearsall, " 'The Late Flagrant Instance of Depravity in My Family': The Story of an Anglo-Jamaican Cuckold", *William and Mary Quarterly* 60 (2003): 582.

12. Metcalf, *Royal Government and Political Conflict in Jamaica,* 79; Trevor Burnard, "Passengers Only: The Extent and Significance of Absenteeism in Eighteenth Century Jamaica", *Atlantic Studies* 1 (2004), 179–89.

13. Sheridan, "Simon Taylor", 287; Sheridan, *Sugar and Slavery,* 385. Cf. Long, *History of Jamaica,* 1: 377–80.

14. Higman, *Slave Population and Economy,* 10–14. See also J. R. Ward, "The Profitability of Sugar Planting in the British West Indies, 1650–1834", *Economic History Review* 31 (1978): 207.

15. J. Stewart, *A View of the Past and Present State of the Island of Jamaica* (Edinburgh: Oliver and Boyd, 1823), 184.

16. Gad J. Heuman, *Between Black and White: Race, Politics, and the Free Coloreds in Jamaica, 1792–1865* (Westport, Conn.: Greenwood Press, 1981), 76.

17. *Journals of the Assembly of Jamaica* 10 (1799): 438; S. D. Smith, "Sugar's Poor Relation: Coffee Planting in the British West Indies, 1720–1833", *Slavery and Abolition* 19 (1998): 68–89; S. D. Smith, "Coffee and the 'Poorer Sort of People' in Jamaica during the Period of African Enslavement", in *Slavery Without Sugar: Diversity in Caribbean Economy and Society since the Seventeenth Century,* ed. Verene A. Shepherd (Gainesville: University Press of Florida, 2002), 109.

18. Brathwaite, *Development of Creole Society,* 12–16; Pitman, "West Indian Absentee Planter", 117.

19. Philip Wright, ed., *Lady Nugent's Journal of Her Residence in Jamaica from 1801 to 1805* (Kingston: Institute of Jamaica, 1966), xxv. Cf. Brathwaite, *Development of Creole Society,* 14.

20. David Patrick Geggus, *Slavery, War, and Revolution: The British Occupation of Saint Domingue 1793–1798* (Oxford: Clarendon Press, 1982), 8. See also Pares, *Merchants and Planters,* 34.

21. Geggus, *Slavery, War, and Revolution,* 257–58, 332–46; Watts, *West Indies,* 353.

22. Stuart B. Schwartz, *Sugar Plantations in the Formation of Brazilian Society: Bahia, 1550–1835* (Cambridge: Cambridge University Press, 1985), 283–84.

23. Carter G. Woodson, *Free Negro Owners of Slaves in the United States in 1830; Together with Absentee Ownership of Slaves in the United States in 1830* (1924; reprint, New York: Negro Universities Press, 1968), 45–78. Cf. Scarborough, *Masters of the Big House,* 6.

24. Orlando Patterson, *The Sociology of Slavery: An Analysis of the Origins, Development and Structure of Negro Slave Society in Jamaica* (London: MacGibbon and Kee, 1967), 278.

25. Pares, *Merchants and Planters,* 38.

26. Percival Spear, *The Nabobs: A Study of the Social Life of the English in Eighteenth Century India* (London: Oxford University Press, 1932); H. V. Bowen, "British India, 1765–1813: The Metropolitan Context", in *The Oxford History of the British Empire,* vol. 2, *The Eighteenth Century,* ed. P. J. Marshall (Oxford: Oxford University Press, 1998), 530–51; James Raven, *Judging New Wealth: Popular Publishing and Responses to Commerce in England, 1750–1800* (Oxford: Clarendon Press, 1992), 231.

27. W. E. Vaughan, *Landlords and Tenants in Mid-Victorian Ireland* (Oxford: Clarendon Press, 1994), 3.

28. J. V. Beckett, "Absentee Landownership in the Later Seventeenth and Early Eighteenth Centuries: The Case of Cumbria", *Northern History* 19 (1983): 87.

29. *Parliamentary Papers,* 1808 (178): 4, "[First] Report from the Committee on the Distillation of Sugar and Molasses", 275, 301–2.

30. Williams, *Capitalism and Slavery,* 85; Richard Pares, *A West-India Fortune* (London: Longmans, 1950); T. M. Devine, "An Eighteenth-Century Business Elite: Glasgow–West India Merchants, *c.*1750–1815", *Scottish Historical Review* 57 (1978): 52–54; Morgan, *Slavery,* 53–54.

31. B. W. Higman, "The West India 'Interest' in Parliament, 1807–1833", *Historical Studies* 13 (1967): 1–19; Lillian M. Penson, "The London West India Interest in the Eighteenth Century", *English Historical Review* 36 (1921): 373–92; C. H. Philips, "The East India Company 'Interest' and the English Government, 1783–4", *Transactions of the Royal Historical Society,* 4th ser., 20 (1937): 83–101; C. H. Philips, *The East India Company, 1784–1834* (Manchester: Manchester University Press, 1940), 23–24, 307–335; Spear, *Nabobs;* Sheridan, *Sugar and Slavery,* 60; Andrew J. O'Shaughnessy, "The West India Interest and the Crisis of American Independence", in *West Indies Accounts: Essays on the History of the British Caribbean and the Atlantic Economy in Honour of Richard Sheridan,* ed. Roderick A. McDonald (Kingston: The Press, University of the West Indies, 1996), 126.

32. Jamaica Act 319, 1731, "An Act for appointing an agent or agents in Great Britain, to solicit the passing of laws, and other the public affairs of this island". Lillian M. Penson, *The Colonial Agents of the British West Indies: A Study in Colonial Administration Mainly in the Eighteenth Century* (London: University of London Press, 1924); Douglas Hall, *A Brief History of the West India Committee* (Barbados: Caribbean Universities Press, 1971), 4.

33. O'Shaughnessy, *Empire Divided*, 15. Cf. Pares, *Merchants and Planters,* 43.

34. Higman, "West India Interest", 1–19; Bowen, "British India", 530–51.

35. Williams, *Capitalism and Slavery,* 92–97; McCusker and Menard, *Economy of British America,* 161–63.

36. See Jones, *Wealth of a Nation to Be,* 319; Lee Soltow, *Distribution of Wealth and Income in the United States in 1798* (Pittsburgh: University of Pittsburgh Press, 1989), 110–13; W. D. Rubinstein, *Men of Property: The Very Wealthy in Britain since the Industrial Revolution* (New Brunswick, NJ: Rutgers University Press, 1981), 43–46, 198–200.

37. O'Shaughnessy, "West India Interest", 128–29; Clayton, "Sophistry", 319–44.

38. Frank Wesley Pitman, *The Development of the British West Indies 1700–1763* (New Haven: Yale University Press, 1917), 51–52; Pitman, "West Indian Absentee Planter", 118–20. See also N. A. T. Hall, "Some Aspects of the Deficiency Question in Jamaica in the Eighteenth Century", *Jamaica Journal* 7, no. 1–2 (1973): 36–41.

39. George Wilson Bridges, *The Annals of Jamaica* (London: John Murray, 1828), 2: 66–67. See also Sheridan, *Sugar and Slavery,* 433.

40. Long, *History of Jamaica,* 1: 386–87; O'Shaughnessy, *Empire Divided,* 20. On Long, see Howard Johnson, "Introduction: Edward Long, Historian of Jamaica", in Edward Long, *The History of Jamaica* (Kingston: Ian Randle Publishers, 2002), 1: i–xxv.

41. Long, *History of Jamaica,* 2: 265–66.

42. Beckford, *Descriptive Account,* 2: 374–75. Cf. Stewart, *View of the Past and Present,* 184; Brathwaite, *Development of Creole Society,* 300–303.

43. Lady Sydney Morgan, *Absenteeism* (London: Henry Colburn, 1825), 1; A. P. W. Malcolmson, "Absenteeism in Eighteenth Century Ireland", *Irish Economic and Social History* 1 (1974): 15; Thomas F. Moriarty, "The Irish Absentee Tax Controversy of 1773: A Study in Anglo-Irish Politics on the Eve of the American Revolution", *Proceedings of the American Philosophical Society* 118 (1974): 370–408.

44. Mary Jean Corbett, "Public Affections and Familial Politics: Burke, Edgeworth, and the 'Common Naturalization' of Great Britain", *ELH* [*English Literary History*] 61 (1994): 883; Maria Edgeworth, *The Absentee,* ed. W. J. McCormack and Kim Walker (Oxford: Oxford University Press, 1988). See also J. V. Beckett, "Landownership and Estate Management", in *The Agrarian History of England and Wales,* vol. 6, *1750–1850,* ed. G. E. Mingay (Cambridge: Cambridge University Press, 1989), 591; G. E. Mingay, *English Landed Society in the Eighteenth Century* (London: Routledge and Kegan Paul, 1963), 59–60.

45. J. R. McCulloch, *Treatises and Essays on Money, Exchange, Interest, The Letting of Land, Absenteeism, the History of Commerce, Manufactures, etc.* (Edinburgh: Adam and Charles Black, 1859), 223, 242. The essay was originally published in the *Edinburgh Review,* November 1825.

46. Mountifort Longfield, *Three Lectures on Commerce and one on Absenteeism, Delivered in Michaelmas Term, 1834, before the University of Dublin* (Dublin: Milliken and Son, 1835), 72; William Ernest Montgomery, *The History of Land Tenure in Ireland* (Cambridge: Cambridge University Press, 1889), 92–93; W. A. Maguire, *The Downshire Estates in Ireland, 1801–1845: The Management of Irish*

Landed Estates in the Early Nineteenth Century (Oxford: Clarendon Press, 1972), 231–32; Vaughan, *Landlords and Tenants,* 2–3.

47. Herman Merivale, *Lectures on Colonization and Colonies* (London: Longman, Green, Longman, and Roberts, 1861), 81–83.

48. Henry Higgs, ed., *Palgrave's Dictionary of Political Economy* (London: Macmillan, 1925), 1: 3–4. Entry by F. Y. Edgeworth. This entry was reprinted without change or addition in John Eatwell, Murray Milgate and Peter Newman, eds., *The New Palgrave: A Dictionary of Economics* (London: Macmillan, 1987), 1: 2–3.

49. Thorstein Veblen, *Absentee Ownership and Business Enterprise in Recent Times: The Case of America* (New York: B. W. Huebsch, 1923); Rick Tilman, *Thorstein Veblen and His Critics, 1891–1963: Conservative, Liberal, and Radical Perspectives* (Princeton: Princeton University Press, 1992), 63, 197–98.

50. David W. Pearce, ed., *The MIT Dictionary of Modern Economics* (Cambridge, Mass.: The MIT Press, 1992), 1; Giovanni Frederico, "Landlordism", in *The Oxford Encyclopedia of Economic History,* ed. Joel Mokyr (New York: Oxford University Press, 2003), 3: 266. For an exception, see C. Daniel Dillman, "Absentee Landlords and Farm Management in Brazil During the 1960s", *American Journal of Economics and Sociology* 37 (1978): 1–8.

51. But see Bryan Edwards, *The History, Civil and Commercial, of the British Colonies in the West Indies* (London: John Stockdale, 1793), 2: 130.

52. Mary Turner, "Planter Profits and Slave Rewards: Amelioration Reconsidered", in *West Indies Accounts: Essays on the History of the British Caribbean and the Atlantic Economy in Honour of Richard Sheridan,* ed. Roderick A. MacDonald (Kingston: The Press, University of the West Indies, 1996), 249. Cf. Hall, *In Miserable Slavery,* 172.

53. Pitman, *Development of the British West Indies,* 30–31, 41; Pitman, "West Indian Absentee", 113–27.

54. Lowell Joseph Ragatz, "Absentee Landlordism in the British Caribbean, 1750–1833", *Agricultural History* 5 (1931): 7, 18–19.

55. Ragatz, "Absentee Landlordism", 20–22. Cf. Gray, *History of Agriculture,* 1: 498.

56. Williams, *Capitalism and Slavery,* 85–86.

57. Pares, *Merchants and Planters,* 42–43. See also Philip D. Curtin, *Two Jamaicas: The Role of Ideas in a Tropical Colony 1830–1865* (Cambridge, Mass.: Harvard University Press, 1955), 16.

58. Hall, "Absentee-Proprietorship", 15–35. See also B. W. Higman, "Ideas and Illustrations in the Historical Thought of Douglas Hall", *Journal of Caribbean History* 35 (2001): 74–75. Cf. Elsa V. Goveia, *Slave Society in the British Leeward Islands at the End of the Eighteenth Century* (New Haven: Yale University Press, 1965), 111; Watts, *West Indies,* 354; Carrington, "Management of Sugar Estates", 27–53.

59. Patterson, *Sociology of Slavery,* 33, 43, 278. See also Richard S. Dunn, *Sugar and Slaves: The Rise of the Planter Class in the English West Indies, 1624–1713* (Chapel Hill: University of North Carolina Press, 1972), 213.

60. Brathwaite, *Development of Creole Society,* 130–31.

61. Richard B. Sheridan, "Planters and Merchants: The Oliver Family of Antigua and London 1716–1784", *Business History* 13 (1971): 113. Cf. Sheridan, *Sugar and Slavery,* 385; Seymour Drescher, *Econocide: British Slavery in the Era of Abolition*

(Pittsburgh: University of Pittsburgh Press, 1977), 39–40, 232; Cateau, "Conservatism and Change", 1–36.

62. Burnard, "Passengers Only", 180, 189.

63. Geggus, *Slavery, War, and Revolution*, 8. See also Dale W. Tomich, *Slavery in the Circuit of Sugar: Martinique and the World Economy, 1830–1848* (Baltimore: Johns Hopkins University Press, 1990), 111; César J. Ayala, *American Sugar Kingdom: The Plantation Economy of the Spanish Caribbean 1898–1934* (Chapel Hill: University of North Carolina Press, 1999), 2, 74–75.

64. Drescher, *Econocide,* 40.

65. P. Roebuck, "Absentee Landownership in the Late Seventeenth and Early Eighteenth Centuries: A Neglected Factor in English Agrarian History", *Agricultural History Review* 21 (1973): 17; Malcolmson, "Absenteeism in Eighteenth Century Ireland", 34; Frank T. Melton, "Absentee Land Management in Seventeenth-Century England", *Agricultural History* 52 (1978): 147–59; Beckett, "Absentee Landownership", 87; David Oldroyd, "Through a Glass Clearly: Management Practice on the Bowes Family Estates *c.*1700–70 as Revealed by the Accounts", *Accounting, Business and Financial History* 9 (1999): 177–78.

66. Malcolmson, "Absenteeism in Eighteenth Century Ireland", 16–17, 23, 28, 35. See also Maguire, *Downshire Estates,* 231–32; Vaughan, *Landlords and Tenants,* 2–3.

67. Cf. Pares, *Merchants and Planters,* 43.

68. Ibid., 44; Cowton and O'Shaughnessy, "Absentee Control", 34–35.

69. *Parliamentary Papers,* 1842 (479): 13, "Report from the Select Committee on West India Colonies", 391.

70. Ibid., 374, 392, 496–503.

71. *Parliamentary Papers,* 1836 (560): 15, "Select Committee on Negro Apprenticeship in the Colonies", 388.

72. Anon., *Marly; or, The Life of a Planter in Jamaica* (Glasgow: Richard Griffin and Co., 1828), 23.

73. F. G. Cassidy and R. B. Le Page, eds., *Dictionary of Jamaican English* (Cambridge: Cambridge University Press, 1967); Long, *History of Jamaica,* 1: 387–89.

74. Richard B. Sheridan, "Letters from a Sugar Plantation in Antigua, 1739–1758", *Agricultural History* 31 (1957): 3.

75. Goveia, *Slave Society,* 110–11, 208; S. G. Checkland, *The Gladstones: A Family Biography 1764–1851* (Cambridge: Cambridge University Press, 1971), 123–24, 185. Cf. J. R. Ward, *British West Indian Slavery, 1750–1834: The Process of Amelioration* (Oxford: Clarendon Press, 1988), 263n10.

76. J. B. Moreton, *West India Customs and Manners* (London: J. Parson, W. Richardson, H. Gardner and J. Walter, 1793), 79. Cf. "Select Committee on Negro Apprenticeship", 352; Goveia, *Slave Society,* 208; Cowton and O'Shaughnessy, "Absentee Control of Sugar Plantations", 39.

77. "Report from the Select Committee on West India Colonies", 362.

78. Douglas Hall, "Absentee-Proprietorship", 23n28. Cf. Cowton and O'Shaughnessy, "Absentee Control of Sugar Plantations", 35.

79. William Kauffman Scarborough, *The Overseer: Plantation Management in the Old South* (Baton Rouge: Louisiana State University Press, 1966), 4, 16–18, 178; Gray, *History of Agriculture,* 1: 548.

80. Gray, *History of Agriculture,* 1: 501; Scarborough, *Overseer,* 3, 181.

81. William Beckford Jr, *Remarks upon the Situation of Negroes in Jamaica* (London: Egerton, 1788), 89; Peter Marsden, *An Account of the Island of Jamaica* (Newcastle: the author, 1788), 22; Anon., *Marly* (1828), 16; Moreton, *West India Customs,* 79. See also Stewart, *View of the Past and Present,* 189; Goveia, *Slave Society,* 208.

82. Hall, *In Miserable Slavery,* 89, 127–28; Bernard Martin Senior, *Jamaica, As It Was, As It Is, and As It May Be* (London: T. Hurst, 1835), 60–62.

83. Gabriel Debien, *Les esclaves aux Antilles Françaises (XVIIe–XVIIIe siècles)* (Basse-Terre: Société d'histoire de la Guadeloupe, 1974), 105–33; Geggus, *Slavery, War, and Revolution,* 10, 406n35.

84. Thomas Roughley, *The Jamaica Planter's Guide* (London: Longman, Hurst, Rees, Orme and Brown, 1823), 68–69; Burnard, *Mastery,* 73–75. Cf. Beckford, *Remarks,* 69.

85. D. R. Hainsworth, *Stewards, Lords and People: The Estate Steward and His World in Later Stuart England* (Cambridge: Cambridge University Press, 1992); Barbara English, *The Great Landowners of East Yorkshire, 1530–1910* (New York: Harvester/Wheatsheaf, 1990), 153–54.

86. Beckett, "Landownership and Estate Management", 591–92; Mingay, *English Landed Society in the Eighteenth Century,* 60.

87. Christopher Clay, "Landlords and Estate Management in England", in *The Agrarian History of England and Wales,* vol. 5, *1640–1750, Part 2, Agrarian Change,* ed. Joan Thirsk (Cambridge: Cambridge University Press, 1990), 243.

88. R. C. Dallas, *The History of the Maroons* (London: T. N. Longman and O. Rees, 1803), 2: 358.

89. F. M. L. Thompson, *English Landed Society in the Nineteenth Century* (London: Routledge and Kegan Paul, 1963), 153.

90. Beckett, "Landownership and Estate Management", 592.

91. Eric Richards, "The Land Agent", in *The Victorian Countryside,* ed. G. E. Mingay (London: Routledge and Kegan Paul, 1981), 2: 439. See also Thompson, *English Landed Society in the Nineteenth Century,* 169; David Spring, *The English Landed Estate in the Nineteenth Century: Its Administration* (Baltimore: Johns Hopkins University Press, 1963), 97.

92. I. H. Adams, "The Agents of Agricultural Change", in *The Making of the Scottish Countryside,* ed. M. L. Parry and T. R. Slater (London: Croom Helm, 1980), 165–68; Eric Richards and Monica Clough, *Cromartie: Highland Life, 1650–1914* (Aberdeen: Aberdeen University Press, 1989), 27–29; Eric Richards, *Patrick Sellar and the Highland Clearances: Homicide, Eviction and the Price of Progress* (Edinburgh: Polygon at Edinburgh, 1999), 63–67.

93. Malcolmson, "Absenteeism in Eighteenth Century Ireland", 31. See also Maguire, *Downshire Estates,* 184–85; Spring, *English Landed Estate,* 98–105.

94. Maguire, *Downshire Estates,* 188, 192. See also Vaughan, *Landlords and Tenants,* 108.

95. *Journals of the Assembly of Jamaica* 12 (1808–15): 808–9, 816.

96. Stewart, *View of the Past and Present,* 183.

97. "Report from the Select Committee on West India Colonies", 338, 362. Cf. Philip Wright, *Monumental Inscriptions of Jamaica* (London: Society of Genealogists, 1966), 297.

98. "Select Committee on Negro Apprenticeship", 327.

99. Ibid., 352.

100. Wright, *Inscriptions,* 59, 244.

101. Beckford, *Remarks,* 68. See also Marsden, *Account,* 19.

102. Senior, *Jamaica,* 89.

103. Andrew Long, *Powers of Attorney and Other Instruments Conferring Authority* (Cambridge: ICSA Publishing, 1987), 1.

104. See, for example, Simon Stevenson, "Open Field or Enclosure? Peasants, Planters' Agents and Lawyers in Jamaica, 1866–1875", *Rural History* 12 (2001): 54n6. Cf. Cowton and O'Shaughnessy, "Absentee Control of Sugar Plantations", 39.

105. Robert Robson, *The Attorney in Eighteenth-Century England* (Cambridge: Cambridge University Press, 1959), 1–12; Michael Miles, " 'A Haven for the Privileged': Recruitment into the Profession of Attorney in England, 1709–1792", *Social History* 11 (1986): 197.

106. Lloyd G. Barnett, *The Constitutional Law of Jamaica* (Oxford: Oxford University Press, 1977), 330–32.

107. Michael Miles, " 'Eminent Practitioners': The New Visage of Country Attorneys c.1750–1800", in *Law, Economy and Society, 1750–1914: Essays in the History of English Law,* ed. G. R. Rubin and David Sugarman (Abingdon, UK: Professional Books, 1984), 470.

108. B. L. Anderson, "The Attorney and the Early Capital Market in Lancashire", in *Liverpool and Merseyside: Essays in the Economic and Social History of the Port and Its Hinterland,* ed. J. R. Harris (London: Frank Cass and Co., 1969), 50–77; B. L. Anderson, "Provincial Aspects of the Financial Revolution of the Eighteenth Century", *Business History* 11 (1969): 20–22; M. Miles, "The Money Market in the Early Industrial Revolution: The Evidence from West Riding Attorneys c.1750–1800", *Business History* 23 (1981): 127–46; Miles, " 'Eminent Practitioners' ", 476–77.

109. Philip Aylett, "Attorneys and Clients in Eighteenth-Century Cheshire: A Study in Relationships, 1740–1785", *Bulletin of the John Rylands University Library of Manchester* 69 (1987): 358.

110. Thompson, *English Landed Society in the Nineteenth Century,* 182. See also Robson, *Attorney,* 86; Aylett, "Attorneys and Clients", 352–53; Edward Hughes, "The Eighteenth-Century Estate Agent", in *Essays in British and Irish History in Honour of James Eadie Todd,* ed. H. A. Cronne, T. W. Moody and D. B. Quinn (London: Frederick Muller, 1949), 185–99; Peter Mathias, "The Lawyer as Businessman in Eighteenth-Century England", in *Enterprise and History: Essays in Honour of Charles Wilson,* ed. D. C. Coleman and Peter Mathias (Cambridge: Cambridge University Press, 1984), 151–67.

111. "Report from the Select Committee on West India Colonies", 364. See also, Accounts Current, Liber 29, f. 195 (Jamaica Archives, Spanish Town).

112. Returns of Registrations of Slaves, Libers 129, 131, 137 (Jamaica Archives, Spanish Town).

113. Roughley, *Jamaica Planter's Guide,* 11; Stewart, *View of the Past and Present,* 184; Anon., *Marly,* 96; Mulgrave to Goderich, 6 Oct. 1832, Ripon Papers, f. 504, Add. Ms. 40879, Part II (British Library). For examples of the use of "planting attorney", see "Select Committee on Negro Apprenticeship", 406.

114. W. J. Gardner, *A History of Jamaica* (1873; reprint London: Frank Cass and Co., 1971), 377.

115. Ward, *British West Indian Slavery*, 265; Carrington, "Management of Sugar Estates", 28; Carrington, *Sugar Industry*, 138.

116. Richard Pares, *Yankees and Creoles: The Trade between North America and the West Indies before the American Revolution* (London: Longmans, Green and Co., 1956), 9.

117. Roughley, *Jamaica Planter's Guide*, 11.

Chapter 3

1. Long, *Powers of Attorney*, 1; Anderson, "Provincial Aspects", 22.

2. Galenson, *Traders, Planters, and Slaves*, 139. See also Sheridan, *Sugar and Slavery*, 362.

3. Higman, *Jamaica Surveyed*, 20–30.

4. Metcalf, *Royal Government*, chapters 3 and 4.

5. Jamaica Act 127, 1740.

6. Sheridan, "Simon Taylor", 287.

7. Jamaica Act 388, 1737.

8. Jamaica Act 184, Clause XIV, of 1751. Pares refers to this as Jamaica Act 25 Geo. II, cap. 19, section 8. See Pares, *Merchants and Planters*, 85n35. In 1752 Act 193 was passed to "explain and amend a clause" in the 1751 act, but this amendment applied only to the commencement date of regulation of the rate of interest.

9. Pares, *Merchants and Planters*, 85n35.

10. Jamaica Act 179, 1751.

11. *The Laws of Jamaica* (1938), vol. 5, 4150–59: cap. 373, The Attorneys, Executors and Trustees (Accounts and General) Law, 30 May 1904. See also Higman, *Slave Population and Economy*, 9–10; Sheridan, "Simon Taylor", 287; Sheridan, "Wealth", 294.

12. K. E. Ingram, *Sources of Jamaican History 1655–1838* (Zug, Switzerland: Inter Documentation Co., 1976), 1: 569–70, 598, 602, 623, 631; 2: 633, 662.

13. J. Maxwell, *Remarks on the Present State of Jamaica* (1848), 15, quoted in Douglas Hall, "Absentee-Proprietorship", 25.

14. Powers of Attorney, 1806–1825 (Jamaica Archives, Spanish Town); Long, *Powers of Attorney*, 1.

15. Senior, *Jamaica*, 89; William Paley, *A Treatise on the Law of Principal and Agent, Chiefly with Reference to Mercantile Transactions* (Philadelphia: John S. Littell, 1840), 78–85; Trevor M. Aldridge, *Powers of Attorney* (London: Longman, 1988); Stephen M. Cretney and Denzil Lush, *Enduring Powers of Attorney* (Bristol: Jordans, 1996).

16. Galenson, *Traders, Planters, and Slaves*, 139–40; Burnard, *Mastery*, 44, 85.

17. Dawkins Papers, vol. 2, f. 43, MS 181 (National Library of Jamaica, Kingston).

18. Ibid., vol. 11, ff. 61–62.

19. Powers of Attorney, 1806–1825, 51. William Rhodes James (1785–1842) was memorialized in Black River parish church, the tablet erected by his widow. He was identified as "of Newell Pen" but his father lived in Trelawny. Wright, *Inscriptions*, 168, 261.

20. Powers of Attorney, 1806–1825, 62.

21. Ibid., 132–34.

22. Ibid., 135. Thomas James Brown (1790–1823) and John Gale Vidal (1792–1850) were located in Spanish Town. Brown died "on his passage to England" but appears to have been a creole, married to a creole woman. He was memorialized on the wall of Spanish Town Cathedral. Wright, *Inscriptions,* 103.

23. Dovaston, "Agricultura Americana", 1: 3–7; Ingram, *Sources,* 2: 727–33; Returns of Registrations of Slaves, Liber 129.

24. Ingram, *Sources,* 1: 602; Grassby, *Kinship and Capitalism,* 281.

25. Richards, "Land Agent", 2: 440; Thompson, *English Landed Society in the Nineteenth Century,* 156–57. In Jamaica, argued Sheridan, "attorneyships were eagerly sought after". Sheridan, "Simon Taylor", 288.

26. Beckford, *Descriptive Account,* 2: 364. See also Anon., *Marly,* 96–97.

27. Moreton, *West India Customs,* 71–72; Senior, *Jamaica,* 89; Beckford, *Descriptive Account,* 2: 368.

28. Beckford, *Descriptive Account,* 2: 361; Stewart, *View of the Past and Present,* 184.

29. Ragatz, "Absentee Landlordism", 20–21; W. L. Burn, *Emancipation and Apprenticeship in the British West Indies* (London: Jonathan Cape, 1937), 36; Sheridan, "Simon Taylor", 287; Carrington, "Management of Sugar Estates", 28.

30. Karras, *Sojourners,* 55–65; Alan Karras, "The World of Alexander Johnston: The Creolization of Ambition, 1762–1787", *Historical Journal* 30 (1987): 58; O'Shaughnessy, *Empire Divided,* 26; Hall, *In Miserable Slavery,* 225.

31. Thompson, *English Landed Society in the Nineteenth Century,* 158–59.

32. Arthur E. Shipley, *Islands, West Indian – Aegean* (London: Martin Hopkinson and Co., 1924), 47.

33. Beckford, *Descriptive Account,* 2: 367. For Beckford, see Brathwaite, *Development of Creole Society,* 131, 139; Sheridan, "Planter and Historian", 56.

34. Roughley, *Jamaica Planter's Guide,* 5–10. See also Leonard Wray, *The Practical Sugar Planter* (London: Smith, Elder and Co., 1848), 62.

35. Sheridan, "Simon Taylor", 288; Sheridan, *Sugar and Slavery,* 386–87; Karras, *Sojourners,* 65.

36. *Parliamentary Papers,* 1831–32 (721): 20, "Report from the Select Committee on the Extinction of Slavery throughout the British Dominions", 439. See also Beckford, *Descriptive Account,* 2: 365; Curtin, *Two Jamaicas,* 16.

37. Curtin, *Two Jamaicas,* 16.

38. Moreton, *West India Customs and Manners,* 70–71.

39. "Report from the Select Committee on the Extinction of Slavery", 32.

40. "Select Committee on Negro Apprenticeship", 389.

41. Burn, *Emancipation and Apprenticeship,* 36.

42. "Select Committee on Negro Apprenticeship", 341.

43. Burnard, *Mastery,* 97–104.

44. Henry Bleby, *Death Struggles of Slavery: Being a Narrative of Facts and Incidents, which occurred in a British Colony, during the two years immediately Preceding Negro Emancipation* (London: Hamilton, Adams and Co., 1853), 3; Philip Wright, *Knibb "the Notorious": Slaves' Missionary 1803–1845* (London: Sidgwick and Jackson, 1973), 68–69; H. P. Jacobs, *Sixty Years of Change, 1806–1866: Progress and*

Reaction in Kingston and the Countryside (Kingston: Institute of Jamaica, 1973), 56–58.

45. Pares, *Yankees and Creoles,* 9.

46. Cf. Sheridan, *Sugar and Slavery,* 387.

47. Hope Masterton Waddell, *Twenty-nine Years in the West Indies and Central Africa* (London: T. Nelson and Sons, 1863), 38. For examples of collections of attorneys' letters and accounts, see Ingram, *Sources,* 1: 590, 594, 2: 648, 727, 778, 784–85, 800, 803; K. E. Ingram, *Manuscripts Relating to Commonwealth Caribbean Countries in United States and Canadian Repositories* (Barbados: Caribbean Universities Press, 1975), 251; B. W. Higman, "The Letterbooks of Isaac Jackson, Jamaican Planting Attorney, 1839–1843", *Journal of Caribbean History* 37 (2003): 317–29; Wood, *Letters of Simon Taylor.*

48. Beckett, "Landownership and Estate Management", 592.

49. Richards, "Land Agent", 439–40. See also Spring, *English Landed Estate,* 105–18.

50. Avner Offer, "Farm Tenure and Land Values in England, *c.*1750–1950", *Economic History Review* 44 (1991): 1.

51. Offer, "Farm Tenure and Land Values", 1; David R. Stead, "Risk and Risk Management in English Agriculture, *c.*1750–1850", *Economic History Review* 57 (2004): 334.

52. Offer, "Farm Tenure and Land Values", 17.

53. Scarborough, *Overseer,* 179.

54. "Report from the Select Committee on the Extinction of Slavery", 465.

55. Stewart, *View of the Past and Present,* 183.

56. Burn, *Emancipation and Apprenticeship,* 35.

57. Carrington, "Management of Sugar Estates", 27.

58. Thomas C. Holt, *The Problem of Freedom: Race, Labor, and Politics in Jamaica and Britain, 1832–1938* (Baltimore: Johns Hopkins University Press, 1992), 424n21.

59. *The Jamaican Censuses of 1844 and 1861,* ed. B. W. Higman (Mona, Jamaica: Social History Project, University of the West Indies, 1980), 57.

60. Anthony Trollope, *The West Indies and the Spanish Main* (1859; reprint, Gloucester: Alan Sutton, 1985), 80.

61. Holt, *Problem of Freedom,* 368; R. W. Beachey, *The British West Indies Sugar Industry in the Late Nineteenth Century* (Oxford: Basil Blackwell, 1957), 73–76; Richard A. Lobdell, "Patterns of Investment and Sources of Credit in the British West Indian Sugar Industry, 1838–97", *Journal of Caribbean History* 4 (1972): 31–53.

62. *Handbook of Jamaica* (1939): 298–301; *Handbook of Jamaica* (1951): 335–39; *Handbook of Jamaica* (1953): 317–19.

63. Kathleen Mary Butler, *The Economics of Emancipation: Jamaica and Barbados, 1823–1843* (Chapel Hill: University of North Carolina Press, 1995), 59.

64. Higman, *Slave Population and Economy,* 68–69.

65. Ibid., 30.

66. The names of the owners are unknown for 28 properties in the hands of attorneys (most of them properties in the hands of mortgagees or under the Court of Chancery). These are included in the total of 473, making this the maximum and 445 the minimum number of owners. The percentages are derived from the known 445 owners.

67. Higman, *Slave Population and Economy,* 13–16 and 282n23. Urban "pens" are excluded here.

68. For maps of estates, pens and plantations, see ibid., 19, 22, 32–33.

69. For a map of population density, see ibid., 54–55.

70. Jean Lindsay, "The Pennants and Jamaica 1665–1808: Part I, The Growth and Organisation of the Pennant Estate", *Transactions of the Caernarfonshire Historical Society* 43 (1982): 62–65; Moreton, *West India Customs and Manners,* 72.

71. "Report from the Select Committee on West India Colonies", 452–55.

72. Heuman, *Between Black and White,* 4; Burn, *Emancipation and Apprenticeship,* 35–36; Curtin, *Two Jamaicas,* 16.

73. Stewart, *View of the Past and Present,* 185.

74. Brathwaite, *Development of Creole Society,* 139. See also Stewart, *View of the Past and Present,* 186–87.

75. Holt, *Problem of Freedom,* 86.

76. The distribution in Table 3.2 depends on the identification of names, which were not always spelled consistently. Notably, James MacDonald and James McDonald might have been one person or perhaps more than two.

77. Wright, *Knibb,* 108; R. R. Madden, *A Twelvemonth's Residence in the West Indies, during the Transition from Slavery to Apprenticeship* (London: James Cochrane and Co., 1835), 1: 212.

78. Dallas, *History of the Maroons,* 2: 373; Gardner, *History of Jamaica,* 320, citing the *Journals of the House of Assembly* 9 (1796).

79. Karras, *Sojourners,* 65n58.

80. Marsden, *Account,* 20; *Parliamentary Papers,* 1807 (65): 3, "Report from the Committee on the Commercial State of the West India Colonies", 9, 12; "[First] Report from the Committee on the Distillation of Sugar and Molasses", 280.

81. *Journals of the Assembly of Jamaica* 12 (1808–15): 804–5.

82. Gardner, *History of Jamaica,* 378; Holt, *Problem of Freedom,* 424n21.

83. Jean Lindsay, "The Pennants and Jamaica 1665–1808: Part II, The Economic and Social Development of the Pennant Estates in Jamaica", *Transactions of the Caernarfonshire Historical Society* 44 (1983): 67.

84. Cf. Hall, *In Miserable Slavery,* 123.

85. "Report from the Committee on the Commercial State of the West India Colonies", 18; "[First] Report from the Committee on the Distillation of Sugar and Molasses", 174.

86. "[First] Report from the Committee on the Distillation of Sugar and Molasses", 166; A. E. Furness, "George Hibbert and the Defence of Slavery in the West Indies", *Jamaican Historical Review* 5 (1965): 56–70; Wright, *Inscriptions,* 280.

87. Matthew Gregory Lewis, *Journal of a West India Proprietor* (London: John Murray, 1834), 359–65.

88. "Select Committee on Negro Apprenticeship", 327.

89. Ibid., 327, 334, 344.

90. *Journals of the Assembly of Jamaica* 12 (1808–15): 814.

91. Madden, *Twelvemonth's Residence,* 1: 220.

92. Beckford, *Descriptive Account,* 2: 360; Curtin, *Two Jamaicas,* 16.

93. *Journals of the Assembly of Jamaica* 12 (1808–15): 810.

94. "Report from the Select Committee on the Extinction of Slavery", 428–32; Ingram, *Sources,* 2: 686.

95. Grassby, *Kinship and Capitalism,* 330–31; Trevor Burnard, "Inheritance and Independence: Women's Status in Early Colonial Jamaica", *William and Mary Quarterly* 48 (1991): 93–114; Trevor Burnard, "Family Continuity and Female Independence in Jamaica, 1665–1734", *Continuity and Change* 7 (1992): 181–98.

96. Wright, *Inscriptions,* 151.

97. Richard B. Sheridan, "The Role of the Scots in the Economy and Society of the West Indies", *Annals of the New York Academy of Sciences* 292 (1977): 94–106; Hall, *In Miserable Slavery,* 124; Karras, *Sojourners,* passim.

98. Wright, *Lady Nugent's Journal,* 29.

99. Sheridan, *Sugar and Slavery,* 387; Sheridan, "Simon Taylor", 289; Anon., *Marly,* 7–9; Karras, "World of Alexander Johnston", 54–57; Burnard, *Mastery,* 88–89.

100. "Report from the Select Committee on the Extinction of Slavery", 473.

101. "Select Committee on Negro Apprenticeship", 387–88.

102. Higman, *Jamaica Surveyed,* 211. John Campbell the attorney may have been John Campbell the coloured retailer of Montego Bay and member of the House of Assembly (1833–34) and the John Campbell who died in Montego Bay in 1834, but the link has not been established firmly. See Heuman, *Between Black and White,* 9, 58; Wright, *Inscriptions,* 222.

103. Jacobs, *Sixty Years of Change,* 105. Cf. Burnard, *Mastery,* 90.

104. "Report from the Select Committee on the Extinction of Slavery", 472; Lewis, *Journal,* 171.

105. Penrhyn 1241, quoted in Lindsay, "Pennants and Jamaica: Part I", 63.

106. *Journals of the Assembly of Jamaica* 12 (1808–15): 808–9.

107. Waddell, *Twenty-nine Years,* 39; Burn, *Emancipation and Apprenticeship,* 35n3.

108. Waddell, *Twenty-nine Years,* 21, 38.

109. Wright, *Inscriptions,* 169, 176.

110. Ibid., 6, 150, 176.

111. Ibid., 268, 278.

112. Ibid., 235.

113. Ibid., 116, 235.

114. Lewis, *Journal,* 171.

115. Moreton, *West India Customs,* 77. Cf. Brathwaite, *Development of Creole Society,* 139.

116. Hall, *In Miserable Slavery;* Burnard, *Mastery.*

117. Ingram, *Sources,* 2: 731; Steel, "Philosophy of Fear", 14.

118. Jacobs, *Sixty Years of Change,* 64; Enid Shields, *Vale Royal: The House and the People* (Kingston: Jamaican Historical Society, *c.*1984), 30–32; Heuman, *Between Black and White,* 61.

119. Ward, *British West Indian Slavery,* 265.

120. Long, *History of Jamaica,* 1: 438; Beckford, *Descriptive Account,* 2: 364; Senior, *Jamaica,* 90.

121. Moreton, *West India Customs,* 73; Roughley, *Jamaica Planter's Guide,* 11; Stewart, *View of the Past and Present,* 185; Gardner, *History of Jamaica,* 377–78.

122. Cf. Burn, *Emancipation and Apprenticeship,* 36; Curtin, *Two Jamaicas,* 16; Sheridan, "Simon Taylor", 288; Sheridan, *Sugar and Slavery,* 387.

123. Beckford, *Descriptive Account,* 2: 364; Dallas, *History of the Maroons,* 2: 359; Stewart, *View of the Past and Present,* 185; "Report from the Select Committee on West India Colonies", 374. Cf. Gardner, *History of Jamaica,* 377–78.

124. Senior, *Jamaica,* 90.

125. Burn, *Emancipation and Apprenticeship,* 36; Curtin, *Two Jamaicas,* 16; Sheridan, *Sugar and Slavery,* 387; Sheridan, "Simon Taylor", 288; Ward, *British West Indian Slavery,* 265.

126. Lindsay, "Pennants and Jamaica: Part I", 73.

127. Dallas, *History of the Maroons,* 2: 359, 370; Thompson, *English Landed Society in the Nineteenth Century,* 153. Cf. Burnard, *Mastery,* 47.

128. Brathwaite, *Development of Creole Society,* 139; Holt, *Problem of Freedom,* 89; Ward, *British West Indian Slavery,* 92; Stewart, *View of the Past and Present,* 185. Cf. Gardner, *History of Jamaica,* 377–78.

129. "Report from the Select Committee on West India Colonies", 374, 455; Holt, *Problem of Freedom,* 424n21.

130. Beckford, *Descriptive Account,* 2: 365–66; Gardner, *History of Jamaica,* 377–78; Curtin, *Two Jamaicas,* 16.

131. Burn, *Emancipation and Apprenticeship,* 36.

132. Curtin, *Two Jamaicas,* 16. See also Sheridan, "Simon Taylor", 288; Sheridan, *Sugar and Slavery,* 387.

133. Curtin, *Two Jamaicas,* 16; Beckford, *Descriptive Account,* 2: 364–65; Anon., *Marly,* 7.

134. Brathwaite, *Development of Creole Society,* 139. See also Holt, *Problem of Freedom,* 89.

135. Gardner, *History of Jamaica,* 320.

136. Beckford, *Descriptive Account,* 2: 366–67; Gardner, *History of Jamaica,* 377–78; Senior, *Jamaica,* 90.

137. Stewart, *View of the Past and Present,* 194; Burn, *Emancipation and Apprenticeship,* 38; Curtin, *Two Jamaicas,* 16; Selwyn H. H. Carrington, " 'Econocide' – Myth or Reality? The Question of West Indian Decline, 1783–1806", *Boletin de Estudios Latinoamericanos y del Caribe* 36 (1984): 23.

138. "Report from the Select Committee on West India Colonies", 374.

139. Cited in Douglas Hall, *Free Jamaica 1838–1865: An Economic History* (New Haven: Yale University Press, 1959), 228.

140. Thompson, *English Landed Society in the Nineteenth Century,* 161; Beckett, "Landownership and Estate Management", 594–95; Maguire, *Downshire Estates,* 188; Vaughan, *Landlords and Tenants,* 109.

141. Moreton, *West India Customs,* 69, 72. See also Anon., *Marly,* pp. 23–27; Dallas, *History of the Maroons,* 2: 361.

142. Burn, *Emancipation and Apprenticeship,* 36.

143. A "George Gordon" did own 5 slaves in Kingston but seems unlikely to be the same person. Cf. "Select Committee on Negro Apprenticeship", 407.

144. "Select Committee on Negro Apprenticeship", 327.

145. Wright, *Inscriptions,* 186.

146. Quoted in Butler, *Economics of Emancipation,* 69; Gardner, *History of Jamaica,* 283–93; Ingram, *Sources,* 1: 359.

147. Butler, *Economics of Emancipation,* 69.

148. Returns of Registrations of Slaves, Libers 126, 135; Butler, *Economics of Emancipation,* 70, 162n18.

149. Quoted in Butler, *Economics of Emancipation,* 70.

150. Wright, *Inscriptions,* 267.

151. Inventories, Liber 159, f. 99 (Jamaica Archives, Spanish Town).

152. *Journals of the Assembly of Jamaica* 12 (1808–15): 812.

153. Returns of Registrations of Slaves, Liber 131.

154. Inventories, Liber 159, f. 71.

155. Returns of Registrations of Slaves, Liber 131. Cf. Jackie Ranston, *The Lindo Legacy* (London: Toucan Books, 2000), 74.

156. Returns of Registrations of Slaves, Liber 136.

157. Inventories, Liber 152, ff. 39–43.

158. Wright, *Inscriptions,* 116, 121.

159. Ibid., 101.

160. Brathwaite, *Development of Creole Society,* 40–43; Hall, *Free Jamaica,* 2–4; Burnard, *Mastery,* 75–79.

161. Mulgrave to Goderich, 2 March 1833, Ripon Papers, f. 22, Add. Ms. 40863; Mulgrave to Goderich, 6 Oct. 1832, Ripon Papers, f. 504, Add. Ms. 40879, Part II (British Library); Burn, *Emancipation and Apprenticeship,* 153, 185; Holt, *Problem of Freedom,* 84–85.

162. Jacobs, *Sixty Years of Change,* 48, 100.

163. Wright, *Inscriptions,* 186.

164. Wright, *Knibb,* 72.

165. "Select Committee on Negro Apprenticeship", 327–28.

166. Wright, *Inscriptions,* 116.

167. Ibid., 72; Jacobs, *Sixty Years of Change,* 67, 81; Alexander Barclay, *A Practical View of the Present State of Slavery in the West Indies* (London: Smith, Elder, 1826).

168. Wright, *Inscriptions,* 169.

169. Wright, *Knibb,* 83, 91.

170. Wright, *Inscriptions,* 186.

171. Ibid., 270.

172. Quoted in Heuman, *Between Black and White,* 120.

173. Wright, *Inscriptions,* 297.

174. Ibid., 287.

175. Ibid., 220.

176. Ibid., 151–52.

177. Ibid., 89, 119, 262.

178. Anon., *Marly,* 74–75.

179. Curtin, *Two Jamaicas,* 47.

180. Burnard, *Mastery,* 61.

181. Beckford, *Descriptive Account,* 2: 366; Gardner, *History of Jamaica,* 377–78; Curtin, *Two Jamaicas,* 16.

182. Beckford, *Descriptive Account,* 2: 366–67.

183. Madden, *Twelvemonth's Residence,* 1: 200.

Chapter 4

1. Galenson, *Traders, Planters, and Slaves,* 139.
2. Cf. Charles W. Wootton and Mary Virginia Moore, "The Legal Status of Account Books in Colonial America", *Accounting History* 5 (2000): 33–58.
3. Richard Laughlin, "Critical Accounting: Nature, Progress and Prognosis", *Accounting, Auditing and Accountability Journal* 12 (1999): 73–78; Richard K. Fleischman, Vaughan S. Radcliffe and Paul A. Shoemaker, eds., *Doing Accounting History: Contributions to the Development of Accounting Thought* (Oxford: Elsevier Science, 2003); Cooke, "Denial of Slavery in Management Studies"; Richard K. Fleischman and Thomas N. Tyson, "Accounting in Service to Racism: Monetizing Slave Property in the Antebellum South", *Critical Perspectives on Accounting* 15 (2004): 376–99; Thomas N. Tyson, Richard K. Fleischman, and David Oldroyd, "Theoretical Perspectives on Accounting for Labor on Slave Plantations of the USA and British West Indies", *Accounting, Auditing and Accountability Journal* 17 (2004): 758–78.
4. Marcia Annisette, "Importing Accounting: The Case of Trinidad and Tobago", *Accounting, Business and Financial History* 9 (1999): 106–7. See also Theresa Hammond, "History from Accounting's Margins: International Research on Race and Gender", *Accounting History* 8 (2003): 15–16; M. Annisette and D. Neu, "Accounting and Empire: An Introduction", *Critical Perspectives on Accounting* 15 (2004): 1–4
5. Ward, *British West Indian Slavery,* 265; McCusker and Menard, *Economy of British America,* 344.
6. Sidney Pollard, *The Genesis of Modern Management: A Study of the Industrial Revolution in Great Britain* (London: Edward Arnold, 1965), 210. Cf. Christopher J. Napier, "Aristocratic Accounting: The Bute Estate in Glamorgan 1814–1880", *Accounting and Business Research* 21 (1991): 165.
7. Napier, "Aristocratic Accounting", 165; Oldroyd, "Through a Glass Clearly", 182–83. See also Haydn Jones, *Accounting, Costing and Cost Estimation: Welsh Industry, 1700–1830* (Cardiff: University of Wales Press, 1985), 39–72; Christopher Nobes, ed., *The Development of Double Entry: Selected Essays* (New York: Garland, 1984); Cowton and O'Shaughnessy, "Absentee Control of Sugar Plantations", 37–38.
8. Thompson, *English Landed Society in the Nineteenth Century,* 153–54. Cf. Napier, "Aristocratic Accounting", 164.
9. Pollard, *Genesis,* 210–12.
10. Higman, *Jamaica Surveyed,* 102–4; Richard K. Ormrod, "The Evolution of Soil Management Practices in Early Jamaican Sugar Planting", *Journal of Historical Geography* 5 (1979): 157–70.
11. Joseph R. Razek, "Accounting on the Old Plantation: A Study of the Financial Records of an Ante-Bellum Louisiana Sugar Planter", *Accounting Historians Journal* 12 (1985): 17–36; Michael J. Mepham, *Accounting in Eighteenth Century Scotland* (New York: Garland, 1988), 253–60. Cf. Alexander Malcolm, *A Treatise of Book-keeping, or, Merchants Accounts: in the Italian Method of Debtor and Creditor* (1731; reprint, New York: Garland, 1986); W. T. Baxter, "Accounting in Colonial

America", in *Studies in the History of Accounting,* ed. A. C. Littleton and B. S. Yamey (London: Sweet and Maxwell, 1956), 272–87; B. S. Yamey, H. C. Edey and Hugh W. Thompson, *Accounting in England and Scotland, 1543–1800: Double Entry in Exposition and Practice* (London: Sweet and Maxwell, 1963); A. C. Littleton, *Accounting Evolution to 1900* (New York: Russell and Russell, 1966), 26–28; Cowton and O'Shaughnessy, "Absentee Control of Sugar Plantations", 36; Annisette, "Importing Accounting", 107.

12. Lindsay, "Pennants and Jamaica: Part I", 62; Mepham, *Accounting in Eighteenth Century Scotland,* 253–60; Michael J. Mepham, "The Scottish Enlightenment and the Development of Accounting", *Accounting Historians Journal* 15 (1988): 151–76.

13. Roughley, *Jamaica Planter's Guide,* 28–29.

14. "Select Committee on Negro Apprenticeship", 334.

15. Braco Estate Journal, 1795–97 (Jamaica Archives, Spanish Town); Rose Hall Journal, 1817–32 (Jamaica Archives, Spanish Town).

16. P. J. Laborie, *The Coffee Planter of Saint Domingo* (London: T. Cadell and W. Davies, 1798), 155.

17. Rose Hall Journal, 1817–32; Higman, *Slave Population and Economy,* 193–96; Fleischman and Tyson, "Accounting in Service to Racism", 386; Richard K. Fleischman, David Oldroyd and Thomas N. Tyson, "Monetizing Human Life: Slave Valuations on United States and British West Indian Plantations", *Accounting History* 9 (2004): 35–62; Cowton and O'Shaughnessy, "Absentee Control of Sugar Plantations", 41.

18. Old Montpelier Estate, Account Book, 1824–28 (MS 217, National Library of Jamaica, Kingston).

19. Isaac Jackson Letterbooks, 1: 167, July 1840.

20. Carrington, *Sugar Industry,* 118.

21. Anderson, "Provincial Aspects", 12–13; V. B. Grant, *Jamaican Land Law* (Master of Laws diss., University of London, 1948, published 1957), 49–57.

22. "Report from the Select Committee on West India Colonies", 360–61.

23. Reports of John W. Cooper, for Anna Susanna Watson Taylor, 18 April 1835, 7/177/1 (Jamaica Archives, Spanish Town).

24. Douglas Hall, "Incalculability as a Feature of Sugar Production during the Eighteenth Century", *Social and Economic Studies* 10 (1961): 343; Best, "Outlines", 305, 312.

25. Ray Bert Westerfield, *Middlemen in English Business, Particularly between 1660 and 1760* (New Haven: Yale University Press, 1915), 357.

26. B. W. Higman, "Patterns of Exchange within a Plantation Economy: Jamaica at the Time of Emancipation", in *West Indies Accounts: Essays on the History of the British Caribbean and the Atlantic Economy in Honour of Richard Sheridan,* ed. Roderick McDonald (Kingston: The Press, University of the West Indies, 1996), 211–31; Verene A. Shepherd and Kathleen E. A. Monteith, "Pen-keepers and Coffee Farmers in a Sugar-Plantation Economy", in *Slavery Without Sugar: Diversity in Caribbean Economy and Society since the Seventeenth Century,* ed. Verene A. Shepherd (Gainesville: University Press of Florida, 2002), 82–101.

27. Beckford, *Descriptive Account,* 2: 353. See also D. W. Thoms, "The Mills Family: London Sugar Merchants of the Eighteenth Century", *Business History* 11 (1969): 5.

28. Richard Pares, "A London West-India Merchant House, 1740–1769", in *Essays Presented to Sir Lewis Namier,* ed. Richard Pares and A. J. P. Taylor (London: Macmillan and Co., 1956), 75–107; David Hancock, *Citizens of the World: London Merchants and the Integration of the British Atlantic Community, 1735–1785* (Cambridge: Cambridge University Press, 1995), 126–31; Sheridan, "Planters and Merchants", 107–8; Sheridan, *Sugar and Slavery,* 282–98; Lindsay, "The Pennants and Jamaica: Part I", 58.

29. Beckford, *Descriptive Account,* 2: 355; Richard Pares, "The London Sugar Market, 1740–1769", *Economic History Review* 9 (1956): 257–58; Westerfield, *Middlemen,* 354.

30. Thoms, "Mills Family", 7; Hancock, *Citizens of the World,* 126.

31. Penrhyn 1354 and 1392, quoted in Lindsay, "Pennants and Jamaica: Part II", 61.

32. Pares, "London Sugar Market", 257–58.

33. Gary M. Walton, "Sources of Productivity Change in American Colonial Shipping, 1675–1775", *Economic History Review* 20 (1967): 71; Lindsay, "Pennants and Jamaica: Part II", 65.

34. Carrington, *Sugar Industry,* 58, 271.

35. Barry Supple, *The Royal Exchange Assurance: A History of British Insurance, 1720–1970* (Cambridge: Cambridge University Press, 1970), 52–53, 186–89; Pares, "London West-India Merchant House", 91.

36. Ralph Davis, *The Rise of the English Shipping Industry in the Seventeenth and Eighteenth Centuries* (London: Macmillan and Co., 1962), 279n2; Kenneth Morgan, *Bristol and the Atlantic in the Eighteenth Century* (Cambridge: Cambridge University Press, 1993), 83; Hancock, *Citizens of the World,* 133.

37. Beckford, *Descriptive Account,* 2: 353–54.

38. A Society of Gentlemen in Scotland, *Encyclopaedia Britannica* (Edinburgh: A. Bell and C. Macfarquhar, 1768–71), 1: 582–620; Mepham, *Accounting in Eighteenth Century Scotland,* 253–60; Malcolm, *Treatise of Book-keeping;* Yamey, Edey and Thompson, *Accounting in England and Scotland;* Littleton, *Accounting Evolution,* 26–28; Baxter, "Accounting in Colonial America", 272–87.

39. Thoms, "Mills Family", 5.

40. Pollard, *Genesis,* 212.

41. Stephen Quinn, "Money, Finance and Capital Markets", in *The Cambridge Economic History of Modern Britain,* vol. 1, *Industrialisation, 1700–1860,* ed. Roderick Floud and Paul Johnson (Cambridge: Cambridge University Press, 2004), 151–53.

42. James Pennington, *The Currency of the British Colonies* (London: Her Majesty's Stationery Office, 1848), 49–51; Charles Victor Callender, *The Development of the Capital Institutions of Jamaica* (Mona, Jamaica: Institute of Social and Economic Research, University of the West Indies, 1965), 2–5.

43. *Encyclopaedia Britannica,* 1: 553; Quinn, "Money, Finance and Capital Markets", 153–54.

44. Jamaica Act 172, 1750, revived 1755. See also Thoms, "Mills Family", 7–8.

45. *Encyclopaedia Britannica,* 1: 588–90.

46. K. G. Davies, "The Origins of the Commission System in the West India Trade", *Transactions of the Royal Historical Society,* 5th ser., 2 (1952): 101; Pares, "London Sugar Market", 254–70; R. B. Sheridan, "The Commercial and Financial

Organization of the British Slave Trade, 1750–1807", *Economic History Review* 11 (1958): 253; Pares, *Merchants and Planters,* 33–38; Lindsay, "Pennants and Jamaica: Part I", 67–68.

47. Pares, *Merchants and Planters,* 38; Carrington, *Sugar Industry,* 121.

48. Carrington, *Sugar Industry,* 129; Heather Cateau, "The New 'Negro' Business: Hiring in the British West Indies 1750–1810", in *In the Shadow of the Plantation: Caribbean History and Legacy,* ed. Alvin O. Thompson (Kingston: Ian Randle Publishers, 2002), 106.

49. Beckford, *Descriptive Account,* 2: 340–43.

50. Cateau, "New 'Negro' Business", 102–4; Carrington, *Sugar Industry,* 184.

51. Penrhyn 1261 and 1263 (26 July 1787), quoted in Lindsay, "Pennants and Jamaica: Part I", 68. Cf. Carrington, *Sugar Industry,* 184, 317n88, citing Penrhyn 1263, Penrhyn to Hering, 29 July 1777. I assume the last date should be 1787, but this letter has a different form of words to that of 26 July to Falconer.

52. Douglas Hall, "Slaves and Slavery in the British West Indies", *Social and Economic Studies* 11 (1962): 306–7; Richard B. Sheridan, " 'Sweet Malefactor': The Social Costs of Slavery and Sugar in Jamaica and Cuba, 1807–1854", *Economic History Review* 29 (1976): 236–57.

53. Hall, "Slaves and Slavery", 308; Hall, "Incalculability", 349; Higman, *Slave Population and Economy,* 1–2.

54. Quoted in Jean Lindsay, *A History of the North Wales Slate Industry* (Newton Abbot: David and Charles, 1974), 48.

55. Cf. Jason Hribal, " 'Animals Are Part of the Working Class': A Challenge to Labor History", *Labor History* 44 (2003): 435–53.

56. Penrhyn 1211, quoted in Lindsay, "Pennants and Jamaica: Part I", 56; Lindsay, *History of the North Wales Slate Industry,* 41–43; Hall, "Incalculability", 351; B. W. Higman, "Slavery and the Development of Demographic Theory in the Age of the Industrial Revolution", in *Slavery and British Society 1776–1846,* ed. James Walvin (London: Macmillan, 1982), 171.

57. Donald W. Jones and John R. Krummel, "The Location Theory of the Plantation", *Journal of Regional Science* 27 (1987): 174–78; B. W. Higman, "The Spatial Economy of Jamaican Sugar Plantations: Cartographic Evidence from the Eighteenth and Nineteenth Centuries", *Journal of Historical Geography* 13 (1987): 17–39; Lindsay, "Pennants and Jamaica: Part I", 57.

58. See Beckford, *Descriptive Account,* 23–25; Roughley, *Jamaica Planter's Guide,* 182–83; Higman, *Jamaica Surveyed,* 82; Michael Chisholm, *Rural Settlement and Land Use: An Essay in Location* (London: Hutchinson University Library, 1962), 21–35; Roger Juchau, "Early Cost Accounting Ideas in Agriculture: The Contributions of Arthur Young", *Accounting, Business and Financial History* 12 (2002): 369; Liam Brunt, "Rehabilitating Arthur Young", *Economic History Review* 56 (2003): 265; D. P. O'Brien, *The Classical Economists* (Oxford: Clarendon Press, 1975), 37–45; Peter Hall, ed., *Von Thünen's Isolated State* (Oxford: Pergamon Press, 1966); P. P. Courtenay, *Plantation Agriculture* (London: G. Bell and Sons, 1965), 87; Jones and Krummel, "Location Theory of the Plantation", 176. Cf. Sheridan, "Samuel Martin", 135.

59. English, *Great Landowners of East Yorkshire,* 148–49.

60. Dawkins Papers (National Library of Jamaica, Kingston). See also Cateau, "Conservatism and Change", 8–9.

61. Susanne Seymour, Stephen Daniels and Charles Watkins, "Estate and Empire: Sir George Cornewall's Management of Moccas, Herefordshire, and La Taste, Grenada, 1771–1819", *Journal of Historical Geography* 24 (1998): 333; Stephen Daniels and Charles Watkins, "Picturesque Landscaping and Estate Management: Uvedale Price at Foxley, 1770–1829", *Rural History* 2 (1991): 141–69.

62. Higman, *Slave Population and Economy,* 196; Lindsay, "Pennants and Jamaica: Part I", 81; Barrett, "Caribbean Sugar Production Standards", 147–70. Cf. Andrew J. Higgins and Russell C. Muchow, "Assessing the Potential Benefits of Alternative Cane Supply Arrangements in the Australian Sugar Industry", *Agricultural Systems* 76 (2003): 623–38.

63. Barrett, "Caribbean Sugar Production Standards", 167.

Chapter 5

1. See David Oldroyd, "John Johnson's Letters: The Accounting Role of Tudor Merchants' Correspondence", *Accounting Historians Journal* 25 (1998): 57–58.

2. Hall, *In Miserable Slavery,* 12–15, 22, 31, 33–37, 42, 58, 60, 78–79, 81, 90, 94, 99–100, 169; Burnard, *Mastery,* 25, 134; Roughley, *Jamaica Planter's Guide,* 68–70.

3. Quoted in Hancock, *Citizens of the World,* 126.

4. "Report from the Select Committee on West India Colonies", 453, 503–7.

5. Old Montpelier Estate, Account Book, 1824–28; Isaac Jackson Letterbooks, 1: 167, July 1840; Hall, *In Miserable Slavery,* 220; *Encyclopaedia Britannica,* 2: 842, 3: 524.

6. Isaac Jackson Letterbooks, 1: 167, July 1840; *Encyclopaedia Britannica,* 3: 456; Albertine Gaur, *A History of Writing* (New York: Cross River Press, 1992), 44–47.

7. See John Armstrong and Stephanie Jones, *Business Documents: Their Origins, Sources and Uses in Historical Research* (London: Mansell, 1987), 60–68; JoAnne Yates, *Control Through Communication: The Rise of System in American Management* (Baltimore: Johns Hopkins University Press, 1989), 25–29.

8. Georgia Estate, St Thomas, Letterbooks and Accounts, 1805–35 (National Library of Jamaica, Kingston); Ingram, *Sources,* 1: 625–26, 2: 778–79; Higman, *Slave Population and Economy,* 203, 209. See also Sheridan, "Letters from a Sugar Plantation in Antigua", 3.

9. Lewis, *Journal,* 203; Isaac Jackson Letterbooks, 1: 167, July 1840; *Encyclopaedia Britannica,* 3: 932.

10. Hancock, *Citizens of the World,* 387; Westerfield, *Middlemen,* 366–68; Brathwaite, *Development of Creole Society,* 31–39. Cf. Richard D. Brown, *Knowledge Is Power: The Diffusion of Information in Early America, 1700–1865* (New York: Oxford University Press, 1989), 36–37.

11. Jamaica Act 127, 1740.

12. Veront M. Satchell and Cezley Sampson, "The Rise and Fall of Railways in Jamaica, 1845–1975", *Journal of Transport History* 24 (2003): 3–5; Hall, *In Miserable Slavery,* 26.

13. Long, *History of Jamaica,* 2: 231–34; Kenneth Ellis, *The Post Office in the Eighteenth Century: A Study in Administrative History* (London: Oxford University Press, 1958), 16.

14. Thomas Foster, *The Postal History of Jamaica* (London: R. Rowe, 1968), 27.

15. Long, *History of Jamaica,* 2: 233.

16. Foster, *Postal History of Jamaica,* 25.

17. James MacQueen, *A General Plan for a Mail Communication by Steam: Between Great Britain and the Eastern and Western Parts of the World* (London: B. Fellowes, 1838), 55.

18. Long, *History of Jamaica,* 1: 466.

19. Hall, *Free Jamaica,* 13. Cf. W. F. Maunder, "Notes on the Development of Internal Transport in Jamaica", *Social and Economic Studies* 3 (1954): 163.

20. Trollope, *West Indies and the Spanish Main,* 36. See also R. H. Super, *Trollope in the Post Office* (Ann Arbor: University of Michigan Press, 1981), 40.

21. Andrew J. O'Shaughnessy, "The Stamp Act Crisis in the British Caribbean", *William and Mary Quarterly* 51 (1994): 215; Foster, *Postal History of Jamaica,* 27.

22. Foster, *Postal History of Jamaica,* 25.

23. MacQueen, *General Plan for a Mail Communication,* 54–56.

24. Drawing 163, Jamaica Scrapbook – William Berryman, 1808–1816, DRWG 1–A-Berryman (Library of Congress, Washington);

25. Drawings 161–165, Jamaica Scrapbook, William Berryman; Foster, *Postal History of Jamaica,* 27.

26. Wright, *Lady Nugent's Journal,* 85, 90, 92.

27. Ibid., 65, 69–70, 95–96; Higman, *Jamaica Surveyed,* 126.

28. Pitman, *Development of the British West Indies,* 307; Frances Armytage, *The Free Port System in the British West Indies: A Study in Commercial Policy, 1766–1822* (London: Longmans, Green and Co., 1953), 42, 63.

29. Long, *History of Jamaica,* 2: 230; Hall, *In Miserable Slavery,* 124; Higman, *Jamaica Surveyed,* 224.

30. Long, *History of Jamaica,* 2: 231.

31. Foster, *Postal History of Jamaica,* 27–28.

32. Lewis, *Journal,* 359–65; Waddell, *Twenty-nine Years,* 29; *Parliamentary Papers,* 1847–48 (167): 23, part 1, "Third Report from the Select Committee on Sugar and Coffee Planting", 4424.

33. Satchell and Sampson, "Rise and Fall of Railways", 1; Gardner, *History of Jamaica,* 164; Foster, *Postal History of Jamaica,* 26.

34. Howard Robinson, *The British Post Office: A History* (Princeton: Princeton University Press, 1948), 163; Howard Robinson, *Carrying British Mails Overseas* (London: George Allen and Unwin, 1964), 24–25; M. J. Daunton, *Royal Mail: The Post Office since 1840* (London: Athlone Press, 1985), 5; Bernard Bailyn, "Communications and Trade: The Atlantic in the Seventeenth Century", *Journal of Economic History* 13 (1953): 378–87; George L. Priest, "The History of the Postal Monopoly in the United States", *Journal of Law and Economics* 18 (1975): 33–80.

35. Hall, *In Miserable Slavery,* 221; Ian K. Steele, *The English Atlantic 1675–1740: An Exploration of Communication and Community* (New York: Oxford University Press, 1986), 113–19; Robinson, *British Post Office,* 164.

36. L. E. Britnor, *The History of the Sailing Packets to the West Indies* (London: British West Indies Study Circle, Paper no. 5, 1973), 3–5, 9; Foster, *Postal History of Jamaica,* 9–12; McCusker and Menard, *Economy of British America,* 341;

Westerfield, *Middlemen,* 364–66; Steele, *English Atlantic,* 168–84; Robinson, *Carrying British Mails Overseas,* 35–37; Ellis, *Post Office in the Eighteenth Century,* 7–8, 17.

37. Quoted in Britnor, *History of the Sailing Packets,* 13.

38. Steele, *English Atlantic,* 183.

39. Britnor, *History of the Sailing Packets,* 29; Hancock, *Citizens of the World,* 223–24.

40. Long, *History of Jamaica,* 2: 233; Foster, *Postal History of Jamaica,* 20–22; Ellis, *Post Office in the Eighteenth Century,* 44; Robinson, *Carrying British Mails Overseas,* 43–47.

41. Steele, *English Atlantic,* 168; Morgan, *Bristol and the Atlantic,* 66–67.

42. Britnor, *History of the Sailing Packets,* 40; Foster, *Postal History of Jamaica,* 21–22; Ellis, *Post Office in the Eighteenth Century,* 112–13, 163; Robinson, *Carrying British Mails Overseas,* 57–58.

43. Britnor, *History of the Sailing Packets,* 132, 135, 167–68; Robinson, *Carrying British Mails Overseas,* 73–74, 95, 106; Foster, *Postal History of Jamaica,* 22–23.

44. J. R. Owen, "The Post Office Packet Service, 1821–37: Development of a Steam-Powered Fleet", *The Mariner's Mirror* 88 (2002): 155–75; Robinson, *British Post Office,* 162.

45. Britnor, *History of the Sailing Packets,* 144–49; Robinson, *Carrying British Mails Overseas,* 109–11.

46. *St George's Chronicle and Grenada Gazette,* 31 July 1824.

47. Armytage, *Free Port System,* 5; Britnor, *History of the Sailing Packets,* 151–53; Robinson, *Carrying British Mails Overseas,* 123–24.

48. Quoted in Rodney Baker and Alan Leonard, *Great Steamers, White and Gold: A History of Royal Mail Ships and Services* (Southampton: Ensign Publications, 1993), 9.

49. MacQueen, *General Plan for a Mail Communication*; Foster, *Postal History of Jamaica,* 29–30.

50. Algernon E. Aspinall, *The British West Indies: Their History, Resources and Progress* (London: Sir Isaac Pitman and Sons, 1912), 344–45; Robinson, *Carrying British Mails Overseas,* 148–53; Britnor, *History of the Sailing Packets,* 154; Baker and Leonard, *Great Steamers,* 16–20; Gardner, *History of Jamaica,* 413; Daunton, *Royal Mail,* 27; C. Ernest Fayle, *A Short History of the World's Shipping Industry* (London: George Allen and Unwin, 1933), 230–31.

51. Edward McGeachy, *Suggestions towards a general plan of Rapid Communication by Steam Navigation and Railways: Shortening the time of transit between the eastern and western hemispheres* (London: Smith, Elder and Co., 1846), 3–4.

52. Ibid., 6–12.

53. Ibid., 8.

54. Trollope, *West Indies and the Spanish Main,* 6, 180–81; Super, *Trollope in the Post Office,* 38–40; Robinson, *Carrying British Mails Overseas,* 148–57; Stephen Hopwood, "Three Hundred Years of Postal Service in Jamaica", *Jamaica Journal* 5, nos. 2–3 (1971): 12; Britnor, *History of the Sailing Packets,* 169.

55. Steele, *English Atlantic,* 274–75.

56. Richard Croson Yates, "The Cost of Ocean Transport between England and Jamaica, 1784–1788" (PhD diss., University of Washington, 1969), 5, 58.

57. Hancock, *Citizens of the World,* 133.

58. Steele, *English Atlantic,* 275. Cf. Kenneth J. Banks, *Chasing Empire Across the Sea: Communications and the State in the French Atlantic* (Montreal: McGill-Queen's University Press, 2002), 78.

59. Hall, *In Miserable Slavery,* 9–12.

60. Wright, *Lady Nugent's Journal,* 3–10, 244–53.

61. Lewis, *Journal,* 2–60.

62. Ibid., 241–309.

63. Ibid., 310–20.

64. David Eltis and David Richardson, "Productivity in the Transatlantic Slave Trade", *Explorations in Economic History* 32 (1995): 477. I am indebted to David Eltis for the Jamaica–London data, based on 126 voyages. See also Herbert S. Klein, *The Middle Passage: Comparative Studies in the Atlantic Slave Trade* (Princeton: Princeton University Press, 1978), 157.

65. Yates, "Cost of Ocean Transport", 27.

66. Wright, *Lady Nugent's Journal,* 149.

67. Morgan, *Bristol and the Atlantic,* 43–45, 52–53; Davis, *Rise of the English Shipping Industry,* 261, 280–81. Cf. H. A. Gemery and J. S. Hogendorn, "Technological Change, Slavery, and the Slave Trade", in *The Imperial Impact: Studies in the Economic History of Africa and India,* ed. Clive Dewey and A. G. Hopkins (London: University of London, 1978), 255.

68. Britnor, *History of the Sailing Packets,* 9.

69. J. R. Harris, "Copper and Shipping in the Eighteenth Century", *Economic History Review* 19 (1966): 567–68; Robinson, *Carrying British Mails Overseas,* 51.

70. Britnor, *History of the Sailing Packets,* 40. Cf. Foster, *Postal History of Jamaica,* 21.

71. Britnor, *History of the Sailing Packets,* 49; Foster, *Postal History of Jamaica,* 22.

72. Wright, *Lady Nugent's Journal,* 139.

73. John Pudney, *London's Docks* (London: Thames and Hudson, 1975), 10–11.

74. Robinson, *Carrying British Mails Overseas,* 67–74.

75. Wright, *Lady Nugent's Journal,* 14.

76. Cf. Cowton and O'Shaughnessy, "Absentee Control of Sugar Plantations", 36.

77. Trollope, *West Indies and the Spanish Main,* 1–7; R. C. Terry, *A Trollope Chronology* (London: Macmillan, 1989), 29.

78. Algernon E. Aspinall, *The Pocket Guide to the West Indies* (Chicago: Rand, McNally and Co., 1914), 35.

79. Wright, *Lady Nugent's Journal,* 47, 80, 84, 107, 135, 166, 234.

80. Karras, *Sojourners in the Sun,* 66–67.

81. Clare Taylor, "The Journal of an Absentee Proprietor, Nathaniel Phillips of Slebech", *Journal of Caribbean History* 18 (1984): 68.

82. Cf. Stuart Bruchey, "Success and Failure Factors: American Merchants in Foreign Trade in the Eighteenth and Early Nineteenth Centuries", *Business History Review* 32 (1958): 285.

83. Robinson, *Carrying British Mails Overseas,* 94.

84. Daniel R. Headrick, *The Tools of Empire: Technology and European Imperialism in the Nineteenth Century* (New York: Oxford University Press, 1981), 130; Brown, *Knowledge Is Power,* 13.

Chapter 6

1. Wood, *Letters of Simon Taylor*.
2. Isaac Jackson Letterbooks (American Philosophical Society, Philadelphia).
3. Sarah M. S. Pearsall, " 'After All These Revolutions': Epistolary Identities in an Atlantic World, 1760–1815" (PhD diss., Harvard University, 2001), 182.
4. James Hakewill, *A Picturesque Tour of the Island of Jamaica, from drawings made in the years 1820 and 1821* (London: Hurst and Robinson, 1825), "Holland".
5. Sheridan, "Simon Taylor", 285–96.
6. Wright, *Lady Nugent's Journal,* 318; Sheridan, "Simon Taylor", 286; Betty Wood and T. R. Clayton, "Slave Birth, Death and Disease on Golden Grove Plantation, Jamaica, 1765–1810", *Slavery and Abolition* 6 (1985): 99. Wood, *Letters of Simon Taylor,* 5, repeats Wright's assessment but attributes it to Sheridan, who did not identify Wright as author.
7. Wright, *Lady Nugent's Journal,* 318.
8. Sheridan, "Simon Taylor", 286. Cf. Wood and Clayton, "Slave Birth, Death and Disease", 117n2.
9. Gardner, *History of Jamaica,* 346–47.
10. Wright, *Lady Nugent's Journal,* 65.
11. Wright, *Inscriptions,* 299; Wright, *Lady Nugent's Journal,* 319. For the intense correspondence between Simon Taylor and Sir Simon, see Pearsall, " 'After All These Revolutions' ", 183–209.
12. Sheridan, "Simon Taylor", 286–88; Shields, *Vale Royal,* 16. Browne, *A New Map of Jamaica* (London, 1755), uses "Archdeacon" and the crop account for 1765 "Arcedecon". Accounts Produce, Liber 4, f. 152 (Jamaica Archives, Spanish Town). Wood, *Letters of Simon Taylor,* uses "Arcedekne" throughout but "Arcedeckne" is by far the most common form.
13. Wood, *Letters of Simon Taylor,* 7n5, 42, 70.
14. Ibid., 101.
15. Wright, *Lady Nugent's Journal,* 70; Lewis, *Journal,* 368; Higman, *Jamaica Surveyed,* 126.
16. Wood, *Letters of Simon Taylor,* 70.
17. Ibid., 101–2. Cf. Long, *History of Jamaica,* 2: 159; Sheridan, "Simon Taylor", 289.
18. Wood and Clayton, "Slave Birth, Death and Disease", 117n2. Cf. Sheridan, "Simon Taylor", 289–95.
19. Pearsall, "Late Flagrant Instance", 574n79. Presumably, this amount includes realty as well as personalty and is in sterling.
20. Rubinstein, *Men of Property,* 43–46, 198–200. For comparison with the North American colonies, see Jones, *Wealth of a Nation to Be,* 319; Soltow, *Distribution of Wealth and Income,* 110–13.
21. Sheridan, "Simon Taylor", 286, 295.
22. Inventories, Liber 123, ff. 252–55 (Jamaica Archives, Spanish Town); Higman, *Jamaica Surveyed,* 228–30; Shields, *Vale Royal,* 15–16.
23. Inventories, Liber 123, ff. 216–17; Higman, *Jamaica Surveyed,* 241–42.
24. Inventories, Liber 123, f. 223; Higman, *Jamaica Surveyed,* 203–4.

25. Higman, *Jamaica Surveyed,* 238–41.

26. Inventories, Liber 123, ff. 227–36.

27. Quoted from Cunninghame-Grahame Muniments, Scottish Record Office, Edinburgh, in Ingram, *Sources,* 1: 594. Cf. Hakewill, *Picturesque Tour,* "Holland"; Ingram, *Sources,* 1: 457.

28. Wright, *Lady Nugent's Journal,* 318.

29. Ibid., 64–71.

30. Wood, *Letters of Simon Taylor,* 76, 78.

31. Wright, *Lady Nugent's Journal,* 241–42.

32. Wood, *Letters of Simon Taylor,* 65.

33. Ibid., 24–25. Michael Craton and James Walvin, *A Jamaican Plantation: The History of Worthy Park 1670–1970* (London: W. H. Allen, 1970), 50, 72, indicate that Rose Price died *circa* 1765. Taylor on 25 July 1768 said "Rose Price died about a month ago": Wood, *Letters of Simon Taylor,* 64 (cf. 24n80).

34. Wood, *Letters of Simon Taylor,* 107–8.

35. Ibid., 125.

36. Pearsall, "Late Flagrant Instance", 567; Pearsall, " 'After All These Revolutions' ", 183.

37. Hall, *In Miserable Slavery,* 297, 312; Higman, "Patterns of Exchange", 226–27.

38. Pearsall, "Late Flagrant Instance", 568, 572; Wright, *Inscriptions,* 258.

39. Sheridan, "Simon Taylor", 294.

40. Power of Attorney by Simon Taylor, of Jamaica, to Robert Taylor and John Taylor, of Great Britain, 27 April 1795, MS 1415 (National Library of Jamaica, Kingston); Sheridan, "Simon Taylor", 294–95; Ingram, *Sources,* 2: 903. Cf. K. E. Ingram, *Manuscript Sources of the History of the West Indies* (Kingston: University of the West Indies Press, 2000), 72.

41. Sheridan, "Simon Taylor", 286.

42. Metcalf, *Royal Government,* 93; Wood, *Letters of Simon Taylor,* 7n1; Brathwaite, *Development of Creole Society,* 40.

43. Arcedeckne Papers, DM 41/92/12, Chancery Case, 1 (University of Bristol, Arts and Sciences Library, Special Collections).

44. Wright, *Inscriptions,* 99; Wood, *Letters of Simon Taylor,* 79.

45. Wood, *Letters of Simon Taylor,* 5 and 7n1; Arcedeckne Papers, DM 41/92/14, Will of Chaloner Arcedeckne, 2 June 1808, 1; Sheridan, "Simon Taylor", 288; Wood and Clayton, "Slave Birth, Death and Disease", 99.

46. Wood, *Letters of Simon Taylor,* 18–19; Clayton, "Sophistry", 344.

47. Wood, *Letters of Simon Taylor,* 34, 39, 47, 49.

48. Ibid., 114.

49. Ibid., 8–9.

50. Ibid., 51. Cf. James E. McClellan III, *Colonialism and Science: Saint Domingue in the Old Regime* (Baltimore: Johns Hopkins University Press, 1992), 71–74; Galloway, *Sugar Cane Industry,* 102–3.

51. Wood, *Letters of Simon Taylor,* 1–164.

52. There are two year-long gaps in the published letters, the first from 9 December 1765 to 29 November 1766, and the second 3 December 1771 to 9 January 1773. The first may be explained by Arcedeckne's travels but the context of the second

clearly suggests that letters are missing. These gaps are both ignored in the calculations of frequency.

53. Wood, *Letters of Simon Taylor,* 42–43.

54. Ibid., 109.

55. Ibid., 56.

56. Ibid., 62.

57. Ibid., 59–60.

58. Ibid., 81.

59. Ibid., 42–43, 46.

60. Ibid., 79–80.

61. Ibid., 22.

62. Ibid., 81.

63. Ibid., 120, 128.

64. Ibid., 134.

65. Yates, "Cost of Ocean Transport", 5, 58; Steele, *English Atlantic,* 275.

66. Wood, *Letters of Simon Taylor,* 12–15.

67. Ibid., 43.

68. Ibid., 27, 54, 81, 98, 100, 106, 107.

69. Ibid., 29, 39, 108, 120, 123.

70. Ibid., 43.

71. Ibid., 72.

72. Ibid., 39.

73. Ibid., 7–8, 26.

74. Ibid., 4, 7, 31.

75. For a description of the Arcedeckne Family papers in the Vanneck MSS., see Ingram, *Manuscript Sources,* 348.

76. For example, Wood, *Letters of Simon Taylor,* 80.

77. Ibid., 75–76, 89.

78. Pearsall, " 'After All These Revolutions' ", 182.

79. See Higman, "Letterbooks of Isaac Jackson", 317–29.

80. B. W. Higman, *Montpelier, Jamaica: A Plantation Community in Slavery and Freedom, 1739–1912* (Kingston: The Press, University of the West Indies, 1998).

81. Wright, *Inscriptions,* 212; Isaac Jackson Letterbooks, 1: 156, Jackson to Lord Seaford, 24 June 1840; ibid., 3: Jackson to Seaford, 4 September 1843 and 5 October 1843.

82. Accounts Produce, Liber 74, f. 27.

83. Returns of Registrations of Slaves, Liber 130; *Jamaica Almanack, 1832* (Kingston), 151.

84. *Jamaica Almanack, 1832,* 124; Wright, *Inscriptions,* 212.

85. Hall, *Free Jamaica,* 51, citing Metcalfe to Russell, 30 March 1840.

86. CO 137/214, f. 292, enclosure No. 300, "Investigations at Montpelier" (Public Record Office, London).

87. Douglas Hall, "Bountied European Immigration with Special Reference to the German Settlement at Seaford Town up to 1850", *Jamaica Journal* 9, no. 1 (March 1975): 9n40.

88. Isaac Jackson Letterbooks, 1: 6, Jackson to Seaford, 14 August 1839. For McNeil, see Higman, *Montpelier,* 59

89. Returns of Registrations of Slaves, Liber 136.

90. Hall, *In Miserable Slavery,* 130, 216–21; Peter Linebaugh and James Rediker, *The Many-headed Hydra: Sailors, Slaves, Commoners, and the Hidden History of the Revolutionary Atlantic* (Boston: Beacon Press, 2000), 287; *Burke's Peerage* (London: Burke's Peerage, 1949), 2091–92; Peter C. Newman, *Caesars of the Wilderness: Company of Adventurers* (Markham, Ontario: Penguin Books Canada, 1987), 2: 133; Iain McCalman, ed., *The Horrors of Slavery and Other Writings by Robert Wedderburn* (New York: Markus Wiener, 1991), 61n1.

91. McCalman, *Horrors of Slavery,* 45, 48. See also Iain McCalman, *Radical Underworld: Prophets, Revolutionaries and Pornographers in London, 1795–1840* (Cambridge: Cambridge University Press, 1988), 50–63; Helen Thomas, *Romanticism and Slave Narratives: Transatlantic Testimonies* (Cambridge: Cambridge University Press, 2000), 255–71.

92. Isaac Jackson Letterbooks, 1: 7, Jackson to James, 14 August 1839; ibid., 1: 23, Jackson to James, 3 September 1839; ibid., 1: 26, Jackson to James, 10 September 1839.

93. Ibid., 1: 1, Jackson to Tinling, 1 Aug. 1839; ibid., 1: 7, Jackson to James, 14 August 1839; ibid., 1: 92, Jackson to Tinling, 18 February 1840; ibid., 1: 18, Jackson to C. Paterson, 21 August 1839.

94. Ibid., 1: 27, Jackson to Seaford, 10 September 1839. Cf. Carrington, "Management of Sugar Estates", 29–30.

95. Isaac Jackson Letterbooks, 1: 26–27, Jackson to Lyon, 10 September 1839.

96. Ibid., 1: 30, Jackson to James, 29 September 1839.

97. Ibid., 1: 32, Jackson to Hawthorn and Shedden, 29 September 1839.

98. Ibid., 1: 33, Jackson to Campbell, 29 September 1839.

99. Ibid., 1: 46, Jackson to Seaford, 23 October 1839.

100. Ibid., 1: 42, Jackson to Lyon, 18 October 1839.

101. Ibid., 1: 44, Jackson to Campbell, 23 October 1839.

102. Ibid., 1: 52, Jackson to Campbell, 14 November 1839.

103. Ibid., 1: 46, Jackson to Seaford, 23 October 1839; ibid., 3: Jackson to Seaford, 17 October 1842 and 27 June 1843.

104. Ibid., 1: 46, Jackson to Seaford, 23 October 1839.

105. Ibid., 1: 47, Jackson to McNeil, 24 October 1839.

106. Ibid., 1: 50, Jackson to Seaford, 1 November 1839.

107. Ibid., 1: 51, Jackson to McNeil, 5 November 1839.

108. Ibid., 1: 56–57, Jackson to McNeil, 19 November 1839.

109. Ibid., 1: 57, Jackson to Clarke, 20 November 1839.

110. Ibid., 1: 132, Jackson to Campbell, 12 May 1840.

111. Ibid., 1: 158–171; ibid., 2: Jackson to Seaford, 29 June 1841.

112. Accounts Produce, Liber 76, f. 183; ibid., Liber 77, f. 177; ibid., Liber 79, f. 126; ibid., Liber 81, f. 31; ibid., Liber 82, f. 94; ibid., Liber 83, f. 94.

113. Isaac Jackson Letterbooks, 2: Jackson to Seaford, 15 June 1840.

114. Ibid., 3: Jackson to Elgin, 6 February 1843.

115. Land Deeds, Liber 880, f. 62 (Island Record Office, Spanish Town). Before this,

Jackson had bought town land in Falmouth for £600. See Land Deeds, Liber 876, f. 134. I am indebted to Swithin Wilmot for the following citations to land deeds.

116.   Land Deeds, Liber 881, f. 162.

117.   Ibid., Liber 902, f. 4.

118.   Ibid., Liber 899, f. 210.

119.   Ibid., Liber 915, f. 121.

120.   Wright, *Inscriptions,* 212; Returns of Registrations of Slaves, Liber 130.

121.   Inventories, Liber 159, ff. 111–12.

122.   Isaac Jackson Letterbooks, 3 vols., 1839–1843.

123.   Ibid., 3: Jackson to Seaford, 10 May 1842.

124.   Ibid., 3: Jackson to Seaford, 27 June 1843.

125.   Ibid., 1: 46, Jackson to Seaford, 23 October 1839.

126.   Ibid., 2: Jackson to Campbell, 16 September 1841.

127.   Ibid., 2: Jackson to Seaford, 26 August 1841.

128.   Ibid., 2: Jackson to Seaford, 28 September 1841.

129.   Ibid., 1: 32, Jackson to Hawthorn and Shedden, 29 September 1839.

130.   Ibid., 2: Jackson to Seaford, 29 October 1841.

131.   Ibid., 3: Jackson to Seaford, 2 August 1842.

132.   Ibid., 3: Jackson to Seaford, 19 August 1842.

133.   Ibid., 3: Jackson to Seaford to Elgin, 3 May 1842 (letter follows 3 January 1843).

134.   Ibid., 1: 46, Jackson to Seaford, 23 October 1839.

135.   Ibid., 3: Jackson to Seaford, 1 November 1842.

136.   Ibid., 3: Jackson to Seaford, 30 May 1843 and 27 June 1843.

137.   Ibid., 1: 30, Jackson to James, 29 September 1839.

138.   Ibid., 1: 32, Jackson to Campbell, 29 September 1839.

139.   Ibid., 1: 41, Jackson to James, 17 October 1839.

140.   Ibid., 3: Jackson to Seaford, 19 May 1842.

141.   Ibid., 3: Jackson to Seaford, 1 December 1842.

142.   Ibid., 3: Jackson to Seaford, 30 May 1843 and 27 June 1843; Baker and Leonard, *Great Steamers,* 15, 22.

143.   Isaac Jackson Letterbooks, 1: 151, Jackson to Seaford, 24 June 1840.

144.   Pares, "London West-India Merchant House", 99; Richard B. Sheridan, *The Development of the Plantations to 1750 and An Era of West Indian Prosperity* (Barbados: Caribbean Universities Press, 1970); Metcalf, *Royal Government,* 167.

Chapter 7

1.   Rafi Ahmad, F. N. Scatena and Avijit Gupta, "Morphology and Sedimentation in Caribbean Montane Streams: Examples from Jamaica and Puerto Rico", *Sedimentary Geology* 85 (1993): 163; Avijit Gupta, "Stream Characteristics in Eastern Jamaica, an Environment of Seasonal Flow and Large Floods", *American Journal of Science* 275 (1975): 825–26.

2.   David Knighton, *Fluvial Forms and Processes: A New Perspective* (London: Arnold, 1998), 231–32; André Robert, *River Processes: An Introduction to Fluvial Dynamics* (London: Arnold, 2003), 143–57. Cf. Alex D. Hawkes, "Plantain Garden Area, Scenic and Impressive", *Daily Gleaner,* 20 November 1975, 3.

3. Michael Chenoweth, *The Eighteenth Century Climate of Jamaica: Derived from the Journals of Thomas Thistlewood 1750–1786* (Philadelphia: American Philosophical Society, 2003), 75; Long, *History of Jamaica*, 2: 167; Lewis, *Journal*, 368–69; Knighton, *Fluvial Forms and Processes*, 174; M. Gordon Wolman and Luna B. Leopold, "Flood Plains", in *Rivers and River Terraces*, ed. G. H. Dury (London: Macmillan, 1970), 166–96.

4. Thomas Craskell and James Simpson, *Map of the County of Surrey in the Island of Jamaica* (London, 1763); Charles Bochart and Humphrey Knollis, *Map of the Island of Jamaica and other the territories depending thereon* [1684], CO700/Jamaica3 (Public Record Office, London).

5. Verene A. Shepherd, "Livestock and Sugar: Aspects of Jamaica's Agricultural Development from the Late Seventeenth to the Early Nineteenth Century", *Historical Journal* 34 (1991): 641–42.

6. Arcedeckne Papers, DM 41/92/12, Chancery Case, 2, 8 (University of Bristol, Arts and Sciences Library, Special Collections); Jamaica Act 217, 1721; Jamaica Act 246, 1723, "An Act for encouraging white people to come over and become settlers in this island, and for the more easy and speedy settling the north-east part thereof"; Jamaica Act 259, 1725, "An Act for the more effectual suppressing rebellious and runaway slaves, and for encouraging parties to be sent out for that purpose; as also for the better securing the settlements at Plantain Garden River, and other out-parts of this island".

7. Wood, *Letters of Simon Taylor*, 8n6, 10, 26, 42; Arcedeckne Papers, DM 41/92/12, Chancery Case, 4.

8. Wood, *Letters of Simon Taylor*, 135; Arcedeckne Papers, DM 41/92/3; "A Plan of Golden Grove Plantation on the Plantain Garden River, Jamaica, the property of Calloner Arcedickne Esquire, 1788" (Plans, St Thomas 12A, National Library of Jamaica, Kingston).

9. Wood, *Letters of Simon Taylor*, 135.

10. Ibid., 8, 130, 135.

11. Ibid., 7, 10.

12. Ibid., 96, 101.

13. Ibid., 7n1.

14. Ibid., 8, 10, 18, 26; Wright, *Inscriptions*, 4.

15. Wood, *Letters of Simon Taylor*, 27–28, 64, 99, 116, 146, 150. The crop accounts, beginning in 1765, identified Taylor both as "attorney" and "one of the attorneys" to Arcedeckne. Accounts Produce, Liber 4, ff. 152–53.

16. Roughley, *Jamaica Planter's Guide*, 10–11; Carrington, *Sugar Industry*, 138.

17. Wood, *Letters of Simon Taylor*, 116.

18. Ibid., 22.

19. Ibid., 31.

20. Ibid., 58n157. Cf. Richard B. Sheridan, *Doctors and Slaves: A Medical and Demographic History of Slavery in the British West Indies, 1680–1834* (Cambridge: Cambridge University Press, 1985), 42–52.

21. Wood, *Letters of Simon Taylor*, 65.

22. Ibid., 136, 149.

23. Ibid., 17, 25, 36.

24. Wood and Clayton, "Slave Birth, Death and Disease", 100–105; Wood, *Letters of Simon Taylor,* 107–8.

25. Wood, *Letters of Simon Taylor,* 14. See also ibid., 36n115.

26. Ibid., 26.

27. Ibid., 84.

28. Ibid., 107–8.

29. Ibid., 27, 70, 74–75. Cf. Returns of Registrations of Slaves, Liber 137.

30. Wood, *Letters of Simon Taylor,* 25n85, 38, 103.

31. Arcedeckne Papers, DM 41/92/12, Chancery Case, 3; Wood, *Letters of Simon Taylor,* 8n7, 17.

32. Arcedeckne Papers, DM 41/92/12, Chancery Case, 3–4. On lease and release, see Anderson, "Provincial Aspects", 12–13; Grant, *Jamaican Land Law,* 49–57.

33. Wright, *Inscriptions,* 99; Burnard, *Mastery,* 107–8; Jack Greene, "Jamaica Privilege Controversy", 31–32; Wood, *Letters of Simon Taylor,* 16n32, 23n68; Arcedeckne Papers, DM 41/92/12, Chancery Case, 4.

34. Wood, *Letters of Simon Taylor,* 40. In his letters, Taylor regularly referred to Robert as Robin, using "Robert" only once, in June 1765. See Wood, *Letters of Simon Taylor,* 16 (and n32). The index to the Letters has separate entries for Robert and Robin but gives matching page references for the two men, though the names in the text vary.

35. Wood, *Letters of Simon Taylor,* 40.

36. Ibid., 16–17.

37. Ibid., 56, 91.

38. Ibid., 41, 50, 71.

39. Ibid., 43–44.

40. Ibid., 52, 62.

41. Ibid., 71, 75.

42. Ibid., 16n32.

43. Ibid., 85, 90. Cf. F. M. L. Thompson, "The End of a Great Estate", *Economic History Review* 8 (1955): 50–52.

44. Wood, *Letters of Simon Taylor,* 101.

45. Ibid., 104–5.

46. Ibid., 112.

47. Wright, *Inscriptions,* 99; Jack Greene, "Jamaica Privilege Controversy", 31–32; Wood, *Letters of Simon Taylor,* 23n68, and 119; Arcedeckne Papers, DM 41/92/12, Chancery Case, 4.

48. Wood, *Letters of Simon Taylor,* 106–7.

49. Ibid., 110.

50. Ibid., 110–11, 118, 122, 128, 135.

51. Mindie Lazarus-Black, "John Grant's Jamaica: Notes Towards a Reassessment of Courts in the Slave Era", *Journal of Caribbean History* 27 (1993): 145.

52. Wood, *Letters of Simon Taylor,* 90–91, 102–3, 133, 141–42; Higman, *Jamaica Surveyed,* 19–28, 49–58.

53. Arcedeckne Papers, DM 41/92/12, Chancery Case, 1.

54. Jamaica Act 375, 1736.

55. Wood, *Letters of Simon Taylor,* 16.

56. Ibid., 32–33, 48–49, 59–60, 70, 84, 99, 103–4.

57. Ibid., 70.

58. Ibid., 101–2, 105, 106, 137.

59. Ibid., 106.

60. Ibid., 110.

61. Ibid., 114–18, 124; Higman, *Jamaica Surveyed*, 31.

62. Wood, *Letters of Simon Taylor*, 78.

63. Ibid., 69, 86.

64. Ibid., 112–13. Cf. 13n22.

65. Edwards, *History, Civil and Commercial*, 2: 227; Higman, "Spatial Economy". See also John Shaw, *Water Power in Scotland, 1550–1870* (Edinburgh: Donald, 1984), 111; John Reynolds, *Windmills and Watermills* (London: Hugh Evelyn, 1974); Terry S. Reynolds, *Stronger than a Hundred Men: A History of the Vertical Water Wheel* (Baltimore: Johns Hopkins University Press, 1983).

66. Wood, *Letters of Simon Taylor*, 13n23, 14n26.

67. Ibid., 64, 71, 85.

68. Ibid., 108.

69. Ibid., 112.

70. Ibid., 146–47.

71. Ibid., 86. Cf. ibid., 90.

72. Long, *History of Jamaica*, 2: 168.

73. Wood, *Letters of Simon Taylor*, 12–13.

74. Ibid., 46, 52–53.

75. Ibid., 54.

76. José Carlos Millás, *Hurricanes of the Caribbean and Adjacent Regions, 1492–1800* (Miami: Academy of the Arts and Sciences of the Americas, 1968), 18–23, 216–45.

77. Wood, *Letters of Simon Taylor*, 67. See also 61, 65.

78. Higman, "Spatial Economy".

79. Brian Cotterell and Johan Kamminga, *Mechanics of Pre-Industrial Technology* (Cambridge: Cambridge University Press, 1990), 43; Higman, *Jamaica Surveyed*, 119.

80. Browne, *New Map of Jamaica*.

81. "A Plan of . . . Batchellors Hall Plantation at Plantain Garden River in the Parish of St. Thomas in the East, . . . April 1741, . . . by Bartholomew Brady, surveyor" (Plans, St Thomas 12A, National Library of Jamaica, Kingston). Parts of this plan are damaged.

82. Arcedeckne Papers, DM 41/92/12, Chancery Case, 2.

83. Ibid., 2–3.

84. Wood, *Letters of Simon Taylor*, 67–69, 74. Cf. Carol Wilcox, *Sugar Water: Hawaii's Plantation Ditches* (Honolulu: University of Hawaii Press, 1996).

85. P. Ph. Jansen, L. van Bendegom, J. van den Berg, M. de Vries, and A. Zanen, eds., *Principles of River Engineering: The Non-Tidal Alluvial River* (London: Pitman, 1979), 378–81.

86. Wood, *Letters of Simon Taylor*, 69, 74. Cf. Zeev Nir, "Hydraulics of Open Channels", in *CRC Handbook of Irrigation Technology*, ed. Herman J. Finkel (Boca Raton, Fla.: CRC Press, 1982), 1: 93–143.

87. Arcedeckne Papers, DM 41/92/12, Chancery Case, 4–6.

88. Wood, *Letters of Simon Taylor,* 114.

89. Ibid., 113.

90. Ibid., 123, 127.

91. Ibid., 127–29.

92. Ibid., 129, 132.

93. Ibid., 130–32.

94. Ibid., 134; Craton and Walvin, *Jamaican Plantation,* 158–69.

95. Wood, *Letters of Simon Taylor,* 136–37.

96. Ibid., 138–44.

97. Ibid., 151, 154–55.

98. Arcedeckne Papers, DM 41/92/4.

99. Arcedeckne Papers, DM 41/92/2. Ryve is the only name located in the area on Bochart and Knollis, *Map of the Island of Jamaica.*

100. Arcedeckne Papers, DM 41/92/3.

101. Arcedeckne Papers, DM 41/92/12, Chancery Case, 10, 15; Ingram, *Sources,* 2: 750–52; "A Plan of Winchester Estate in the Parish of St. Thomas in the East, Jamaica, the property of Mrs. Catherine Lambert, 1829/30" (Plans, St Thomas 15, National Library of Jamaica, Kingston).

102. "A Sketch drawn to show the course of the Plantain Garden River and the position of a weir made by Winchester Estate to turn the water into the canal of that Estate, done in June 1846 by Alexander R. Carter for McGeachy and Griffiths, surveyors" (Plans, St Thomas 3A, National Library of Jamaica, Kingston); Higman, *Jamaica Surveyed,* 126. Robertson in 1804 showed a lengthy "aqueduct" running all the way from Plantain Garden River Estate, through Winchester and on, but this seems fanciful. James Robertson, *Map of the County of Surrey in the Island of Jamaica* (London, 1804).

103. Craskell and Simpson, *Map of the County of Surrey.*

104. Wood, *Letters of Simon Taylor,* 21–22, 25, 36.

105. Ibid., 74, 83.

106. Ibid., 78–79, 87–88.

107. Ibid., 25.

108. Ibid., 34, 49.

109. Ibid., 47, 49–50, 63.

110. Ibid., 55, 57.

111. Ibid., 58, 59, 61, 63, 65.

112. Ibid., 78, 81, 88, 96.

113. Plan of Golden Grove, 1788.

114. Wright, *Lady Nugent's Journal,* 68.

115. Among the "views taken in Jamaica" but not published in Hakewill's *Picturesque Tour,* the first listed was "Arcedeckne, C. Esq. – Mill yard and works, Golden Grove, St. Thomas in the East. – Batchelor's Hall, Penn, Ditto". The location of these works is not known.

116. Wood, *Letters of Simon Taylor,* 84, 94; Arcedeckne Papers, DM 41/92/3.

117. Wood, *Letters of Simon Taylor,* 14.

118. Ibid., 87.

119. Cf. ibid., 67.

120. Ibid., 65, 67.

121. Ibid., 114, 125; Pares, *West-India Fortune,* 105, 113–14; Noel Deerr, *Cane Sugar: A Textbook on the Agriculture of the Sugar Cane, the Manufacture of Cane Sugar, and the Analysis of Sugar-House Products* (London: Norman Rodger, 1921), 159; A. C. Barnes, *The Sugar Cane* (London: Leonard Hill, 1964), 277–78.

122. Wood, *Letters of Simon Taylor,* 21.

123. Long, *History of Jamaica,* 2: 167; Ormrod, "Evolution of Soil Management Practices"; J. H. Galloway, "Tradition and Innovation in the American Sugar Industry, *c.*1500–1800", *Annals of the Association of American Geographers* 75 (1985): 334–51; Pares, *West-India Fortune,* 113.

124. Wood, *Letters of Simon Taylor,* 22.

125. Ibid., 27.

126. Ibid., 105.

127. Ibid., 27. See also Shepherd, "Livestock and Sugar", 641–42.

128. Wood, *Letters of Simon Taylor,* 36, 43, 55.

129. Ibid., 70, 74–75, 154.

130. Bryan Edwards, *The History, Civil and Commercial, of the British Colonies in the West Indies,* 2nd ed. (London: John Stockdale, 1794), 2: 128;

131. Burnard, *Mastery,* 139–52.

132. Wood, *Letters of Simon Taylor,* 29–30. See also Burnard, *Mastery,* 140; Hall, *In Miserable Slavery,*

133. Wood, *Letters of Simon Taylor,* 10.

134. Ibid., 11.

135. Ibid., 14.

136. Ibid., 11.

137. Ibid., 14.

138. Ibid., 21.

139. Ibid., 22.

140. Ibid., 27–28.

141. Ibid., 34, 36; Wood and Clayton, "Slave Birth, Death and Disease", 101.

142. Wood, *Letters of Simon Taylor,* 37.

143. Ibid., 53.

144. Ibid., 55. See also Burnard, *Mastery,* 181–82.

145. Long, *History of Jamaica,* 2: 168–69.

146. Wood, *Letters of Simon Taylor,* 56.

147. Ibid., 64–65.

148. Ibid., 71.

149. Ibid., 77.

150. Ibid., 83.

151. Ibid., 11, 86–87. See also Anon., *Marly,* 152–53.

152. Cassidy and Le Page, *Dictionary of Jamaican English,* 92 (cf. 138–39). The first citation in Cassidy and Le Page is 1790 (Moreton, *Manners and Customs in the West India Islands,* 47), making Taylor's use in 1770 an earlier example. "Capoose" does not appear in the *Oxford English Dictionary.*

153. Wood, *Letters of Simon Taylor,* 87; Edwards, *History, Civil and Commercial* (1793

ed.), 2: 227; Edwards, *History, Civil and Commercial* (1801 ed.), 2: 223; Roughley, *Jamaica Planter's Guide,* 190. For an example of the problems when a gudgeon snapped, see the next chapter on Montpelier, and Isaac Jackson Letterbooks, 2: Jackson to Seaford, 4 February 1842. Cf. Deerr, *Cane Sugar,* 218–23; Noel Deerr, "The Evolution of the Sugar Cane Mill", *Transactions of the Newcomen Society* 21 (1940–41): 3; John Daniels and Christian Daniels, "The Origin of the Sugarcane Roller Mill", *Technology and Culture* 29 (1988): 530–32.

154. Wood, *Letters of Simon Taylor,* 86–87. Cf. B. W. Higman, *Slave Populations of the British Caribbean, 1807–1834* (Baltimore: Johns Hopkins University Press, 1984), 179–88.

155. Wood, *Letters of Simon Taylor,* 87.

156. Ibid., 93.

157. Ibid., 99.

158. Ibid., 105. See also Heather Cateau, "New 'Negro' Business", 100; Burnard, *Mastery,* 129–31, 258; Srividhya Swaminathan, "Developing the West Indian Proslavery Position after the Somerset Decision", *Slavery and Abolition* 24 (2003): 46.

159. Wood, *Letters of Simon Taylor,* 116; Cateau, "New 'Negro' Business", 108.

160. Wood, *Letters of Simon Taylor,* 118–19.

161. Ibid., 125–27, 135.

162. Ibid., 145–46.

163. Ibid., 152.

164. Ibid., 154.

165. David Beck Ryden, "Does Decline Make Sense? The West Indian Economy and the Abolition of the British Slave Trade", *Journal of Interdisciplinary History* 31 (2001): 357–58.

166. Long, *History of Jamaica,* 1: 461–63.

167. Accounts Produce, Liber 5, ff. 22–23.

168. Ibid., Liber 5, ff. 76–77.

169. Wood, *Letters of Simon Taylor,* 18, 21, 55; Higman, *Slave Population and Economy,* 21.

170. Wood, *Letters of Simon Taylor,* 130.

171. Ibid., 138.

172. Ibid., 21–22.

173. Ibid., 138. See also Clayton, "Sophistry", 330.

174. Wood, *Letters of Simon Taylor,* 148–49, 153.

175. Accounts Produce, Liber 5, ff. 22–23.

176. Ibid., Liber 5, ff. 76–77.

177. Wood, *Letters of Simon Taylor,* 7–8.

178. Ibid., 27. Cf. Pares, "London Sugar Market, 1740–1769", 257.

179. Wood, *Letters of Simon Taylor,* 59–60.

180. Ibid., 93.

181. Ibid., 146.

182. Ibid., 84.

183. Ibid., 100.

184. Ibid., 11–12, 15, 41, 61.

185. Ibid., 12.

186. Pares, "London Sugar Market, 1740–1769", 257; Hancock, *Citizens of the World*, 126; Thoms, "Mills Family", 7.

187. Wright, *Lady Nugent's Journal*, 68.

188. Wood, *Letters of Simon Taylor*, 8, 18, 77, 97.

189. Ibid., 81–82.

190. Ibid., 89.

191. Ibid., 91, 105–6.

192. Ibid., 32, 34–35, 48.

193. Ibid., 7, 61.

194. Ibid., 22.

195. Ibid., 154.

196. Ibid., 145.

197. Ibid., 151.

198. Ibid., 138.

199. Ibid., 77, 100, 126.

200. Ibid., 144–45.

201. Ibid., 26, 35.

202. Ibid., 58.

203. Ibid., 59–61.

204. Ibid., 66.

205. Drogging Bonds (Jamaica Archives, Spanish Town); Higman, *Slave Population and Economy*, 40.

206. Wood, *Letters of Simon Taylor*, 66–67.

207. Ibid., 68, 70.

208. Ibid., 76–77, 81.

209. Ibid., 109.

210. Ibid., 121, 146.

211. Accounts Produce, Liber 4, f. 152.

212. Higman, *Slave Population and Economy*, 235–39; John J. McCusker, "Weights and Measures in the Colonial Sugar Trade: The Gallon and the Pound and Their International Equivalents", *William and Mary Quarterly* 30 (1973): 599–624.

213. Accounts Produce, Liber 6, f. 157.

214. Wood, *Letters of Simon Taylor*, 36, 39, 55.

215. Accounts Produce, Liber 5, ff. 22–23. When the crop account for 1765 was posted is unknown because there is a gap in the correspondence between 9 December 1765 and 29 November 1766.

216. Wood, *Letters of Simon Taylor*, 66.

217. Ibid., 16, 18.

218. Ibid., 83.

219. Ibid., 28.

220. Ibid., 34–38.

221. Ibid., 56.

222. Ibid., 60–62.

223. Ibid., 66.

224. Ibid., 56.

225. Ibid., 62–63.

226. Ibid., 68–69.

227. Ibid., 10.

228. Ibid., 12–13.

229. Accounts Produce, Liber 4, f. 152; Wood, *Letters of Simon Taylor,* 22.

230. Wood, *Letters of Simon Taylor,* 27; Accounts Produce, Liber 5, ff. 22–23.

231. Wood, *Letters of Simon Taylor,* 32.

232. Ibid., 36–37, 46, 52.

233. Accounts Produce, Liber 5, ff. 76–77.

234. Wood, *Letters of Simon Taylor,* 63, 69.

235. Cf. ibid., 70.

236. Ibid., 66–67.

237. Ibid.

238. Ibid., 85–86.

239. Ibid., 86.

240. Ibid., 95.

241. Ibid., 134.

242. Ibid., 150.

243. For prices, see Deerr, *History of Sugar,* 2: 530–31.

244. Wood, *Letters of Simon Taylor,* 23, 29; O'Shaughnessy, "Stamp Act Crisis", 203–5; Metcalf, *Royal Government,* 164.

245. Wood, *Letters of Simon Taylor,* 148–49, 152.

246. Ibid., 152–53.

247. Richard B. Sheridan, "The Crisis of Slave Subsistence in the British West Indies during and after the American Revolution", *William and Mary Quarterly* 33 (1976): 632; Selwyn H. H. Carrington, *The British West Indies during the American Revolution* (Dordrecht, Holland: Foris Publications, 1988); Carrington, *Sugar Industry,* 58–59.

248. Wood and Clayton, "Slave Birth, Death and Disease", 105; "[Third] Report from the Committee on the Distillation of Sugar and Molasses", 383–84, 388; Accounts Produce, Liber 6, f. 157.

249. Clayton, "Sophistry", 332–33.

250. Accounts Produce, Liber 15, ff. 13–14; Wood and Clayton, "Slave Birth, Death and Disease", 106; Cateau, "New 'Negro' Business", 108. Note, however, that Hayward appears on the plan of Golden Grove dated 1788 (Figure 7.3).

251. Wood and Clayton, "Slave Birth, Death and Disease", 107, 110.

252. Arcedeckne Papers, DM 41/92/14, Will of Chaloner Arcedeckne, 2 June 1808, 3–4.

253. Ibid., 5; Sheridan, "Simon Taylor", 294.

254. Returns of Registrations of Slaves, Liber 136; Ingram, *Manuscript Sources,* 56, 82; *Gentleman's Magazine* (London) (1810): 89; *Gentleman's Magazine* (London) (1849): 430.

255. *Parliamentary Papers,* 1837–38 (215): 48, " Accounts of Slave Compensation Claims", 48.

256. Returns of Registrations of Slaves, Liber 137.

257. Accounts Produce, Liber 15, ff. 13–14; Liber 73, f. 197. See also Shepherd, "Livestock and Sugar", 641–42; Higman, *Slave Population and Economy,* 235–36. The hogsheads were probably larger in 1832.

258. Roughley, *Jamaica Planter's Guide,* 182–83; Higman, "Spatial Economy", 17–39; Higman, *Jamaica Surveyed,* 80–84.

259. Veront Satchell, "Early Use of Steam Power in the Jamaican Sugar Industry, 1768–1810", *Transactions of the Newcomen Society* 67 (1995–96): 221–31; Noel Deerr and Alexander Brooks, "The Early Use of Steam Power in the Cane Sugar Industry", *Transactions of the Newcomen Society* 21 (1940–41): 11–21; Higman, *Jamaica Surveyed,* 149–51.

260. Calculated on the assumptions that field slaves worked 18 hours every day for eight months, during crop, and 8 hours per day on twenty-two days of each of the other four months of the year. This gives a total of 5,083 hours. The first part of the calculation is based on Wood, *Letters of Simon Taylor,* 87.

261. Higman, *Slave Populations,* 188.

262. Long, *History of Jamaica,* 1: 461–63.

263. Wood, *Letters of Simon Taylor,* 65, 87.

Chapter 8

1. For the history of Montpelier, see Higman, *Montpelier.*

2. Ibid., 106–8, 258–62; Catherine Hall, *Civilising Subjects: Metropole and Colony in the English Imagination, 1830–1867* (Cambridge: Polity Press, 2002).

3. *Great Britain, Parliamentary Debates,* House of Lords (17 April 1832): 615–16; Higman, *Montpelier,* 35.

4. Seaford to Frederick William, Earl and Marquess of Bristol, 16 August 1832, Hervey Family Archives, 941/56/30 (Bury St Edmunds and West Suffolk Record Office, microfilm at University of the West Indies Library, Mona).

5. Probate of Will, Manton and Hart Papers, 4/82/46 (Jamaica Archives, Spanish Town).

6. Accounts Produce, Liber 76, f. 183; ibid., Liber 77, f. 177; ibid., Liber 79, f. 126; ibid., Liber 81, f. 31; ibid., Liber 82, f. 94; ibid., Liber 83, f. 94.

7. Higman, *Montpelier,* 35–59. Jackson was last listed as attorney for Montpelier and Shettlewood in the Accounts Produce of 1849, and in the years following, only the overseer's name was given, until 1853 when George Cunningham is identified as the attorney. See Accounts Produce, Liber 95, f. 121.

8. Isaac Jackson Letterbooks, 1: 46, Jackson to Seaford, 23 October 1839.

9. Ibid., 1: 129, Jackson to Seaford, 17 April 1840; ibid., 1: 145, Jackson to Seaford, 4 June 1840.

10. Ibid., 2: Jackson to Seaford, 15 June 1841; ibid., 3: Jackson to Seaford, 3 January 1843.

11. Ibid., 1: 136, Jackson to Seaford, 12 May 1840; ibid., 1: 129, Jackson to Seaford, 17 April 1840.

12. *Jamaica House of Assembly Votes,* (1833): 492; Higman, *Slave Population and Economy,* 189; Higman, *Montpelier,* 238–39, 274.

13. Isaac Jackson Letterbooks, 3: Jackson to Seaford, 21 June 1842; Accounts Produce, Liber 88, f. 212.

14. Isaac Jackson Letterbooks, 2: Jackson to Seaford, 23 July 1841.

15. Returns of Registrations of Slaves, Liber 30, f. 49.

16. Isaac Jackson Letterbooks, 3: Jackson to Seaford, 25 April 1843.

17. Hall, *Free Jamaica,* 26.

18. Isaac Jackson Letterbooks, 2: Jackson to Seaford, 21 March 1842.

19. Ibid., 3: Jackson to Seaford, 7 July 1842.

20. Hall, *Civilising Subjects,* xiii.

21. Isaac Jackson Letterbooks, 2: Jackson to Seaford, 23 July 1841; Returns of Registrations of Slaves, Liber 30, f. 49; CO 137/214, f. 293.

22. Isaac Jackson Letterbooks, 2: Jackson to Seaford, 28 September 1841; James Pennington, *The Currency of the British Colonies* (London: Her Majesty's Stationery Office, 1848), 49–50; Callender, *Development of the Capital Market Institutions,* 4; Barnes, *The Sugar Cane,* 230.

23. Isaac Jackson Letterbooks, 2: Jackson to Seaford, 28 September 1841; Jackson to Seaford, 4 December 1841; Jackson to Seaford, 4 February 1842; Returns of Registrations of Slaves, Liber 30, f. 42; CO 137/214, f. 294.

24. Isaac Jackson Letterbooks, 1: 41, Jackson to Philip Haughton James, 17 October 1839.

25. Ibid., 1: 35, Jackson to Heaven and Co., 1 October 1839.

26. James Spedding, "The Jamaica Question", *Edinburgh Review* 69, no. 140 (July 1839): 555; D. J. Murray, *The West Indies and the Development of Colonial Government, 1831–1834* (Oxford: Clarendon Press, 1965), 226–28.

27. Higman, *Montpelier,* 58.

28. Isaac Jackson Letterbooks, 1: 110, Jackson to Gardiner, 25 March 1840.

29. Ibid., 1: 140, Jackson to Campbell, 4 June 1840.

30. Ibid., 2: Jackson to Campbell, 28 June 1841.

31. Long, *History of Jamaica,* 1: 384–404; Brathwaite, *Development of Creole Society,* 86–91; Hall, "Bountied European Immigration", 2–9; Higman, *Montpelier,* 55.

32. Isaac Jackson Letterbooks, 3: 28 March 1843.

33. Ibid., 2: Jackson to Seaford, 29 October 1841.

34. *Cornwall Chronicle,* 20 October 1841, 2; Gardner, *History of Jamaica,* 410–11.

35. Isaac Jackson Letterbooks, 2: Jackson to Seaford, 29 October 1841.

36. Ibid., 3: Seaford to Elgin, 3 May 1842, located at 6 February 1843. See Monica Schuler, *"Alas, Alas, Kongo": A Social History of Indentured African Immigration into Jamaica, 1841–1865* (Baltimore: Johns Hopkins University Press, 1980), 17–23.

37. Isaac Jackson Letterbooks, 3: Jackson to Seaford, 6 February 1843.

38. Ibid., 3, Jackson to Seaford, 7 February 1843.

39. Spedding, "Jamaica Question", 551; Holt, *Problem of Freedom,* 85.

40. See Swithin Wilmot, "Emancipation in Action: Workers and Wage Conflict in Jamaica 1838–40", *Jamaica Journal* 19, no. 3 (1986): 55–62; Hall, *Free Jamaica,* 43–51; Holt, *Problem of Freedom,* 123–28.

41. Isaac Jackson Letterbooks, 1: 52, Jackson to Campbell, 14 November 1839.

42. Ibid., 1: 96, Jackson to Campbell, 25 February 1840.

43. Ibid., 3: Jackson to Seaford, 27 June 1843.

44. Accounts Produce, Liber 82, f. 109.

45. Isaac Jackson Letterbooks, 1: 77, Jackson to Seaford, 1 January 1840.

46. Ibid., 1: 41, Jackson to H. James, 17 October 1839.

47. Ibid., 1: 108–109, Jackson to Seaford, 17 March 1840; ibid., 1: 136, Jackson to Seaford, 12 May 1840; 1: 145, Jackson to Seaford, 4 June 1840.
48. Ibid., 2: Jackson to Seaford, 14 January 1842.
49. Ibid., 3: Jackson to Seaford, 19 May 1842.
50. Ibid., 3: Jackson to Seaford, 21 March 1842.
51. Ibid., 1: 77, Jackson to Seaford, 1 January 1840.
52. Ibid., 2: Jackson to Seaford, 4 December 1841.
53. Ibid., 3: Jackson to Seaford, 2 and 19 August 1842.
54. *Great Britain, Parliamentary Debates,* 3rd ser., 17: 1230; 19: 1252–56; 20: 588; *Jamaica House of Assembly Votes* (1833): 271, 479–92; B. W. Higman, "Slavery Remembered: The Celebration of Emancipation in Jamaica", *Journal of Caribbean History* 12 (1979): 59.
55. McNeil to Seaford, 8 January 1839, in Jamaica Agent (William Burge), *Copies of any communications addressed to the Secretary of State by the Agent for the Island of Jamaica, relative to the conduct of the Negro population in that Island* (*Parliamentary Papers,* 1839), 49. For fuller accounts of this period, see Higman, *Montpelier,* 57–61; B. W. Higman, " 'To Begin the World Again': Responses to Emancipation at Friendship and Greenwich Estate, Jamaica", in *Jamaica in Slavery and Freedom: History, Heritage and Culture,* ed. Kathleen E. A. Monteith and Glen Richards (Kingston: University of the West Indies Press, 2002), 291–306.
56. Isaac Jackson Letterbooks, 1: 62, Jackson to Alexander Campbell, 3 December 1839; 1: 63, Jackson to Edmund Gardiner, 4 December 1839.
57. Ibid., 2: Jackson to Campbell, 16 September 1841.
58. Ibid., 1: 140, Jackson to Campbell, 4 June 1840.
59. Seaford to Lady Holland, 11 November 1844, Holland House Papers, Add. Ms. 51818, f. 165 (British Library, London).
60. Isaac Jackson Letterbooks, 3: Jackson to Seaford, 17 October 1842.
61. Ibid., 1: 26, Jackson to David Lyon, 1 August 1839.
62. Ibid., 1: 99–100, Jackson to Seaford, 25 February 1840; 1: 145, Jackson to Seaford, 12 May 1840.
63. Ibid., 1: 99–100, Jackson to Seaford, 25 February 1840; Curtin, *Two Jamaicas,* 57.
64. Isaac Jackson Letterbooks, 1: 116, Jackson to Seaford, 25 March 1840.
65. Ibid., 1: 150–51, Jackson to Seaford, 24 June 1840.
66. Ibid., 3: Jackson to Seaford, 21 June 1842.
67. Hall, *Free Jamaica,* 51; Higman, *Slave Population and Economy,* 238; Higman, *Slave Populations of the British Caribbean,* 180.
68. Seaford to Holland, 7 May 1832, Holland House Papers, Add. Ms. 51818, ff. 35–36.
69. Seaford to Lord Holland, n.d. [late 1838 or early 1839], Holland House Papers, Add. Ms. 51818, f. 104.
70. Isaac Jackson Letterbooks, 1: 26, Jackson to Lyon, 10 September 1839.
71. Ibid., 1: 32, Jackson to Campbell, 29 September 1839.
72. Ibid., 1: 1, Jackson to Tinling, 1 August 1839.
73. Ibid., 1: 20, Jackson to Stirling Gordon and Co., 27 August 1839.
74. Ibid., 1: 35, Jackson to Heaven and Co., 1 October 1839.
75. Hall, *Civilising Subjects,* 120–21; Holt, *Problem of Freedom,* 134–39; Hall, *Free Jamaica,* 20–21.

76. Isaac Jackson Letterbooks, 1: 50, Jackson to Seaford, 1 November 1839.

77. List of instructions for Friendship and Greenwich, n.d. [1839], Holland House Papers, Add. Ms. 51819, ff. 132–33; Seaford to Holland, n.d. [1839], Holland House Papers, Add. Ms. 51818, ff. 84–85. The British Library wrongly dates the letter to 1837. Cf. Holt, *Problem of Freedom,* 135.

78. Isaac Jackson Letterbooks, 1: 65, Jackson to Seaford, 3 December 1839.

79. Ibid., 1: 77, Jackson to Seaford, 1 January 1840.

80. Ibid., 1: 87, Jackson to Seaford, 29 January 1840.

81. Ibid., 1: 77, Jackson to Seaford, 1 January 1840; 1: 79, Jackson to G. C. Ricketts, 4 January 1840.

82. Ibid., 1: 99–100, Jackson to Seaford, 25 February 1840; Curtin, *Two Jamaicas,* 57.

83. Isaac Jackson Letterbooks, 1: 145, Jackson to Seaford, 4 June 1840; Accounts Produce, Liber 78, f. 138; ibid., Liber 80, f. 152; ibid., Liber 82, f. 105; ibid., Liber 83, f. 147; ibid., Liber 85, f. 190; ibid., Liber 86, f. 97.

84. Returns of Registrations of Slaves, Liber 27, f. 37.

85. Isaac Jackson Letterbooks, 1: 108, Jackson to Seaford, 17 March 1840.

86. Ibid., 1: 108–9, Jackson to Seaford, 17 March 1840.

87. CO 137/248, ff. 174–77, Metcalfe to Russell, 30 March 1840. See also Swithin Wilmot, ed., *Adjustments to Emancipation in Jamaica* (Mona, Jamaica: Social History Project, University of the West Indies, 1994), 7–17.

88. Isaac Jackson Letterbooks, 1: 105, Jackson to Alexander Campbell, 16 March 1840.

89. Returns of Registrations of Slaves, Liber 40, f. 83, where he is named Cuffie.

90. Isaac Jackson Letterbooks, 1: 117, Jackson to Seaford, 25 March 1840.

91. Ibid., 1: 117, Jackson to Seaford, 25 March 1840.

92. Ibid., 1: 128, Jackson to Seaford, 17 April 1840.

93. The Accounts Produce records roughly confirm these amounts. For the period from 20 November 1839 to 30 September 1840 (ten months and ten days) the labourers paid for rent and pasturage £334 at Montpelier Estate and £495 at Montpelier Pen. At Shettlewood they paid £279 for the period 1 November 1839 to 30 September 1840. Accounts Produce, Liber 84, ff. 154–55, 164. For 1838/39, see Accounts Produce, Liber 83, ff. 147–48, 153.

94. Isaac Jackson Letterbooks, 1: 135–36, Jackson to Seaford, 12 May 1840.

95. Accounts Produce, Liber 85, f. 190; ibid., Liber 87, f. 213; ibid., Liber 88, f. 212; Isaac Jackson Letterbooks, 3: Jackson to Seaford, 19 August 1842.

96. Isaac Jackson Letterbooks, 3: Jackson to Seaford, 20 September 1842 and 3 January 1843.

97. Ibid., 1: 145, Jackson to Seaford, 4 June 1840.

98. Ibid., 1: 150–51, Jackson to Seaford, 24 June 1840.

99. Ibid., 1: 140, Jackson to Tinling, 2 June 1840.

100. Ibid., 2: Jackson to Campbell, 16 September 1841; Douglas Hall, "The Flight from the Estates Reconsidered: The British West Indies, 1838–1842", *Journal of Caribbean History* 10–11 (1978): 7–24.

101. Hall, *Civilising Subjects,* 120–39; Holt, *Problem of Freedom,* 154; Higman, *Jamaica Surveyed,* 280–85.

102. Isaac Jackson Letterbooks, 3: Jackson to Seaford, 27 June 1843.

103. Ibid., 1: 151, Jackson to Seaford, 24 June 1840.

104. Accounts Produce, Liber 84, ff. 154–55, 164; ibid., Liber 85, ff. 190, 205; ibid., Liber 86, ff. 96–97.
105. Isaac Jackson Letterbooks, 2: Jackson to Seaford, 15 June 1841.
106. Ibid., 2: Jackson to Seaford, 4 February 1842.
107. Ibid., 3: Jackson to Seaford, 19 May 1842; Higman, *Montpelier,* 105–6
108. Isaac Jackson Letterbooks, 3: Jackson to Seaford, 19 May 1842; Higman, *Montpelier,* 90–93.
109. Isaac Jackson Letterbooks, 3: Jackson to Seaford, 21 June 1842, 17 October 1842 and 1 December 1842.
110. Accounts Produce, Liber 86, f. 97; ibid., Liber 87, f. 213.
111. Isaac Jackson Letterbooks, 3: Jackson to Seaford, 7 February 1843.
112. Higman, *Montpelier,* 89–92.
113. Isaac Jackson Letterbooks, 3: Jackson to Seaford, 28 March 1843.
114. Ibid., 3: Jackson to Seaford, 9 May 1843.
115. Accounts Produce, Liber 83, f. 147; ibid., Liber 85, f. 190; ibid., Liber 87, f. 213; Isaac Jackson Letterbooks, 3: Jackson to Seaford, 19 May 1842 and 6 June 1842.
116. Isaac Jackson Letterbooks, 1: 33, 29 September 1839; ibid., 1: 63–65, Jackson to Seaford, 3 December 1839; Higman, *Montpelier,* 37–50.
117. Isaac Jackson Letterbooks, 1: 87, Jackson to Seaford, 29 January 1840; ibid., 1: 100, Jackson to Seaford, 25 February 1840; ibid., 1: 128, Jackson to Seaford, 17 April 1840.
118. Accounts Produce, Liber 84, f. 154. Some small quantities, in eccentric containers, are omitted from these totals.
119. In Jackson's letter "third ratoons" is repeated but it is assumed the first use should be "second ratoons". Isaac Jackson Letterbooks, 1: 63–67, Jackson to Seaford, 3 December 1839; Higman, *Montpelier,* 89–91.
120. Isaac Jackson Letterbooks, 2: Jackson to Seaford, 21 March 1842, and 12 April 1842. Both Old and New Montpelier had a "First cut" piece, and other pieces cannot be identified on the plan of 1821 (namely Brote, Beauman and Still house). See Higman, *Montpelier,* 89–93.
121. Isaac Jackson Letterbooks, 1: 150, Jackson to Seaford, 24 June 1840.
122. Ibid., 1: 150–51, Jackson to Seaford, 24 June 1840.
123. Ibid., 2: Jackson to Seaford, 26 August 1841; Accounts Produce, Liber 85, f. 190.
124. Ibid., 2: Jackson to Seaford, 12 April 1842; Inventories, Liber 157, ff. 185–87.
125. Ibid., 2: Jackson to Seaford, 4 December 1841.
126. Ibid., 2: Jackson to Seaford, 14 January 1842.
127. Ibid., 2: Jackson to Seaford, 4 February 1842.
128. Ibid., 2: Jackson to Seaford, 4 February 1842 and 12 April 1842; ibid., 3: Jackson to Seaford, 10 May 1842.
129. Accounts Produce, Liber 86, f. 97; Isaac Jackson Letterbooks, 3: Jackson to Seaford, 6 June 1842.
130. Isaac Jackson Letterbooks, 3: Jackson to Seaford, 6 June 1842; Accounts Produce, Liber 86, f. 97.
131. Isaac Jackson Letterbooks, 2: Jackson to Seaford, 15 June 1841 and 6 June 1842.
132. Ibid., 3: Jackson to Seaford, 3 January 1843.
133. Ibid., 3: Jackson to Seaford, 28 March 1843.

134. Accounts Produce, Liber 87, f. 213. Cf. Isaac Jackson Letterbooks, 3: Jackson to Seaford, 25 April 1843, 30 May 1843 and 27 June 1843.

135. Isaac Jackson Letterbooks, 3: Jackson to Seaford, 4 August 1843 and 20 October 1843.

136. Ibid., 3: Jackson to Seaford, 4 August 1843.

137. Ibid., 3: Jackson to Seaford, 4 September 1843.

138. Ibid., 3: Jackson to Seaford, 18 November 1843; Accounts Produce, Liber 88, f. 212.

139. Ibid., 3: Jackson to Seaford, 28 February 1843, 20 October 1843 and 4 August 1843.

140. Ibid., 3: Jackson to Seaford, 4 September 1843. Cf. Hall, *Free Jamaica,* 47; Liam Brunt, "Mechanical Innovation in the Industrial Revolution: The Case of Plough Design", *Economic History Review* 56 (2003): 463–64.

141. Isaac Jackson Letterbooks, 3: Jackson to Seaford, 5 and 20 October 1843.

142. Ibid., 3: Jackson to Seaford, 28 February 1843.

143. Ibid., 2: Jackson to Seaford, 21 March 1842.

144. Ibid., 1: 65–67, Jackson to Seaford, 3 December 1839. Jackson gave the total as 1,286, but adding the units gives 1,298.

145. Ibid., 1: 151, Jackson to Seaford, 24 June 1840.

146. Ibid., 3: Jackson to Seaford, 19 May 1842.

147. Ibid., 3: Jackson to Seaford, 6 and 21 June 1842.

148. Ibid., 3: Jackson to Seaford, 20 September 1842; Higman, *Montpelier,* 89–90.

149. Isaac Jackson Letterbooks, 3: Jackson to Seaford, 17 October 1842.

150. Ibid., 3: Jackson to Seaford, 3 January 1843.

151. Ibid., 3: Jackson to Seaford, 3 January 1843, 28 February 1843, 25 April 1843 and 4 August 1843.

152. Ibid., 2: Jackson to Seaford, 28 September 1841.

153. Ibid., 3: Jackson to Seaford, 2 August 1842.

154. Ibid., 1: 129, Jackson to Seaford, 17 April 1840.

155. Ibid., 3: Jackson to Seaford, 9 May 1843.

156. Ibid., 3: Jackson to Seaford, 28 September 1841, 19 August 1842, 27 June 1843 and 5 October 1843.

157. Ibid., 1: 65–66, Jackson to Seaford, 3 December 1839. See also Verene A. Shepherd, "Alternative Husbandry: Slaves and Free Labourers on Livestock Farms in Jamaica in the Eighteenth and Nineteenth Centuries", *Slavery and Abolition* 14 (1993): 58–59.

158. Isaac Jackson Letterbooks, 2: Jackson to Seaford, 15 June 1841.

159. Ibid., 2: Jackson to Seaford, 23 July 1841.

160. Ibid., 2: Jackson to Seaford, 28 September 1841.

161. Ibid., 2: Jackson to Seaford, 4 February 1842.

162. Ibid., 1: 65–66, Jackson to Seaford, 3 December 1839; ibid., 1: 78, Jackson to Seaford, 1 January 1840. See also Shepherd, "Alternative Husbandry", 58–59.

163. Isaac Jackson Letterbooks, 1: 99, Jackson to Seaford, 25 February 1840.

164. Ibid., 2: Jackson to Seaford, 4 February 1842 and 21 March 1842.

165. Ibid., 3: Jackson to Seaford, 10 May 1842.

166. Ibid., 3: Jackson to Seaford, 21 June 1842.

167. Ibid., 3: Jackson to Seaford, 28 February 1843. See also ibid., 3: Jackson to Seaford, 25 April 1843, 27 June 1843, 5 October 1843, 18 November 1843.

168. Ibid., 1: 129, Jackson to Seaford, 17 April 1840.

169. Ibid., 1: 56–57, Jackson to McNeil, 19 November 1839.

170. Ibid., 1: 63–67, Jackson to Seaford, 3 December 1839; ibid., 2: Jackson to Seaford, 11 April 1842.

171. Ibid., 3: 19 May 1842; Accounts Produce, Liber 87, f. 213.

172. Ibid., 3: Jackson to Seaford, 19 May 1842.

173. Ibid., 1: 161–67.

174. Ibid., 3: Jackson to Seaford, June 1842, List of supplies required; ibid., 2: Jackson to Seaford, 23 July 1841.

175. Ibid., 1: 49–50, Jackson to Seaford, 1 November 1839.

176. Ibid., 2: Jackson to Seaford, 15 and 29 June 1841. In 1842 Jackson observed to Seaford that there was a difference between the land area of the properties as measured by Morris' plat of 1837. He could not offer any reason for the difference. Ibid., 2: Jackson to Seaford, 14 January 1842.

177. Ibid., 3: Jackson to Seaford, 2 August 1842.

178. Ibid., 2: Jackson to Seaford, 14 January 1842.

179. Ibid., 2: Jackson to Seaford, 26 August 1841; ibid., 3: Jackson to Seaford, 9 May 1843.

180. Ibid., 3: Jackson to Seaford, 30 May 1843 and 4 August 1843.

181. Ibid., 2: Jackson to Seaford, 4 January 1842.

182. According to Howard de Walden's evidence, in "Third Report from the Select Committee on Sugar and Coffee Planting", 4–7; Higman, *Montpelier,* 51.

183. Isaac Jackson Letterbooks, 2: Jackson to Seaford, 4 January 1842.

184. Ibid., 2: Jackson to Seaford, 29 June 1841 and 28 September 1841.

185. Ibid., 2: Jackson to Seaford, 26 August 1841 and 28 September 1841.

186. Ibid., 3: Jackson to Seaford, 19 May 1842, 1 November 1842, 20 October 1843

187. Ibid., 3: Jackson to Seaford, 17 October 1842. Cf. "Third Report from the Select Committee for Sugar and Coffee Planting", Minutes of Evidence, 4.

188. Isaac Jackson Letterbooks, 3: Jackson to Seaford, 28 February 1843.

189. Ibid., 3: Jackson to Seaford, 20 October 1843.

190. Ibid., 1: 46, Jackson to Seaford, 23 October 1839.

191. Ibid., 3: Jackson to Seaford, 17 October 1842.

192. Ibid., 3: Jackson to Seaford, 27 June 1843.

193. Ibid., 2: Jackson to Seaford, 28 September 1841.

194. Ibid., 2: Jackson to Seaford, 15 June 1841 and 29 June 1841.

195. Ibid., 2: Jackson to Seaford, 26 August 1841.

196. Ibid., 3: Jackson to Seaford, 21 March 1842, 19 May 1842, 4 August 1843. All of these were drawn on Charles Robinson, whose identity is unknown. Jackson's clerk was identified as "C.R." and it is possible, though unlikely, that he would also have served as Jackson's agent for these funds.

197. Ibid., 3: Jackson to Seaford, 18 November 1843; Accounts Produce, Liber 88, f. 212.

198. Hall, *Free Jamaica,* 23; Richard B. Sheridan, "Changing Sugar Technology and the Labour Nexus in the British Caribbean, 1750–1900, with Special Reference to Barbados and Jamaica", *New West Indian Guide* 63 (1989): 76–77; Curtin, *Two Jamaicas,* 122; Holt, *Problem of Freedom,* 131.

199. Accounts Produce, Liber 92, f. 157; Higman, *Montpelier,* 44–45, 50–51.

200. Trollope, *West Indies and the Spanish Main,* 169.

201. Lord Howard de Walden, *General Instructions for Montpelier and Ellis Caymanas Estates in Jamaica* (private print, June 1852), 3; Accounts Produce, Liber 95, f. 121; "Third Report from the Select Committee for Sugar and Coffee Planting", Minutes of Evidence, 4.

202. Howard de Walden, *General Instructions,* 3–4.

203. Ibid., 57.

204. Ibid., *General Instructions,* 41.

205. Hall, "Absentee-Proprietorship", 25.

206. Isaac Jackson Letterbooks, 3: Jackson to Seaford, 6 June 1842. See Deerr, *Cane Sugar,* 473–97; Barnes, *Sugar Cane,* 352–55.

207. Higman, *Jamaica Surveyed,* 151–55.

208. Isaac Jackson Letterbooks, 2: Jackson to Seaford, 28 September 1841.

Chapter 9

1. Brathwaite, *Development of Creole Society,* 139–40.

2. Cf. "Select Committee on Negro Apprenticeship", 50, evidence of Richard Robert Madden.

3. On the ethics of "honour among thieves", see Martin Hollis, *Reason in Action: Essays in the Philosophy of Social Science* (Cambridge: Cambridge University Press, 1996), 114–15. On the broader issues, see Daniel M. Hausman and Michael S. McPherson, *Economic Analysis and Moral Philosophy* (Cambridge: Cambridge University Press, 1996); Pierre Force, *Self-Interest Before Adam Smith: A Genealogy of Economic Science* (Cambridge: Cambridge University Press, 2003); Amartya Sen, *Development as Freedom* (Oxford: Oxford University Press, 1999).

4. David Sunderland, *Managing the British Empire: The Crown Agents, 1833–1914* (Woodbridge, UK: The Boydell Press, for the Royal Historical Society, 2004), 8–12.

5. Carrington, "Management of Sugar Estates", 27.

6. Ward, *British West Indian Slavery,* 263.

7. Anon., *Marly,* 23–24.

8. Taylor, "Journal of an Absentee Proprietor", 68; Watts, *West Indies,* 354. Similarly, in England: Mingay, *English Landed Society in the Eighteenth Century,* 59; Thompson, *English Landed Society in the Nineteenth Century,* 154. Cf. Bruchey, "Success and Failure Factors", 272.

9. Sheridan, *Sugar and Slavery,* 385.

10. Ward, *British West Indian Slavery,* 264; Ward, "Profitability of Sugar Planting", 207–8. See also Hall, "Absentee-Proprietorship", 21; Keith Mason, "The World an Absentee Planter and His Slaves Made: Sir William Stapleton and His Nevis Sugar Estate, 1722–1740", *Bulletin of the John Rylands University Library of Manchester* 75 (1993): 119.

11. Veront Satchell, "Pattern of Abandonment of Sugar Estates in Jamaica during the Late Nineteenth Century", *Caribbean Geography* 2 (1989): 251–67.

12. "Report from the Select Committee on West India Colonies", 389.

13. *Jamaica House of Assembly Votes* (1847): Appendix 57, 373–90. The lists do not indicate attorneys, only plantation names. The attorneys have been identified from the Returns of Registrations of Slaves.

14. Schuler, *"Alas, Alas, Kongo"*, 46, 61–62; Gad Heuman, *"The Killing Time": The Morant Bay Rebellion in Jamaica* (London: Macmillan, 1994), 20–25.

15. *Handbook of Jamaica*, 1881–82 and 1890; Anon., "The Industrialisation of Jamaica: Sugar, Part Two", *West Indian Review*, 12 July 1952, 27–28; Kenneth Street, "The Estates of Jamaica: Jamaica Sugar Estates Ltd.", *West Indian Review*, 16 October 1954, 1–14; Michelle Barrett, "Golden Grove Residents Desperate for New Homes", *Gleaner*, 27 October 1994, 32.

16. "[First] Report from the Committee on the Distillation of Sugar and Molasses", 281. See also Carrington, *Sugar Industry*, 236.

17. Higman, *Montpelier*, 65–74.

18. Ward, *British West Indian Slavery*, 263.

19. Craton and Walvin, *A Jamaican Plantation*, 169–75; Michael Craton, *Searching for the Invisible Man: Slaves and Plantation Life in Jamaica* (Cambridge, Mass.: Harvard University Press, 1978), 268.

20. Penrhyn 1329, quoted in Jean Lindsay, "Pennants and Jamaica: Part II", 61.

21. *Parliamentary Papers*, 1847–48 (184): 23, part 2, "Fourth Report from the Select Committee on Sugar and Coffee Planting", 1, 6, 16. See also Geddes evidence in 1842, "Report from the Select Committee on West India Colonies", 465–87.

22. "[First] Report from the Committee on the Distillation of Sugar and Molasses", 300.

23. Lowell Joseph Ragatz, *The Fall of the Planter Class in the British Caribbean, 1763–1833* (New York: American Historical Association, 1928); Williams, *Capitalism and Slavery*; John J. McCusker, *Essays in the Economic History of the Atlantic World* (London: Routledge, 1997), 330; Ryden, "Does Decline Make Sense?", 373–74; Ward, "Profitability of Sugar Planting", 209; Carrington, *Sugar Industry*, 2–6, 243, 285–86. See also Higman, *Slave Population and Economy*, 224.

24. Checkland, *Gladstones*, 123.

25. Ibid., 199–200, 277, 321–26, 414–15.

26. Ward, *British West Indian Slavery*, 266–70; Cateau, "Conservatism and Change", 10–14; R. Keith Aufhauser, "Slavery and Technological Change", *Journal of Economic History* 34 (1974): 36–50; W. A. Green, "The Planter Class and British West Indian Sugar Production, before and after Emancipation", *Economic History Review* 26 (1973): 448–63; Ormrod, "Evolution of Soil Management Practices", 157–70; Galloway, "Tradition and Innovation", 334–51.

27. Cateau, "Conservatism and Change", 30–31. See also Aufhauser, "Slavery and Technological Change", 36–50. Cf. Eric Richards, "Land Agent", 455; Thompson, *English Landed Society in the Nineteenth Century*, 183.

28. Mason, "World an Absentee Planter and His Slaves Made", 115.

29. Holt, *Problem of Freedom*, 86.

30. Satchell, "Early Use of Steam Power", 221–31.

31. Lindsay, "Pennants and Jamaica: Part I", 78–79; Lindsay, *History of the North Wales Slate Industry*, 40, 45–54.

32. Mason, "World an Absentee Planter and His Slaves Made", 118–21; Carrington, *Sugar Industry,* 168–69.

33. Cateau, "Conservatism and Change", 15–16.

34. First recorded by Rampini, as a proverb, in 1873. Cited in Cassidy and Le Page, *Dictionary of Jamaican English,* 443.

35. Gardner, *History of Jamaica,* 157.

36. Craton, *Searching for the Invisible Man,* 268. See also Patterson, *Sociology of Slavery,* 44; Watts, *West Indies,* 355–56.

37. Cf. Maureen Harkin, "Matthew Lewis's Journal of a West India Proprietor: Surveillance and Space on the Plantation", *Nineteenth-Century Contexts* 24 (2002): 139–50.

38. Ursula Halliday, "The Slave Owner as Reformer: Theory and Practice at Castle Wemyss Estate, Jamaica, 1808–1823", *Journal of Caribbean History* 30 (1996): 66.

39. Srividhya Swaminathan, "Developing the West Indian Proslavery Position after the Somerset Decision", *Slavery and Abolition* 24 (2003): 49–50; David Turley, "British Antislavery Reassessed", in *Rethinking the Age of Reform,* ed. Arthur Burns and Joanna Innes (Cambridge: Cambridge University Press, 2003), 183. Cf. David Patrick Geggus, *Slavery, War, and Revolution,* 25, 43.

40. Lewis, *Journal,* 369–70.

41. Quoted in Pearsall, "Late Flagrant Instance", 569. Cf. Madden, *Twelvemonth's Residence,* 1: 223.

42. The same applied in England and Ireland. See Richards, "Land Agent", 440; Maguire, *Downshire Estates,* 183.

43. Cf. Beckford, *Descriptive Account,* 2: 368–69.

44. Lewis, *Journal,* 115–18; Lindsay, "Pennants and Jamaica: Part II", 67–68.

45. Higman, *Slave Population and Economy,* 133–36; Higman, *Slave Populations of the British Caribbean,* 328–29.

46. Mason, "World an Absentee Planter and His Slaves Made", 124–25.

47. Higman, *Slave Population and Economy,* 102; Higman, *Slave Populations of the British Caribbean,* 314–29; Ward, *British West Indian Slavery,* 185.

48. Dallas, *History of the Maroons,* 2: 370–72.

49. Roughley, *Jamaica Planter's Guide,* 29–32.

50. Ibid., 33–36.

51. Ward, *British West Indian Slavery,* 92.

52. "Report from the Select Committee on West India Colonies", 436.

53. Pares, *Merchants and Planters,* 43.

54. Woodville K. Marshall, "A 'Valued Pamphlet': Henry James Ross's Rationale for Sharecropping in the West Indies", *Slavery and Abolition* 24 (2003): 82–111; Stead, "Risk and Risk Management in English Agriculture", 334.

55. Raphael Klapinsky, *Cane Sugar: The Small-Scale Processing Option* (London: Intermediate Technology Publications, 1989).

56. Tilman, *Thorstein Veblen,* 63, 197–98.

57. Sunderland, *Managing the British Empire*; Simon Ville, *The Rural Entrepreneurs: A History of the Stock and Station Agent Industry in Australia and New Zealand* (Cambridge: Cambridge University Press, 2000).

58. Gardner, *History of Jamaica,* 84–85; Burnard, "Failed Settler Society", 64.

Bibliography

Manuscripts

Jamaica Archives, Spanish Town

Accounts Current.
Accounts Produce.
Braco Estate Journal, 1795–97.
Drogging Bonds.
Inventories.
Manton and Hart Papers.
Powers of Attorney, 1806–25, 1B/11/23/15.
Reports of John W. Cooper, for Anna Susanna Watson Taylor, 1834–35, 7/177/1.
Returns of Registrations of Slaves, 1817–32.
Rose Hall Journal, 1817–32.

Island Record Office, Spanish Town

Land Deeds.

National Library of Jamaica, Kingston

Dawkins Papers, 1660–1812. 17 volumes. MS 181.
Georgia Estate, St Thomas, Letterbooks and Accounts, 1805–1835. 3 vols.
Hermitage Estate, St Elizabeth, Letterbook, 1819–24. MS 250.
Old Montpelier Estate, Account Book, 1824–28. MS 217.
Power of Attorney by Simon Taylor, of Jamaica, to Robert Taylor and John Taylor, of
    Great Britain, 27 April 1795. MS 1415.

University of the West Indies Library, Mona

Hervey Family Archives, 941/56/30. Microfilm. Original at Bury St Edmunds and West
    Suffolk Record Office, UK.

British Library, London

Holland House Papers. Add. Mss. 51816, 51817, 51818, 51819.
Ripon Papers. Add. Mss. 40863, 40879.

Public Record Office, London

CO 137 Despatches of Jamaica Governors.

University of Bristol, Arts and Sciences Library, Special Collections

Arcedeckne Papers. DM 41/92/2–14.

American Philosophical Society, Philadelphia

Isaac Jackson Letterbooks.

John Carter Brown Library, Providence, Rhode Island

Dovaston, John. "Agricultura Americana, or Improvements in West-India Husbandry Considered, wherein the present system of Husbandry used in England is applied to the Cultivation or growing of Sugar canes to advantage". Codex Eng 60.

Library of Congress, Washington

Jamaica Scrapbook – William Berryman, 1808–1816. DRWG 1–A-Berryman.

Maps and Plans

Bochart, Charles, and Humphrey Knollis. *Map of the Island of Jamaica and other the territories depending thereon.* [1684]. CO700/Jamaica3 (Public Record Office, London).

Browne, Patrick. *A New Map of Jamaica.* London, 1755.

Craskell, Thomas, and James Simpson. *Map of the County of Surrey in the Island of Jamaica.* London, 1763.

"A Plan of All the Level Cane Pieces on Potosi Estate, in the Parish of St. Thomas in the East, Jamaica; All said cane pieces bounding on Plantain Garden River, the former and present courses of which are represented and also the quantity of cane land carried away by it, since the year 1813 but more especially in 1815 and the subsequent years to the present date, surveyed by Francis Ramsay, December 1818". National Library of Jamaica, St Thomas 12C.

"A Plan of . . . Batchellors Hall Plantation at Plantain Garden River in the Parish of St. Thomas in the East, . . . April 1741, . . . by Bartholomew Brady, surveyor". National Library of Jamaica, St Thomas 12A.

"A Plan of Golden Grove Plantation on the Plantain Garden River, Jamaica, the property of Calloner Arcedickne Esquire, 1788". National Library of Jamaica, St Thomas 12A.

"A Plan of Holland Plantation in the Parish of St. Thomas in the East the property of the Honourable Simon Taylor Esquire, surveyed in September 1780 by Smellie and Sheriff". National Library of Jamaica, St Thomas 12A.

"Plan of Old Montpelier and New Montpelier Estates, 1821". National Library of Jamaica, St James 12.

"A Plan of Shettlewood Pen", n.d. National Library of Jamaica, Hanover 17.

"A Plan of Shettlewood Pen Situated in the Parish of Hanover and Island of Jamaica, the Property of the Honourable Lord Seaford, performed with alterations August 1830 [by] Morris and Cunningham, Surveyors". National Library of Jamaica, Hanover 17.

"A Plan of Winchester Estate in the Parish of St. Thomas in the East, Jamaica, the property of Mrs. Catherine Lambert, 1829/30". National Library of Jamaica, St Thomas 15.

Robertson, James. *Map of the County of Cornwall in the Island of Jamaica.* London, 1804.

Robertson, James. *Map of the County of Surrey in the Island of Jamaica.* London, 1804.

"A Sketch drawn to show the course of the Plantain Garden River and the position of a weir made by Winchester Estate to turn the water into the canal of that Estate, done in June 1846 by Alexander R. Carter for McGeachy and Griffith, surveyors". National Library of Jamaica, St Thomas 3A.

Official Publications

Great Britain, Parliamentary Debates.
Handbook of Jamaica.
Jamaica Almanack.
Jamaica House of Assembly Votes.
Journals of the House of Assembly of Jamaica.
Laws of Jamaica.

Parliamentary Papers (Great Britain)

1807 (65) Vol. III, "Report from the Committee on the Commercial State of the West India Colonies".

1808 (178) Vol. IV, "Report from the Committee on the Distillation of Sugar and Molasses".

1831–32 (721) Vol. XX, "Report from the Select Committee on the Extinction of Slavery throughout the British Dominions".

1836 (560) Vol. XV, "Select Committee on Negro Apprenticeship in the Colonies".

1837–38 (215) Vol. XLVIII, "Accounts of Slave Compensation Claims".

1842 (479) Vol. XIII, "Report from the Select Committee on West India Colonies".

1847–48 (167) Vol. XXIII, Part 1, "Third Report from the Select Committee on Sugar and Coffee Planting".

1847–48 (184) Vol. XXIII, Part 2, "Fourth Report from the Select Committee on Sugar and Coffee Planting".

Newspapers and Periodicals

Cornwall Chronicle (Montego Bay).
Edinburgh Review.
Gentleman's Magazine (London).
St. George's Chronicle and Grenada Gazette.

Books and Articles

Adams, I. H. "The Agents of Agricultural Change". In *The Making of the Scottish Countryside,* edited by M. L. Parry and T. R. Slater, 155–75. London: Croom Helm, 1980.

Ahmad, Rafi, F. N. Scatena and Avijit Gupta. "Morphology and Sedimentation in Caribbean Montane Streams: Examples from Jamaica and Puerto Rico". *Sedimentary Geology* 85 (1993): 157–69.

Aldridge, Trevor M. *Powers of Attorney.* London: Longman, 1988.

Allen, Robert C. "Progress and Poverty in Early Modern Europe". *Economic History Review* 56 (2003): 403–43.

Allsopp, Richard, ed. *Dictionary of Caribbean English Usage.* Oxford: Oxford University Press, 1996.

Anderson, B. L. "Provincial Aspects of the Financial Revolution of the Eighteenth Century". *Business History* 11 (1969): 11–22.

Anderson, B. L. "The Attorney and the Early Capital Market in Lancashire". In *Liverpool and Merseyside: Essays in the Economic and Social History of the Port and Its Hinterland,* edited by J. R. Harris, 50–77. London: Frank Cass and Co., 1969.

Annisette, Marcia. "Importing Accounting: The Case of Trinidad and Tobago". *Accounting, Business and Financial History* 9 (1999): 103–33.

Annisette, M., and D. Neu. "Accounting and Empire: An Introduction". *Critical Perspectives on Accounting* 15 (2004): 1–4.

Anon. *Marly; or, The Life of a Planter in Jamaica.* 2nd ed. Glasgow: Richard Griffin and Co., 1828.

Anon. "The Industrialisation of Jamaica: Sugar, Part Two". *West Indian Review,* 12 July 1952, 24–28.

Armstrong, John, and Stephanie Jones. *Business Documents: Their Origins, Sources and Uses in Historical Research.* London: Mansell, 1987.

Armytage, Frances. *The Free Port System in the British West Indies: A Study in Commercial Policy, 1766–1822.* London: Longmans, Green and Co., 1953.

A Society of Gentlemen in Scotland. *Encyclopaedia Britannica.* Edinburgh: A. Bell and C. Macfarquhar, 1768–71.

Aspinall, Algernon E. *The British West Indies: Their History, Resources and Progress.* London: Sir Isaac Pitman and Sons, 1912.

Aspinall, Algernon E. *The Pocket Guide to the West Indies.* Chicago: Rand, McNally and Co., 1914.

Aufhauser, R. Keith. "Slavery and Scientific Management". *Journal of Economic History* 33 (1973): 811–24.

Aufhauser, R. Keith. "Slavery and Technological Change". *Journal of Economic History* 34 (1974): 36–50.

Ayala, César J. *American Sugar Kingdom: The Plantation Economy of the Spanish Caribbean 1898–1934.* Chapel Hill: University of North Carolina Press, 1999.

Aylett, Philip. "Attorneys and Clients in Eighteenth-Century Cheshire: A Study in Relationships, 1740–1785". *Bulletin of the John Rylands University Library of Manchester* 69 (1987): 326–58.

Bailyn, Bernard. "Communications and Trade: The Atlantic in the Seventeenth Century". *Journal of Economic History* 13 (1953): 378–87.

Baker, Rodney, and Alan Leonard. *Great Steamers, White and Gold: A History of Royal Mail Ships and Services.* Southampton: Ensign Publications, 1993.

Banks, Kenneth J. *Chasing Empire Across the Sea: Communications and the State in the French Atlantic, 1713–1763.* Montreal and Kingston: McGill–Queen's University Press, 2002.

Barclay, Alexander. *A Practical View of the Present State of Slavery in the West Indies.* London: Smith, Elder, 1826.

Barnes, A. C. *The Sugar Cane.* London: Leonard Hill, 1964.

Barnett, Lloyd G. *The Constitutional Law of Jamaica.* Oxford: Oxford University Press, 1977.

Barrett, Michelle. "Golden Grove Residents Desperate for New Homes". *Gleaner,* 27 October 1994, 32.

Barrett, Ward. "Caribbean Sugar Production Standards in the Seventeenth and Eighteenth Centuries". In *Merchants and Scholars: Essays in the History of Exploration and Trade,* edited by John Parker, 147–70. Minneapolis: University of Minnesota Press, 1965.

Baxter, W. T. "Accounting in Colonial America". In *Studies in the History of Accounting,* edited by A. C. Littleton and B. S. Yamey, 272–87. London: Sweet and Maxwell, 1956.

Beachey, R. W. *The British West Indies Sugar Industry in the Late 19th Century.* Oxford: Basil Blackwell, 1957.

Beckett, J. V. "Absentee Landownership in the Late Seventeenth and Early Eighteenth Centuries: The Case of Cumbria". *Northern History* 19 (1983): 87–107.

Beckett, J. V. "Landownership and Estate Management". In *The Agrarian History of England and Wales.* Vol. 6, *1750–1850,* edited by G. E. Mingay, 545–640. Cambridge: Cambridge University Press, 1989.

Beckford, George L. *Persistent Poverty: Underdevelopment in Plantation Economies of the Third World.* New York: Oxford University Press, 1972.

Beckford, William, Jr. *Remarks upon the Situation of Negroes in Jamaica.* London: Egerton, 1788.

Beckford, William. *A Descriptive Account of the Island of Jamaica.* London: T. and J. Egerton, 1790.

Beckles, Hilary McD. " 'The Williams Effect': Eric Williams's Capitalism and Slavery and the Growth of West Indian Political Economy". In *British Capitalism and Caribbean Slavery: The Legacy of Eric Williams,* edited by Barbara L. Solow and Stanley L. Engerman, 302–16. Cambridge: Cambridge University Press, 1987.

Best, Lloyd. "Outlines of a Model of Pure Plantation Economy". *Social and Economic Studies* 17 (1968): 283–326.

Blackburn, Robin. *The Making of New World Slavery: From the Baroque to the Modern 1492–1800.* London: Verso, 1997.

Blackford, Mansel G., and K. Austin Kerr. *Business Enterprise in American History.* Boston: Houghton Mifflin Co., 1990.

Bleby, Henry. *Death Struggles of Slavery: Being a Narrative of Facts and Incidents, which occurred in a British Colony, during the two years immediately Preceding Negro Emancipation.* London: Hamilton, Adams and Co., 1853.

Bowen, H. V. "British India, 1765–1813: The Metropolitan Context". In *The Eighteenth Century.* Vol. 2, *The Oxford History of the British Empire,* edited by P. J. Marshall, 530–51. Oxford: Oxford University Press, 1998.

Brathwaite, Edward. *The Development of Creole Society in Jamaica, 1770–1820.* Oxford: Oxford University Press, 1971.

Bridges, George Wilson. *The Annals of Jamaica.* London: John Murray, 1828.

Britnor, L. E. *The History of the Sailing Packets to the West Indies.* London: British West Indies Study Circle, Paper No. 5, 1973.

Brown, Richard D. *Knowledge Is Power: The Diffusion of Information in Early America, 1700–1865.* New York: Oxford University Press, 1989.

Brown, Vincent. "Spiritual Terror and Sacred Authority in Jamaican Slave Society". *Slavery and Abolition* 24 (2003): 24–53.

Bruchey, Stuart. "Success and Failure Factors: American Merchants in Foreign Trade in the Eighteenth and Early Nineteenth Centuries". *Business History Review* 32 (1958): 272–92.

Brunt, Liam. "Rehabilitating Arthur Young". *Economic History Review* 56 (2003): 265–99.

Brunt, Liam. "Mechanical Innovation in the Industrial Revolution: The Case of Plough Design". *Economic History Review* 56 (2003): 444–77.

Burke's Peerage. London: Burke's Peerage, 1949.

Burn, W. L. *Emancipation and Apprenticeship in the British West Indies.* London: Jonathan Cape, 1937.

Burnard, Trevor. "Inheritance and Independence: Women's Status in Early Colonial Jamaica". *William and Mary Quarterly* 48 (1991): 93–114.

Burnard, Trevor. "Family Continuity and Female Independence in Jamaica, 1665–1734". *Continuity and Change* 7 (1992): 181–98.

Burnard, Trevor. "A Failed Settler Society: Marriage and Demographic Failure in Early Jamaica". *Journal of Social History* 28 (1994): 63–82.

Burnard, T. G. " 'Prodigious Riches': The Wealth of Jamaica before the American Revolution". *Economic History Review* 54 (2001): 506–24.

Burnard, Trevor. " 'The Grand Mart of the Island': The Economic Function of Kingston, Jamaica in the Mid-Eighteenth Century". In *Jamaica in Slavery and Freedom: History, Heritage and Culture,* edited by Kathleen E. A. Monteith and Glen Richards, 225–41. Kingston: University of the West Indies Press, 2002.

Burnard, Trevor. *Mastery, Tyranny, and Desire: Thomas Thistlewood and His Slaves in the Anglo-Jamaican World.* Chapel Hill: University of North Carolina Press, 2004.

Burnard, Trevor. "Passengers Only: The Extent and Significance of Absenteeism in Eighteenth Century Jamaica". *Atlantic Studies* 1 (2004): 178–95.

Butler, Kathleen Mary. *The Economics of Emancipation: Jamaica and Barbados, 1823–1843.* Chapel Hill: University of North Carolina Press, 1995.

Callender, Charles Victor. *The Development of the Capital Institutions of Jamaica.* Mona, Jamaica: Institute of Social and Economic Research, University of the West Indies, 1965.

Canny, Nicholas. "The Origins of Empire: An Introduction". In *The Origins of Empire:*

British Overseas Enterprise to the Close of the Seventeenth Century. Vol. 1, *The Oxford History of the British Empire,* edited by Nicholas Canny, 1–33. Oxford: Oxford University Press, 1998.

Carrington, Selwyn H. H. " 'Econocide' – Myth or Reality? The Question of West Indian Decline, 1783–1806". *Boletin de Estudios Latinoamericanos y del Caribe* 36 (1984): 13–48.

Carrington, Selwyn H. H. *The British West Indies during the American Revolution.* Dordrecht, Holland: Foris Publications, 1988.

Carrington, Selwyn H. H. "Management of Sugar Estates in the British West Indies at the End of the Eighteenth Century". *Journal of Caribbean History* 33 (1999): 27–53.

Carrington, Selwyn H. H. *The Sugar Industry and the Abolition of the Slave Trade, 1775–1810.* Gainesville: University Press of Florida, 2002.

Cassidy, F. G., and R. B. Le Page, eds. *Dictionary of Jamaican English.* Cambridge: Cambridge University Press, 1967.

Cateau, Heather. "Conservatism and Change Implementation in the British West Indian Sugar Industry 1750–1810". *Journal of Caribbean History* 29 (1995): 1–36.

Cateau, Heather. "The New 'Negro' Business: Hiring in the British West Indies 1750–1810". In *In the Shadow of the Plantation: Caribbean History and Legacy,* edited by Alvin O. Thompson, 100–120. Kingston: Ian Randle Publishers, 2002.

Chandler, Alfred D., Jr. *The Visible Hand: The Managerial Revolution in American Business.* Cambridge, Massachusetts: Harvard University Press, 1977.

Chandler, Alfred D., Jr., and Herman Daems, eds. *Managerial Hierarchies: Comparative Perspectives on the Rise of the Modern Industrial Enterprise.* Cambridge, Massachusetts: Harvard University Press, 1980.

Checkland, S. G. *The Gladstones: A Family Biography 1764–1851.* Cambridge: Cambridge University Press, 1971.

Chenoweth, Michael. *The 18th Century Climate of Jamaica: Derived from the Journals of Thomas Thistlewood 1750–1786.* Philadelphia: American Philosophical Society, 2003

Chisholm, Michael. *Rural Settlement and Land Use: An Essay in Location.* London: Hutchinson University Library, 1962.

Clay, Christopher. "Landlords and Estate Management in England". In *The Agrarian History of England and Wales.* Vol. 5, *1640–1750, Part 2, Agrarian Change,* edited by Joan Thirsk, 119–251. Cambridge: Cambridge University Press, 1990.

Clayton, T. R. "Sophistry, Security, and Socio-Political Structures in the American Revolution; or, Why Jamaica Did Not Rebel". *Historical Journal* 29 (1986): 319–44.

Coelho, Philip R. P. "The Profitability of Imperialism: The British Experience in the West Indies, 1768–1772". *Explorations in Economic History* 10 (1973): 253–80.

Cooke, Bill. "The Denial of Slavery in Management Studies". *Journal of Management Studies* 40 (2003): 1895–1918.

Corbett, Mary Jean. "Public Affections and Familial Politics: Burke, Edgeworth, and the 'Common Naturalization' of Great Britain". *ELH* [English Literary History], 61 (1994): 877–97.

Cotterell, Brian, and Johan Kamminga. *Mechanics of Pre-Industrial Technology.* Cambridge: Cambridge University Press, 1990.

Courtenay, P. P. *Plantation Agriculture.* London: G. Bell and Sons, 1965.

Cowton, Christopher J., and Andrew J. O'Shaughnessy. "Absentee Control of Sugar Plantations in the British West Indies". *Accounting and Business Research* 22 (1991): 33–45.

Craton, Michael. *Searching for the Invisible Man: Slaves and Plantation Life in Jamaica.* Cambridge, Massachusetts: Harvard University Press, 1978.

Craton, Michael, and James Walvin. *A Jamaican Plantation: The History of Worthy Park 1670–1970.* London: W. H. Allen, 1970.

Cretney, Stephen M., and Denzil Lush. *Enduring Powers of Attorney.* Bristol: Jordans, 1996.

Curtin, Philip D. *Two Jamaicas: The Role of Ideas in a Tropical Colony 1830–1865.* Cambridge, Massachusetts: Harvard University Press, 1955.

Dallas, R. C. *The History of the Maroons.* London: T. N. Longman and O. Rees, 1803.

Daniels, John, and Christian Daniels. "The Origin of the Sugarcane Roller Mill". *Technology and Culture* 29 (1988): 493–535.

Daniels, Stephen, and Charles Watkins. "Picturesque Landscaping and Estate Management: Uvedale Price at Foxley, 1770–1829". *Rural History* 2 (1991): 141–69.

Daunton, M. J. *Royal Mail: The Post Office since 1840.* London: Athlone Press, 1985.

Davies, K. G. "The Origins of the Commission System in the West India Trade". *Transactions of the Royal Historical Society,* Fifth Series, 2 (1952): 89–107.

Davis, David Brion. *Slavery and Human Progress.* New York: Oxford University Press, 1984.

Davis, Ralph. *The Rise of the English Shipping Industry in the Seventeenth and Eighteenth Centuries.* London: Macmillan and Co., 1962.

Debien, Gabriel. *Les esclaves aux Antille Françaises (XVIIe–XVIIIe siècles).* Basse-Terre: Société d'histoire de la Guadeloupe, 1974.

Deerr, Noel. *Cane Sugar: A Textbook on the Agriculture of the Sugar Cane, the Manufacture of Cane Sugar, and the Analysis of Sugar-House Products.* London: Norman Rodger, 1921.

Deerr, Noel. "The Evolution of the Sugar Cane Mill". *Transactions of the Newcomen Society* 21 (1940–41): 1–9.

Deerr, Noel. *The History of Sugar.* London: Chapman and Hall, 1949–50.

Deerr, Noel, and Alexander Brooks. "The Early Use of Steam Power in the Cane Sugar Industry". *Transactions of the Newcomen Society* 21 (1940–41): 11–21.

Devine, T. M. "An Eighteenth-Century Business Elite: Glasgow–West India Merchants, *c.*1750–1815". *Scottish Historical Review* 57 (1978): 40–67.

Dillman, C. Daniel. "Absentee Landlords and Farm Management in Brazil during the 1960s". *American Journal of Economics and Sociology* 37 (1978): 1–8.

Drescher, Seymour. *Econocide: British Slavery in the Era of Abolition.* Pittsburgh: University of Pittsburgh Press, 1977.

Dunn, Richard S. *Sugar and Slaves: The Rise of the Planter Class in the English West Indies, 1624–1713.* Chapel Hill: University of North Carolina Press, 1972.

Dury, G. H., ed. *Rivers and River Terraces.* London: Macmillan, 1970.

Eatwell, John, Murray Milgate, and Peter Newman, eds. *The New Palgrave: A Dictionary of Economics.* London: Macmillan, 1987.

Edgeworth, Maria. *The Absentee.* Edited by W. J. McCormack and Kim Walker. Oxford: Oxford University Press, 1988.

Edwards, Bryan. *The History, Civil and Commercial, of the British West Indies.* 5th ed. London: G. and W. B. Whittaker, 1819.

Eisner, Gisela. *Jamaica, 1830–1930: A Study in Economic Growth.* Manchester: Manchester University Press, 1961.

Ellis, Kenneth. *The Post Office in the Eighteenth Century: A Study in Administrative History.* London: Oxford University Press, 1958.

Eltis, David. "The Slave Economies of the Caribbean: Structure, Performance, Evolution and Significance". In *General History of the Caribbean.* Vol. 3, *The Slave Societies of the Caribbean,* edited by Franklin W. Knight, 105–37. London: UNESCO Publishing/Macmillan Education, 1997.

Eltis, David, and Stanley L. Engerman. "The Importance of Slavery and the Slave Trade to Industrializing Britain". *Journal of Economic History* 60 (2000): 123–44.

Eltis, David, Frank D. Lewis, and Kenneth L. Sokoloff. Introduction to *Slavery in the Development of the Americas,* edited by David Eltis, Frank D. Lewis and Kenneth L. Sokoloff. Cambridge: Cambridge University Press, 2004.

Eltis, David, and David Richardson. "Productivity in the Transatlantic Slave Trade". *Explorations in Economic History* 32 (1995): 465–84.

Engerman, Stanley L. "The Slave Trade and British Capital Formation in the Eighteenth Century: A Comment on the Williams Thesis". *Business History Review* 46 (1972): 430–43.

Engerman, Stanley L., and B. W. Higman. "The Demographic Structure of the Caribbean Slave Societies in the Eighteenth and Nineteenth Centuries". In *General History of the Caribbean.* Vol. 3, *The Slave Societies of the Caribbean,* edited by Franklin W. Knight, 45–104. London: UNESCO Publishing/Macmillan Education, 1997.

English, Barbara. *The Great Landowners of East Yorkshire, 1530–1910.* New York: Harvester/Wheatsheaf, 1990.

Fayle, C. Ernest. *A Short History of the World's Shipping Industry.* London: George Allen and Unwin, 1933.

Field-Hendrey, Elizabeth B., and Lee A. Craig. "The Relative Efficiency of Free and Slave Agriculture in the Antebellum United States: A Stochastic Production Frontier Approach". In *Slavery in the Development of the Americas,* edited by David Eltis, Frank D. Lewis, and Kenneth L. Sokoloff, 236–57. Cambridge: Cambridge University Press, 2004.

Finkelman, Paul. *Slavery and the Founders: Race and Liberty in the Age of Jefferson.* New York: M. E. Sharpe, 2001.

Finley, M. I. *Economy and Society in Ancient Greece.* Harmondsworth: Penguin, 1983.

Fleischman, Richard K., David Oldroyd, and Thomas N. Tyson. "Monetizing Human Life: Slave Valuations on United States and British West Indian Plantations". *Accounting History* 9 (2004): 35–62.

Fleischman, Richard K., and Thomas N. Tyson. "Accounting in Service to Racism: Monetizing Slave Property in the Antebellum South". *Critical Perspectives on Accounting* 15 (2004): 376–99.

Fleischman, Richard K., Vaughan S. Radcliffe, and Paul A. Shoemaker, eds. *Doing Accounting History: Contributions to the Development of Accounting Thought.* Oxford: Elsevier Science, 2003.

Fleisig, Heywood. "Comment on Paper by Aufhauser". *Journal of Economic History* 34 (1974): 79–83.

Fogel, Robert William. *Without Consent or Contract: The Rise and Fall of American Slavery.* New York: W. W. Norton and Co., 1989.

Fogel, Robert William. *The Slavery Debates, 1952–1990: A Retrospective.* Baton Rouge: Louisiana State University Press, 2003.

Fogel, Robert William, and Stanley L. Engerman. *Time on the Cross: The Economics of American Negro Slavery.* Boston: Little Brown, 1974.

Force, Pierre. *Self-Interest Before Adam Smith: A Genealogy of Economic Science.* Cambridge: Cambridge University Press, 2003.

Foster, Thomas. *The Postal History of Jamaica.* London: R. Rowe, 1968.

Frederico, Giovanni. "Landlordism". In *The Oxford Encyclopedia of Economic History,* edited by Joel Mokyr, 3: 264–66. New York: Oxford University Press, 2003.

Furness, A. E. "George Hibbert and the Defence of Slavery in the West Indies". *Jamaican Historical Review* 5 (1965): 56–70.

Galenson, David W. *Traders, Planters, and Slaves: Market Behavior in Early English America.* Cambridge: Cambridge University Press, 1986.

Gallman, Robert E. "Economic Growth and Structural Change in the Long Nineteenth Century". In *The Cambridge Economic History of the United States.* Vol. 2, *The Long Nineteenth Century,* edited by Stanley L. Engerman and Robert E. Gallman, 1–55. Cambridge: Cambridge University Press, 2000.

Galloway, J. H. "Tradition and Innovation in the American Sugar Industry, *c.*1500–1800: An Explanation". *Annals of the Association of American Geographers* 75 (1985): 334–51.

Galloway, J. H. *The Sugar Cane Industry: An Historical Geography from Its Origins to 1914.* Cambridge: Cambridge University Press, 1989.

Gardner, W. J. *A History of Jamaica.* 1873. Reprint, London: Frank Cass and Co., 1971.

Gaur, Albertine. *A History of Writing.* New York: Cross River Press, 1992.

Geggus, David Patrick. *Slavery, War, and Revolution: The British Occupation of Saint Domingue 1793–1798.* Oxford: Clarendon Press, 1982.

Geggus, David. "The Enigma of Jamaica in the 1790s: New Light on the Causes of Slave Rebellions". *William and Mary Quarterly* 44 (1987): 274–99.

Gemery, H. A., and J. S. Hogendorn. "Technological Change, Slavery, and the Slave trade". In *The Imperial Impact: Studies in the Economic History of Africa and India,* edited by Clive Dewey and A. G. Hopkins, 243–58. London: University of London, 1978.

Genovese, Eugene D. *Roll, Jordan, Roll: The World the Slaves Made.* New York: Pantheon Books, 1974.

George, Claude S., Jr. *The History of Management Thought.* Englewood Cliffs, NJ: Prentice-Hall, 1968.

Gordon, William. *The Universal Accountant, and Complete Merchant.* Edinburgh: Alexander Donaldson, 1765.

Goveia, Elsa V. *Slave Society in the British Leeward Islands at the End of the Eighteenth Century.* New Haven: Yale University Press, 1965.

Grant, V. B. *Jamaican Land Law.* Master of Laws diss., University of London, 1948. Published 1957.

Grassby, Richard. *Kinship and Capitalism: Marriage, Family, and Business in the English-Speaking World, 1580–1740*. Cambridge: Cambridge University Press, 2001.

Gray, Lewis Cecil. *History of Agriculture in the Southern United States to 1860*. Washington: Carnegie Institution of Washington, 1933.

Green, W. A. "The Planter Class and British West Indian Sugar Production, before and after Emancipation". *Economic History Review* 26 (1973): 448–63.

Greene, Jack P. "The Jamaica Privilege Controversy, 1764–66: An Episode in the Process of Constitutional Definition in the Early Modern British Empire". *Journal of Imperial and Commonwealth History* 22 (1994): 16–53.

Gupta, Avijit. "Stream Characteristics in Eastern Jamaica, an Environment of Seasonal Flow and Large Floods". *American Journal of Science* 275 (1975): 825–47.

Hainsworth, D. R. *Stewards, Lords and People: The Estate Steward and His World in Later Stuart England*. Cambridge: Cambridge University Press, 1992.

Hakewill, James. *A Picturesque Tour of the Island of Jamaica, from drawings made in the years 1820 and 1821*. London: Hurst and Robinson, 1825.

Hall, Catherine. *Civilising Subjects: Metropole and Colony in the English Imagination, 1830–1867*. Cambridge: Polity Press, 2002.

Hall, Douglas. *Free Jamaica 1838–1865: An Economic History*. New Haven: Yale University Press, 1959.

Hall, Douglas. "Incalculability as a Feature of Sugar Production during the Eighteenth Century". *Social and Economic Studies* 10 (1961): 340–52.

Hall, Douglas. "Slaves and Slavery in the British West Indies". *Social and Economic Studies* 11 (1962): 305–18.

Hall, Douglas. "Absentee-Proprietorship in the British West Indies, to about 1850". *Jamaican Historical Review* 4 (1964): 15–35.

Hall, Douglas. *A Brief History of the West India Committee*. Barbados: Caribbean Universities Press, 1971.

Hall, Douglas. "Bountied European Immigration with Special Reference to the German Settlement at Seaford Town up to 1850". *Jamaica Journal* 9, no. 1 (1975): 2–9.

Hall, Douglas. "The Flight from the Estates Reconsidered: The British West Indies, 1838–42". *Journal of Caribbean History* 10–11 (1978): 7–24.

Hall, Douglas. *In Miserable Slavery: Thomas Thistlewood in Jamaica, 1750–86*. London: Macmillan, 1989.

Hall, N. A. T. "Some Aspects of the Deficiency Question in Jamaica in the Eighteenth Century". *Jamaica Journal* 7, nos. 1–2 (1973): 36–41.

Hall, Peter, ed. *Von Thünen's Isolated State*. Oxford: Pergamon Press, 1966.

Halliday, Ursula. "The Slave Owner as Reformer: Theory and Practice at Castle Wemyss Estate, Jamaica, 1808–1823". *Journal of Caribbean History* 30 (1996): 65–82.

Hammond, Theresa. "History from Accounting's Margins: International Research on Race and Gender". *Accounting History* 8 (2003): 9–24.

Hancock, David. *Citizens of the World: London Merchants and the Integration of the British Atlantic Community, 1735–1785*. Cambridge: Cambridge University Press, 1995.

Harkin, Maureen. "Matthew Lewis's Journal of a West India Proprietor: Surveillance and Space on the Plantation". *Nineteenth-Century Contexts* 24 (2002): 139–50.

Harris, J. R. "Copper and Shipping in the Eighteenth Century". *Economic History Review* 19 (1966): 550–68.

Hausman, Daniel M., and Michael S. McPherson. *Economic Analysis and Moral Philosophy.* Cambridge: Cambridge University Press, 1996.

Hawkes, Alex D. "Plantain Garden Area, Scenic and Impressive", *Daily Gleaner,* 20 November 1975, 3.

Headrick, Daniel R. *The Tools of Empire: Technology and European Imperialism in the Nineteenth Century.* New York: Oxford University Press, 1981.

Heuman, Gad J. *Between Black and White: Race, Politics, and the Free Coloreds in Jamaica, 1792–1865.* Westport, Connecticut: Greenwood Press, 1981.

Heuman, Gad. *"The Killing Time": The Morant Bay Rebellion in Jamaica.* London: Macmillan, 1994.

Higgins, Andrew J., and Russell C. Muchow, "Assessing the Potential Benefits of Alternative Cane Supply Arrangements in the Australian Sugar Industry". *Agricultural Systems* 76 (2003): 623–38.

Higgs, Henry, ed. *Palgrave's Dictionary of Political Economy.* London: Macmillan, 1925.

Higman, B. W. "The West India 'Interest' in Parliament, 1807–1833". *Historical Studies* 13 (1967): 1–19.

Higman, B. W. *Slave Population and Economy in Jamaica, 1807–1834.* Cambridge: Cambridge University Press, 1976.

Higman, B. W. "Slavery Remembered: The Celebration of Emancipation in Jamaica". *Journal of Caribbean History* 12 (1979): 55–74.

Higman, B. W., ed. *The Jamaican Censuses of 1844 and 1861.* Mona, Jamaica: Social History Project, University of the West Indies, 1980.

Higman, B. W. "Slavery and the Development of Demographic Theory in the Age of the Industrial Revolution". In *Slavery and British Society 1776–1846,* edited by James Walvin, 164–94. London: Macmillan, 1982.

Higman, B. W. *Slave Populations of the British Caribbean, 1807–1834.* Baltimore: Johns Hopkins University Press, 1984.

Higman, B. W. "The Spatial Economy of Jamaican Sugar Plantations: Cartographic Evidence from the Eighteenth and Nineteenth Centuries". *Journal of Historical Geography* 13 (1987): 17–39.

Higman, B. W. *Jamaica Surveyed: Plantation Maps and Plans of the Eighteenth and Nineteenth Centuries.* Kingston: Institute of Jamaica Publications, 1988.

Higman, B. W. "Patterns of Exchange within a Plantation Economy: Jamaica at the Time of Emancipation". In *West Indies Accounts: Essays on the History of the British Caribbean and the Atlantic Economy in Honour of Richard Sheridan,* edited by Roderick A. McDonald, 211–31. Kingston: The Press, University of the West Indies, 1996.

Higman, B. W. *Montpelier, Jamaica: A Plantation Community in Slavery and Freedom, 1739–1912.* Kingston: The Press, University of the West Indies, 1998.

Higman, B. W. "Demography". In *A Historical Guide to World Slavery,* edited by Seymour Drescher and Stanley L. Engerman, 168–74. New York: Oxford University Press, 1998.

Higman, B. W. "The Sugar Revolution". *Economic History Review* 53 (2000): 213–36.

Higman, B. W. "Ideas and Illustrations in the Historical Thought of Douglas Hall". *Journal of Caribbean History* 35 (2001): 66–79.

Higman, B. W. " 'To Begin the World Again': Responses to Emancipation at Friendship and Greenwich Estate, Jamaica". In *Jamaica in Slavery and Freedom: History, Heritage and Culture,* edited by Kathleen E. A. Monteith and Glen Richards, 291–306. Kingston: University of the West Indies Press, 2002.

Higman, B. W. "The Letterbooks of Isaac Jackson, Jamaican Planting Attorney, 1839–1843". *Journal of Caribbean History* 37 (2003): 317–29.

Hollis, Martin. *Reason in Action: Essays in the Philosophy of Social Science.* Cambridge: Cambridge University Press, 1996.

Holt, Thomas C. *The Problem of Freedom: Race, Labor, and Politics in Jamaica and Britain, 1832–1938.* Baltimore: Johns Hopkins University Press, 1992.

Hopwood, Stephen. "Three Hundred Years of Postal Service in Jamaica". *Jamaica Journal* 5, nos. 2–3 (1971): 11–16.

Howard de Walden, Lord. *General Instructions for Montpelier and Ellis Caymanas Estates in Jamaica.* Privately printed, June 1852.

Hribal, Jason. " 'Animals Are Part of the Working Class': A Challenge to Labor History". *Labor History* 44 (2003): 435–53.

Hudson, Pat. "Industrial Organisation and Structure". In *The Cambridge Economic History of Modern Britain.* Vol. 1, *Industrialisation, 1700–1860,* edited by Roderick Floud and Paul Johnson, 28–56. Cambridge: Cambridge University Press, 2004.

Hughes, Edward. "The Eighteenth-Century Estate Agent". In *Essays in British and Irish History in Honour of James Eadie Todd,* edited by H. A. Cronne, T. W. Moody and D. B. Quinn, 185–99. London: Frederick Muller, 1949.

Ingram, K. E. *Manuscripts Relating to Commonwealth Caribbean Countries in United States and Canadian Repositories.* Barbados: Caribbean Universities Press, 1975.

Ingram, K. E. *Sources of Jamaican History 1655–1838.* Zug, Switzerland: Inter Documentation Co., 1976.

Ingram, K. E. *Manuscript Sources for the History of the West Indies.* Kingston: University of the West Indies Press, 2000.

Inikori, Joseph E. *Africans and the Industrial Revolution in England: A Study in International Trade and Development.* Cambridge: Cambridge University Press, 2002.

Jacobs, H. P. *Sixty Years of Change, 1806–1866: Progress and Reaction in Kingston and the Countryside.* Kingston: Institute of Jamaica, 1973.

Jansen, P. Ph., L. van Bendegom, J. van den Berg, M. de Vries, and A. Zanen, eds. *Principles of River Engineering: The Non-Tidal Alluvial River.* London: Pitman, 1979.

Johnson, Howard. "Introduction: Edward Long, Historian of Jamaica". In Edward Long, *The History of Jamaica,* 1: i–xxv. Kingston: Ian Randle Publishers, 2002.

Jones, Alice Hanson. *Wealth of a Nation to Be: The American Colonies on the Eve of the Revolution.* New York: Columbia University Press, 1980.

Jones, Donald W., and John R. Krummel. "The Location Theory of the Plantation". *Journal of Regional Science* 27 (1987): 157–82.

Jones, Haydn. *Accounting, Costing and Cost Estimation: Welsh Industry, 1700–1830.* Cardiff: University of Wales Press, 1985.

Juchau, Roger. "Early Cost Accounting Ideas in Agriculture: The Contributions of Arthur Young". *Accounting, Business and Financial History* 12 (2002): 369–86.

Karras, Alan. "The World of Alexander Johnston: The Creolization of Ambition, 1762–1787". *Historical Journal* 30 (1987): 53–76.

Karras, Alan L. *Sojourners in the Sun: Scottish Migrants in Jamaica and the Chesapeake, 1740–1800*. Ithaca: Cornell University Press, 1992.

Karsten, Peter. *Between Law and Custom: "High" and "Low" Legal Cultures in the Lands of the British Diaspora – The United States, Canada, Australia, and New Zealand, 1600–1900*. Cambridge: Cambridge University Press, 2002.

Klapinsky, Raphael. *Cane Sugar: The Small-Scale Processing Option*. London: Intermediate Technology Publications, 1989.

Klein, Herbert S. *The Middle Passage: Comparative Studies in the Atlantic Slave Trade*. Princeton: Princeton University Press, 1978.

Knighton, David. *Fluvial Forms and Processes: A New Perspective*. London: Arnold, 1998.

Laborie, P. J. *The Coffee Planter of Saint Domingo*. London: T. Cadell and W. Davies, 1798.

Laughlin, Richard. "Critical Accounting: Nature, Progress and Prognosis". *Accounting, Auditing and Accountability Journal* 12 (1999): 73–78.

Lazarus-Black, Mindie. "John Grant's Jamaica: Notes Towards a Reassessment of Courts in the Slave Era". *Journal of Caribbean History* 27 (1993): 144–59.

Lewis, Matthew Gregory. *Journal of a West India Proprietor*. London: John Murray, 1834.

Lindsay, Jean. *A History of the North Wales Slate Industry*. Newton Abbot: David and Charles, 1974.

Lindsay, Jean. "The Pennants and Jamaica 1665–1808: Part I, The Growth and Organisation of the Pennant Estate". *Transactions of the Caernarfonshire Historical Society* 43 (1982): 37–82.

Lindsay, Jean. "The Pennants and Jamaica 1665–1808: Part II, The Economic and Social Development of the Pennant Estates in Jamaica". *Transactions of the Caernarfonshire Historical Society* 44 (1983): 59–96.

Linebaugh, Peter, and James Rediker. *The Many-headed Hydra: Sailors, Slaves, Commoners, and the Hidden History of the Revolutionary Atlantic*. Boston: Beacon Press, 2000.

Littleton, A. C. *Accounting Evolution to 1900*. New York: Russell and Russell, 1966.

Lobdell, Richard A. "Patterns of Investment and Sources of Credit in the British West Indian Sugar Industry, 1838–97". *Journal of Caribbean History* 4 (1972): 31–53.

Long, Andrew. *Powers of Attorney and Other Instruments Conferring Authority*. Cambridge: ICSA Publishing, 1987.

Long, Edward. *The History of Jamaica*. London: T. Lowndes, 1774.

Longfield, Mountifort. *Three Lectures on Commerce and one on Absenteeism, Delivered in Michaelmas Term, 1834, before the University of Dublin*. Dublin: Milliken and Son, 1835.

McCalman, Iain. *Radical Underworld: Prophets, Revolutionaries and Pornographers in London, 1795–1840*. Cambridge: Cambridge University Press, 1988.

McCalman, Iain, ed. *The Horrors of Slavery and Other Writings by Robert Wedderburn*. New York: Markus Wiener, 1991.

McClellan, James E., III. *Colonialism and Science: Saint Domingue in the Old Regime*. Baltimore: Johns Hopkins University Press, 1992.

McCulloch, J. R. *Treatises and Essays on Money, Exchange, Interest, the Letting of Land, Absenteeism, the History of Commerce, Manufactures, etc.* Edinburgh: Adam and Charles Black, 1859.

McCusker, John J. "Weights and Measures in the Colonial Sugar Trade: The Gallon and the Pound and Their International Equivalents". *William and Mary Quarterly* 30 (1973): 599–624.

McCusker, John J. *Essays in the Economic History of the Atlantic World.* London: Routledge, 1997.

McCusker, John J., and Russell R. Menard. *The Economy of British America, 1607–1789.* Chapel Hill: University of North Carolina Press, 1985.

McGeachy, Edward. *Suggestions towards a general plan of Rapid Communication by Steam Navigation and Railways: Shortening the time of transit between the eastern and western hemispheres.* London: Smith, Elder and Co., 1846.

Mackay, David. "Banks, Bligh and Breadfruit". *New Zealand Journal of History* 8 (1974): 61–77.

MacQueen, James. *A General Plan for a Mail Communication by Steam: Between Great Britain and the Eastern and Western Parts of the World.* London: B. Fellowes, 1838.

Madden, R. R. *A Twelvemonth's Residence in the West Indies, during the Transition from Slavery to Apprenticeship.* London: James Cochrane and Co., 1835.

Maguire, W. A. *The Downshire Estates in Ireland, 1801–1845: The Management of Irish Landed Estates in the Early Nineteenth Century.* Oxford: Clarendon Press, 1972.

Malcolm, Alexander. *A Treatise of Book-keeping, or, Merchants Accounts; in the Italian Method of Debtor and Creditor.* London: J. Osborn and T. Longman, 1731. Reprint, New York: Garland, 1986.

Malcolmson, A. P. W. "Absenteeism in Eighteenth Century Ireland". *Irish Economic and Social History* 1 (1974): 15–35.

Marglin, Stephen A. "What Do Bosses Do? The Origins and Functions of Hierarchy in Capitalist Production". In *The Division of Labour: The Labour Process and Class-Struggle in Modern Capitalism* edited by André Gorz, 13–54. Atlantic Highlands, NJ: Humanities Press, 1976.

Marsden, Peter. *An Account of the Island of Jamaica.* Newcastle: The author, 1788.

Marshall, Woodville K. "A 'Valued Pamphlet': Henry James Ross's Rationale for Sharecropping in the West Indies". *Slavery and Abolition* 24 (2003): 82–111.

Marx, Karl. *Capital.* London: Dent, Everyman's Library, 1972 [1867].

Mason, Keith. "The World an Absentee Planter and His Slaves Made: Sir William Stapleton and His Nevis Sugar Estate, 1722–1740". *Bulletin of the John Rylands University Library of Manchester* 75 (1993): 103–31.

Mathias, Peter. "The Lawyer as Businessman in Eighteenth-Century England". In *Enterprise and History: Essays in Honour of Charles Wilson,* edited by D. C. Coleman and Peter Mathias, 151–67. Cambridge: Cambridge University Press, 1984.

Maunder, W. F. "Notes on the Development of Internal Transport in Jamaica". *Social and Economic Studies* 3 (1954): 161–85.

Melton, Frank T. "Absentee Land Management in Seventeenth-Century England". *Agricultural History* 52 (1978): 147–59.

Mepham, Michael J. *Accounting in Eighteenth Century Scotland.* New York: Garland, 1988.

Mepham, Michael J. "The Scottish Enlightenment and the Development of Accounting". *Accounting Historians Journal* 15 (1988): 151–76.

Merivale, Herman. *Lectures on Colonization and Colonies.* London: Longman, Green, Longman, and Roberts, 1861.

Metcalf, George. *Royal Government and Political Conflict in Jamaica 1729–1783.* London: Longmans, 1965.

Metzer, Jacob. "Rational Management, Modern Business Practices, and Economies of Scale in the Ante-Bellum Southern Plantations". *Explorations in Economic History* 12 (1975): 123–50.

Miles, M. "The Money Market in the Early Industrial Revolution: The Evidence from West Riding Attorneys *c.*1750–1800". *Business History* 23 (1981): 127–46.

Miles, Michael. " 'Eminent Practitioners': The New Visage of Country Attorneys *c.*1750–1800". In *Law, Economy and Society, 1750–1914: Essays in the History of English Law,* edited by G. R. Rubin and David Sugarman, 470–503. Abingdon, UK: Professional Books Limited, 1984.

Miles, Michael. " 'A Haven for the Privileged': Recruitment into the Profession of Attorney in England, 1709–1792". *Social History* 11 (1986): 197–210.

Millás, José Carlos. *Hurricanes of the Caribbean and Adjacent Regions, 1492–1800.* Miami: Academy of the Arts and Sciences of the Americas, 1968.

Mingay, G. E. *English Landed Society in the Eighteenth Century.* London: Routledge and Kegan Paul, 1963.

Mintz, Sidney W. *Sweetness and Power: The Place of Sugar in Modern History.* New York: Viking Penguin, 1985.

Montgomery, William Ernest. *The History of Land Tenure in Ireland.* Cambridge: Cambridge University Press, 1889.

Moreton, J. B. *West India Customs and Manners.* London: J. Parson, W. Richardson, H. Gardner and J. Walter, 1793.

Morgan, Kenneth. *Bristol and the Atlantic in the Eighteenth Century.* Cambridge: Cambridge University Press, 1993.

Morgan, Kenneth. *Slavery, Atlantic Trade and the British Economy, 1660–1800.* Cambridge: Cambridge University Press, 2000.

Morgan, Lady Sydney. *Absenteeism.* London: Henry Colburn, 1825.

Moriarty, Thomas F. "The Irish Absentee Tax Controversy of 1773: A Study in Anglo-Irish Politics on the Eve of the American Revolution". *Proceedings of the American Philosophical Society* 118 (1974): 370–408.

Murray, D. J. *The West Indies and the Development of Colonial Government 1801–1834.* Oxford: Clarendon Press, 1965.

Napier, Christopher J. "Aristocratic Accounting: The Bute Estate in Glamorgan 1814–1880". *Accounting and Business Research* 21 (1991): 163–74.

Newman, Peter C. *Caesars of the Wilderness: Company of Adventurers.* Vol. 2. Markham, Ontario: Penguin Books Canada, 1987.

Nir, Zeev. "Hydraulics of Open Channels". In *CRC Handbook of Irrigation Technology,* edited by Herman J. Finkel, 1: 93–143. Boca Raton, Fla.: CRC Press, 1982.

Nobes, Christopher, ed. *The Development of Double Entry: Selected Essays.* New York: Garland, 1984.

O'Brien, D. P. *The Classical Economists.* Oxford: Clarendon Press, 1975.

Offer, Avner. "Farm Tenure and Land Values in England, *c.*1750–1950". *Economic History Review* 44 (1991): 1–20.

Oldroyd, David. "John Johnson's Letters: The Accounting Role of Tudor Merchants' Correspondence". *Accounting Historians Journal* 25 (1998): 57–72.

Oldroyd, David. "Through a Glass Clearly: Management Practice on the Bowes Family Estates *c.*1700–70 as Revealed by the Accounts". *Accounting, Business and Financial History* 9 (1999): 175–201.

Ormrod, Richard K. "The Evolution of Soil Management Practices in Early Jamaican Sugar Planting". *Journal of Historical Geography* 5 (1979): 157–70.

O'Shaughnessy, Andrew J. "The Stamp Act Crisis in the British Caribbean". *William and Mary Quarterly* 51 (1994): 203–26.

O'Shaughnessy, Andrew J. "The West India Interest and the Crisis of American Independence". In *West Indies Accounts: Essays on the History of the British Caribbean and the Atlantic Economy in Honour of Richard Sheridan,* edited by Roderick A. McDonald, 126–48. Kingston: The Press, University of the West Indies, 1996.

O'Shaughnessy, Andrew J. *An Empire Divided: The American Revolution and the British Caribbean.* Philadelphia: University of Pennsylvania Press, 2000.

Owen, J. R. "The Post Office Packet Service, 1821–37: Development of a Steam-Powered Fleet". *Mariner's Mirror* 88 (2002): 155–75.

Paley, William. *A Treatise on the Law of Principal and Agent, Chiefly with Reference to Mercantile Transactions.* Philadelphia: John S. Littell, 1840.

Pares, Richard. *War and Trade in the West Indies, 1739–1763.* Oxford: Clarendon Press, 1936.

Pares, Richard. *A West-India Fortune.* London: Longmans, 1950.

Pares, Richard. *Yankees and Creoles: The Trade between North America and the West Indies before the American Revolution.* London: Longmans, Green and Co., 1956.

Pares, Richard. "The London Sugar Market, 1740–1769". *Economic History Review* 9 (1956): 254–70.

Pares, Richard. "A London West-India Merchant House, 1740–1769". In *Essays Presented to Sir Lewis Namier,* edited by Richard Pares and A. J. P. Taylor, 75–107. London: Macmillan and Co., 1956.

Pares, Richard. *Merchants and Planters. Economic History Review* supplement No. 4, 1960.

Patterson, Orlando. *The Sociology of Slavery: An Analysis of the Origins, Development and Structure of Negro Slave Society in Jamaica.* London: MacGibbon and Kee, 1967.

Pawson, Michael, and David Buisseret. *Port Royal, Jamaica.* Oxford: Clarendon Press, 1975.

Pearce, David W., ed. *The MIT Dictionary of Modern Economics.* Cambridge, Massachusetts: The MIT Press, 1992.

Pearsall, Sarah M. S. " 'The Late Flagrant Instance of Depravity in My Family': The Story of an Anglo-Jamaican Cuckold". *William and Mary Quarterly* 60 (2003): 549–82.

Pennington, James. *The Currency of the British Colonies.* London: Her Majesty's Stationery Office, 1848.

Penson, Lillian M. "The London West India Interest in the Eighteenth Century". *English Historical Review* 36 (1921): 373–92.

Penson, Lillian M. *The Colonial Agents of the British West Indies: A Study in Colonial Administration mainly in the Eighteenth Century.* London: University of London Press, 1924.

Phillips, C. H. "The East India Company 'Interest' and the English Government, 1783–4". *Transactions of the Royal Historical Society,* 4th ser., 20 (1937): 83–101.

Phillips, C. H. *The East India Company, 1784–1834*. Manchester: Manchester University Press, 1940.

Pitman, Frank Wesley. *The Development of the British West Indies 1700–1763*. New Haven: Yale University Press, 1917.

Pitman, Frank W. "The West Indian Absentee Planter as a British Colonial Type". *American Historical Association Pacific Coast Branch Proceedings* (1927): 113–27.

Plantation Systems of the New World. Washington, DC: Pan American Union, 1959.

Pollard, Sidney. *The Genesis of Modern Management: A Study of the Industrial Revolution in Great Britain*. London: Edward Arnold, 1965.

Priest, George L. "The History of the Postal Monopoly in the United States". *Journal of Law and Economics* 18 (1975): 33–80.

Pudney, John. *London's Docks*. London: Thames and Hudson, 1975.

Quinn, Stephen. "Money, Finance and Capital Markets". In *The Cambridge Economic History of Modern Britain*. Vol. 1, *Industrialisation, 1700–1860,* edited by Roderick Floud and Paul Johnson, 147–74. Cambridge: Cambridge University Press, 2004.

Ragatz, Lowell Joseph. *The Fall of the Planter Class in the British Caribbean, 1763–1833*. New York: American Historical Association, 1928.

Ragatz, Lowell Joseph. "Absentee Landlordism in the British Caribbean, 1750–1833". *Agricultural History* 5 (1931): 7–24.

Ranston, Jackie. *The Lindo Legacy*. London: Toucan Books, 2000.

Raven, James. *Judging New Wealth: Popular Publishing and Responses to Commerce in England, 1750–1800*. Oxford: Clarendon Press, 1992.

Razek, Joseph R. "Accounting on the Old Plantation: A Study of the Financial Records of an Ante-bellum Louisiana Sugar Planter". *Accounting Historians Journal* 12 (1985): 17–36.

Reynolds, John. *Windmills and Watermills*. London: Hugh Evelyn, 1985.

Reynolds, Terry S. *Stronger than a Hundred Men: A History of the Vertical Water Wheel*. Baltimore: Johns Hopkins University Press, 1983.

Richards, Eric. "The Land Agent". In *The Victorian Countryside,* edited by G. E. Mingay, 2: 439–56. London: Routledge and Kegan Paul, 1981.

Richards, Eric. *Patrick Sellar and the Highland Clearances: Homicide, Eviction and the Price of Progress*. Edinburgh: Polygon at Edinburgh, 1999.

Richards, Eric, and Monica Clough. *Cromartie: Highland Life, 1650–1914*. Aberdeen: Aberdeen University Press, 1989.

Robert, André. *River Processes: An Introduction to Fluvial Dynamics*. London: Arnold, 2003.

Robinson, Howard. *The British Post Office: A History*. Princeton: Princeton University Press, 1948.

Robinson, Howard. *Carrying British Mails Overseas*. London: George Allen and Unwin, 1964.

Robson, Robert. *The Attorney in Eighteenth-Century England*. Cambridge: Cambridge University Press, 1959.

Roebuck, P. "Absentee Landownership in the Late Seventeenth and Early Eighteenth Centuries: A Neglected Factor in English Agrarian History". *Agricultural History Review* 21 (1973): 1–17.

Roughley, Thomas. *The Jamaica Planter's Guide*. London: Longman, Hurst, Rees, Orme and Brown, 1823.

Rubinstein, W. D. *Men of Property: The Very Wealthy in Britain since the Industrial Revolution.* New Brunswick, NJ: Rutgers University Press, 1981.

Ryden, David Beck. "Does Decline Make Sense? The West Indian Economy and the Abolition of the British Slave Trade". *Journal of Interdisciplinary History* 31 (2001): 347–74.

Samper, Mario, and Radin Fernando. "Historical Statistics of Coffee Production and Trade from 1700 to 1960". In *The Global Coffee Economy in Africa, Asia, and Latin America, 1500–1989,* edited by William Gervase Clarence-Smith and Steven Topik, 411–62. Cambridge: Cambridge University Press, 2003.

Satchell, Veront. "Pattern of Abandonment of Sugar Estates in Jamaica during the Late Nineteenth Century. *Caribbean Geography* 2 (1989): 251–67.

Satchell, Veront M. "Early Use of Steam Power in the Jamaican Sugar Industry, 1768–1810". *Transactions of the Newcomen Society* 67 (1995–96): 221–31.

Satchell, Veront M., and Cezley Sampson. "The Rise and Fall of Railways in Jamaica, 1845–1975". *Journal of Transport History* 24 (2003): 1–21.

Scarborough, William Kauffman. *The Overseer: Plantation Management in the Old South.* Baton Rouge: Louisiana State University Press, 1966.

Scarborough, William Kauffman. *Masters of the Big House: Elite Slaveholders of the Mid-Nineteenth-Century South.* Baton Rouge: Louisiana State University Press, 2003.

Schuler, Monica. *"Alas, Alas, Kongo": A Social History of Indentured African Immigration into Jamaica, 1841–1865.* Baltimore: Johns Hopkins University Press, 1980.

Schwartz, Stuart B. *Sugar Plantations in the Formation of Brazilian Society: Bahia, 1550–1835.* Cambridge: Cambridge University Press, 1985.

Sen, Amartya. *Development as Freedom.* Oxford: Oxford University Press, 1999.

Senior, Bernard Martin. *Jamaica, As It Was, As It Is, and As It May Be.* London: T. Hurst, 1835.

Seymour, Susanne, Stephen Daniels and Charles Watkins. "Estate and Empire: Sir George Cornewall's Management of Moccas, Herefordshire, and La Taste, Grenada, 1771–1819". *Journal of Historical Geography* 24 (1998): 313–51.

Shaw, John. *Water Power in Scotland, 1550–1870.* Edinburgh: Donald, 1984.

Shepherd, Verene A. "Livestock and Sugar: Aspects of Jamaica's Agricultural Development from the Late Seventeenth to the Early Nineteenth Century", *Historical Journal* 34 (1991): 627–42.

Shepherd, Verene A. "Alternative Husbandry: Slaves and Free Labourers on Livestock Farms in Jamaica in the Eighteenth and Nineteenth Centuries". *Slavery and Abolition* 14 (1993): 41–66.

Shepherd, Verene A., and Kathleen E. A. Monteith. "Pen-Keepers and Coffee Farmers in a Sugar-Plantation Economy". In *Slavery Without Sugar: Diversity in Caribbean Economy and Society since the Seventeenth Century,* edited by Verene A. Shepherd, 82–101. Gainesville: University Press of Florida, 2002.

Sheridan, Richard B. "Letters from a Sugar Plantation in Antigua, 1739–1758". *Agricultural History* 31 (1957): 3–23.

Sheridan, R. B. "The Commercial and Financial Organization of the British Slave Trade, 1750–1807". *Economic History Review* 11 (1958): 249–63.

Sheridan, Richard B. "Samuel Martin, Innovating Sugar Planter of Antigua, 1750–1776". *Agricultural History* 34 (1960): 126–39.

Sheridan, Richard B. "Planter and Historian: The Career of William Beckford of Jamaica and England, 1744–1799". *Jamaican Historical Review* 4 (1964): 36–58.

Sheridan, Richard B. "The Wealth of Jamaica in the Eighteenth Century". *Economic History Review* 18 (1965): 292–311.

Sheridan, Richard B. "The Wealth of Jamaica in the Eighteenth Century: A Rejoinder". *Economic History Review* 21 (1968): 46–68.

Sheridan, Richard B. *The Development of the Plantations to 1750 and An Era of West Indian Prosperity 1750–1775.* Barbados: Caribbean Universities Press, 1970.

Sheridan, Richard B. "Planters and Merchants: The Oliver Family of Antigua and London 1716–1784". *Business History* 13 (1971): 104–13.

Sheridan, R. B. "Simon Taylor, Sugar Tycoon of Jamaica, 1740–1813". *Agricultural History* 45 (1971): 285–96.

Sheridan, Richard B. *Sugar and Slavery: An Economic History of the British West Indies, 1623–1775.* Barbados: Caribbean Universities Press, 1974.

Sheridan, Richard B. " 'Sweet Malefactor': The Social Costs of Slavery and Sugar in Jamaica and Cuba, 1807–1854". *Economic History Review* 29 (1976): 236–57.

Sheridan, Richard B. "The Crisis of Slave Subsistence in the British West Indies during the American Revolution". *William and Mary Quarterly* 33 (1976): 615–41.

Sheridan, Richard B. "The Role of the Scots in the Economy and Society of the West Indies". *Annals of the New York Academy of Sciences* 292 (1977): 94–106.

Sheridan, Richard B. *Doctors and Slaves: A Medical and Demographic History of Slavery in the British West Indies, 1680–1834.* Cambridge: Cambridge University Press, 1985.

Sheridan, Richard B. "Captain Bligh, the Breadfruit, and the Botanic Gardens of Jamaica". *Journal of Caribbean History* 23 (1989): 28–50.

Sheridan, Richard B. "Changing Sugar Technology and the Labour Nexus in the British Caribbean, 1750–1990, with Special Reference to Barbados and Jamaica". *New West Indian Guide* 63 (1989): 59–93.

Shields, Enid. *Vale Royal: The House and the People.* Kingston: Jamaican Historical Society, [1984].

Shipley, Sir Arthur E. *Islands, West Indian – Aegean.* London: Martin Hopkinson, 1924.

Smith, Adam. *An Inquiry into the Nature and Causes of the Wealth of Nations.* 1776. Edited by Edwin Cannan, London: Methuen, 1961.

Smith, S. D. "Sugar's Poor Relation: Coffee Planting in the British West Indies, 1720–1833". *Slavery and Abolition* 19 (1988): 68–89.

Smith, S. D. "*Merchants and Planters* Revisited", *Economic History Review* 55 (2002): 434–65.

Smith, S. D. "Coffee and the 'Poorer Sort of People' in Jamaica during the Period of African Enslavement". In *Slavery Without Sugar: Diversity in Caribbean Economy and Society since the Seventeenth Century,* edited by Verene A. Shepherd, 102–28. Gainesville: University Press of Florida, 2002.

Soltow, Lee. *Distribution of Wealth and Income in the United States in 1798.* Pittsburgh: University of Pittsburgh Press, 1989.

Spear, Percival. *The Nabobs: A Study of the Social Life of the English in Eighteenth Century India.* London: Oxford University Press, 1932.

Spedding, James. "The Jamaica Question". *Edinburgh Review* 69, no. 140 (July 1839): 527–56.

Spring, David. *The English Landed Estate in the Nineteenth Century: Its Administration.* Baltimore: Johns Hopkins University Press, 1963.

Stead, David R. "Risk and Risk Management in English Agriculture, *c.*1750–1850". *Economic History Review* 57 (2004): 334–61.

Steel, M. J. "A Philosophy of Fear: The World View of the Jamaican Plantocracy in a Comparative Perspective". *Journal of Caribbean History* 27 (1993): 1–20.

Steele, Ian K. *The English Atlantic 1675–1740: An Exploration of Communication and Community.* New York: Oxford University Press, 1986.

Stevenson, Simon. "Open Field or Enclosure? Peasants, Planters' Agents and Lawyers in Jamaica, 1866–1875". *Rural History* 12 (2001): 41–59.

Stewart, J. *A View of the Past and Present State of the Island of Jamaica.* Edinburgh: Oliver and Boyd, 1823.

Street, Kenneth. "The Estates of Jamaica: Jamaica Sugar Estates Ltd.". *West Indian Review,* 16 October 1954, 1–14.

Sturge, Joseph, and Thomas Harvey. *The West Indies in 1837.* London: Hamilton, Adams and Co., 1838.

Sunderland, David. *Managing the British Empire: The Crown Agents, 1833–1914.* Woodbridge, UK: The Boydell Press, for the Royal Historical Society, 2004.

Super, R. H. *Trollope in the Post Office.* Ann Arbor: University of Michigan Press, 1981.

Supple, Barry. *The Royal Exchange Assurance: A History of British Insurance, 1720–1970.* Cambridge: Cambridge University Press, 1970.

Swaminathan, Srividhya. "Developing the West Indian Proslavery Position after the Somerset Decision". *Slavery and Abolition* 24 (2003): 40–60.

Taylor, Clare. "The Journal of an Absentee Proprietor, Nathaniel Phillips of Slebech". *Journal of Caribbean History* 18 (1984): 67–82.

Terry, R. C. *A Trollope Chronology.* London: Macmillan, 1989.

Thomas, C. Y. "A Model of Pure Plantation Economy: Comment". *Social and Economic Studies* 17 (1968): 339–48.

Thomas, Helen. *Romanticism and Slave Narratives: Transatlantic Testimonies.* Cambridge: Cambridge University Press, 2000.

Thomas, Robert Paul. "The Sugar Colonies of the Old Empire: Profit or Loss for Great Britain?" *Economic History Review* 21 (1968): 30–45.

Thompson, F. M. L. "The End of a Great Estate". *Economic History Review* 8 (1955): 36–52.

Thompson, F. M. L. *English Landed Society in the Nineteenth Century.* London: Routledge and Kegan Paul, 1963.

Thoms, D. W. "The Mills Family: London Sugar Merchants of the Eighteenth Century". *Business History* 11 (1969): 3–10.

Tilman, Rick. *Thorstein Veblen and His Critics, 1891–1963: Conservative, Liberal, and Radical Perspectives.* Princeton: Princeton University Press, 1992.

Tomich, Dale W. *Slavery in the Circuit of Sugar: Martinique and the World Economy, 1830–1848.* Baltimore: Johns Hopkins University Press, 1990.

Trollope, Anthony. *The West Indies and the Spanish Main.* 1859. Reprint, Gloucester: Alan Sutton, 1985.

Turley, David. "British Antislavery Reassessed". In *Rethinking the Age of Reform: Britain 1780–1850,* edited by Arthur Burns and Joanna Innes, 182–99. Cambridge: Cambridge University Press, 2003.

Turner, Mary. "Planter Profits and Slave Rewards: Amelioration Reconsidered". In *West Indies Accounts: Essays on the History of the British Caribbean and the Atlantic Economy in Honour of Richard Sheridan,* edited by Roderick A. McDonald, 232–52. Kingston: The Press, University of the West Indies, 1996.

Tyson, Thomas N., Richard K. Fleischman, and David Oldroyd. "Theoretical Perspectives on Accounting for Labor on Slave Plantations of the USA and the British West Indies". *Accounting, Auditing and Accountability Journal* 17 (2004): 758–78.

Vaughan, W. E. *Landlords and Tenants in Mid-Victorian Ireland.* Oxford: Clarendon Press, 1994.

Veblen, Thorstein. *Absentee Ownership and Business Enterprise in Recent Times: The Case of America.* New York: B. W. Huebsch, 1923.

Ville, Simon. *The Rural Entrepreneurs: A History of the Stock and Station Agent Industry in Australia and New Zealand.* Cambridge: Cambridge University Press, 2000.

Waddell, Hope Masterton. *Twenty-nine Years in the West Indies and Central Africa.* London: T. Nelson and Sons, 1863.

Wagley, Charles. "Plantation-America: A Culture Sphere". In *Caribbean Studies: A Symposium* edited by Vera Rubin, 3–13. Seattle: University of Washington Press, 1960.

Walton, Gary M. "Sources of Productivity Change in American Colonial Shipping, 1675–1775". *Economic History Review* 20 (1967): 67–78.

Ward, J. R. "The Profitability of Sugar Planting in the British West Indies, 1650–1834". *Economic History Review* 31 (1978): 197–213.

Ward, J. R. *British West Indian Slavery, 1750–1834: The Process of Amelioration.* Oxford: Clarendon Press, 1988.

Watts, David. *The West Indies: Patterns of Development, Culture and Environmental Change since 1492.* Cambridge: Cambridge University Press, 1987.

Westerfield, Ray Bert. *Middlemen in English Business, Particularly between 1660 and 1760.* New Haven: Yale University Press, 1915.

Wilcox, Carol. *Sugar Water: Hawaii's Plantation Ditches.* Honolulu: University of Hawaii Press, 1996.

Williams, Eric. *Capitalism and Slavery.* Chapel Hill: University of North Carolina Press, 1944.

Williamson, Oliver E., and Sidney G. Winter, eds. *The Nature of the Firm: Origins, Evolution, and Development.* New York: Oxford University Press, 1991.

Wilmot, Swithin. "Emancipation in Action: Workers and Wage Conflict in Jamaica 1838–40". *Jamaica Journal* 19, no. 3 (1986): 55–62.

Wilmot, Swithin, ed. *Adjustments to Emancipation in Jamaica.* Mona, Jamaica: Social History Project, University of the West Indies, 1994.

Wolman, M. Gordon, and Luna B. Leopold. "Flood Plains". In *Rivers and River Terraces* edited by G. H. Dury, 166–96. London: Macmillan, 1970.

Wood, Betty, ed., with the assistance of T. R. Clayton and W. A. Speck. *The Letters of Simon Taylor of Jamaica to Chaloner Arcedekne, 1765–1775.* London: Cambridge University Press, for the Royal Historical Society, Camden Miscellany, Vol. 35, 2002.

Wood, Betty, and T. R. Clayton, "Slave Birth, Death and Disease on Golden Grove Plantation, Jamaica, 1765–1810". *Slavery and Abolition* 6 (1985): 99–121.

Woodson, Carter G. *Free Negro Owners of Slaves in the United States in 1830; Together with Absentee Ownership of Slaves in the United States in 1830.* 1924. Reprint, New York: Negro Universities Press, 1968.

Wootton, Charles W., and Mary Virginia Moore. "The Legal Status of Account Books in Colonial America". *Accounting History* 5 (2000): 33–58.

Wray, Leonard. *The Practical Sugar Planter.* London: Smith, Elder and Co., 1848.

Wright, Philip, ed. *Lady Nugent's Journal of Her Residence in Jamaica from 1801 to 1805.* Kingston: Institute of Jamaica, 1966.

Wright, Philip. *Monumental Inscriptions of Jamaica.* London: Society of Genealogists, 1966.

Wright, Philip. *Knibb "the Notorious": Slaves' Missionary 1803–1845.* London: Sidgwick and Jackson, 1973.

Yamey, B. S., H. C. Edey and Hugh W. Thompson. *Accounting in England and Scotland, 1543–1800: Double Entry in Exposition and Practice.* London: Sweet and Maxwell, 1963.

Yates, JoAnne. *Control Through Communication: The Rise of System in American Management.* Baltimore: Johns Hopkins University Press, 1989.

Dissertations

Pearsall, Sarah M. S. " 'After All These Revolutions': Epistolary Identities in an Atlantic World, 1760–1815". PhD diss., Harvard University, 2001.

Yates, Richard Croson. "The Cost of Ocean Transport between England and Jamaica, 1784–1788". PhD diss., University of Washington, 1969.

Index

Abandonment: of coffee, 282–83, 285; of estates, 19, 244, 261, 277, 282–84; of sugar, 235, 265, 273–76, 282, 285

Abolition. *See* Slavery; Slave trade

Absenteeism: and abolition of slavery, 55; and accountability, 94, 268, 292; and attorneys, 15–29, 41–42, 280; and communication, 123, 133, 147; critique of, 22–29, 41, 84, 222, 290–92; decline of, 18–19; defence of, 24–25, 27–28, 54; and enslaved people, 289–90; and government, 16–17, 19, 21–22; growth of, 18–19; and long-term investment, 111, 222, 280–81, 287; and management, 11, 15–29, 280–81, 290–92; of merchants, 16–17, 21; and modern historians, 26–29; and morality, 289–91; origins of, 7, 17–19; of proprietors, 7, 10, 17–22; of workers, 25–26

Absentees: and aristocracy, 20, 53; and attorneys, 41–43, 46–47, 51–53, 108–9, 140, 146, 164–65, 168, 280–82; British-born, 17–18; and communication, 53, 94–95, 97, 113–14; creole, 17, 140, 164; and ideas of home, 18, 21, 220; as innovators, 28–29, 287–88; knowledge of, 111–12, 249, 274; motivations of, 17–18; networks of, 46–47, 132; numbers of, 18–22, 55; merchant, 16–17, 21; permanent, 7, 17–18, 228; as planters, 36–37, 40; as politicians, 20–22, 42; as proprietors, 7, 36–37, 46–47, 52–53, 57, 64, 102–3, 106, 286; and slavery, 287–89; temporary, 7, 17, 22; transnational, 17–18; types of, 17–18; wealth of, 17–22, 159, 220, 274, 279, 281–82, 285–89

Accountability, 16–17, 31, 94, 97, 112–13, 268, 280, 292

Account books, 97–100, 174, 267

Accounting: and abolition of slavery, 95; and absenteeism, 28–29; and attorneys, 53, 83, 97–98; and book-keepers, 34; and correspondence, 113, 148; cost, 112, 246; critical, 94–95; efficiency, 93, 112; failures, 41–42, 100–101, 157, 267, 270–71; and management, 35, 102, 215; of merchants, 100–108; methods, 95–99, 106–8, 212–14, 267–69; and morality, 94; in plantation economy, 95–102; professional, 36; projections, 109; and slavery, 94–95; theory, 28–29. *See also* Charge and discharge; Double-entry; Master and steward

Accounts Current, 89, 97, 100, 151, 214, 267, 271–73

Accounts Produce: and absenteeism, 42–44, 281; and accounts current, 267–68, 270–71; and attorneys, 53; contents of, 42–43, 100, 206, 212–14; and internal exchange, 99, 109; as public records, 89, 97, 212, 267; required by law, 42–44, 212, 214

Administrators, 39, 42, 84, 98, 160

Admiralty (British), 121–22, 125–27, 130

Africans: indentured, 276, 238, 283; in Jamaica, 2, 6, 172, 217, 224, 233, 238, 293; languages of, 114; liberated, 238. *See also* Enslaved people; Slave trade

Agents: of absentees, 16, 18, 24, 43, 51, 55, 95; as attorneys, 22, 44, 51; defined, 35, 38, 42; distant, 10, 133; and enslaved people, 26; estate, 39; land, 36, 47, 54; local, 18, 40, 49, 163, 272; and management, 22, 26–27, 37, 205; and

Agents (*continued*)
  marketing, 10; metropolitan, 10, 271;
  and monitoring problem, 16, 281;
  planters', 38; professional, 33, 35–36; as
  representative, 38, 41; travelling, 292.
  See also Commission agents; Principal-
  agent problem
Agriculture: crops, 1–4, 19; exhibitions,
  265; output, 1–5; resources for, 1–6, 112,
  166–67, 195, 227–28; Jamaican system
  of, 4–5, 19; knowledge of, 27, 35,
  47–48, 92, 222; and management, 47,
  49–54, 111–12, 273–74; and
  monoculture, 15; plantation, 1-10,
  39–40, 53–54, 111, 194–97, 257–62;
  techniques in, 35, 288, 292
Albion: Estate, 143; Pen, 86
Allen, Robert, 153, 158
Allsopp, Richard, 32–33
Amelioration, 90, 197, 225, 290
American Revolution: and Jamaican
  planters, 6–7, 21, 152, 165, 217–18, 221,
  227, 274, 287; and post, 124; and
  starvation, 219; and trade, 40, 152, 219
Amity Hall Estate, 180, 187–88, 283
Anglesea Pen, 85, 88
Annisette, Marcia, 95
Antigua, 32, 122
Appleton, Raines Waite, 159
Apprentices, 51, 153
Apprenticeship, 81, 84, 86, 90, 152, 231,
  243, 258, 287
Aqueducts, 183, 228, 329n102
Arcedeckne, Andrew (father of
  Chaloner), 140, 147, 168, 173–75, 177,
  215–16, 220, 225
Arcedeckne, Andrew (son of Chaloner),
  220, 283
Arcedeckne, Anne, 147, 168, 173
Arcedeckne, Chaloner: as absentee, 137,
  140, 147–48, 164, 175, 193, 221, 280;
  attorneys of, 170–71, 272; biography of,
  147–48, 168, 170; correspondence of,
  140, 147–51, 161, 322n52; as entrepreneur, 164–65, 180, 196, 198–200, 222–26,
  287; and Golden Grove Estate, 168–226,

329n115; and management, 216–20;
  name of, 321n12; and risk, 209–10, 223;
  and slavery, 172, 225, 228, 280; wealth
  of, 173–74, 204–5, 280
Arcedeckne, Nicholas, 173
Arcedeckne, Robert, 173–75, 177, 327n34
Arcedeckne, Robin. *See* Robert
  Arcedeckne
Aristocracy, 20, 22, 29, 53, 141, 228, 271,
  278
Assembly. *See* House of Assembly
Atherton, William, 61
Atlantic: British, 18, 20; shipping, 1, 114,
  117, 121–33, 149–50; slave trade, 63, 68,
  105, 116–17, 129, 145, 165, 172, 199–201,
  219–20, 225, 274; system, 3, 28, 69
Attorneys: and abolition of slavery, 55,
  84; and abolition of slave trade, 63;
  acting, 44–45; appointment of, 44–47;
  authority of, 44, 54, 109, 171–72,
  194–201, 204–9, 219, 221–26, 273, 278,
  280; birthplaces of, 77–78; children of,
  80–81, 143, 160, 164; and
  communication, 113–33; deference of,
  278; defined, 32–40; demography of,
  75–81, 164; domains of, 51, 65–75;
  education of, 78; employers of, 59–64,
  65, 68; estate, 15, 35, 40; families of,
  79–81, 144–45, 160, 164; functions of,
  40–41, 49–54, 92, 112, 158, 170–71,
  197–212, 221–27, 231–32, 240–44,
  247–48, 261–62, 274–76, 280;
  geographical distribution of, 57–61; of
  Jamaica, 11, 15–93; joint, 68, 70–71, 73,
  87, 154–55, 170–71, 221–22, 278;
  landownership of, 85, 140–42, 159–60,
  164, 168, 277, 286; large, 64–68, 83, 85,
  92–93, 288, 291; as lawyers, 34, 36–38,
  51, 173, 176; managing, 40; mercantile,
  39–40, 50, 52, 68, 72–73, 103, 146,
  170–71, 208, 278; multiple, 41, 57, 59,
  61, 63, 221–22; networks of, 72–75,
  277; numbers of, 55–69; plantation, 15,
  36, 138; planting, 15, 17, 39–93, 95, 100,
  103, 113, 146, 170, 208, 278;
  qualifications of, 47–49, 277;

recruitment of, 46–47, 77; regulation of, 41–44, 94; remuneration of, 41–43, 81–84, 156–57, 159, 171, 215, 222, 271, 277; residences of, 73, 75, 83, 85, 158–59, 276–77; rise and decline of, 55–56, 65; as slave owners, 85–88, 141–42, 164–65; status of, 88–91, 215, 271; success as managers, 221–26, 272–93; or travelling agents, 292; visits by, 50–51, 140, 151, 154, 156, 168, 170, 222, 276–77, 280; wealth of, 83–88, 164–65, 222, 271, 277

Attorneys-general, 64, 147, 244

Auditors, 35–36

Aylett, Philip, 39

Bachelors Hall Estate, 159

Bahamas, 125–26

Bailiffs, 33, 35–36, 54

Balance sheets, 96–97

Balcarres, Earl of, 69

Banks, 90, 95, 107, 272

Bankers, 84, 103, 146

Bankruptcy, 49, 280

Baptists, 90, 228, 233, 243

Barbados, 2, 17, 68, 122, 125–26, 130–31, 291

Barclay, Alexander, 89

Barrett, Richard, 86

Barrett, Samuel Gooding, 30, 282

Barristers, 38–39, 147

Batchelors Hall Pen, 167, 172, 184–85, 196, 206, 220, 228, 329n115

Bath, 166–67, 184

Bayley, Alexander, 85

Beans Estate, 153, 158–59

Beaumont, Augustus Hardin, 30, 37, 51, 77–78

Beckett, J. V., 20, 35–36, 53

Beckford, Francis Love, 220

Beckford, Harriet, 220

Beckford, William, 23, 33–34, 37, 47–49, 73, 81, 83, 92, 104–6, 108

Beeston Long and Company, 207

Belvidere Estate, 153, 158–59

Bernal, Ralph, 63, 114–15

Bernard, Thomas James, 70, 80, 85

Berryman, William, 120

Bills of exchange, 102–4, 106–9, 146, 170, 207, 214–15

Bills of lading, 99, 101, 103, 148–49, 151, 158, 207, 209, 160, 272

Blackburn, John, 65, 285

Black River, 90, 118, 120, 128–29

Blair, John, 85

Bleby, Henry, 51

Blue Mountains, 1, 57, 140, 166

Boiling-house books, 97–99

Bona Vista, 80, 237–38

Bonds, 39, 88, 145, 220

Book-keepers: and book-keeping, 33–34, 116; defined, 33–34; education of, 49; free coloured, 78; housing of, 192; mobility of, 152, 172; as plantation supervisors, 33–34, 116; as planters, 37, 91; qualifications of, 49; recruitment of, 50; remuneration of, 99, 265–66; status of, 91, 113–14, 217

Book-keeping. See Accounting

Boston, 17, 283

Boulton and Watt, 224, 288

Boundaries, property, 51, 176–81, 186, 188–90, 22

Bourke, Nicholas, 173–75

Brathwaite, Kamau, 28, 63, 83, 280

Brazil, 3, 6, 19

Bridges, Rev. George Wilson, 22

Bristol, 20, 130, 145, 150, 158, 207

British Guiana, 6, 32, 291

British North America: absentees from, 21; and attorneys, 44; and management, 11; politics in, 6, 22; population of, 1–2, 23; and post, 123–24, 132; product of, 2; trade of, 40, 108, 165, 206, 213, 218–19; visited, 174–75, 180; wealth of, 1, 22. See also American Revolution

British West Indies: and absenteeism, 19–21, 25–26; attorneys in, 32–33, 55; and British Army, 36; and British Empire, 3, 6; historiography of, 9, 26–28, 95, 272; as plantation colonies,

British West Indies (*continued*)
6, 10, 264, 281, 288; and politics,
21–22; and post, 122–33; trade of, 100,
208; wealth of, 3, 20–21, 287
Brown, Hamilton, 77, 87–88, 90
Brown, Thomas James, 46, 307n22
Browne, Patrick, 166, 184
Brutality, 3–5, 7, 27, 51–52, 165, 197–98,
221, 241, 277, 280, 287, 290
Brydon, James, 78
Buildings: burned, 152, 197; for enslaved
people, 193–94 ; for book-keepers, 192;
on estates, 4, 27, 52, 88, 111, 190–94,
269; on pens, 88; public, 27; works, 4,
167, 190–91, 199, 216–17, 223. *See also*
Houses
Buisseret, David, 16
Burchell, Thomas, 233, 243, 257
Burke, Edmund, 24
Burn, W. L., 48, 55, 63, 78, 82–83, 85
Burnard, Trevor, 28, 91
Burnt Ground Pen, 158–59
Butcheries, 196, 231–32, 265, 267, 270–71
Butler, Kathleen Mary, 56, 86
Byndloss, Matthew, 196

Cacoon Castle Pen, 157, 159–60
Campbell, Alexander, 152–53, 155, 158–59,
163, 237, 243, 247, 251, 258
Campbell, John, 153, 159, 310n102
Canals, 180–81, 184, 186, 190, 208
Capital: and absenteeism, 29, 220, 293;
accounting, 96, 100; of attorneys, 159,
222; British, 3, 39, 55; and labour, 272,
293; and planters, 11, 93, 108; enslaved
people as, 5, 108, 110, 198; investment
of, 8, 100, 198, 275, 281; sources of, 29,
279
Capitalism: 9, 11; aristocratic, 20
Capooses, 201–2, 225, 330n152
Carawina Estate, 85, 87–88
Carey, William, 85
Cargill, James Farmer, 89
Carrington, Selwyn H. H., 9, 48–49, 55,
100, 108, 281, 287–88
Cash book, 106

Cassidy, F. G., 32, 330n152
Cateau, Heather, 9, 287–89
Catherine Mount Estate, 85, 87
Cattle: for draft, 167, 181, 196, 262–63; of
enslaved people, 99; herds, 110, 140,
263–65, 285; imported, 265, 267; for
meat, 262–65, 270; mills, 167, 180, 190,
201–2, 224, 262; sale of, 196–97, 265,
270–71; working, 204–5, 231, 262–65
Caymanas, 139, 275
Central mills, 235, 275, 283, 292
Chandler, Alfred D., Jr, 8
Chapelton, 77, 91
Chapplin, Johny, 172
Charge and discharge, 95–96, 98
Charleston, 17, 211
Checkland, S. G., 287
Chisholm, Alexander, 283
Chisholm, Captain, 210–11
Churches, 75, 77–79, 86, 88, 90–91, 117,
138, 228, 254, 269, 272
Church of Scotland Missionary Society,
78
Clarke, Sir Simon Haughton, 69
Clarendon parish, 45, 47, 61, 73, 77–79,
97, 109, 118, 179, 286, 288
Clark, Dugald, 224
Clarke, Sir Simon Haughton, 155, 157
Clay, Christopher, 35
Clayton, T. R., 138
Clergy, 48–49, 84, 158
Clerks, 36, 49, 78, 83, 95, 116, 132, 151,
162, 212, 234
Climate, 1, 6, 112, 144, 164, 167, 204, 292
Coffee: accounts, 98, 102–3; and
attorneys, 46, 57–61; cultivation, 1;
expansion of, 119; mills, 2; production,
1, 5–6, 19, 43, 118; trade, 219
Collins, Dr, 144, 172
Collins, Edward Kidvallede, 172
Collins, Isaac, 172
Colonial agents, 21
Colonial Church Union, 90
Colonial Office, 89, 234, 251, 272
Colvile, Andrew, 126, 154
Colville and Company, 88

Commission agents, 100–101, 103, 105–9, 145, 207–10, 214, 286

Commissioners, 35–36

Commissions: of attorneys, 16, 34, 42–44, 81–84, 94, 141, 164, 171, 213, 222, 285, 291; of brokers, 103; of factors, 102, 285–86

Committee of West India Planters and Merchants, 126

Compensation, 56, 86, 153, 273

Complexity, 5, 10, 15–17, 31–32, 35, 53, 97, 106, 112, 223, 292

Cooper, John W., 101

Cooper, Wilkin, 70

Copse Estate, 152–54, 156, 158–60, 162, 231, 247, 253, 258

Copying: of documents, 117, 132, 174; of letters, 115–16, 132, 150–51, 161–62

Cost analysis, 96, 100

Council. See Legislative Council

Counting-houses, 95, 103, 106

Courts, 35, 38–39, 50–51, 82, 89, 93, 117, 156, 173, 187–88, 247, 249–51; Appeal, 270; Assize, 89–90; Chancery, 19, 42, 72, 87, 89, 100, 173–74, 177, 308n66; Common Pleas, 138; Grand, 186; Martial, 152; Slave, 152; Supreme, 43, 89

Cowell, Benjamin, 148–51, 168, 171, 184, 191–92, 199–200, 207, 209–11, 214–15

Cowper, Ann, 45

Cowper, Thomas, 45

Cox, Henry, 86

Craskell and Simpson, 167, 191

Craton, Michael, 289

Credit, 16, 43, 94, 103–4, 108, 199–200, 215, 265

Creoles, 17–19, 23–24, 36, 77–79, 92, 114, 137, 143, 164

Cron, Robert, 80

Crop Accounts. See Accounts Produce

Crown, British, 19, 21, 89

Cuba, 2–3, 6, 127

Curtin, Philip, 50, 63, 82–83, 273

Cussans, Thomas, 180, 184, 186–90, 221

Custodes, 81, 89–90, 93, 117, 138, 143

Dallas, R. C., 35, 81–82, 291

Daly, James, 79

Dams, 183–84, 187, 189, 228

Davies, K. G., 108

Davy, John, 64

Dawkins, Henry, 45, 97, 177, 179, 187

Dawkins, James, 57, 70

Dawkins Papers, 111, 179

Days of work, 239, 240–42, 246, 248, 250, 252, 334n260

Debauchery, 143–44, 280

Debt: and attorneys, 50, 88, 160, 163; bad, 266, 270; book, 94; imprisonment for, 35; merchant, 45, 107–8, 145; payment of, 43; planter, 23, 100, 105–8, 140, 174, 199, 215–18, 221, 292; recovery of, 17

Deffell, John Henry, and Company, 46

Deficiency Acts, 22, 41, 98, 224, 237

Delacree Pen, 75, 87

Demerara, 32, 287

Demography: of attorneys, 55–56, 75–81; of enslaved, 56–57, 59, 110, 203, 217, 219–20, 291; and fertility, 220; geographical patterns, 18, 59, 235, 238–39; and mortality, 47, 200, 220, 225; of occupations, 55; populations, 1–6, 18, 235–36, 275, 294n4; of whites, 22, 41. See also Immigration; Slave trade

Diaries, 97–99

Distilleries, 88, 97, 99, 191–92, 224, 234

Doctors, 48, 78–79, 154, 171–72, 193, 224, 244

Donne, Grace, 145

Double-entry, 96–97, 100, 106

Dovaston, John, 47

Drescher, Seymour, 28, 287

Drivers, 33–34, 51–52, 114, 142, 172, 234, 289

Duckenfield Hall Estate: attorney of, 170–71, 180, 222; canals, 180–81, 186–87, 208; central mill at, 283; disputed boundaries of, 177, 181; doctor at, 171–72; location of, 167; and

Duckenfield Hall Estate (*continued*) shipping, 212; trade of, 206; water rights of, 184, 186–87, 189–90; windmill on, 224

Dummer, Edmund, 122

Duperly, Adolphe, 193

Duties, 82, 99, 104–5, 219, 270, 273

East India interest, 21

Economies of scale, 3–5, 8–9, 15–16, 25, 95, 111–12, 223, 235, 281

Edgar, Alexander, 46

Edgeworth, Maria, 24

Education, 23, 28, 49, 78

Edwards, Bryan, 201–2

Efficiency: and absenteeism, 28; and accounting, 94–96, 100; of attorneys, 53, 70, 82, 93–94, 221–26, 279–82; of communication, 117, 133; and complexity, 16, 112; economic, 9, 203; of management, 4, 11, 28, 30–31, 100; and morality, 9; of wealth transfer, 7

Eisner, Gisela, 294n4

Ejectments, 39, 179, 184, 186–88, 247

Elgin, Earl of, 162, 233, 238

Ellis Charles Rose, 227–28

Ellis, John, 227–28

Ellis Caymanas Estate, 275

England: absenteeism in, 20, 24, 28–29; accounting in, 96; agriculture in, 53–54, 235, 261; attorneys from, 16–17, 49, 77, 101; attorneys in, 37–39, 44; estate management in, 33, 35–36, 53–54, 82, 84; gentry in, 145; legal education in, 49; medieval, 38; output in, 2; people of, 5, 17–18, 25, 143; ports of, 105; provincial, 39; schooling in, 23, 80, 137, 147, 228; society in, 292; wealth in, 141

Enslaved people, 3–4, 7–8, 11, 18–20, 26, 30, 50–52, 56, 59–61, 80, 84–85, 95, 98–99; and absenteeism, 289–90; and attorneys, 279, 282, 289–91; and communication, 113–14; and doctors, 171; on estates, 141–42, 152–53, 172, 175, 197–205, 217, 221–26; female, 154;

hired, 170; management of, 197–205, 290–91; and post, 119–20; purchase of, 107–10, 197–201, 203–05, 214–15, 218–20, 222, 286, 288–89; and reproduction, 203, 219–20, 291; and resident proprietors, 279, 282

Entrepreneurship, 15, 164

Estate agent, 39

Estates: attorneys of, 35, 37, 40, 55–57, 64, 65, 139–42, 153–54, 159; British, 95–96, 111; defined, 4; and plantations, 42, 269; rum, 55

Eton, 23, 147

Europe, 5, 11, 78, 122, 180, 211, 237 38

Executions, 34–35, 197

Executors, 39, 42, 84, 154, 159–60, 175–76

Factors. *See* Merchants

Fairweather, Robert, 69, 71, 85

Falconer, Alexander, 61, 109

Falmouth (England), 122, 124–27, 130–31

Falmouth (Jamaica), 57, 71, 85, 120, 230–31, 260, 265, 276–77, 324n115

Farquharson, Matthew, 39

Fearon, Angelina Israel, 79

Fearon, Elizabeth, 173

Fearon, Rowland, 68, 104

Fearon, Thomas, 173

Fearon, William Wheeler, 79

Fences, 253, 262–64, 274

Ferguson, Thomas, 158, 231

Field labour, 4, 34, 142, 224, 240, 246, 251–52, 289

Finlayson, Mr (Stipendiary Magistrate), 249, 252

Flint River Estate, 153, 158–60, 236

Floodgates, 181–84, 186, 189

Floods, 150, 166–67, 172, 181–84, 186, 188, 190, 194–95, 198, 216–17

Florida, 127, 129

Fogel, Robert William, 9–10

Food: and absenteeism, 290; animal, 4, 196–97, 263; of attorneys, 101, 143; of enslaved people, 3–4, 6, 196–97, 219, 290; of planters, 101, 143, 263; production, 4, 99, 195–96, 263–65; and provision grounds, 4, 196, 244–45; security, 6, 195–96, 199; shortages, 219; and transition to freedom, 244, 263

Forsyth, Alexander, 69

Forsyth, James, 85

Fowles, John, 87

France, 2, 25, 28, 34, 123, 125, 148–49, 207, 218

Fraud, 42, 82–83, 92, 94, 101–2, 179, 188, 222, 277, 281, 289

Free people, 3, 50; of colour, 77–80, 224, 310n102; of United States, 157

Free villages, 233, 238, 254

Freight, 99, 101, 104–5

Friendship Estate (Hanover), 155, 158–59, 162

Galenson, David W., 16, 41, 94

Gang labour, 4, 33, 109, 142, 197, 199, 203, 225, 239, 243

Gardens. *See* Houses

Gardiner, Edmund, 153, 158, 236

Gardner, Thomas Patterson, 231, 258, 260, 272

Gardner, Rev. W. J., 40, 65, 81, 83, 138, 289, 292–93

Gayleard, James, 88–89

Geddes, Alexander, 286

Geggus, David, 19, 28

Georgia Estate, 116

Germany, 138, 153, 237

Gibraltar Estate, 153, 155, 158–59

Gladstone, John, 32, 273, 287

Glasgow, 20, 145, 158

Golden Grove Estate (Hanover), 153, 158–59

Golden Grove Estate (St Thomas-in-the-East): agriculture at, 169, 194–97, 212–20, 283, 285; attorneys of, 37, 89–90, 101, 137, 147–48, 151, 164–72, 221–26, 276; boundaries of, 176–80; doctors at, 144, 171–72, 333n250; environment of, 150, 166–67, 181–82, 227–28, 262, 275, 285; management of, 164–228, 286–88; overseers of, 37, 90, 101, 168–72, 278; owners of, 137,

147–48, 164–65, 168–76, 283, 287–88; profits from, 212–16, 221–26, 257; rent of lands, 140; religion at, 89, 230; settlement pattern of, 169, 190–94, 329n115; slavery at, 197–205, 235, 240; trading of, 205–12; water resources of, 180–90; women of, 143–44

Good Hope Estate, 145

Goodwin, (Thomas) Lewis, 234

Gordon, George, 64, 70, 85, 311n143

Gordon, George William, 81, 90

Gordon, Joseph, 64, 73, 81, 87, 261

Gordon, William, 69

Goveia, Elsa V., 32

Governors: and absenteeism, 22, 42, 230; and attorneys, 89, 143, 147, 158, 162–63, 243, 250–51; and government, 42, 88–89; and planters, 147, 162–63, 230, 233, 243, 251; salaries of, 3; and workers, 233, 250–51

Graham, Francis, 65, 116

Graham, Robert, 140, 175, 207

Grant, Alexander, 114

Gravesend, 128–30

Great Britain: absentees in, 7, 18–29, 32, 46, 55, 144–45, 147, 207; agriculture in, 15, 33, 288; aristocracy of, 22, 164; attorneys in, 38, 46, 148; estate management in, 33, 35–36, 47, 53–54, 111; government of, 42, 65, 86; industry in, 3–4, 21, 288; investment in, 88, 103, 145, 220; merchants in, 21, 105–6; newspapers of, 116; people of, 17–18, 25; postal system of, 117, 121–33; prices in, 43, 82, 104; productivity in, 3–4; radical thought in, 110; and sailing times, 113, 128–31, 149–50. *See also* England

Great houses. *See* Houses

Great River, 160, 227–29, 249, 258, 263

Green, Joseph, 37

Green Island, 119, 158

Gregory, Dr Matthew, 187–88

Grenada, 125–26

Grignon, Colonel William Stanford, 51–52, 90

Ground provisions, 194–96, 199, 219, 255. *See also* Provision grounds
Guadeloupe, 28
Guardians, 39, 42, 56, 174
Gudgeons, 201–2, 225, 259, 331n153
Gunn, John, 69, 90

Haiti, 126–27
Hakewill, James, 137
Hale, Smart, 47
Hall, Douglas, 15, 27–28, 30, 33, 102, 110, 119, 272, 274
Hamilton, George William, 73–74, 116
Hamilton, Thomas B., 72
Hanover parish, 18, 69–70, 75, 115, 141, 152–53, 159–60, 228, 236, 261, 265, 269
Harris, Frances, 170–71, 173, 176, 221
Harris, Robert William, 37
Harvey, George, 250
Haughton Court Estate, 141
Haughton Hall Estate, 158–59
Hawthorn and Shedden, 155–56, 158–59, 162
Hayward, Dr, 171–72, 193, 219, 333n250
Headmen, 31, 114, 142, 232–34, 239, 243, 245–46, 250, 252–53, 269
Health: of enslaved, 98, 199–200, 203–4, 217, 240, 256, 269; of whites, 7, 17, 30, 157, 175
Heaven, William H., 153, 158
Heuman, Gad, 18, 63
Hibbert, George, 68
Hibbert, Thomas, 68
Hierarchies, 4–5, 7, 9, 11, 15–40, 91–92, 106, 114, 232, 234
Hilton and Biscoe, 207
Hind, Richard, 160
Hine, Thomas, 71
Hire of workers: absentees' objections to, 109, 204, 218, 226, 286, 288; and accounts, 109, 206; by attorneys, 52, 109, 198, 201, 218, 226; cost of, 100, 224, 243, 288–89; by overseers, 109, 170–71, 198–99, 203; by plantations, 206, 223; and productivity, 288–89; and self-hire, 243

Hislop, Lawrence, 69
Hodgson, Abraham, 86
Holidays, 242, 259, 266, 290
Holland, Lady, 244
Holland, Lord, 231, 247
Holland Bay, 167, 180
Holland Estate, 101, 140, 142–43, 145, 151, 170, 177, 179–80, 188, 222, 224
Holt, Thomas, 55, 64, 273
Honesty, 29, 43, 48, 50, 94, 138, 210, 280
Hordley Estate, 69, 85, 140, 187–88, 290
Horses, 34, 69, 253, 259, 262–63
Hours of work, 225, 239, 240–41, 243, 261, 277, 290, 334n260
Housekeepers, 143, 145, 147
House of Assembly: and absenteeism, 19, 22, 37, 65; attorneys in, 63, 81, 88–90, 93, 138, 147, 173–74, 291, 310n102; and currency, 106; legislation of, 42–44, 89, 168, 238; merchants in, 42, 147, 170; planters in, 30, 42, 86, 147, 165, 170, 173
Houses: building of, 255, 257; of enslaved, 167, 170, 181, 193–94, 203–4; on estates, 283; great, 30, 142, 148, 192–93, 199; and households, 248; repair of, 252–53; and rents, 247–48, 273; valuation of, 250, 252–53
Howard de Walden, Lord, 273–75
Hudson's Bay Company, 154
Hughan, Thomas, 20
Humanity, 26, 28, 110, 165, 199, 225
Humphrey, 172
Hurricanes, 10, 42, 165–66, 182, 199, 207, 211, 219
Hyde Hall Estate, 70, 232

Imperial College of Tropical Agriculture, 49
Immigration, 153, 157–58, 235, 237–38, 251, 254, 276, 283
Incalculability, 102, 280
Indentured workers: African, 276, 283; Indian, 276, 283, 287; white, 23, 30, 48, 103, 224, 232
India, 1, 20, 25, 133

Indians, indentured, 276, 283, 287

Indulgence, 30, 142

Industrial Revolution, 3, 21, 288

Inheritance: and absentees, 17, 29, 164, 173–76, 220, 227; and attorneys, 84, 140, 145, 160, 173–76, 222; hazards of, 84, 111, 173–76; by planters, 140, 146–47, 164, 173–76, 227; rules of, 174, 220; settlement of, 173–74, 217

Innovation, 8, 11, 27, 29, 96, 112, 180, 224, 262, 273, 287–88

Insurance: accounting for, 99; and attorneys, 53, 105, 151, 158, 209–10, 260; by commission agents, 103, 209–10; and hurricanes, 105, 182, 207; limits of, 10; Lloyd's, 105; and overseers, 209–10; and planters, 105, 151, 209–12; rates, 105, 182; on slaves, 110; on shipping, 10, 53, 209

Interest, 43, 101, 103, 105

Interest groups, 20–22, 165

Inventories, 86–88, 98, 111, 141–42, 151, 160, 214

Invoice books, 106

Ireland, 17, 20, 173–74; absenteeism in, 20, 24–25, 29; attorneys from, 77; attorneys in, 44; estate management in, 35, 84; lawyers from, 147; post to, 125

Irrigation, 2, 148, 180–81, 288

Island secretary, 42–44, 53, 89, 100, 146, 174, 212, 267

Isle of Wight, 128–29

Italy, 148–50, 162, 212, 217, 238

Jackson, Ann, 160

Jackson, Isaac: and absentees, 152, 154–55, 165, 288; as attorney, 50, 133, 137, 152–60, 227–78, 280, 334n7; biography of, 151–60, 164; correspondence of, 132–33, 152–65; employers of, 152–59, 164–65, 227–31, 287; and enslaved people, 152–53, 160; family of, 160; as land owner, 153, 159–60, 324n115; and metropolitan merchants, 155–59; as overseer, 152, 158, 271; and overseers,

157, 231–32; remuneration of, 156–57, 159; and transition to freedom, 152, 156, 165, 227, 272–73; wealth of, 159–60; and workers, 232–46

Jackson, William, 87

Jacobs, H. P., 78, 89–90

Jamaica: agriculture in, 1-10, 18–19, 31–32; attorneys in, *passim*; creole society in, 28; economy of, 100–110; exports of, 1-10; government of, 41–44, 88–89, 94, 120, 128, 148; migration from, 23; plantation accounting in, 95; planters of, 1-11, 17–18, 21–22, 111, 116; population of, 2, 55, 75–76; postal system of, 117–21, 151; production of, 1-10, 208; productivity in, 2–5, 8–10, 287, 294n4; resources of, 1–2, 6, 93, 285; and sailing times, 113, 128–31, 149–51; society in, 3, 17, 25, 228, 272, 292–93; trade of, 68, 82, 103–6, 115

Jamaicans: as absentees, 17–19, 21–29, 32, 51; attitudes to Jamaica, 292–93; as attorneys, 77–78, 91; as creoles, 142–43, 164; and idea of home, 18–19, 23–24, 28–29, 152, 188; languages of, 114; proverbs of, 289; schooling of, 23; women, 79

Jamaica Sugar Estates Limited, 283

James, Patrick Haughton, 154–55, 163

James, Philip Haughton, 159

James, William Rhodes, 46, 306n19

Jobbing, 50, 52, 170, 199, 203–4, 217, 224, 240, 243, 246, 288

Journals, 95–98, 106–7

Karras, Alan, 49, 65

Kearsey, Elizabeth, 147, 151, 170–71, 173, 175–76, 180, 187, 196, 199, 201, 213, 221

Kelly, John: as attorney, 170–71, 181, 187, 221–22; as overseer, 151, 168, 170–72, 180, 194–99, 206, 216–17, 219, 221–22, 278, 286; and shipping, 208–10; as slave owner, 170–71, 203–4, 217, 224

Kelsall, Charles, 175–76

Kennion, John, 144, 177, 180

Kingston: attorneys in, 87, 222, 261, 277; merchants, 20, 30, 68, 78–79, 86, 103, 139, 147, 151, 174, 207, 212–13, 215; newspapers, 117; pens in, 57, 141; port of, 1, 19, 103, 120, 211; and postal system, 117–21, 125, 127–31, 163; prices in, 208, 210; representation of, 88; roads from, 167; shipping from, 207; and slave trade, 203

Knibb, William, 292

Kynaston, Roger, Jr, 153, 158

Laborie, P. J., 98

Labour: absenteeism, 25; and attorneys, 52; bargaining, 155–56, 239–40, 242–43, 247–48, 251–52, 276; as capital, 110; cost, 100, 110, 204, 246, 270; discipline, 10, 34, 197, 225, 277, 290; division of, 4, 9; hired, 100, 109, 198, 201, 203, 223–24, 226, 240, 288–89; industrial, 10; and management, 7–10, 111–12, 197–205, 223–27, 233–34, 277; mobility, 238–39, 254–55; and morality, 94, 201; productivity of, 3–5, 7–9, 195, 203–5, 218–21, 223–25, 235, 288; seasonal, 240–42; shortage, 235–37, 261, 275–76; slave, 3–5, 7, 54, 108–10, 195–205, 218–21, 223–27; specialization, 9; supervision of, 7, 197, 233; wage, 165, 234–51, 268, 272; withdrawal of, 240–41, 245, 247, 250

Laing, Malcolm, 170–71, 173, 180, 188, 198–99, 206, 210, 221

Lambie, William, 79, 85

Land: purchase of, 159, 165, 179–80, 223, 238, 287; sale of, 29–30, 39, 50–51, 84–85, 146, 254, 269, 282; valuation, 269–70. *See also* Rents

Land agents, 36, 39, 47, 49, 53–54, 84

Landlordism, 25–27, 29, 35–36, 53–54

Land surveys: 35–36, 41, 51, 84, 94, 127, 176–79, 184, 194, 255, 340n176

Land tenure, 4–5, 7, 24–25, 53–54, 111, 173–79, 227, 238–39, 244, 254, 277–78

Lawyers, 35–39, 47–49, 173, 176, 179

Ledgers, 96, 100, 106–7

Lee, Robert Cooper, 173

Leeward Islands, 32, 125–26

Legislative Council, 42, 88–90, 93, 144, 152, 270, 291

Leisure, 113, 131, 217, 280–81, 289

Le Page, R. B., 32, 330n152

Letters: of absentees, 113–15, 131–32, 247; as accounts, 94–95; of attorneys, 53, 113–15, 131, 137; duplicate, 115–16, 132; of Isaac Jackson, 152–61, 238, 245, 248, 254, 277; and management, 114–15; monthly, 122; and post, 117–33; ship, 121; of Simon Taylor, 147–51, 168, 170, 176, 187, 204, 210, 217, 322n52

Letters of attorney. *See* Powers of attorney

Lewis, Matthew Gregory, 69, 78, 80, 85, 116, 128–29, 289–90

Lightfoot and Robson, 157

Lime Savanna, 118, 120

Literacy, 31, 34, 42, 47, 92, 113–16, 247

Liverpool, 20, 150, 287

Livestock: and attorneys, 52, 157, 209; and enslaved people, 98–99, 110; as food, 4, 262–63, 265–66; imported, 263, 265; planter's, 263; production, 4–5, 19, 228, 262–65, 267, 274–75; small, 262; stray, 253, 259, 274; trade, 43, 209, 262–64; working, 4, 195, 262–63, 265. *See also* Cattle; Pens

Llanrumney Estate, 140–42

Loans, 16, 39, 100, 103

London: absentees in, 37, 45, 158; agents in, 35, 106, 145, 155–56, 168, 207; City of, 18, 130; and gentry, 20; merchants, 20–21, 45–46, 63, 68, 99, 101, 105, 114, 145–47, 151, 157; and politics, 21, 86; and postal system, 122, 125, 128–30, 151; prices in, 208, 210, 218; shipping to, 207, 237; sugar brokers, 154, 208, 259; theatre, 28

Long, Andrew, 38

Long, Beeston, 207

Long, Edward: on absenteeism, 23–24, 32; on attorneys, 32, 81; on creoles, 23; on education, 23; on Plantain Garden

River, 167, 181, 200; on post, 117, 120–21; on productivity, 225; on roads, 119; on white population, 23, 32, 237

Long Drake and Long, 147, 207, 210

Lowndes, Henry, 39, 82, 84

Lucea, 120, 156, 260, 277

Lyon, David, 154–56

Lyssons Estate, 101, 138, 140, 143, 151, 170, 222

McCallum, Duncan, 79

McCook, Francis, 63

McCornock, Thomas, 33, 37, 77, 88–90, 101

McCraugh, Dennis, 186

McCreath, John, 77

McCulloch, J. R., 24–25

McCusker, John J., 287

McDonald, James, 87, 309n76

McGeachy, Edward, 127–28

MacGlashan, Charles, 78

McKenzie, Colin, 73–74, 77

McKenzie, John, 116

McNeil, Thomas: and accounts, 157, 267; as attorney, 154–57, 231, 247, 250, 264; and ejectment, 247; memorialized, 88; as township commissioner, 237; and transition to freedom, 243, 247–48, 277

MacPherson, Evan, 77

MacQueen, James, 120, 126

Madden, R. R., 92

Mafoota, 159, 255, 257

Magistrates, 48, 89, 152, 158, 247, 249–50. See also Stipendiary magistrates

Maguire, W. A., 36

Mais, John, 86–87

Malcolm, Neill, 57, 70, 115

Malcolmson, A. P. W., 29, 36

Management: and absenteeism, 7, 10–11, 17–29, 115; accounting, 94–95, 106, 109; and capital, 11; delegated, 7; efficiency, 4, 27, 94–95, 279–82; of enslaved people, 197–205; extravagant, 27; hierarchical, 4, 7–8, 15–40, 106; modern, 8–9, 11, 95, 293; and

ownership, 9, 11; planning, 216–27, 287; plantation, 8–9, 46–49, 114, 152, 176; and profit, 4, 7–8, 216–27; and scale, 3–4; scientific, 8; and slavery, 3–5, 201; and supervision, 232; systems, 3–4, 29–32, 292; theory, 8–10

Managers, 33, 37, 49–51, 55, 90, 153, 172

Managing attorneys. See Attorneys

Manchester parish, 30, 64, 69, 79, 266–67

Manchioneal, 119, 143, 151, 206, 208

Manumission, 81, 144, 172

Manure, 97, 100, 195, 224, 262, 274

Maps, 97, 111–12, 167, 179, 184, 194

Marketing, 9–10, 29, 31, 45–46, 55, 103–4

Markets: British, 21, 103–4, 108; capital, 20, 39; internal, 4, 102, 106, 108, 205, 266, 293; slave, 98; sugar, 1, 102–4, 108, 205, 208

Marly, 31, 34, 40, 91, 281

Maroons, 152, 227, 291

Marrett, George, 70, 85

Marriage: and absenteeism, 17, 29, 220, 231; and attorneys, 79–81, 93, 147, 160, 164; and business networks, 140; and plantation whites, 172; plantation workers, 240, 244–45; of planters, 144–45, 174–75, 205; and wealth, 174–75, 218

Marronage, 8, 26, 34, 168, 172

Marsden, Peter, 34, 65

Martinique, 28

Marx, Karl, 279

Mason, Keith, 288

Master and steward, 95

Mendes Plantation, 87

Mercantile attorneys. See Attorneys

Merchants, 1, 6, 11, 16–17, 19–22, 29–30, 32, 34, 39–40, 42, 46, 48–50, 52, 55, 68, 83–84, 86, 94–95, 97, 100–102; agents of, 102; and communication, 113–14; and factors, 102, 104; Kingston, 103, 139–40, 147, 164, 174–75, 213–14; local, 277; metropolitan, 103, 105–9, 145–47, 151, 158, 207, 213, 268, 271, 286–87, 291; travelling, 102

Merivale, Herman, 25

Metcalf, George, 147, 165

Metcalfe, Sir Charles, 91, 243, 250–51

Miles, Michael, 39

Miles, Philip John, 57

Militia, 90, 93, 138, 152

Miller, Guy, 231

Miller, William: correspondence of, 98, 228; as large attorney, 37, 40, 51, 64, 65, 152; as member of Council, 89; and Montpelier, 230–32, 257–58; origins of, 78; partnerships of, 70–73, 277; residence of, 73, 276; as slave owner, 37, 85

Milligan, Robert, 20

Mills. *See* Cattle; Steam; Sugar; Water; Wind

Milner, David, 179

Missionaries, 78, 138, 228, 254

Mitchell, William, 65

Molasses, 42, 108, 206, 213, 219, 260

Mole St Nicholas, 126–27

Moncrieffe, Benjamin Scott, 78

Money: in accounts, 96–98, 106, 214; allowances, 265–66; currency, 106–7, 213; flows, 95; in internal trade, 106, 214, 257; and rent, 253, 257; in sugar trade, 104, 213–14; and wages, 253, 263, 268, 272

Monitoring problem, 16–17, 93–95, 268

Montego Bay, 80, 118, 120–21, 150, 158, 162, 233, 237, 260, 268, 271, 277, 310n102

Montpelier Estate: account books of, 99, 115; attorneys of, 154, 157–59, 163, 231–34, 272–78, 285–86, 334n7; environment of, 227–29; livestock on, 262–67; management of, 137, 165, 227–78; owners of, 152, 273–75; profits from, 267–72; rebellion at, 90; rent of houses and land on, 247–57, 337n93; sugar production at, 257–62, 285; water resources of, 228–30; workers of, 234–46, 289. *See also* Old Montpelier; New Montpelier; Shettlewood

Montpelier Farm, 99, 255, 257

Montpelier Pen, 250, 253, 255, 262–64, 266–67, 269–71, 337n93

Montpelier Wharf, 158, 237, 267–71

Montrose Pen, 141–42, 233

Montserrat, 122

Morality, 9, 11, 25, 94–95, 201, 221, 234, 279–81, 289–90

Morant Bay, 138, 170, 210, 283

Moreton, J. B., 33–34, 48, 51, 80–81, 84

Morgan, Kenneth, 130

Moro Pen, 140

Mortgages, 16, 39, 42, 46, 50, 84, 100, 146, 159, 173, 216, 265, 308n66

Mount Edgecombe Pen, 154–55

Mulgrave, Earl of, Governor, 40, 230

Murder, 7, 164, 197, 203, 283

Murray, William, 73

Nabobs, 20–21, 83, 92

Napier, Christopher J., 96

Napoleonic Wars, 84, 105, 125, 130

Navy, 21, 78, 122, 128

"Negroes" as slaves, 42–43, 46, 77, 110, 200–201, 203, 225

Nevis, 122

New Montpelier Estate: enslaved people of, 233; and internal exchange, 99, 267; livestock on, 262–63; sugar production at, 257–58, 262–63, 269, 338n120; woodland on, 255; workers of, 234, 249; works established, 228; works restored, 230–31, 257. *See also* Montpelier Estate

"New Negroes", 196–98

New York, 127, 132, 174–75

Newspapers, 116–17, 126, 228

Nisbetts, 171, 181

North America. *See* British North America

North Britain, 77, 79

Nova Scotia, 127

Nugent, Governor George, 130, 138, 143

Nugent, Lady Maria, 77, 120, 128–30, 138, 141, 143–44, 193, 208

O'Connor, Charles, 90

Offer, Avner, 53

Old Harbour: Bay, 118, 120; Market, 118

Old Montpelier Estate: account books of, 98–99, 232, 267–68; chapel at, 254; overseers of, 232; as a pen, 231, 240, 262, 282; provision grounds on, 245, 255–56; sugar production at, 257–58, 269, 282, 338n120; workers of, 249; works abandoned, 230–31

Oldham, John, 85

Oldroyd, David, 96

O'Shaughnessy, Andrew Jackson, 21, 49

Overlookers, 34

Overseers: and accounting, 94–95; and attorneys, 53, 109, 143, 157, 171–72, 194, 219, 221–22, 273; as attorneys, 48, 152, 158, 168, 170, 208–10; correspondence of, 113–14, 151; defined, 32–34; education of, 49; efficiency of, 27, 51, 258, 261, 286; and enslaved people, 26–27, 50, 197, 289–90; functions of, 30, 42, 52, 56, 99, 102, 197, 208–10, 219, 242, 245, 247, 250–51, 269; houses of, 141–42; monitoring of, 16, 268, 270–72; murdered, 283; as planters, 37, 287; recruitment of, 50, 78, 155, 231–33; remuneration of, 83–84, 101, 265–66, 285–86; as slave owners, 170–71, 203–4, 217, 224; status of, 80, 91, 143, 278

Pacific Ocean, 6, 127

Packet boats, 122–28, 130–31, 149–50, 154, 161–63, 233, 272

Palmer, Charles, 251

Paradise Pen, 154–55, 231

Pares, Richard, 20, 27, 40, 43, 52, 108, 165

Parliament, British, 18, 20–21, 54, 75, 164, 219–20, 228, 230, 282

Partnerships, 17, 29, 57, 59, 68, 71–73, 140, 155, 292. See also Attorneys, joint

Pasturage, 205, 232, 245–46, 252–53, 337n93

Pastures, 172, 179, 194, 196, 205, 228, 245–46, 250–53, 258, 263–65, 283, 285

Patent offices, 19

Patents, 173, 177, 184–85, 189, 224

Paterson, C., 154, 156

Patterson, Orlando, 20, 28

Pawson, Michael, 16

Payne, Edward, 232–33

Peasantry, 233, 235, 274, 292–93

Pennant, Edward, 45

Pennant, John, 61, 97

Pennant, Richard, 78, 97, 109–10

Pen-keepers, 19, 172, 196, 232, 265

Pens: and absenteeism, 19; defined, 4–5; managed by attorneys, 30, 56–57, 64, 65, 153–54, 159, 167, 262–63; and meat market, 4, 262–67; and merchants, 102; owned by attorneys, 85–88, 140–42; and plantations, 5, 37, 64; and production of working livestock, 4, 172, 228, 262–65; and sugar estates, 4–5, 167, 172, 228, 262–63, 285; trade of, 4–5, 102, 262–63; valuation of, 269; workers on, 240, 263, 265

Penrhyn, Lord, 68, 104, 109, 286, 288. See also Richard Pennant

Petgrave, Mrs, 257, 267

Philadelphia, 206

Philander, 172

Philip, 172

Phillipson, Rev. Richard Burton Burton, 144–45

Pimento, 43

Pitman, Frank Wesley, 26–28

Planning, 50, 52, 109–12, 194–97, 216–20, 223, 230–31, 257, 288

Plantain Garden River: and absenteeism, 57; discharge of, 166–67, 184, 186, 290; district, 57, 140, 168, 283; and fertility, 57, 166–67, 181, 195; floodplain, 166–67, 181–84, 195, 285; mouth, 177–79, 187, 208, 211–12; plantations along, 140, 166, 179–80, 187–88, 190, 227; and soils, 57, 166–67, 181, 195; unhealthy, 200; water for mills, 183–84, 186–88, 190, 329n102; weirs on, 184, 186–88, 190–91

Plantains, 140, 179, 184, 194, 196, 199, 206

Plantation America, 19, 32, 35

Plantation Jamaica, 7, 11, 121, 293
Plantations: and absenteeism, 7, 11; and
  accounting, 95–102; and attorneys, 15,
  37, 56–57, 64, 65; and colonization, 5;
  defined, 5, 42; economy of, 2; labour
  on, 4–5, 7; management of, 7–9, 11, 15,
  165, 292; and modern enterprise, 5,
  8–10; productivity of, 4, 6, 11; rise and
  decline of, 5–6; sale of, 29, 51; scale of,
  4; as sugar estates, 4, 184. *See also* Coffee
Planters, 5–10, 15, 17–20, 29, 34, 37–39,
  42, 55, 83, 91, 95–102, 114, 139–40
Planters' Bank, 90
Plantership, 15, 23, 37, 48
Planting attorneys. *See* Attorneys
Ploughs, 232, 246, 258, 261–63
Plummer, Henry Waite, 69
Police, 249
Pollard, Sidney, 96, 106
Population. *See* Demography
Port Antonio, 118–20
Port Maria, 118–19
Port Morant, 167, 208, 210–12
Port Royal, 16–17, 88, 127, 140
Port Royal parish, 87
Portland parish, 90
Ports, 1, 6, 21, 73, 105, 120, 126, 207
Portsmouth, 128–29
Post, 94, 117–33, 149–51, 161–63, 277
Potosi Estate, 181–82
Powers of attorney: defective, 176;
  executed outside Jamaica, 44–45, 176;
  form of, 46; functions of, 11, 17, 44–45,
  55, 155–57, 162–63, 208, 221–22;
  general, 44, 170, 221; legal status of, 17,
  38, 44; and merchants, 81, 102, 145–46,
  174; specific, 46
Price, Sir Charles, 144
Price, Rose, 144, 286, 289
Prices: of beef, 266–67; of exports, 10, 43,
  100–104, 165; of land, 45, 269; local,
  205, 208; metropolitan, 205, 213; of
  slaves, 45, 98, 199, 203–4; of
  plantations, 29; of sugar, 2, 6, 101–4,
  165, 204, 208, 213, 218, 261, 273, 294n4;
  and uncertainty, 10, 100–102

Principal-agent problem, 16, 31, 38, 41,
  54, 102, 133, 137
Prisons, 35, 239
Productivity: and absenteeism, 24–25,
  281–82, 288–90; and attorneys, 225–26,
  274–75, 288–91; in Jamaican economy,
  1–10, 262–63; of labour, 201, 203, 221,
  225–27, 235, 265; and management,
  3–4, 8–11, 197, 201, 203, 221, 225;
  marginal, 111; measurement of, 100,
  111–12; per capita, 2, 197; and slavery,
  3–4, 8, 164, 197, 201–3, 225
Professionalism: of attorneys, 15–16, 39, 41,
  49, 84, 92, 161, 164–65, 271, 277; in
  England, 35–36, 49, 84; of estate-
  attorneys, 15; of land agents, 36, 49; of
  land surveyors, 41; of managers, 15, 35,
  84; of planters, 7, 37, 39; of stewards, 84
Profit and loss accounts, 96, 107
Profitability: and absenteeism, 54,
  280–81, 289–90; and accounting, 96,
  100, 111; and attorneys, 52, 93, 199, 216,
  278–82, 289–90; and communication,
  93; of plantation system, 7, 216, 278,
  293
Proprietors: and absenteeism, 7–8, 41, 95,
  222–25; accounts required by, 95–97,
  101–2, 108; and attorneys, 55, 57,
  68–70, 84–85, 160, 222–26, 235,
  279–81, 286; average, 83;
  correspondence of, 114; defined, 7–9;
  distinguished from planters, 7, 9, 37;
  domains of, 70; families of, 174, 176,
  274–75; large, 70, 83; and
  management, 7–8, 11, 52–53, 95,
  209–10, 222–26, 235; planter, 17, 34,
  160, 279; residence choices of, 7–8;
  status of, 7, 9, 34–35, 41. *See also*
  Absentees; Resident proprietors
Prospect Pen, 141, 143, 151
Provision grounds: crop cycle in, 248;
  defined, 4; and enslaved people, 4; and
  internal marketing, 4; on estates,
  194–96, 236–37, 240–41, 243, 251, 283;
  and ground provisions, 194–96, 199,
  219, 255; and peasantry, 293; rental of,

245, 248, 252, 257, 273; trespass, 251; and wage labour, 244, 246–47, 250, 276

Punishment, 34, 51–52

Pusey, Richard, 46

Ragatz, Lowell Joseph, 26–28, 48, 287

Railways, 121, 127–28

Rainfall, 1, 112, 166–67, 180–82, 216, 241–42

Ramble Pen, 153, 158–59, 266

Ratoons, 52, 99, 111, 195, 223, 257–58, 261

Razek, Joseph R., 97

Rebellions: of 1765, 197–98; of 1831, 6, 51, 90, 152, 228, 230, 232–33, 257–58; Demerara, 287; Morant Bay, 283; of enslaved people, 8, 168, 197, 200, 217. *See also* American Revolution; St Domingue

Receivers, 39, 84, 154, 159

Receivers general, 35–36, 89–90

Reeves, William, 70

Reisset, Jaffray and Yelloly, 215

Renny, James, 145

Rents: accounting for, 268, 270, 337n93; collected by attorneys, 43, 45–46, 146, 156, 158; in England, 24, 35–36, 39, 54; of free workers, 50, 52, 232, 240–41, 243, 245, 247–57, 276–77; in Ireland, 84; negotiation of, 114, 155, 243, 248–52, 276–77; peppercorn, 187; of plantations, 29, 47, 218, 292; of provision ground, 273; sued for, 156, 158, 245, 249, 253; and tenancy, 24, 43, 45–46, 140, 179, 255–57, 267; and wages, 52, 247–57, 273, 276–77

Residence, rights of, 238–40, 247–48, 272, 276–78

Resident proprietors: and abandonment, 282–83; and absentees, 17, 21, 280–81; and attorneys, 30, 47–48, 59, 91, 147, 243, 285–86; in Brazil, 19; and coffee, 19, 283; and complexity, 16; and commission agents, 103, 109; as creoles, 23–24; and enslaved people, 289–90; as failures, 17; and innovation,

288; and management, 16, 25–28, 30, 222, 280–81, 285–86; and partnership, 29; part-time, 23, 290; and pens, 19; plantations of, 57, 59, 140, 173; in politics, 21–22, 42; and sugar, 19, 282–83; and tenancy, 292; in the United States, 19–20; virtues of, 27–28

Retirement Estate, 157, 159

Returns of Registrations of Slaves, 56, 78, 85, 89, 99, 220, 342n13

Reynolds, William, 85, 87

Richards, David, 75

Richards, Eric, 36, 47, 53

Richmond Hill, 257, 267

Ridgard, William, 77

Risk, 9–10, 30, 54, 105, 110, 112, 209–10, 223, 265

Roads, 69, 112, 117–21, 167–68, 181, 192

Robertson, Bridget, 79

Robertson, Duncan, 64, 79–80, 88, 90

Robertson, Elizabeth Frances, 79

Robertson, James, 329n102

Robinson, Charles, 340n196

Rodney, Admiral, 188, 219

Roehampton Estate, 159–60, 238, 255, 257, 259

Roman Catholics, 147

Rome, John, 179

Roughley, Thomas, 39–40, 49–51, 81, 97–98, 291–92

Royal Mail Steam Packet Company, 126–27, 154, 163

Ruinate, 194, 255, 258, 263–64, 267, 282, 285

Rum: in accounts, 42, 97, 99, 213–14; and attorneys, 52, 205–6; and commission agents, 46; estates, 55; exported, 46, 52, 103, 108, 206, 213, 219, 260; insurance of, 209; local sale of, 102, 108, 199, 205–6, 213, 260; production of, 18, 205, 213, 216, 260–61, 281, 294n4; retailed, 257

Ryden, David Beck, 187

St Andrew parish, 75, 79, 81, 85–87, 141, 224

St Ann parish, 57, 65, 70, 79, 86

St Ann's Bay, 119–20

St Catherine parish, 85, 147

St Croix, 126

St David parish, 143, 173

St Domingue, 2, 6, 19, 28, 34, 148, 291

St Dorothy parish, 63, 85, 87

St Elizabeth parish, 59, 64, 79, 85, 267

St George parish, 30, 59, 69, 75

St James parish, 51, 57, 69–70, 73, 75, 80, 85, 90, 152, 159, 237, 269

St John parish, 87

St Kitts, 47, 122

St Mary parish, 59, 69, 85–86, 118, 140–41, 143, 173, 175, 197, 228, 264

St Thomas, 126, 131

St Thomas-in-the-East parish, 37, 57, 69, 75, 85, 89, 116, 118, 138, 140–41, 143, 147, 151, 224

St Thomas-in-the-Vale parish, 39, 57, 170, 228

St Vincent, 125–26

Sailing times, 53, 69, 121–33, 161, 163

Salaries: of attorneys, 82, 84, 156–57, 159, 164, 271, 274, 277, 285–86; of book-keepers, 99; of clerks, 116; in Britain, 84; and commissions, 82; of distillers, 234; of overseers, 50, 84, 99, 101, 203, 232, 285–86; of professionals, 84; ranking of, 84; of tradesmen, 99, 101, 234

Sales book, 106

Salmon, John, Jr, 64, 69, 85

Salt Spring Estate, 51, 90

Santo Domingo, 267

Savanna-la-Mar, 90, 118–20, 127

Scale. See Economies of scale

Scarborough, William K., 33

Schools, 23, 103, 137, 147, 228, 257

Schusmidt, Bernard, 70

Scientific management, 8–9

Scotland: absentees in, 46, 79–80; accounting in, 97; attorneys from, 49, 77–79, 92, 139–40; companies in, 283; doctors from, 154; estate management in, 35–36, 54; migrants from, 237; and

legal system, 49; people of, 17, 20, 77–79, 126; schooling in, 23, 80; tradesmen from, 172

Scotland, George, 84

Scott, Charles, 69, 85, 116

Seaford, Lord, 137, 152–53, 156–57, 160–65, 227–78, 280, 286–87. See also Charles Rose Ellis

Seaford Township, 153, 237, 254

Seasonality, 241–42, 248, 261

Senior, Bernard Martin, 38, 44, 48, 81, 83

Senior, Nassau, 25

Settlements, 5, 42, 56, 254–57, 276

Settler colonies, 5, 17–18, 292–93

Seven Years War, 123–24, 165

Sex, 80, 143–44

Shand, William, 37, 50, 54, 75, 77–78

Sharecropping, 54, 235, 292

Sheridan, Richard B., 15–16, 28, 31–32, 42, 48, 77, 138, 145–46, 273, 281

Shettlewood Pen: in accounts, 99, 232, 260, 267–68, 271; attorneys of, 152, 157–59, 231–35, 276, 334n7; butchery, 232, 238, 266, 270–71; livestock on, 262–67; management of, 231–35, 250, 252, 262–71; overseers of, 231–32; owners of, 228, 231; rentals at, 248, 254, 337n93; squatting on, 156; valuation of, 269; workers on, 156, 234–35, 238, 240, 242, 248, 250

Shickle, John, 61

Ship captains, 101, 103, 120–23, 143, 151, 207–10, 213–14, 260, 277

Shipping: in accounts, 100, 103; and attorneys, 50, 52–53, 103, 205–13, 260, 277; coastal, 120, 211–12; by convoy, 207; by droggers, 211; and insurance, 105, 182, 207, 209–12; merchant, 121, 128–30, 151, 207; and metropolitan merchants, 103–5; naval, 121, 128; northward, 206, 219; and overseers, 52, 208–9; ownership of, 103, 141, 210–12; ports, 1, 103, 151, 260, 277; and post, 120–33; and proprietors, 52, 103, 209; reliability of, 121, 124–25, 130, 132–33,

150, 210–12; speed of, 114, 124–33; steam, 126–28; wharves, 1, 103, 158, 180

Shops, 23, 77, 257

Shortridge, Samuel, 283

Silver Grove Estate, 153, 158–59

Simpson Taylor and Company, 87

Sinclair, Daniel, 115

Slavery: abolition in Cuba, 6; and absenteeism, 7; and accountancy, 94–95; advocates of, 68, 90, 142–43, 287; and attorneys, 52, 89; British abolition of, 84, 86, 106, 119, 152; Caribbean, 2; and literacy, 113; and management, 3–4, 112, 293; and merchants, 68, 109; opponents of, 110; plantation, 3–6, 94; and productivity, 2–4, 9, 112; and slave courts, 152; and slave owners, 3–8, 56, 85–88; and sugar, 6, 22; and transition to freedom, 11, 19, 52, 55, 89, 152, 235, 243; and wealth, 165, 217

Slaves. *See* Enslaved people

Slave society. *See* Society

Slave trade: abolition of, 6, 63, 105, 110, 116, 145, 220; from Africa, 6, 68, 117, 129, 165, 199–200, 203, 217, 219, 281; and attorneys, 109, 197–200; and commission agents, 214–15; voyages, 129

Sligo, Lord, 86

Smallpox, 171–72

Smuggling, 219

Society: and absenteeism, 25–26, 54; alternative models, 24, 292–92; colonial, 5, 25–26, 54; creole society, 8, 28; plantation, 7, 25, 33; settler, 5, 17–18, 292–93; slave, 3, 20, 25, 28, 91, 138, 144, 164, 228

Soils, 1, 104, 112, 166–67, 181, 195, 224, 261–62, 285

Sojourners, 18, 20, 289

Solicitors, 35–36, 38–39, 173

Southampton, 127, 130

Spain, 2, 25, 34, 163

Spalding, Hinton, 30

Spanish Main, 263, 265

Spanish Town, 42, 45–46, 57, 80, 88, 117, 119, 121, 146–48, 151, 170, 174–75, 214, 228, 267, 307n22

Specialization, 7–9, 16, 90, 95, 197

Spedding, James, 234

Speed. *See* Travel times

Squatting, 156, 238

Stamp Act, 22, 120

Starvation, 219

Steam power: for mills, 112, 180, 224, 275, 288; for railways, 127; for ships, 125–27, 131, 161, 163

Steele, Ian K., 128

Sterling, William, 159

Stewards, 33, 35–36, 39, 53–54, 82, 84, 96

Stewart, John, 18, 37, 39, 48, 55, 63, 81–82

Stewart, John (millwright), 224

Stewart, Walter George, 70, 85, 88–89

Still-house books, 97, 99

Stipendiary magistrates, 243, 249

Stockbrokers, 39, 93

Stokes, John, 234

Stokes Hall Estate, 167

Stores: plantation, 10, 88, 142, 180; provision, 257, 270; retail, 80, 257

Strikes, 156, 240, 243–44, 247

Sugar: brokers, 101, 103–4, 154; cultivation, 1–6, 40, 48, 52, 97, 100, 111–12, 155, 157, 166, 169, 181, 194–97, 201, 240, 245, 257–62, 274–75; crop, 182, 198, 241–42, 250, 256, 261; decline of, 6, 262–63, 283; diseases, 195; duties, 21, 219, 273; expansion, 52, 179, 198, 218, 282; exports, 1–2, 6, 103, 207–13, 260; grocers, 103; lodged canes, 195, 260; and management, 9, 15–16, 30, 37–40, 50–52, 55, 97–100; manufacturing, 10, 48, 52, 99, 155, 198, 275; marketing, 46, 55, 102, 155, 205–6; mills, 2, 4–5, 8, 140, 167, 223–24, 275; and mortality, 291; profits from, 18, 165, 214–20, 223–25, 267–72; prices, 2, 6, 43, 165, 204, 208, 213, 218, 261, 273, 294n4; production, 1–7, 140, 201, 205–6, 216–20, 223–24, 234–35, 257–62, 281, 286, 288, 294n4; refiners,

Sugar (*continued*)
103; qualities, 104, 207, 213, 259, 275; and society, 25; yields, 97, 112, 181, 195, 197, 200–201, 225, 261
Suicide, 8, 89, 188–89
Supervision, 11, 16, 30, 34, 52, 86, 92, 142, 172, 197, 224, 232, 289
Sustainability, 279–82, 287
Swamps, Estate, 173

Task work, 225, 235, 243, 245–46, 289
Taxes, 22–24, 42, 98, 162, 224, 269–70
Taylor, Anne, 140
Taylor, Clare, 132, 281
Taylor, Henry, 234
Taylor, John, 145–46
Taylor, Sir John, 138–39
Taylor, Patrick, 139–40, 147
Taylor, Robert, 145–46
Taylor, Simon (1740–1813): as attorney, 50, 133, 138, 140, 147–51, 153, 164–65, 167–228, 274, 276, 278, 280, 286–88; biography of, 137–40, 164; correspondence of 132–33, 147–51, 161; family of, 80, 138–39, 143–45; as merchant, 139–40, 145–46, 175, 205–12, 277; in partnership, 175; politics of, 138–39, 143–44; as proprietor, 140–43, 228; and religion, 230; sexuality of, 80, 143–45; and slavery, 197–205, 232, 235; vulgarity of, 138, 143; wealth of, 138, 140–42, 145–46, 271
Taylor, Simon (fl. 1832), 87
Taylor, Sir Simon Richard Brissett (1785–1815), 138–39
Taylor, William, 51
Taylor and Graham, 140, 148, 151
Technology: and absenteeism, 28–29; and attorneys, 158, 223–24, 235, 274–75, 280; communication, 94, 112–17; and innovation, 28–29, 96, 112, 261–62, 292; shipping, 130; and slavery, 1–5, 9, 287; and sugar, 1–5, 8, 112, 273–74
Tenancy, 24, 29, 35, 39, 53–54, 274, 292
Tharp, Ann, 144–45
Tharp, Charles Lawrence, 233, 250

Tharp, John, 57, 70, 141, 144–45, 290
Tharp, William, 70, 85
Theft, 16, 34, 281, 289–91
Thistlewood, Thomas, 80, 113, 128–29
Thompson, F. M. L., 36, 39, 96
Thomson, Thomas, 90
Tinling, Nicholas, 155
Topography, 1–2, 4, 6, 112, 166–67, 183, 224, 227, 285
Townships, 254–55, 272, 292
Trade: accounts, 97, 100; free, 24; internal, 1, 4–5, 43, 50, 52, 55, 99–100, 102, 205–7, 213, 260, 268; international, 1–5, 10, 16–17, 20, 40, 42–43, 50, 52, 55, 106–7, 114, 205–13, 219, 268
Tradesmen: free, 101, 234, 246; recruitment of, 50, 103, 172, 191, 194, 224; slave, 142, 191, 194, 224; white, 103, 172, 191–92, 217–18, 224
Travel times: on land, 63–75, 111, 113–14, 117–21, 132, 154–55, 167, 208; on sea, 116, 120–33
Treatment, of slaves, 8, 27, 165, 197–205
Trelawny, Edward, 42
Trelawny parish, 57, 69–70, 75, 89, 145, 153, 155, 159
Trinidad and Tobago, 49, 95
Trollope, Anthony, 55, 119, 128, 273
Trust, 36, 42, 281
Trustees, 39, 42, 56, 154, 173–74, 220
Tryall Estate, 153, 158–59
Tullideph, Dr Walter, 32
Turner, James Wright, 77, 91
Turner, Mary, 26

Uncertainty: and absenteeism, 30, 112, 132, 148, 287; and accounting, 112; and commission system, 106; and communication, 112, 114, 132, 161; economic, 9–10; and incalculability, 102, 280; and information, 10, 112, 132; and management, 9–10, 30, 112; and measurement, 10; and prediction, 216, 257, 278, 280; of trade, 114
United States: absenteeism in, 19–20;

business, 8; free blacks in, 157; North, 3; plantation management in, 53–54; South, 3, 33, 54

Vagrancy Act, 238
Vanneck Papers, 151, 323n75
Veblen, Thorstein, 25
Vere parish, 57, 73, 79, 118, 181, 291
Vestries, 89, 98, 117, 162, 269
Vidal, John Gale, 46, 88, 307n22
Villages, 254, 257, 272, 278, 285, 292

Waddell, Hope Masterton, 78–79
Wages: competitive, 156, 275–76; and money supply, 106, 163, 241, 253, 263, 268; negotiated by attorneys, 50, 52, 114, 155, 158, 239, 242–43, 276–77; rates of, 245–46, 254; reduction of, 243–44; and rent, 242–43, 247–50, 273; and salaries, 232; and transition to freedom, 165, 235–50, 266
War, 105, 205, 219. *See also* Napoleonic Wars; Seven Years War
Ward, J. R., 40, 81–82, 95, 281, 287, 292
Waste book, 106
Water, 1–2, 4, 52; competition for, 180–90; and cooperation, 180, 184, 186, 189; flow dynamics, 166–67, 183–84, 186; for irrigation, 2, 148, 180–81; mills, 112, 140, 166, 180–84, 187, 189–91, 224, 228, 241, 259–60, 275; for ponds, 263–64; rights, 180–81, 186–89, 222; wheels, 183, 258–59
Watt, James, 224
Watts, David, 281
Way, Benjamin, 45
Wealth: and abolition, 18–19, 55; and absenteeism, 7–8, 17–18, 23, 25, 55, 145, 164–65; of attorneys, 76, 83–88, 93, 138, 140, 146, 160, 164–65; British, 22, 84, 138, 141; consumption of, 20–21, 23, 286; and debt, 140–41; inequality, 5; inherited, 140, 174–75, 220; investment of, 21, 141, 145–46, 220; and management, 279, 286; of merchants, 140, 146, 164; North American, 22; of

planters, 5–8, 18, 22, 25, 140, 147, 164; and protection, 7, 21–22; and slavery, 5, 141–42, 146; and sugar, 5, 18, 22; transfer, 7, 18, 145–46, 220
Wedderburn, Andrew, 68–69
Wedderburn, James, 154
Wedderburn, Robert, 154
Wedderburn properties, 154–56
Weirs, 183–84, 186–88, 190–91
Welcome Estate, 260
Westerfield, Ray Bert, 102
Western Interior Regiment, 90, 152, 238
West India Dock, 6, 130
West India interest, 21–22, 86, 105, 220, 228, 230
West Indians, 23–28
West Indies Sugar Company, 55
Wesleyans, 138
Westmoreland parish, 69–70, 88–89, 154, 220, 231, 237, 260–61
Westphalia Plantation, 87
Wharves, 1, 6, 56, 103, 158, 208, 267, 270–71
Wheelerfield Estate, 179, 206
Whipping, 34, 51–52
White people: as absentees, 7, 22–23, 281; creole, 18, 23; and fear, 7, 30; female, 18, 28, 143; indentured, 23, 224; as labourers, 237–38, 276; male, 91, 143, 217; as proportion of population, 2, 22, 41; and punishment, 34–35; and slavery, 7, 91, 224; and social structure, 91, 171–72, 232, 281, 292; as tradesmen, 23, 172, 217, 224, 232; transient, 289; transnational, 28. *See also* Demography
Wildman, James Beckford, 39
Williams, Eric, 3, 27, 287
Williams, Joseph Stone, 85, 87–90, 154
Wills, 144, 173, 175–76
Wilmot, Swithin, 159, 324n115
Winchester Estate, 190–91, 329n102
Winchester Pen, 179–80, 184, 189–90
Winde, Mr, 180–81
Windmills, 140, 180, 224
Windward Islands, 33, 37, 208

Women: as head people, 232; as managers, 76; white, 18, 28, 143; as wives, 79, 93; workers, 156, 198, 203, 219, 240

Wood, Betty, 138, 148, 151

Woodland, 4, 52, 206, 254–56, 264, 269, 283, 285

Woodson, Carter G., 19–20

Woollery, Edward, 202

Workhouses, 239

Worthy Park Estate, 144, 188, 286, 289

Wright, Philip, 75–76, 90, 138

Writing, 113–17, 131–33, 149, 155, 161–62, 176, 209

Written documents, 42, 44, 51, 53, 94–95, 111, 113–15, 124, 174, 179, 252

Young, Edward James, 231–32, 271